Urban Anthropology

Urban Anthropology

Cross-Cultural Studies of Urbanization

EDITED BY
AIDAN SOUTHALL
University of Wisconsin

New York
OXFORD UNIVERSITY PRESS
London Toronto 1973

Library of Congress Catalogue Card Number: 73-76911
Printed in the United States of America

Contents

Acknowledgements

I wish to thank Ed Bruner for co-parenthood of the idea which led to this volume, conceived on a convivial occasion at the University of Chicago in 1961 while I was teaching courses in urban anthropology there. Most of all I wish to express the collective gratitude of all the contributors, as well as myself, to the Wenner-Gren Foundation for Anthropological Research and especially its Director of Research, Dr. Lita Osmundsen, for the generosity with which the Foundation supported our seminar at Burg Wartenstein on "Cross-Cultural Similarities in the Urbanization Process," and for assisting the editor in preparing this manuscript for publication.

It is a melancholy obligation to record that two of our number are no longer with us, Oscar Lewis and Rusi Nayacakalou. To them I dedicate this volume in respectful tribute to a long and distinguished career of scholarship in this field and to a brief career of promise sadly cut short.

Urban Anthropology

Introduction

Aidan Southall

The new emphasis on urban anthropology is an inevitable aspect of the dialectic growth of anthropology, but the strength of the demand for teaching urban anthropology and the extent to which younger scholars are turning towards it as their main focus of interest has been remarkable. As a major aspect of the equally new concern with complex societies, the study of urban anthropology marks an important step in implementing the traditional claim of anthropology to deal with man everywhere and as a whole. Further, it requires a radical change in the usual public image of anthropology. Although there is no denying the depth of the intellectual stimulus which continues to flow from study of the rich variety of man's cultural arrangements at both social and cognitive levels, anthropologists have long been aware that an exclusive interest in small, isolated, exotic cultures was a quicksand which would engulf them if they could not realize the broader relevance of their insights. They had every incentive to become more and more concerned with the transformation of erstwhile countrymen and peasants into city dwellers, industrial workers, and national elites. This turning towards urbanized aspects of foreign cultures has recently merged with the desperate search for more meaningful data on and interpretations of the deepening crisis of urban culture in America and other Western countries. To provide quick, easy, almost magic answers to the problems of urbanization is a naive hope, neither possible nor the best contribution for anthropology to make.

The best contribution of anthropology is, as always, to provide convincing accounts of what is happening to people in varied real life situations and to set these in a broader framework of time and space. To understand how urbanization is taking place among non-Western peoples to whom it is an entirely new experience, as in much of Africa and Oceania, and how it is spreading in its industrial form to those acquainted only with its earlier manifestations, as in Asia, is vital to Western peoples for a number of reasons. It is important for the richer urban industrial nations of the West to realize the implications of their galloping consumption of the world's resources for the poor masses of non-Western nations and for the increasingly urban society into which these people are being irresistibly drawn. It is also important for the Western nations to study with care and humility the new urban forms emerging in the non-Western world, to see if they offer any lessons as yet unthought of in Western ethnocentric assumptions.

The following accounts of urban data and urban theory, arising from studies mainly in Africa, Latin America, Japan, India, Indonesia, and the Pacific, confront us with the diversity of the subject but reveal a number of common themes. As is the way with anthropologists, all the contributors have intensive knowledge of particular localities and regions, acquired through research on the spot and prolonged study, which they have striven to relate to a wider and more universal framework. Through reading the written record and continued intellectual wrestling with colleagues who have been interested in similar problems, but in different places, they have been moving toward generalization.

The relation of urban to rural and of city to nation and state is one of the oldest human themes; it is illustrated here by a range of situations and views. The links between the institutions of town and country, between urban and rural populations, and between urban and rural phases in the careers of individuals have to be distinguished.

Anthony Leeds properly insists upon the intertwining of local and supra-local, or urban and national, institutions. The conventional analogy between the self-contained tribe (itself a concept of very dubious validity) and the local community as viable autonomous units of study is false to him. It is better to treat any convenient locality within an urban area heuristically as an arena of action and interests. These may have some significant concentration and coherence within it, but assuredly run beyond it in diverse directions and contexts that must equally be studied if the picture is not to be falsified. Both the impact of locality power on the centers of power and local impact on the power centers have to be taken into account. The typical *favela* of Rio de Janeiro does harbor and nurture its own distinctive way of life, but it also generates power and impels the representatives of supralocal institutions, which it confronts, to curry favor with it. The same is true of the *barriada* in Lima, the *vecindad* in Mexico City, the *jopadi* in Bangalore, the *bidonvilles* and housing estates in African cities, and localities in urban areas all over the world.

Oscar Lewis shows how the urban locality in Mexico City can retain many features of behavior which its inhabitants brought with them from more rural areas, despite the different institutional framework in which they find themselves. Secondary relationships may be more numerous but have only a minor psychological effect, whereas primary relationships are successfully maintained and even deepened in significance. Correcting the implications of Robert Redfield's urban secularization hypothesis, Lewis finds no general drift to anomie. The urban poor even strengthen their participation in the Catholic Church rather than become secularized; their family and *compadrazgo* ties are not noticeably weakened; and many traditional practices remain as significant for the urban as the rural poor. The retention of solidary relationships by the urban poor is a necessity for survival and has been widely noted, not only in Asia and Africa, but in the North American ghettoes. At different status levels the opposite process is now taking place in Western countries; urban middle- and upper-status persons are carrying city ways, city outlooks, and city involvements with them out into the countryside, either by residence there or by the decentralized establishment of distinctly urban functions and institutions in what was the countryside. As a result of both processes the former countryside is in many respects ceasing to be rural in a sociological sense.

This brings rich possibilities of further confusion and misunderstanding as to what various writers mean by "urban." Many eschew further debate on the definition as barren, assuming that it is easy enough to know by common sense whether what we are studying is urban, even if we cannot agree on a definition. It is doubtful whether such an amateur view is adequate when anthropologists attempt, as they must, to work towards valid generalizations over wide ranges of time and space. Some assume that "urban" refers to population aggregates of a certain size, at a certain level of density, others that it means major dependence on occupations other than agriculture or direct subsistence production; while still others relate it to some general kind of social complexity. Peter Lloyd's examination of the nature of Yoruba cities from this point of view provides as good an empirical test as any. He shows that Yoruba cities were large by preindustrial standards, with populations running into tens of thousands, and they were certainly dense. They were also heterogeneous in the number of specialized craft occupations, as well as political positions and titles, which they contained. Trading was highly developed, not only in the large internal markets, but between cities and city-states, and embraced neighboring peoples as well. Indeed this long-distance trade was probably more noticeable before the colonial period, since colonial institutions tended to supersede it. Still, most of the men were partly engaged in agriculture, going out of the city to outlying farms and staying on them at busy seasons.

In my article, I argue that any adequate urban definition will have to be rather abstract, probably echoing and drawing upon the ideas of some of the founding fathers of social science, such as Durkheim, Simmel, and Toennies, but with modifications to avoid the pitfalls into which some of these ideas led. I think any such definition must essentially concentrate upon the high spatial density of social interactions, rather than as heretofore upon the mere physical density of bodies or buildings. By high spatial density of social interaction I mean quite simply the extremely large number of interactions of different kinds between very large numbers of persons going on within a certain limited range of space and time. Cities and urban life have been distinguished in all times and places by a high density of social interaction relative to the wider society in which they were situated.

No moral component enters into this idea of density. It purposely raises many questions, but it does not mislead when applied across time and space as other definitions do. The minimal definition of social interaction is one problem. The potential frequency and multiplicity of social interaction has been vastly increased by communications technology. People interact socially not only on buses and jet planes, but in and through letter-writing, telephoning, radio, television, and even satellites. This is what generates unprecedentedly high density of social interaction in the urban life of today, which still has to be considered in spatial terms but certainly not in the outdated spatial terms of the city limits on the ground. A large part of these multitudinous social interactions may be very shallow and fleeting, but that is the whole point. Such multitudinous, shallow, and fleeting interactions are an essential aspect of urban life; but they are not the whole of it, as some have made the serious mistake of supposing. For another, equally important, aspect of the same high density and communications technology is that it also permits and facilitates the emergence and maintenance of profoundly personal relationships, as Lewis has emphasized.

The spatial mobility which means a fairly frequent turnover of population in many cities feeds into this definition by still further increasing the number of people in social interaction over a period of time. Also, difficult to define or quantify as they are, we have to include those forms of mass participation which have always been characteristic of cities and cannot occur to the same extent except in cities: football matches, circuses, political rallies, national ceremonies, mobs, and riots. All these are intrinsically urban. Woodstock and other contemporary mass festivals in the countryside are an interesting exception but cannot reverse the trend. In any case they are of urban people. Peasant revolts end up in the city. Anonymous social interaction is characteristically urban. Loneliness is more intense against the background of fleeting mass interaction. There has rightly been a reaction against the exaggeration of urban anomie, recognizing that most members of the urban masses everywhere achieve quite effective solidary relationships with a few neighbors, kinsfolk, and friends. But account still has to be taken of the fact that they must do this in the context and against the background of fleeting mass interaction.

It is important to note that Michael Banton adds the moral connotation of consensus and agreement on norms and conformity with customary patterns of behavior in his discussion of density. This moral density is higher in villages than towns, and higher in small towns than large cities. While also recognizing that towns are not self-contained units, Banton suggests that the more a city constitutes an independent set of roles, the tighter is the social network and the higher the moral density. Marked cleavages in a city, or extreme and all-embracing pressure from monolithic institutions, may generate a high level of consensus and moral density, as in the case of South African mine compounds or American black ghettoes. The objective of urban anthropology is to bridge the gap between microsocial studies of interpersonal relations and macrosocial studies of urban structures. Empirical studies of interpersonal relations in non-Western cities are still extremely few and far between, as a result of which the conclusions drawn from sample surveys and macrosocial studies are superficial and liable to misinterpretation.

Takeo Yazaki concisely documents the long, unbroken continuity of the Japanese urban tradition, undoubtedly the most significant non-Western urban tradition for the contemporary world, because it is the only one in which the problems of industrialization were successfully mastered while maintaining autonomy from the West. It is the only case to date of industrialization without Westernization, though no doubt another example is now emerging in China. The Japanese urban tradition began rather suddenly in the eighth century with adoption of the already ancient Chinese urban model. The intertwining urban, political, and economic evolution of Japan over a thousand years shows certain formal parallels with the West—the alternation of centralization and decentralization, of feudal and bureaucratic structure—but striking contrasts too—the place of merchants in the urban system, the fact that the cities linked to the castles of the feudal barons were never themselves walled or fortified, and the extraordinarily detailed and meticulous efficiency of administrative control over cities, extending to every ward and every individual household and family. One startling aspect of this was the capacity to organize and maintain a level of individual and family mobility between town and country otherwise quite unheard of anywhere in the world before the industrial era. Robert J. Smith's remarkable research demonstrates this mobility and in the process shows the astonishing detail and accuracy of the Japanese urban demographic record at a time when comparable data were quite unavailable in the West. Eighteenth-century travelers noted the Japanese cities and the traffic on the highways as greater than anything they had seen in Europe. Despite the dramatic suddenness with which the transformation seemed to take place after the Meiji Restoration of 1868, Smith notes that in many important respects Japan was prepared for this transformation long before.

In India, on the other hand, despite its own ancient and extensive urbanization, the greatest contemporary cities derive from the colonial impact rather than from the indigenous urban tradition. They have been fed by a huge stream of migration, which has become a permanent feature. The percentage of the Bombay population born elsewhere has remained between 64 and 84 for over a century without any clear trend up or down. The caste ecology of cities has largely remained, despite this high migration rate. William L. Rowe recognizes that the urban and rural aspects are simply parts of a single system. The city enables the village to survive through migrants' cash remittances. Many northern migrants to Bombay come without their wives and families. They suffer caste indignities and humiliation in the city, which they are able to hide from their rural kin generation after generation (as Rowe has informed me in personal communication). They keep their two lives separate but succeed in retaining their status and land rights in the village. On the other hand, many southern migrants to Bangalore are so destitute that retaining village ties is hardly worth their while, so that they are more likely to move to the city permanently, complete with wives and families (personal communication).

Caste associations have provided a bridge between the solidarities and the institutions of the migrants' home places and the cities to which they have gone in search of greater opportunities, just as ethnic associations have done in Africa or in the United States. Up to a certain point the caste associations continue to play the caste game, by struggling to better the relative status of their members within local systems of caste relations. But beyond that point they have begun to play a more purely political or economic game by acting as pressure groups and reservoirs of power and support which can maneuver to secure for their members political privileges, or monopolistic control over certain sections of industry, outside and beyond mere caste considerations. At the same time many associations with quite secular names, as in the field of labor organization, remain none the less mainly channels for the expression of particular caste interests.

In Suva City, the capital of Fiji, where immigrant Indians outnumber Fijians in the urban population by more than two to one, Rusiate R. Nayacakalou not surprisingly finds a great retention of Fijian customary behavior between kin and affines in the city. It is true that urban housing is differently designed, so that the expression of rank differences through the spatial positioning of persons in the house has become more difficult; and, since fewer kin are available to each Fijian than in his home village, he is inclined to draw neighbors and fellow employees into joint activities which used to be restricted to kinsfolk. But the village also is having to accommodate to the presence of non-kin; while, at the same time, many villagers commute daily to work in town, so that we find a continuity, rather than a polarity, between urban and rural relationships.

The Toba Batak migrants to Medan, the large capital city of Sumatra, also succeed in utilizing rural kinship obligations with some modification in the urban context, so that Edward M. Bruner sees the greatest change not in kin relations but in those with non-kin. For, as is the case with many of those African peoples whose traditional structure was stateless, positive relationships with non-kin, except as enemies, were simply not possible unless they could be approximated to some kinship category. The minimal lineage binds together its members both in town and country. Circumstances restrict the usual urban residential unit to the nuclear family, as opposed to the rural extended family. It is a question of the urban transformation of kin ties, not of mere persistence, but not of breakdown, either. Bruner has made the important general point that, where the institutions and controls of the state are shaken to their foundations and remain in doubt for considerable periods, as has been the case in postwar Indonesia, ethnic groups in the cities are forced to rely more heavily upon the adaptation of their own local and traditional institutions (personal communication). This applies to a number of other countries, as for example Zaïre, and, more horrifyingly, to the new nations of Indo-China.

The great cities of Southeast Asia represent an important part of the world's urbanization. The nineteenth and twentieth centuries have seen a massive increase of the older migrations of Indians eastwards to Rangoon and Singapore and of Chinese to Saigon, Manila, Bangkok, and Djakarta. Before the fifteenth century, when the advent of the Portuguese heralded the European empires in Asia, the great cities had for a millennium been either the inland temple capitals of divine kings, symbolically planned to represent the universe, as at Angkor, or had been port cities controlling the trade between China and India to the West, like Malacca or Palembang. The colonial cities of the nineteenth century were described as parasitic, funneling wanted products out to the West without inducing economic transformation. Now that most of them have become the capital cities of independent countries, local elites have been co-opted alongside the white elites, who remain in even greater numbers than before, though they have retreated from open political dominance to more subtle diplomatic, commercial, military, and general aid-to-development dominance. Considering that the gap between urban luxury and both urban and rural poverty is also greater than before, and that they serve as channels through which the United States alone consumes 60 per cent of the world's natural resources—ten times its share by population size—these Asian cities can hardly be considered less parasitic than before. The spatial segregation and social solidarity of the immigrant ethnic communities of Chinese and Indians remain marked and, in the conditions of extreme overcrowding and underemployment, doubtless necessary to survival.

Ethiopia provides another case of the continuing importance of ethnic ties in its capital city, Addis Ababa. Most of the country's ethnic groups were only conquered by the dominant Amhara at the end of the nineteenth century; and the city owes its origin to the military camps of various generals, whose huge followings consisted of the particular ethnic groups whom they had subdued and brought into service. The distaste of the dominant ethnic groups for manual work has led to a certain identification of types of occupation with ethnicity. William A. Shack suggests historical parallels between the urbanization of Ethiopia and Japan, based on the dominance in both cases of an imperial, feudal, and military structure. Indeed, Japan and Ethiopia are two of the very few countries which have successfully resisted colonial conquest, both suffering military defeat but being rather soon reinstated without loss of cultural continuity. This is clearly associated in both cases with a determination to preserve this cultural autonomy; but in other respects the Ethiopian urban tradition differs markedly from that of Japan, since Ethiopia had no large permanent cities till the end of the nineteenth century and even now is only very slightly industrialized. Furthermore, the great ethnic heterogeneity of Ethiopia, contrasted with the basic homogeneity of Japan, leads to profound differences in the structure of urban life.

While large-scale migration is a ubiquitous feature of contemporary urban growth, it is obvious that it has ethnic importance only where the source of migration is ethnically heterogeneous, as in most of Africa, Sumatra, or Fiji. However, the great metropolis everywhere now draws upon such a wide and international catchment area that ethnic problems are also appearing everywhere. Their long history includes the extremely diverse migration to the United States, the vast migration of Indians eastward and Chinese westward or southward to the huge cities of Southeast Asia, the West Indian or Pakistani communities in English cities, Algerians in French cities, or Chinese in Rangoon, Bangkok, Singapore, and Saigon. But the importance of ethnic diversity, if present, depends upon the type of stratification and degree of industrialization, as well as the particular characteristics of certain ethnic groups. The basic orientation of the receiving society affects the implications of ethnicity, as in the persistence of ethnic and racial discrimination in the United States, as compared with most Latin American countries, where status distinctions are mainly expressed in other ways.

Kenneth Little states that in the new mining town of Lunsar in Sierra Leone, the Temne miners aim at bettering and educating themselves, rather readily adopting the idea of the nuclear family based on monogamy and companionate marriage, allowing their ties with extended family and clan, as well as their belief in ancestral spirits, to weaken; whereas the Fulani in Lunsar, with an aristocratic background, keep aloof and to themselves, concentrating on activities such as cattle trading which are compatible with the retention of much traditional behavior despite urban residence. On the other hand, in the mining and industrial areas of Southern Africa the oppression by white minority governments cements all Africans together and damps down the expression of ethnic differences except as convenient categories of social classification; and employment by huge, monolithic enterprises accentuates this effect by necessitating the use by Africans of effective labor organization which largely ignores ethnic differences. Distance from home is another relevant factor. It had been shown by Mayer in East London, South Africa, that migrants whose homes were so near that they could visit them frequently at weekends did not need to stress their kinship and ethnic solidarity in town because the rural actuality of it was so readily accessible as to remain real to them without such reinforcement. J. Clyde Mitchell tests this idea further in a sophisticated statistical study of migrants to the Zambian Copperbelt towns. He confirms the East London study by showing that "the degree to which an individual is able to become caught up in urban life depends upon the extent to which he is able to maintain his participation in events and affairs in his rural home without finding it necessary to absent himself completely from the town for long periods." The more distant the migrant's rural home, the lower his urban involvement, as measured by the presence of his wife in town, the spending of more time in town than in country (especially of long unbroken periods in town), and the expectation of long continuous future residence there. Although the more distant migrants had spent less time in town, their wages and skill were somewhat higher on the average than those of nearer migrants.

The reasons for migrants leaving distant homes are explored in a different way by Stillman Bradfield in his study of Peruvian migration from the highlands to the coastal boom town of Chimbote or the capital city of Lima. Only a minority of the migrants, or even their fathers, had previously been farmers. Most came from intermediate small towns or cities. In one study, three quarters of those who had completed primary education (as only 11 per cent of the population had) became migrants and were living away from home (the spread of schooling in Africa has been equally closely connected with an increase in migration). Bradfield finds, in effect, that it is those best equipped to do so who migrate to the big cities. Those who do not make a successful adjustment often return home, but those who stay tend to drop most of their characteristically home traits and identify fully with the city (personal communication). This situation is clearly different (perhaps a further stage in the process) from the situation revealed by studies of either Africa or northern India, but perhaps more similar to that of Southern India in the rather complete break which many make with their past. However, while it is true of very low-status migrants in South India, in Peru it is both the more educated and those of somewhat higher status who seem most likely to leave permanently. Of course, this reflects the great differences of general social structure in the two cases.

William Mangin's study relates to another aspect of Peruvian migration, in which some dwellers in the central slums of Lima had the courage to reject the intolerable living conditions to which they were subjected, sieze public land outside the city, hold it steadfastly in the face of brutal attacks by the police, and create new communities out of nothing, with no outside assistance and in the face of official hostility and misrepresentation. The new communities now account for a fifth of the population of Greater Lima. We are thus led back to another variant of the evidence from all continents on how urban masses generate their own solidarities and defeat the threatened anomies of large cities. It also leads us on to some of the most intractable problems which will haunt the world's great cities for decades to come. These are the problems of how to humanize big city life for the poor in their frighteningly growing numbers, how to help through official programs without stifling the initiative and dignity of the people themselves and actually undermining their lives through blundering policies; how to understand, accept, and facilitate the people's own efforts, which at present seem always to alarm the Establishment as subversive.

The Peruvian elite, according to Mangin, sees the *barriada* residents as landless, lawless, jobless, recently arrived, rural, Quechua-speaking Indians. He shows them as well-established, Spanish-speaking, coming from provincial towns rather than rural areas, successfully establishing their own system of law and order where none was offered to them, and energetically aiming at secure employment and good neighborly respectability. Allowing for the cultural and structural variations which we have been noting, a similar picture emerges in any part of the world where social investigators have come to terms with urban masses as human beings and persons. In this basic respect, Anthony Leeds has presented the *favelas* of Rio de Janeiro in a similar light, and has elsewhere drawn attention to the growing horrors of the huge high-rise apartment complexes being constructed for the poor of Rio as much as forty miles from the city center. Urban experts are now calling these "slumscrapers." Chicago's

South Side, St. Louis, and parts of New York City have known slum-scrapers for several decades, and they are now invading the teeming cities of Asia, such as Singapore, Bangkok, and Hongkong. An alternative and equally deadening model may be found in the tens of thousands of utterly standardized one-story cement bungalows which house the half million Africans of Soweto township outside Johannesburg. Urban renewal in the United States is said to destroy more homes than it creates. Everywhere in the world mushrooming cities are posing an agonizing dilemma between physically unsightly and often officially illegal settlements, which none the less represent some positive achievement and adjustment by their inhabitants despite lamentably inadequate services, and, on the other hand, mass-produced official schemes of astronomical cost. These are technically modern and efficient on the drawing board but often disastrous in practice, through ignorance of the real needs and convenience of the people at whom they are aimed and rapid deterioration and breakdown resulting from bad maintenance and the impossibility of paying rents which are always higher than those of the previous accommodation, from which the inhabitants were involuntarily removed. The counter-approach which is beginning to emerge is, of course, that the inhabitants themselves must be involved at all stages and must have some say and responsibility for their own destiny. Since anthropology became a field-work discipline rather than an armchair hobby, this has been an implicit principle; and it is here that urban anthropology may perhaps bring together both theoretical and practical concerns of the greatest moment.

Locality Power in Relation to Supralocal Power Institutions

Anthony Leeds

Introduction[1]

This paper is an effort to develop some concepts and a model to deal with (a) the institutions of the territorial state, (b) the social unit—the community, and (c) the human-geographical unit—the locality, in a single frame of reference and as a single, systemic totality.

In former days, anthropology dealt almost exclusively with sociocultural entities loosely called "tribes." These were "natural" units in the sense that they usually possessed a distinctive language or dialect; comprised socioeconomic systems or subsystems; had a series of discrete characterizing customs; and, finally, recognized themselves and were recognized by the use of some name as being separate. Such tribes are mark-

1. The paper stands essentially as written in 1964 with, however, expansion of theoretical considerations, clarification and tightening of definitions, and the like. The paper, elaborated deductively as a model, was intended as a theoretical work and a kind of position paper growing out of theoretical work on the nature of cities I had been doing for several years. It is also concerned, though this has not been underscored, with epistemological problems, particularly the status of our units of study. It was *not* intended as a data paper or abbreviated monograph. The favela material is only exemplary; it was not, then, properly field data at all, being based on three very brief visits to favelas combined with some reading. Subsequent fieldwork of about twenty months not only confirmed what I was arguing deductively from scraps of data but indicate that I underemphasized the argument. Data from the fieldwork are beginning to appear as indicated in the bibliography but are not germane, in the mass, to the ends of this paper. The responsibility is mine for retaining the original form, despite criticism at the seminar and several suggestions to build the theory out of the data. This was an inductive procedure I deliberately eschewed because I thought—and think—it has consistently tended to block fruitful theoretical vision.

edly constituted by autonomous locality groups (e.g. bands, villages, etc.), parallel as to ecology, institutions, culture content, and so on. The parallelism and autonomy permitted the intensive study of one as a representative sample of all belonging to the same tribe (or so it was thought), because they were putatively complete communities.[2] From samplings of this sort, it was believed to be possible to describe a "total culture"[3] or a total society.

Anthropologists transferred this "method" to the study of complex societies when they were led to study them by the exigencies of the science and the times. They continued to focus on *localities, a priori* assumed to be communities and supposed to be representative samples of the total culture and society (e.g. Dollard, 1937; Embree, 1939; Lynd and Lynd, 1929; Oberg, 1960; Pierson, 1949; Powdermaker, 1939; Shirley, 1971; Wagley, 1953; Warner and Lunt, 1941; West, 1945; Willems, 1947; and many others).

When it began to become clear that such "units" of study in complex societies are not analogs of the tribal local units and do not indeed give a picture of the totality,[4] anthropologists began to try treating sociocultural totalities in ways which were extensions of older methods, especially trait distribution and pattern analyses (cf. Benedict, 1946 a and b; Embree, 1945; Mead, 1942; etc.). These, nevertheless (and necessarily), still failed to give descriptions of the functional dynamics of change and resistance to change.

For such problems of dynamics of change, resistance, etc., the older

2. The data on the Yaruro Indians, collected by Falla (personal communication), Le Besnerais (1954), Leeds (1964c), Petrullo (1939), and Rootes (personal communication), clearly demonstrate what appear to be microecological variations of some significance from village to village across a number of geographical gradients of the area; furthermore, the Yaruro are in interlocking relations with other linguistic groups or "tribes" which each have specialized ecological relations within the larger ecological system of the llanos in which all of them exist. This sort of data, for which parallels may be found elsewhere in the world, suggest that the representativeness of single communities in "primitive" society should long have been questioned and sampling procedures used to control this kind of variation.

3. For the concept of "total culture" see Kroeber, 1948:316-18; also Leeds, in preparation, "Conclusions."

4. Cf. Steward, 1950; Steward, ed., 1956; and the series of studies carried out by the Columbia University–State of Bahia project in 1950-52, cf. Harris, 1956; Hutchinson, 1957; Wagley, ed. 1952. In connection with this the following comments by T. Lynn Smith (1947:587) are striking: ". . . the Brazilian rural community is not readily visualized and defined; . . . the village is by no means identical with the community; . . . the Brazilian countryman might have been called 'the man without a community.' " Cf., also, Leeds, in preparation.

conceptions, models, and methods were inadequate because they did not in fact deal with the sociocultural "unit" of the complex society; that is, with the more or less clearly delimitable unit called a territorial state or country, the proper analog to the tribal locality-community.

Thus, neither anthropologists nor anyone else has presented models of an entity, for example, the United States, the community studies of which were supposed to constitute societal representatives or microcosmic reproductions of it. Far less have they presented what the relationships *among* the communities studied might be. For instance, what kind of structural, dynamic relationships might be said to exist between Plainville, U.S.A., and Yankee City or Middletown or Elmtown or even Hollywood? Where is the locus of such relationships? Are they to be studied in the respective localities? Are they, indeed, exemplified in the internal relationships of the ostensible "communities?" If so, how? Are the only constraining parameters governing the organization and characteristics of these "communities" the local ecological conditions and the internally self-perpetuating cultural values and options, or do the constraining parameters stem from a more comprehensive order, in fact, that order which *includes* locality A—Plainville, U.S.A.—and locality B—Yankee City, U.S.A. —in a single system? If the latter is the case, as this paper assumes, then we have, as anthropologists, virtually no extant methodological tools to deal with the relationships between Plainville and Yankee City, because we have not dealt anthropologically with the empirical social structure of the state and other large-scale orders in modern complex nations. This paper deals with certain aspects of these questions.[5]

The Community

By most common definitions or usages,[6] the community, especially as an

5. I have dealt with other aspects elsewhere. My 1964a paper gives a case study of how constitutive elements of social structure link localities of coordinate and hierarchic levels into national and even international networks as well, and construct social nodes of various scale which cross-cut all sorts of locality. 1964b relates local ecology, local political events, and national political events in an interactive system. 1967b gives part of the theoretical framework underlying both. In Leeds, in preparation, the relationship between national legal systems and local social structure is extensively discussed. See also treatments of the connections of various "parts" and social loci, including "communities," in Adams, 1970; Leeds, 1969, 1971; Leeds and Leeds, 1972.

6. Note, for example, Murdock's statement (1949:79): "[The community] has been defined as 'the maximal group of persons who normally reside together in face-to-face

object of study, is held to be a minimal social structural unit of some kind. It has generally been considered some sort of microcosm of some sort of macrocosm called the total-society, or an equivalent term. Thus, students doing community studies have assumed that the study of the community would of itself tell one about the total society.

A number of major fallacies are involved in these assumptions. First, it is not self-evident that the macrocosm is structured like the microcosm. Indeed, were anthropologists less illiterate in other social sciences, especially political science, economics, and geography, as well as the formidable political economy of the nineteenth century, it would be immediately evident on empirical grounds and impellingly clear on logical grounds that this could in no case be so. Also, on general axiomatic grounds, there would be every reason to suppose the opposite, at least for complex, state-organized societies.[7] It would seem more likely, *axiomatically,* that the localities studied in so-called community studies constitute specialized, differentiated, and variously interrelated entities of a total society possessing institutionalized mechanisms for tying them together. From such an axiom it is clear that the organization of the microcosm cannot be homologous with that of the macrocosm.

It would follow from this that the "community study" cannot possibly, in any usable definition of community, give us a description of the macrocosm; hence, that the ostensible ends of community studies were *always* off the mark. Herein lies the second great fallacy of the community study method.

It would follow, still further, that even if we had exemplary studies, one each from every category of community in a total-society or macrocosm, we would still not have such a description. A sampling from the community types of a nation, such as we now have for Brazil,[8] still gives us no picture of the interrelationships of these localities, that is, of macro-

association.'" Firth (1951:27-28) says, "The term community emphasizes the space-time component, the aspect of living together. It involves a recognition, derived from experience and observation, that there must be minimum conditions of agreement on common aims, and inevitably, some common ways of behaving, thinking, and feeling. Society, culture, community, these involve one another. . . ." It is interesting that Bredemeier and Stephenson (1964) do not even deal with the community!

7. But also, I think, for tribal societies, except perhaps for the simplest band-organized types whose locality units are, for the most part, largely autonomous.

8. Cf. Forman, 1970; Harris, 1956; Hutchinson, 1957; Leeds, in preparation; Oberg, 1960; Pierson, 1949; Shirley, 1971; Wagley, 1953; Wagley, ed., 1952; Willems, 1947; Willems and Mussolini, 1957; etc., and from an historical point of view, Morse, 1951, 1958; Poppino, 1953; Stein, 1957.

cosmic *structures* and *dynamics*. All that can be derived from them are traits held in common. These may then be listed as an entirely static trait inventory characterizing the entire territorial unit of the macrocosm. On the basis of such an inventory, no prediction as to future conditions of either the macrocosm or the microcosm can be made. The inventory proves as sterile as most trait-listing, culture-area analyses, so common in the 1920's and 1930's, were to prove by the late 1940's when they substantially disappeared from modern anthropology as a major interest.

In short, the community study method is wholly inadequate to the study of state-organized societies, nations, complex societies, countries, or whatever one wants to call them.

We must, then, discover and analyze the direct and indirect forms of interrelationships among so-called communities or localities. This is not entirely virgin territory: political economy, political science, historical jurisprudence, and economics have been dealing with a number of such institutions for some centuries. These disciplines, however, have, for the most part, dealt only with the *forms* of interrelationship as such—with what I shall call here "supralocal institutions"—and then only with selected ones. For the most part, these have been considered without regard to the nature of their interdigitation with the "communities" and localities and without regard for the influence, in turn, of these latter on the institutions. Put another way, these disciplines have dealt with a restricted number of institutions which have been selected from among all social institutions and treated as if they operated entirely independently of local foundations. For example, economists deal with taxation, but I know of no instance in which the mobilization of local social organization to handle tax problems engendered by a given national taxation policy has been explored. I state the case extremely, but in the main the assertion is true.

Since it appears to be axiomatic among anthropologists that they are to deal with total societies or whole systems, they have been committed to attempting, and have indeed ventured, descriptions of the macrocosm.[9] But they have not been able to deal adequately with the supralocal institutions in themselves. Much less adequately, if at all, have they been able to deal with the interrelations between these institutions and the individual communities or localities with which they articulate. There are few descriptions of such relationships in the literature, with the possible exception of the sinological material, and virtually no general propositions,

9. Cf. Adams, *et al.*, 1960; Adams, 1970; Benedict, 1946; Embree, 1945; Lowie, 1945; Mead, 1942, 1955; Steward, ed., 1956; Wagley, 1949; and many others.

hypotheses, or models as to the nature of such interrelations (cf., however, Lopes, 1964; Adams, 1967). In what follows, I propose one such general model.

The Locality

For present purposes, I shall use the term 'locality' rather than "community" because of the prevailing confusions regarding the latter term as it has been used to designate the ethnographies of particular places. If one accepts Arensberg's definition (1961) or the rather different one given by Murdock (1949:79), it is clear that most so-called community studies are only dubiously studies of communities at all; they are rather studies of localities. The status of the locus of study in these field researches as an actual unit of the social order is most ambiguous in the sense of Arensberg's definition of community. In any case, he defines at best a unit conceived in isolation, not one which acts with respect to other units in a total system.

The term 'locality,' however, refers, in the context of human geographic distributions, to sensorily distinct loci of settlement characterized by such things as more or less stable aggregates of people or inventories of houses, generally surrounded by and including relatively empty, though not unused, spaces. Thus, what we ordinarily call a city, a town, a village, but also oil drilling platforms and mining camps, are localities. Visually distinct subareas of a city, sharply marked off like squatter settlements or a cathedral close, also fall under the definition. No matter how simple the locus, this still holds true. Even a farmstead, probably the simplest kind of locus of all, is a locality by the definition given.

It can be shown on theoretical grounds that localities comprise nodes of interaction (cf. Leeds, 1970, in press), the points of greatest density and widest variety of categories of behavior in the area, but not necessarily having an exhaustive array of such categories of behavior as are required for the community by Arensberg's definition. This comment applies not only to towns and villages, but even to the cathedral close and to the farmstead mentioned above. They are places of greatest density and widest variety of categories of human behavior when seen in contrast to the space in between them and the next locality; economic, social, religious, etc., transactions and behaviors all are concentrated there.

Long-term and customary face-to-face interaction and personalized relationships of all kinds are preponderantly locality interactions, but not exclusively so. It must be noted, however, that the definition does *not* imply that all relationships in localities are of these types; they may be impersonal and secondary ones. Indeed, it is the specific intent of the definition to be neutral in this respect so that the nature of the relationships becomes an empirical question rather than a definitional one: it may be the case, ideally, that *no* personalized relationships exist in the locality; that there are solely impersonal and secondary ones without community characteristics or feeling.

Thus, use of the term "locality" does not commit us to postulating a minimal or maximal unit of organization like the "community" (see MacIver and Page, 1949, Ch. 12, pp. 281-309), nor to arguing about its ontological status. We need only develop adequate and relevant tools to deal with its empirical description.

It does not commit us to assuming that the locality in which we have lived and done research as anthropologists is also a community. It often is not or is only partially so. The fact that the localities anthropologists and sociologists have studied are so often not communities is, of course, another major ambiguity of the community study method in its attempt to deal with the macrocosmic society of which the communities are a part.

Characteristics of the Locality

Localities as loci of interaction, as I have noted above, are characterized, even in very simple localities, by a highly complex web of divers types of relationships. The most active kinship ties—those within the nuclear family and, often, those with close relatives—are largely to be found in the locality, especially a small one. The most immediate, numerous, and lively (if not the deepest) friendships tend to be in the locality. The majority of one's ritual kinfolk tend to be in the locality where they may be mobilized more or less instantaneously. One's neighbors whom one may call on for various ends are by definition in the locality. The ambience, as defined by Caplow (1955), is in great part necessarily a locality phenomenon. A plethora of informal groups such as cliques, gangs, work groups, and the like, as well as small associations whose interests and range of action are necessarily rather limited (e.g., a town band or a samba school) are phenomena of localities.

In contrast to kinship, ritual kinship, friendship, ambience, neighbor, informal group, and small associational personalized face-to-face relationships, countless impersonal face-to-face and secondary relationships also may characterize localities as loci of transaction and interaction (cf. Leeds, 1967b, 1970, in press). The vast array includes mass services (such as are rendered by subway change-makers or restaurant cashiers), one-time services (like those of department-store sales clerks), buying and selling in the impersonal market, memberships in secondary groups (such as corporate bodies like a university or, more strikingly, mail-order book or record "clubs"), support from welfare agencies, and so on. Such relationships as these plainly do not fall under Murdock's definition of community and do not clearly relate to Arensberg's.

Inhabitants of localities interrelate by means of modes of action falling into many or all of these categories and hold them in readiness for meeting the contingencies and exigencies of daily life. Individuals choose among these modes, mobilizing now one, now another, as occasion and utility warrant. It is of greatest significance that, for most occasions or ends, two or more types of relationships might well be useful and mobilizable.

On one hand, to help in a moment of financial crisis one might call on friends, neighbors, kin, and ritual kin. To give support at sudden death, the same types of personnel might be called upon. To resist taxation or other external impositions, these types, as well as work groups and cliques, perhaps, may be called into play to serve as informal and undetectable distributive networks moving wealth away from the hand of the tax collector. All of these forms of organization may also facilitate the active preservation of valued cultural traditions and orientations against encroachments from outside.

On the other hand, localities, depending on size, may possess formal, institutional modes of action, in greater or smaller number, which may also be used to deal with such problems as financial crisis, sudden death, or others. Again, the question is an empirical one, not to be handled by assumptions which include or exclude these links from consideration.

The same kinds of relationships may be called upon to handle the extraordinary exigencies of life, especially those not arising from the daily routine characteristic of, or imposed by, the institutionalized economic, political, or social features of the locality. The most typical exigencies of this sort are external, imposed from outside the locality by supralocal agencies, and may include taxation, draft, military coercion, and others; these are discussed below. Among the most effective kinds of relationships to handle such exigencies are the informal and personalized ones, facilitated by proximity in the locality.

In sum, the social organization of the locality may be seen as a highly flexible system of human adaptation. Its very flexibility and looseness of organization, its unchartered and unspecified (or, one might say, unrationalized and unbureaucratized) complexity, permits it a wide range of responses to an almost infinite variety of events, contexts, and exigencies. Its flexibility permits rapid mobilization of its social and economic resources for different ends and in diverse forms, often under the most extreme stress, in a way not achievable by any other system of organization. It is limited only by the extent of the total available resources in land, matériel, personnel, and finances. These, of course, vary greatly in kind and amount in different kinds of localities, as, for example, between a college town and a proletarian slum in Rio de Janeiro. The extent of the limitations is itself an important factor in giving form to the power and institutional interrelationships of locality and supralocal agencies.

In this connection, it is of utmost importance to note that all localities are also in some way ecological entities. That is, they are populations related to some tract of territory, possessing some resources, however minimal, including human labor. They are themselves differentially ordered into specialized areas and activities, often at least partly related to territorial differences and to the point of impingement of external influences (e.g. gas stations at the road entrances to towns, entry points of power lines, etc.).

Further, since the system of organization is so flexible, we should expect to observe not only long-term physical continuities of such localities, but also continuities of their characteristic orderings of the various types of ties, both internally and with respect to changing supralocal structures encroaching from the outside. Thus, though the government or even the state may change, the locality continues. Near Eastern villages, as Braidwood somewhere has remarked, Bolivian and other corporate communities, the Russian *mir,* the Indian village "community," and many other forms of locality are cases in point.

Two other features of localities may be noted. First, individuals are identified by their residence in and/or origin from some locality, e.g. an Edinburgher living in Kensington, London, or a Recifense living in favela Tuiutí, in Rio de Janeiro. Residential identification involves no specification as to membership in a community or group, although such membership may actually exist. Again it is an *empirical* question, not a definitional one.

Second, the definition of locality allows for different levels of locality, one including the other; a kind of nested hierarchy, as for example in Rio de Janeiro: favela Babilônia, within the area called Lido, within the area called Copacabana, within the Regional Administration of Copacabana, within the area called the South Zone, within Rio de Janeiro City, within Greater Rio de Janeiro, and so on. Each of these levels is relevant to some set of supralocal institutions, which also occur as a nested hierarchy; or several levels of the one may be in relation to several of the other at the same time.

The amorphousness, multiplicity, and kaleidoscopic quality of the organization of localities, which give rise to the flexibility I have mentioned, are very difficult to grasp intellectually, even by the specially trained. By the same token, they are virtually impossible to legislate for (or against) or to control by uniform sets of sanctions. The only fully effective control over localities, one which would affect all forms of organization, would be total coercion through major application of force. Because of these conditions, localities are almost always found to be characterized by a certain autonomy from external agencies and institutions, a certain ability to enter into relationships with them as independent bodies. This independence is maintained by the "padding" provided by the complex of social relationships in the locality against the impact of these supralocal entities. In this independence and its social and ecological bases is found a locus of power for cooperation with—but especially for resistance against the encroachments of—the supralocal institutions, as will be seen. It is also the basis for the emergence of the true community: a cross-section of all major institutions of society transected by a local, self-maintaining boundary.

The Structure and Resources of Power

Before developing the argument further, we must turn briefly to the subject of power. The literature on power is monumental, but one thing appears to be increasingly clear. A definition of power which narrowly limits itself, on one hand, to the special prerogatives of the state or its personnel or to the institutions of state, or, on the other hand, to the control of strategic resources (which may also be wholly or partly state prerogatives) is entirely inadequate. The essential dimensions of the notion of power appear to be the exercise of some control, as individual or group, over one's own situation and the exercise of some effect on the situation of others. To speak of the *potential* to exercise such controls seems to me useless because it is neither observable nor measurable.

The only intelligible sense in which one might speak of power as potential is by considering the dimensions indicated above simply as the expression in action of a subset of empirically describable attributes among the many possible attributes that statuses, roles, or status and role networks may possess (see Leeds, 1967b: 335-36, note, for definition of these terms). The attributes in question appear to be of two main types: (a) an explicit right or privilege belonging to the status, role, or network by its cultural definition; and (b) a tactical location achieved by virtue of one's position in a status or role network (without any right being defined). Both the right and the tactical location are used to protect interests and prerogatives of the statuses and roles, and their networks and incumbents, by the application of sanctions, however these may be formulated.

The observation and measurement of power involve, then, on one hand, the description of situations in which controls are being exercised and for which the resources involved can be specified, and, on the other, the statuses, roles, and status and role networks, whose attributes are rights and privileges or tactical locations (see Mills, 1956).

When such rights are differentially distributed among two (or more) groups, both of which agree to the right of one of the groups to exercise sanctions, a stable, peaceable arrangement exists. Where each group defines its own right of sanction, it is likely that conflict and opposition exist, and a constant tension and oscillation of power between the groups occur. If tactical locations are differentially distributed among two (or more) groups, relations may be peaceable or antagonistic, depending on whether the group controlling the locations and the non-controlling group do or do not recognize the possession of the tactical location. Where the non-controlling group does not cognize the existence of the tactical location, relations are likely to be peaceable (note, here, the role of ideology); where it does cognize the location, relations are likely to be antagonistic unless no countervailing rights or tactical locations are available to the group.

With respect to the resources of power, we may refer as a point of departure to Bierstedt (1967), who argues that power has three major sources: (a) the control of material resources; (b) the use of organization; and (c) mobilizable masses of persons. He argues that these three sources of power generally correspond to three great classes, respectively an upper, resource-controlling class; a middle class marked by endless arrays of large and small-scale associations; and a lower class represented simply by quantity of personnel—the masses.

Extending Bierstedt's remarks, it is plain that each class in a class system possesses some degree of control over each source, though one of them may predominate. Thus, the groups of people who control strategic resources are also highly organized (e.g. the National Association of Manufacturers, the NAM; thc Chamber of Commerce; the National Farm Bureau), probably *necessarily* so. The organized middle "classes," in the United States at least, are also extremely numerous, perhaps outnumbering the "masses" themselves, that is, those social levels supposedly characterized mainly by large numbers.

It is extremely useful to examine the distribution of Bierstedt's sources of power in the population at large in order to be able to map out power relations. Here we shall examine the distribution of such sources in localities and in the external, or supralocal, institutions which they confront.

Localities and the Sources of Power

The tenor of the preceding discussion has been that localities are in fact highly organized segments of the total population and are characterized by varying degrees of control over certain resources, especially those of territory and personnel, as well as a certain amount of capital, however small (Fried, 1962). Most important, however, is that they are organized, indeed highly organized, but in the very special way I have described; that is, in a multifold, flexible, complex structure. By virtue of their possession of these sources of power, however limited, localities can be considered loci of power in the society at large, varying according to their unique histories, their geographical bases, their position in the locality hierarchy, and so on.

As loci of power, they can, therefore, enter into various sorts of interrelationships with other loci of power, characterized by different conjunctures of power sources. These relationships can be quite dynamic and may be of various sorts, e.g. cooperative, hostile, competitive, autonomous, or *several of these at once.* Actual interrelationships observed between a locality and supralocal institutions are usually of several kinds at one time. The modalities of interaction obtaining at a given moment will depend on the various interests of both parties to the relationship and the social structure of the relationship itself. Where several different localities, especially if of different types, are interacting with several different types of supralocal structures in several different ways, the actual situation may be most complex and its description extremely difficult.

Supralocal Structures and Institutions

We may now turn to supralocal structures and institutions. The term 'supralocal structures' refers to social bodies to whose organizational principles any given set of local and ecological conditions is irrelevant; that is, in their fundamental principles of action, supralocal structures confront any locality, any sociogeographical subunit of the total system or its subdivisions, with uniform, generalized, organizational and operational norms or equipment. "Supralocal institutions" refers to principles and manners of operation of supralocal structures. Any structure whose form is not governed by, or related to, a given locality, and which confronts a number of localities identically, is a supralocal structure operating with supralocal institutions.

Among such supralocal structures and institutions are business organizations of national scale, the banking system, the price-making market or indeed the national economy itself, national political organizations (notably parties), labor unions, large-scale professional and private-interest associations (the NAM; the American Medical Association, the American Anthropological Association), paragovernmental associations (like the association of U.S. state governors or of secretaries of agriculture), and the state itself, including parts of the electoral system, the judiciary, the educational system, monetary agencies, administrative bureaucracies, and so on.

Together, the decision-making personnel of these structures comprise, either directly or indirectly, the major controllers of strategic resources—that is, of one of the significant sources of power. They are themselves highly organized, thereby utilizing another source of power, though availing themselves of only a narrow range of forms of organization. Many of the organizations involve significant masses of people, for example the large labor unions.

It should be noted, in terms of a general model, that supralocal structures such as national business organizations, labor unions, and political parties are recent evolutionary phenomena. Throughout recent evolutionary history, the most widespread supralocal structure has been the state (as opposed to sibs or age-sets, for example, which often would better be designated as "translocal"). For the present, I shall consider only the state and its generic relations to localities, especially in its hostile interactions, returning later to other supralocal institutions like national business organizations and parties.

The State and Localities

The state and its agencies, as social bodies or systems, exercise modes of control over their own situation and especially, of course, over the situations of others by means of a variety of institutions. The ends of state are dual: first, the public coordination, administration, and maintenance of order in the entire polity, and second, its own private self-maintenance as a special-interest group, usually composed of a dominating class or its representatives.

The first, the public end of state—that is, the supervision of the interests of the polity—is itself ambivalent because often the interests of the polity may correspond, for different reasons, to the private interest of the state in maintaining itself. This is the situation in contemporary Mexico where every sector of the polity—business, labor, peasantry, Church, etc.—each for its own reasons, works in the general interest of the polity to foster growth, increase consumption, widen distribution, and maintain order. But the state, in aggrandizing its own power, aims, and control as a private interest group, covertly operates just like the other sectors in the pursuit of its own goals by manipulating the overt—that is, public—ends of state so as to achieve those goals.

This duality of the ends of state entails, in its relationships with localities, a corresponding duality or perhaps, even better, polarity, one end of which involves clear-cut, cooperative relationships arising out of common interests and the other clear-cut antagonisms and struggle. Intermediate stages involve more ambiguous cooperations growing out of *different* goals which may be achieved by common means; rather neutral relations of ambivalent coexistence or generalized autonomy; resistance without overt antagonism, and so on.

These various types of relationship may be seen as a kind of scale. When the pressures of supra-local institutions on localities grow greater, relationships tend to drift toward the antagonistic end of the polarity. As the pressures of the supralocal institutions grow less vigorous or fewer, cooperation and autonomy tend to increase. The semi-autonomous villages or communities described for the Guatemala of twenty or thirty years ago, the Indian village community, and the Russian *mir* are perhaps examples of the latter. Though in each of these cases the pressures were doubtless considerable, yet for the most part they were restricted to a very narrow range of institutions, particularly taxation in money, kind, or labor. In other respects, the localities tended to be left to themselves to manage their own affairs internally. Only in special circumstances or at moments of crisis in the state or the locality did the state exert many and great pressures, including military sanctions, on the locality.

There is, then, always a dual tendency. On one hand, there is the pull towards common assent to the state's policy ends and their associated operations, simply because they contribute to the viability or well-being of the locality in terms of public order, welfare, relief, handling of foreign relations, etc. On the other hand, there is the tendency to antagonism towards the private ends of the state and their associated operations (which may merely be intensifications of the same operations that are used for the public policy ends but to a point beyond endurance), because they deny or curtail the interests, welfare, well-being, etc., of the locality.

A word must be said about the emergence of national business and political structures as supralocal entities. Both of these, for intrinsic structural reasons, require access to large numbers of people for mass labor, memberships, votes, and the like, a condition *not* necessarily characteristic of the structures of the state. It becomes critical for the national business and political structures (though each in its own way) to have direct access to, control over, and use of masses of people. As the structures evolve, they require new forms of articulation between themselves, especially their supralocal decision-making bodies, and the masses of people, whose daily lives are largely locality-oriented in work, homes, schools, and so on. In other words, as society evolves, new types of complementary and dual relationships between localities and supralocal institutions emerge and old ones disappear. Any given historical situation displays combinations of both new and old types, but, of course, the kinds of combinations possible in a given society will vary sequentially as it evolves.

Further, the supralocal decision-makers of each of these types of national structures, while distinct from the mass of personnel of their own organizations, are linked with each other. The linkage is necessary because access to decision-making is itself a resource, and, for both value and operational reasons, must be kept among restricted groups of people.

Not only are the decision-makers linked with one another, even where they are competitive, but also they must, to some minimal degree, be channeled into the state in its role as coordinator of the polity. These linkings may pivot around common ends or around discrete goals—in general, cooperatively achievable. Both conditions are presently observable in Mexico in the relations between the state and parties, business, and labor, all of which tend to become supralocal structures in various complementary, multivalent relationships of opposition, cooperation, and neutrality with localities.

The state, therefore, occupies a key role as a set of supralocal institutions; first, because it is a channel and coordinator for the rest of the supralocal institutions of the society at large, and second, because it does not necessarily depend directly on masses for its resources but can exercise control over resources, numbers, and organizations by virtue of its public polity purposes, in a relatively autonomous and indirect way.

In general the evolution of society involves a continuous adjustment and readjustment between locality and supralocal power institutions. Any shift in resources or the institutions of control brings about shifts in the power relations, shifts which may be responded to by still further adjustments to compensate for the shifts. Power systems, as conceived here, may thus be seen as moving equilibria, occasionally passing into disequilibria or, through quantum leaps, from one equilibrium state to another.

State and Locality—The Favela Case

The dual or multiple relationships between the locality, on one hand, and the state and non-state supralocal institutions, on the other, may be illustrated by the interactions between a special type of locality and a number of supralocal structures. I speak of the urban slum, and shall refer here especially to data on Brazilian favelas[10] and agencies of state.

In brief, the favela is a human-geographic unit, easily observable, possessing all of the forms of organization mentioned above as characteristic of localities. The favela has an ecology, that is, a distribution of social activities across its territory responding to topography, soils, and other

10. Strictly speaking favelas are not slums, but are discussed here as such because they are generally so conceived and treated. If one defines a slum as an area of a city with decaying housing, relatively high rents (in proportion to the salaries of residents), virtually no home ownership, substandard facilities, and high population density, where buildings are ordinarily officially docketed in the appropriate registry of titles, then a favela is not a slum. Favelas, for the most part, are areas of improvement occurring by means of the private investment of generally poor but independent homeowners who are squatters on the lands of others, on which, over time, the facilities tend to improve, though they tend also to be substandard. Population density, as in the slums, is quite high, but this is also true of some solid "middle" and "upper-middle" class areas of Rio de Janeiro, like parts of the south end of Copacabana, with up to about 3000 persons per hectare (CEDUG, 1965:152, 153). What is true of favelas in Rio is also true of Lima's barriadas (see Mangin, 1967; Turner and Mangin, 1963) and squatter settlements in other parts of Latin America.

geographic conditions. This distribution is often governed by, for example, the rain forests on the saddles of the hills dividing Rio de Janeiro into segments, which provide hideouts for criminals, while the thoroughfares at the base of the hills are sites for stores and other economic activities and for the entry of power lines and water supply. Thus, the territorial favela is subdivided into socially specialized zones which pattern daily activities.

On the whole favelas maintain their own order, a truly community-like endeavor. Bringing in the police—a supralocal organization—is rigorously avoided. Yet crime is not rampant in the favela, and even in the absence of the police, agents of the state, public order is generally well-established.

The favela is very complexly organized by kinship, pseudo-kinship, ambience, friendship, workgroup, clique, neighborhood, associational, and other ties. The social behavior of the favela consists of a constant flux among these, at least insofar as interaction takes place within the locality, a point I return to below. The importance of associational life is not to be underestimated, at least in Brazil. Recent evidence indicates that many favelas have an extraordinarily elaborate structure revolving about Carnaval clubs. Presently, many favelas, at least in Rio, also have favela civic associations which provide centralizing nodes of organization. All favelas have several kinds of church associations, as well.

Nevertheless, it should be noted that the social relations occurring in a favela are preeminently of a face-to-face and personal sort, a fact which has led so many writers to speak of the urban "slums" (meaning squatter settlements) of Latin America as being "rural" in social and value structure (cf. Bonilla, 1961, 1962; Pearse, 1957; etc.; also Leeds and Leeds, 1970). The attribute of rurality is made even though the "slum" dwellers have immigrated not from rural areas but from towns where, presumably, the immigrants *should* have learned urban ways. The attribution is even made in instances where the favela dwellers and the favela itself have been *in situ* for two, three, four, and more generations. Descriptions of Rio slums, or *cortiços*, from the mid to late nineteenth century (cf. Azevedo, ca. 1891)[11] are remarkably like those of the mid twentieth century. Observers

11. The *cortiço* no longer exists in Rio, with one or two exceptions. It was a multi-unit rooming house, built by building speculators for low-income rentals, laid out, usually, in a double row with a group of toilets at one end or in the middle of the courtyard where, too, were found the water faucets and laundry tubs which serviced the entire set of rooms. A good deal of community life centered in these rooming house-enclosures and around the wash tubs and water faucets. The *cortiço* residents

have spoken of the favelas as rural enclaves in the city, despite much significant data which makes such descriptions misleading or entirely erroneous.

In this regard, I have already spoken of the existence of associational life in the favela, which is a feature not widely characteristic of rural or peasant areas of Brazil. I have mentioned a fair degree of ecological and social specialization. There are, however, other evidences against this rurality as well. For example, it seems that among those favela dwellers who have indeed come directly from rural areas a rapid shift of values in the direction of an urban orientation often takes place (cf. Cate, 1962, 1963, 1967, and others). Second, there is much evidence that family structure changes (cf. Hammel, 1961, 1964), e.g. towards serial common-law marriages, towards matri-centered family groups, towards a narrowing of the generational range (largely to two, rather than three or even four generations as in the country). Another way of saying this is that the demographic distribution according to age and sex is sharply changed from rural patterns. Other evidence will be discussed below in connection with the external relations of the favela.

Under all these circumstances, the question arises why the face-to-face —the ostensibly "rural" relationships—exist, or, according to current thinking, persist, in the favela. It seems to me that part of the answer to this question lies not in origins (i.e. persistences), but in the fact that these relationships, given the ecology and demography of the favela, must perforce be face-to-face. The other part of the answer, the more important one, lies in the relationships of the favela to its supralocal environment. I am, then, arguing that the long-term continuity of those aspects of the favelas that observers have called "rural" is a functional question and only incidentally a question of origins (or history), and especially so when the favela is considered in the context of supralocal structures and institutions, as I shall try to show.

Favelas as Localities vs. Supralocal Structures and Institutions

How shall we look at these ecological, social, and legal characteristics of the favela (or also of a slum) which we have been discussing? The con-

---

appear to have been one of the pools of people from which the favela populations began to be drawn around the turn of the century and afterwards as the decaying *cortiços* were gradually destroyed, mostly to be replaced by higher-rent housing. With respect to the question of the urbanness of the favela residents, see Leeds and Leeds, 1970.

ceptions of locality power, supralocal power institutions, and their relationships are useful here.

Favelas, as well as slum localities, in Brazil and undoubtedly generally in Latin America and other parts of the world, confront a highly organized set of structures which control strategic resources, make decisions, and operate with respect to the nation as a whole, that is, supralocally. The structures operate both singly, in their own right, and linked together, especially through the state.

The supralocal demands on the favela appear in the form of taxes, ground rents, charges for utilities, draft, police pressure or interference, and, of course, vote solicitation and labor recruitment. Taxes, rents, utility charges, and like institutions are all supralocal institutions which drain notably scarce resources from the locality, whether favela or slum. As a rule, favela social organization apparently mitigates—that is to say, exerts a certain power of resistance against—these drains, unless the demands are too oppressively enforced. Unbeknownst to the supralocal agencies, the social organization may serve to redistribute the meager resources among the favela and slum dwellers by means of mutual aid devices and the like, in such a way as to decrease the take of the agencies. It may operate to make "illicit" uses of utilities. It may help to reduce or evade the payment of rents by keeping all information about unapproved construction tightly within the favela community, entry into which by rentier types for inspection purposes is difficult or unsalutary.

Favela and slum social organization serves as a highly complex but effective communications system which, however limiting the conditions under which it operates, helps to maximize the advantages to be extracted from the external agencies and their personnels, and to reduce stress (cf. pp. 21-22 above). These and a host of other procedures can only be carried out by forms of organization operating specifically within the local ecological units.

However, favela and slum resistance may be more active, as in Brazil today, where favelas, often through their favela civic associations, have moved judicially against unjustified rent practices. The law has also been used for other purposes in recent times. That is, the favela, as a locality, acts as a juridical person against outside pressure. To do so, it makes use of institutions arising from the polity ends of state, against both nonstate supralocal interests and against the interests of the state-as-private-person.

However, from an external point of view, the most important resource of the favela or slum locality is, of course, masses of people: in a place like Rio, where perhaps 20-25 per cent of the city's population lives in "unsightly" favelas, they constitute significant parts of the electorate and of the labor force. They also comprise potentially large forces of riot and rebellion. As an electorate and labor force, from the point of view of the supralocal structures, they are to be mobilized as means to achieve ends of supralocal personnel; as a potential force for riot and disorder, they are to be contained or actively repressed—contradictory tasks of the supralocal agents, between which these agents must necessarily oscillate. These relationships are characteristic of certain types of societies in which mass exploitation is important to the economy and polity—capitalist societies, and possibly others based on private gain from resource control.

These contradictory tasks enjoin a series of relationships with the locality which the locality, in turn, exploits as much as possible or evades by means of its own forms of organization and by use of its available power resources, extremely limited as most of them may be. Thus, for example, the parties, on one hand, and the state in its polity role, on the other, are brought into the position of doing favors for, carrying out public works in, providing public welfare and relief to, the residents of the favelas. In other words, a distribution of resources of the supralocal structures to the locality occurs, which, however limited it may be, nevertheless helps insure the viability of the locality whose sanctions are riot, disorder, non-cooperation or opposition by means of voting, legal recourse, and so on. A response to both status attributes and tactical location—in other words, to power—is made.

On the other hand, when supralocal agencies attempt actively to repress, stress may be minimized by using the flexible organization of the favela or slum. The locality can, for example, use its social structure to spirit away the person or persons sought by the police, make wanted goods and material disappear, withhold information, deceive and mislead with great consistency, and so forth. No one and nothing can be found. The only solution for the supralocal agency is the elimination of the locality itself. In Brazil, there have been instances of this, as when a Rio favela was burned to the ground on the grounds that it was harboring criminals.

In sum, with respect to favela locality organization, it may be said that the viability and long-term continuity of favelas as phenomena can, in considerable part, be accounted for in terms of their effectiveness as loci of power in countering, evading, or making use of pressures of supralocal institutions in the interests of the locality, especially under highly stressful conditions. It may be said, too, that their so-called rural attributes are not necessarily rural at all but the functionally most effective organizational adaptations in the *urban* context in view of their economic, social, and institutional resources and the constraints operating on them. Any other organizational alternative for the larger mass of favela dwellers is likely to put most of them in much worse condition, given the exploitative foundations of the society referred to above, than that which they are constrained to when living in the favela—a fact that must be kept in mind in all development and housing or urban renewal schemes.

Generalizations and Conclusions

Generalizing from the favela material, I would propose that many, if not all, long-term continuities of localities (such as Bolivian corporate communities, the Near Eastern villages Braidwood speaks of as being continuous with ancient times, or the village communities of India), in contrast with the relative changeability of states which have come and gone, may be accounted for in terms of the conception of locality power presented here. The explanation seems to me the more powerful when land resources for food production and military action are involved in the locality situation (cf. Leeds, 1962).

In this regard, as an example, it seems easier to understand the slowness of Soviet agricultural development despite (or better, because of) constant, vigorous, and sometimes violent supralocal pressures. The agricultural populations which have been developing so slowly are locality groupings under pressure, variously resisting supralocal blandishments while preserving their own interests (as yet undescribed[12]). Real revolution in agriculture involves demolition of old forms of locality power and their replacement either by new forms or by total supralocal control.[13]

12. Soviet social scientists have only in the past few years begun to recognize that there is indeed a need here and that "value" and "psychological" aspects play a more active role in society than they had been willing to allow. The German Democratic Republic early recognized this and permitted more local interest openly to operate in agriculture by attempting to preserve, at least in part, the local social arrangements of work even though property was made largely collective (interview with collective farm administrative committee, near Leipzig, G.D.R., August 1964).

13. Most schemes for agrarian reform are not revolutionary in this sense at all but tend rather to foster the ossification of old forms of locality organization. Most of the schemes seem to me, then, preordained to fail from the very beginning. Since the schemes are almost entirely formulated by personnel of the supralocal agencies, one may well ask about the function of such failures.

The institution of the Chinese communes by the Red Chinese supralocal agencies was just such a demolition of old forms and replacement by new, just as the Cultural Revolution destroyed locality features and translocal extensions of the archaic, patriarchal, capital-holding extended family. The implications of this sort of analysis for agrarian reform and community development seem to me numerous but cannot be developed here.

In sum, localities may be looked at as loci of certain forms of power, often in highly attenuated condition; supralocal structures as loci of other forms of power whose intensity of concentration and application may vary greatly over time. Localities and supralocal structures, with their respective forms of power, enter into a variety of oppositional, cooperative, complementary, and other types of relationship which constitute some of the most important structures of the total society, though they have largely been neglected in the literature. They require a great deal of fundamental research. Doing such research requires specification of those forms of national structures and institutions which are almost always, at best, treated peripherally in anthropological studies, though it is specifically the supralocal or national character of these entities that ties communities or localities into a single system. One needs, then, conceptually well-formulated anthropological descriptions of national institutions, of localities and communities, and of the arrangements of their interrelationships. Only then will we be able to develop adequate theories of change and resistance to change.

References Cited

Adams, Richard N.

1967. *The Second Sowing: Power and Secondary Development in Latin America.* San Francisco: Chandler.

1970. *Crucifixion by Power: Essays on Guatemalan National Social Structure, 1944-1966.* Austin: University of Texas Press.

Adams, Richard N., *et al.*

1960. *Social Change in Latin America Today.* New York: Random House, Vintage Books.

Arensberg, Conrad M.

1961. "The Community as Object and Sample." *American Anthropologist* 63(2):241-64.

Azevedo, Aluísio

ca. 1891. *O Cortiço.* São Paulo: Martins (1965). Trans. by Harry W. Brown as *A Brazilian Tenement,* New York: Robert M. McBride, 1926.

Benedict, Ruth F.
1946a. *The Chrysanthemum and the Sword: Patterns of Japanese Behavior.* Boston and New York: Houghton-Mifflin.
1946b. *Thai Culture and Behavior* (mimeo). New York: Institute for Intercultural Studies.
Bierstedt, Robert
1967. "Power and Social Class." In A. Leeds, ed., 1967a, pp. 77-83.
Bonilla, Frank
1961. "Rio's Favelas: The Rural Slum Within the City." *Reports Service* 8(3):1-15. New York: American Universities Field Staff.
1962. "Rio's 'Favelas': The Rural Slum Within the City." *Dissent* 9(4): 383-86.
Bredemeier, Harry C., and R. M. Stephenson
1964. *The Analysis of Social Systems.* New York: Holt, Rinehart, and Winston.
Caplow, Theodore
1955. "The Definition and Measurement of Ambiences." *Social Forces* 34 (1):28-33.
Cate, Katherine Royal
1962. Final Report to the Technical Secretary of the O.A.S. Fellowship Program. Typescript, July 15.
1963. Letter to Dr. Vera Rubin, Director, Research Institute for the Study of Man. September 11.
1967. *O Folclore no Om Carnaval no Recife.* Rio de Janeiro: Ministério da Cultura e Educação, Divisão da Cultura Popular. Published under the name of Katherina Real.
CEDUG
1965. *Guanabara: A Plan for Urban Development.* Athens: Doxiadis Associates for the Comissão Executiva Para o Desenvolvimento Urbano, Guanabara.
Dollard, John
1937. *Caste and Class in a Southern Town.* New York: Harper.
Embree, John F.
1939. *Suye Mura: A Japanese Village.* Chicago: University of Chicago Press.
1945. *The Japanese Nation: A Social Survey.* New York: Rinehart.
Firth, Raymond
1951. *Elements of Social Organization.* London: Watts.
Forman, Shepard
1970. *The Raft Fishermen: Tradition and Change in the Brazilian Peasant Economy.* Bloomington: Indiana University Press.
Fried, Morton H.
1962. "Power Relations Between Local and Translocal Institutions: Centrifugal and Centripetal Tendencies in Chinese Society." Paper read at Annual Meeting, American Anthropological Association. Chicago, November.

Hammel, Eugene A.

1961. "The Family Cycle in a Coastal Peruvian Slum and Village." *American Anthropologist* 63(5):989-1005.

1964. "Some Characteristics of Rural Villages and Urban Slum Populations on the Coast of Peru." *Southwestern Journal of Anthropology* 20: 346-58.

Harris, Marvin

1956. *Town and Country in Brasil.* New York: Columbia University Press.

Hutchinson, Harry W.

1957. *Village and Plantation Life in Northeastern Brazil.* Seattle: University of Washington Press.

Kroeber, A. L.

1948. *Anthropology*. New York: Harcourt, Brace.

Le Besnerais, Henri

1954. "Contribution a l'Etude des Indiens Yaruro." *Journal de la société des Américanistes, Paris* 43:109-22.

Leeds, Anthony

1962. "Borderlands and Elite Circulation: Locality Power Versus Central Power Institutions." Paper read at Annual Meeting, American Anthropological Association. Chicago, November.

1964a. "Brazilian Careers and Social Structure: an Evolutionary Model and Case History." *American Anthropologist* 66(6):1321-47.

1964b. "Brazil and the Myth of Francisco Julião. In Joseph Maier and Richard W. Weatherhead, eds., *Politics of Change in Latin America,* pp. 109-204, 224-47. New York: Praeger.

1964c. "Some Problems of Yaruro Ethnohistory." *Actas y Memorias del 35° Congresso Internacional de Americanistas, Mexico, 1962,* pp. 157-75. Mexico: I.C.A.

1967a. (ed.) *Social Structure, Stratification, and Mobility.* Washington: Pan American Union.

1967b. "Some Problems in the Analysis of Class and the Social Order." In A. Leeds, ed., 1967a, pp. 327-61.

1969. "The Significant Variables Determining the Character of Squatter Settlements." *América Latina* 12(3):44-86.

1970. "Informal Author's Summary." In A. J. Field, ed., *City and Country in the Third World,* pp. 273-76. Cambridge, Mass.: Schenkman.

1971. "The Culture of Poverty—Conceptual, Logical, and Empirical Problems with Perspectives from Brazil and Peru." In E. Leacock, ed., *The Culture of Poverty: A Critique,* pp. 226-84. New York: Simon and Schuster.

In press. "Urban Society Subsumes Rural: Specialties, Nucleations, Countryside, and Networks—Metatheory, Theory, and Method." *Acts, International Congress of Americanists,* Rome, September 1972.

In preparation. *Class and Economy in Brasil: A Total Culture Pattern.* Austin: University of Texas Press. Revision of *Economic Cycles in Brasil,* PhD thesis, Columbia University. Ann Arbor: University Microfilms.

Leeds, Anthony, and Elizabeth Leeds

1970. "Brasil and the Myth of Urban Rurality: Urban Experience, Work, and Values in 'Squatments' of Rio de Janeiro and Lima." In Arthur J. Field, ed., *City and Country in the Third World.* Cambridge, Mass.: Schenkman.

1972. "Favelas and Polity: The Continuity of the Structure of Social Control." *LADAC Occasional Papers,* Series 2, No. 5. Austin: University of Texas, Institute of Latin American Studies.

Lopes, Juarez R. B.

1964. *Relações Industriais na Sociedade Tradicional Brasileira; Estudo de duas Comunidades Mineiras.* Faculdade de Filosofia, Ciências, e Letras de São Paulo. PhD thesis (mimeo).

1965. *Desenvolvimento e Mudança Social: A Formação da Sociedade Urbana-Industrial no Brasil.* São Paulo: Companhia Editôra Nacional.

Lowie, Robert H.

1945. *The German People: A Social Portrait to 1914.* New York: Rinehart.

Lynd, Robert S., and Helen M. Lynd

1929. *Middletown: A Study in American Culture.* New York: Harcourt, Brace.

MacIver, Robert M., and Charles H. Page

1949. *Society: An Introductory Analysis.* New York: Rinehart.

Mangin, William

1967. "Squatter Settlements." *Scientific American.* 217(4):21-29.

Mead, Margaret

1942. *And Keep Your Powder Dry: An Anthropologist Looks At America.* New York: Morrow.

1955. *Soviet Attitudes Towards Authority: An Interdisciplinary Approach Towards Problems of Soviet Character.* New York: William Morrow.

Mills, C. Wright

1956. *The Power Elite.* New York: Oxford University Press.

Morse, Richard

1951. "A Cidade de São Paulo no Período 1855-1870." I: *Sociologia* 13 (3):230-51; II: *Sociologia* 13(4):341-62.

1958. *From Community to Metropolis: A Biography of São Paulo, Brazil.* Gainesville: University of Florida Press.

1965. "The Sociology of San Juan: An Exegesis of Urban Mythology." *Caribbean Studies* 5(2):45-55.

Murdock, George Peter

1949. *Social Structure.* New York: Macmillan.

Oberg, Kalervo, and Thomas Jabiu

1960. *Toledo: um Município da Fronteira Oeste do Paraná.* Rio de Janeiro: Serviço Social Rural.

Pearse, Andrew

1957. "Integração Social das Famílias de Favelados." *Educação e Ciências Sociais* 2(6):245-77.

1958. "Notas Sobra a Organização Social de Uma Favela do Rio de Janeiro." *Educação e Ciências Sociais* 3(7):9-32.

1961. "Some Characteristics of Urbanization in the City of Rio de Janeiro." In Philip Hauser, ed., *Urbanization in Latin America.* New York: UNESCO.

Petrullo, Vicenzo

1939. "The Yaruros of the Capanaparo River, Venezuela." *Bulletin* No. 123, Bureau of American Ethnology, pp. 161-290. Washington: Government Printing Office.

Pierson, Donald

1949. *Cruz das Almas: A Brazilian Village.* Smithsonian Institution, Institute of Social Anthropology, Publication No. 12. Washington: Government Printing Office.

Poppino, Rollie

1953. *Princess of the Sertão: A History of Feira de Santana.* Ph.D. Thesis, Stanford University. Ann Arbor: University Microfilms.

Powdermaker, Hortense

1939. *After Freedom: A Cultural Study of the Deep South.* New York: Viking.

Shirley, Robert W.

1971. *The End of a Tradition: Culture Change and Development in the Municipio of Cunha, São Paulo, Brazil.* New York and London: Columbia University Press.

Smith, T. Lynn

1947. *Brazil: People and Institutions.* Baton Rouge: Louisiana State University Press.

Stein, Stanley

1957. *Vassouras: A Brazilian Coffee County, 1850-1900.* Cambridge: Harvard University Press.

Steward, Julian H.

1950. *Area Research: Theory and Practice.* New York: Social Science Research Council.

1956. (ed.) *The People of Puerto Rico: A Study in Social Anthropology.* Urbana: University of Illinois Press.

Turner, John, and William Mangin

1963. "Dwelling Resources in South America: Urbanization Case Study in Peru." *Architectural Design,* August, pp. 360-93. London.

Wagley, Charles

1949. "Brazil." In Ralph Linton, ed., *Most of the World: the Peoples of Africa, Latin America, and the East Today,* pp. 212-70. New York: Columbia University Press.

1952. (ed.) *Race and Class in Rural Brazil.* Paris: UNESCO.

1953. *Amazon Town: A Study of Man in the Tropics.* New York: Macmillan.

Warner, W. Lloyd, and Paul S. Lunt

1941. *The Social Life of a Modern Community.* New Haven: Yale University Press.

West, James
1945. *Plainville, U.S.A.* New York: Columbia University Press.
Willems, Emílio
1947. *Cunha: Tradição e Transição em uma Cultura Rural do Brasil.* São Paulo: Secretaria da Agricultura do Estado de São Paulo: Directoria de Publicidade Agrícola.
Willems, Emílio, and Giaconda Mussolini
1952. *Buzios Island: A Caiçara Community in Southern Brazil.* American Ethnological Society Monograph XX. Locust Valley, N.Y.: J. J. Augustin.

Urbanization and Role Analysis

Michael Banton

From the very beginnings of anthropological writing there has been a tension between the particularistic descriptions of single tribes or peoples, and the universalistic aspirations of those who would direct scholarly activity to the discovery of general laws. Exponents of both tendencies have needed the contributions of others if their work was not to be meaningless; but the argument about the proper emphasis to be given to these two aspects of research has been continuous and often heated. Urban anthropology is heir to this tension as to other strains in the parent discipline. Some cultural anthropologists have concentrated upon building up comprehensive ethnographies of particular peoples, but to try and assemble the same sort of ethnography of towns would be futile. Towns are not self-contained units of study, for they need to be considered in their human and economic environment. The complexity of urban phenomena is so daunting that the urban anthropologist has a special need for theoretical schemes which will guide investigations and facilitate the comparison of results obtained in different urban centers.

This essay has two starting points, one fairly particular, the other highly generalized. The particular one has been to account for the discrepancies between the interpretation I offered of the structure of social relations in Freetown, Sierra Leone, and that of the urban social system on the Copperbelt of Northern Rhodesia (now Zambia) which was put forward at the same time by social anthropologists associated with the Rhodes-Livingstone Institute. How far were the discrepancies to be attributed to the theoretical approaches employed, and how far were they a consequence of actual differences in the two situations? The subsequent publication of more studies carried out in African and other tropical towns has only increased the importance of this problem. A framework for the comparative analysis is needed if we are to ask why one investigator's results do not resemble those of other workers in this field. The other, more general, starting point has been my interest in the concept of role. A theory which attempts to account for the special characteristics of social life in towns cannot build a definition of the town into its assumptions but must use as units of analysis features of social life in general. The analytical performance of the role concept over the past thirty years has never equaled its apparent promise, and few authors have tried to disperse the surrounding terminological fog to use it in theoretical studies of urban life; nevertheless the feeling persists that it has more potential usefulness than most other units of analysis available. The expression "role theory" can be used in both narrow and broad senses. The narrow usage restricts its application to the more psychological aspects of conduct. The broad usage makes role analysis basically similar to much structural theory in social anthropology. If the rephrasing of structural theory in role concepts adds any further understanding, or links one understanding with others, then there is a case for translating familiar ideas into the language of role analysis. It is with role theory in the broad sense that this essay is concerned.

One strand in the discussion that follows is the argument that two of the most important variables for the comparative analysis of urban social relations are rural-urban continuity and the strength of structural oppositions. The other main strand is the contention that these factors can be brought within the scope of role analysis. This second argument is the more difficult to advance because in places it runs contrary to ideas widely held among anthropologists and sociologists that derive from the work of two notable scholars: Emile Durkheim and Ralph Linton. Durkheim presented urban social systems as more integrated than rural ones. Linton presented the notion of role as a way of conceptualizing the tasks allocated to separate individuals. I seek to point out alternative approaches which are not in conflict with Durkheim's and Linton's views but which may, for some readers, require a reorientation of the way they have thought about familiar topics. Therefore I have had to begin at the beginning with a suggestion as to how we may avoid the usual impasse in the definition of role and a review of Durkheim's conclusion about the "moral density" of society. The next task has been to show how an analysis of roles from the standpoint of their differentiation from one another has very different implications from the more usual approach to roles in terms of their content. It is possible that my argument is incomplete or that the objections to it are more serious than I envisage, but if I have found a new way to approach these questions it is certain to need further refinement. Having, in the first portion of the essay, tried to lay these theoretical foundations, I pass next to a review of some of the ways in which social changes affect the differentiation of roles and then to discussion of how variations in rural-urban continuity and in the strength of structural opposition in urban systems influence the definition of roles within those systems. In the final section these two variables are presented as the axes for a schematic representation of comparative social density. A conceptual framework of this kind might constitute a bridge between microsociological studies of interpersonal relations and macrosociological studies of the characteristics of total urban structures. The importance of the goal is a partial justification for the presumptuous and speculative nature of the attempt to reach it.

Defining "Role"

It is relatively easy to define a particular role—to determine, say, the characteristics of the role of warder for the purpose of analyzing prison organization. It is much more difficult to define the concept of role. Is all social behaviour to be ascribed to some role-relationship? Is there a finite number of roles in any one community—and if not, how can roles be the units in any kind of scientific theory? What kind of consensus must obtain in any population as to the obligations of a given position before it can be counted a role? Some anthropologists regard these as the sort of questions that must be answered at the beginning of an investigation. They attempt to define role in a particular manner and to keep to the definition, but find that if they are to be consistent they have to ignore interesting features of their data. Other writers hold that these questions are the kind that can be answered only at the end of a long series of varied investigations. Not until we have discovered what we can *do* with the notion of role can we know how best to shape it. Having considerable sympathy for this latter viewpoint, I do not propose to summarize or review the recent literature concerning this problem of definition,[1] instructive though it is, but to use the concept in the simplest possible sense as denoting "a set of rights and obligations." This usage is in line with Linton's initial proposal, except that it favours more neutral terms than "duties," which implies moral imperatives as well as socially sanctioned expectations. Furthermore, such a simple definition does not attempt to establish Linton's distinctions between position, status, and role at the outset of the enquiry, though they can be introduced if the analysis requires them.

Roles do not exist apart from social situations. In many situations unmarried girls aged twenty and twenty-one occupy one role, yet there are times when a young woman who has attained her legal majority has rights and obligations that are not extended to someone twelve months her junior. Where a research worker draws the boundaries of particular roles must therefore depend upon the topic he is investigating, and inventories of the numbers of roles can be compiled only with reference to specific problems.

Many avenues of enquiry do not require very delicate prior determination of the content of roles; indeed, it is probably just these lines of work which are the most rewarding at present. Of all the studies in this field conducted by social psychologists in the last fifteen years, probably the most interesting have been the analyses of role conflicts. These studies have concentrated upon situations where people felt two roles to be partially incompatible; behavior was analyzed from the standpoint of two sets of expectations only, and the question of whether it might also belong with yet other roles was excluded by the very nature of the enquiry. These studies dealt with the implications for the actor of conflicting role expectations and the ways in which particular individuals resolved them. Hitherto there has been no explicit and systematic treatment of the implications of role conflict (or absence of conflict) for the social structure, though this offers the sociologist or anthropologist a similar opportunity to get round the difficulties of defining role content comprehensively. Why is it that women (in Britain) can be ministers of religion in certain denominations and not others? What would be the consequences of permitting an individual to occupy both the female role and the priestly role? In struc-

1. See Gross *et al.* (1958) for a concise review by social psychologists that pays particular attention to the question of variations in consensus on role obligations; Rocheblave-Spenlé (1962) for a historical study; Biddle and Thomas (1966), which appeared after this essay had been drafted; Dahrendorf (1964) and Goode (1960) for sociological reviews of the field; for an application to problems germane to those discussed here, note Reader (1964).

tural analysis it is frequently possible to postpone the problems of definition and to investigate empirically why certain roles have to be combined, why others have to be kept apart, and what happens when these principles are not, or cannot be, followed.

Social Density

A sociological interpretation of urbanization must attempt to identify and explain the differences in the quality of social relations in urban and rural surroundings. There have been two chief approaches to this problem; the one stressing changes in economic interdependence, the other changes in the interdependence of social relationships.

The first approach is associated with Durkheim's *Division of Labor in Society*, in which the simpler forms of society are depicted as congeries of small self-sufficient communities. With economic development, they are absorbed into a larger society, and "the progress of the division of labor is in direct ratio to the moral or dynamic density of society" (Durkheim, 1893: 257). According to this view, urban and industrial life is characterized by the interdependence that stems from the division of labor: thus, if the public transport workers go on strike the whole city may be thrown into chaos, and if one group of workers down tools they may endanger the employment of thousands of others. This line of argument has been brought to bear upon the present problem by Aidan Southall. He emphasizes the increase in the number of roles associated with the progressive division of labor and the variety of role relationships that can subsist between city-dwellers. He concludes that "the passage from rural to urban conditions is marked by a rise in the density of role texture" (Southall, 1959: 29).

The second approach starts from a recognition that in small village societies people know one another as individuals and are dependent upon one another for social reputation. One person interacts with another on the basis of several different role relationships, giving rise to a tightly interlocking network of social ties. In the city, on the other hand, many kinds of social relationships are confined in separate compartments and the urbanite has scope to choose his associates; there is much less chance that his partner in one relationship will be his partner in another. From this standpoint urban society reveals a lower social density. Such an approach, though never systematized in a way comparable to Durkheim's, has been implicit in a variety of writings: Simmel (1955: 125-95); Malinowski (1926: 125); Homans ("the effectiveness of control lies in the large number of evils a man brings down on himself when he departs from a group norm," 1951: 289); Nadel ("The advantages of role summation lie in the strengthening of social integration and of social control. For the more roles an individual combines in his person, the more he is linked by relationships with persons in other roles. . . ." 1957: 71); and other writers, especially some of those associated with the Manchester school of social anthropology. This line of argument differs from the Durkheim-Southall approach chiefly in that it focuses upon interpersonal relations and tries to build upwards to a model of the society, where the other view works downward from a macrosociological starting point.

To reconcile the two approaches it is necessary first to take account of a qualification which Durkheim inserted in his own analysis but which he never developed adequately. The passage runs: "It is not enough that society take in a great many people, but they must be, in addition, intimately enough in contact to act and react on one another. If they are, on the contrary, separated by opaque milieux, they can only be bound by rare and weak relations, and it is as if they had small populations." (Durkheim, 1893: 262). While economic advance unites people previously separated, it divides them up again in new ways. The relation of the industrial worker with his employer may be more impersonal even than the relation of the plantation owner with his slave. Great areas of industrial cities are segmented almost exactly in Durkheim's sense; large numbers of people of similar occupation and social status occupy separate territories and are related to other groups only in a relatively few restricted role-relationships. The spheres of the factory and of the home are milieux separated by opaque partitions. Within a particular milieu there may be a dense network of social relations, the various groups being bound together by cross-cutting ties, but between milieux there may be only standardized role-relationships. The level of social interdependence is not uniform throughout an urban society: it tends to be patchy, rising fairly high in certain social islands, falling quite low between them, and being in general lower than in village society.

Even when allowance is made for the segmentary elements in urban life, a conceptual difference between the two approaches remains to be explained. The economic interdependence which impressed Durkheim springs from what people do as occupants of roles, especially work roles. "Moral or dynamic density" is a function of the *content* of roles. The other approach focuses upon how one person occupies several roles; in village society many roles have a wide social significance and custom dictates what combinations of roles are socially appropriate. In the transition to urban living many roles are subdivided and all sorts of new combinations become possible. The lower social density in the city is a consequence of this greater *differentiation* of roles. This distinction should not be used in an inflexible manner, for role content and differentiation are interrelated, but I believe it may be rewarding to try and concentrate on the latter. To take an example, for some years now it has been a sociological commonplace that economic advance is accompanied by role specialization. This is undeniable, but it attracts attention to the content of the roles and away from the central sociological issues. When the sociologist studies the role of physician he is not concerned with medical skill *per se*, but with the implications of professional skills for the organization of medicine, the relations of the doctor to his colleagues, his collaborators (technicians, nurses, etc.), and his patients; the relations of patients to hospital staff, to one another, to their families, etc. The content of a role is usually among the data that the sociologist has to take as given; he considers the implications of different ways of arranging tasks rather than the tasks themselves. Economic advance is equally dependent upon the process of role differentiation, whereby a more flexible social structure is developed which can respond to and exploit technological change.

The technologically primitive society tends to be founded upon a small repertory of undifferentiated roles which are so interrelated that the level of control is high and there are few rewards for innovation. The social order is suffused with moral judgments about the propriety of different modes of conduct, so that problems of technical expediency may not be openly acknowledged. The role structure makes little allowance for individual peculiarities; everyone has to be allocated unequivocally to one of the basic categories, and anomalies such as homosexuals, unmarried mothers, barren wives, and spinsters are forced into the nearest appropriate category even if their case does not quite fit. Thus in primitive society there is frequently appreciable role strain[2] which has to be eased by role-reversal ceremonials like carnavalia. Urbanization breaks up the system of social categories, building up a complex but loose structure of independent roles overlying a pattern of fairly diffuse basic roles. The

2. Cf. Goode (1960a), where role strain is defined as a "felt difficulty in fulfilling role obligations"; for our purpose it is not necessary to limit consideration of role strain to those difficulties of which the actor is conscious.

sheer number of acknowledged roles increases greatly. Important roles continue to be filled by ascription, and kinship is not necessarily weakened, but the old pattern loses significance relative to the new structure of achieved and independent roles. The vetoes upon certain role combinations are lifted and new kinds of choice are forced upon people. The simplest role system would show a single hierarchy of rank, the man at the summit being top in every field of social activity. As societies increase in scale and specialization, the range of choice is such that even the richest and ablest man cannot engage in everything: he must choose the kinds of activity that interest him and allow others to score in the remaining fields. Consequently the strains of urban living do not flow from the restrictions of the role structure but from its very flexibility, which generates problems of adjustment. European observers of African and Middle Eastern towns have been inclined to comment upon the squalor and misery frequently found there. This judgment often stems from the observers' unexamined assumptions about the arcadian qualities of a bucolic existence. The immigrants generally believe themselves to be better off in the town. Whatever their standard of living as measured by, say, calorie intake, they value the freedom and variety of urban living. I suggest that this feeling springs in part from the greater differentiation of roles and that the new social opportunities can be as much a source of stimulus as of strain.

Measuring Role Differentiation

The foregoing argument assumes that roles can be placed along a continuum varying from one extreme, where they are little differentiated, to another, where they are interdependent. It is not possible to construct such a scale with any precision, but the idea of one is, I submit, useful as a sort of mental exercise in clarifying the issues and suggesting propositions on a less abstract level which could possibly be put to empirical test. Relatively undifferentiated roles are ones that are relevant to behavior in a wide range of situations. Sex and age roles are obvious examples. A person's sex role usually affects the way people respond to him or her more than does any other role; in almost any interpersonal situation norms of propriety are associated with sex roles and usually supported by sanctions of some kind. This wide situational relevance of sex roles is expressed in the restrictions that prohibit the incumbent from taking up certain roles and oblige him or her to interpret many other roles in a particular manner (note, for example, the norms of seemliness governing a married woman's relations with other men). Relatively undifferentiated roles have implications for the actor's incumbency of most other roles. Independent roles are ones that have few such implications; many leisure roles are of this kind. Elsewhere (Banton 1965: 33-35) I have envisaged a scale of differentiation divided roughly into three sections: basic roles, general roles and independent roles, like this:

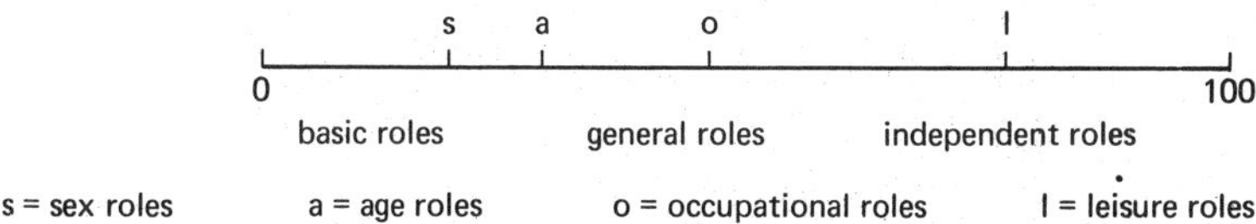

As societies advance in productive and technological sophistication the behavioral relevance of age and sex roles is restricted and declines in importance. The social structure of industrial societies is founded on a complex system of independent roles which overlies the pattern of basic roles. The two kinds of society may be compared as follows:

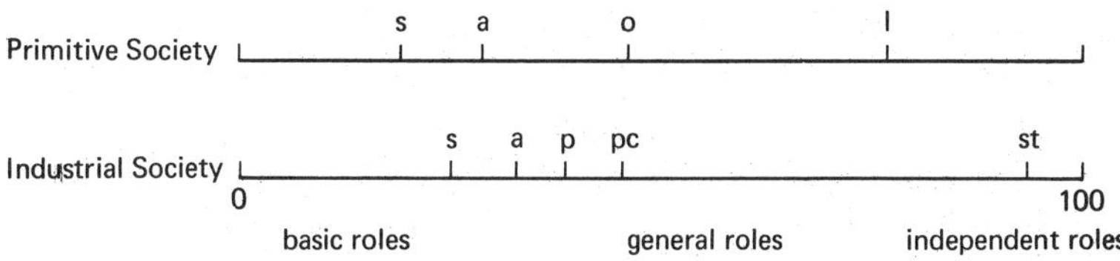

In primitive society sex (s) and age (a) roles are little differentiated; occupational roles (o) provide some liberty of choice, and leisure roles (l) somewhat more. In industrial society sex and age roles are more differentiated; certain occupations, e.g. priest (p) and policeman (pc), are hedged round with varied restrictions and expectations limiting incumbents' social liberty, but many others, e.g. student (st), can be combined with almost all other roles in the social repertory.

There are difficulties in any such comparison. Are the items strictly comparable? To compare a category of roles, like age roles, with a specific role, like policeman, is scarcely legitimate. Similarly, a category like "sex roles" is not homogeneous: the role of female tends to be less independent of other roles than that of male. Since the scale tries to order the extent to which incumbency of one role has implications for the same person's incumbency of other roles, it does not deal directly with role behavior, i.e. a person's conduct towards someone occupying a reciprocal role. This belongs with role content. To exclude considerations of content creates special difficulties in respect of kinship roles, for their interpersonal significance lies principally in their content, the way they signalize social obligations. Incumbency of one kinship role excludes the possibility of the individual's occupying certain others; but this problem is best approached by the traditional methods of anthropological analysis. Some kinship roles can be given meaningful positions on a scale of differentiation—for example, the role of mother may confer prestige and give a woman the privilege of associating with the matrons—but many kinship roles like niece and nephew are of little social significance except in relation to specific partners (i.e. aunts and uncles). While these difficulties do not invalidate the approach outlined, they indicate one of its limitations. Another snag is that, as we have seen, urban societies divide up into relatively independent social realms and a role which is important in one may have no significance in another. The obstacles which a general theory of role differentiation must overcome if it is to be of use in the analysis of interpersonal behaviour are quite forbidding, but nevertheless the idea of such a scale may suggest particular research problems of a manageable kind. For example, the differentiation of the same role in different places can be measured: the role of schoolteacher may be more independent in the town than in nearby villages, and analysis of such variations might find them related to job satisfaction and turnover. Changes in the implications of a role over a period of years can be investigated or two fairly similar roles compared.

How Differentiation Occurs

The spread of new social norms is in part a psychological process of learning and of the adaptation of cognitive structure. But learning occurs within social contexts, and while some of these force individuals to change their ideas quite rapidly, other contexts make less pressing demands. It is therefore of the greatest importance to avoid thinking of social change as the gradual spread of ideas through a society. It is more fruitful to visualize societies as divided into partially independent compartments or sectors which change at different rates. Conduct in one sector may be organized completely in terms of the new values, while an adjacent sector is scarcely affected by them. A suitable illustration of this may be found in studies of the introduction of cash transactions into subsistence economies. In many parts of Africa, young men have gone off to the towns to earn money to meet tax obligations and obtain trade goods: blankets, clothing, household utensils, guns, bicycles. To have spent their money on subsistence goods would, in their view, have been to waste it: such things were exchanged or given as an expression of social obligation, not in return for cash. The next step is to use money to substitute for goods given to meet social obligations, as with bridewealth or feast-giving. Only later do cash transactions come in as payment for foodstuffs or shelter (Reining, 1959, cf. Bohannan, 1955). Change often occurs by new situations being added to the customary pattern: in these new situations people observe norms which to an outside observer might seem inconsistent with those acknowledged elsewhere. Thus Bruner observes that the Batak elite in Medan have not modified their traditional marriage ceremony. They have added a church service as the opening phase and a western-style reception as the closing phase. This last is an urban innovation. Guests at the traditional ceremony are seated according to their position in the genealogical structure and the values of kinship receive full recognition. But the reception is a gathering of elite personnel from different ethnic groups organized in terms of the participants' social status. The two fields of social relationships are compartmentalized (Bruner, 1961: 517).

That social change progresses sector by sector is most evident when urban influences spread out into the countryside, but the same principle holds for changes within the urban community. Migrants may accept the old norms of propriety as valid but circumscribe them by asserting that they hold only in the villages; or European-style norms may be endorsed in the workplace while traditional ones retain their influence over domestic relations. Nevertheless, there are limits to the extent to which adjacent sectors can be organized on conflicting principles. Individuals may come to feel that the inconsistency is intellectually disturbing and seek to reduce the level of normative dissonance. Or there may be a direct feedback from one social field into another. For example, young men in industrial employment regularly earn more money than their elders, which brings them increased influence in other spheres of social life, and therefore tends to erode one of the traditional bases of authority.

In the simplest role systems the role of adult male specifies the conduct expected of incumbents in most fields of activity. As societies increase in scale and complexity this role is split up, step by step, into a multiplicity of roles, many of which are alternatives or specializations. A similar process is apparent in the case of the female role. In traditional African society a woman has usually to live in the household of some male; she cannot take much initiative in communal life unless, by a jural fiction, she is allowed to assume a male role. In parts of West Africa a woman is expected to make a contribution to the household economy; in the country she can do this by farming, in the city the best opening may be through petty trade. But her activities as a trader give the woman a financial and personal independence of her husband that farm work never could. Those who have established their independence through some extra-familial role lead the way in resisting polygamy, assuming leadership roles, and in building up matrifocal households. In Freetown, Sierra Leone, I thought it notable that very many of the important older women—section chiefs, senior officials of companies, etc.—lived singly and had not remarried after losing their husbands (Banton, 1957: 197-98). A Nigerian study emphasizes that the independence of urban women is based upon their enlarged opportunities to acquire a personal income (Baker and Bird, 1959: 103-6 and 109). A recent survey from the Republic of South Africa shows that the pattern of disorganization, promiscuity, and marital instability in the city obscures a new tendency which permits urban Xhosa women to run their own households and support their own children. The social price they pay for their independence and for the absence of a legitimate husband is only loss of esteem—and this may be worth it (Pauw, 1962: viii, 146-49, and 153-59). These observations relate chiefly to working-class women. As in Latin America (Gillin, 1960: 49), even more dramatic changes are occurring where middle-class women are entering public employment.

A kind of situation which illustrates better than most how the compartmentalization of different milieux affects changes in the woman's role is highlighted in a report from Zaïre.[3] Congolese politicians have found it embarrassing to take their wives to diplomatic functions, and so a new and relatively well-rewarded role of *femme libre* or female consort has been recognized. The wives seem content to make over their new and unwelcome social obligations to these women, provided they keep to their role of consort. This is reminiscent of the situation in Japan, where traditionally the role of wife and mother was sharply set off from that of the geisha, whose obligations were those of courtesan, consort, and entertainer. The geisha still serves as a device helping the Japanese business-

3. *Vide* correspondent's report in *New Society*, 21 xi 1963, pp. 4-5.

man maintain traditional domestic relations, but in urban industrial Japan she is now vastly outnumbered by bar-girls, hostesses, and other women who play a role which in this respect is similar to hers. In other social structures, however, it seems as if there is no room for any new intermediate role. In West Africa, men who have risen in the social scale have often felt obliged either to divorce an illiterate wife in order to seek an educated spouse who can play the roles of hostess and consort, or to relegate the illiterate wife to a subordinate position and marry a new one (Busia, 1950: 42-43; Little, 1965: 120). Similar pressures upon Zambian trades-union leaders have been mentioned (Epstein, 1958: 237). In some countries, therefore, pressure for change in the wife's role is met by the creation of a new in-between role, but elsewhere this solution is not possible and in the groups most exposed to change the wife's role is redefined fairly radically within one generation.

What determines the strength and timing of the pressure upon the traditional role of wife? First, there may be a time gap in the impact of new influences upon the two sex roles. In Africa it has been the men who have had to assume leadership roles in response to challenges generated by world political and economic forces. Their wives did not have to make a comparable response to changing circumstances so early. In West Africa, where there has long been a Westernized middle class, the time interval was smaller than in the Congo, and the process of adjustment had been at work over a much longer period. Second, when it is difficult to compartmentalize different spheres of social relations, changes must be made more quickly. In the West African countries Western influences had affected traditional life deeply, so that the whole society was in the process of change. In the Congo, the occupational life of the urban elite formed a sphere of social life relatively separate both from traditional life in the countryside and from the domestic life of the politicians in question. Third, it is relevant to note that urban industrial society places a new value upon informal sociability as a counterweight to high mobility and to the restrictions stemming from the formally-structured organizations in which most people work. In some occupations—diplomatic posts are a striking example—there is less distinction between work and leisure spheres; informal contacts are used to supplement and test out people's behavior in their formal roles (cf. Banton, 1965: 144-45). People who have to represent their countries or their organizations cannot conceal their private lives so easily, and their dependents must share some of the burden of representation.

Changes in age roles follow lines similar to the changes in sex roles. Several studies document the emergence of the Western-oriented young men as a distinctive social grouping with their own styles of living. In the political sphere opposition between old and new may be very noticeable. One of the Copperbelt studies shows how tribal elders were first utilized as labor representatives because men with traditional authority were thought of as the legitimate leaders in the mining community also. When an industrial dispute developed, the old men were disavowed by the strikers and a new, industry-based pattern of labor leadership developed (Epstein, 1958). The nationalist movements of Africa illustrate time and again the separation of political leadership from the earlier pattern of basic roles. Yet in examining the role structure of urban communities it is necessary to note not only the progressive differentiation and splitting up of the old role interdependencies based upon sex, age, and descent, but also the crystallizing of new lines along which roles are clustered. Newcomers to a city are often forced into new role combinations. When Jewish and Christian minorities have been introduced into caste societies, they have taken on the characteristics of castes. (Strizower, 1959, Hutton, 1946: 2). In the same way, ethnic minorities in class societies are characterized in class terms. With urbanization and increased social mobility in Brazil there seems to have been a stronger tendency to emphasize racial characteristics as criteria of social status. (Wagley, 1952: 155; Bastide, 1957: 502-12). The African data show that membership in tribal or ethnic groupings does not remain relevant to behavior in urban, or any other, surroundings unless it is vested with significance by the social structure. In many situations it is given such significance. People acquire a tribal identity only when they meet persons ascribed to other tribal groups, so that "tribalism" as a feature of interpersonal relations is a product of the city and the labor camp. Tribal roles remain important in the cities as a basis for categoric interaction and because they often become associated with stereotyped beliefs about group customs, social status, etc. When political movements acquire a tribal foundation, this may lead to a major split such that tribal affiliation becomes the mark of a basic role relevant in a great variety of situations. One of the most important new kinds of role combinations associated with urbanization is the formation of social classes. A recent study of rehousing in Lagos, Nigeria, found that whereas most of the Yoruba residents of the central district found life in an outlying estate unattractive, a minority welcomed the independence it gave them. By comparison with the central area the population of the estate included a significantly higher proportion of non-Yoruba, Christians, young men, and wage-earners, especially clerks. "It attracted above all the employees of Government and commercial firms, men from the Eastern Region whose close family ties in Lagos were few, the young rebel escaping from a domineering family." (Marris, 1961: 100) Some of the factors affecting the formation of classes and the significance of such groupings are discussed in subsequent sections of this essay.

Rural-Urban Continuity

Many of the earlier studies of life in African towns were organized round the concept of "detribalization," which emphasized psychological changes in the individual and distracted attention from the way social systems can oblige people to conform to their norms without necessarily undergoing any fundamental psychological change. Opposing this tendency, Max Gluckman has argued that from the sociological standpoint it is more appropriate to see rural and urban life as constituting two distinct social systems, and to trace out the implications of each system for the behavior of people who participate in it. An African miner is to be seen as a miner first, and as an African second. When he is working in the town he is a townsman; when he goes back to his family village he becomes a countryman again (Gluckman, 1960, 1961). In an analysis of some of the concepts used by Gluckman and his associates which helps clarify their argument, Philip Mayer shows that everything occurring within the town is not equally urban, and that the most interesting contrast is between typically urban sets of social relations and other sets which, even though they may be town-located, could develop in other surroundings (Mayer, 1962: 584-85). He goes on to show from his own material concerning East London, South Africa, how the demands of the urban system require urban behavior of the migrant at work but leave him with a range of choice in other situations. In his leisure time he can choose to follow rural or urban models or compromise at some point along the scale. Moreover, he may, in the course of time, move along the scale until he becomes what the people themselves recognize as a "real townsman" (Mayer, 1962: 588-89).

These analyses successfully distinguish the ongoing nature of the urban system from the nature of the migrant personnel, but they do not yet provide us with a basis for comparing the phenomena of urbanization in different localities. Gluckman's statement about the distinctive character of urban living can be viewed either as a methodological principle instructing us to examine the interconnections of urban institutions or as an empirical proposition asserting that rural and urban social systems are radically different. The former implication is excellent advice but the latter requires closer examination. In Zambia there is a striking contrast between the two systems, but elsewhere the difference is less marked. In East London a "Red" migrant is in the city but not of the city. In Medan, Sumatra, he may lead a life unaffected by urban institutions. The vast majority of the urban lower class in Brazilian cities do not acknowledge urban values but are "peasants living in the city" (Wagley, 1960: 211). In West Africa the countryside has been permeated by urban values to a greater extent than in Zambia, and the nature of the urban system with respect to employment and housing discourages the perpetuation of rural social patterns to a lesser extent (e.g. Banton, 1957; Frankel, 1964; Lloyd, 1959). The degree of continuity between the rural and the urban social systems is therefore a factor that should be subjected to empirical examination. It is also important to any explanation of many variations in the social structure of different cities (Southall, 1961: 6-11, 19).

While it is not possible to adopt any particular index of rural-urban continuity, some of the relevant factors can be readily distinguished. Continuity will be high where there are many migrants from the same ethnic division or local group because they will then reinforce one another's attitudes. This will be especially strong where the migrants are interrelated by pre-migration ties of kinship or neighborhood and where the immigrant community has a balanced age and sex structure. Mutual reinforcement will be stronger where they can inhabit the same urban locality and where they can buy their own housing. Such migrant concentrations are more frequent in rapidly-growing towns than in mature industrial cities. Where migrants are able to obtain employment in the same kind of work under supervisors from their own group, these ties of community are further strengthened. A final factor is one that recalls the "laws of migration" propounded by Ravenstein eighty years ago.[4] He showed, from European population figures, that while the current of migration was towards the cities, it tended to go stage by stage for short distances only (Ravenstein, 1885: 198-99). Where this law holds, the migrants learn city ways relatively gradually and there is less chance of

4. The author was reminded of the relevance of Ravenstein's work by J. Clyde Mitchell.

the two social systems being completely different. The town of Chimbote, described in this volume by Stillman Bradfield, exemplifies this, for it is a *mestizo* town populated by migrants who have moved stage by stage. The social life of a Peruvian town with a high proportion of Indians in its population would show different features.

Rural-urban continuity will be low when migrants from the same rural social groups are few in number, not interrelated, unevenly distributed with respect to age and sex, scattered throughout a large city, etc. It will be further reduced when, as on the Copperbelt, they are living in a mine compound in houses allocated them by their employers and they work under the supervision of Europeans or boss-boys who are prevented from recognizing social ties declared irrelevant by the formal structure of the concern. In East London religious ethic seems also to play a part, Christian migrants being less involved in home-based groups—though the evidence on this score from Cape Town suggests that this inference should be regarded with caution (Mayer, 1964). The pattern of migration is also relevant. Ravenstein specified, as an exception to his law, that where a town was growing much more rapidly than the surrounding region it had to draw migrants from further afield (1885: 214-18). The Copperbelt towns exemplify this: because the migrants come straight there from distant regions, the difference between rural and urban social patterns is greater, and they have less in common with other migrants who have come equal distances but from other directions. Rural-urban continuity is therefore lower. It is in such circumstances that an urban identity (such as the idea of the "real townsman" described by Mayer) is most likely to develop. In some circumstances there may be considerable pressure on a migrant to adopt an urban identity *vis à vis* his country cousins.

In the traditional village, a man interacts with the same individuals over and over again. One of his chief concerns is to maintain his reputation with his peer group. Very rarely does he have to worry about managing a relationship with a stranger; in fact, the more tightly integrated is his society, the more resolutely will it rebuff strangers. Where rural-urban continuity is high, the migrant will maintain something of the same outlook, taking his relatives and former neighbors as a positive reference group. But the general effect of migration is to remove individuals from the controls exerted by their old peer groups and to give them new scope for choice. Where rural-urban continuity is low, a worker is more likely to live entirely within the city, both physically and psychologically. He has continually to deal with strangers, and their standards have in many cases to be taken as models. He cannot rely upon peer group sanctions but must develop interpersonal controls on a new basis. Therefore the greater the discontinuity between an urban social system and the way of life of the surrounding region, the more highly integrated will that system be; or to express the same proposition in a different way, to the extent that town life constitutes an independent set of social relations, so much will these relations constitute a tighter social network displaying a higher level of social density.

Structural Opposition in the Urban Social System

Another major factor determining the roles open to an urban migrant and the kinds of role-combinations that are standardized is the pattern of relations between social groupings. In the town of Luanshya studied by Epstein, migrant workers in the mines were faced by the monolithic power of the mining company. They were obliged to organize in a similarly monolithic fashion in defense of their own interests (Epstein, 1959: 123-24). The opposition between the company and the Mine Workers' Union (made sharper by the pressure on company policies exerted by white supervisory workers) influenced workers' roles *vis à vis* one another. The miner was forced by his peers to be a trade unionist. The demands of fraternal solidarity helped define his roles at work and in situations of political tension; sanctions upon deviant behavior could be powerful and could override ethnic ties. But within the African community other divisions—of tribe and class—opened up when internal issues were under discussion and there was no sense of pressure from Europeans, suggesting that the stronger the solidarity a group shows in response to external threat, the more readily it divides internally when the threat is absent. In many other towns—both in Africa and in other regions—the social cleavages either have not gone so deep or have not yet developed to the point at which they have so diverse an effect upon social relations. This question therefore requires explicit consideration in comparative analysis.

Three factors seem to be of chief importance in determining the extent and strength of structural opposition: the stability of the cleavages; the balance of the opposed units; and the location of power.

Where a population is divided into social categories based upon stable and relatively visible criteria like race, caste, and ethnic group (especially when the latter is associated with linguistic, religious, and customary differences), this makes for a rigidity in the structure and for the allocation of many important roles by ascription. Such distinctions lend themselves to categoric interaction across group lines, to a high level of group opposition, and therefore to a greater degree of social density within groups. Because people cannot—within the space of two generations—move out of such a group, they may seek to make membership a source of strength by organizing other activities on the basis of it. They have stronger sanctions over deviants when these cannot resign from their race, caste, or ethnic group. Thus where economic growth is relatively low and much employment is not related to technical skills, ethnic differences may be projected into the labor market and the phenomena of "urban tribalism" or ethnicity analyzed by Shack (in this volume) make their appearance. An extreme example of how racial cleavages may prevent role differentiation and preserve certain combinations is provided by the Bantu clerk in South Africa. The attitudes of the whites prevent his developing his administrative skills, while peer group pressures from fellow Bantu (and his sympathies with them) militate against his assuming a dispassionate bureaucratic role (Sherwood, 1958: 298-99). Similar conflicts arise for headmasters and nursing sisters (Wilson and Mafeje, 1963: 148-49).

Where the major social cleavages are based upon unstable characteristics, notably economic class or social status reckoning, the position is otherwise. Intergroup relations occur mostly within the context of work institutions organized on a formal basis, which distracts attention from social features belonging to other realms of activity. In the residential and leisure sphere, classes and status groups tend to be segregated, and contacts between groups are minimized. Upwardly mobile members of lower-status groups do not threaten the social order because they are assimilated into groups higher up the scale. Thus in Monrovia, the capital of Liberia, where racial cleavages are absent and the caste-like division between the Americo-Liberians and the tribal people has been replaced by a continuous pattern of social differentiation which permits an appreciable degree of mobility, there are no sharp conflicts of interest or outlook identified with particular groups. The social structure of the city can be represented as forming a homogeneous pyramid in which the political elite is the economic elite and is also the social elite (Fraenkel 1964). Proletarian immigrants do not form groups in any politically significant pattern of structural opposition. Similarly, in Latin American cities much of the political power is located in informal structures based on clientage in which benefits are handed down in return for votes and loyalty. One author refers to this as "populism" and states that it "does not favour the organization of common interest groups or co-operative groups, and power is usually delegated downwards rather than upwards." He describes populism as being, from the standpoint of the propertied classes, "an attempt to maintain traditional privilege and authority in face of the institution of constitutional democracy . . ." (Pearse, 1961: 201-2). Unless class differences are tied tightly to economic opportunities and the underprivileged groups become sharply conscious of their subordination, class or status cleavages do not constitute so pervasive an organizing principle of interpersonal relations as racial or ethnic divisions.

The important question, however, is not whether the lines of social division run vertically along ethnic or horizontally along class lines, but the significance vested in the divisions by felt opposition, whatever its source. This is illustrated by the contrast Epstein draws between the patterns of social relations in the mining compound at Luanshya and in the nearby municipal location. Because of the miners' sense of opposition *vis à vis* the company, "the province of Union activity is not confined to the issues of wages and working conditions . . . it is to a large extent co-extensive with life on the mine itself . . ." (1958: 126). To the "unitary" structure of the compound he contrasts the "atomistic" structure of the location. The residents in the location work for a variety of employers, and there are hardly any situations which bring them together as a solidary bloc opposed to a comparable grouping. Consequently the internal structure "is marked by a higher degree of flux" and is "less integrated" (Epstein, 1958: 191; 1964: 87-94). The racial, tribal, and class differentiae are the same in the two communities; in the former they are utilized to structure a wide range of social situations in an unequivocal fashion, but in the latter they are not tied so closely to economic interests, so that the structure is loose, more ambiguous, and more open to manipulation. The East London locations, while showing a similar pattern of racial and tribal differentiation, also reveal an "atomistic" structure. Their inhabitants work for many different employers and live (as owners or as lodgers) in privately owned dwellings in shantytowns, so they are not even direct tenants of the only monolithic power on the White side—the municipal corporation (Mayer, 1962: 583). Again, in East London the birth-determined ethnic categories are overlaid by the choice between a migrant or an urban identity. In many situations what matters most is whether someone presents himself as a "real townsman" rather than as a Red or School migrant (Mayer, 1962: 588). Consequently, less force lies behind opposition between Red and School Xhosa. Nevertheless it is always easier to breathe life into ethnic divisions when circumstances change. It is interesting that Mangin (essay in this volume) should report that there is a growing Quechua nationalism in Peru, everywhere evident in Lima, and nurtured by regional associations. Ethnicity may become more important in Latin American cities; its continuing strength in towns such as New York, Quebec, and Brussels shows that urbanism does not necessarily weaken ethnic grouping.

On the Copperbelt at the time the relevant studies were conducted, there was a sharp cleavage between the black and white groups and a relative balance of power between them. The intermediary groups, such as Coloureds and Indians, were politically unimportant. In situations involving no opposition between blacks and whites, the white group divided along lines of class and political loyalty. In similar situations the African group divided along lines of class or tribal affiliation. Within a group of people of similar class background, dissensions coinciding with tribal groupings attracted most attention, and all sorts of oppositions tended to be phrased in terms of tribalism. Within a group of people from the same tribe splits occurred more readily along class lines (Mitchell, 1956: 43). Of the two, it seems as if tribal divisions were the more readily appreciated in the early fifties, for Epstein shows how a conflict of interests within the Mine Workers' Union aligned with emerging class distinctions was interpreted by Africans as an expression of intertribal hostility (Epstein, 1958: 235-36). But class and tribal divisions were obliterated when next the Africans found themselves in a situation evoking racial loyalties. This degree of balance and equilibrium is relatively rare in urban populations, even when ethnic distinctions are relatively important. In Freetown, the non-European population was, at the time of my research, divided between the Creoles and the tribal people, who, in some situations, felt more opposition towards each other than towards the British. Intermediary groups, notably the Lebanese, though not powerful politically, played more important parts than any comparable groups in Central Africa. Moreover class distinctions within the African population were much greater and the economic basis of national life was more diversified. Consequently cross-cutting ties between groups were stronger and there was no clear pattern of balanced opposition (Banton, 1957: 77-78, 97-98, 107-8).

In East London opposition is muted for a different reason: the Government has effectively prevented the Africans from combining. The position in this town, however, is of crucial interest because it enables us to study the implications of rural-urban continuity for group opposition. Continuity is higher in respect of the "School" migrants, for school and urban people have in common many basic institutions, and school people do not necessarily disapprove of their fellows "becoming townspeople" (Mayer, 1961: 76-78, 207-8). The Red migrants came from a similar physical but a different cultural environment: they cultivate traditional Xhosa values and depreciate the value of education. The continuity between the rural and urban social systems is therefore lower in their case. There is a choice: either they can abandon traditional values as poor guides to conduct in a new social system, or they can draw together—incapsulate themselves, in Mayer's terminology—to preserve their culture as an island in the urban sea. Where the latter choice is adopted, opposition between the ethnic minority and other groups is likely to be higher: social density within the ethnic group will also be higher. This is, perhaps, a commonsense inference, but illustrative detail is available from a study of Red and School migrants' conceptions of prestige (Mayer, 1961: 66, 77) and from generalizations about the close-knit nature of the Reds' social networks by comparison with the loose networks of the School migrants (Mayer, 1961: 287-93). Similarly in Freetown the Hausa migrant traders from Nigeria, and other trading groups from the interior, tended to form tightly integrated minorities by comparison with the peoples from the immediate hinterland.

In the post-colonial situation of many African towns, the white-black opposition has been robbed of its strength by political change, social stratification has become more significant, and the government has wished to obviate intertribal conflicts. Outside Africa ethnic distinctions sometimes attain considerable significance, as with the Batak, who were originally reviled as pig-eaters and cannibals by the Muslim majority in Medan. Even today there is no way for a matrilineal Minangkabau Moslem to marry a patrilineal Batak Christian (Bruner, 1963: 511, 514). The opposition which the Batak feels between his group and the remainder is relatively high and must reinforce the internal structure of his group. But a Minangkabau Moslem may not have the same sense of belonging to a minority, so the pattern of structural opposition is probably less inclusive than on the Copperbelt. In many of the South American cities opposition appears to be low. Indian ethnic groups do not organize on a communal basis; many of their more enterprising members pass into intermediate groups like the *mestizo*; as in East London, social classification depends chiefly upon personal identification and achievement.

A further factor to be considered is the location of power. In Luanshya the strongest opposition was between the mining company and the miners resident in the mine compound. Disputes over pay and conditions of work could be settled on the spot, which must have been a stimulus to combination on the workers' part. In some towns this is not the case. Bradfield explains that in Chimbote, for example, all disputes have to be referred to Lima: conflicts escalate up the structure to the center of power where they are fought out by the representatives of decentralized interests. In such circumstances there is presumably less incentive to combine, and groups do not achieve solidarity so readily.

The effect of a developed structure of opposed groups is to regulate social relations over a much wider range than can be achieved on the basis of ties of personal acquaintance and neighborliness. It provides members of the society with social categories in which they can place most of the people they meet and tells them something of the behavior appropriate to these relationships.

Social Density and Role Differentiation

I have argued that the study of variations in social density is of particular relevance to the urban anthropologist because this is one of the chief dimensions distinguishing the texture of social relations in town and country and in different towns or sections of towns. Two of the chief determinants of social density in towns seem to be rural-urban continuity and structural opposition, and in the adjacent diagram I have represented my arguments schematically. The diagram seeks to clarify the kind of social network in which a representative member of a given group within a particular town is likely to be involved. Probably the variations in this respect for persons playing different roles are too great, and the splits between different social realms—such as those of work and leisure—are too deep, for such a schema to have any general validity, but it may nevertheless suggest problems for further research and analysis.

It would be valuable to have more comparative data on the social networks of different groups of migrants in the same towns and upon similar groups of migrants in different towns. When clerks in Medan, Addis Ababa, and General Benavides invite guests to a celebration, is their selection biased towards people of similar ethnic background or similar

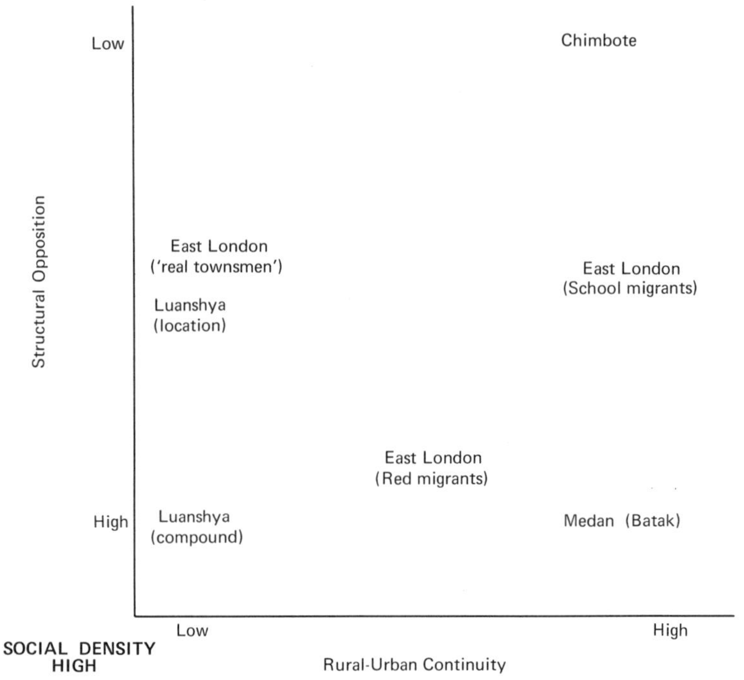

Characteristics of Social Relations in Selected Urban Milieus

social status? Can variations in the cross-tribal marriage rate in African cities be related to the emergence of social strata? Is there, in Latin American cities, any functional equivalent of cross-tribal marriage? Then it would be useful to examine the ways in which different networks are mobilized (it should not be forgotten that even the corporate lineage in a traditional society following unilineal descent is a collection of people who combine only when some incident activates the system of group relations). Bradfield describes voluntary associations which rarely assemble but which have a *directoria* that meets frequently; the committee services the network and activates it when necessary. Observers of community life on housing estates in Britain have often advanced similar observations: tenant activity is intense when there is a dispute over rents but as soon as an issue is settled tenants' associations relapse into indifference. In places where intergroup conflict is frequent, however, ties of allegiance are continually tested.

This is where the discussion of social density relates to role theory in a narrower sense. The more frequently people are called upon to play distinctive roles, the more necessary is it that these roles should be articulated with the other ones constituting the network. The greater the density, the clearer must be the definition of roles. This conclusion was reached in the course of a comparison of the roles of police officer in Scotland and the United States. The Scottish police officer, working in a more closely textured society, has to be more careful to keep his occupational role uncontaminated by off-the-job associations; in dealing with citizens, especially those of higher social class, he is assisted by a relatively elaborate etiquette. By comparison with his American counterpart, the role of the Scottish police officer is much more closely defined; what he may not do is specified in detail and the rules are enforced; what people expect of him shows a higher level of consensus. These differences are apparently related to differences in the integration of social relations in the two countries (Banton, 1964: 215-43). The same relation should presumably hold in comparative urban studies: a higher level of consensus and a greater degree of role differentiation is to be expected in towns like Luanshya than in one like Chimbote.

Comparative studies of the organization of social relations in different towns are badly needed. It seems reasonable to believe that the elaboration of role theory for this purpose will be facilitated by the use and refinement of a conception of social density different from Durkheim's. On the microsociological level it can be linked with studies of social networks; on the macrosociological level it is necessary to explore how the overall structure of the town causes role differentiation to follow particular lines and for networks to be based upon different kinds of relationship.

References Cited

Adams, Richard N. *et al.*
1960. *Social Change in Latin America Today*. New York: Vintage Books.
Banton, Michael
1957. *West African City: A Study of Tribal Life in Freetown*. London: Oxford University Press for International African Institute.
1964. *The Policeman in the Community*. London: Tavistock Publications.
1965. *Roles: An Introduction to the Study of Social Relations*. London: Tavistock Publications.
Biddle, Bruce J., and Edwin J. Thomas, eds.
1966. *Role Theory: Concepts and Research*. New York: John Wiley & Sons.

Bohannan, Paul
1955. "Some Principles of Exchange and Investment among the Tiv." *American Anthropologist* 57:60-70.
Bruner, Edward S.
1961. "Urbanization and Ethnic Identity in North Sumatra." *American Anthropologist* 63:508-21.
Busia, K. A.
1950. "Report on Social Survey of Sekondi-Takoradi." London: Crown Agents for the Colonies.
Dahrendorf, Ralf
1964. *Homo Sociologicus: ein Versuch zur Geschichte, Bedeutung und Kritik der Kategorie der sozialen Rolle.* 4th ed. Köln und Opladen: Westdeutscher Verlag.
Durkheim, Emile
1893. *The Division of Labor in Society.* Trans. 1947. Glencoe, Ill.: Free Press.
Epstein, A. L.
1958. *Politics in an Urban African Community.* Manchester: Manchester University Press, for the Rhodes-Livingstone Institute.
1964. "Urban Communities in Africa." In *Closed Systems and Open Minds: The Limits of Naivety in Social Anthropology,* ed. Max Gluckman, pp. 83-102. Edinburgh: Oliver and Boyd.
Fraenkel, Merran
1964. *Tribe and Class in Monrovia.* London: Oxford University Press for International African Institute.
Gillin, John
1960. "Some Signposts for Policy." In Adams *et al.*, 1961, pp. 14-62.
Gluckman, Max
1960. "Tribalism in Modern British Central Africa." *Cahiers d'études Africaines,* 1, 55 ff.
1961. "Anthropological Problems Arising from the African Industrial Revolution." In *Social Change in Modern Africa,* A. Southall, ed., pp. 67-82. London: Oxford University Press for International African Institute.
Goode, William J.
1960a. "A Theory of Role Strain." *American Sociological Review* 25:483-96.
1960b. "Norm Commitment and Conformity to Role-Status Obligations." *American Journal of Sociology* 66:246-58.
Gross, Neal, Ward S. Mason, and Alexander W. McEachern
1958. *Explorations in Role Analysis: Studies of the School Superintendency Role.* New York: Wiley.
Hauser, Philip M., ed.
1961. *Urbanization in Latin America.* Paris: UNESCO.
Holleman, J. F. *et al.*, eds.
1964. *Problems of Transition.* Durban: University of Natal Press.

Homans, George C.
1951. *The Human Group*. London: Routledge; New York: Harcourt, Brace.
Hutton, J. H.
1946. *Caste in India*. Cambridge, Eng.: Cambridge University Press.
Little, Kenneth
1965. *West African Urbanization*. Cambridge, Eng.: Cambridge University Press.
Lloyd, P. C.
1959. "The Yoruba Town Today." *The Sociological Review* n.s. 7:45-63.
Marris, Peter
1961. *Family and Social Change in an African City*. London: Routledge.
Mayer, P.
1961. *Townsmen or Tribesmen*. Cape Town: Oxford University Press for Rhodes University Institute of Social and Economic Research.
1962. "Migrancy and the Study of Africans in Towns." *American Anthropologist* 64:576-92.
1964. "Sociological aspects of Labour Migration." *In* Holleman *et al.*, 1964.
Mitchell, J. Clyde
1956. "The Kalela Dance." Rhodes-Livingstone Paper No. 27. Manchester: Manchester University Press.
Nadel, S. F.
1957. *The Theory of Social Structure*. London: Cohen and West.
Pauw, B. A.
1962. *The Second Generation*. Cape Town: Oxford University Press for Rhodes University Institute of Social and Economic Studies.
Pearse, Andrew
1961. "Some Characteristics of Urbanization in the City of Rio de Janeiro." In Hauser, 1961.
Ravenstein, E. G.
1885. "The Laws of Migration." *Journal Statistical Society* 48:167-227.
Reader, D. H.
1964. "Models in Social Change, with Special Reference to Southern Africa." *African Studies* 23:11-33.
Reining, Conrad
1959. "The Role of Money in Zande Economy." *American Anthropologist* 61:39-43.
Rocheblave-Spenlé, Anne-Marie
1962. *La notion de Role en psychologie sociale; étude historico-critique*. Paris: Presses Universitaires de France.
Sherwood, Ray
1958. "The Bantu Clerk: A Study of Role Expectations." *Journal Social Psychology* 47:285-316.
Simmel, Georg
1955. "The Web of Group Affiliations" (trans.). In *Conflict: The Web of Group Affiliations*. Glencoe, Ill.: Free Press.

Southall, Aidan
1959. "An Operational Theory of Role." *Human Relations* 12:17-34.
1961. "Introductory Summary." In *Social Change in Modern Africa,* ed. Aidan Southall. London: Oxford University Press for International African Institute.

Strizower, Shifra
1959. "Jews as an Indian Caste." *Jewish Journal of Sociology* 1:43-57.

Wagley, Charles
1960. "The Brazilian Revolution: Social Change Since 1930." In Adams, 1960, pp. 177-284.

Wilson, Monica, and Mafeje, Archie
1963. *Langa: A Study of Social Groups in an African Township.* London: Oxford University Press.

The Density of Role-Relationships as a Universal Index of Urbanization

Aidan Southall

The Problem of Definition

Social scientists who study cities are often troubled by the difficulty of defining their subject matter, unless they stay comfortably within an ethnocentric, unicultural niche with an arbitrary, partial solution. Such different entities in time and space are labeled cities, towns, or urban settlements that many have despaired of formulating any meaningful definition to cover such a wide range of cases.[1] The question has been debated so often, with such inadequate results, that for many it has become sterile. The usual compromise is to agree that on a commonsense level it is obvious what is and is not urban; only marginal instances cause confusion, so the question can be put aside while more fruitful matters are discussed. But the marginal cases turn out to be rather pervasive in any comparative study, and the lack of an agreed definition results in ambiguity and confusion. Many hotly debated hypotheses depend upon differing, unspoken assumptions on this very issue, in which the meaning of crucial terms varies from one scholar to another, so that the hypotheses themselves are equivocal and cannot be proved or disproved to any general satisfaction. Many an argument turns and founders upon the question as to whether a certain situation or population aggregate is "truly urban," whether it is a "true city" (Sjoberg, 1960: 34; Coe, 1961: 85), or on the

1. "The word city has been used to designate almost every type and size of living settlement except the pastoral band and the small village whose primary ecological function is self-subsistence." John Gulick (1962-63), New York Academy of Sciences, *Transactions*, Series II, 25:445-48.

determination of "specifically urban factors" which relate to "urbanism as such" (Mitchell, 1966: 51). But how on earth can such determinations be made if that which is urban cannot be satisfactorily defined, at least to the agreement of the majority? If the debate concerns American cities only, the ambiguity is not too serious. Even if archeologists argue as to whether Jericho was urban eight millennia ago, it is a question of facts rather than of definitions. But when industrial and pre-industrial cities are compared, when the Yoruba cities are considered, or when the question arises as to whether the small market town and the great metropolis have anything in common sufficient to justify the application of the adjective urban to them both, the ground of systematic analysis becomes quicksand. Nor do neologisms like "rurban" or openly contradictory designations such as "rural city" (Lynch, 1967) provide an acceptable solution.

The enormous range in size, function, and culture of cities might well lead to the conclusion that they cannot all be fitted onto any absolute measure but only onto a continuum. But how can a continuum distinguish that which is urban from that which is not? Will not the appropriate point of distinction on any continuum be bound to vary with time and place? The continua based on the polarities formulated by Durkheim, Toennies, and others have contributed much to integrative understanding but little to empirical analysis. They have not been rendered into satisfactorily quantifiable components; but any future index is likely to owe a great deal to them.

Steward's levels of sociocultural integration were too closely tied to archeological perspectives and to the small-scale folk and tribal end of the continuum. They did not seem relevant to contemporary urban situations, and the units of analysis were not sufficiently clear or precise to assist in systematic, rigorous, and detailed cross-cultural comparisons.

The Contribution of Role Analysis

The concept of role as developed by Linton (1936: 113-14; 1945: 137), Nadel (1951: 93), Levy (1952: 102-3), and Parsons (1952: 38-39) seemed to offer further possibilities, which I explored in a preliminary paper (1956). By the time this was published (1959), I found that major new contributions had been made by Nadel (1957) and Merton (1957). Since then there have been no major new departures in role theory which are particularly relevant to its use in the appraisal and comparison of urban and non-urban situations, nor has any other more attractive formulation appeared. This may indicate that, indeed, it is not a very productive line of enquiry, or at least that current fashion directs interest elsewhere. The present attempt is to apply role theory more systematically to the cross-cultural study of urban forms, claiming not so much that a final answer to the problem can be given as that "our gain lies in the application of the appropriate analytical methods, not in gathering together, schematically, the results. For it is in the course of this application that we achieve a penetrating insight into the working of society" (Nadel, 1957: 154).

The general idea is that a certain type of role analysis, at least as a conceptual approach, will probably yield about as clear, valid, and comprehensive a cross-cultural appraisal of urban communities, both in relation to one another and also to that which is non-urban, as is possible at present. Diagnostic aspects of roles and role-relationships on the one hand, and the role structure of the whole community on the other, are related together in a formula whose basic components are:

1. Area (A): the spatial extent of a city, community, or social system. This is highly relevant in the context of technology and communication, but begs the question of the basis of definition. How to establish the spatial limits of urban communities objectively and consistently for scientific study, rather than (as is usual) in a fashion which is quite arbitrary from this point of view, is one of the crucial questions.

2. Number (N): the number of persons in the population inhabiting the area. This remains ambiguous unless "inhabiting" is defined strictly and in a manner which is sociologically meaningful. The length of the period of habitation must also be included. Some people may be in the city by day, others by night, and some both; some on weekends, some only during the week; some for the summer, some for the winter; some in their childhood, some only as students, young adults, middle-aged, or retired persons.

3. Roles (R): The number of culturally differentiated roles recognized in the population aggregate.

4. Role-Relationships (r): the number of relationships entered into by the persons in the population on the basis of such differentiated roles.

This part of the formula, which may be briefly referred to as (ANRr), deals with a progressively narrowing series, relating space to persons, to the types of roles they play, and to the number of relationships engaged in by them on the basis of such roles.

Types of Role-Relationships or Domains of Action

It is convenient to distinguish between predominantly kinship or ethnic (K), economic and occupational (E), political (P), ritual or religious (L), and recreational, leisure time, or voluntary (V) role-relationships. These five domains (KEPLV) refer to institutional spheres of action which are popularly distinguished, although they are subject to considerable overlap and frequent ambiguity. The domains also refer to five aspects of social action which may be more or less separate or combined in the definition of roles within a particular cultural system.

Qualities of Roles and Role-Relationships:

5. Broad/Narrow (B): this is concerned with the range of domains of social action comprised in the role. Some cultures frequently combine K and E in role definition. Similarly P and L may be combined, or P, L, and E. Some cultures distinguish very few V roles, others very many. Such differences are closely associated with urbanization. It has been claimed that K cannot occur alone, but only in the other domains (Beattie, 1964), although the difficulties and inconsistencies of this view have also been stressed (Schneider, 1964).

6. Diffuse/Specific (D): whether the range of action comprised in the role is vaguely or precisely defined. This is closely related to B but not isometric with it. The role of bricklayer is usually, though not of necessity, defined quite specifically as E, whereas that of musician may be E with diffuse extension into V or L. Friend is a characteristically diffuse role. It is difficult to establish when and which friendships have the degree of formality to qualify as role-relationships.

7. Manifest/Latent (M): a role-relationship may be inactivated for a longer or shorter period, and more or less in abeyance during that time. This matter was first effectively explored by Merton (1957).

8. Time duration (T): apart from the intermittency or latency of a role-relationship, there is the question of the length of time it lasts before being terminated.

9. Inequality of distribution (I): this is concerned with the pattern of distribution of role-relationships throughout the population concerned.

Area and number, of course, repeat Wirth's items of size and density, while his heterogeneity is, from our point of view, more adequately dealt with under the general heading of role. Role is understood as a differentiated and named structural position in a particular social system. Such a position involves a collection of rights and duties (cf. Goodenough's social identities, 1965: 2), which may be more or less precisely defined. From one point of view, all institutions are made up of an interlocking cluster of such roles. Every role, then, is a culturally recognized and named position. It is structural in the sense that it is expected to be occupied by someone. If it is vacated by one incumbent it should be occupied by another, or else there is recognition of a vacancy. While certain roles such as King, President, or Chief Justice occur only once in a society—as mayor occurs only once in a city—most roles, such as father, bricklayer, farmer, or priest occur very many times. For this reason we have to distinguish not only the presence of the idea of a particular role in a culture, but also the number of times that it is played. Most roles are played many times, not only because many different persons are playing the same role in different parts of the society (in every family, town, or business firm), but because each person often plays the same role to many different people. It is the conceptual idea of the particular, defined, structural position which I call role, and every instance in which it is played, whether by different persons, or by the same person to a number of others, I call a role-relationship.

This is a most important distinction. It does not, of course, refer to each of a person's separate "role-acts," but to the sequence of one person's role-acts to one other person, in terms of a single role, which taken together constitute a role-relationship. To some it is quite obvious that most roles, as named positions, are played out innumerable times by many persons to many others. It seems equally self-evident that each of these numerous instances is a different concrete relationship. I am forced to insist on the distinction between role and role-relationship for two reasons. First that, however obvious it may be, it is frequently ignored and its significance missed. Second, that a role-relationship is a relationship of a particular, formal kind. Social relationship is a rather vague idea, usually only involving the fact that two or more people should react to one another in terms of it. I assume that most societies contain a certain number, and often an innumerable host, of such merely interactive relationships, which fall short of the structural definition and formality of a role-relationship. They are either too informal, their rights and obligations too undefined, or they are too fleeting, to constitute the enactment of a role. From the point of view of comparative urban studies I would much rather it were possible to take into account the totality of social relationships, not only those which have the formality of role-relationships. But at present it is not feasible because relationships as such are too variable and too ill-defined, at least until network studies have proceeded much further than at present. We restrict ourselves to the more formal level of role relationships, not because it is ideal, but because it is the furthest feasible point to which this type of analysis can be pushed. In the small-group laboratory it is feasible to push it further to the level of unit acts, but not usually in real life. After all, a few years ago, social anthropologists would not go beyond corporate groups, and even congratulated themselves on this limitation.

The basic data consist of culturally named roles and the number of times each one is played as a role-relationship by different persons in a particular group or community such as a city. But these roles, proper to each culture, need to be measured and classified against some cross-cultural yardstick. The one we adopt is the distinction between K (kinship and ethnic), E (economic and occupational), P (political), L (ritual or religious), and V (recreational, leisure time, or voluntary). These conventional domains of action have the advantage of familiarity. Nadel used a different classification in his role chart (1957: 53), based on the distinction between recruitment and achievement roles, and, within each of these two categories, between independently and dependently defined roles. He also speaks of status, leadership, expressive, occupational, age, religious, kinship, and other kinds of roles (1957: 73). He brings out many important logical aspects of roles which are not of major relevance to our present problem. He cites such examples as able-bodied or cripple, brave or coward, which I would not consider as necessarily roles at all, basing my conclusion on the incumbency test and the cultural recognition of named distinctiveness.

Banton adapts Nadel and uses a scale with basic (sc. dependent) roles at the left and independent roles at the right, with general roles in between (1965: 33). He marks off sex, age, occupational, and leisure roles successively from left to right. I do not consider sex or age as roles for my present purpose, because neither is a universal generator of role-relationships. There is no question of the importance of sex and age in qualifying performance and attitude, but they do not in themselves give rise to basic role-relationships. The fact that particular societies do have specialized age roles only emphasizes this. Age and sex are subsumed as the primary bases of other roles, especially those of kinship, in most societies. Mother and daughter are expected to be female and father and son to be male, but their kinship roles are defined in terms of motherhood and daughterhood, fatherhood and sonship, not sex or age. The fact that social definition of sex determines whether parents count a newborn baby as son or daughter does not reduce kinship roles to a question of sex and age. A female lawyer does not have a different kind of set or sequence of relationships *qua* lawyer, because she is a woman; but she will play other roles, such as daughter, wife, mother, or member of some women's organization, which a male lawyer could not play because of his sex. For the present argument, the role of lawyer is the same, and one not two, whether played by male or female. Banton has explored the restriction of priesthood to men (1965: 32). This makes the nearest role to priest which a woman can play a different and distinct role, such as that of deaconess in some churches. But these roles are not properly thereby defined as sex roles.

As Banton says (1965: 29), many classifications are needed for different purposes; and I retain the simple KEPLV classification for this particular analysis because it seems serviceable and illuminating. Kinship refers to the social evaluation of blood relationships and their fictional or metaphorical extension. Ethnic associations will be included here, for the bond felt between those recognizing common ethnic origin over against a wider community of strangers is quite similar to extended kinship and is even treated specifically as such, and in that idiom, by those concerned. This is of wide relevance to heterogeneous, cosmopolitan, or metropolitan cities, which are important to the argument as including individuals conditioned by the extremes of urban and rural ways of life. Economic roles are concerned with the allocation of goods and services and with getting a living. Political roles are those primarily concerned with the allocation and use of power. By religious and ritual roles I refer to all kinds of cult service, including the complex organization of highly institutionalized religions, and also the phenomena of ancestor worship, spirit possession, sorcery, witchcraft, divination, and various other symbolic activities in particular societies. Recreational, leisure, or voluntary roles are by definition those not primarily concerned with kinship, economy, polity, or religion. It is thus a residual category, which is also highly diagnostic because of its immense importance in some societies and its almost complete absence from others.

Roles do not necessarily fall neatly within one of the categories. Indeed, the purpose of the categories is to reveal which roles fall neatly within one, which straddle several, and whether their spread is vaguely or precisely defined. We assign a role to one category if its dominant content clearly belongs there, but it may include other minor aspects which belong to other categories. The categories help to reveal the other qualities and aspects of role relationships which we have specified: broad/narrow (B); diffuse/specific (D); manifest/latent (M); time duration (T); and inequality of distribution (I).

Roles which are purely or primarily political are narrow, while those which have, say, political, ritual, and kinship significance are broad. Roles whose range of rights and duties seems ill-defined and indeterminate, extensible by circumstance yet of uncertain force, are diffuse; but those whose range of application is quite clearly delimited are specific. The role player will usually be aware of role-relationships which are continuously or constantly activated; these are manifest roles. At certain phases of the family cycle there is hardly any break in the continuity of a mother's role. But second cousins may forget one another's existence for long periods, during which their role-relationship is latent, being occasionally activated and manifested by special circumstances. Latency has become especially characteristic of associational membership. Such role-relationships have a markedly intermittent quality. The actual time duration of a role-relationship is most significant, and here the distinction between role and role-relationship is vital. For example, a corporation director may play this role for decades, but constantly be changing the particular corporations he directs and consequently also the collection of other directors with whom he interacts. Here the continuity of the role itself and the frequent change of role-relationships in which it is expressed are both important, but the latter is most significant for the present argument. Furthermore, underlying the change of directorships by the director, and in the long run contributing to it, is the change and turnover or proliferation of the corporations and directorship positions themselves.

The empirical allocation and distribution of role-relationships among the members of a community may be more or less unequal. In general, a person acquires more role relationships, both in type and number, during the passage from infancy to adulthood, beyond which there may again be a decline towards old age. More importantly, persons of different status levels have markedly different numbers of role-relationships. This multiple role-playing is an important criterion of certain types of social structure and is directly connected with the acquisition and maintenance of status and power.[2]

The A/N/R/r formula simply relates the number of role-relationships to a certain space. In a social demographic sense we may justifiably call this the density of role-relationships. Variations in this density are correlated with variations in the B/D/M/T/I qualities of role relationships which we have outlined. There are also correlated variations in the relative importance and frequency of the K/E/P/L/V types of role-relationship. The purpose of spelling out all these aspects is to give a determinate basis for either agreement or disagreement with the point of view adopted, and to impart a determinate content to such concepts as social complexity, density, heterogeneity, specialization, differentiation, and the division of labor. In the absence of such commitment to a determinative content it is possible for some of these concepts to be understood in diametrically opposed senses.

Density, Complexity and Heterogeneity

The most important concept to keep clear is density. I use it throughout only to indicate the number of role-relationships activated by an aggregate of persons within a particular space. This is clearly analogous to demographic density. Given a large number and therefore a high density of role-relationships within a particular space, it is possible to conceptualize the situation in sociometric fashion, drawing a line to represent each dyadic role-relationship between the two parties who are linked by the line. If drawn out diagrammatically, or so envisaged, a situation of high density in role-relationships will reveal itself by the large number of criss-crossing lines, which beyond a certain level of density are bound to coalesce into a solid mass. This solidity arising from high density attaches most properly to the persons upon whom a very large number of role-

2. Perhaps the most striking example of all is the multiple interlocking relationships of the Japanese elite (Yanaga, 1968: passim). But indeed the same point could be illustrated from any country (see, for example, Sampson, 1962). The major interlocking directorates constitute an international urban network, as in the case of the oil industry; the copper, tin, gold, and diamond mining rings; or the mammoth international construction consortia.

relationships converge, but it also attaches to the institutions incorporating the roles which are played out in the most numerous role-relationships. Here it is vital to keep clear the distinction between R (roles) and r (role-relationships). Both are abstractions. R is the ideational abstraction which results from interaction between the abstract cognitive formulation of the role and the innumerable instances in which it is played out in relationships between persons. r is the abstraction which sums up the current experience of two persons who interact in terms of a single R. This latter interaction must in some degree be lasting, repetitive, and regular, despite the phenomenon of latency, otherwise it cannot amount to the enactment of R in r. It would be a relationship of a merely informal or fleeting kind.

Density has also been applied to what is, in fact, the opposite situation, in the sense of high moral density, or consensus, associated with a high level of conformity with customary patterns of behavior, a high degree of acceptance and agreement on the definition of norms, and often a relatively high degree of resistance to change (Banton, 1965: 203-4). This moral density is "higher in villages than in towns, and higher in small towns than in large cities" (*ibid.*). Banton accepts Durkheim's moral density as referring "to what people do in their roles rather than to the way their roles are arranged" (1965: 207). Durkheim's association of high moral density with large populations and organic solidarity has never been very convincing (Barnes, 1966: 167). Indeed Banton's suggestion is more satisfactory—that high moral density is associated with small population groups, where everyone knows everyone else, so that deviance in role performance by one person affects all the rest. Barnes had added another dimension to the concept with his precise definition of network density, which he takes to be the proportion of all possible links between persons which are actually realized in a network consisting of a given number of people (1968: 118). On this basis, networks in tribal society are typically dense and relations multiplex, whereas the tendency in industrial society is for networks to be sparse and relationships single-stranded (1968: 127; Gluckman, 1955: 18-19).

It is nonetheless necessary to recognize that high density of role-relationships is associated typically with large population groups in cities and industrial societies. It is here that the sheer number of role-relationships generated within a certain space is greatest in the usual demographic sense. In counting the links in a network, Barnes does not differentiate between different kinds of links or their components, though he recognizes this distinction in Gluckman's contrast between multiplex and single-stranded relationships. But in estimating the density of role-relationships, we endeavor to count the number of strands involved. If A is linked to B as cousin, as fellow director on a company board and fellow member of a country club, he is linked by three strands, or role-relationships, not one, just as in another case X might be linked to three or more different persons by role-relationships of these three different kinds. Investigation of the sociological significance of demographic density should be taken beyond the mere mechanical counting of heads.

The distinction between simplicity and complexity in social structure is often taken for granted and not defined (Eisenstadt, 1962: 201; Despres, 1968: 4); or the fundamental problem of social complexity is avoided by scaling communities according to economic complexity alone (Frankenberg, 1966: 135). Both Leach (1961: 214) and Schneider (1961: 215) take Eisenstadt to task for failure to state the criteria of distinction and for the futility of debating the nature of an undefined entity. Like other terms, simplicity and complexity may legitimately apply to a number of different things. Simple technology does not mean that the problems of social life are simple for the individual; perhaps quite the contrary. It is obvious that in a sense the man who lives in a small-scale subsistence society has to be far more resourceful to survive than the industrial worker who repeats standardized procedures within a specialized context. In whatever sense small-scale subsistence society is simple, it is certainly not easy. Recognizing the importance of all these nuances, the arbitrary, but, I hope, clear and unequivocal usage adopted here is that complexity refers to high density of role-relationships and simplicity to low. On the other hand, multiplexity refers to low density of role-relationships and the playing of most available roles with the same set of persons, a situation characterized as high moral density by Banton with reference to role and by Barnes with reference to network (while Durkheim would appear to have been mistaken in associating it with organic solidarity).

Confusion often occurs in connection with statements as to that which is personal and that which is individual in different types of social system. The contrast that I shall make is between the personal quality of simple, multiplex societies and the individual quality of complex societies. In simple societies nearly all relationships are face to face between persons who all know one another in an all-round fashion. In complex societies much social interaction is between individuals, not necessarily face to face, who only know particular limited aspects of one another.[3]

Although social life is thus on a very personal basis in simple societies, it does not mean that the system encourages unlimited development of personal originality. On the contrary, the system imposes a certain basic conformity which it is dangerous for ordinary people to transgress. A great deal of social life in complex societies is much more impersonal, but the large number of choices available in social interaction, and the limited extent of multiplex relationships—the low level of moral density—allows greater scope to the development and expression of individual differences. There is no question that the members of a simple society are very real persons with distinctive character traits and a certain number of deviants, who may sometimes even acquire distinction as prophets, diviners, or outstanding leaders. Equally unquestionably, the most complex societies are the most individualistic and also permit a profound kind of voluntary intimacy, beyond convention, among small numbers of people, which is less developed in small-scale societies. This makes the study of networks beyond the limits of formal role-relationships particularly important. While personal relationships in depth are possible, there are insidious new pressures to conformity and superficiality in the growing proliferation of mechanical and electronic mass media. There is a strong strain of conformity in the other-directed type of person, which Riesman relates to the conditions of metropolitan centers in advanced industrial countries generally, but finds most at home in America (1954: 35). The general contrast remains true, despite the standardizing influence of routine, monotonous jobs, and mass media on the one hand or the conventional intimacy of age-mates on the other. The complexity of complex societies is above all a characteristic of urban situations. It has seemed unavoidably necessary to clear up these points of ambiguity, but it is most important to escape from the crude polarity of simple and complex, still echoing Maine, Durkheim, Toennies, Simmel, and Redfield, and to examine the ground in between.

From a sociological point of view, heterogeneity must surely be considered the most important component of Wirth's celebrated definition of

3. Thus, in connection with the hijacking of planes, newspapers have reported the distant, invisible intimacy of the role-relationship between flight controller X in the control tower of Miami airport and "José," his counterpart in Havana. Or again, when the President of the United States was asked recently when he was going to get rid of a certain official, he replied that he did not know the gentleman but would take steps to do so. He had, however, appointed the official to his position.

the city (1964: 66), yet its meaning has been left strangely vague. Wirth speaks of social heterogeneity, of "variety of personality types" (1964: 75), and of the city as not only tolerating but rewarding individual differences, as the "melting-pot of races, peoples and cultures,"—"a most favorable breeding ground of new biological and cultural hybrids." Heterogeneity seems to imply vague individual differences of all kinds, with special emphasis on ethnicity and personality types. The heterogeneity with which I am concerned here does not include personality type; and ethnicity is only one aspect of it. Most accurately, it is the result of progressive role differentiation. In this formulation urban communities are more heterogeneous than rural communities in the sense that they comprise a larger number and greater variety of differentiated roles and also a larger number of role-relationships played in terms of them. Ethnic roles, which we consider close to kinship roles, have been of great historical importance, but not necessarily in every case. The great proliferation of differentiated roles has in the long run been more in the field of economic and occupational roles than anywhere else, with voluntary associations next in importance; so it is in these fields that the greatest heterogeneity of the urban social person has developed. It is also a product of the heterogeneous, complex situation that a larger number of roles can be played by the same person than is possible in simple, multiplex societies. This is not only because a larger number of roles are differentiated, but also because there are fewer rules of incompatibility. Thus a person can play the role of teacher as well as student during the same period of his life.

To envisage a continuum from rural to urban social structure is to envisage a special case of the continuum from simple to complex society. It is necessary to consider, as far as possible, the whole range of rural social structures and the whole range of urban social structures, not just the extreme instances of either. Furthermore, this needs to be done first within single societies, taking examples of each major type of contemporary society, and similarly of past societies, onwards from the time of the first appearance of cities, and finally considering how far there is an overall continuum to which all of these can be fitted cross-culturally. The basis of the continuum is the density of role-relationships, the significance of which is amplified by the changes in the balance of qualitative aspects and types of role-relationships which accompany increasing density. It is assumed that increasing density of role-relationships accompanies any transition, temporal or spatial, from rural to urban social structure. This density is further accompanied by qualitative changes in the majority of role-relationships towards narrowness, specificity, latency, short duration, and unequal distribution, and by changes in the frequency of predominant content or type of role-relationships away from kinship to the four other types—and, secondarily, away from ritual to the other three, with the greatest eventual increase in voluntary leisure role-relationships. I have spelled this out in some detail before (1959: 29-33) and would like now to pay fuller attention to the range of variation in urban social forms.

Frankenberg successfully applied my criteria, supplemented by some others, in calibrating a range of rural and small urban communities in Britain (1966: 132). Along the scale from rural to urban,

> roles cease to splay across the five major type categories. . . . Roles become specialized in one or other of these fields. . . . they also become less diffuse and more specific in the behaviour described as appropriate to them. Father/employer/ritual-leader/teacher becomes father and employer and priest and teacher. In the traditional English countryside one must plough and sow and reap and mow to be a farmer's boy. . . . Roles in the countryside are mediated by direct face-to-face relationships. In the town—the roles of fellow-members in a voluntary association may never bring their incumbents face to face. . . . Each individual in the countryside has equal access to roles which he can fill and to role relationships which he can take part in. The stratification and above all spatial segregation of strata in the non-rural situation ensure that this is not the case. . . . Status at the rural end tends to be total and ascribed and at the other partial and achieved. . . . This is closely related to the fact that at the rural end of the continuum status determines *how* people behave when they meet; at the non-rural end *whether* they meet at all!

Frankenberg adds the point from Bott (1957) and Barnes (1954) that networks can be close-knit, small-meshed, and self-contained in the rural setting; but in the non-rural are more likely dispersed, large-meshed, and loose-knit. The metaphor of mesh has often proved ambiguous, but is clarified in Barnes' more recent treatment (1968).

The Range of Cities and Urban Situations

If we consider the earliest forms of urban life known, such as the Sumerian cities, or for the New World those of Mexico and Guatemala, there are virtually no data available from direct social observation. But it can hardly be doubted that these early cities represented a higher density of role-relationships than the surrounding countryside. The ingenious and scholarly attempt of Adams (1966) to wring sociological evidence from indirect sources, with his convincing exposition of the many new urban-based roles which developed, fully supports our interpretation.

The archeological record at present still leaves us with the picture of Sumeria as the first known area of emergence of a system of cities. The extraordinary case of Jericho shows that similar developments may have occurred even earlier, each, not surprisingly, in a rather special ecological and politico-economic niche in relation to its contemporary culture. As with all periods we regard as transitional—from anthropoid to human, from food-collecting to farming, or paleolithic to neolithic—the transition from rural to urban was no doubt adumbrated in many places and over long periods. The transition was always longer, more gradual, and less revolutionary than we are inclined to assume. Hence the importance of always relating the rural-urban distinction to a relative index, not to some fanciful climacteric marking off the "true" city from all else.

The question assumes particular importance for the second major case of the independent emergence of cities. The early Maya concentrations are usually referred to as ceremonial centers. Some experts call them cities, others do not. The latter assume that the impressive architectural concentrations were occupied mainly by political and ritual specialists, rather than by a general urban population. These centers were surrounded by a dense agricultural countryside from which quite large populations could gather on great occasions. Uaxactun is estimated to have had a population of about 12,000 within an eight-kilometer radius. The great center of Tikal itself covered sixteen square kilometers. In the Belize Valley there may have been minor centers almost every kilometer and major centers ten to fifteen kilometers apart (Willey *et al.*, 1965: 572-73). "This overall design of Maya settlement of community units arranged in an ascending hierarchy suggests a parallel structure of organization in society, of similarly ascending foci of authority with minor leaders in minor centers and paramount rulers governing from major centers" (1965: 580). Willey concludes that the Maya centers were "non-urban, at least in the formal sense of the densely populated metropolis," until a definite trend towards urbanism set in with the late classic period (*ibid.*). There may have been a progressive urbanization at Tikal. In Northern Yucatan, by the late post-classic period, the walled city of Mayapan probably contained 12,000 people in its heyday from 1260-1460 A.D. There are other, similar cases (1965: 10-11). But by this late stage there may well have been Mexican influence. The great Mexican centers such as Teotihuacan may have been urban in the conventionally accepted sense as early as 300 A.D. (Coe, 1961: 82). Teotihuacan seems to have been roughly contemporary with Tikal in its general development, or slightly earlier, and almost twice as large.

Adams stresses that Maya civilization was as distinctive an entity within Mesoamerica as Egypt was within the Near East as a whole (1965: 24). The Maya remain enigmatic, but there is no doubt for most scholars that urban civilization evolved independently in Mesoamerica some four millennia after it had first done so in Mesopotamia. The classic Maya centers have been interestingly compared with those of Angkor in Cambodia, which was almost coeval but a little later (Coe, 1961). Both arose in areas which were regionally undifferentiated, lacking extensive trade or transportation "because of the area-wide uniformity of crops and the difficult terrain" (1961: 85). But they could produce a surplus of food and labor, which through religious sanctions could be used to create and support huge cult centers.

All this is relevant to the present argument because it emphasizes a number of important and partly independent aspects of the concept of city. According to the usual interpretation, the Maya and Khmer had architectural cities but not human cities. It is likely that many specialized roles were differentiated in the process of organizing the population for the construction and maintenance of the ceremonial centers and their rulers. There were obviously specialized economic tasks here, as well as political and ritual, but there may not have been that important extra proliferation of economic roles arising from extensive trade between different areas producing complementary products. Nor were those roles stimulated which would have been required for the permanent organization and maintenance of a large resident population in the centers. But the centers were clearly created for human activity involving large numbers. So they were also concentrations of population, for non-agricultural purposes, within and around permanent buildings, and in this sense urban by several generally accepted criteria. The question is, how frequently, and for how long? How frequently did priest and congregation, prince and subject, tax and tribute collector, and farmer, steward, and temple suppliers, meet and interact? How manifest were their role-relationships? Clearly Tikal or Angkor Wat were different types of cities from those of Sumeria, or China, if they had no permanent mass resident population. But perhaps attendance at ceremonies and the bringing of supplies for them and for the politico-ritual elite residents were so frequent, even rotating between one sector of the surrounding countryside and another, that the presence of a highly organized concourse of people in the ceremonial center was almost constant, and must have been quite "urban" in appearance and in the form of interaction, even if they did not sleep there. The same, or similar, arguments apply to any great market center, which draws a large and frequent attendance from the surrounding countryside. In other words, differences should be recognized, but hard conceptual frontiers may be misleading and misplaced. The index of the density of role-relationships would place Tikal and Angkor Wat at the appropriate point on the scale of passage from rural to urban forms. The question as to whether they are "true" cities or not can be left to those who know what the significance of the answer would be.

It seems necessary to draw the same conclusion—that to ask whether they are "true" cities is meaningless, but that their place on the scale of role-relationship density would be meaningful and could be assessed if the facts were available—for all the major historical urban civilizations: Sumeria, the Indus Valley, Egypt, Phoenicia, China, classical Greece and Rome, the Hellenistic cities, Hindu India, Indonesia and Southeast Asia, Islamic cities, medieval Europe, Japan, the Renaissance cities of Italy, the Low Countries and the Hanseatic League, Mexico, Guatemala and the Andes, Yoruba, and Benin.

We have here many examples of long urban evolution within distinctive cultures. The density of role-relationships index applies conceptually to the gradual increase in the size and complexity of cities which occurred, with ups and downs, in all these instances, accompanied by the continuing contrast with the countryside. The matter remains fairly straightforward as long as only one urban cultural sequence is considered. But many of them reacted with one another, so that cities did not simply grow, or on occasion decline, within a single cultural tradition, but reflected the influence and even conquest of one urban society by another. Japan borrowed an urban culture almost ready-made from China. The Phoenicians moved to Carthage and Spain, but suffered defeat from the Romans, who had conquered and absorbed the urban Etruscans. The Mexican Teotihuacan was partially abandoned before 750 A.D. (Adams, 1965: 132), and the Maya cities mysteriously collapsed.

Even within one cultural tradition it is false to assume a continuous growth in the number, size, and density of cities. It is more difficult to conceptualize the pattern of urban evolution arising from the interaction of several traditions, at times stimulating and at times destructive. It would seem, however, that during the four millennia preceding the industrial revolution there was such a continuous growth for the world as a whole. Although the Indus cities, like the Maya cities, came to a mysterious end, urbanization was still proceeding steadily in many other parts of the world. The Dark Ages of Europe, which were certainly a regional relapse in urbanization, were more than balanced by the flowering and spread of cities throughout the Islamic world and in Japan and much of Asia, as well as by the Mexican and Guatemalan centers.

If we look at those cities which seem to have attained the greatest size, the temporal pattern is much more irregular. The greatest pre-industrial cities appeared at particular points in regional cultural development, but not in any meaningful overall sequence. Consider, for example, ancient Rome, Constantinople, Teotihuacan, Baghdad, Peking, Vijayanagar in South India, and Edo (Tokyo). Steward's Formative, Regional Florescent, and Cyclical Conquest phases (1955: 93-94) would not apply effectively to the problem of urban climax. The "social features" compared (1955: 196-98) were admittedly tentative with respect to complex societies. They are too vaguely defined and composite to be used in testing correlations between sequences of development in different regions and at different periods, as Steward himself seems to have recognized (1955: 199).

Only an index at a rather high level of abstraction, such as that of the density of role-relationships, can be expected to reveal the underlying common difference between rural and urban social life and between small and great cities. It follows that this is achieved by concentrating on the abstract characteristics of the social relationships involved, to the exclusion of cultural differences. The same density of role-relationships can be expressed in a variety of cultural forms. It is unlikely that there is a satisfactory single cultural scale to which all cities could be meaningfully related. In so far as analysis is based upon spelling out detailed aspects of the relative density of role-relationships, it is possible to specify the common characteristics which all cities possess in different balance and degree. But when analysis is extended to cultural forms, it must take account of a number of different types.

When the whole field of contemporary urbanization is brought into consideration, the variety in size and in the particular balance of social structure is vastly increased. Whether there are certain technical characteristics of the contemporary metropolitan city, which will tend in time to iron out cultural differences between cities, is one of the great questions of our time. Enormous cultural diversity remains in great cities, but it could be argued that much of this is residual from the past and from other situations whence urban migrants have come. Will the homogenization process ever be completed, or are great cities in any case following several divergent paths rather than a single one?

Many contemporary cities outside the Western world present a confusingly composite appearance because of two main historical processes: the movement of European peoples out into all other continents between the sixteenth and twentieth centuries, and the change in the technological base and economic function of urban communities since the industrial revolution. The two processes became interwoven. The first has come to be known as colonialism, in its widest sense, and largely coincides with the confrontation between white and non-white peoples. The second constitutes the least ambiguous component of the process of modernization and largely coincides with the basis of confrontation between rich nations and poor nations. Although it is difficult to achieve precision at the margin and to state the exact degree of overlap and divergence, it is quite clear that the phenomena of colonialism, Westernization, industrialization, and modernization[4] have so much in common and have been so intertwined that the constant confusion among them is hardly surprising. Likewise, the confrontation of rich and poor nations, and of white and non-white peoples, do not wholly coincide, but so nearly do so as to make this approximate identification a paramount factor in the contemporary world.

It is necessary to distinguish economic industrialization from social industrialization, and of course varying degrees of either. A city which is economically industrialized is one whose prime function is industrial. A city which is socially industrialized is one whose prime function is not industrial, but whose whole fabric and population presupposes and depends upon the technology and products of industrialization brought to it from elsewhere. While in the West industrialization was first economic and later social, in the rest of the world it was usually the other way round. In the West it is also becoming increasingly the case that even the countryside and its population are socially industrialized in this sense. If Washington is a political and administrative city, not industrialized in primary economic function, it is none the less socially industrialized.

4. There are many fallacies in this concept as so far presented in the literature, but they cannot be explored further here.

All these matters can become more intelligible and more meaningfully related if the density of role-relationships index is used as a yardstick to assess them in a systematic way. It may seem at first sight that by attempting to substitute this yardstick for other efforts to establish universal categories which would distinguish urban from non-urban, we are simply obliterating the distinction altogether and saying that the only universally valid distinction to be made in this field is one between different levels in the density of role-relationships. In a sense this is exactly what we mean. Much of the conventional distinction between urban and rural turns out to be invalid and false when looked at historically and cross-culturally. It may derive from the mental image of leaving the green fields and entering the gates of the city. In more contemporary fashion, it may derive from the sense of leaving scattered settlements and entering a continuously built up area, the unbroken succession of man-made buildings and enclosures. For many, this now takes the particular cultural form of entering the unbroken lines of motels and gas stations. But we realize that there is no one-to-one relationship between buildings and people. With modern means of transport and communication, buildings do not precisely determine the spatial distribution of people's social lives. The density of buildings is no longer a reliable measure of the density of people and of social relationships, at least if we take proper account of the spatial distribution of persons throughout their sleeping and waking lives. Unfortunately none of the conventional statistical measures of urbanization do this, and admittedly it is difficult. But if it is too difficult or costly to achieve practically, it is all the more important to give it full weight conceptually. The urban distinction may also arise from accurate knowledge of its legal and administrative definition. But we know that this too can be quite misleading, since it is not based consistently on demographic or social density, but rather on a host of other special considerations.

There is thus a good deal of excuse for concluding that conventional rural-urban distinctions are sociologically and cross-culturally invalid. It would be less misleading if, instead of describing studies as urban, we described them as relating to particular levels in the density of role-relationships. It would draw attention to the fact that neither the point nor the extent of social discontinuity between rural and urban can be taken for granted, but is always a matter to be determined by research. Indeed, it may be that the distinction between rural and urban is not wholly obliterated by this approach; and that the only way to establish such a distinction cross-culturally is to determine whether there is always a degree of discontinuity, or perhaps change in gradient, on the density of role-relationships index. This would approximate the sort of relative boundary between rural and urban which we need. If it were possible to plot samples of the density of role-relationships from the center to the periphery of some obviously dense aggregation, we might find that there is a relatively steep fall in this density at a certain point all round, which does mark the boundary between urban and rural social systems. This would be a genuinely sociological definition. It would be not a line, but a zone of relative discontinuity. Geographers have plotted demographic density in this way for some cities. Here too, no absolute density should be taken as boundary; the boundary should be marked by a relatively sudden fall in density.

It is rather unfortunate for general theory that the formulation of rural-urban differences has often reflected the influence of local or regional circumstances combined with the attempt to bolster particular theories. Redfield's studies in Yucatan are a well-known case. Another is Gluckman's strong insistence on the distinctness of urban and rural social systems in central and southern Africa (1960: 56-57). The aim here was to counter the fallacious interpretation of differences in African rural and urban life as different degrees of detribalization. Indeed, there is some analogy between detribalization in this sense and Redfield's secularization. On the other hand, Gluckman's stress diverts attention from the very process of urbanization itself (Epstein, 1967: 276). Furthermore, the peculiar gulf between rural and urban situations in the major mining centers of southern Africa is somewhat exceptional. The gulf has political, economic, social, and even spatial aspects. It is characteristic of long-distance, large-scale, temporary labor migration in a special type of colonial situation. It is less marked in other regions of Africa where the urban tradition is longer, or where the demand for African labor by huge foreign enterprises does not dominate the whole situation to the same extent. Nor is it so marked where well-established stratification systems incorporate both urban and rural populations.

Pre-Industrial Cities

In terms of this yardstick there cannot be any absolute distinction between pre-industrial cities and those which are economically or socially industrialized. Obviously the one form grew into the other, in a historical sense. For the same reason there cannot be a single model type of all pre-industrial cities, since any such single model would inevitably include particular cultural forms belonging only to some, not all, regions and epochs. This is the fallacy of Sjoberg's "constructed type," with all its provisos (1960: 321-28). It should go without saying that these cultural forms are important, and perhaps much more interesting than a laborious tracing of density in role-relationships. But acceptance of some such yardstick as the only universal basis for the calibration of urban forms might leave us free to study diverse urban cultures more accurately and more fruitfully, identifying common elements where they really are, rather than having to twist the facts to fit chimerical models.

Anthropologists and sociologists owe a great debt to Sjoberg for edging pre-industrial cities onto the map of contemporary interest and knowledge, and at least initiating the process of correcting the myopic view of urban life as a general human phenomenon, which ethnocentric American sociology in particular has foisted upon the world. Weber's more monumental work failed to achieve this for many English speakers because they were unable to read it until it was translated in 1958. Criticism of Sjoberg's "capsule form" of the pre-industrial city must be taken as a tribute to the wide influence of his work, which is so important that it must be taken up in some detail. He insists that all pre-industrial cities, from the fourth millennium B.C. onwards (1960: 321-23), "evince a startling degree of communality." While conceding that they do not all display every trait delineated, he builds up a composite type from the following features: the center of the city is the hub of governmental and religious activity and of elite residence, rather than of commerce. Low-status and outcaste groups are regarded as defiling and are residentially peripheral. Ethnic quarters constitute isolated little worlds. Land use is unspecialized and multipurpose. The small, centralized elite is ascribed by birth. It avoids and even "negates" economic activity, which is poorly developed, and more the sphere of low-status and outcaste groups. Elite individuals, especially, are subordinated to the extended family, which is the socialization agency. There is dominance by the men and by the old, with a rigid sexual division of labor. Upper-class women are secluded, lower-class women more unrestricted. Recruitment to office depends on kinship and personal more than objective and universalistic criteria. Division of labor is more complex than in folk society, but "from the industrial city's vantage point is surprisingly simple." Guilds dominate the economic realm, with specialization in product rather than in process. There is little standardization in price, type, or quality, with bargaining and adulteration prevalent, and meagre sources of credit and capital. The upper class is "in command of the key governmental positions," with the sovereign exercising autocratic power through hierarchical yet imprecise lines of authority, since decisions are made on the basis of personal considerations rather than impersonal rules, and salaries are not fixed. Religion is also "rent" by class divisions, and the lower strata deviate from the ideal norms. Only the elite get formal education, which is also dominated by religion and geared to perpetuate rather than to remake the social order.[5]

The list is comprehensive, covering all major aspects of social life. The components are perspicaciously drawn, and many of them are clearly interrelated. The questions that arise are: do they, as a whole, sufficiently characterize all pre-industrial cities; do they distinguish them from industrial cities and from non-urban communities? It would be pedantic and unfair to insist that the whole list should be represented in every pre-industrial city, and not in any other situation. But unless the majority of features are found in the majority of pre-industrial cities and not normally anywhere else, the list is hard to justify. If it is markedly inapplicable to pre-industrial cities of any region or epoch, or if it applies in large part to any industrial cities, the whole thesis of "striking communality" falls to the ground.

The list can be divided into some forty points, a number of which are clustered into composite syndromes. It would be easy to cite a whole host of exceptions. This is not the fairest method of appraisal, but some exceptions are so important as to demand notice. Full comparative testing would involve another treatise as long as the original. For example, where is it that low-status groups do not deviate from establishment norms? Certainly both poor whites and poor blacks do so in American cities. Where is it that formal educational institutions do not tend to perpetuate rather than remake the social order? Where is it that upper-status groups are not in command of key governmental positions? All these characteristics belong to human society as such, not just to pre-industrial cities. The black ghettoes of American cities also amount to ethnic quarters which are little worlds of their own in terms of their general way of life and segregation from the rest of the community. If they do not actually have gates which are shut at night, the frequent curfews imposed by armed guards amount to much the same thing. What percentage of American senators and congressmen, priests and ministers of religion, judges and

5. Sjoberg (1960: 323-28) sets out the list in fuller detail.

attorneys, corporation presidents, police and firemen, sanitation workers, university deans, presidents and trustees, builders and contractors, miners and steelworkers, or musicians in jazz and rhythm bands are women? What proportion of typists and secretaries, supermarket cashiers, nurses, and domestic servants are men? Does this not amount to a pervasive division of labor by sex?

The mass media present Washington as a man's world, expressing the current popular view of the sex division of labor, in which politics and diplomacy are virtually reserved to men. The appointment of women as advisers on consumer interests only amplifies the point, as also does the presence of a special category of Washington hostesses, who win glamor and status, but throw parties for the purposes and on the instructions of men. Cannot the churches and religious sects in every American city be largely ranked according to class and ethnic status? Can it be doubted that white American urban society has regarded black Americans as defiling? There is plenty of bargaining and little price standardization in many important and widely diverse sectors of the American market, such as business and finance, housing, used cars, supermarket competition, and the whole enormous field of defense contracts. Indeed the system of named, branded goods, with daily, weekly, and seasonal commercial advertising stunts and the flood of discount coupons reduces the idea of standardization in price, type, or quality to an absurdity. Home visiting, face-to-face hard-selling techniques for encyclopaedias, carpet cleaners, cosmetics, magazines, and a host of other products all emphasize the same point. Very large numbers are also employed on salaries which conform to no fixed scale, fluctuate, and are subject to constant bargaining and political influence. In Great Britain during at least the first half century of industrialization, formal education was dominated and largely provided by religious bodies. The personal considerations entering into the appointments made in the corridors of power are surely notorious. Nor can it be said that discrimination against blacks in employment is based on objective and universalistic criteria. Thus fourteen out of the forty criteria supposedly distinctive of pre-industrial cities turn out to apply completely or partially to American industrial cities. On this basis the distinction would seem to be very much one of degree.

In the great industrial cities of South Africa, such as Johannesburg, the white rulers have forced the low-status, and virtually outcaste, majority population of Africans out to the periphery. They are certainly regarded as defiling and clearly constitute separate ethnic worlds. Family and kinship ties remain extremely important in elite circles, both economically and politically, in Japan, India, Brazil, and many non-Western countries. To dismiss this exception as a passing phase would be to substitute unproven forecasts of the future for present facts. The great cities of these countries cannot possibly be classified as pre-industrial.

Most of Sjoberg's criteria of distinction are very much a matter of degree. He remarks himself on differentiation of land use according to occupation in pre-industrial cities (1960: 101). The combination of religious, educational, and cultural activities on one site seems as common in the United States as in pre-industrial cities (1960: 323). At first sight business activities do seem to be excluded in the former case; but account must be taken of the frequent church bazaars and fairs, which are certainly concerned with buying and selling, so that the only valid distinction may be that such activities are confined to securing financial support for the religious institution itself.

Capital cities such as Washington, Westminster, Canberra, and New Delhi all conform to the pre-industrial characteristic of being hubs of governmental and religious rather than commercial ventures. In dozens of the newer developing countries the capital is also the primate city, so that this phenomenon is very widespread. In most countries there is still a central elite ascribed by birth more than achievement. The real distinction here is perhaps that in the most advanced industrial countries the upper middle class of achieved status has unprecedented dominance in urban and public life generally.

Another matter of great significance treated by Sjoberg is the place of merchants and traders in the urban stratification system. He states boldly that "businessmen, or merchants, fall into the lower class or the outcaste groups" (1960: 136). Later, in recognizing the occurrence of exceptions, he insists that nonetheless they do not invalidate the general picture (1960: 183). But within the model there is no means of judging the exceptions less significant than the conformities. In Early Dynastic Sumeria, intercity trade was "either subject to royal demand or under direct royal control" (Adams, 1966: 155), and the merchants held an official status under a head who ranked high in the order of precedence. Later imperialist rulers such as Sargon were most closely concerned with trade and tribute. In Aztec Mexico, also, trade and tribute were major military objectives, and though distinct from the military nobility, traders were a powerful group (1966: 160). They were represented in the governing councils of some cities and also began to acquire land (1966:

168). Trade and kingship were so closely connected in the ancient cities of the Near East that it would be meaningless to assign a low status to trading. Solomon gave Hiram, king of Tyre, twenty thousand measures of wheat and twenty measures of pure oil in exchange for the fir and cedar trees which the king sent him (I Kings, 5:11). Byblos, Tyre, Sidon, Damascus, Carthage, and New Carthage in Spain represent a continuous tradition of the political dominance of trade in the cities of the Near East and Mediterranean.

The Sherifian lineage of the Prophet Muhammad was descended from the Quraishite merchants of the city of Mecca and held the highest status throughout the Islamic world. There was no strict official ranking of occupations; in fact, there was ambivalence. "The littérateur aligned the commercial and artisan groups with the nameless scum" (just as the aristocracy in nineteenth-century Europe regarded trade and industry as defiling), but it was not the general nor the theological view (Von Grunebaum, 1961: 215-16). "Pagan Mecca had been a state of merchants, Mohammed had been engaged in trade, and Islam favored commerce as well as the crafts" (*ibid.*). Market, merchant, and craftsmen were honorable essentials in the fundamental Islamic concept of the city. Indeed, Muslim traders founded, ruled, and maintained cities all down the east coast of Africa and along the southern shores of Asia, as well as along the internal caravan routes.

In the medieval and Renaissance cities of Europe, merchants achieved the highest rank and power. The nobility had been above them, but as the guilds gave way to entrepreneurs, the cities fell under the rule of rich merchants and bankers (Origo, 1957: xv). In Venice, Florence, Genoa, and countless other Italian cities, bankers, merchants and professionals, favorable to trade, took over supreme power. In Bruges, Ghent, and the other cities of Flanders a similar process occurred. The nobility retained greater hold over the countryside than in Italy, and in this sense complete city-states, with control over rural hinterlands, did not emerge (Nicholas, 1968), yet the town magistrates wielded absolutely independent power and the nobles became "little more than the hired mercenaries of the great towns" (*ibid.*, 458). Merchants bought land and acquired noble titles; nobles sought status in the city to avoid extinction. The Hanseatic towns of northern Europe, the city of London and other independently chartered English cities and boroughs, all showed the same merchant dominance.

It was mainly in Hindu India, Confucian China, and Japan that merchants were assigned a particularly low ritual and social ranking, often in contradiction with their economic power. In China, according to Eberhard (1956: 267), merchants were often not the lowest class because big business and financial organization in medieval China was often in the hands of adventurous junior sons of gentry families. They tended to be penalized for this by their gentry kin and, if successful, bought their sons back into gentry titles. In Japan, also, merchants were officially ranked below farmers (including ordinary peasants), but being kept a despised and separate group did not prevent them from becoming a major force in Japanese society. They acquired a very special position of their own in the great merchant city of Osaka. Towards the end of the Tokugawa period the nobles and samurai became increasingly indebted and dependent upon them, so that accommodation, cooperation, and even a kind of fusion between some samurai sections and merchants became a major thread in the transformation accomplished under the Meiji Restoration. As elsewhere, there was also profound borrowing of values and life styles between merchants and samurai over the centuries, as Smith (1960) has shown.

In India the Vaisya, popularly Baniya, merchant castes traditionally ranked below the priests and warriors, but above the Sudra, service castes. They were the lowest element among the high-caste "twice born" (Carstairs, 1961: 24), and it is wrong to call them low-caste, let alone outcaste. These upper castes are "interrelated in a system structured on 'mutual repulsion' (to use C. Bouglé's term)" (Fox, 1969: 88).

If the description of merchants as low-caste or outcaste is untrue or dubious for so many regions in such important periods, it cannot be accepted as a criterion of the social system in pre-industrial cities. It is an indication that the category is not homogeneous and cannot be made so this way. Greater refinement of categories, greater discrimination of time and place, greater attention to changing social processes over such long periods of time are required. It may be possible to sort out a larger number of types with historical depth within the pre-industrial category, as Tilly suggests (1967: 112), but it is doubtful whether this is the most fruitful line of analysis except as a preliminary descriptive approach. Rather, the factors themselves should be constantly refined as comparative study proceeds, and the varying combinations of such factors in different regions, and changes in them over time, analyzed.

In the case of merchants and trade, it is clearly their relation to the political structure of cities and the degree of autonomy which cities win within a wider state, largely as a result of merchant efforts, which is the relevant factor. A very large number of cities in the ancient and medieval worlds, indeed in the colonial world also, were founded for political rather than economic reasons, as Sjoberg correctly argued. They remained predominantly political and administrative rather than commercial—let alone industrial—in function, without acquiring their own legal identity or administrative autonomy. Even so, in important instances the governing elites of cities were themselves closely involved in trade (Polanyi, 1957). Furthermore, the cases in which cities did achieve partial or complete autonomy as city-states are so widespread in time and place, so crucial for an understanding of world urbanization as a vast process of social change, that they cannot be brushed aside to tidy up a false model which excludes them. Such misconceptions could not possibly occur if the structure of cities and processes of change within them were studied with a proper attention to the progressive differentiation of roles and role-relationships and the variable balance between them.

The capsule form of the constructed type does not apply completely or consistently enough to pre-industrial cities, while at the same time too many of its components apply much too widely outside the pre-industrial category, either to industrial cities or to rural folk and tribal societies. It is not that the criteria selected are wrong, but that they are all clearly not absolutes, but essentially graded continua with, at the most, a marked change in gradient indicating the distinction between urban and rural, or industrial and pre-industrial. Nearly all the criteria stated by Sjoberg apply widely and in varying degrees to cities in industrialized and industrializing societies on the one hand, or to folk societies on the other. They are not clearly distinctive of pre-industrial cities on a global basis.

Contemporary Urban Trends

Many pre-industrial cities are looked upon as rather marginal by many of those more immersed in the study of mass industrial urban life, either because they seem minimal in size or because they contain so much agricultural land and rural occupations within them. But, in a complementary way, those who now look at the rural and agricultural hinterlands of great industrial and metropolitan cities see the countryside itself becoming in many essential ways urban rather than rural. Some have coined the ugly neologism "rurban" to evade the need for clarity on this issue. Mechanized high-farming areas have become as industrial in their technology, their capital-intensive and labor-saving production, and their narrowly specialized occupations as urban areas. The ever-expanding resort areas which cater essentially for the urban dwellers are becoming equally specialized in technology and occupation, mobile and fleeting in the interactions of a great part of the population. Some areas may relapse into a more recognizably isolated, immobile, and rural life during the off-season, whether this be summer when the winter sporters or sun-chasers are gone, or winter when the summer vacationers are gone, and the rump population consists of longer-term residents who know one another face-to-face and remember simpler days. However, resort and farming areas necessarily remain less dense in population and in role-relationships, although their technology and their role inventory may be little different from that of conventional urban areas. When Surajit Sinha (1966: 189) studied an American Midwest community, he expressed this ambiguity by calling it "Mapletown" yet referring to it as a village (which, legally, it was). However, he goes on to say that it had no characteristics of a village except population size (2972). It had all modern amenities: electricity, telephones, television, radio, supermarkets, automatic laundry, hotels, and restaurants. It had numerous industries employing about 1700 people: 3 wineries, 2 juice processing companies, 2 canning companies, 2 fish bait companies, 1 electronics factory, 1 plating company, 1 fruit packaging company, 1 cement products company, 1 notebook and loose-leaf binder company, and 1 dairy processing plant. The example could be replicated thousands of times.

To debate whether such cases are urban or rural, village or town, is futile. They can be related and compared to other situations at the abstract level of their role-relationship density, or they can be portrayed in their various activities according to any cultural view of what constitutes urban or rural activity. Simmel contrasts metropolitan life not with rural but with small-town life (1964: 410-15), attributing to the latter the qualities often associated with rural or even subsistence communities (everyone knows everyone else, everyone has a positive relationship to almost everyone else). This is obviously the multiplex pole of the familiar polarity. It would seem confusing in terms of the conventional folk-urban continuum, but need not seem so in relation to the index of density in role-relationships.

It is necessary to distinguish what various writers mean by urban or rural, town or village, in such ambiguous situations without becoming tied to concepts which have no cross-cultural meaning. There is no conceptual difficulty involved if the quality, quantity, spread, duration, and distribution of role-relationships are studied as suggested. It is pointless to debate whether a situation of this sort is urban or rural. Taken in its entirety, it can be put on a scale of the overall density of role-relationships. Taken in its analytic aspects, it can be related to each component of the index with more refinement. An area whose basic economic activity is mechanized corn production may display a very high degree of role differentiation, while the presence of agricultural land keeps the quantitative density of role-relationships lower than it would otherwise be. Thus, social relationships could be called more urban in some ways and more rural in others. The effective contrast between metropolis and small town may be greater than between small town and rural community.

Modern urban communications technology raises increasing complications for any theory of social interaction, including role theory. The possibility of latency in role-relationships and of fleeting superficiality reaches undreamed-of extremes. The whole new dimension of distant electronic communication, auditory and visual, one-way and two-way, radically affects the field of social interaction. While it has been extensively written about (McLuhan, 1962, 1964), it has not been systematically incorporated into role-theory. Letter writing has provided a genuine extension of the range and frequency of role-relationships for millennia already, greatly magnified more recently by the telephone. But writers in books, magazines, and newspapers and their readers, performers on radio and television and their listening and viewing audiences, cannot be excluded from consideration. All involve great frequency of social interaction, which cannot fail to generate its own formal rules of behavior. The sheer volume of social interaction is vastly magnified in quantity and variety, yet alarmingly attenuated in quality. Here it is difficult not to recognize the validity of Simmel's multiplication of contacts (1964: 415), while still recognizing that urban situations do offer the possibility of profound, intimate, and long-term contacts also.

The new electronic field of role-relationships, like earlier technologically based changes, began in the cities and spread to the countryside. In parts of the Western world the latter process is almost complete, but in poorer regions and countries it is barely begun. In fact, despite the extreme rapidity of recent population growth, it is misleading to regard urban areas in the poorer countries as either following after or destined to catch up with the cities of the West. For in the most crucial sociological respects they differ fundamentally, and perhaps increasingly, both in structure and process, from Western cities.

A contemporary city in a poor country may have a population size and density comparable to that of a city in a rich country, but the two are radically different in the distribution of technological equipment throughout the population and the distribution of material resources as a whole. The contextual meaning of poverty and deprivation is quite different in the two cases. Both the relative frequency of different types of role-relationships and the pattern of their distribution throughout the population are also different. Quite false comparisons are often made between the situation of some city in a poor country today and that of cities in rich Western countries two centuries or so ago. Furthermore, the trend in stratification, in family composition and patterns of behavior, or in the relation between economic, political, and religious activity not only differs in rich and poor countries, but in many important respects hardly seems to be moving in the same direction. This is true for a comparison of Calcutta and New York, despite the crisis situation of both. In most respects other than the purely technological, the history of Western cities during the last two centuries is a completely misleading example for the poor cities of the non-Western world, because, although many common processes can be identified, their combination, direction, and hence their meaning are radically different.

Industrialization inevitably leads to or increases urbanization, but the converse proposition does not hold. In this respect urbanization in poor countries occurs in a situation virtually opposite to that in rich countries. In the latter, recent urbanization reflected and accompanied technological dominance and control of all major world markets. Furthermore, these two factors guaranteed the major advantage in exploitation of all new natural resources, whether discovered by geographical exploration or by technological development. In all these respects the cities of poor countries are in a precisely opposite situation. The cities of the rich countries began their modern growth in the context of laissez-faire capitalism with relatively small governmental bureaucracies. The cities of poor countries are growing in the context of politically planned economies, with very large bureaucracies in relation to their resources and total population. In these circumstances, it is reasonable to argue that even if certain indices of urban population growth are similar for cities in poor and rich countries, their sociological significance is nonetheless radically different. The poor cities reflect economies for which the terms of trade for their mainly primary products are generally disadvantageous to them compared with the terms of trade for the mainly manufactured products of rich cities.

That the rich cities increasingly regard themselves as faced with a seemingly insoluble crisis of finance and services, traffic, noise, pollution, and public disorder, is a further irony. The services, traffic, noise, pollution, and disorders of the poor cities remain different from those of the rich cities in their impact on the general population. The flight to the suburbs is becoming a major characteristic of big Western cities. Central London, New York, Manchester, and Copenhagen actually lost population from 1950 to 1960 (Hoyt, 1969), but no such phenomenon is reported from the big cities of poor countries, despite their high densities and overcrowding.

To divide countries, and hence cities, into rich and poor, and their cities accordingly, is very crude but involves fewer fallacies and concealed value judgments than the use of any other terms in a brief treatment. There are some intermediate cases between these two categories, but surprisingly few.[6] The rich countries are primarily those of the Euro-American Western world, together with Russia and the major non-European exception of Japan. Since the standard of living of the masses in the poor countries is hardly improving, while their populations are rising, there seems to be a widening rather than a narrowing gap between them and the rich countries, which have more stable populations and constantly proliferating technologies. Since the situation of cities in poor and rich countries is so different, so, it would appear, must their processes of evolution be. The density of role-relationships is likely to remain somewhat lower in poor cities, with slower proliferation of economic roles and greater retention of kinship and ethnic roles. Meanwhile, despite the spread of new technologies to cities in poor countries before they can be integrated in their own productive systems, the overall level and

6. In the recent Lester Pearson report to the World Bank, six countries are seen as possibly catching up with the general material standards of the rich Western countries and Japan, within sixty or seventy years if present progress is maintained. These are Mexico, Chile, Venezuela, Gabon, Greece, and Cyprus. Most developing countries achieved annual growth rates of 2 per cent or less during the "Development Decade," thus falling lamentably short of the mark set at 5 per cent. Since these rates are not at constant prices, the real standard of living of the masses in most of these countries has not noticeably bettered (*Jeune Afrique,* no. 460, Oct. 1969, "Miracle au Sud," the Pearson Commission, Partners in Development, New York: Praeger).

intensity of social interaction generated by new mass transport and communication media will remain much lower than in the cities of rich countries.

Although we have restricted formal consideration to roles and role-relationships, it is likely that the sheer number of social interactions or relationships of all kinds is also the diagnostic mark of different degrees of urban living. Such interactions are not only very often fleeting and ephemeral, but also ineluctable as a whole, despite the apparent choices available with respect to the direction and timing of each particular one. Simmel stressed the mental correlates of this with his "intensification of nervous stimulation" (1964: 410), but satisfactory and comparative demonstration of this has never been forthcoming. The qualities of intelligence, calculation, and reserve are undoubtedly present, as Simmel noted, but apply in a much more limited, sectional, and unintegrated manner than Simmel realized. The intensity characterizes those who work the system most actively. Others can retire and segregate themselves from it to an extent impossible where interactional density is lower and moral density higher.

References Cited

CA: *Current Anthropology*.
CSSH: *Comparative Studies in Society and History*.
ED & CC: *Economic Development and Cultural Change*.

Adams, R. McC.
1966. *The Evolution of Urban Society: Early Mesopotamia and Prehispanic Mexico*. Chicago: Aldine.

Banton, Michael
1965. *Roles: An Introduction to the Study of Social Relations*. New York: Basic Books.

Barnes, J. A.
1966. "Durkheim's Division of Labour in Society." *Man*, 1, (2):158-75.
1968. "Networks and Political Process." In Swartz, ed., 1968.

Carstairs, G. M.
1961. *The Twice Born*. London: Hogarth.

Coe, Michael D.
1961. "Social Typology and the Tropical Forest Civilizations." *CSSH* 4(1): 65-85.

Despres, L. A.
1968. "Anthropological Theory, Cultural Pluralism, and the Study of Complex Societies." *CA*, 9:3-26.

Eberhard, W.
1956. "Data on the Structure of the Chinese City in the Pre-Industrial Period." *ED & CC* 4(3):253-68.
Eisenstadt, S. N.
1961. "Anthropological Studies of Complex Societies." *CA* (2)3:201.
Fox, R. J.
1969. *From Zamindar to Ballot Box: Community Change in a North Indian Market Town.* Ithaca, N.Y.: Cornell University Press.
Frankenberg, R.
1966. *Communities in Britain.* London: Penguin Books.
1966. *"British Community Studies: Problems of Synthesis."* In ASA 4, *The Social Anthropology of Complex Societies.* London: Tavistock.
Gluckman, M.
1955. *The Judicial Process among the Barotse.* Manchester: Manchester University Press.
1960. "Tribalism in Modern British Central Africa." Cahiers d'Etudes Africaines, 55 ff.
Goodenough, W. H.
1965. "Rethinking 'Status' and 'Role': Toward a General Model of the Cultural Organization of Social Relationships." In ASA 1, *The Relevance of Models for Social Anthropology.* New York: Praeger.
Gulick, J.
1963. "Urban Anthropology: Its Present and Future." New York Academy of Sciences, *Transactions,* Series II, vol. 25, 445-48.
Hoyt, H.
1969. "Growth and Structure of Twenty-One Great World Cities." In Breese, G., ed. *The City in Developing Countries.* Englewood Cliffs, N.J.: Prentice-Hall.
Leach, E. R.
1961. "Comment on Eisenstadt." *CA* 2(3):214.
Levy, Marion J.
1952. *The Structure of Society.* Princeton, N.J.: Princeton University Press.
Linton, Ralph
1936. *The Study of Man.* New York: Appleton-Century.
1945. *The Cultural Background of Personality.* New York: Appleton-Century.
Lynch, Owen
1967. "Rural Cities in India: Continuities and Discontinuities." In Mason, Philip, ed. *India and Ceylon: Unity and Diversity.* New York: Oxford University Press.
McLuhan, M.
1962. *The Gutenberg Galaxy.* Toronto: University of Toronto Press.
1964. *Understanding Media.* New York: McGraw-Hill.
Merton, R. K.
1957. *Social Theory and Social Structure,* rev. ed. Glencoe, Ill.: Free Press.

Mitchell, J. C.
1966. "Theoretical Orientations in African Urban Studies." In Banton, Michael, ed. *The Social Anthropology of Complex Societies.* London: Tavistock.
Nadel, S. F.
1951. *The Foundations of Social Anthropology.* London: Cohen and West.
1957. *The Theory of Social Structure.* London: Cohen and West.
Nicholas, D. M.
1968. "Town and Countryside: Social and Economic Tensions in Fourteenth Century Flanders." *CSSH,* 10, 458-85.
Origo, Iris
1957. *The Merchant Of Prato.* New York: Knopf.
Parsons, Talcott
1952. *The Social System.* London: Tavistock.
Polanyi, Karl, *et al.*
1957. *Trade and Markets in the Early Empires.* Glencoe, Ill.: Free Press.
Riesman, D., N. Glazer, and R. Denney
1954. *The Lonely Crowd.* New York: Doubleday. (Yale 1950.)
Sampson, A.
1962. *Anatomy of Britain.* London: Hodder & Stoughton.
Schneider, D. M.
1961. "Comment on Eisenstadt." *CA,* 2(3):215.
Simmel, Georg, see Kurt H. Wolff.
Sinha, Surajit
1966. "Religion in an Affluent Society." *CA* 7(2):189-95.
Sjoberg, Gideon
1960. *The Pre-Industrial City, Past and Present.* Glencoe, Ill.: Free Press.
Smith, R. J.
1960. "Pre-Industrial Urbanization in Japan: A Consideration of Multiple Tradition in a Feudal Society." *ED & CC* 9, 1(2):246.
Southall, Aidan
1959. "An Operational Theory of Role." *Human Relations* 12 (1):17-34.
Steward, J. H.
1955. *Theory of Culture Change.* Urbana: University of Illinois Press.
Swartz, M. J., ed.
1968. *Local-Level Politics.* Chicago: Aldine.
Thrupp, Sylvia L.
1961. "The Creativity of Cities: A Review Article." *CSSH,* 4(1):53-64.
Tilly, Charles
1967. "The State of Urbanization." *CSSH,* 10.
Von Grunebaum, G. E.
1961. *Medieval Islam.* Chicago: University of Chicago Press.
Willey, G. R., W. R. Bullard, J. B. Glass, and J. C. Gifford
1965. "Prehistoric Maya Settlements in the Belize Valley." Peabody Museum of Archeology, Harvard University, vol. 54.

Wirth, Louis
1964. *On Cities and Social Life.* Chicago: University of Chicago Press.
Wolff, Kurt H.
1964. *The Sociology of Georg Simmel.* Glencoe, Ill.: Free Press.
Yanaga, Chitoshi
1968. *Big Business in Japanese Politics.* New Haven: Yale University Press.

The Yoruba: An Urban People?

Peter C. Lloyd

The economic development of twentieth-century Nigeria has produced its new towns, bustling with recently arrived immigrants from rural and tribal areas. Such are Enugu, the administrative capital and coal-mining center of the Eastern Region; Kaduna, capital of the Northern Region; Sapele, dominated by its modern plywood factory; and many others. But an equal number of Nigerian towns are of considerable antiquity: the Hausa towns such as Kano, Zaria, and Katsina were described by medieval Arab travelers; Benin astounded the first Portuguese who visited it at the end of the fifteenth century (when it was already, in all probability, two centuries old). Yoruba towns too were mentioned by the Portuguese, though we have no record of their visits to any of them; but, again from oral evidence, we suppose the existence of sizable towns at least in the twelfth or thirteenth centuries and perhaps earlier (Bascom, 1955, 1959).

These towns, as we know them at the present time and in the immediate pre-colonial period of the late nineteenth century, are not of a single type. The Hausa towns are the capitals of kingdoms of considerable size, whose populations range today from 250,000 to 4 million; they are market centers serving the predominantly rural hinterland of their kingdoms. Dominated by a ruling Fulani aristocracy, these towns have much in common with towns of early medieval Europe. The Yoruba towns are, in contrast, much larger. Ibadan today has a population of over one million, three towns have populations exceeding 100,000, and several others are only slightly smaller. In the past, the population of the capitals of Yoruba kingdoms probably did not exceed 50,000. But in the early nineteenth century, civil wars and Fulani attacks in the savanna north of their territory destroyed many towns, driving their inhabitants southward to swell the population of existing settlements along the forest margins. It is in this area, now designated Ibadan Province, that 60 per cent of the people live in towns with populations greater than 20,000. The origin of towns in this part of West Africa is speculative. Their walls and their location on or near rocky eminences suggest a need for defense. Oral history suggests that their development may be attributed to political growth consequent upon domination by immigrant peoples, probably a millennium ago. Although individual towns have had their vicissitudes, many have a continuous history spanning several centuries: they are definitely not temporary phenomena (P. C. Lloyd, 1960a; Lloyd, Mabogunje, and Awe, 1967; Mabogunje, 1968; Krapf-Askari, 1969; Wheatley, 1970).

Several factors seem likely to have facilitated the development of towns: (a) kingship; (b) a high density of population (where there are 150 people per square mile, the population of a town of 20,000 can farm within a day's walking distance); (c) permanent workplaces of certain crafts (weavers' and blacksmiths' sheds); (d) long-distance trade routes which "fixed" the location of towns; (e) the fact that men could do all the farmwork, so their wives were released for petty trading, thus coping with the problems of distribution created by town dwelling.

Every Yoruba town was enclosed by a high wall or a rampart and ditch, broken only by the gates on the main routes radiating from the central marketplace, which was usually sited at the gates of the palace, itself a walled enclosure extending over several acres, only a few of which would be occupied by the buildings—the remainder being devoted to shrines and sacred groves. Few other public buildings existed in the town (Frobenius, 1913). Circling the palace were the vast compounds of rectangular courtyards belonging to the descent groups composing the towns.

Today the appearance of the towns is changing. The walls have crumbled, and the earth from the ramparts has been taken to build the new houses which are extending beyond the former limits of habitation. As the old courtyards grow derelict they are replaced by single- or two-storey houses which increasingly tend to face the newly constructed roads. Shops and gas stations spring up around the main market and the new truck parking lots. The built-up area of these towns now has a density of population of over 75 persons per acre—a figure no doubt higher than that prevailing in the nineteenth century but sufficiently high, nevertheless, to indicate the crowded aspect of Yoruba living even then.

Yet these towns are settlements of agricultural people. Over 70 per cent of the adult Yoruba men are farmers, 9 per cent are traders, and 8 per cent are craftsmen (1952 census).[1] These proportions are substantially repeated in each of the large towns. In fact, in some towns lacking modern administrative or commercial functions (for example, Ikere-Ekiti, pop. ca. 36,000), the proportion of farmers is as high as 80 per cent. Even in Ibadan, capital of the Region and its leading commercial center, the proportion of farmers exceeds 50 per cent. The farmlands of the large towns extend for several miles from their walls—from 20 to 30 miles in the case of Ibadan. Blocks of land are held corporately by the members of the descent groups comprising the town, and individual farmers commute between their town compound and the hamlet on the farm. Some men spend most of the year in the hamlet, returning to the town only for the major religious feasts or for important funerals; craftsmen or clerks may visit their farms on weekends or in slack periods of work. In the smaller towns (say from 5,000–25,000 inhabitants) it is possible to walk daily from the compound to the farm, and the number of dependent hamlets is much smaller. The hamlet has no independent political status—it has no hierarchy of chiefs; important marriages or burials always take place in the town compound.

A few of the larger Yoruba towns were themselves independent but lacked any independent settlements. In most cases, however, they were the capitals of kingdoms which comprised a number of towns individually (or, in some cases, collectively) smaller than the metropolis. Yet the differences in size were not matched by any great difference in social structure or occupational distribution; the dependent towns usually had fewer traders and craftsmen. In towns of all sizes is found a fairly uniform distribution of persons by age and sex. It is thus almost impossible to speak of Yoruba country in terms of a rural-urban dichotomy.

1. A later census was held in 1962-63, but many of the figures for individual towns and districts are believed to be too high. Comparative deductions from them are therefore unreliable. The census figures became, in fact, a major political issue. The figures for the 1952 census, while generally low at the present time, have thus been retained. A new census has been announced for 1973.

Urbanism Defined

One wonders, in fact, whether the term "urban" is aptly used in describing the Yoruba town. If we decide that the pre-colonial towns do not merit this designation, we may still ask, first, whether the structure of the towns facilitated contemporary economic development and second, whether this development has made the towns significantly more urban than before. These questions are significant, for it is often stated that the urban centers of the pre-industrial era have fostered those values necessary for rapid economic development—the take-off stage for sustained growth.

But what is an urban area? Urbanism, we are told, is a way of life distinguished from the folk or rural life. The dichotomy may, however, be interpreted in two ways. Either all towns have certain features in common which are not shared by rural areas, or towns may differ from one another, but each will differ from its rural hinterland in a similar manner and degree. One might apply the second interpretation to the Hausa emirates but, as I have just noted, its application is impossible in most parts of Yoruba country.

Two criteria are most commonly used to define an urban area. First, the size of the settlement: whether one takes census definitions of 2000 or 5000 inhabitants or a more realistic figure of 20,000, for example, it is clear that many Yoruba settlements will fall within the category. If, on the other hand, one defines an urban settlement as one with less than half its adult male working population engaged in farming, one excludes most, if not all, Yoruba towns. Such towns as Ibadan and Abeokuta become marginal, for while the total population of the descent groups with compounds in the town is predominantly agricultural, the majority of the population usually resident there (and counted there in the census period) is non-agricultural. (Thus all the 300,000 Egba belong to compounds in Abeokuta; yet of this town's census population of 80,000, only 15 per cent of the adult men were farmers; the remaining 220,000 Egba were enumerated in the hamlets).

Thus there exists some confusion in the definition of an urban settlement and in the meaning of the urban-rural dichotomy; in addition one finds considerable ambiguity in many of the concepts which are used in characterizing the urban area. Furthermore many of the attributes ascribed to the urban area would seem to be more properly correlated either with a stage of industrial development or with the early stages of rapidly growing towns. For, in the African context, the urbanization process usually involves the sudden movement of rural tribesmen into modern towns and the structure and social problems of these towns.

The Yoruba are certainly anomalous in having such large towns while practicing near-subsistence agriculture and possessing a social structure based on descent and age groups. Their towns certainly do not have much in common with Sjoberg's (1960) pre-industrial (and basically feudal) towns. If, however, we hold that the important attributes of urbanism derive from the dense settlement of people in large towns, then we must expect to find these attributes present in the Yoruba towns. If the attributes are absent here, we must endeavor to ascribe them to factors other than settlement size and density.

In the following pages, I shall examine the Yoruba towns with respect to criteria commonly ascribed to urban areas.

Elsewhere in this book Southall and Banton describe the rural-urban dichotomy in terms of role theory, the one emphasizing the content of roles, the other their interdependence. In the urban area far more roles are open to the individual actor, consequent upon the higher degree of specialization. Superficially this statement seems acceptable. But how is a single role being defined? Are we being ethnocentric in listing every occupation recognized in a census in an industrial country as a separate role while lumping together the numerous degrees of blood and affinal relationships into a few kinship roles? Inasmuch as more roles exist in the urban area, a greater choice among them is said to exist for the individual actor—emphasizing the importance of achieved status in the town. But are all these roles open to the individual in practice? Could not his adult status still be determined largely by his origins? The distinction between the numbers of roles existing in the town and those open to an individual, and in fact chosen by him, is often missed. Urban man may in some cases fill no more roles than his rural counterpart. Urban roles are said to be more specific, less diffuse. Occupational roles tend to be so —but not those of friend or neighbor. Multiplex relationships predominate in the rural areas—roles are more independent in the town. Yet a high degree of interdependence of roles may exist within certain urban communities—in industrial slums or the Latin American *favelas*.

The heterogeneity of towns is often stressed, sometimes in the context of role theory, elsewhere in an ethnic or religious sense. It is not clear what types of heterogeneity are important. Should one apply the term to Yoruba towns because their constituent descent groups claim origins from different Yoruba kingdoms and have in consequence a variety of individual customs and deities?

Furthermore, one may examine the integration of the urban area—in Durkheim's terms, the relative mechanical or organic solidarity in the community.

Traditional Yoruba Society

In the light of these concepts, whatever their merits or their precision, let us look at some of the attributes of Yoruba society. Only a bare outline is given of some salient features; further details are contained in the references (for general descriptions see B. Lloyd, 1967; P. C. Lloyd, 1962, 1965).

Economy

The majority of Yoruba men are farmers who produced, in the past, for the needs of their own polygynous families. They showed considerable skill in evaluating the allocation of land to various crops and varieties. For Yoruba agriculture has several stable crops—cassava, yam, maize, plantain, and cocoyam, including in some cases many known varieties (thirty for instance of yam); a wide range of minor crops is also cultivated. There was little cooperation among men outside the family group. Rights to the land of the descent group were held corporately by all members of the group, the individual being allocated usufructuary rights over land sufficient for his needs. Thus every man had his own land and no man could accumulate land beyond the capacity of himself and his sons to cultivate. There was little deliberate specialization but a considerable quantity of farm produce did enter the markets. This could be ascribed to several factors: the supply of foodstuffs to the non-agricultural workers, chiefs, traders, craftsmen; the adjustment of surpluses and shortages in single crops, e.g. a man might have a bumper maize harvest but his yams might be late in maturing; transport difficulties in conveying food from the farm to the town compound, forcing the residents in the latter to buy in the town markets.

Yoruba men and women practice a wide variety of crafts. All of these are technologically simple: they do not involve the use of the wheel, of non-human power, or of writing. Some relate to the royal courts and chieftaincy like the making of regalia, others to goods of everyday use, like blacksmithery (men), weaving (men and women), pottery (women). Most of the traditional men's crafts are hereditary, and where the market is large enough to sustain a large number of men, one finds that the men of a descent group follow a single occupation (as with weaving or blacksmithing in the larger towns). Thus the economic organization of these crafts—the maintenance of the workplace, the fixing of prices—is achieved within the patrilineage organization (Calloway, 1965). Craftsmen differ in their skills, but most men produce the full range of items known to their craft. However one does find a considerable specialization if one traces the stages through which raw material passes from producer to consumer. Thus cotton passes, in turn, through the hands of farmer, trader, spinner (woman), trader, dyer, trader, weaver, tailor and embroiderer, and consumer. Where the manufactured goods are to be of a special design or quality the consumer orders them directly from the maker. Absent from the Yoruba towns is the entrepreneur who controls several stages of manufacture. (An important exception, but perhaps a recent one, is the development of entrepreneurship in the Iseyin cloth trade; many of the town's 2000 weavers work in their own sheds at piece rates for the capitalist who buys the yarn in Ibadan and Lagos and wholesales the finished garments in the same markets.)

Yoruba markets often number several hundred sellers (mostly women, for they do no farm work). But here too one finds no large-scale organization, though a highly complex one. Each woman is independent save perhaps for the assistance of a daughter or junior relative. Each works within a limited sphere, being limited to a single commodity (or group of related commodities) and moving over a regular route. The market women's guilds protect their members against trespass by non-members or sharp practice within their own group. A woman may, however, change her trade as she accumulates capital; today the wealthiest women are the imported-cloth sellers. The complexity of the trading pattern lies in the number of hands through which a yam, for instance, passes between the farmer and the consumer, as it is sold successively in a rural market, the town's wholesale market, and the ward market (Hodder, 1962).

An unexpected feature of the contemporary Yoruba market is the extensive sale of cooked food. The economy of buying in bulk and the small return expected by the cooks makes it cheaper for a housewife to buy some food ready cooked than to prepare it herself with small quantities of the raw material purchased in the market.

The Yoruba economy is thus characterized by a simple technology within which a considerable degree of skill may be shown, as for instance that displayed by the farmer, or by the trader in evaluating the state of local markets. Specialization is coordinated not by entrepreneurs but through the marketing system.

Furthermore, craftsmen and traders are not set apart from the society which they serve. They all live in the compounds of their own descent groups and are subject to such sanctions as are operated by these groups. In addition they have face-to-face relationships with their customers, and their business success depends as much on their popularity as on their financial acumen. The wealthy trader is thus usually a generous man —his generosity resulting in a quick turnover of capital but in an inability to accumulate it. Thus neither traders nor craftsmen have been in a good position to flout local norms and values to extend or develop their enterprises. (Traditionally, much of a man's profits went into acquisition of wives, a source of prestige and valuable in extending his circle of kin. Yet the increased number of resultant children guaranteed the fragmentation of his wealth at his death.) In Yoruba towns chieftaincy titles conferring high political office are usually available to all adult men. The principal prerequisite for election or selection to office is the support of a large number of kinsmen. Wealth is important too and it seems common among the Yoruba that a successful trader should seek political office; if he is successful in politics, his business activities decline as the new office yields a steady income in gifts and tribute.

Whether wealth may be gained through trade or political office, it is widely distributed upon the death of its creator. A man's self-acquired property is divided into as many equal parts as he has wives with children. Such a fragmenting distribution renders it difficult to maintain the business organization of the deceased. It is rare to encounter a wealthy man in traditional society who has started life with considerable inherited wealth.

The Family

The development of the nuclear family is one of the most frequently cited concomitants of urbanism. The compounds of the Yoruba descent group, however, often average, in a moderately sized town, a thousand persons; some may be considerably larger. The members of the group are bound by their corporate rights in land and in chieftaincy titles held by the group, and by their worship of ancestors and deities peculiar to the group (P. C. Lloyd, 1955a).

The members of the descent group are ranked by age. The most frequently used kinship terms for siblings differentiate those older from those younger than oneself, irrespective of sex. The seniority of women married into the group is determined by their date of marriage.

In spite of the appearance of communal living that may be presented by the traditional compound, since most daily tasks were carried out on its open verandahs, the domestic unit was the polygynous family. A man was expected to provide each of his wives with food sufficient for them to feed him (in turn) and their own children. The proximity of members of the extended family in particular, and of the descent group in general has made it possible to accommodate a number of by no means abnormal situations—the care of a child whose mother is dead or away trading, the feeding of a man whose wife is temporarily absent.

Family life, in these circumstances, has attributes diametrically opposed to those associated with the nuclear family of modern industrial society. They are sufficiently obvious and can be stated simply. Marriage involves the descent groups of the two parties and the couple are constrained by these groups throughout their lives. The wife retains her membership of her own group, and is not alienated from it to any marked degree; romantic love plays little part in her relationship with her husband. Most occupations are carried on within or from the compound and there is no separation of family and occupational roles. The child, growing up in the compound, is surrounded by a large number of kin who participate in the socialization process (Levine, 1967).

In the urban area, it is said, the family is bilateral or omnilineal—the bonds with kin through both father and mother are similar. The recently arrived immigrant to the town will wish to exploit those kin ties which promise most advantage, through whichever parent they lie. It is postulated therefore that men from those tribal societies with cognatic descent groups will adjust more quickly to urban life than those from rigidly patrilineal societies. The descent groups of the northern Yoruba are patrilineages, while those of the Ijebu are cognatic (Lloyd, 1966). The stereotype of Ijebu is of aggressive business activity and a high sense of achievement; but these attributes have yet to be demonstrated by psychological tests, and even if they are shown to exist may well derive more from land shortage in the Ijebu area than from family structure. In patrilineal Yoruba societies, married women retain close relationships with their own descent groups and, through them, their sons can obtain (though not claim or demand) valuable rights in land and political office. Yoruba family structure thus casts little light on the proposition stated at the beginning of the paragraph. Nor can one assert that the Yoruba pattern is derived from town living, except insofar as a woman's relationship with her own descent group is more easily maintained when her natal compound is in the same town as, and perhaps within a few hundred yards of, that of her husband.

Within the descent groups roles are multiplex, or highly interdependent, since so much of a man's social, economic, and political activity takes place within the compound, its farmland, and the regular meetings of its members. Within the town the constituent descent groups stand in a relationship of competition with one another, and this intensifies the interdependence of roles within each group. Yet matrilineal and affinal ties do relate men of different groups. Such ties, too, can be exploited in other contexts—for instance, trade or political support—and thus the multiplexity of relationships within the Yoruba town is intensified.

Social Stratification

The rural-urban dichotomy is often paralleled by that of ascribed and achieved status. A class structure develops in societies where status is achieved. It is even postulated that a peasant, coming from such a stratified society, will make a better adjustment to urban life than the tribal migrant from a "classless" society. An element of achievement and competition in tribal life seems often to be overlooked.

A Yoruba man cannot change his descent group nor alter his age. (An Ijebu can, of course, choose which group he will identify himself with—a choice limited in practice to one set of grandparents or the other.) But positions of great wealth and political power were open to those with the requisite talents. Wealth came mainly from trading, but also from farming, and was open to all; few traders inherited wealth from their fathers and each was a self-made man. Where chieftaincy titles were held by descent groups, one could of course strive only for the title of one's own group (or more rarely that of one's mother's group). Yet all male members of the lineage were equally eligible. Thus quite intense competition can exist within a tribal society; and this quality is functional in the modern African town to which the tribesman migrates.

Here again we must stress that, in the traditional Yoruba town, the achieved statuses of wealth or power were gained by those who substantially upheld the norms of the society—the trader relying on his popularity with his customers, the chief on the support of the members of his descent group (his constituents). Each stood at the apex of a pyramidal network of social relationships. Interaction between the chiefs and the wealthy did not extend much beyond formal meetings. They formed a category; they were scarcely a status group and certainly not a social class. It is, incidentally, a very similar image of a classless society that contemporary Yoruba politicians, in common with those of other African territories, are endeavoring to propagate.

The Integration of the Town

Without the king there would be no town, say the Yoruba, meaning that in the absence of his mediation the descent groups could not cohere in a single settlement. Some form of centralized government would indeed seem to be a *sine qua non* of town dwelling (P. C. Lloyd, 1954; 1960b).

Each Yoruba town, in the belief of its people, was founded by its first king. Subsequent immigrants, the founders of the descent groups, made pacts with the reigning ruler defining their own position and that of their descendants in the town. All groups are thus equally members of the town and there is little ranking among them. All members of a town participate in its government through their descent- and age-group meetings, their opinions being reported by their chiefs in the king's council. Annual rituals re-emphasize the relationship between the sacred king and his chiefs and people (Wheatley, 1970). The Yoruba man has a feeling of belonging to his town quite unlike that of the recent migrant to an industrial city or the lowly citizen in a medieval city.

Yet this integration is of a segmental type. Each of the constituent descent groups has the same general structure and characteristics. Every quarter of the traditional Yoruba town presented the same appearance. The emigration of a few descent groups (of farmers) would have little effect on the remainder of the town—less tribute for the king, a smaller market for craftsmen and traders. The town would shrink in response but its structure would remain the same. Similarly the town seems to be able to absorb large numbers of immigrants without structural change. One sees little basic difference in the structures of Ibadan, in the million-inhabitant range, the towns with 100,000 people, and those with 10,000-

20,000. It is possible that certain types of political structure may have maximum population limits, but this has not yet been explored. Much more probable is that rapid immigration might in the past have been exploited by an astute king to alter his relationship with his chiefs and thus produce a permanent change in the political structure.

In the pre-colonial period there does seem to have been quite a considerable movement of people from one town and kingdom to another. But this seems to have been absorbed into the existing structures of the recipient towns. The single migrant, perhaps a craftsman or professional, would lodge with his host who would guarantee his good behavior and find him land for farming. The immigrant would probably marry into his host's descent group and his children would become adopted into their mother's lineage. Larger groups of immigrants, the losing faction in a kingship dispute for instance, would approach the king of the recipient town and be granted land and perhaps ultimately a title; they would become new descent groups in the town. The Yoruba town had no place in its structure for the permanent stranger. (Slaves were numerous and did lack some civil rights; but Yoruba slavery was of the domestic type.)

Review

The attributes of the traditional Yoruba town here described seem far removed from those qualities of impersonality, transiency, superficiality, and anonymity often ascribed to urban areas but appearing most appropriate to the middle-class suburbs of mid-twentieth-century, highly industrialized societies. In some respects the attributes of the Yoruba town are the very opposite of those cited by Wirth. Some of them are, indeed, shared by pre-industrial towns, but in their totality they constitute an anomalous correlate with town settlement. There would seem to be much closer parallels between the structure of Yoruba society and that of the neighbouring Ibo, who live mostly in dispersed settlements in areas of very high population density.

The main difference between the Yoruba and the Ibo lies perhaps in the greater number of specialized crafts known to the Yoruba and their possession of sacred kingship. The Yoruba have had these attributes for several centuries, and although they have undoubtedly contributed to the complexity of Yoruba culture, they do not seem to have provided the impetus for sustained economic development.

The Yoruba Town Today

The impetus to economic development came to Yoruba country with colonial rule. Yet the development has taken such a form as to have maintained the indigenous social structure to a relatively high degree (P. C. Lloyd, 1959; Schwab, 1962).

The growing of cocoa, a cash crop, has spread throughout the forest areas. But there were no vast areas of suitable but unused land, and the new crop is cultivated on a peasant scale on land already allocated to the farmer by his descent group. Thus there has been no displacement of the farming population. The wealth from cocoa has led to the development of modern crafts—tailoring, building (of modern houses), furniture-making, etc. But these craftsmen too tend to live in the towns of their birth, often working from their own compound. The men of one craft are unrelated to one another and are associated into guilds, which on the one hand seem very similar to those of medieval Europe, but on the other hand derive obviously from indigenous forms of association. After two to five years' training the apprentice becomes his own master; there is very little cooperation in production among master-craftsmen (P. C. Lloyd, 1953). Entrepreneurship is developing in the building trades, where men of little or no technical skill, a minimum of capital, and rather more enterprise act on behalf of the customer in coordinating the activities of wall builder, plasterer, glazier, carpenter, and the like. Trading has greatly increased in intensity but not in the scale of organization.

Few industries have been established in Yoruba towns. Ibadan has a large tobacco factory, a plastic factory, and soft-drink bottling plants—none of them indigenous developments. Other towns go no further than posession of small bakeries and soft drink plants employing less than twenty persons. Only 6 per cent of the adult male population of Western Nigeria are wage earners, most of whom employed by the public services and the expatriate trading firms.

Thus, although the proportion of farmers in the Yoruba town is slowly declining, many of the attributes of these towns remain. Most men still live in the compounds of their descent groups; the cash value of land for development purposes and its growing scarcity as the population rises have probably resulted in a strengthening of the descent group in its capacity as a corporate landholder. Again, the values of the new craftsmen and traders are little different from their pre-colonial counterparts;

they too rely on their personal popularity in their face-to-face relationships with their customers.

During the colonial period the British administration ostensibly sought to preserve and govern through the indigenous political authorities. Thus the kingship and chieftaincy have been maintained to the present; and in maintaining chieftaincy, the solidarity of the descent groups has been upheld. These traditional institutions are, indeed, threatened by modern local and central government, with elections by adult suffrage. But ward and constituency boundaries often follow those of the compounds and quarters, and various local rivalries often develop into political factions and form the basis of membership of rival parties. Sometimes an election is contested between a nominee of party headquarters, a native of the constituency but not well known there, and the popular local trader or teacher, active in the welfare of his people; it is usually the latter who is successful (P. C. Lloyd, 1955b).

Thus the contemporary Yoruba town, in spite of its modern-looking houses, new shops, gas stations, and public buildings, is still far from possessing those features usually attributed to the urban area. Two processes are, however, producing a more rapid change.

In the years since national independence and its constitutional preludes, the size of the well-educated (in the Western sense) elite has multiplied several fold. The recruits to this category come from all types of homes many being children of illiterate farmers. Upward social mobility has been extremely rapid for a few men, and the image of an open society has been easily maintained. The men and women of this elite are endeavoring, however, through their understanding and manipulation of the educational system, to ensure elite status for their own numerous issue. If the economy should fail to expand at the same rapid rate as during the past decade, this elite will become an almost closed group (B. Lloyd, 1967; P. C. Lloyd, 1967).

Secondly, the establishment of free primary education by the Action Group government, in an attempt to satisfy the educational aspirations of the electorate, is producing an increasing flow to the larger towns of school leavers with job aspirations that are not likely to be met. These unemployed youths are, today, feared by the politicians as an incipient proletariat capable of manipulation by radical leaders.

The development of corporate sentiments among the elite and of class consciousness among the unskilled and perhaps unemployed primary-educated youth is impeded by their continuing loyalties to their home towns.

Today the Yoruba living in a town other than his own is still treated as a stranger. He has voting rights in local and national elections but is debarred from traditional political office. He is not absorbed into a local descent group. He tends to find his recreation among other strangers—the local people are fully occupied with the affairs of their own kin. As a public servant he is subject to frequent transfer from one town to another. Thus few Yoruba migrants seem to put down any roots in their new, and probably temporary, domiciles.

More important, however, is the fact that, by their emigration, they have lost none of their rights as members of the descent group. At any time they may return and claim land for farming and such prestige as their age entitles them to. Thus the poor man returns home seeking the security of his group; the wealthy man returns believing that his affluence and education will give him greater prestige among his own people than in the alien town. Every Yoruba hopes to retire and to die in his own compound, or at least in his own town.

The Yoruba example would certainly support a proposition that close ties will continue to bind the migrant with his home area when his status there is based upon age and membership of descent groups and when the rights deriving from those criteria are not lost by his emigration. In these circumstances one will find town and village associations most strongly developed among migrants.

Yoruba town associations are, of course, not confined to Yoruba country but are found wherever Yoruba have settled. Similarly Yoruba towns contain branches of associations formed by other ethnic groups, most especially by Ibo and Edo. These associations all have the dual function of socializing the immigrant into town life and maintaining his ties with his home. For the poor it is the social security provided that is most important; for the affluent the associations provide avenues for leadership and service which will yield prestige and, perhaps, political office when the migrant returns home. Almost every Yoruba migrant belongs to his town association; few are brave enough to risk the ostracism that would meet the non-participant when he returns home. All are, to some extent, subject to the social control exercised through the association.

To conclude: in spite of a limited degree of economic development—the introduction of permanent cash crops and of craft industries—the traditional social structure of Yoruba towns has strongly persisted. This is undoubtedly due to the relatively small displacement of population which has occurred and the patterns of migration resulting in the maintenance of loyalties to the home area. In some respects modernizing factors may even have reinforced the solidarity of the descent groups—as corporate owners of valuable town land and as electoral units in modern government. On the other hand, the towns contain an increasing number of non-natives as the primary-school leavers migrate in search of work, and these men and women will form new associations in the town, notwithstanding their membership of their ethnic associations. As men gain more secure types of employment, as increased social services are provided by the state, so will a man's dependence on his descent group decrease, and in corresponding measure his feelings of obligation to it.

References Cited

Bascom, W. B.
1955. "Urbanization among the Yoruba." *American Journal of Sociology* 60:446-54.
1959. "Urbanism as a traditional African pattern." *Sociological Review* 7: 29-43.
1969. *Ifa Divination.* Bloomington: Indiana University Press.
Calloway, A.
1965. "From Traditional Crafts to Modern Industries." *Odu* 2(1):28-51.
Frobenius, L.
1913. *The Voice of Africa.* London: Hutchinson.
Goddard, S.
1965. "Town-Farm Relations in Yorubaland—Oyo." *Africa* 35(1):21-29.
Hodder, B. W.
1962. "Yoruba Markets." In *Markets in Africa,* ed. P. J. Bohannan and G. Dalton. New York: The Natural History Press.
Krapf-Askari, E.
1969. *Yoruba Towns and Cities.* Oxford: Clarendon Press.
Leighton, A., *et al.*
1963. *Psychiatric Disorder among the Yoruba.* Ithaca: Cornell University Press.
Levine, R. A.
1967. "Father-Child Relationships in Ibadan." In *The City in Modern Africa,* ed. H. Miner. New York: Praeger.
Lloyd, B.
1966. "Education and Family Life in the Development of Class among the Yoruba." In *The New Elites of Tropical Africa,* ed. P. C. Lloyd. London: Oxford University Press, for International African Institute.

1967. "Oje: A Traditional Quarter of Ibadan." In *City of Ibadan,* eds. P. C. Lloyd, A. Mabogunje, and B. Awe. Cambridge, Eng.: Cambridge University Press.

Lloyd, P. C.

1953. "Craft Organisations in Yoruba Towns." *Africa* 23:30-44.

1954. "The Traditional Political Systems of the Yoruba." *Southwestern Journal of Anthropology* 10(4):366-84.

1955a. "The Yoruba Lineage." *Africa* 25:235-51.

1955b. "The Development of Political Parties in Western Nigeria." *American Political Science Review* 49:693-707.

1959. "The Yoruba Town Today." *Sociological Review* 7:45-63.

1960a. "Yoruba Towns." *Ibadan* 10:18-22.

1960b. "Sacred Kingship and Government among the Yoruba." *Africa* 30: 221-37.

1962. *Yoruba Land Law.* London: Oxford University Press for Nigerian Institute of Social and Economic Research.

1965. "The Yoruba." In *Peoples of Africa,* ed. J. Gibbs. New York: Holt, Rinehart & Winston.

1966a. "Agnatic and Cognatic Descent among the Yoruba." *Man,* N.S. 1(4): 484-500.

1966b. "Class Consciousness among the Yoruba." In *The New Elites of Tropical Africa.*

ed. 1966. *The New Elites of Tropical Africa.* London: Oxford University Press for International African Institute.

1967. "The Elite of Ibadan." In *The City of Ibadan.*

Lloyd, P. C., A. Mabogunje, and B. Awe, eds.

1967. *The City of Ibadan.* Cambridge, Eng.: Cambridge University Press.

Mabogunje, A. L.

1968. *Urbanization in Nigeria.* London: University of London Press.

Schwab, W. B.

1962. "Continuity and Change in the Yoruba Lineage System." *Ann. N.Y. Acad. Sci.* 96:590-605.

1965. "Oshogbo—An Urban Community." In *Urbanization and Migration in West Africa,* ed. H. Kuper. Berkeley: University of California Press.

Sjoberg, G.

1960. *The Preindustrial City.* Glencoe, Ill.: Free Press.

Wheatley, Paul

1970. "The Significance of Traditional Yoruba Urbanism." *Comparative Studies in Society and History* 12:390-419.

Some Perspectives on Urbanization with Special Reference to Mexico City

Oscar Lewis

My interest in studies of urbanism and the urbanization process in Mexico City has been a direct outgrowth of my earlier study of Tepoztlan. In that work I suggested that the folk-urban continuum was an inadequate theoretical model for the study of culture change and needed drastic revision.[1] Later, in my follow-up study of Tepoztecans who had migrated to Mexico City, I found evidence which strengthened this conviction, this time viewing the problem from the urban pole.[2]

The terms folk, rural, and urban each encompass a wide range of phenomena with multiple variables which have to be carefully sorted out, ordered, dissected, and perhaps redefined, if we are to establish meaning-

1. Oscar Lewis, *Life in a Mexican Village: Tepoztlan Restudied.* Urbana. University of Illinois Press, 1951.

2. There has been a growing literature of criticism of the folk-urban and rural-urban dichotomies by urban sociologists. See for example, Theodore Caplow, "The Social Ecology of Guatemala City," *Social Forces* 28, December 1949; Philip M. Hauser, "The Urban-Folk and Urban-Rural Dichotomies as Forms of Western Ethnocentrism," mimeographed paper for the SSRC Committee on Urbanization, 1959; William L. Kolb, "The Social Structure and Function of Cities," *Economic Development and Culture Change,* October 1954; Duncan and Reiss, *Social Characteristics of Urban and Rural Communities,* 1950, New York: John Wiley and Sons, 1956, Part IV; Gideon Sjoberg, "Comparative Urban Sociology," in *Sociology Today,* New York: Basic Books, 1959, 334-59. Horace Miner has attempted to defend the Redfield position in what seems to me to be a rather apologetic article. A careful reading will show that he accepts most of the criticism although he swallows hard. See his "The Folk-Urban Continuum" in Hatt and Reiss, *et al., Cities and Society,* Glencoe, Ill.: The Free Press, 1957, pp. 22-34.

ful, causal relationships among them. Each of these terms implies relatively high-level abstractions intended for the characterization of whole societies or large segments thereof. While such characterizations are attractive because of their simplicity and may be useful in distinguishing gross stages or types in societal evolution, they confuse issues in the study of short-run changes, and their heuristic value as research tools has never been proven.

Hauser has put this criticism admirably. He writes,

> There is evidence, by no means conclusive as yet, that both parts of these dichotomies [i.e., folk-urban and rural-urban] represent confounded variables and, in fact, complex systems of variables which have yet to be unscrambled. The dichotomizations perhaps represent all too hasty efforts to synthesize and integrate what little knowledge has been acquired in empirical research. The widespread acceptance of these ideal type constructs as generalizations, without benefit of adequate research, well illustrates the dangers of catchy neologisms which often get confused with knowledge.[3]

In his elaboration of the folk-urban continuum, Robert Redfield sought to achieve greater sophistication than earlier societal typologies by utilizing traits or variables which were of a general, more abstract nature. For example, whereas Hobhouse, Wheeler, and Ginsburg distinguished between food-gathering, hunting and fishing, agricultural, and pastoral economies, and sought to establish their social and juridical correlates, Redfield's definition of the folk society as an ideal type never specified a type of technology or economy beyond stating that it was simple, subsistence motivated, without money, familial, etc.

In his later work Redfield showed some important but subtle changes in his thinking which have not been given sufficient emphasis by his disciples. Here I should like to mention two such changes. First, he seemed to be less sanguine about the possibility of deriving sound general propositions concerning social and cultural change and gave more stress to descriptive integration, "understanding," and the element of art in the social sciences. Compare for example his *Folk Culture of Yucatan* with *The Village That Chose Progress.* In the former, he was still optimistic about finding regularities in culture change. In the latter, he gave us a brilliant description of changes in Chan Kom but made no attempt to relate these changes to the theoretical framework of the folk-urban continuum.

3. Hauser, *op. cit.*, p. 14.

A second change is to be seen in *The Primitive World and Its Transformations,* where he no longer conceives of the folk society exclusively as an ideal type. Rather, he treats it as a type of real society. In this book Redfield takes a frank neo-evolutionary stance, identifying the folk society with the pre-agricultural and early Neolithic period and with the tribal (and I would add pre-tribal) level. In an effort to find common elements he paints with a big brush, lumping together all the peoples of the world prior to the Neolithic, irrespective of whether they were food gatherers, fishers or hunters, whether they had rich or poor resources, whether they were starving or produced some surplus. In the very nature of the case, this approach glosses over the more refined archeological distinctions, between the Lower and Upper Paleolithic, each with subdivisions based upon new technologies and inventions.

True, we have little evidence about societal types for the prehistoric periods. However, a theoretical scheme must somehow take into account many levels and types of societal development prior to the rise of cities. Otherwise, there are unexplained and sudden breaks in the postulated evolutionary sequence from folk to urban. Indeed, if one had to choose between evolutionary schemes, there is still a good deal to be said in favor of Morgan's *Ancient Society* despite its many factual errors and crude technological determinism. Fortunately, we have other, more sophisticated, alternatives, such as the multilinear evolution of Julian Steward[4] and the very suggestive and stimulating work of Irving Goldman.[5]

The identification of the folk society with the pre-Neolithic seems to me to invalidate, or at least to raise serious questions about, Redfield's work in *The Folk Cultures of Yucatan,* since all of the Yucatan communities were agricultural peasant societies, which, by his own definition, are part societies subject in varying degree to urban influences. Even his most "folk-like" community of Quintana Roo was producing hennequin for the world market.

Similarly, some of my own criticism of his Tepoztlan work, as well as Sol Tax's criticism based upon the Guatemalan studies, would seem to be beside the point since both Tax and I were dealing with communities which had left the folk stage (if they were ever in it) for at least a few

4. Julian H. Steward, *Theory of Culture Change,* Urbana: University of Illinois Press, 1947.

5. Irving Goldman, "Status Rivalry and Cultural Evolution in Polynesia," *American Anthropologist* 57 (4):680-97; "Evolution and Anthropology," in *The Journal of Victorian Studies,* Sept. 1959, pp. 55-75; "Variations in Polynesian Social Organization," *Journal of the Polynesian Society* 66 (4):374-90.

thousand years. To this extent, Ralph Beals' comment that Tepoztlan was not a crucial case for evaluating the transition from folk to peasant to urban has considerable merit, because Tepoztlan was already a well-advanced peasant society in pre-Hispanic days. But by the same token, I know of no other contemporary community study in Meso-America which would serve this purpose any better. Actually, Redfield had assumed a survival of folk, that is Paleolithic, elements in Tepoztlan; but we have no evidence in that village for this period.

The traditional contrast between societies based on kinship and those based on non-kinship or contract is not only inaccurate but of so broad and general a nature as to be of little help in the analysis of the process of change. To say of a society that it is organized on a kinship basis doesn't tell us enough for purposes of comparative analysis. It may be a nuclear family system as among the Shoshone Indians, a lineage system as in Tikopia, or a clan system as among the Zuni Indians. We still have a lot to learn about the more modest problem of how and under what conditions in a given society a simple nuclear, bilateral system turns into a unilateral clan system, and the social, economic, and psychological concomitants thereof. As a general proposition I would like to suggest that we may learn more about the processes of change by studying relatively short-run sequential modifications in particular aspects of institutions in both the so-called folk and urban societies, than by global comparisons between folk and urban.

Pre-urban and pre-industrial societies have been capable of developing class stratification, elaborate priesthoods, status rivalry, and many other phenomena which are implicitly and unilaterally attributed to the growth of cities, according to the folk-urban conception of social change. Tonga, the Maori, and native Hawaii are good examples of this. Even among a fishing and hunting people like the Kwakiutl Indians, we find class stratifications, slavery, and war. The Kwakiutl case illustrates the importance of including natural resources as a significant variable in evolutionary schemes. I find no such variable in the folk-urban continuum.

In place of, or in addition to, the handy designations folk society, peasant society, urban society, we need a large number of sub-types based upon better-defined variables and perhaps the addition of new ones.[6]

6. I have made this point in an earlier paper, "Peasant Culture in India and Mexico," in *Village India* (ed. Mckim Marriott), *AA* 57 (3), Part 2. Memoir No. 83, June 1955, "For both applied and theoretical anthropology we need typologies of peasantry for the major culture areas of the world. . . . Moreover, within each area we

Hauser's observations on the Western ethnocentrism implicit in the folk-urban and rural-urban dichotomies is well taken. Redfield's firsthand research experience in Mexican communities, which were essentially endogamous, tended to confirm his preconception of the folk society as "inward-looking." The thinking of Simmel, Toennies, Durkheim, and others, which influenced Redfield, was also based on experience with the endogamous peasant communities of Europe. Had these men done fieldwork with the Nuer of Africa, with the Australian aborigines, or with the north Indian peasants, it is quite possible that Redfield's ideal type model of the folk society would have been different.

Before turning to an examination of some of the assumptions of the Simmel-Wirth-Redfield axis regarding urbanism, I would like to present in brief some of my own research findings in Mexico which can serve as a starting point for the discussion. The relevant findings of my first Mexico City study of 1951 can be summarized as follows. (1) Peasants in Mexico City adapted to city life with far greater ease than one would have expected, judging from comparable studies in the United States and from folk-urban theory. (2) Family life remained quite stable and extended family ties increased rather than decreased. (3) Religious life became more Catholic and disciplined, indicating the reverse of the anticipated secularization process. (4) The system of *compadrazgo* continued to be strong, albeit with some modifications. (5) The use of village remedies and beliefs persisted.

In the light of these findings I wrote at the time, ". . . this study provides evidence that urbanization is not a single, unitary, universally similar process but assumes different forms and meanings, depending upon the prevailing historic, economic, social, and cultural conditions."[7]

---

need more refined subclassifications. Only after such studies are available will we be in a position to formulate broad generalizations about the dynamics of peasant culture as a whole" (p. 165).

7. Oscar Lewis, "Urbanization Without Breakdown: A Case Study," in *The Scientific Monthly* 75 (1), July 1952. In this article I have suggested a number of specific Mexican conditions which might explain the special findings. More recently Joseph A. Kahl has restated and elaborated upon some of these points in his article "Some Social Concomitants of Industrialization and Urbanization," *Human Organization* 18 (2):53-74 (1959). See also Ralph L. Beals, "Urbanism, Urbanization and Acculturation," *AA* 53 (1), Jan.-Mar. 1951; William Mangin, "Mental Health and Migration to Cities: A Peruvian Case," *Annals of the New York Academy of Sciences* 84, Article 17, pp. 911-17, Dec. 1960; Douglas S. Butterworth, "A Study of the Urbanization Process Among Mixtec Migrants from Tilaltongo in Mexico City," *America Indigena* 22(3), July 1962, pp. 257-74.

Because of the unusual nature of my findings, I decided to test them in 1956-57 against a much wider sample of non-Tepoztecan city families. I selected two lower-class housing settlements or *vecindades,* both located in the same neighborhood within a few blocks of the Tepito market and only a short walk from the central square of Mexico City. In contrast with the Tepoztecan city families, who represented a wide range of socioeconomic levels and were scattered in twenty-two colonias throughout the city, my new sample was limited to two settlements whose residents came from over twenty-four of the thirty-two states and territories of the Mexican nation.[8]

On the whole, our research findings tended to support those of the earlier study. The findings suggested that the lower-class residents of Mexico City showed much less of the personal anonymity and isolation of the individual which had been postulated by Wirth as characteristic of urbanism as a way of life. The *vecindad* and the neighborhood tended to break up the city into small communities which act as cohesive and personalizing factors. It was found that many people spend most of their lives within a single *colonia* or district, and even when there were frequent changes of residence, they were usually within a restricted geographical area determined by low rentals. Lifetime friendships and daily face-to-face relations with the same people were common, and resembled a village situation. Most marriages also occurred within the *colonia* or adjoining *colonias.* Again, we found that extended family ties were quite strong, as measured by visiting, especially in times of emergency, and that a relatively high proportion of the residents of the *vecindades* were related by kinship and *compadrazgo* ties.

In spite of the cult of *machismo* and the overall cultural emphasis upon male superiority and dominance, we found a strong tendency toward matricentered families, in which the mother plays a crucial role in parent-child relations even after the children are married. In genealogical studies we found that most people recalled a much larger number of relatives on the mother's side than on the father's side.

We also found that the *vecindad* acted as a shock absorber for the rural migrants to the city because of the similarity between its culture and that of rural communities. Both shared many of the traits which I have elsewhere designated as the culture of poverty. Indeed, we found no sharp

8. Oscar Lewis, "The Culture of the Vecindad in Mexico City: Two Case Studies," *Actas de III Congresso Internacional de Americanistas,* Tomo I, San José, Costa Rica, 1959, pp. 387-402.

differences in family structure, diet, dress, and belief systems of the *vecindad* tenants according to their rural-urban origins. The use of herbs for curing, the raising of animals, the belief in sorcery and spiritualism, the celebration of the Day of the Dead, illiteracy and low level of education, political apathy and cynicism about government, and the very limited membership and participation in both formal and informal associations, were just as common among persons who had been in the city for over thirty years as among recent arrivals. Indeed, we found that *vecindad* residents of peasant background who came from small land-holding families showed more middle-class aspirations in their desire for a higher standard of living, home ownership, and education for their children, than did city-born residents of the lower income group.

These findings suggest the need for a reexamination of some aspects of urban theory and for modifications which would help explain the findings from Mexico City and other cities in underdeveloped countries, as well as those from Chicago.

Wirth defines a city as "a relatively large, dense, and permanent settlement of socially heterogeneous individuals." By "socially heterogeneous" he had in mind primarily distinctive ethnic groups rather than class differences. Wirth defines urbanism as the mode of life of people who live in cities or who are subject to their influence. Because Wirth thinks of the city as a whole, as a community (and here, I believe, is one of his errors), he assumes that all people who live in cities are affected by this experience in profound and similar ways, namely, the weakening of kinship bonds, family life, and neighborliness, and the development of impersonality, superficiality, anonymity, and transitoriness in personal relations. For Wirth, the process of urbanization is essentially a process of disorganization.[9]

This approach leads to some difficulties. For one thing, as Sjoberg has pointed out, ". . . their interpretations [i.e. those of Park, Wirth and Redfield] involving ecology have not articulated well with their efforts to explain social activities."[10] Wirth himself showed some of the contradictory aspects of city life without relating them to his theory of urbanism. He writes of the city as the historic center of progress, of learning, of higher standards of living and all that is hopeful for the future of mankind, but he also points to the city as the locus of slums, poverty, crime,

9. Louis Wirth, "Urbanism As A Way of Life," *American J. of Sociology* 44 (July, 1938), pp. 1-24.
10. Sjoberg, *op. cit.*, p. 340.

and disorganization. According to Wirth's theory, both the carriers of knowledge and progress (the elite and the intellectuals) and the ignorant slum dwellers have a similar urban personality, since presumably they share in the postulated urban anonymity, etc.

It is in the evaluation of the personality of the urban dweller that urban theory has gone farthest afield. It leaps from the analysis of the social system to conjecture about individual personality; it is based not upon solid psychological theory but upon personal values, analogies, and outmoded physio-psychological concepts. Some of the description of the modern urbanite reads like another version of the fall of man. The delineation of the urbanite as blase, indifferent, calculating, utilitarian, and rational (presumably as a defensive reaction to preserve his nervous system from the excessive shocks and stimuli of city life), suffering from anonymity and anomie, being more conscious and intellectual than his country brother yet feeling less deeply, remain mere statements of faith.[11]

Besides the lack of an adequate personality theory, it seems to me that some of the difficulty stems from the attempt to make individual psychological deductions from conditions prevailing in the city as a whole. The city is not the proper unit of comparison or discussion for the study of social life because the variables of number, density, and heterogeneity as used by Wirth are not the crucial determinants of social life or of personality.[12] There are many intervening variables. Social life is not a mass phenomenon. It occurs for the most part in small groups, within the family, within households, within neighborhoods, within the Church, formal and informal groups, etc.

Any generalizations about the nature of social life in the city must be based upon careful studies of these smaller universes rather than upon *a priori* statements about the city as a whole. Similarly, generalizations about urban personality must be based on careful personality studies. The delineation of social areas within cities and a careful analysis of their characteristics would take us a long way beyond the over-generalized formulations of "urbanism as a way of life."

Basic to this Simmel-Wirth-Redfield approach are the supposed consequences of the predominance of primary relations in small rural com-

11. Louis Wirth, "Urbanism As A Way of Life," in *Community Life and Social Policy,* pp. 119-20. Chicago: University of Chicago Press, 1964.

12. Sjoberg has correctly criticized the logic of comparison inherent in the writings of Redfield and Wirth on folk-urban theory on the ground that they were comparing a whole society with a part society. Here my criticism is that Wirth treated the city as a whole society for purposes of social relations and personality.

munities versus the predominance of secondary relations in large cities. It seems to me that the psychological and social consequences of primary versus secondary relations have been misunderstood and exaggerated for both the country and the city. I know of no experimental or other good evidence to indicate that exposure to large numbers of people *per se* makes for anxiety and nervous strain or that the existence of secondary relations diminishes the strength and importance of primary ones. Primary group relations are just as important psychologically for city people as they are for country people, and sometimes they are more satisfying and more profound. And while the sheer number of secondary relations in the city is much greater than in the country, these relations can also be said to be secondary in the sense that their psychological consequences are minor.

The number of profound warm and understanding human relationships or attachments is probably limited in any society, rural or urban, modern or backward. Such attachments are not necessarily or exclusively a function of frequency of contact and fewness of numbers. They are influenced by cultural traditions which may demand reserve, and mind-your-own business attitude, a distrust of neighbors, fear of sorcery and gossip, and the absence of a psychology of introspection.

George Foster's comparative analysis of the quality of interpersonal relations in small peasant societies, based upon anthropological monographs, shows that they are characterized by distrust, suspicion, envy, violence, reserve, and withdrawal.[13] His paper confirms my earlier findings on Tepoztlan.

In some villages, peasants can live out their lives without any deep knowledge or understanding of the people whom they "know" in face-to-face relationships. By contrast, in modern Western cities, there may be more give and take about one's private, intimate life at a single "sophisticated" cocktail party than would occur in years in a peasant village. But seriously, I suspect there are deeper, more mature human relationships among sympathetic, highly educated, cosmopolitan individuals who have chosen each other in friendship, than are possible among sorcery-ridden, superstitious, ignorant peasants, who are daily thrown together because of kinship or residential proximity.

It is a common assumption in social science literature that the process of urbanization for both tribal and peasant peoples is accompanied by a

13. George Foster, "The Personality of the Peasant," paper read at the 58th Annual Meeting of the American Anthropological Assn., Mexico City, 1959.

change in the structure of the family, from an extended to a nuclear family. It is assumed that the rural family is extended and the urban nuclear. It must be pointed out that not even all primitive or pre-literate people are characterized by a preponderance of the extended family as the residential unit. The Eskimo is a good example. Among peasantry, also, one finds a wide range of conditions in this regard. In most highland Mexican villages the nuclear family predominates as the residence unit. Very often and without any evidence, this fact is interpreted as a symptom of change from an earlier condition.[14] In India, one finds a remarkable difference in family composition by castes within a single village. For example, in Rampur village in the State of Delhi, the Jats and Brahmans, both of whom own and work the land, have large extended families, whereas the landless lower-caste Sweepers and Leatherworkers have small nuclear families.

I suggest that we must distinguish much more carefully between the existence of the extended family as a residence unit and as a social group. In Mexico, the extended family is important as a social group in both rural and urban areas where the nuclear family predominates as the residence unit. In Mexico, the persistence of extended family bonds seems compatible with urban life and increased industrialization. Moreover, the *compadre* system, with its extension of adoptive kinship ties, is operative, though in somewhat distinctive ways, on all class levels. I suspect that increased communication facilities in Mexico, especially the telephone and the car, may strengthen rather than weaken extended family ties.

One of the most distinctive characteristics of cities, whether in the industrial or pre-industrial age, is that they provide, at least potentially, a wider range of alternatives for individuals in most aspects of living than is provided by the non-urban areas of the nation or total society at a given time. Urbanism and urbanization can be defined as the availability of a wide range of services and alternatives in terms of types of work, housing, food, clothing, educational facilities, medical facilities, modes of travel, voluntary organizations, types of people, etc.

If we were to accept these criteria we could develop indices of the degree of urbanization of different sectors of the population within cities. For example, if the population of any subsector of a city had fewer alter-

14. Pedro Tarasco's analysis (1962) of a population census of Tepoztlan of 1550 showed a much higher incidence of the extended family than I found in 1950. However, even in 1550 the majority of families were of the simple, nuclear type!

natives in types of clothing, foods, etc., either because of traditional ethnic sanctions or lack of economic resources, we could designate this population sector as showing a lower degree of urbanization than some other sector. This does not apply to the city alone; the scale of urbanization can also be applied to villages, towns, and to their respective populations.

As I see it, therefore, there are two sides to the urbanization coin: one, the amount and variety of services, etc., to be found in any city, and two, the extent to which different sectors of the city residents can partake of these services. For this distinction it follows that two cities may show the same urbanization index in terms of the number and variety of services per capita but may be very different in terms of the degree of urbanization (cosmopolitanism) of the various sectors of its inhabitants.

It also follows that there are many ways of life which may coexist within a single city. This is particularly evident in the underdeveloped countries, where class or caste differences are sharp. In Mexico City, for example, there are approximately a million and a half people who live in one-room *vecindades* or in primitive *jacales,* with little opportunity to partake of the great variety of housing facilities available for the tourists and the native bourgeoisie. Most of this large mass still have a low level of education and literacy, do not belong to labor unions, do not participate in the benefits of the Social Security system, make very little use of the city's museum, art galleries, banks, hospitals, department stores, concerts, airports, etc. These people live in cities—indeed, a considerable portion were born in the city—but they are not highly urbanized. From this point of view, then, the poor in all cities of the world are less urbanized, that is less cosmopolitan, than the wealthy.

What I have called the culture or subculture of poverty is a provincial, locally oriented culture, both in the city and in the country.[15] In Mexico, it is characterized by a relatively higher death rate, a higher proportion of the population in the younger age groups (less than 15 years), a higher proportion of gainfully employed in the total population, including child labor and working women. Some of these indices for poor *colonias* (districts) of Mexico City are much higher than for rural Mexico as a whole.

On another level the culture of poverty in Mexico, cutting across the rural and the urban, is characterized by the absence of food reserves in the home, the pattern of frequent buying of small quantities of food many

15. See my Introduction in *The Children of Sanchez,* New York: Random House, 1961.

times a day as the need occurs, borrowing money from money lenders at usurious interest rates, the pawning of goods, spontaneous informal credit devices among neighbors, the use of secondhand clothing and furniture, particularly in the city, which has the largest secondhand market in Mexico, a higher incidence of free unions or consensual marriages, a strong present-time orientation, and a higher proportion of pre-Hispanic folk beliefs and practices.

In the preoccupation with the study of rural-urban differences there has been a tendency to overlook or neglect basic similarities of people everywhere. In a recent paper Bruner[16] has illustrated this point for Indonesia, where he found that the urban and rural Toba Batak are essentially part of a single social and economic ceremonial system.

Mexico-India contrasts also illustrate his point. In Mexico, Catholicism gives a similar stamp to many aspects of life in both rural and urban areas. The nucleated settlement pattern of most Mexican villages with the central church and plaza and the barrio subdivisions, each in turn with its respective chapel, makes for a distinctive design which is in marked contrast to the north Indian villages where Hinduism and the caste system have made for a much more segmented and heterogeneously organized type of settlement pattern. It is my impression that a similar contrast is to be seen in some of the cities of these two countries, and I believe this merits further study. Taking another example from India, we find that the way of life of the urban and rural lower castes, such as Washermen and Sweepers, have much more in common with each other than with the higher-caste Brahmans in their respective urban and rural contexts.

Although I agree that number, density, permanence of settlement, and heterogeneity of population is a workable definition of a city, I believe we need an additional, more elementary, set of variables, with a narrower focus, to explain what goes on within cities. The sheer physical conditions of living have a considerable influence on social life, and I would include, among the variables, such factors as stability of residence, the settlement pattern, types of housing, the number of rooms per family, property concepts, etc.

A type of housing settlement like the *vecindad,* which brings people into daily face-to-face contact, in which people do most of their work

16. Edward M. Bruner, "Urbanization and Culture Change: Indonesia," paper read at the 58th Annual Meeting of the AAA in Mexico City, December 28, 1959.

in a common patio, share a common toilet and a common washstand, encourages intensive interaction, not all of which is necessarily friendly. It makes little difference whether this housing and settlement pattern is in the city or the country, indeed whether it occurs among the tribal peoples of Borneo or the Iroquois Indians. In all cases it produces intense interaction, problems of privacy, quarrels among children and among their parents.

Stability of residence too has many similar social consequences wherever it occurs. As I have already shown, in Mexico City the *vecindades* make for a kind of community life which has greater resemblance to our stereotyped notions of village life than to Wirth's description of urbanism. Stability of residence may result from a wide variety of factors, both in rural and urban areas. Nor can we assume that it is a necessary concomitant of non-urban societies; witness the nomadism of the Plains Indians or of agricultural workers in parts of the Caribbean.

Certain aspects of the division of labor stand up well as an elementary narrow-focus variable. When the family is the unit of production, and the home and the work place are one, certain similar consequences follow for family life, both in the country and the city. I have in mind similarities in family life of small artisans in Mexico City and in rural villages. In both, husband and wife spend most of the day together, children are early recruited into useful work, and there is much interaction between family members. Thus, in terms of the amount of time husbands spend away from home, there is much more similarity between a peasant and a factory worker than between either of these and an artisan.

What we need in comparative urban studies as well as in rural-urban comparisons, within a single culture and cross-culturally, are carefully controlled, narrow-focus comparisons of subunits. Here I will list what seem to me to be priorities in research, with special reference to the underdeveloped countries.

1. The delineation of distinctive regions within cities in terms of their demographic, ecological, economic, and social characteristics with the objective of developing measures of urbanization for distinctive population sectors as well as for the city as a whole.

2. Cross-cultural studies of comparable population sectors within cities. For example, we might compare lower-class areas in cities of Japan, India, England, and Mexico, utilizing a common research methodology, so that we could check the role of distinctive cultural factors on comparable urban sectors.

3. Comparisons of the economic, social, and psychological aspects of an equal number of families with the same full-time non-agricultural occupations in a village and in the city within a single country. One objective would be to test the influence of rural versus urban milieu and the many theories associated with same.

4. Studies of the socioeconomic and psychological consequences of the introduction of factories in villages and towns in predominantly peasant countries. A crucial methodological point in such studies would be to select communities prior to the introduction of the factory so that we could have a solid baseline against which changes can be measured.

   One of the weaknesses of most studies to date is that they have had to reconstruct the pre-factory conditions of the community. For example, Manning Nash in his excellent study of a Guatemalan community had to reconstruct the village culture as it was seventy years before, when the factory was first introduced. Similarly, Burlison in his study of Zacapu, Michoacan, Mexico, on the effects of a Celanese rayon factory, had to reconstruct the town conditions as they were fourteen years ago. In the interim the population had grown from about 6,000 to 25,000.

4a. Most studies of the influence of factories have dealt with light industries such as textiles or rayons. It would be good to have studies on the effects of heavy industries such as steel or mining, or chemical plants which demand more skilled labor and continuous operation.

5. Intensive case studies of individuals and families who have moved from tribal communities to urban centers, focusing on the problems of adjustment and the process of acculturation. In terms of method, it would be important to select families from communities which have been carefully studied.

6. Similar studies should be done for peasants and plantation workers who move to the city. The objective of studying subjects from different backgrounds is to learn what different effects, if any, this will have upon the urbanization process. I suspect that the greater disorganization reported by Kahl in his review of African materials as compared to Mexican data can be explained by the fact that the African studies reported on tribal peoples moving to the city, whereas in Mexico we are dealing with peasants. On purely theoretical grounds I would expect that culture shock would be greater for tribal peoples.

The History of Urbanization in Japan

Takeo Yazaki

The Transformation of Early Japanese Social Life and the Rise of the Ancient City

Long after people first settled the Japanese Islands, until about 200 B.C., society remained small, isolated, non-literate, homogeneous, and classless, with a strong sense of group solidarity. Kinship relations and institutions were the categories of experience, the familial group was the main unit of action, and the sacred prevailed over the secular.

As wetland rice cultivation diffused from continental China and spread throughout Japan (200-100 B.C.), local clusters of families cooperating in this new form of production began to take on the structure of villages. Each grouping of families living and working on the same tract of land and united under the names of the same ancestors and deity was called *uji*. Its hierarch or priest-ruler, called the *uji-no-kami*, mediated between the deity and the people—the *uji-bito*. Lesser hierarchs and their villages were subject to more powerful hierarchs, in a subordinate and servile status.

By the latter half of the third century A.D., the local kinship groups had been integrated into a larger state focused upon the Yamato Court[1] in central Japan. Through a system of tribute and compulsory labor, the *uji-no-kami* were able to develop their own military support, bringing previously isolated villages within the expanding structure of the Ya-

1. The Yamato state, centered upon the plain east of present Osaka and south of Kyoto, is the first central and centralizing kingdom of the Japanese tradition. It was from this base that the whole of Japan was gradually brought under control, and from which the long line of emperors claims continuity. From the beginning it shows the strong influence of Chinese culture, constantly transformed by the Japanese.

mato state. But religious, political, and military functions all attached, with little differentiation, to each level of the *uji-no-kami.* Communities tended to be self-sufficient and rather insular, and the economic surplus drawn from the peasants was small. Power was not highly centralized, and at this stage no city appeared as the locus of large-scale central institutions or of a concentrated population; the development of a capital city came only as the Yamato regime undertook to regulate international relations and to define the rights of the *uji-no-kami* over land and people, bringing them all more directly under the control of the emperor.

With the achievement of a legally defined state based on the Taika[2] reforms of A.D. 645, politics and religion were institutionally separated, although the emperor remained at the apex of both structures. While in principle the Ritsuryo system[3] provided for the recruitment of able men into the bureaucracy regardless of their family standing, in practice the influence of powerful families tended to prevail, for it was they who had put the emperor on the throne, and they who still ruled. The ordinary population consisted of two status groups only—the peasants (*ryomin*), and the servants and slaves (*senmin*).

The first Japanese city was Heijokyo (Nara), political and religious capital of the Yamato regime. It did not emerge spontaneously; men and materials were purposefully brought together through the political and religious power of the emperor and supported by the organized influence of the shrines and temples. The geographical center of Japan, traditionally the cultural center of the country, was chosen as the capital site.

2. The Taika reforms were a major landmark in the series of efforts to formalize and codify the structure of the state. They reflected the increasing adoption of Chinese civilization by Japan, which was already becoming Buddhist and using Chinese writing. They endeavored to turn the semi-autonomous local lords and chieftains into state officials and the land into a national patrimony instead of a series of private estates. Fields and households were to be registered, taxes and contributions defined and allocated, central and local government agencies established and their jurisdictions fixed, officers appointed and a system of communications between them maintained. The construction of a permanent capital city was also envisaged for the first time.

3. The Ritsuryo system marks the early climax in the struggle to formalize and regularize the state structure. From 701 A.D. onwards, with revisions in 718 A.D., the Ritsuryo code was embodied in many volumes, laying down civil and penal codes, the whole legal and administrative system of central ministries, and the elaborate hierarchy of territorial units, all of which remained basically unchanged in principle for nearly 1200 years. It was an ideal structure, rarely implemented in practice, but constantly appealed to and never losing its theoretical legitimacy and prestige.

Spatially Heijokyo was fashioned after the Chinese model, being laid out on the pattern of a checkerboard. Government buildings were located on the northern edge of the city—a sacred location, according to Chinese tradition. To the south the trading posts of the nobility ran on an east-west axis, then the residential plots, allotted according to the stratification sequence from nobles to commoners, with corresponding distinctions in the size and shape of houses. In size, design, and buildings, it was a splendid city, with a population estimated at about 200,000.

A hierarchical network of institutions linked Heijokyo to seventy provincial capitals (*kokufu*), bringing the most distant rural communities into an integrated system. The *kokufu,* however, were but small towns, and it may safely be said that Heijokyo and Heiankyo (Kyoto), which became the capital in A.D. 794, were the only cities worthy of the name in ancient Japan.[4]

Feudal Cities

The eighth-century attempt to establish a centralized state on the Chinese model did not fully succeed. The Japanese did not seriously adopt the Chinese bureaucratic system, and the struggle between the emperor and ambitious nobles continued. The gay and splendid life of the capital and its court continued through the ninth, tenth, and eleventh centuries, but was increasingly threatened by the power of nobles in outlying parts of the realm. The state was unable to establish a centralized organization of order and control over the whole country, so local lords inevitably had to rely upon their own military forces, which gave them virtual political autonomy. One noble after another strove to maintain supremacy in the name of the emperor. Instead of the low Chinese valuation of military culture, the warlike nobles and their soldiers developed into the separate warrior caste of the *samurai,* warring with one another yet all united in the same strict code of honor and chivalry. The supreme ritual status of the emperor was never challenged and the court life in Kyoto continued, but his political power was nominal. It became the practice for him

4. The celebrated city of Heijokyo (Nara) was only occupied from A.D. 710 till about 784, when the Emperor Kwammu is said to have built the new capital of Nagaoka, thirty miles away, with over 300,000 forced laborers. The reason for the move is uncertain, but may have been partly an escape from the excessive political dominance of the Buddhist monks of Nara. After violent intrigues in which the emperor's son assassinated the chief minister and was himself in turn exiled, the emperor moved again, but only a few miles away from Nagaoka, establishing Heiankyo (Kyoto) in 794 as the capital city, it remained so till 1869.

to confirm the dominant noble of the moment as head of the military government of the state (*bakufu*).

The central institutions and constitution of the state were thus accepted in principle and could always be appealed to effectively when circumstances were propitious, but the main power lay with the competing dynasties of large fief-holding nobles (*daimyo*) whose fortunes rose and fell with the changing economic and political situation. From the outbreak of the Onin war in 1467 until the end of the sixteenth century the whole country was involved in local warfare. There was an almost complete changeover of dominant families, in which many able and adventurous people of quite humble origins rose to the top. However, most of the supreme contestants were descended from the old feudal families and were often originally offshoots of the imperial family itself. By the end of the sixteenth century, Ieyasu came out finally on top and established the hereditary Tokugawa Shogunate which lasted till 1868.

During this long period there was a gradual increase in farm productivity and in commerce. Local market and temple towns began to grow up, inducing the military to leave their rural estates and concentrate in the towns while still keeping strict control over the peasants. The great *daimyo* who governed the major fiefs into which the whole country was divided began to found castle towns as the capitals of their domains. Artisans and merchants concentrated in the castle towns to meet the needs of the warriors (*samurai*) congregated there. Temples and shrines were also gathered into these centers, so that each castle town became the political, military, economic, and religious focus for a large surrounding area. The castle itself stood in the center, but the residential areas around it were mixed, for the differentiation between merchants, artisans, and farmers was not yet complete. Although the peasants were, in feudal fashion, fixed to the land and not allowed to move except when specifically required to do so in the service of their lords, there was considerable movement about the country by the feudal lords and their huge retinues,[5] by military detachments, merchants, and transporters of local community surpluses. Thus, as castle towns grew up at the feudal lords' headquarters, travel towns developed at the nodes of the communication routes, where the facilities were very highly organized to ensure transport between the headquarters themselves as well as with the capital;

5. At least in the later feudal period it was normal for retinues of as many as 30,000 persons to be moving regularly along the routes between the feudal headquarters and the capital as the great lords fulfilled their obligatory alternate year's residence there.

and similarly, harbor towns grew at the points where main routes linked up with the major ports, as transhipment centers for both coastal and overseas trade.[6]

Japanese feudal society differed considerably from the unitary system of modern states. The *daimyo* kept land and people subjugated at the local level, but at the same time they obediently served the emperor and his military government (*bakufu*), which was charged with maintaining the feudal power system. Because the strength of the *bakufu* rested largely on its ability to control the rural community, it had been granted the power to claim one quarter of the national rice crop at each harvest. It ensured its share of that crop and sought to increase yields by assigning quotas and regulating sales. By confining farmers to the land and prohibiting changes in residence, the *bakufu* was further able to control the rural populace. Feudal rural communities thus became fixed, isolated units exploited by the *daimyo* and the *bakufu* and condemned to poverty by the feudal scheme of rule.

Still, the rural populace was able to evolve a system of mutual support concentrated in kinship and lineage groups. By sharing their difficulties the people managed to alleviate the exploitation of feudal lords and threats of natural disaster. And despite insularity, poverty, and traditional ways that made the introduction of new technology extremely difficult, crop surpluses gradually increased and population began to grow.

The growth of the castle, harbor, and travel towns was simultaneous, both reflecting and leading to further expansion of the commodity economy. In order to raise the funds needed to support growing numbers of unproductive military men, the feudal government and *daimyo* began to make use of the newly emerging high-interest money lenders, who, together with the merchants, wholesalers, and artisans provided vital services to the *daimyo* and *samurai* and were thus drawn into networks of patron-client relationships and accorded special protection and privileges. Travel facilities were improved and the currency unified, allowing the commodity economy to spread throughout the country. The regional division of labor was intensified, and in general the political unification of the country became more effective. Commercial activity, however, was confined to the towns and from the early seventeenth to the mid-nine-

6. Apart from occasional periods of major political upheaval or foreign invasion there was an increase both of coastal trade between the different regions of the Japanese islands and, at least until the sixteenth century, of overseas trade with Korea and the coasts of China.

teenth century a closed-door policy was imposed on international trade, preventing the free development of business.[7]

After 1603, when the Tokugawa Shogunate became firmly established, the government reorganized the fiefs, investing some 260 greater and lesser lords with them and establishing Edo (Tokyo) as the administrative capital of the feudal military government. Osaka, the great merchant city and largest harbor, served as the supply center to Edo, while Kyoto (Heiankyo) remained the city of imperial residence. Osaka was exceptional in not being the city of a feudal lord. Despite their low official status, its merchants and financiers became more and more indispensable, so that although Osaka never had any formal charter as a recognized corporate entity, in practice its citizens were self-governing to a considerable degree and even enjoyed some judicial autonomy. In this way it bore a distinct empirical similarity to the free cities of medieval Europe. By the eighteenth century there were probably over a million people living in Edo, making it the largest city in the world, while both Osaka and Kyoto exceeded half a million.[8] Around this nucleus, castle towns served as provincial capitals under the strict control of the Shogunate. They varied in population from about 10,000 to 120,000, their size being largely determined by the size of the rice yield in each domain. The huge size of Edo was very unusual for a feudal society, but as the center of government it supported large numbers of military men, merchants, artisans, and workers; its population was further greatly augmented by the requirements that every *daimyo* and his retinue reside in the capital each alternate year.

7. In the second half of the sixteenth century the Portuguese developed a lively trade with Japan, sending large fleets annually from Europe and almost taking over the highly lucrative trade between Japan and China. After 1600 British and Dutch rivalry with Spain and Portugal began to spoil Portugal's relations with the Japanese; and the fear that rapidly spreading conversions to Christianity would lead to political interference with internal affairs and the threat of conquest finally led by 1640 to a complete ban on Christianity and on any foreign trader landing in Japan or any Japanese trading overseas, apart from a very few rigorously controlled licenses from the central government.

8. Despite the remarkable records kept by the Japanese, it is difficult to establish comparable figures for urban populations. The population which was meticulously counted as the "normal" population seems to have included permanent residents only, excluding not only large numbers of seasonal laborers, but also the *daimyos'* huge retinues of warrior-retainers, servants, and their families, which, though mobile, were more and more concentrated in the cities. Thus, at the height of famine in 1786, Edo had a "normal" population of 475,000, yet 1,300,000 were registered for famine relief (Irene Taeuber, *The Population of Japan*, Princeton University Press, 1958, p. 27).

Throughout Japan's feudal period, the size and number of cities was limited by the fact that only small groups of non-agricultural people could be supported in one place. Primitive agricultural methods limited possible food surpluses, and the isolation and cultural rigidity of the whole society imposed a low level of social and territorial mobility. In this sense the cities were rather stagnant.

Looking to their natural resources and the available means of transportation and defense, the feudal *daimyo* had chosen town sites that offered a level area for the central part of the town, a hill commanding a full view of the plain for the castle, or perhaps a river to serve as the castle moat. The ancient and medieval cities of Europe and China, like city-states, were usually surrounded by walls. In Europe the lord of the fief served as protector to the citizens; in Japan the people were gathered together solely to meet the needs of the *daimyo*, and apart from the castle no defense was provided for them. Thus the difference in relations between lord and inhabitants found expression in the ecological structure of the city.

City plans retained the traditional checkerboard pattern as the framework of residential areas and as an expression of the status system, but subdivisions were decided in the light of defense needs and current technology. The principle of accessibility contrasted decidedly with that of modern cities, in which economic factors predominate: accessibility to castle towns was planned primarily in terms of political power. Thus each stratum of the population was segregated according to its proximity to the source of power.

The feudal power system was tightly knit and constituted an insular, fixed formation with relatively constant values. The *daimyo* was at the center, residing in the castle, ruling the town through the military caste of *samurai*. The higher-ranking *samurai* lived within easy access of the castle and the more numerous *samurai* of lower rank occupied the surrounding area for the defense of the town. All this area was self-governed by the military caste occupying it; they supplied from among themselves the officials to administer all the other quarters of the town, including the temple and shrine precincts. Thus the civilian townsmen of first rank, such as rich merchants, wholesalers, and noble families, lived towards the center, in the finest houses and enjoying the highest privileges, though under the administration of the military officials. Somewhat further out were the lesser merchants and the artisans, who performed important work for the régime, living on the main streets and owning their own houses. Here also resided rural landowners who shared in the responsibilities and tax program of the feudal administration. Further out still were the laborers; the ones who were better off in rented houses as tenants (*omotetanakari*) on the main streets, and the masses of the poor (*uratanakari*) occupied the crowded back-street tenements (*uranagaya*), with the outcaste *eta* in hovels on the periphery, performing tasks considered especially degrading.

Each of these categories, differing in rank and function, with correspondingly graded rights as townsmen, was segregated in its own spatial and ecological niche, recognizable by its dress, speech, and manners, as well as by the distinctive architectural style and quality of its dwelling accommodation. The significant feature of the stratification was the dichotomy between two groups: a small minority supported by exploiting a large mass which positively accepted its role. Administratively each ward was controlled as a separate unit, with its own walls and gates which were shut every night. There was no residential mobility. Among the ordinary townsfolk dwellings also served as workshops, and most of the activities of daily life centered upon neighborhoods, which formed well-defined groups sanctioning behavior between families and in the home.

Every occupation had its guilds (*nakama*), which for a certain sum could buy monopoly rights from the feudal lords. Business transactions outside the guilds were forbidden; membership was controlled through the apprenticeship system. Even within the guilds there was a fixed status system of master above and apprentice below, with little specialization of work. Strict adherence to convention was demanded at all times. Thus every occupation had its status, and within a vocational organization the status of members was fixed according to family ranking, sex, and age.

The emergence and expansion of cities depends upon the size and number of their organized institutions for politics and administration, defense, economics, and religion. The larger and more numerous the organizations, the larger the city in which they are clustered and the more intense its urban character. In castle towns the military government was overwhelmingly large in comparison with other institutions. Next in importance were the temples and shrines, then the wholesalers—the chief commercial expression of the era. This last group had expanded considerably, yet it was still much smaller than the military and religious complexes. Other institutions were numerous, but of lesser importance. We shall limit our description to the general elements of the military government and the wholesalers' groups, which together constituted the core of the castle town.

The military government developed gradually from the specialization of the *daimyo*'s rule, which at first was mediated through familial, domestic, and primary relationships and consisted of generalized roles without any clear or simple differentiation of duties. Eventually he came to monopolize authority and all the rights that go with it. On the other hand, as the scale enlarged and a more formal system of administration became indispensable, cabinets were formed and subordinate functions were separately allocated. However, it remained common for one person to shoulder a number of responsibilities. Lords commanded their vassals with absolute authority; and in view of their strictly prescribed family status, both close and distant relatives stood in important relations of dependence upon them and were their personal subordinates.

Military command depended upon the personal capabilities of the *daimyo* and upon the complete subservience of his retainers; no statutory law evolved to replace these ascribed personal relationships of subordinate and superordinate. With the increasing complexity of the military government, new subsystems of command emerged and expanded, but these were shifted on a monthly basis; while in crucial matters a system of councils was employed in such a way as to prevent any power accruing outside the sphere of the *daimyo*.

The kinship group structure of the warrior families was closely allied with the political power structure. Every individual was bound by the status authority of the family, which defined his standing in the hierarchy. Feudal authority depended upon this hierarchy, which presupposed the loyalty of followers and required the complete subordination of their personalities.

The family and not the individual was the basis of social status, and it was ranked in terms of its standing within the total system; occupations were hereditary, as was family property. The family name was considered very important and each family drew up its own set of rules as a kind of constitution to guide its members and to strengthen and perpetuate itself. The continued existence of the family was the first consideration of all its members. This attitude was profoundly sanctioned and reinforced by the enshrining of the ancestors in the house, thus constantly reminding all members of its sacred importance and strengthening the concept of the family itself. Successful families established branches which became residentially separate but for many purposes remained under the control and authority of the main, or stem, family and its head.

Although the guilds were subordinate to the military and were granted rights of monopoly by it, they were fundamentally important to the formation and development of cities. Wholesale merchants formed a series of interconnected kinship groups based upon the ramifying structure of "stem and branch" families. The stem and the branches were connected not only in economic relations, but also in other social relations, and especially through mutual aid. Fixed networks for buying and selling existed, and a merchant family with considerable capital resources was accorded the social and commercial standing of a large corporation (*katoku*), for which the family name and trademark had earned trust and respect. The main house of a *katoku* could announce a *norenwake* (loaning of the cloth bunting hung in front of a house with the trademark written on it) to set someone up in business. The relations between the main house and the new business would then be modeled upon those of a stem and branch family, whether there was in fact a blood relationship between them or only one of business. Admission to the system required the payment of an entrance fee, but in time of distress loans were advanced from common assets. Regular meetings were held to strengthen the stem and branch family relationship.

Master-employee relations also followed a set pattern. Those who went into service included members of the family and relatives, clients, and friends. They began work at seven or eight years of age, receiving training in elementary matters of business. At fifteen or sixteen they were recognized as semi-trained (*hangenpuku*) and were assigned to assist the apprentice clerks (*tedai*) in the stores. From the age of about twenty-two they themselves could become *tedai* and so become eligible for the full status of regular clerks (*banto*) by their thirtieth year. At the age of fifty or fifty-five they might enter retirement (*inkyo*) and leave their immediate responsibilities to their eldest sons. Thus, a clerk in training who had a marriage arranged for him while he was in his early twenties might have a son who had reached the full status of clerk and was able to take over from his father by the time the latter was in his mid-fifties. For the younger sons of the master, as well as for the other apprentice clerks, there was obviously a limit to the expansion of the market and the funds available, especially within the monopolistic guild structure, which was more concerned with stability of business and ensuring the support of its members than with expanding the market. So not all the younger sons of the master, let alone the other apprentice clerks, could be set up in branches on their own, but many of them had to content themselves with remaining as clerks within the existing structure of the business. Even when independent branch houses were set up, the subordinates who ran them always labored to support the business of the head house of the main stem family in return for the protection they received from it. Thus the master-servant relationship, cast in the kinship idiom of father-son and strongly loaded with sanctions of complementary obligation and loyalty, permeated the entire system. One of its greatest strengths was that the ablest apprentices, even if they were not members of the family, could be fully adopted into it as if they were, even in place of less able sons. The women of the guild families could only be employed as kitchen servants. They were not paid for their services, but their master assumed responsibility for all their needs: housing, food, clothing, and education.

Although urban life was dependent on the rural community, a money economy developed in the city and gradually infiltrated the countryside. City and rural community, however, were ordained to provide a clearcut division of labor, and the separation of the military, the merchants, and the artisans of the city from the village heads and farmers was strongly enforced. Rural people were forbidden to change occupation and residence, or to manufacture goods for social purposes. They were driven to peak production while living on a minimum subsistence level, since almost all surplus production was absorbed by the military rulers.[9]

9. During the middle ages many warriors were also farmers, but they gradually came to be distinct, until under the Tokugawa they approximated to rigidly separate castes, with *samurai* at the top, followed by farmers, then artisans, merchants, and finally outcastes. This corresponded less and less with economic realities. The supreme rank of the *samurai* justified their collective exploitation of the rest of the society. The high rank accorded to farmers (including peasants) expressed the complete economic dependence of the early Japanese state upon them, while perhaps hardly compensating for their oppressed condition. The low official status of merchants was increasingly at variance with the real influence which their growing wealth inevitably enabled them to exert, although they remained politically at the mercy of arbitrary exactions by the government. Feudal Japan never had, or aimed at, a unified legal system, and jurisprudence was of minor importance. The whole structure depended upon the relative relationships of superordination and subordination between master and man throughout the hierarchy. It was an expression of evolving ancient principles, rather than of laws. Every *daimyo* could promulgate his own laws or decrees, as long as he presented no threat to the Shogun, who merely encouraged some increasing conformity without attempting any general codification. This related to the fact that executive, legislative, and judicial functions were never clearly separated and were performed in conjunction by the *daimyo* at their various levels.

The Creation of a Modern State and the Emergence of Modern Cities

Although it was a gradual development, the beginning of the modern city in Japan can be sought in the Meiji Restoration of 1868. The commodity economy, established some time before, continued to develop, and as the regional division of labor progressed, the fixed, insular character of the feudal villages started to weaken, and individual householders gained more and more independence. Eventually the financial structure supporting the military classes was undermined, causing a partial breakdown in relations between the military and the feudal regimes, as well as a lowering of morale among the military themselves. Thus the fixed status system and the regional order of feudal society entered the first stage of dissolution.

During the time that Japan was isolated from international society, merchants accumulated capital primarily by absorbing farm surpluses and charging high interest rates on loans to the military that allowed them to continue living in their accustomed style. But since the merchants were dependent upon the military class, they could not themselves undertake the creation of a new society.

If Japan was to enter the competitive world of the industrialized Western nations and escape imminent colonization, she was forced to modernize and industrialize rapidly from within. These processes were initiated and sustained by the new bureaucrats who had been bred in feudal society as members of the military class. They made use of the authority of the emperor to introduce the legal, political, economic, military, and educational institutions of the West in forms applicable to Japan and pushed through a system of centralized authority that extended from the imperial residence in Tokyo to the smallest villages in the land.

Since Japan was relatively poor in natural resources, and the low standard of living of the farming majority of the population provided a poor domestic market, the energies of the Japanese industrial revolution erupted in the military and territorial expansion of the Sino-Japanese War (1894), the Russo-Japanese War (1904), and the First World War (1914). Overall changes in the social structure were accompanied by the legal dissolution of insular barriers and by rapid progress in technology. As the rural community was thus gradually emancipated from the restrictions of social custom and natural environment, its productivity increased; correspondingly the cities changed from consuming to producing communities.

The country was then able to support a much larger population, and the fertility rate rose in response. From 34,800,000 in 1872, the Japanese population swelled to 56,960,000 in 1920.

Within this new social order the old social structure and value systems were for the most part preserved. A combination of traditional religion, emperor worship, and ancestor worship, together with the kinship and family system, supplied the background necessary for the nationalism that served to integrate the new society and provide the props for a new state system. The bureaucrats drew on taxes taken from the rural populace to nurture the merchants who organized monopolistic financial cliques (*zaibatsu*, or kinship groups) that were to grow to mammoth proportions in the absence of free competition during the Taisho era (1912-26). As the industrial revolution progressed, the merchants rose to a position of dominance not only over industry but over politics as well.

The rural community, drawn into a capitalist system of commodity economy, was disadvantaged by an ever-widening difference in the exchange value between urban and rural products. Although rural households continued to concentrate on subsistence production, their managerial independence was strengthened as mutual-aid systems began to break down. Population rose sharply, and soon there was not enough arable land to support the increased numbers of people. This and the increasingly visible advantages of urban employment led to an exodus of the rural population. As a result of land reforms after World War II, the number of rich farmers decreased and the authority of landowners over rural communities began to disintegrate. Even then, migration from the farm to the city continued to increase.

During the Meiji period, continued population growth, accompanied by rapid industrialization and modernization, led to a sudden increase in both the number and the size of cities. In 1879 only 11 per cent of the population lived in communities of more than 10,000 people; by 1920 this figure had increased to 32 per cent. Power remained highly centralized, with the controlling institutions both of government and big business concentrated mainly in large cities. Indeed, as industrialization proceeded, the concentration of population in cities such as Tokyo and Osaka became even more pronounced. Thus, by 1920 Tokyo had a population of 1,920,000 despite the abolition of the system of alternate years' residence, which had concentrated great numbers of the *samurai* in the capital. Similarly, the population of the commercial and industrial center of Osaka swelled from 290,000 in 1872 to 1,670,000 in 1920.

With the abolition of the feudal system, many of the old castle towns declined. But many of them managed to survive the changes. Built as the political centers of the self-sufficient domains, they had through time become transportation and communication centers also. In addition, many of the former *samurai*, who now provided the bureaucratic leadership of the new society, had lived in the old feudal towns and found them convenient as political centers for the new regime.

For similar reasons some of the former harbor towns remained as suitable integrating centers in the context of modern technology. Thus many modern cities developed on the sites of former castle and harbor towns, doubling and tripling their populations in the course of industrialization and modernization. In 1920, of the 81 largest cities, 61 were old castle towns and 5 were old harbor towns. But if feudal centers did not fit the pattern of the changing politico-economic structure, they remained as purely local centers or fell into decay.

Yet new forces were at work, too. Advances in technology and new methods of exploiting natural resources, matched by competitive involvement in the world market and in foreign wars, introduced new considerations of siting and strategy that required the planned growth of cities. Industrial cities were planned mainly by the government, often in conjunction with the great pioneering entrepreneurs, according to the accessibility of natural resources, the availability of labor and capital, and the convenience of land and sea routes. Transportation centers and trading and military cities were all planned according to their functions; thus they were able to develop relatively free from feudal traditions.

Modernization of the bureaucracy, however, was only partial. Just as the ruling military classes were closely allied with the merchant classes during the feudal era, under the Meiji Restoration the administrative and social ties of new government agencies and financial and commercial houses were a maze of interconnections. The bureaucracy, still drawing upon the feudal tradition and abiding in the authority of the emperor, was able to organize a huge and powerful system of privileges, and despite the adoption of many nominal forms of democracy, little democracy actually penetrated its workings.

Among the men of cabinet rank in the Meiji period were many feudal lords, and many former *samurai* filled posts in the middle level of bureaucracy; thus was the feudal system of status values transferred to the modern system of business management. Patron-client relationships and special connections common to the kinship groups and families of feudal times gave the entire system the aura of an elite club, with little place for individual independence. This elite thought of their public positions as private privileges and demanded personal submission from the lower classes because of their status.

The entire bureaucracy was absolutist; the creation of government offices, determining of salaries, appointment and dismissal of officials were all carried out by "imperial mandate" in order to separate the privileged status of government officials from the somewhat more democratic control of the Diet. Court rank and orders of merit were awarded to officials on the basis of seniority or simply by virtue of their being government officials.

Because the people could not overcome their ingrained attitude toward the *samurai* of feudal society and continued to bow submissively before authority, the patterns of coercion and oppression within the bureaucracy led to the same patterns of relations between the system and the people. The bureaucracy, working on the premise of an absolute state, cast its net of rule over the whole country, leaving even the smallest villages almost devoid of local autonomy.

Yet as the industrial revolution proceeded, the character of the bureaucracy changed in some measure. Family status and other traditional restrictions were gradually eliminated, so that men were more frequently judged on the basis of their professional qualifications and abilities, and the absolute power of some officials was lessened. It was not until after World War II, however, that the special power of the bureaucracy was abolished and that it began to serve the welfare of the people.

Next in importance to the government agencies in the development of the modern Japanese cities were the large banks and commercial concerns. Once subordinate to the military, they now took over leadership positions in the new society in concert with the bureaucracy, and under its patronage developed into large monopolistic enterprises. During the industrial revolution and the years of foreign wars, they were able to buttress their power more and more; from Tokyo and Osaka their system of economic control spread across the nation.

Semi-government chartered companies were organized along the lines of the *Konzern*,[10] and with these as the core the *zaibatsu* expanded even

10. The typical German *Konzern* was an industrial trust controlling a diversity of financial and industrial operations through a pyramidal holding-company structure. It

more. In addition to enormous physical capital, they commanded extensive financial capital and not only concerned themselves with industry but also came to exercise considerable political power. With their vast holdings interlocked through marriages and directorates, they commanded all financial and industrial capital in Japan. The *zaibatsu* differed from large corporations in Western countries, which were realized through capital accumulation and free competition, in that they were nurtured and protected by the government and faced virtually no competition. Although persisting feudal customs were strongly intertwined in their structure, the *zaibatsu* managed to achieve a modern form of organization and administration indispensable to the progress of their industries.

The largest *zaibatsu* was Mitsui. In the central office (*omotokata*) were the heads of each family of the Mitsui group, with the head of the most powerful family at the top. This office made large capital loans to branch offices, which in turn made regular payments to the corporate account. Overall profits were divided among the various families with a certain proportion retained for the *omotokata*. Accumulated capital was the common possession of the whole kinship group. At first, stockholding was limited to members of the kinship group, but attractive opportunities during World War I led to some relaxation of *zaibatsu* exclusiveness. Stockholders were then recruited from among the general public as a means of increasing the supply of capital; but since total capital can be controlled by possessing only a fraction, the power of the *zaibatsu* became, if anything, more extensive.

As management became more complex, large numbers of personnel were required, and direct family rule was inevitably lessened. Managers were chosen from among loyal subordinates and some authority necessarily passed into their hands. But the relationships of the top executives to their subordinates were of the master-servant type, and the final decision-making power remained concentrated at the top.

Some of the previously independent medium and small industries were absorbed by the expansion of large industries; others remained independent in form, but subordinate to the large ones, clustering around them in the crowded conditions of the city. In fact, by keeping wages low and through issuing subcontracts, the large industries were able to

---

particularly resembled the *zaibatsu* in the gigantic size which it sometimes attained and in the monopolistic cooperation of business and the government, which permitted the *Konzern* to operate free from the threat of trust-busting in favor of the competitive ideals of liberal capitalism.

gain almost complete control over the smaller concerns. Thus it was possible to keep costs down, products cheap, and profits high. The traditional familialism of the Japanese firm favored strong loyalties, which were reinforced by a system of life-long employment and the low mobility associated with such employment. Thus little sense of community or common interest existed between the workers of one firm and another.[11]

After World War II brought reforms in the family and property system, the *zaibatsu* system began to dissolve. Technology and industry advanced rapidly, and social mobility started to increase. Labor unions gained the right of collective bargaining; and through joint labor-management conferences they were able to lessen the exclusive and absolute power of the managerial group. Population growth and an increasing division of labor, manifested in the progressive differentiation of many new roles, led to highly intricate patterns of stratification throughout Japanese society, producing many new arenas of possible cooperation or conflict.

The expansion of the bureaucratic framework in the early period of modern Japan had been due to the purposeful and continual interference of the bureaucracy in all fields of national and daily life, patterned after the feudal tradition and backed by the supernatural authority of the emperor. As government powers were curtailed, an untrammeled monopolistic capitalism developed under the protection of the government bureaucracy. The industrial power of financial capital then grew so strong that many small and medium industries were enveloped by the large corporations, while the financial cliques which controlled them came to have a dominating influence in politics as well as the economy.

The great *zaibatsu* had been built by men of extraordinary ability and energy, some of *samurai*, some of merchant, and some of extremely humble background, but all effectively recruited into the new elite, so that those who did not originally belong to the actual *zaibatsu* families soon came to do so. The *zaibatsu* had government support and even specific guarantees in major undertakings of national importance; and there were

11. This was reinforced by the fact that labor unions are related to the enterprise rather than to a whole industry. They are said to adopt a left-wing ideology as a psychological mechanism for avoiding company domination. They include all non-manual as well as manual employees. Strikes are rare, employment is secure, each employee enjoys regular annual rises of salary without bargaining, and labor-management relations are such that no resistance is offered to the adoption of new techniques, thus favoring further rises in both productivity and wages.

very close relationships of alliance and mutual support between *zaibatsu* and major national leaders. Thus not only was national independence maintained, but the economic strength was built up which provided the essential base as well as the encouragement to the reassertion of military ambitions and dominance both at home and abroad. As there had been a major reshuffle in the leadership of the whole society, harnessing remarkable new human resources of energy and enterprise yet retaining a very firm foundation of continuity, so there had been a re-orientation of old values without any radical break. Isolation was abandoned in order to ensure national autonomy and survival. The balance of old institutional structures (of emperor, army and government, agriculture and industry, town and country) was redressed and reformed, with the integration of new and old roles and the recruitment of new blood and ability from wherever it appeared. Thus the emergence of the emperors from seclusion was the reinforcement of tradition, and the ablest and most influential Elder Statesmen (*Genro*) were direct descendants of the highest nobility, yet the new establishment as a whole was a fusion of some of the strongest and most successful qualities of both merchants and *samurai*, well symbolized by the merchants already buying *samurai* status before it was formally abolished and by the *samurai* putting on the aprons of merchants to organize *zaibatsu* such as Mitsubishi. Enterprise, wealth, and ruthless courage were fused in the name of the emperor. Despite the forms of responsible and representative government, the command of the revivified armed forces was never clearly subordinated to the civilian government; and after 1930 the latter was progressively taken over by the former. Not only did cliques, factions, personal alliances, and family connections ramify across the gaps between the theoretically distinct institutional complexes of army, navy, politics, civil service, big business, and even scholarship and education, but major figures played multiple roles in many of these fields simultaneously or in succession. After the catastrophic military defeat the same heroic virtues and disciplines, with the same integration of major institutional structures by interpersonal networks, have been wholeheartedly devoted to the equally fierce battle of economic reconstruction and expansion.

While the whole society has been transformed in the interrelationship of its parts, by reaching the point at which an actual majority of the population is urbanized, the central focus and the fastest growth remains concentrated upon the great urban regions of Tokyo and Osaka, increasingly closely linked. Tokyo is the main apex of institutional hierarchies, political, governmental, bureaucratic, commercial, and industrial, although Osaka is still the greatest port and some *zaibatsu* such as Sumitomo make their headquarters there. This central part of the country, already tending in the direction of becoming a national megalopolis, is obviously the main locus of the intricate networks of personal relationships which, through the fluctuating rivalry and regrouping of factions, always reinforced by kinship, adoption, and affinity, control and integrate the key institutions of Japanese society in all domains of activity. Such central urban concentration is fostered and indeed required by this kind of social system.

The modern transformation of society and the urban explosion are reflected in a much expanded upper class of diverse occupation, with a large new urban bureaucratic middle class of managers and technocrats as well as the ubiquitous sales and advertising personnel. The entrepreneurs of medium and small industries, the self-employed merchants, and the artisans constitute a more independent middle class, while at the lower end of the social scale are the still-immense numbers of owner-operators of small family businesses and the masses of poor workers constantly swelled by new recruits from the farm villages.

Until World War II the urban neighborhoods remained clearly marked and bounded, as well as multifunctional. They were in fact deliberately kept so, as the basic units of the national military structure. Most urban residents still lived where they worked, and the physical sense of neighborhood and social sense of neighborliness both continued strongly. These neighborhood units were maintained throughout the war, but shortly afterwards the system was officially dissolved and neighborhoods began to get more specialized. With an increase of residential mobility, some Japanese urban dwellers have begun to experience a little of that lack of neighborliness which is said to characterize contemporary Western cities.

In Tokyo the old Tokugawa fortress has become the imperial residence, while in the other main towns the feudal castles were taken over by government offices, military headquarters, schools, or public parks. The former commercial centers support banks, wholesale houses, retail shops, hotels, and theaters. Rising pressure of land values and high rents, together with the continuing force of historical tradition and the need to maintain easy communication, has led to the concentration of many similar agencies in the same localities, forming streets of government offices, finance streets, newspaper alleys, retail avenues, wholesale blocks, and restaurant, entertainment, and recreation quarters.

In the larger cities, with increasing specialization, there is even a greater intensity of concentration, although at the same time the increased urban population is necessarily spread over a much larger area, as is permitted by improved modern communications. In feudal times the concentration of controlling institutions was the main urbanizing force, and though it still remains strong today, it naturally provokes some reaction towards decentralization, with people moving out to suburbs and satellite cities. Older communities have been swallowed up, as well as new ones generated, and new residential areas have formed somewhat separately for the upper class, the middle class (including apartment house areas), laborers' tenements and slums, areas for transients and lodging houses, hotel districts, and foreigners' settlements. These local ecological distinctions are much more varied, more loosely controlled, and less centrally planned and determined than the rigid caste and occupational zones of the feudal city. Service functions have had to be extended to the needs of the dispersed population. Schools, stores, religious and recreational institutions are now distributed with more concern for convenience and accessibility to the whole population. Some large factories have moved out in search of space in outlying areas where land is cheap yet transportation easily available. Small factories have followed the large ones as subcontractors, but many still cling to the old central locations, using obsolete commercial and residential buildings.

Despite all the changes, in the major cities with a long history the main residential areas still retain many characteristics of the old feudal city. Although new men take up residence as big businessmen, captains of industry, military leaders, and government officials, they inherit and carry on many of the old traditions and values, drawing upon the same heritage as a source of prestige. Where industrialization has been most intense, the change to new urban forms has naturally been the most rapid, reflecting the new techniques of construction and the new technology of communications. Constraints on social and spatial mobility do, however, still exist; traditional patterns of land use tend to overlap with new ones and a similar culture pervades the whole, so that the differences between communities are not so distinct as in the United States. Thus in the process of expansion, the drive towards optimum accessibility is modified by the strength of historical tradition, which attaches special values to particular areas. Wherever there is relative fixation it is mainly because of tradition. Nevertheless, the residential areas of the new elite are tending to follow the decentralization trend to the periphery. Once a new elite residential area is established, high value attaches to it, and its ability to draw the elite class forms a new dimension in the urban process.

The unfolding history of urbanization in Japan obviously confronts us with a unique series of events and in many ways a unique combination of forces; but if we are bold enough to analyze at all, the underlying factors must seem to suggest some stimulating and fruitful comparisons and contrasts, complex though they are, as is immediately implied by the use of such broad categories as feudal and industrial, with however many cautious provisos. In sheer size, Japan seems to have been able to support larger cities than any other feudal society and now bids fair to achieve the equivocal distinction of industrial cities larger than any elsewhere. Whatever the future of megalopolis in the United States, Tokyo is for the moment the largest urban community under unified administration.

The unique example of a non-Western and non-European country which, by its own superhuman efforts, successfully developed a large-scale, highly efficient urban and industrial society from within, Japan achieved this against the background of a national experience significantly different from that of all other industrial nations. It has maintained a continuity which so far has precluded the experience of any revolution comparable either to the English seventeenth-century Commonwealth or the eighteenth-century French or American revolutions, let alone the twentieth-century upheavals of Russian Communism, Italian Fascism, or German Nazism. The most revolutionary experience of Japan in modern times is called, significantly enough, the Restoration. It did involve the revolutionary dissolution of pre-existing institutions, though, as is perhaps the case with other revolutions, these had already been turned almost topsy-turvy by previous events, such as the widespread purchase of *samurai* status by wealthy commoners, the bankruptcy of high-ranking nobles at the hands of low-ranking merchants, and the energetic prosecution of trade, mining, and emergent industries by the more enterprising noble families. The Japanese defeat in World War II and the resultant Allied Occupation must have been a shattering experience, but remarkably brief, since the most radical changes first attempted were soon reversed.

For all these reasons the alignment of Japan with the Western capitalist world, admittedly without real choice, is somewhat anomalous, since her successful development of modern technology and capitalist production was achieved within a social framework essentially different from that of any Western country. Not that it was static, for besides the adoption and adaptation of many Western-sounding institutions, such as the forms of parliamentary and party organization, joint stock companies, trade unions and even orders of nobility, Japan had always recruited the best talent to the top very effectively by the practice of family adoption and the identification of lord and vassal, master-servant, and patron-client relationships with the emotionally charged kinship idiom of father and son.

Thus a technological and productive system that can hardly be judged any less efficient than those of Western countries has been built up with many Western-seeming forms, which in fact work very differently and retain important characteristics of Japanese society which are often rather misleadingly described as traditional.

The extent to which high-level policy in business and politics is run through selective manipulation of kinship, marriage, adoption, and extensions of clientship and dependence in the kinship idiom as aforementioned may have its counterparts in Western practice but is certainly counter to the prevalent Western theory. The low mobility of labor and very low level of unemployment, amounting to considerable career security, are in equally marked contrast to Western ideas of the mobility and flexibility required for industrial efficiency, with obvious implications for the whole relationship of capital and labor and the pattern of urban living. The enormous number of small family firms, which still maintain the identity of work place and residence, is another feature usually regarded as traditional. It has its counterpart in other countries with ancient craft traditions, such as Italy, and although its relative importance has diminished it remains a tenacious element of the whole.[12]

The flexible interpenetration and lack of rigidly separate institutional specialization of different domains of activity, such as business and politics, or (before the war) the army and politics, or work and residence thus show great continuity and stability in Japan. Despite the extraordinary capacity to mobilize talent and exploit opportunity, the continuing emphasis and efficacy of authority, hierarchy, discipline, and loyalty, in

12. Once again, one must note the Western tendency to regard other ways of doing things as the conservative retention of dysfunctional traditional elements inevitably due to be swept away in the tide of progress. The persistence of small industries is often regarded in this light, but it has been remarked that many items of advanced technology consist of innumerable separate parts (e.g. 10,000 for automobiles or 200,000 for planes); therefore a very important place remains for small-scale industries, whose presence is essentially modern and progressive rather than traditional and conservative. Small, specialized, capital-intensive businesses, in which parts are manufactured by skilled and experienced engineers, thus provide quite as efficient a system of production as any other in this situation.

business and politics and in social and domestic life alike, contrast strongly with the West and indeed appear clearly distasteful to dominant Western aspirations, yet on the other hand are combined with an effective care for human problems of family and career security which Western countries fail to solve despite their apparent deep concern. The contemporary Japanese urban and industrial experiment therefore still raises a haunting question, not only because it is incomplete but because the data are not sufficiently refined. Meanwhile, there is no justification for regarding contemporary Japanese urban civilization as being gradually forced by the requirements of the industrial system into the standardized Western mold, hindered only by lingering traditional elements. Rather, it would seem plausible to conclude tentatively that Japan has been able to exercise alternative options which may produce different long-term solutions—options derived from her own cultural experience and therefore not necessarily available to other countries, but nonetheless options which raise fundamental questions about the range of alternative choices in contemporary urbanization and justify rethinking of many rooted assumptions.

Reference Cited

Takeo Yazaki
1968. *Social Change and the City in Japan.* Tokyo: Japan Publications Trading Co.

Town and City in Pre-Modern Japan: Small Families, Small Households, and Residential Instability[1]

Robert J. Smith

Introduction

The history of urbanism in Japan begins with the building of the capital city of Nara in the early eighth century A.D. Both Nara and its successor Kyoto, built late in the same century, are examples of a phenomenon currently imagined to be peculiar to highly developed technological systems like our own—the "instant city." They were architectural expressions of

1. As others who have worked in the documentary sources of the closing period of the Tokugawa can testify, the foreign scholar inevitably incurs debts among his Japanese colleagues which can be acknowledged but not repaid. I should like to express my deepest gratitude to Professor Nakano Takashi of the Tōkyō Kyōiku University, who unwittingly led me into the investigation and subsequently provided much sensible advice. For invaluable assistance in locating and securing the materials on Tennōji, I should like to thank Mr. Enju Reiichirō, Mr. Tokoro Mitsuo, and Miss Asai Junko, all of the Reference Library of the Ministry of Education; Mr. Kanai Madoka of the University of Tokyo's Historiographical Institute; and Professor Hirai Naofusa of the Department of Shinto, Kokugakuin University, Tokyo. For equally essential assistance with the Nishinomiya materials, I must express my debt to Professor Yagi Akihiro of Kobe University, the members of the staff of the Nishinomiya City Office responsible for the compiling and writing of the history of that city, and Mr. Matsuoka Takashi, an *amateur* of local history. (All names are given in the Japanese order, surname first.)

For financial assistance, I am indebted to the Wenner-Gren Foundation for Anthropological Research, the Faculty Research Grants Committee of Cornell University, the Comparative Studies of Cultural Change, Department of Anthropology, Cornell University (Contract AID/csd-296 with the Agency for International Development), and the United States Educational Commission in Japan. I alone am responsible for the interpretations made of the materials. A shorter version of this article appears in Peter Laslett (ed.), *Household and Family in Past Time,* Comparative studies in the size and structure of the domestic group over time, Cambridge University Press, 1972.

the centralization of political and economic power and were created by fiat on the plan of the capital of T'ang China.

By the Tokugawa period (1615-1868), with which we are here concerned, there were hundreds of castle towns, post-towns, shrine and temple towns, marketing centers, and port towns, many of them scattered along the great highways which served to connect the geographical and political fragments making up the country. There were in this period three great cities as well: Edo, capital of the *shōgun*, with a population of about one million; Kyoto, capital of the emperors, with a population ranging up to one-half million; and Osaka, commercial and trade center, "kitchen of the world," with a population between three and four hundred thousand.

Assuming that the term "pre-industrial city" has some utility, I suppose it to be a convenient label for any urban concentration of a pre-industrial society, for I find it difficult to believe that there really are any substantial number of ways in which "pre-industrial cities" are a homogeneous phenomenon. In any event, it is now possible to put into the record some scattered demographic information on Tokugawa Japan. These data have direct bearing upon a variety of questions of some importance:

1. What was the size of the family and the household in the townsmen's (*chōnin*) quarters of these towns and cities? Were they the large households so often imagined in today's "invented history" of the period or were they rather more like the "modern" family and household with respect to size? What was the structure of the residence unit and how does it compare with that of present-day Japan? The issue of invented history is an interesting one which cannot detain us here. By it I mean simply that current explanations of any contemporary phenomenon often are made in terms of an imagined past condition from which change is believed to have occurred. That this procedure often falsifies the past in an effort to render the present more readily comprehensible cannot be denied.[2]

2. How stable was the population of the wards of town and city in Tokugawa Japan? If population turnover proves to be high, how shall we interpret the common view that the wards were village-like in quality as well as structure? Dore (1958: 255) is quite right when he writes:

> In the Tokugawa period, the towns had something of the same system of formal neighborhood relations as the country. The small wards into

2. See the engaging exposé by Francisco Benet, "Sociology Uncertain: The Ideology of the Rural-Urban Continuum," *Comparative Studies in Society and History* 6(1): 1-23, October 1963, of the fallacious nature of the standard presentation of the historical relations of urban centers and rural regions in the United States. See also Richard C. Wade, *The Urban Frontier*, Cambridge: Harvard University Press, 1959.

> which Tokyo is still divided had their origin in the Edo of Tokugawa times. They exercised a certain measure of self-government albeit under the distant supervision of samurai magistrates, and as such their organization resembled that of the villages.

Bellah (1957: 43), in discussing the ward organization of Tokugawa cities and drawing a parallel with the barrio system in Latin America, writes in a similar vein:

> Even in the cities a strong particularistic nexus of relationships was maintained for purposes of social control. The city only to a limited extent represented a new form of social organization, that connected with the market and a differentiated economy. For many purposes it was merely a congeries of "villages" in close geographical contiguity.

I shall try to deal with an issue not raised by either of the two authors cited because it is not central to their argument, and shall offer the following proposition: The structuring of the urban ward of Tokugawa times along the lines of village organization was not, as is so often mistakenly assumed, simply the natural outgrowth of the village-like quality of the units making up an urban agglomeration, but an administrative response to an incredibly high rate of population turnover. I shall also suggest that the relative stability of the *total* population figures for the wards produces the illusion of stability of residence within the wards, an assumption at great variances with the facts (Smith, 1963; Taeuber, 1960).

The Shūmon-Nimbetsu-Chō

Since the Tokugawa government was dedicated to the proposition that the good society was the stable society, its agents at the local level directed the most intense scrutiny at the residents of the unit for which they held administrative responsibility. One of the means by which periodic checks on the population were made was the *Shūmon-nimbetsu-chō* (at some periods, *Shūmon-aratame-chō*). Inasmuch as our data are drawn from these documents, it is necessary to say something about their intent and their quality.[3]

The *Shūmon-aratame-chō* are literally the "Registers of the Investigation of Religious Sects"; the *Shūmon-nimbetsu-chō* are "Census Registers by Religious Sect." They are simply variants of a form of registration

3. Here I draw heavily on the paper by Naganuma Kenkai, "Shūshi nimbetsu aratame no hattatsu" ("Development of the Investigation of Religious Sects"), *Shigaku-zasshi* (*The Journal of History*) 40(11): 13-62, 1929. See also the very important paper by Nomura (1953).

which was originally instituted in 1616 in connection with the suppression of Christianity. This early registry system was revised in 1626, instituting a procedure whereby two appointed officials conducted an investigation of the religious affiliations of all persons living in a village or ward, and the head (*shōya*) endorsed the report as an accurate accounting of the residents of his unit. This accounting required that every household list its temple affiliation, a development which greatly affected the fortunes of Buddhism in Japan. Prior to the instituting of these registers, the poor farmer, the small merchant, and the servant seem not to have had regular temple affiliation, but with the new requirement most of them joined the great popular sect of Shin Buddhism whose regulations were simple and whose fees were modest. Furthermore, early registers show that while the members of one family often did not belong to the same temple in the early seventeenth century, later in the century all members of one family listed the same temple affiliation. What was at first instituted as the result of an administrative system later became the custom of the land.

Around 1638 the persecutions of the Christians became increasingly severe and the Tokugawa government undertook to collect information about the concealed Christians in an effort to stamp out the religion. With the formal adoption of the national seclusion policy (*sakoku*) in 1639, a variety of other steps were taken with a view to ferreting out Christian converts and forcing them to recant. In 1640 a board of inquiry, the *Shūmon Aratame* (Investigation of Sects), was established in Edo; and in 1664 all feudal lords (*daimyo*) with an income greater than 10,000 *koku* of rice were ordered to institute analogous offices in their fiefs (Sansom, 1963: 42).

Among the various measures undertaken against the Christians the only one which concerns us here is the registers (*Shūmon-aratame-chō*) themselves. What had been devised as a means of checking on the religious affiliation of the population soon became a census register of commoners. The registers also were aimed at identifying a variety of people with irregular status: renegade *samurai* (the *rōnin*, members of the warrior class with neither fixed fealty nor residence), criminals, and floaters without passports for travel or certificates permitting change of residence.

It would appear that the registry system was generally more severely enforced in urban than in rural areas, probably because of the mobility of the population of the towns and cities. As the system became better organized, the central government realized its possibilities, and a 1726 edict established a national census of commoners to be conducted every six years. Until 1776 the registers in many districts were kept on an annual basis, and a report of the total by category of residents of ward or village submitted to the authorities every sixth year. After 1776, in the wards subdivided by Buddhist sect, so that what was earlier simply one catalog with which we are dealing, the volumes of the census were kept by ward, of all households of a ward later became groupings of the households by their sect of affiliation. This style of register persisted until the opening of the Meiji period in 1868, when the modern system of household registers (*koseki-chō*) was introduced.

I have dwelt on the origins and development of the *Shūmon-nimbetsu-chō* in some detail in order to defend my position that they are reasonably accurate, with the single exception that they do not report consistently the number of children below the age of ten. Certainly it was the intent of the government to have available a head-count of people actually resident in a given place. Unlike the modern *koseki-chō*, which do not enumerate the actual residents of a place, the *nimbetsu-chō* offer what was intended to be a population census. The enumerations found in them, therefore, more nearly reflect the facts of population composition and movement than do the post-Meiji registers.[4]

4. Kaempfer, whose descriptions of the highways and cities of Japan in the seventeenth century are referred to below, was interested in the organization of the wards of Nagasaki. In discussing the duties of the officials of these "streets" as he called them, he makes several references to the population registers which they were required to maintain:

> [The *otona*] keeps books and registers, wherein he enters, what persons are born in the street, how many die, or marry, or go a travelling, or leave the street, as also what new inhabitants come in, along with their names, birth, religion, trade, and so on (i, 279). [The "secretary" is said to be responsible for maintaining all manner of records] such as, the list of all the houses in the street, and of their Inhabitants, along with their names, age, trade, religion, and so on, a book, wherein are enter'd the names of all the persons that die in the street . . . , a register book containing what passports have been issued out of his office, with the names of the persons to whom they were granted, the business which call'd them abroad, the time of their departure, and their return . . . (i, 281).

He closes with the observation that in the last month of every year, the "Street's-messenger" performs the "*hito-aratame*":

> . . . that is, he takes down in writing the names of all the inhabitants of every house, old and young, with the time and place of their birth, and the . . . religion of the landlords. . . . Women are only counted in this inquisition, and 'tis added to the last how many there are (i, 287).

Nagasaki was, to be sure, something of a special case, for the coming and going of foreign vessels, as well as the continuing presence of foreigners, put local authorities on the strictest guard against unauthorized intercourse between them and the Japanese, such an anathema was Christianity. Kaempfer also has an account of the street-by-street check of residents upon the occasion of the departure of a Dutch or a Chinese ship, noting how the names of the inhabitants of each dwelling are read out. Clearly

The make-up of the *nimbetsu-chō* is simple, direct, and informative. The residents of a given house are listed together, identified by name, age, and in terms of the following list of categories:

1. Relationship to house-head	Expressed as a kin-term
2. *genin*	Servant; sometimes given as *genan*, male servant, and *gejō*, female servant.
3. *dōke*	Co-resident, an ambiguous category which is discussed below.
4. *inkyō*	A retired family member, i.e. a family member who has withdrawn from active participation in household affairs, usually at the age of 60.
5. *dōshinsha* or *deshi*	Acolyte or disciple (Buddhist)
6. *ama*	Nun (Buddhist)

Two sample household listings follow:

Sawaraya (house-name)		
Chōbei	35	Head of house
Tone	27	Wife
Ishimatsu	3	Son
Kane	Newborn	Daughter
Tami	62	Mother
Jirōbei	16	*genan* (male servant)
Kō	22	*gejō* (female servant)
Sumiyoshiya (house-name)		
Jihei	50	Head of house
Sato	19	Daughter
Chōjirō	33	*dōke* (co-resident)
Kin	26	Chōjirō's wife
Awa	14	*gejō* (female servant)

These are our data. For each household we have the name, age, and relation to house-head of every resident. In scattered registers annotations appear concerning births, deaths, and migration, but for the most part the fact of movement must be deduced by a matching of registers for consecutive years. I shall present below an analysis of the scale of movement suggested by matching by name all households of a given ward for a run of however many years they last, over a period of time, yielding a running tally of residential continuity and turnover.

---

these population registers were kept current with a view to continuous use, at least in Nagasaki. At another place in his journals, however, Kaempfer (i, 486ff) deals at length with the strictness with which the registers of Kyoto were maintained in his time.

The Data

The registers with which we shall deal are from two wards in each of two urban communities and are of two kinds—those of the house-owners (*iemochi*) and those of the renters/tenants (*shakuya*). The scope of the data is shown in the following summary chart:

Name of Community	*Name of Ward*	*Category of Register*	*Number of Registers*	*Span of Years*
Nishinomiya	Hama-kubo-chō	House-owners	12	1771-1866
Nishinomiya	Hama-kubo-chō	Renters/Tenants	10	1771-1868
Nishinomiya	Hama-issai-chō	House-owners and Renters/Tenants combined	6	1713-1774
Nishinomiya	Hama-issai-chō	House-owners	7	1784-1861
Nishinomiya	Hama-issai-chō	Renters/Tenants	5	1787-1861
Tennōji	Kubo-machi	House-owners	36	1757-1858
Tennōji	Kubo-machi	Renters/Tenants	36	1757-1858
Tennōji	Horikoshi-machi	House-owners	36	1757-1858
Tennōji	Horikoshi-machi	Renters/Tenants	36	1757-1858

This represents a total of 164 annual registers from four wards for a period of 156 years (1713-1868), with a complete enumeration of the residents of 9,973 households.

History of Nishinomiya[5]

Two of the wards are located in what is now Nishinomiya-shi (city), lying on the northern coast of the Inland Sea midway between Osaka to the east and Kobe to the west on the island of Honshu. In the earliest of the registers it is called Nishinomiya-mura (village), although it was already a town. Not until the middle of the Tokugawa period does it officially become Nishinomiya-chō (town). This detail of the community's history is of some importance, because it is my contention that for the entire period of the registers Nishinomiya was indeed a town. Why, then, was it called a village? In the time of Hideyoshi, at the establishment of the four-class system of Tokugawa Japan (warrior, farmer, artisan, merchant, in descending order, with the nobility and the outcastes at either extreme), there appears to have been some effort made to classify as much as possi-

5. These historical materials are drawn from Volume 2 of the superb multi-volume *Nishinomiya-shi-shi* (*History of Nishinomiya City*), edited by Uozumi Sōgorō and published by the Municipal Office in 1960.

ble of the population of the country as either warriors (the small ruling group) or farmers (the largest class, viewed as the only productive class of the governed). There was little place in the system for either artisans or merchants, and throughout the period the latter were defined as a purely parasitic class. The logic of the classification of the registers was unassailable: since farmers live in villages, the simplest means of achieving the division of society into two major groups was to classify virtually all towns (*chō*) as villages (*mura*). This meant that there were, by administrative fiat, few people classified as townsmen (*chōnin*); thus the agricultural village (*nōson*) population is proportionally exaggerated in the records.

Nishinomiya grew up originally around two Shinto shrines which retain their importance today. They are Hirota-jinja and Nishinomiya-jinja, the latter given over to the worship of Ebisu, the sea-god. In the Sengoku period, the period of the warring states (1490-1600), a local strongman built a fort at Koshimizu between 1504 and 1520 and established hegemony over the area. In 1617, shortly after the unification of the country under the Tokugawa Shogunate, Nishinomiya was made part of the Amagasaki fief, whose castle was in the town of Amagasaki, and Nishinomiya declined in political importance while prospering economically. In 1769 the central government assumed direct control of Nishinomiya, chiefly to obtain the substantial revenues deriving from the great *sake* breweries and because of the key position of the community as a post-town (*shukuba-machi*).

The town has a complex history which does not fit neatly into the typology preferred by Japanese historians. It combines some features of the shrine-centered town (*monzen-machi*), the post-town (*shukuba-machi*), the port-town (*minato-machi*), and the entrepôt (*shūsan-chi*). Furthermore, in the Tokugawa period, it was already a center for the development of light industry. Although it did not function as a castle-town (*jōka-machi*) during its incorporation into the Amagasaki fief, it was nonetheless the trading center of the domain and much of the business of the fief was carried on there.

Let us consider briefly the various functions of Nishinomiya. As a shrine-centered town, its importance is marked by the great "tenth-day Ebisu" market, attracting fishmongers, peddlers, merchants, and entertainers. Hirota-jinja, which, like the Ebisu Shrine, had a market, shared in the support given the important shrines by the lord of the fief, which was chiefly in the form of gifts of rice. Additional revenue was gained by the imposition of a surtax on the market vendors. The gateway of the Ebisu Shrine was a famous landmark from which distances along the post-road were reckoned.

As a post-town, Nishinomiya occupied a crucial position. Two major highways of the Tokugawa period still transect the city. One is the Chūgoku Highway, a continuation of the famed Tōkaidō (known to Westerners chiefly through the series of prints by Andō Hiroshige, "The Fifty-Three Stations of the Tōkaidō"), which carried traffic from the southern terminus of the Tōkaidō into the western part of the country. The second great road is the Saikoku Highway, which leads from Kyoto, the Imperial capital until 1868, through Itami to Nishinomiya on the coast. Two lesser roads from Arima and Tambaji carried the agricultural produce and craft items of the area into the town. Major inns in the center of Nishinomiya were designated official posting-houses catering to the great when they stopped over between Osaka and Kobe, and a large number of lesser official posting-houses were reserved to travelers of lesser rank. In addition, there was a concentration of stables, eating places, and supply houses. Taeuber (1958: 25)writes:

> *Shukuba-machi* . . . were located each eight to twelve kilometers along these great roads. Town lots were prepared along each side of the highway . . . sufficient for some agriculture. Hotels for *daimyo* and *samurai* were located in the central section, as was the traffic center that handled passengers and freight. Inns for general travelers and shops were located at the peripheries. As the number of travelers and the movement of commodities increased, these *shukuba-machi* assumed more of the characteristics of towns than of villages.

We have a fascinating glimpse into both the post-towns and the highways of Japan in the journals of Engelbert Kaempfer (1727), whose history and reports deserve some comment here. Kaempfer, well-educated and an excellent observer, was a Westphalian physician who, following his service as secretary to a Swedish mission to the court of the Ottoman Empire, signed on with the Dutch East-India Company in the capacity of surgeon to the fleet. He arrived in Japan in 1690 and left in 1692, having made two round-trip journeys from Nagasaki to Edo in 1691 and 1692. He commented on the highways on which his company traveled:

> To accommodate travellers, there is in all the chief villages and hamlets a Post-house belonging to the Lord of the place, where at all times they may find a competent number of horses, porters, footmen, and what else they might be wanting to continue the journey in readiness, at certain settled prices (i, 419). They lie at one and half to four miles distance

> from each other, but generally not so good, nor so well furnished upon *Kiusju* [Kyushu], in the way from *Nagasaki* to *Kokura,* as we found them upon the great Island *Nipon* [Honshu], where we came to 56, going from *Osacca* [Osaka] to *Jedo* [Edo] (i, 419).

Kaempfer refers then to the great number of specialists, including clerks, bookkeepers, and messengers, to be found in these places, and continues:

> There are innumerable smaller Inns, Cook-shops, *Sacki* [sake] or Ale-houses, Pastry-cook's, and Confectioner's shops, all along the road . . . (i, 426). I could not help admiring the great number of shops we met in all the cities, towns and villages, whole large streets being scarce any thing else but continued rows of shops on both sides, and I own, for my part, that I could not well conceive, how the whole country is able to furnish customers enough, only to make the proprietors get a livelihood, much less to enrich them (i, 414). It is scarce credible, what numbers of people daily travel on the roads in this country, and I can assure the reader from my own experience, having passed it four times, that *Tokaido,* which is one of the chief . . . great roads in Japan, is upon some days more crowded, than the publick streets in any the most populous town in Europe. . . . The train of some of the most eminent among the Princes of the Empire fills up the road for some days. Accordingly tho' we travell'd pretty fast ourselves, yet we often met the baggage and fore-troops, consisting of the servants and inferior officers for two days together, dispers'd in several troops, and the Prince himself follow'd but the third day attended with his numerous court. . . . The retinue of one of the chief *Daimios* [daimyō: lord of a fief] as they are call'd, is computed to amount to about 20,000 men . . . (i, 429).

As a port-town and entrepôt Nishinomiya was heavily involved in fishing and in the Inland Sea trade. Numerous guilds were established to handle the manufacture, transport, and wholesale and retail trade in a great variety of products. Of prime importance was the *sake* industry, and direct shipment from Nishinomiya to the *shōgun*'s capital at Edo began as early as 1704. Rape-seed and rape-oil, cotton, fish and fish products, fertilizer, and rice were all handled through the Nishinomiya guilds. Other merchant guilds (*shōnin-nakama*) dealt in clothing, notions, and pawn.

The *sake* industry, established here in the Muromachi period (1392-1490), was the key to the town's prosperity; its guild was so powerful that it occasionally registered opposition to government policy, a most unusual occurrence in this society. The manufacture of *sake* naturally made for a very active rice trade, and as the breweries expanded their activities with the growth of the fame of their still-famous product, there developed an extremely active labor market. Involved in the industry were the manufacturers of a great variety of technical equipment as well as the longshoremen's associations and shipping companies.

This, in rough outline, is the nature of the town of Nishinomiya from which two sets of our registers come. By 1661 it was already possible to rent both land and houses, and the town spread rapidly south from the highways toward the shore (*hama*). Both our wards' names are prefaced by this word (Hama-kubo-chō and Hama-issai-chō), and both appear on a map prepared in 1684. Certainly by the Genroku period (1688-1715), the heyday of the townsmen's culture, the *hama* areas were firmly integrated into the town. Our two wards appear again only slightly altered on a map dated 1769.

Between 1710 and 1868, the population of the wards (*chō*) of Nishinomiya ranged from over 2,000 in the largest to less than 100. The two wards with which we shall be concerned were in the medium range—between 900 and 1,000 in Hama-kubo-chō and between 700 and 800 in Hama-issai-chō. We have only a small amount of evidence concerning migration during the period covered by our registers. Certainly one of the most important aspects of migration was the movement north, usually on a temporary basis, to the famed fishing area of what is now Chiba Prefecture, then called Awashimoosa. During the Tempō era (1830-1843), many individuals and families from the Nishinomiya area appear to have remained in Chiba over a period of years, apparently with the intention of earning money and returning to their native place. The extent of this kind of migration was such that in some years of the first half of the nineteenth century a separate register was kept in Chiba for these temporary Nishinomiya "expatriates." The pattern seems to have been established early in the seventeenth century with the decision of the central government to build its own capital at Edo, a massive undertaking which required the importing of great numbers of skilled and unskilled workers. Many went from Nishinomiya to explore the great fishing grounds off Chiba and stayed on as processors of fish, with the result that many successful merchants of Edo and Chiba trace their ancestry back to Nishinomiya.

History of Tennōji

Historical materials relating to the second community, Tennōji, are extremely scarce. Like Nishinomiya it was designated a village (*mura*) in early Tokugawa, but appears to have been much more than that, for it lies only two miles to the south of the Osaka castle, well within the boundaries of that great city. Sansom (1963: 112) remarks that the castle towns of this region were less important than the

> expanded village in the environs of Osaka. These ancient rural settlements were spread over a large area in the provinces of Settsu, Kawachi, and Izumi, and, being separated by only short distances from one another, they tended to coalesce and form an urban conglomeration. . . . country towns, such as Hirano, Tennōji, Sumiyoshi, and Sakai, developed close relations and towards the end of the [seventeenth] century had coalesced to form the great national market of which Osaka was the axis.

Unlike the two wards of Nishinomiya, those of Tennōji for which we have registers appear no longer even to exist. Apparently the vast modern complex of the Tennōji subway, railway station, and yards has completely obliterated them, although the great Tendai Buddhist temple remains. It is fairly clear, however, that the growth of the community was due in large part to its association with this temple, which gives the town its name. The temple of Tennōji was first built in 587 A.D. by the Imperial Regent, Shōtoku Taishi, to whom the firm establishment of Buddhism in Japan is credited. It was removed to roughly its present location by the Empress Suiko in 593. From the eleventh to the sixteenth century it was governed by an imperial prince; it was destroyed in 1802 and finally reconstructed in 1812.

The ubiquitous Kaempfer was himself in Tennōji once and perhaps twice in the course of his two journeys. He writes:

> The water, which is drunk at *Osacca,* tastes a little brackish. But in lieu thereof they have the best *Sacki* in the Empire, which is brew'd in great quantities in the neighboring village *Tenusij* [Tennōji], and from there exported into most other Provinces, nay by the Dutch and Chinese out of the country (1727: i, 477).

This passage appears in his account of 1691 and his plan to visit Tennōji in 1692 to see the processing of *sake* was foiled "through the moroseness and ill nature of the commanding officers of our retinue (i, 554)" on the way up to Edo. On his return to Nagasaki in that year, however, he notes in passing that he and his party "were carried to *Symmios* (Sumiyoshi), and from thence back again to *Tenosi* (Tennōji) . . . (i, 603)."

We are fortunate in having a Japanese map of Osaka printed in 1691, the first year that Kaempfer visited that city. This map (reproduced in

Nishioka and Hattori 1956: 208-9) shows Tennōji just at the edge of the settled part of the city, and we may safely assume that in the more than sixty years which elapse before our register of 1757 the city had engulfed the "village" of Tennōji. Kaempfer (1727: i, 472) writes of the expanding city of Osaka in 1691:

> We pass'd by several new villages and small towns, or rather suburbs of Osacca, which had been built along the banks of [the] river for these several years last past, and amidst upwards of a thousand boats we enter'd the city it self.

He returns to this theme at the close of his journals:

> The country is populous beyond expression, and one would scarce think it possible, that being no greater than it is, it should nevertheless maintain, and support such a vast number of inhabitants. The highways are an almost continued row of villages and boroughs: You scarce come out of one, but you enter another; and you may travel many miles, as it were, in one street, without knowing it to be composed of many villages, but by the differing names, that were formerly given them, and which they afterwards retain, though joined to one another. It hath many towns, the chief whereof may vy with the most considerable in the world of largeness, magnificence, and the number of inhabitants (Appendix, 55-56). . . . it is scarce credible, how much trade and commerce is carried on between the several provinces and parts of the Empire! How busy and industrious the merchants are every where! How full their ports of ships! How many rich and flourishing mercantile towns up and down the Country! There are such multitudes of people along the coasts, and near the sea-ports, such a noise of oars and sails, such numbers of ships and boats, both for use and pleasure, that one would be apt to imagine the whole nation had settled there, and all the inland parts of the Country were left quite desart and empty (Appendix, 62).

We have population figures for Osaka (Sekiyama 1958: 220-21, 230-31) which place our registers in context. In the Keichō era (1596-1614) the residents of the city numbered about 200,000. By 1709 the population had grown to 380,000. Figures are available for the period 1711 to 1765, at which time there were about 420,000 residents of the city. From this year on there are fluctuations, but the population hovers around the 380,000 mark until 1834, after which it declines steadily until 1858 to approximately 300,000, the level of two hundred years before. The reason for the marked decline in the 1830's and 1840's is not far to seek. It has been estimated that of the population of townsmen of Edo between 1843 and

Table 1. Registers of All Categories in All Wards, 1713-1868: Size and Composition c

Ward	Number of House-holds	Family Members Male	Female	Total	No./House
*Combined**					
Nishinomiya					
Hama-issai-chō (1713-1774)	841	1,793	1,814	3,607	4.282
House-owners					
Nishinomiya					
Hama-issai-chō (1771-1868)	1,176	2,128	2,252	4,380	3.675
Hama-issai-chō (1784-1861)	707	1,204	1,364	2,568	3.632
Tennōji					
Kubo-machi (1757-1858)	1,729	3,244	2,883	6,127	3.543
Horikoshi-machi (1757-1858)	805	1,610	1,548	3,158	3.922
Totals	4,417	8,186	8,047	16,233	3.675
Renters/Tenants					
Nishinomiya					
Hama-kubo-chō (1771-1868)	1,615	2,325	2,544	4,869	3.015
Hama-issai-chō (1787-1861)	503	647	807	1,454	2.890
Tennōji					
Kubo-machi (1757-1858)	1,119	1,862	1,780	3,642	3.254
Horikoshi-machi (1757-1858)	1,478	2,569	2,348	4,917	3.326
Totals	4,715	7,403	7,479	14,882	3.156
Grand Totals	9,973	17,382	17,340	34,722	3.481

* No distinction is drawn in these registers between "House-owner" (*Iemochi*) anc

1867, about one-quarter were people born in the rural areas who had migrated there. Osaka, a very busy port, seems also to have attracted large numbers of migrants from rural regions. In the Tempō era (1830-1843) the central government made a concerted effort to force these people back to their home villages through enforcement of "repatriation edicts." The population of Osaka alone declined by 18,000 between the censuses of 1842 and 1843 as a result of this program, and the edicts appear to have had a continuing effect.[6]

6. Sekiyama (1958: 231) is of the opinion that another reason lies in the fact that a purely commercial city such as Osaka could, in what he calls a "feudal society like that of Tokugawa Japan," sustain a population of not much more than 300,000, a figure to which the totals for Osaka return after two hundred years of abnormal growth in the eighteenth and early nineteenth centuries. For an independent analysis of the Tennōji registers see Sasaki (1967).

Family and Households

Quasi-Family Members				*Status Unknown*			*All Household Residents*			
Male	*Female*	*Total*	*No./ House*	*Male*	*Female*	*Total*	*Male*	*Female*	*Total*	*No./ House*
112	30	142	.169	20	22	42	1,925	1,866	3,791	4.508
199	261	460	.391	31	43	74	2,358	2,556	4,914	4.178
78	99	177	.250	13	13	26	1,295	1,476	2,771	3.919
648	400	1,048	.606	2	1	3	3,894	3,284	7,178	4.151
534	294	828	1.028	3	1	4	2,147	1,843	3,990	4.956
1,459	1,054	2,513	.568	49	58	107	9,694	9,159	18,853	4.268
165	191	356	.220	47	56	103	2,537	2,791	5,328	3.299
30	49	79	.157	6	12	18	683	868	1,551	3.083
54	52	106	.094	1	1	2	1,917	1,833	3,750	3.351
143	104	247	.167	–	2	2	2,712	2,454	5,166	3.494
392	396	788	.167	54	71	125	7,849	7,946	15,795	3.349
1,963	1,480	3,443	.345	123	151	274	19,468	18,971	38,439	3.855

"Renters/Tenants" (*Shakuya*).

The two wards of Tennōji with which we shall deal were smaller than those of Nishinomiya. The population of Kubo-machi was between 250 and 350 for most of the period 1757-1858, and Horikoshi-machi was somewhat smaller.

Analysis of the Registers

In the following pages are given tables which show complete information on the size of families and households in the four wards. The data are ungrouped, i.e. figures are given for each of the 164 registers over the 156 years covered in the study. Some comments on a few of the terms used are in order here: "quasi-family members" in Tables 1 and 3-9 include all individuals listed in the censuses for whom a kin-relationship to

Table 2. Registers of All Categories in All Wards, 1713-1868: Number of

Ward			*Number of* 1	2	3	4	5	6
*Combined**								
Nishinomiya								
Hama-issai-chō (1713-1744)	Family	No.	67	100	140	170	144	105
	Household		59	82	141	163	150	107
	Family	%	8.0	11.9	16.6	20.2	17.1	12.5
	Household		7.0	9.8	16.8	19.4	17.8	12.7
House-owners								
Nishinomiya								
Hama-kubo-chō (1771-1866)	Family	No.	179	172	218	212	182	110
	Household		140	156	206	198	177	128
Hama-issai-chō (1784-1861)	Family	No.	99	129	145	118	104	49
	Household		80	125	131	119	102	67
Tennōji								
Kubo-machi (1757-1858)	Family	No.	436	195	254	300	217	170
	Household		343	148	217	289	255	192
Horikoshi-machi (1757-1858)	Family	No.	164	64	94	145	161	87
	Household		163	31	51	106	113	102
Totals	Family	No.	878	560	711	775	664	416
	Household		726	460	605	712	647	489
	Family	%	19.9	12.7	16.1	17.5	15.0	9.4
	Household		16.5	10.4	13.7	16.1	14.6	11.1
Renters/Tenants								
Nishinomiya								
Hama-kubo-chō (1771-1868)	Family	No.	419	292	314	263	162	86
	Household		352	291	303	273	165	107
Hama-issai-chō (1787-1861)	Family	No.	132	112	96	78	44	22
	Household		120	104	89	88	50	27
Tennōji								
Kubo-machi (1757-1858)	Family	No.	213	221	215	180	158	105
	Household		191	224	216	174	163	113
Horikoshi-machi (1757-1858)	Family	No.	232	300	324	297	161	82
	Household		194	284	316	312	182	89
Totals	Family	No.	996	925	949	818	525	295
	Household		857	903	924	847	560	336
	Family	%	21.1	19.6	20.1	17.4	11.1	6.3
	Household		18.2	19.1	19.6	18.0	11.9	7.1
Grand Totals	Family	No.	1,941	1,585	1,800	1,763	1,333	816
	Household		1,642	1,445	1,670	1,722	1,357	932
	Family	%	19.5	15.9	18.0	17.7	13.4	8.2
	Household		16.5	14.5	16.7	17.3	13.6	9.3

* No distinction is drawn in these registers between "House-owner" (*Iemochi*) and

'amily Members Compared with Number of Residents per Household

ersons											
7	8	9	10	11	12	13	14	15	16	*Total*	%
62	32	15	3	1	2	–	–	–	–	841	
70	38	15	9	3	3	1	–	–	–	841	
7.4	3.8	1.8	.4	.1	.2	–	–	–	–		100
3.3	4.5	1.8	1.0	.4	.4	.1	–	–	–		100
65	21	9	6	2	–	–	–	–	–	1,176	
90	41	16	12	7	2	3	–	–	–	1,176	
34	15	9	4	1	–	–	–	–	–	707	
45	15	11	7	5	–	–	–	–	–	707	
62	61	20	9	1	4	–	–	–	–	1,729	
07	80	59	25	8	6	–	–	–	–	1,729	
55	22	13	–	–	–	–	–	–	–	805	
98	55	37	23	13	4	5	1	2	1	805	
16	119	51	19	4	4	–	–	–	–	4,417	
40	191	123	67	33	12	8	1	2	1	4,417	
4.9	2.7	1.2	.4	.1	.1	–	–	–	–		100
7.7	4.3	2.8	1.54	.73	.27	.18	.02	.04	.02		100
38	29	8	4	–	–	–	–	–	–	1,615	
55	34	23	7	2	3	–	–	–	–	1,615	
10	6	2	1	–	–	–	–	–	–	503	
14	6	4	1	–	–	–	–	–	–	503	
18	7	2	–	–	–	–	–	–	–	1,119	
28	7	2	1	–	–	–	–	–	–	1,119	
52	19	7	3	1	–	–	–	–	–	1,478	
64	23	9	4	1	–	–	–	–	–	1,478	
18	61	19	8	1	–	–	–	–	–	4,715	
61	70	38	13	3	3	–	–	–	–	4,715	
2.5	1.3	.4	.18	.02	–	–	–	–	–		100
3.4	1.5	.80	.28	.06	.06	–	–	–	–		100
396	212	85	30	6	6	–	–	–	–	9,973	
571	299	176	89	39	18	9	1	2	1	9,973	
3.9	2.08	.9	.3	.06	.06	–	–	–	–		100
5.7	3.0	1.8	.9	.4	.17	.09	.01	.02	.01		100

'Renters/Tenants" (*Shakuya*).

the house-head is not indicated (servants, co-residents, and other non-kin); "status unknown" in these same tables includes those individuals for whom no identifying term is given at all; "family members" in all the tables which follow includes only those individuals for whom a kin-relationship with the house-head is indicated.

Table 1 presents a breakdown of the registers by ward and by category (whether house-owner, renter/tenant, or combined), showing the average family and household sizes. Although there is no doubt an under-reporting of small children, the totals reveal residential units of very small average size. The smallest figure is 2.9 persons per family of renters/tenants in the Nishinomiya ward of Hama-issai-chō in the period 1787-1861; the largest is the household size (4.5) of the combined registers of that same community in the period 1713-1774. In no case is the size of the average household unit markedly greater than that of the average family unit of the same community. (Detailed data are presented in Tables 3 through 9.) The average size of the 9,973 households in these registers is 3.9.

How do these figures compare with more recent data from Japan's "modern" period? Taeuber (1958: 107-8), writing of the "ordinary households" of Japan, i.e. excluding residents of factory dormitories, military barracks, etc., gives the average size as 4.89 in 1920, 4.98 in 1930, 4.99 in 1940, and 4.97 in 1950 and 1955. All these figures are, of course, larger than the 3.9 average of our registers, but I have included in the calculations which yield this average the very large percentage of single-person households (16.5% of the total). Correcting for this factor brings the average size of ordinary households in the registers from 1713 through 1868 very close to that for the 1920-1955 period.

In Table 2 are given the total number of family and household units having a given number of residents. Of the 9,973 residence units in our registers, the largest household (and there is only one of these) had sixteen members. Grouping of the data presented in this table, and in Tables 10 through 21, will be found in Table 22. The contention expressed in the title of this paper is clearly borne out in respect to size of residential units. For the entire period of 156 years and for the 9,973 units appearing in the registers, 96.6 per cent of the families had seven members or less. Nor was the large household a feature of these town and city wards, for 93.6 per cent of the households had seven or fewer residents. It is of interest, furthermore, to note that single-person households account for 16.5 per cent of the total appearing in all the registers.

Table 3. Nishinomiya, Hama-kubo-chō. Registers of the *Iemochi* (House-owners), 1771-1866: Size and Composition of Family and Household

	Number of	Family Members				Quasi-Family Members				Status Unknown			All Household Residents			
Year	*House-holds*	*Male*	*Female*	*Total*	*No./House*	*Male*	*Female*	*Total*	*No./House*	*Male*	*Female*	*Total*	*Male*	*Female*	*Total*	*No./House*
1771	113	257	225	482	4.265	33	33	66	.584	5	7	12	295	265	560	4.955
1782	112	231	243	474	4.232	23	32	55	.491	2	4	6	256	279	535	4.775
1786	106	208	203	411	3.877	23	27	50	.471	7	5	12	238	235	473	4.462
1795	99	210	193	403	4.070	25	24	49	.494	–	–	–	235	217	452	4.565
1806	100	176	188	364	3.640	13	13	26	.260	1	4	5	190	205	395	3.950
1810	106	172	183	355	3.349	15	16	31	.292	4	9	13	191	208	399	3.764
1816	101	134	193	357	3.534	9	23	32	.316	4	3	7	177	219	396	3.920
1818	103	170	200	370	3.592	14	25	39	.378	2	3	5	186	228	414	4.019
1822/3	97	162	188	350	3.575	11	21	32	.322	–	1	1	173	210	383	3.910
1843/4	86	145	156	301	3.525	14	24	38	.441	5	5	10	164	185	349	4.066
1865	74	112	137	249	3.364	10	10	20	.270	1	2	3	123	149	272	3.675
1866	79	121	143	264	3.341	9	13	22	.278	–	–	–	130	156	286	3.620
Totals	1,176	2,128	2,252	4,380	3.724	199	261	460	.391	31	43	74	2,358	2,556	4,914	4.179

Table 4. Nishinomiya, Hama-kubo-chō. Registers of the *Shakuya* (Renters/Tenants), 1771-1868: Size and Composition of Family and Household

	Number of	*Family Members*				*Quasi-Family Members*				*Status Unknown*			*All Household Residents*			
Year	*House-holds*	*Male*	*Female*	*Total*	*No./House*	*Male*	*Female*	*Total*	*No./House*	*Male*	*Female*	*Total*	*Male*	*Female*	*Total*	*No./House*
1771	113	203	165	368	3.256	9	4	13	.115	20	13	33	232	182	414	3.664
1781	135	222	221	443	3.281	9	9	18	.133	3	4	7	234	234	468	3.466
1806	174	262	280	542	3.114	10	15	25	.143	6	18	24	278	313	591	3.396
1810	165	252	255	507	3.072	17	18	35	.212	5	6	11	274	279	553	3.351
1816	173	246	275	521	3.011	29	26	55	.317	3	1	4	278	302	580	3.355
1819	172	238	277	515	2.994	20	21	41	.238	1	–	1	259	298	557	3.238
1822/3	172	241	291	532	3.093	17	16	33	.190	2	2	4	260	309	569	3.308
1843/4	209	271	316	587	2.805	31	32	63	.283	2	2	4	304	350	654	3.108
1865	154	186	232	418	2.714	14	27	41	.266	2	9	11	202	268	470	3.051
1868	148	204	232	436	2.945	9	23	32	.216	3	1	4	216	256	472	3.189
Totals	1,615	2,325	2,544	4,869	3.015	165	191	356	.220	47	56	103	2,537	2,791	5,328	3.299

Table 5. Nishinomiya, Hama-issai-chō. Registers of All Categories, 1713-1861: Size and Composition of Family and Household

Year	*Number of House-holds*	*Family Members*				*Quasi-Family Members*				*Status Unknown*			*All Household Residents*			
		Male	*Female*	*Total*	*No./House*	*Male*	*Female*	*Total*	*No./House*	*Male*	*Female*	*Total*	*Male*	*Female*	*Total*	*No./House*
Combined*																
1713	131	291	296	587	4.480	62	9	71	.537	5	4	9	358	309	667	5.091
1733	136	297	300	597	4.389	7	3	10	.073	6	5	11	310	308	618	4.544
1737	157	318	321	639	4.070	9	3	12	.076	1	4	5	328	328	656	4.178
1744	138	315	298	613	4.442	4	2	6	.043	0	2	2	319	302	621	4.500
1757	175	366	381	747	4.268	9	5	14	.080	2	4	6	377	390	767	4.382
1774	104	206	218	424	4.076	21	8	29	.278	6	3	9	233	229	462	4.442
Totals	841	1,793	1,814	3,607	4.289	112	30	142	.169	20	22	42	1,925	1,866	3,791	4.508
House-owner																
1784	108	200	211	411	3.805	13	5	18	.166	2	5	7	215	221	436	4.037
1788	112	193	218	411	3.669	20	25	45	.401	–	–	–	213	243	456	4.071
1792	109	195	217	412	3.779	9	16	25	.229	–	–	–	204	233	437	4.009
1800	105	135	218	403	3.838	15	20	35	.333	4	2	6	204	240	444	4.229
1820	97	138	180	318	3.278	7	12	19	.195	2	–	2	147	192	339	3.495
1847	94	158	166	324	3.446	10	8	18	.191	5	6	11	173	180	353	3.755
1861	82	135	154	289	3.524	4	13	17	.207	–	–	–	139	167	306	3.731
Totals	707	1,204	1,364	2,568	3.632	78	99	177	.250	13	13	26	1,295	1,476	2,771	3.919
Renters/Tenants																
1787	98	118	171	289	2.948	8	14	22	.224	3	1	4	129	186	315	3.214
1792	109	140	177	317	2.908	4	10	14	.128	1	–	1	145	187	332	3.045
1820	101	136	154	290	2.871	8	10	18	.178	–	–	–	144	164	308	3.049
1847	103	139	160	299	2.902	5	4	9	.087	2	9	11	146	173	319	3.097
1861	92	114	145	259	2.815	5	11	16	.173	–	2	2	119	158	277	3.010
Totals	503	647	807	1,454	2.890	30	49	79	.157	6	12	18	683	868	1,551	3.083

* No distinction is drawn in these registers between "House-owner" (*Iemochi*) and "Renters/Tenants" (*Shakuya*).

Table 6. Tennōji, Kubo-Machi. Registers of the *Iemochi* (House-owners), 1757-1858: Size and Composition of Family and Household

	Number of	Family Members				Quasi-Family Members				Status Unknown			All Household Residents			
Year	*House-holds*	*Male*	*Female*	*Total*	*No./ House*	*Male*	*Female*	*Total*	*No./ House*	*Male*	*Female*	*Total*	*Male*	*Female*	*Total*	*No./ House*
1757	55	92	79	171	3.109	18	16	34	.618	–	1	1	110	96	206	3.745
1760	58	101	91	192	3.310	26	17	43	.741	–	–	–	127	108	235	4.051
1761	58	108	89	197	3.396	28	18	46	.793	–	–	–	136	107	243	4.189
1762	59	110	86	196	3.322	25	17	42	.711	–	–	–	135	103	238	4.033
1763	58	110	87	197	3.396	23	17	40	.689	–	–	–	133	104	237	4.086
1765	57	111	90	201	3.526	21	13	34	.596	–	–	–	132	103	235	4.122
1766	57	110	91	201	3.526	24	16	40	.701	–	–	–	134	107	241	4.228
1767	58	109	89	198	3.413	28	17	45	.775	–	–	–	137	106	243	4.189
1784	51	95	87	182	3.568	35	19	54	1.058	–	–	–	130	106	236	4.627
1785	51	101	94	195	3.823	33	19	52	1.019	–	–	–	134	113	247	4.843
1788	51	93	85	178	3.490	35	24	59	1.180	–	–	–	128	109	237	4.647
1795	51	95	92	187	3.666	29	23	52	1.019	1	–	1	125	115	240	4.705
1797	54	104	92	196	3.629	32	17	49	.907	–	–	–	136	109	245	4.537
1798	50	93	93	186	3.720	34	20	54	1.080	–	–	–	127	113	240	4.800
1802	50	95	92	187	3.740	32	23	55	1.100	–	–	–	127	115	242	4.840
1805	49	98	96	194	3.959	34	17	51	1.040	–	–	–	132	113	245	5.000
1806	51	96	96	192	3.764	29	22	51	1.000	1	–	1	126	118	244	4.784
1816	47	89	90	179	3.808	25	17	42	.893	–	–	–	114	107	221	4.702
1817	47	93	91	184	3.914	22	16	38	.808	–	–	–	115	107	222	4.723
1831	46	96	85	181	3.934	20	10	30	.652	–	–	–	116	95	211	4.586
1834	48	104	94	198	4.125	15	8	23	.479	–	–	–	119	102	221	4.604
1837	45	95	81	176	3.911	12	6	18	.400	–	–	–	107	87	194	4.311
1838	46	93	77	170	3.695	8	6	14	.304	–	–	–	101	83	184	4.000
1840	44	88	82	170	3.863	7	3	10	.227	–	–	–	95	85	180	4.090
1843	43	80	72	152	3.534	5	3	8	.186	–	–	–	85	75	160	3.720
1844	42	78	73	151	3.595	6	2	8	.190	–	–	–	84	75	159	3.785
1847	42	75	59	134	3.190	4	3	7	.166	–	–	–	79	62	141	3.357
1848	42	71	61	132	3.142	4	3	7	.166	–	–	–	75	64	139	3.309
1849	39	70	61	131	3.358	4	1	5	.128	–	–	–	74	62	136	3.487
1850	41	75	62	137	3.341	4	1	5	.121	–	–	–	79	63	142	3.463
1851	39	75	59	134	3.435	5	1	6	.153	–	–	–	80	60	140	3.589
1852	40	75	64	139	3.475	5	1	6	.150	–	–	–	80	65	145	3.625
1854	42	72	70	142	3.380	4	1	5	.119	–	–	–	76	71	147	3 500
1855	38	62	60	122	3.210	4	1	5	.131	–	–	–	66	61	127	3.342
1856	40	65	58	123	3.075	4	1	5	.125	–	–	–	69	59	128	3.200
1858	40	67	55	122	3.050	4	1	5	.125	–	–	–	71	56	127	3.175
Totals	1,729	3,244	2,883	6,127	3.543	648	400	1,048	.606	2	1	3	3,894	3,284	7,178	4.151

Table 7. Tennōji, Kubo-Machi. Registers of the *Shakuya* (Renters/Tenants), 1757-1858: Size and Composition of Family and Household

Year	Number of House-holds	Family Members				Quasi-Family Members				Status Unknown			All Household Residents			
		Male	Female	Total	No./House	Male	Female	Total	No./House	Male	Female	Total	Male	Female	Total	No./House
1757	32	30	31	61	1.906	–	–	–	–	–	–	–	30	31	61	1.906
1760	33	40	39	79	2.393	–	–	–	–	–	–	–	40	39	79	2.393
1761	30	48	44	92	3.066	–	–	–	–	–	–	–	48	44	92	3.066
1762	31	47	50	97	3.129	–	–	–	–	–	–	–	47	50	97	3.129
1763	37	53	53	106	2.864	–	–	–	–	–	–	–	53	53	106	2.863
1765	35	45	48	93	2.657	–	–	–	–	–	–	–	45	48	93	2.657
1766	31	43	47	90	2.903	–	–	–	–	–	–	–	43	47	90	2.903
1767	28	37	48	85	3.035	1	–	1	.035	–	1	1	38	49	87	3.107
1784	43	72	66	138	3.209	3	5	8	.186	–	–	–	75	71	146	3.395
1785	39	67	59	126	3.230	1	3	4	.102	–	–	–	68	62	130	3.333
1788	35	59	54	113	3.228	3	1	4	.114	–	–	–	62	55	117	3.342
1795	42	66	57	123	2.928	6	4	10	.238	–	–	–	72	61	133	3.166
1797	41	65	52	117	2.853	4	1	5	.121	–	–	–	69	53	122	2.975
1798	44	72	50	122	2.772	1	2	3	.068	–	–	–	73	52	125	2.840
1802	42	65	59	124	2.952	1	–	1	.023	–	–	–	66	59	125	2.976
1805	51	78	84	162	3.176	2	3	5	.098	1	–	1	81	87	168	3.294
1806	53	85	92	177	3.339	2	4	6	.113	–	–	–	87	96	183	3.452
1816	27	55	44	99	3.666	6	5	11	.407	–	–	–	61	49	110	4.074
1817	24	50	38	88	3.666	3	1	4	.142	–	–	–	53	39	92	3.833
1831	20	27	25	52	2.600	3	3	6	.300	–	–	–	30	28	58	2.900
1834	26	41	41	82	3.153	3	6	9	.346	–	–	–	44	47	91	3.500
1837	18	36	36	72	4.000	1	1	2	.111	–	–	–	37	37	74	4.111
1838	16	28	32	60	3.750	2	–	2	.125	–	–	–	30	32	62	3.875
1840	23	45	40	85	3.695	–	–	–	–	–	–	–	45	40	85	3.695
1843	22	35	36	71	3.227	1	–	1	.043	–	–	–	36	36	72	3.272
1844	26	45	49	94	3.615	–	1	1	.038	–	–	–	45	50	95	3.653
1847	26	52	51	103	3.961	2	2	4	.153	–	–	–	54	53	107	4.115
1848	30	57	59	116	3.866	2	1	3	.100	–	–	–	59	60	119	3.966
1849	27	52	59	111	4.111	1	–	1	.037	–	–	–	53	59	112	4.148
1850	28	53	54	107	3.821	1	1	2	.071	–	–	–	54	55	109	3.892
1851	29	53	54	107	3.689	1	1	2	.074	–	–	–	54	55	109	3.448
1852	24	48	47	95	3.958	–	1	1	.041	–	–	–	48	48	96	4.000
1854	23	46	36	82	3.565	1	–	1	.043	–	–	–	47	36	83	3.608
1855	22	44	45	89	4.045	–	–	–	–	–	–	–	44	45	89	4.045
1856	29	63	54	117	4.034	1	3	4	.137	–	–	–	64	57	121	4.172
1858	32	60	47	107	3.343	2	3	5	.156	–	–	–	62	50	112	3.500
Totals	1,119	1,862	1,780	3,642	3.254	54	52	106	.094	1	1	2	1,917	1,833	3,750	3.351

Table 8. Tennōji, Horikoshi-Machi. Registers of the *Iemochi* (House-owners), 1757-1858: Size and Composition of Family and Household

	Number of House-holds	Family Members				Quasi-Family Members				Status Unknown			All Household Residents			
Year		*Male*	*Female*	*Total*	*No./ House*	*Male*	*Female*	*Total*	*No./ House*	*Male*	*Female*	*Total*	*Male*	*Female*	*Total*	*No./ House*
1757	28	45	44	89	3.178	20	10	30	1.034	–	–	–	65	54	119	4.250
1760	24	44	36	80	3.333	16	11	27	1.080	–	–	–	60	47	107	4.458
1761	25	47	43	90	3.600	17	11	28	1.120	1	–	1	65	54	119	4.760
1762	25	46	41	87	3.480	15	6	21	.840	–	–	–	61	47	108	4.320
1763	23	42	43	85	3.695	15	8	23	1.000	–	–	–	57	51	108	4.695
1765	22	46	38	84	3.818	19	11	30	1.363	–	–	–	65	49	114	5.181
1766	22	47	43	90	4.090	20	7	27	1.227	–	–	–	67	50	117	5.318
1767	22	48	44	92	4.181	18	10	28	1.272	1	1	2	67	55	122	5.545
1784	24	41	45	86	3.583	30	15	45	1.875	–	–	–	71	60	131	5.458
1785	25	40	43	83	3.320	25	17	42	1.680	1	–	1	66	60	126	5.040
1788	27	43	47	90	3.333	24	17	41	1.518	–	–	–	67	64	131	4.851
1795	21	37	45	82	3.904	33	17	50	2.380	–	–	–	70	62	132	6.285
1797	19	34	36	70	3.684	31	16	47	2.473	–	–	–	65	52	117	6.157
1798	19	33	38	71	3.736	33	18	51	2.684	–	–	–	66	56	122	6.421
1802	17	33	34	67	3.529	29	21	50	2.941	–	–	–	62	55	117	6.882
1805	18	36	35	71	3.789	28	19	47	2.611	–	–	–	64	54	118	6.555
1806	19	38	40	78	4.105	28	14	42	2.210	–	–	–	66	54	120	6.315
1816	19	33	39	72	3.789	27	17	44	2.315	–	–	–	60	56	116	6.105
1817	20	36	44	80	4.000	28	17	45	2.250	–	–	–	64	61	125	6.250
1831	22	42	42	84	3.819	27	14	41	1.863	–	–	–	69	56	125	5.681
1834	23	49	50	99	4.304	9	3	12	.521	–	–	–	58	53	111	4.826
1837	24	50	48	98	4.083	8	4	12	.500	–	–	–	58	52	110	5.583
1838	25	51	46	97	3.880	7	3	10	.400	–	–	–	58	49	107	4.280
1840	26	52	52	104	4.000	7	3	10	.384	–	–	–	59	55	114	4.384
1843	25	53	50	103	4.120	2	1	3	.120	–	–	–	55	51	106	4.240
1844	23	50	50	100	4.347	7	3	10	.434	–	–	–	57	53	110	4.782
1847	23	48	49	97	4.217	7	1	8	.347	–	–	–	55	50	105	4.565
1848	21	46	48	94	4.476	1	–	1	.047	–	–	–	47	48	95	4.523
1849	22	47	44	91	4.136	1	–	1	.045	–	–	–	48	44	92	4.181
1850	20	48	40	88	4.400	1	–	1	.050	–	–	–	49	40	89	4.450
1851	21	47	39	86	4.095	–	–	–	–	–	–	–	47	39	86	4.095
1852	22	49	39	88	4.000	–	–	–	–	–	–	–	49	39	88	4.000
1854	21	49	42	91	4.333	1	–	1	.047	–	–	–	50	42	92	4.380
1855	22	52	42	94	4.272	–	–	–	–	–	–	–	52	42	94	4.272
1856	21	53	41	94	4.476	–	–	–	–	–	–	–	53	41	94	4.476
1858	25	55	48	103	4.120	–	–	–	–	–	–	–	55	48	103	4.120
Totals	805	1,610	1,548	3,158	3.922	534	294	828	1.028	3	1	4	2,147	1,843	3,990	4.956

Table 9. Tennōji, Horikoshi-Machi. Registers of the *Shakuya* (Renters/Tenants), 1757-1858: Size and Composition of Family and Household

	Number of	*Family Members*				*Quasi-Family Members*				*Status Unknown*			*All Household Residents*			
Year	*House-holds*	*Male*	*Female*	*Total*	*No./ House*	*Male*	*Female*	*Total*	*No./ House*	*Male*	*Female*	*Total*	*Male*	*Female*	*Total*	*No./ House*
1757	24	33	26	59	2.458	–	–	–	–	–	–	–	33	26	59	2.458
1760	48	72	66	138	2.875	1	1	2	.041	–	–	–	73	67	140	2.916
1761	51	76	75	151	2.960	2	5	7	.137	–	–	–	78	80	158	3.098
1762	46	72	66	138	3.000	2	1	3	.065	–	–	–	74	67	141	3.065
1763	52	82	74	156	3.000	1	1	2	.036	–	–	–	83	75	158	3.038
1765	40	73	46	119	2.975	1	1	2	.050	–	1	1	74	48	122	3.050
1766	42	68	46	114	2.714	3	–	3	.071	–	–	–	71	46	117	2.758
1767	43	73	51	124	2.883	1	2	3	.069	–	1	1	74	54	128	2.976
1784	36	61	58	119	3.305	1	1	2	.055	–	–	–	62	59	121	3.361
1785	39	62	71	133	3.410	1	1	2	.051	–	–	–	63	72	135	3.461
1788	37	62	73	135	3.648	3	2	5	.135	–	–	–	65	75	140	3.783
1795	38	72	69	141	3.710	7	1	8	.210	–	–	–	79	70	149	3.921
1797	41	84	86	170	4.146	5	2	7	.170	–	–	–	89	88	177	4.317
1798	43	87	85	172	4.000	7	2	9	.209	–	–	–	94	87	181	4.209
1802	45	90	80	170	3.777	6	2	8	.177	–	–	–	96	82	178	3.955
1805	56	112	98	210	3.750	6	2	8	.142	–	–	–	118	100	218	3.892
1806	51	103	94	197	3.862	6	3	9	.176	–	–	–	109	97	206	4.039
1816	49	107	78	185	3.775	4	4	8	.163	–	–	–	111	82	193	3.938
1817	47	100	68	168	3.574	4	3	7	.148	–	–	–	104	71	175	3.723
1831	43	62	67	129	3.000	10	3	13	.302	–	–	–	72	70	142	3.302
1834	49	78	69	147	3.000	11	3	14	.285	–	–	–	89	72	161	3.285
1837	40	69	69	138	3.450	7	5	12	.300	–	–	–	76	74	150	3.750
1838	39	63	56	119	3.051	2	3	5	.128	–	–	–	65	59	124	3.179
1840	41	71	61	132	3.219	2	4	6	.146	–	–	–	73	65	138	3.365
1843	30	54	52	106	3.500	4	5	9	.300	–	–	–	58	57	115	3.833
1844	36	57	64	121	3.361	6	9	15	.416	–	–	–	63	73	136	3.777
1847	34	62	61	123	3.617	3	5	8	.235	–	–	–	65	66	131	3.852
1848	34	65	68	133	3.911	5	6	11	.323	–	–	–	70	74	144	4.235
1849	35	58	60	118	3.371	2	4	6	.171	–	–	–	60	64	124	3.542
1850	37	66	58	124	3.351	5	4	9	.243	–	–	–	71	62	133	3.594
1851	40	68	67	135	3.375	5	3	8	.200	–	–	–	73	70	143	3.575
1852	43	71	65	136	3.162	6	4	10	.232	–	–	–	77	69	146	3.395
1854	42	67	60	127	3.023	4	6	10	.238	–	–	–	71	66	137	3.261
1855	38	62	58	120	3.157	4	2	6	.157	–	–	–	66	60	126	3.315
1856	36	55	52	107	2.972	4	2	6	.166	–	–	–	59	54	113	3.138
1858	33	52	51	103	3.121	2	2	4	.121	–	–	–	54	53	107	3.242
Totals	1,478	2,569	2,348	4,917	3.326	143	104	247	.167	–	2	2	2,712	2,454	5,166	3.494

Table 10. Nishinomiya, Hama-kubo-chō. Registers of the *Iemochi* (House-owners), 1771-1866: Number of Houses with Given Number of Family Members

Year	*Number of Family Members* 1	2	3	4	5	6	7	8	9	10	11	*Total No. of Houses*
1771	6	14	19	28	23	9	7	4	1	2	–	113
1782	12	13	20	21	14	15	8	6	2	1	–	112
1786	10	15	30	13	18	9	6	2	2	1	–	106
1795	10	8	22	17	24	10	5	1	1	–	1	99
1806	17	16	15	20	15	10	4	1	1	1	–	100
1810	24	19	12	22	14	7	7	1	–	–	–	106
1816	18	18	16	19	13	10	4	2	–	1	–	101
1818	16	21	16	18	14	9	7	1	–	–	1	103
1822/3	17	10	19	19	18	9	4	1	–	–	–	97
1843/4	18	9	19	16	10	6	6	2	–	–	–	86
1865	15	15	13	9	9	9	3	–	1	–	–	74
1866	16	14	17	10	10	7	4	–	1	–	–	79
Total No.	179	172	218	212	182	110	65	21	9	6	2	1,176
%	15.2	14.6	18.5	18.0	15.5	9.4	5.5	1.8	.8	.5	.2	100

Nishinomiya, Hama-kubo-chō. Registers of the *Shakuya* (Renters/Tenants), 1771-1868: Number of Houses with Given Number of Family Members

Year	*Number of Family Members* 1	2	3	4	5	6	7	8	9	10	11	*Total No. of Houses*
1771	19	26	26	18	10	6	4	3	1	–	–	113
1781	23	32	22	29	13	7	5	4	–	–	–	135
1806	47	30	37	22	14	14	2	6	2	–	–	174
1810	38	39	35	22	16	3	4	3	2	3	–	165
1816	51	23	39	27	14	10	5	3	–	1	–	173
1819	49	27	30	34	19	4	5	4	–	–	–	172
1822/3	46	28	34	28	22	6	4	3	1	–	–	172
1843/4	67	36	36	30	26	10	2	2	–	–	–	209
1865	38	23	27	32	11	18	4	–	1	–	–	154
1868	41	28	28	21	17	8	3	1	1	–	–	148
Total No.	419	292	314	263	162	86	38	29	8	4	–	1,615
%	26.0	18.1	19.5	16.3	10.0	5.3	2.4	1.8	.4	.2	–	100

Table 11. Nishinomiya, Hama-kubo-chō. Registers of the *Iemochi* (House-owners), 1771-1866: Number of Households with Given Number of Residents

	Number of Residents													*Total No. of*
Year	*1*	*2*	*3*	*4*	*5*	*6*	*7*	*8*	*9*	*10*	*11*	*12*	*13*	*Houses*
1771	4	12	18	27	23	8	6	6	2	2	3	1	1	113
1782	9	11	16	19	17	17	10	7	2	1	1	1	1	112
1786	8	16	26	11	13	10	13	2	3	3	1	–	–	106
1795	8	7	22	13	20	11	8	6	2	–	1	–	1	99
1806	13	14	15	21	14	13	7	1	–	2	–	–	–	100
1810	20	15	14	21	13	10	8	4	–	1	–	–	–	106
1816	15	17	15	15	15	11	7	3	2	1	–	–	–	101
1818	13	19	15	17	13	12	7	3	1	2	1	–	–	103
1822/3	14	9	16	21	15	13	7	1	1	–	–	–	–	97
1843/4	8	11	18	19	11	7	6	5	1	–	–	–	–	86
1865	13	14	13	7	11	8	5	2	1	–	–	–	–	74
1866	15	11	18	7	12	8	6	1	1	–	–	–	–	79
Total														
No.	140	156	206	198	177	128	90	41	16	12	7	2	3	1,176
%	11.9	13.3	17.4	16.8	15.1	10.9	7.6	3.5	1.4	1.0	.6	.2	.3	100

Nishinomiya, Hama-kubo-chō. Registers of the *Shakuya* (Renters/Tenants), 1771-1868: Number of Households with Given Number of Residents

	Number of Residents													*Total No. of*
Year	*1*	*2*	*3*	*4*	*5*	*6*	*7*	*8*	*9*	*10*	*11*	*12*	*13*	*Houses*
1771	16	25	25	17	8	7	6	5	2	–	1	1	–	113
1781	17	31	25	32	11	9	5	4	1	–	–	–	–	135
1806	37	31	36	27	14	12	8	5	4	–	–	–	–	174
1810	31	41	32	23	17	6	3	3	6	2	1	–	–	165
1816	45	20	39	27	16	10	6	4	4	2	–	–	–	173
1819	41	26	34	32	21	5	8	3	2	–	–	–	–	172
1822/3	41	30	28	31	20	11	2	5	1	2	–	1	–	172
1843/4	59	37	32	30	25	13	8	4	–	1	–	–	–	209
1865	30	22	26	29	17	21	6	–	2	–	–	1	–	154
1868	35	28	26	25	16	13	3	1	1	–	–	–	–	148
Total														
No.	352	291	303	273	165	107	55	34	23	7	2	3	–	1,615
%	21.8	18.0	18.8	16.9	10.2	6.6	3.4	2.1	1.4	.5	.1	.2	–	100

Table 12. Nishinomiya, Hama-issai-chō. Registers of All Categories, 1713-1861: Number of Houses with Given Number of Family Members

Year	1	2	3	4	5	6	7	8	9	10	11	12	Total No. of Houses
	Number of Family Members												
*Combined**													
1713	9	21	16	24	23	16	10	4	5	1	–	2	131
1733	11	13	21	28	28	16	10	5	2	1	1	–	136
1737	15	17	29	33	27	21	11	3	1	–	–	–	157
1744	14	9	22	28	25	18	11	7	3	1	–	–	138
1757	10	20	32	41	32	16	14	7	3	–	–	–	175
1774	8	20	20	16	9	18	6	6	1	–	–	–	104
Total													
No.	67	100	140	170	144	105	62	32	15	3	1	2	841
%	8.0	11.9	16.6	20.2	17.1	12.5	7.4	3.8	1.8	.4	.1	.2	100
House-owners													
1784	11	21	20	17	22	6	7	2	1	1	–	–	108
1788	13	21	22	21	15	13	4	2	1	–	–	–	112
1792	14	20	24	14	16	7	7	4	3	–	–	–	109
1800	13	22	13	22	17	4	6	5	2	1	–	–	105
1820	17	16	22	22	11	4	4	1	–	–	–	–	97
1847	14	18	26	9	16	5	3	–	1	2	–	–	94
1861	17	11	18	13	7	10	3	1	1	–	1	–	82
Total													
No.	99	129	145	118	104	49	34	15	9	4	1	–	707
%	14.0	18.2	20.5	16.7	14.7	6.9	4.8	2.1	1.3	.6	.2	–	100
Renters/Tenants													
1787	25	20	18	19	9	2	4	–	1	–	–	–	98
1792	31	24	18	17	7	8	1	2	–	1	–	–	109
1820	23	22	26	12	14	2	1	1	–	–	–	–	101
1847	26	28	14	17	9	4	2	3	–	–	–	–	103
1861	27	18	20	13	5	6	2	–	1	–	–	–	92
Total													
No.	132	112	96	78	44	22	10	6	2	1	–	–	503
%	26.2	22.3	19.1	15.5	8.7	4.4	2.0	1.2	.4	.2	–	–	100
Grand Totals													
No.	298	341	381	366	292	176	106	53	26	8	2	2	2,051
%	14.5	16.6	18.6	17.8	14.2	8.6	5.2	2.6	1.3	.4	.1	.1	100

* No distinction is drawn in these registers between "House-owner" (Iemochi) and "Renters/Tenants" (Shakuya).

Table 13. Nishinomiya, Hama-issai-chō. Registers of All Categories, 1713-1861: Number of Houses with Given Number of Residents

	Number of Family Members													*Total No. of*
Year	*1*	*2*	*3*	*4*	*5*	*6*	*7*	*8*	*9*	*10*	*11*	*12*	*13*	*Houses*
*Combined**														
1713	8	12	18	16	26	17	14	7	5	4	2	2	–	131
1733	9	11	21	28	30	16	11	6	–	3	1	–	–	136
1737	14	18	25	32	31	20	10	5	2	–	–	–	–	157
1744	14	8	22	29	23	20	10	7	4	–	–	1	–	138
1757	9	19	32	41	31	17	15	6	3	1	–	–	1	175
1774	5	14	23	17	9	17	10	7	1	1	–	–	–	104
Total														
No.	59	82	141	163	150	107	70	38	15	9	3	3	1	841
%	7.0	9.8	16.8	19.4	17.8	12.7	8.3	4.5	1.8	1.0	.4	.4	.1	100
House-owners														
1784	9	19	20	18	17	11	10	1	2	1	–	–	–	108
1788	11	23	17	19	13	13	8	3	2	2	1	–	–	112
1792	13	16	24	11	19	11	8	4	3	–	–	–	–	109
1800	9	20	14	20	20	6	6	4	1	2	3	–	–	105
1820	14	17	18	25	9	8	4	2	–	–	–	–	–	97
1847	9	19	22	13	16	7	4	–	2	2	–	–	–	94
1861	15	11	16	13	8	11	5	1	1	–	1	–	–	82
Total														
No.	80	125	131	119	102	67	45	15	11	7	5	–	–	707
%	11.3	17.7	18.7	16.8	14.4	9.4	6.4	2.1	1.6	.9	.7	–	–	100
Renters/Tenants														
1787	24	16	16	21	10	4	5	–	2	–	–	–	–	98
1792	30	22	19	16	8	8	2	2	1	1	–	–	–	109
1820	20	22	22	16	16	2	2	1	–	–	–	–	–	101
1847	22	28	12	20	9	7	2	3	–	–	–	–	–	103
1861	24	16	20	15	7	6	3	–	1	–	–	–	–	92
Total														
No.	120	104	89	88	50	27	14	6	4	1	–	–	–	503
%	23.9	20.6	17.7	17.5	9.9	5.4	2.8	1.2	.8	.2	–	–	–	100
Grand Totals														
No.	259	311	361	370	302	201	129	59	30	17	8	3	1	2,051
%	12.6	15.2	17.6	18.1	14.7	9.8	6.2	2.9	1.5	.8	.4	.15	.05	100

* No distinction is drawn in these registers between "House-owner" (Iemochi) and "Renters/Tenants" (Shakuya).

Table 14. Tennōji, Kubo-machi. Registers of the *Iemochi* (House-owners), 1757-1858: Number of Houses with Given Number of Family Members

Year	*Number of Family Members*												*Total No. of Houses*
	1	*2*	*3*	*4*	*5*	*6*	*7*	*8*	*9*	*10*	*11*	*12*	
1757	9	8	17	12	7	2	–	–	–	–	–	–	55
1760	14	4	14	11	11	1	2	–	1	–	–	–	58
1761	13	6	14	9	8	5	1	1	1	–	–	–	58
1762	14	6	13	12	7	3	2	2	–	–	–	–	59
1763	12	5	14	12	9	4	–	2	–	–	–	–	58
1765	12	4	11	11	13	5	–	1	–	–	–	–	57
1766	10	6	12	13	8	6	1	1	–	–	–	–	57
1767	9	7	13	15	11	1	1	1	–	–	–	–	58
1784	8	12	3	12	8	5	1	2	–	–	–	–	51
1785	7	12	3	11	6	5	5	2	–	–	–	–	51
1788	10	10	5	11	7	4	2	2	–	–	–	–	51
1795	12	6	8	7	6	9	1	1	–	–	–	1	51
1797	14	10	4	5	8	7	4	1	–	–	–	1	54
1798	12	8	8	3	5	7	5	1	–	–	–	1	50
1802	10	3	11	10	7	3	3	3	–	–	–	–	50
1805	10	4	8	7	8	5	3	3	1	–	–	–	49
1806	13	4	7	8	8	4	3	3	1	–	–	–	51
1816	12	6	5	6	8	4	1	3	1	–	–	1	47
1817	11	5	7	8	5	1	4	4	1	1	–	–	47
1831	11	6	6	4	5	6	3	3	2	–	–	–	46
1834	11	7	5	5	5	6	1	4	2	2	–	–	48
1837	12	6	3	7	5	4	2	2	4	–	–	–	45
1838	12	6	6	7	4	3	3	4	1	–	–	–	46
1840	14	2	5	3	7	8	1	2	1	1	–	–	44
1843	15	1	4	10	2	6	4	–	1	–	–	–	43
1844	14	2	4	7	6	4	3	–	2	–	–	–	42
1847	17	2	3	8	5	4	1	2	–	–	–	–	42
1848	17	3	4	7	3	4	2	2	–	–	–	–	42
1849	13	2	5	7	5	5	–	2	–	–	–	–	39
1850	14	3	7	5	4	5	–	2	–	1	–	–	41
1851	13	3	4	7	2	7	1	2	–	–	–	–	39
1852	12	4	4	7	3	8	–	2	–	–	–	–	40
1854	13	5	4	9	2	5	2	1	1	–	–	–	42
1855	11	6	4	9	2	5	–	–	–	–	1	–	38
1856	13	6	4	9	2	5	–	–	–	1	–	–	40
1858	12	5	5	6	5	4	–	–	–	3	–	–	40
Total													
No.	436	195	254	300	217	170	62	61	20	9	1	4	1,729
%	25.2	11.3	14.7	17.4	12.6	9.8	3.5	3.5	1.2	.5	.1	.2	100

Table 15. Tennōji, Kubo-machi. Registers of the *Iemochi* (House-owners), 1757-1858: Number of Houses with Given Number of Residents

	Number of Residents												*Total No. of*
Year	*1*	*2*	*3*	*4*	*5*	*6*	*7*	*8*	*9*	*10*	*11*	*12*	*Houses*
1757	9	5	15	8	7	5	4	1	1	–	–	–	55
1760	13	3	6	12	10	6	1	6	1	–	–	–	58
1761	11	5	7	9	11	6	4	2	3	–	–	–	58
1762	10	5	12	9	7	7	4	4	1	–	–	–	59
1763	8	5	12	9	11	5	2	6	–	–	–	–	58
1765	7	7	6	13	14	3	2	3	2	–	–	–	57
1766	6	8	7	10	12	7	2	3	2	–	–	–	57
1767	3	10	8	14	10	6	3	3	1	–	–	–	58
1784	5	9	4	8	8	7	3	–	4	3	–	–	51
1785	2	8	8	6	9	3	8	3	2	2	–	–	51
1788	8	4	3	7	12	8	5	1	–	2	1	–	51
1795	9	1	2	11	11	8	4	2	1	–	1	1	51
1797	12	3	3	9	7	11	2	4	1	–	1	1	54
1798	9	2	5	7	7	7	8	1	1	1	–	2	50
1802	7	1	4	10	9	6	8	3	–	1	1	–	50
1805	7	2	5	7	11	2	5	5	3	1	–	1	49
1806	9	1	6	10	7	3	6	3	5	–	1	–	51
1816	10	4	2	8	7	2	4	4	4	1	–	1	47
1817	9	3	4	8	7	3	3	4	3	3	–	–	47
1831	8	5	4	6	7	5	4	2	2	3	–	–	46
1834	7	6	7	6	5	5	3	4	2	2	1	–	48
1837	8	3	9	7	3	6	2	3	4	–	–	–	45
1838	9	4	9	5	3	4	5	5	2	–	–	–	46
1840	11	1	7	5	7	7	2	1	2	1	–	–	44
1843	13	2	4	10	2	7	2	2	1	–	–	–	43
1844	11	3	5	7	7	4	3	–	1	1	–	–	42
1847	14	4	3	8	6	4	1	1	1	–	–	–	42
1848	14	5	4	7	4	4	2	1	1	–	–	–	42
1849	12	2	5	7	6	5	–	1	1	–	–	–	39
1850	13	3	7	5	5	5	–	1	1	1	–	–	41
1851	12	3	4	7	3	7	1	–	2	–	–	–	39
1852	11	4	5	5	5	8	–	–	2	–	–	–	40
1854	13	3	6	8	3	5	1	1	2	–	–	–	42
1855	10	5	6	8	3	4	1	–	–	–	1	–	38
1856	12	5	6	8	3	4	1	–	–	–	1	–	40
1858	11	4	7	5	6	3	1	–	–	3	–	–	40
Total													
No.	343	148	217	289	255	192	107	80	59	25	8	6	1,729
%	19.8	8.6	12.6	16.7	14.8	11.1	6.2	4.6	3.4	1.4	.5	.3	100

Table 16. Tennōji, Kubo-Machi. Registers of the *Shakuya* (Renters/Tenants), 1757-1858: Number of Houses with Given Number of Family Members

	Number of Family Members									*Total No. of Houses*
Year	*1*	*2*	*3*	*4*	*5*	*6*	*7*	*8*	*9*	
1757	15	8	6	3	–	–	–	–	–	32
1760	10	10	7	3	2	1	–	–	–	33
1761	6	8	5	4	4	2	1	–	–	30
1762	8	4	7	5	2	5	–	–	–	31
1763	8	9	9	5	3	3	–	–	–	37
1765	10	9	6	4	5	1	–	–	–	35
1766	6	7	8	5	4	1	–	–	–	31
1767	6	4	8	6	1	3	–	–	–	28
1784	6	12	9	5	8	2	–	–	1	43
1785	6	11	7	6	4	3	1	1	–	39
1788	3	7	11	9	4	–	1	–	–	35
1795	9	12	5	9	4	2	1	–	–	42
1797	10	14	5	2	5	4	1	–	–	41
1798	12	9	12	2	6	3	–	–	–	44
1802	9	9	8	8	7	1	–	–	–	42
1805	10	12	7	10	8	2	1	1	–	51
1806	12	8	7	12	7	5	1	1	–	53
1816	5	2	4	7	3	6	–	–	–	27
1817	6	1	2	6	4	5	–	–	–	24
1831	8	2	3	5	2	–	–	–	–	20
1834	5	4	7	4	4	2	–	–	–	26
1837	3	1	3	2	5	3	1	–	–	18
1838	2	3	2	2	4	3	–	–	–	16
1840	2	5	4	4	4	3	1	–	–	23
1843	3	7	3	1	7	1	–	–	–	22
1844	3	5	5	4	6	1	2	–	–	26
1847	2	4	4	5	5	6	–	–	–	26
1848	1	5	8	5	6	4	1	–	–	30
1849	–	4	6	5	8	4	–	–	–	27
1850	2	4	7	5	5	4	–	1	–	28
1851	2	6	6	5	7	2	1	–	–	29
1852	1	4	7	3	3	5	1	–	–	24
1854	5	4	4	2	3	3	1	–	1	23
1855	3	2	4	5	2	3	2	1	–	22
1856	5	2	3	7	3	8	–	1	–	29
1858	9	3	6	5	3	4	1	1	–	32
Total										
No.	213	221	215	180	158	105	18	7	2	1,119
%	19.0	19.8	19.2	16.1	14.1	9.4	1.6	.6	.2	100

Table 17. Tennōji, Kubo-machi. Registers of the *Shakuya* (Renters/Tenants), 1757-1858: Number of Houses with Given Number of Residents

Year	*Number of Residents* 1	2	3	4	5	6	7	8	9	10	*Total No. of Houses*
1757	15	8	6	3	–	–	–	–	–	–	32
1760	10	10	7	3	2	1	–	–	–	–	33
1761	6	8	5	4	4	2	1	–	–	–	30
1762	8	4	7	5	2	5	–	–	–	–	31
1763	8	9	9	4	4	3	–	–	–	–	37
1765	10	9	6	4	5	1	–	–	–	–	35
1766	6	7	8	5	4	1	–	–	–	–	31
1767	5	5	8	6	1	3	–	–	–	–	28
1784	5	8	13	5	9	2	–	–	1	–	43
1785	4	11	9	6	4	3	1	1	–	–	39
1788	3	6	12	8	3	2	1	–	–	–	35
1795	6	12	7	8	6	2	1	–	–	–	42
1797	8	15	6	1	4	6	1	–	–	–	41
1798	10	11	11	2	6	3	1	–	–	–	44
1802	9	9	8	8	6	2	–	–	–	–	42
1805	9	13	7	9	7	3	2	1	–	–	51
1806	10	9	7	14	7	3	3	1	–	–	53
1816	4	3	2	6	3	7	–	–	1	–	27
1817	5	1	2	6	5	5	–	–	–	–	24
1831	7	3	2	4	3	1	–	–	–	–	20
1834	4	3	7	4	4	4	–	–	–	–	26
1837	3	1	3	1	5	4	1	–	–	–	18
1838	2	3	2	1	4	4	–	–	–	–	16
1840	2	5	4	4	4	3	1	–	–	–	23
1843	3	6	3	1	6	2	1	–	–	–	22
1844	2	6	5	4	6	1	2	–	–	–	26
1847	1	5	4	4	5	6	1	–	–	–	26
1848	1	5	7	4	8	4	1	–	–	–	30
1849	–	4	6	4	9	2	2	–	–	–	27
1850	2	4	5	7	6	3	–	1	–	–	28
1851	2	6	4	7	5	4	1	–	–	–	29
1852	1	4	7	4	2	3	3	–	–	–	24
1854	5	4	4	2	3	3	1	–	–	1	23
1855	3	2	4	5	2	3	2	1	–	–	22
1856	4	2	3	7	4	8	–	1	–	–	29
1858	8	3	6	4	5	4	1	1	–	–	32
Total											
No.	191	224	216	174	163	113	28	7	2	1	1,119
%	17.1	20.0	19.3	15.5	14.6	10.1	2.5	.6	.2	.1	100

Table 18. Tennōji, Horikoshi-machi. Registers of the *Iemochi* (House-owners), 1757-1858: Number of Houses with Given Number of Family Members

Year	*Number of Family Members* 1	2	3	4	5	6	7	8	9	*Total No. of Houses*
1757	6	4	7	5	3	2	1	–	–	28
1760	5	3	5	5	3	2	1	–	–	24
1761	6	3	4	3	3	3	3	–	–	25
1762	6	3	3	4	5	3	1	–	–	25
1763	3	5	1	6	5	2	–	1	–	23
1765	4	3	3	3	5	2	–	2	–	22
1766	4	3	3	1	6	2	1	–	2	22
1767	3	3	4	–	6	4	–	1	1	22
1784	5	5	1	3	8	–	1	–	1	24
1785	7	4	1	4	7	1	–	1	–	25
1788	10	1	4	2	5	2	3	–	–	27
1795	2	2	4	4	6	3	–	–	–	21
1797	2	2	4	5	4	2	–	–	–	19
1798	2	1	6	4	4	1	1	–	–	19
1802	1	3	4	2	4	2	–	1	–	17
1805	2	1	4	5	3	1	2	–	–	18
1806	3	–	4	4	3	3	2	–	–	19
1816	4	1	5	1	2	5	1	–	–	19
1817	3	4	1	2	4	4	2	–	–	20
1831	5	1	4	3	5	1	2	1	–	22
1834	5	–	2	4	6	2	2	2	–	23
1837	6	–	2	5	6	2	1	1	1	24
1838	7	–	2	6	5	3	–	1	1	25
1840	6	1	2	6	4	4	1	2	–	26
1843	6	1	1	4	8	1	3	–	1	25
1844	4	1	2	4	6	2	3	–	1	23
1847	5	1	2	4	4	3	2	2	–	23
1848	3	1	1	7	3	2	2	1	1	21
1849	4	1	–	9	3	3	1	–	1	22
1850	3	1	–	7	4	2	2	–	1	20
1851	5	–	1	6	4	2	2	1	–	21
1852	5	1	1	6	4	2	2	1	–	22
1854	5	1	–	4	4	3	2	2	–	21
1855	6	1	1	3	2	4	4	–	1	22
1856	5	1	2	2	2	3	4	1	1	21
1858	6	1	3	2	5	4	3	1	–	25
Total										
No.	164	64	94	145	161	87	55	22	13	805
%	20.4	8.0	11.7	18.0	20.0	10.8	6.8	2.7	1.6	100

Table 19. Tennōji, Horikoshi-machi. Registers of the *Iemochi* (House-owners), 1757-1858: Number of Houses with Given Number of Residents

	Number of Residents																Total No. of
Year	*1*	*2*	*3*	*4*	*5*	*6*	*7*	*8*	*9*	*10*	*11*	*12*	*13*	*14*	*15*	*16*	*Houses*
1757	6	3	3	5	3	4	1	1	–	–	1	–	1	–	–	–	28
1760	5	1	1	7	1	5	3	–	–	–	–	–	1	–	–	–	24
1761	6	1	1	3	3	5	3	1	1	–	–	–	1	–	–	–	25
1762	6	2	1	2	7	1	4	1	–	1	–	–	–	–	–	–	25
1763	3	3	–	4	5	6	–	1	–	–	–	–	–	1	–	–	23
1765	4	1	1	3	4	2	3	3	–	–	–	–	–	–	–	1	22
1766	4	1	1	1	6	2	3	1	2	–	–	–	–	–	1	–	22
1767	4	1	1	1	3	4	4	2	1	–	–	–	–	–	1	–	22
1784	5	2	2	–	3	4	1	–	2	3	2	–	–	–	–	–	24
1785	7	3	1	1	1	2	2	3	–	4	1	–	–	–	–	–	25
1788	10	1	2	–	–	2	5	2	1	3	1	–	–	–	–	–	27
1795	2	–	2	1	3	1	5	2	3	1	1	–	–	–	–	–	21
1797	2	1	–	2	1	4	3	3	2	–	–	–	1	–	–	–	19
1798	2	–	2	–	–	6	1	4	2	1	1	–	–	–	–	–	19
1802	1	–	3	–	–	3	4	2	–	1	1	2	–	–	–	–	17
1805	2	–	2	1	1	1	4	2	2	2	–	1	–	–	–	–	18
1806	2	1	1	1	2	2	2	4	1	2	–	1	–	–	–	–	19
1816	4	–	1	1	1	2	2	1	5	1	1	–	–	–	–	–	19
1817	3	1	1	2	–	–	4	4	3	–	2	–	–	–	–	–	20
1831	5	–	1	1	2	4	4	2	1	1	1	–	–	–	–	–	22

Table 19. (*Continued*)

Year							*Number of Residents*										*No. of Total*
	1	*2*	*3*	*4*	*5*	*6*	*7*	*8*	*9*	*10*	*11*	*12*	*13*	*14*	*15*	*16*	*Houses*
1834	4	1	2	3	5	2	2	2	1	–	–	–	1	–	–	–	23
1837	6	–	1	5	5	2	1	2	1	–	1	–	–	–	–	–	24
1838	7	–	2	4	5	2	2	1	1	1	–	–	–	–	–	–	25
1840	6	1	2	4	4	3	3	2	–	1	–	–	–	–	–	–	26
1843	6	1	1	3	7	3	3	–	1	–	–	–	–	–	–	–	25
1844	4	–	3	2	6	2	4	–	1	1	–	–	–	–	–	–	23
1847	5	–	2	3	4	4	2	3	–	–	–	–	–	–	–	–	23
1848	3	–	2	7	3	2	2	1	1	–	–	–	–	–	–	–	21
1849	4	–	1	9	3	3	1	–	1	–	–	–	–	–	–	–	22
1850	3	1	–	7	4	1	3	–	1	–	–	–	–	–	–	–	20
1851	5	–	1	6	4	2	2	1	–	–	–	–	–	–	–	–	21
1852	5	1	1	6	4	2	2	1	–	–	–	–	–	–	–	–	22
1854	5	1	–	4	4	3	2	1	1	–	–	–	–	–	–	–	21
1855	6	1	1	3	2	4	4	–	1	–	–	–	–	–	–	–	22
1856	5	1	2	2	2	3	4	1	1	–	–	–	–	–	–	–	21
1858	6	1	3	2	5	4	3	1	–	–	–	–	–	–	–	–	25
Total																	
No.	163	31	51	106	113	102	98	55	37	23	13	4	5	1	2	1	805
%	20.2	3.9	6.3	13.2	14.1	12.7	12.2	6.8	4.6	2.9	1.6	.5	.6	.1	.2	.1	100

Table 20. Tennōji, Horikoshi-machi. Registers of the *Shakuya* (Renters/Tenants), 1757-1858: Number of Houses with Given Number of Family Members

	Number of Family Members											*Total No. of Houses*
Year	*1*	*2*	*3*	*4*	*5*	*6*	*7*	*8*	*9*	*10*	*11*	
1757	6	5	9	4	–	–	–	–	–	–	–	24
1760	7	15	10	10	6	–	–	–	–	–	–	48
1761	9	17	7	8	5	5	–	–	–	–	–	51
1762	10	12	5	10	5	4	–	–	–	–	–	46
1763	10	13	10	9	6	4	–	–	–	–	–	52
1765	9	6	12	5	7	1	–	–	–	–	–	40
1766	14	5	8	9	6	–	–	–	–	–	–	42
1767	11	5	13	9	3	2	–	–	–	–	–	43
1784	4	8	7	10	5	2	–	–	–	–	–	36
1785	4	5	12	10	7	–	–	1	–	–	–	39
1788	2	8	7	11	5	2	1	1	–	–	–	37
1795	–	11	7	7	8	5	–	–	–	–	–	38
1797	1	6	8	12	6	2	5	1	–	–	–	41
1798	2	5	9	13	8	2	3	1	–	–	–	43
1802	5	5	16	6	5	–	6	2	–	–	–	45
1805	9	10	10	9	7	3	4	3	1	–	–	56
1806	10	8	5	10	8	2	4	3	1	–	–	51
1816	4	7	15	10	4	2	6	1	–	–	–	49
1817	9	5	11	11	3	3	3	1	–	1	–	47
1831	7	15	6	8	3	2	1	1	–	–	–	43
1834	12	12	9	7	3	2	3	1	–	–	–	49
1837	7	10	5	4	8	3	2	1	–	–	–	40
1838	8	12	5	3	8	2	–	1	–	–	–	39
1840	7	8	13	4	3	4	1	1	–	–	–	41
1843	5	2	9	8	3	1	1	–	–	1	–	30
1844	7	5	8	10	1	3	1	–	–	1	–	36
1847	5	3	11	5	5	3	1	–	1	–	–	34
1848	2	4	13	5	5	2	1	–	1	–	1	34
1849	4	6	11	8	2	3	–	–	1	–	–	35
1850	7	6	8	8	3	3	1	–	1	–	–	37
1851	5	9	8	10	4	2	1	–	1	–	–	40
1852	6	11	11	6	4	4	1	–	–	–	–	43
1854	7	13	7	9	1	3	2	–	–	–	–	42
1855	6	10	7	10	–	2	3	–	–	–	–	38
1856	5	11	7	9	1	3	–	–	–	–	–	36
1858	6	7	5	10	3	1	1	–	–	–	–	33
Total												
No.	232	300	324	297	161	82	52	19	7	3	1	1,478
%	15.7	20.3	21.9	20.1	10.9	5.5	3.5	1.3	.5	.2	.1	100

Table 21. Tennōji, Horikoshi-machi. Registers of the *Shakuya* (Renters/Tenants), 1757-1858: Number of Houses with Given Number of Residents

Year	*Number of Residents* *1*	*2*	*3*	*4*	*5*	*6*	*7*	*8*	*9*	*10*	*11*	*Total No. of Houses*
1757	6	5	9	4	–	–	–	–	–	–	–	24
1760	7	14	9	12	6	–	–	–	–	–	–	48
1761	8	15	8	9	6	5	–	–	–	–	–	51
1762	9	13	4	11	4	5	–	–	–	–	–	46
1763	9	14	9	10	6	4	–	–	–	–	–	52
1765	7	7	13	4	8	1	–	–	–	–	–	40
1766	13	6	8	8	6	1	–	–	–	–	–	42
1767	11	5	11	8	6	2	–	–	–	–	–	43
1784	4	6	7	7	10	2	–	–	–	–	–	36
1785	4	5	12	9	7	1	–	1	–	–	–	39
1788	2	7	6	12	5	3	1	1	–	–	–	37
1795	–	10	5	9	8	5	–	1	–	–	–	38
1797	1	6	8	10	5	4	4	2	–	–	–	41
1798	2	5	9	12	6	5	4	–	1	–	–	43
1802	5	5	15	6	3	2	6	3	–	–	–	45
1805	7	11	9	10	6	4	5	3	1	–	–	56
1806	6	10	6	7	10	3	4	4	1	–	–	51
1816	3	7	14	9	6	2	7	1	–	–	–	49
1817	9	5	11	8	4	3	5	1	–	1	–	47
1831	7	10	7	11	3	2	2	–	1	–	–	43
1834	8	14	8	7	5	2	3	2	–	–	–	49
1837	4	10	6	5	8	3	2	2	–	–	–	40
1838	7	11	5	5	8	2	–	1	–	–	–	39
1840	6	6	14	6	3	4	1	1	–	–	–	41
1843	4	2	6	10	5	1	1	–	–	1	–	30
1844	5	5	6	12	3	3	1	–	–	1	–	36
1847	3	5	7	8	6	2	2	–	1	–	–	34
1848	1	5	10	7	5	1	2	–	1	1	1	34
1849	3	5	12	8	3	2	1	–	1	–	–	35
1850	4	7	8	9	4	2	2	–	1	–	–	37
1851	3	8	10	10	4	3	1	–	1	–	–	40
1852	4	9	13	8	4	2	3	–	–	–	–	43
1854	6	8	11	11	1	2	3	–	–	–	–	42
1855	6	8	6	12	1	2	3	–	–	–	–	38
1856	5	8	9	8	3	3	–	–	–	–	–	36
1858	5	7	5	10	4	1	1	–	–	–	–	33
Total												
No.	194	284	316	312	182	89	64	23	9	4	1	1,478
%	13.1	19.2	21.4	21.1	12.3	6.0	4.3	1.6	.6	.3	.1	100

Comparison of these figures with more recent data on number of persons per household is also possible. Toda (1937: 217), citing the 1920 census, reports that 95.4 per cent of all households in Japan had seven members or less. For Tokyo and Osaka in the same year, households with seven members or less accounted for 88.1 per cent and 90.6 per cent, respectively. In a study done in 1956 and 1957, Koyama (1960: 57) reports that 97.2 per cent of non-farm households in the former village of Komae, engulfed by the spreading Tokyo metropolis, had seven members or less, while 98.8 per cent of the households in a large Tokyo apartment complex had fewer than seven members.[7]

7. The following table from Toda (1937: 217) is relevant:

Table 9: Size of Household (1920 Census)

Number of Persons	*All Japan*	*Tokyo*	*Osaka*
1	5.77%	6.16%	6.94%
2	12.52	15.84	18.26
3	15.20	18.81	19.79
4	15.27	16.79	16.42
5	14.57	13.70	12.77
6	12.56	10.00	9.20
7	9.53	6.83	6.17
8	6.32	4.26	3.80
9	3.76	2.60	2.37
10	2.16	1.79	1.53
11 & above	2.34	3.21	2.76

as is the information from Koyama's (1960: 57) study of an isolated farming community ("Rural"), a Tokyo suburban fringe community ("Komae: Farm" and Komae: Non-Farm"), and a Tokyo apartment complex ("Apartment"):

Table 3: Number of Persons Per Household

Number of Persons	*Rural*	*Komae: Farm*	*Komae: Non-Farm*	*Apartment*
1	3.9%	0.0	11.1%	0.6
2	4.7	1.4	13.9	18.3
3	7.8	8.3	23.6	20.7
4	15.5	6.9	16.7	29.0
5	18.6	11.1	18.1	20.7
6	14.7	15.3	9.6	5.9
7	17.0	23.6	4.2	3.6
8	9.3	16.8	1.4	0.0
9	5.4	8.3	1.4	1.2
10 & above	3.1	8.3	0.0	0.0

Table 22. Percentage of Houses with Given Number of Persons per Family and Household, 1713-1868: All Wards and All Categories of Register—9,973 Households

		Number of Persons						
		1	2-3	4-5	6-7	8-12	13-16	%
Registers Combining House-owners and	*Family*	8.0	28.5	37.3	19.9	6.3	–	100
Renters/Tenants	*Household*	7.0	26.6	37.2	21.0	8.1	.1	100
Registers of the House-owners	*Family*	19.9	28.8	32.5	14.3	4.5	–	100
	Household	16.5	24.1	30.7	18.8	9.64	.26	100
Registers of the Renters/Tenants	*Family*	21.1	39.7	28.5	8.8	1.9	–	100
	Household	18.2	38.7	29.9	10.5	2.7	–	100
Registers of All Categories: Totals	*Family*	19.5	33.9	31.1	12.1	3.4	–	100
	Household	16.5	31.2	30.9	15.0	6.27	.13	100

Let us now turn to the question of residential stability. I have done an annual tally of the rate of turnover of households (*not* individuals) for the registers of the Tennōji wards, Horikoshi-machi and Kubo-machi, for the years 1757 through 1858. The duration of households is analyzed separately for house-owners and for renter/tenants in Tables 23 and 24. The nature of the registers is such that it is possible to trace succession; therefore, households of long duration may have had several heads as son succeeded father, widow took over upon the death of husband, etc. A word of explanation is in order concerning the somewhat cumbersome double entries under each category in Table 23. We do not have complete consecutive runs of registers for these wards, but only the registers for 36 of the 102 years between 1757 and 1858. In each tabulation in the odd-numbered columns (labeled "Minimum"), I have given the number of households of a given number of years duration as actually shown in the scattered registers available. In the even-numbered columns (labeled "Maximum") I have given the number of households of a given number of years duration, calculating the maximum number of years in which they theoretically could have appeared if there were a register available for every one of the 102 years.

For example, we do have the registers for 1757 and 1760, but not for the two intervening years. For any given household appearing in the

Table 23. Tennōji, Horikoshi-machi and Kubo-machi: Duration of Households 1757-1858

Number of Years Duration	*Horikoshi-machi*								*Kubo-machi*							
	House-owner				*Renter/Tenant*				*House-owner*				*Renter/Tenant*			
	Col. 1 Minimum		*Col. 2 Maximum*		*Col. 3 Minimum*		*Col. 4 Maximum*		*Col. 5 Minimum*		*Col. 6 Maximum*		*Col. 7 Minimum*		*Col. 8 Maximum*	
	No.	*%*	*No.*	*%*	*No.*	*%*	*No.*	*%*	*No.*	*%*	*No.*	*%*	*No.*	*%*	*No.*	*%*
1	38	38.8	8	8.2	159	36.9	62	14.4	37	19.5	11	5.8	155	41.2	54	14.3
2	3	3.1	5	5.1	64	14.9	40	9.3	20	10.5	8	4.2	57	15.2	19	5.1
3	–	–	14	14.4	23	5.3	61	14.2	6	3.2	19	10.0	21	5.6	70	18.6
4	7	7.1	7	7.1	24	5.6	26	6.0	9	4.7	7	3.7	30	8.0	41	10.9
5	2	2.0	2	2.0	28	6.5	17	3.9	6	3.2	8	4.2	23	6.1	10	2.6
1-5	50	51.0	36	36.8	298	69.2	206	47.8	78	41.1	53	27.9	286	76.1	194	51.5
6-10	14	14.3	24	24.6	48	11.1	61	14.2	16	8.4	22	11.6	32	8.5	62	16.5
11-20	4	4.1	5	5.1	53	12.3	99	22.9	28	14.8	26	13.7	41	10.9	75	20.0
21-30	11	11.2	10	10.2	22	5.1	45	10.4	15	7.9	32	16.8	10	2.6	36	9.5
31-40	3	3.1	7	7.1	7	1.6	15	3.5	11	5.7	12	6.3	4	1.1	4	1.1
41-50	2	2.0	2	2.0	3	.7	5	1.2	12	6.3	10	5.3	2	.5	4	1.1
51-60	–	–	–	–	–	–	–	–	3	1.6	8	4.2	1	.3	1	.3
61-70	3	3.1	2	2.0	–	–	–	–	8	4.2	7	3.7	–	–	–	–
71-80	–	–	1	1.0	–	–	–	–	3	1.6	4	2.1	–	–	–	–
81-90	1	1.0	–	–	–	–	–	–	5	2.6	5	2.6	–	–	–	–
91-100	1	1.0	1	1.0	–	–	–	–	8	4.2	8	4.2	–	–	–	–
101	–	–	1	1.0	–	–	–	–	–	–	–	–	–	–	–	–
102	9	9.2	9	9.2	–	–	–	–	3	1.6	3	1.6	–	–	–	–
Totals	98	100	98	100	431	100	431	100	190	100	190	100	376	100	376	100
Average duration in years	20.5		23.2		6.1		9.9		23.0		27.2		5.1		8.8	
Median duration in years	5		7		2		3		11		17		2		4	

Table 24. Tennōji, Horikoshi-machi and Kubo-machi, 1757-1858: Duration of House-owners and Renters/Tenants Households Compared with Duration of All Households

Number of Years Duration	*All House-owners* Col. 1 Minimum No.	%	Col. 2 Maximum No.	%	*All Renters/Tenants* Col. 3 Minimum No.	%	Col. 4 Maximum No.	%	*All Households* Col. 5 Minimum No.	%	Col. 6 Maximum No.	%
1	75	26.0	19	6.6	314	38.9	116	14.4	389	35.5	135	12.3
2	23	7.9	13	4.5	121	15.0	59	7.3	144	13.2	72	6.6
3	6	2.1	33	11.4	44	5.5	131	16.2	50	4.6	164	15.0
4	16	5.6	14	4.9	54	6.7	67	8.3	70	6.4	81	7.4
5	8	2.8	10	3.5	51	6.3	27	3.3	59	5.4	37	3.4
1-5	128	44.4	89	30.9	584	72.4	400	49.5	712	65.1	489	44.7
6-10	30	10.4	46	16.0	80	9.9	123	15.2	110	10.0	169	15.4
11-20	32	11.1	31	10.8	94	11.7	174	21.6	126	11.5	205	18.7
21-30	26	9.1	42	14.6	32	4.0	81	10.1	58	5.3	123	11.2
31-40	14	4.9	19	6.6	11	1.3	19	2.4	25	2.3	38	3.5
41-50	14	4.9	12	4.2	5	.6	9	1.1	19	1.7	21	1.9
51-60	3	1.0	8	2.8	1	.1	1	.1	4	.4	9	.8
61-70	11	3.8	9	3.1	–	–	–	–	11	1.0	9	.8
71-80	3	1.0	5	1.7	–	–	–	–	3	.3	5	.5
81-90	6	2.1	5	1.7	–	–	–	–	6	.5	5	.5
91-100	9	3.1	9	3.1	–	–	–	–	9	.8	9	.8
101	–	–	1	.3	–	–	–	–	–	–	1	.1
102	12	4.2	12	4.2	–	–	–	–	12	1.1	12	1.1
Totals	288	100	288	100	807	100	807	100	1,095	100	1,095	100
Average duration in years	22.2		25.8		5.7		9.4		10.0		13.9	
Median duration in years	8		14		2		6		3		7	

1757 register, but not in the 1760 register, the "Minimum" duration would be one year. The "Maximum" possible duration, however, would be calculated at three years, since it is theoretically possible that this household appears also in the registers for 1758 and 1759, only to drop out in 1760.

The truth probably lies somewhere between the two, for I would guess that the former underestimates actual duration, while the latter overestimates it.

The evidence for a very high degree of turnover in these Tennōji wards accords nicely with the findings of Yokoyama (1949) for a ward in Kyoto for the period 1786-1867 (Smith, 1963: 419-20). Yokoyama found that of the 343 households listed in the registers of the ward Koromo-no-tana-chō during this eighty-two-year period, 70 per cent appeared for five years or less and 87 per cent for ten years or less, while five households (1.5 per cent) persisted throughout the entire period. In Tennōji's two wards, 1,095 households appear in the 102-year period. Taking our "Maximum" figures, 44.7 per cent appeared for five years or less; 60.1 per cent for ten years or less; twelve households (1.1 per cent) persisted throughout the entire period.

The figures given in Tables 23 and 24 show that the duration of house-owner households is very much greater than that of the renters/tenants. Using the "Maximum" figures for Horikoshi-machi, we see that whereas no renter/tenant household has a span greater than fifty years, nine house-owner households (9.2 per cent of the total) persist throughout the entire 102 years. In Kubo-machi, the story is much the same; only one renter/tenant household has a span of more than fifty years, while only three house-owner households (1.6 per cent of the total) persist throughout the entire 102 years. I have not tabulated the Nishinomiya wards, but careful inspection of the registers suggests that the situation was essentially like that of Tennōji and Kyoto.

Implications

The outcome is clear. These wards were far from stable communities. When one is reminded that it is *household,* not *individual* mobility which is under consideration, the implications can be seen even more clearly. The people who lived in these communities and the officials responsible for their administration were all exposed to a social environment of constantly shifting composition. Although the continuity of the house-owners is more marked than that of the renters, even they move as households with great frequency. The "Maximum" median span of households of house-owners in Horikoshi-machi was only seven years; in Kubo-machi it was only seventeen years. The renter/tenant households in both wards for this same period had a span of three and four years, respectively. The average "Maximum" duration was in every case higher than the median case, but was only 27.2 years at the longest (for the house-owners of Kubo-machi). The median "Maximum" duration was only seven years for households of all types.

Faced with such rates of in- and out-migration, it is hardly surprising that the administrative structure of the urban wards was based on the village prototype. Only through incessant checking on residents and frequent enumeration could the Tokugawa government retain a degree of control over the population of the cities. That the administrators were faced not merely with a declining or rising population is evident. If we take the overall population figures for the four wards under consideration, we find that even the variation in these figures does not reveal with any clarity the fluidity of the actual composition of the wards. When it is further stressed that the individuals enumerated in one annual census of a ward may be almost entirely replaced within the decade, the scale of the problem faced by the Tokugawa government can be better appreciated.

Conclusions

I do not know that the size of the family and household was equally small in urban communities in the pre-industrial periods of other societies, nor am I certain that their rates of turnover were so extraordinarily high. For the Japanese case, however, it is possible to offer some generalizations.

The situation which I have outlined here had, I think, become typical of the wards of city-dwelling commoners in Japan's towns and cities by the early eighteenth century. At least three features of the system strongly predisposed the Japanese to swift and easy urbanization on the "early industrial" model. First, commercial and small manufacturing endeavors were, well before the 1870's and 1880's, already in the hands of small households with small-family nuclei made possible by the general practice of single-heir inheritance. Whether expressed through primogeniture, ultimogeniture, or "adopted husband" marriage (so that the daughter of a house is used to guarantee continuity of the line through adoption of a husband for her who takes her family name and assumes the status of legitimate heir), it was the custom to select only one child as successor to the name and property and custodian of the ancestral tablets of the house. The first Meiji civil code simply regularized this custom by giving preference before the law to first-son succession.

Second, the small size of the residential unit appears to have facilitated mobility, or at least not to have inhibited it. Our data, as well as Yokoyama's (1949), show quite clearly that urban mobility was not limited to single individuals, and that families moved in and out of cities as units well before the "modern period."[8] Further analysis may reveal whether they were simply circulating about the city or back and forth between the city and the countryside. Wherever their residents came from and whatever their destination, the fluidity of the composition of the wards cannot be denied.[9]

8. In this connection, it is instructive to find Dickinson (1961: 171-83) discussing one instance of a high rate of population turnover as a feature of modern urbanism. Writing of Rotterdam, which had a population of over 600,000 in 1939, he says of two new districts of that city:

> These new districts are occupied by people of low income, who find the rent of their former dwelling too high. . . . The residents in these new outer districts are not "settled in." On the contrary, a high proportion shift quickly and there are many removals after a short period of those who seek cheaper and better houses in a more desirable neighborhood. Thus, the new district of Bergpolder at the end of 1934, scarcely one and a half years after the construction of the first houses, had already changed many of the tenants. Of 2,552 dwellings, in October 1934 no less than 380 had second, and 37 third, tenants, and there had been no less than 464 removals! Of the removed families, only one-third remained in the district, a sixth left Rotterdam (for a neighboring sub-urban district). . . .
>
> In Rotterdam on the average there were 50,000 removals annually. Without exaggeration, we can say that a third of the total population is involved in this "nomadic" movement. This mobility, however, in the outer districts is greatest in the tenement districts where there is attachment neither to dwelling nor to neighbourhood (1961: 176).
>
> The movement of population indicates that there is a lack of attachment to home or neighborhood. A habit of moving from one house to another develops. This psychological feature is especially marked in the new and monotonous, characterless multi-storeyed apartment blocks. That type of dwelling does not foster any attraction for hearth, home or neighbourhood This aspect of our present urban society, in effect a sort of "modern nomadism," is one that deserves very thorough attention from social psychologists; it is tied up with many of the problems of neurosis and the family . . . (1961: 183).

9. Taeuber (1958: 27) makes the interesting observation that "the urbanization of the population increased in the modern period, but the great city was not a product of that period. And movements of surplus youth from the rural areas to the cities were adjustments of population to resources and employment opportunities that antedated modern industrialization by some centuries." A useful discussion of a local situation in the Tokugawa period will be found in Hanley (1968). Our understanding of

Third, I would maintain that the nature of Japanese kinship terminology also has important bearing on the ease with which transition to the urban-industrial style was made. Japanese terminology, as first recorded in the tenth century A.D., was and remains bilateral (Smith, 1962a; 1962b). "Yankee" in type, it differs from contemporary American usage in only one important particular; there is an age distinction in sibling terms. Members of these small families, then, identified an extremely limited range of kin by specific terms, and "cousin" usages appear to have been as ambiguous in eighteenth-century Japan as they are in contemporary Britain and the United States. In the registers with which we have dealt, the number of kin terms which appear is extremely small, and all terms used are of the modern Japanese bilateral system.

The Japanese were early possessed of what some writers have claimed is a kin terminology closely associated with modern urbanized industrial societies which have highly developed commerce, attenuation of kin ties, high rates of mobility, and increasingly universalistic relationships. The terminology itself is far older than the development of such a state of affairs in Japan, suggesting that caution must be exercised in proposing an inevitable connection between the two. Nevertheless, its prior existence would, I feel, have greatly facilitated the adjustment of the family to the changes required at the start of Japan's emergence as a modern state. Our data show that many of the features of that country's emergence, so often ascribed to the Meiji period (1868-1912), were in fact well developed by the early part of the eighteenth century.

References Cited

Bellah, Robert N.
1957. *Tokugawa Religion*. Glencoe, Ill.: Free Press.

Benet, Francisco
1963. "Sociology Uncertain: The Ideology of the Rural-Urban Continuum." *Comparative Studies in Society and History* 6(1):1-23.

Dickinson, Robert E.
1962. *The West European City*. 2d ed., rev. London: Routledge & Kegan Paul.

the social history of the Japanese city has been immeasurably extended by the two remarkable books by Yazaki (1963, 1968) which make available to Western readers for the first time the rich detail to be found in the Japanese-language sources. The analysis of the Tokugawa population has been the subject of an important series of papers by Hayami (1966-67, 1968a, 1968b), to cite only some of those published in English.

Dore, Ronald P.
1958. *City Life in Japan.* Berkeley and Los Angeles: University of California Press.

Hanley, Susan
1968. "Population Trends and Economic Development in Tokugawa Japan: The Case of Bizen Province in Okayama." *Daedalus* 97 (2):622-35.

Hayami, Akira
1966-67. "The Population at the Beginning of the Tokugawa Period: An Introduction to the Historical Demography of Pre-Industrial Japan." *Keio Economic Studies* 4:1-28.
1968a. "The Demographic Analysis of a Village in Tokugawa Japan: Kando-Shinden of Owari Province, 1778-1871." *Keio Economic Studies* 5: 50-88.
1968b. "Demographic aspects of a village in Tokugawa Japan." In Paul Deprez (ed.), *Population and Economics,* pp. 109-25. Winnipeg: University of Manitoba Press.

Kaempfer, Engelbert
1727. *The History of Japan* (trans. J. G. Scheuchzer). London, 2 vols. (The first printing of Kaempfer's Japan journals of 1690-92.)

Koyama, Takashi (ed.)
1960. *Gendai kazuko no kenkyū (A Study of the Modern Family).* Tokyo: Kōbundō.

Naganuma, Kenkai
1929. "Shūshi nimbetsu aratame no hattatsu" ("Development of the Investigation of Religious Sects"). *Shigaku-zasshi (Journal of History)* 40(11):13-62.

Nishioka, Toranosuke, and Hattori Korefusa (eds.)
1956. *Nihon rekishi chizu (Historical Maps of Japan).* Tokyo: Kenkoku Kyōiku Tosho.

Nomura, Kanetarō
1953. *On Cultural Conditions Affecting Population Trends in Japan.* Tokyo: Science Council of Japan, Division of Economics and Commerce, Economic Series No. 2.

Sansom, George B.
1963. *History of Japan,* vol. 3. Stanford: Stanford University Press.

Sasaki, Yoichirō
1967. "Tokugawa jidai koki toshi jinkō no kenkyū—Settsu no kuni, Nishinari gun, Tennōji mura" ("An Urban Population in the Later Tokugawa Period—Tennōji, Nishinari, Province of Settsu"). *Shikai* 14.

Sekiyama, Naotarō
1958. *Kinsei nihon no jinkō kōzō (Demographic Structure of "Early Modern" Japan).* Tokyo: Yoshikawa Kobunkan.

Smith, Robert J.
1962a. "Japanese Kinship Terminology: The History of a Nomenclature." *Ethnology* 1(3):349-59.
1962b. "Stability in Japanese Kinship Terminology: The Historical Evi-

dence." In Robert J. Smith and Richard K. Beardsley (eds.), *Japanese Culture: Its Development and Characteristics*. Viking Fund Publications in Anthropology #34:25-33.

1963. "Aspects of Mobility in Pre-Industrial Japanese Cities." *Comparative Studies in Society and History* 5(4):416-23.

Taeuber, Irene B.

1958. *The Population of Japan*. Princeton: Princeton University Press.

1960. "Urbanization and Population Change in the Development of Modern Japan." *Economic Development and Cultural Change* 9(1), Pt. 2:1-28.

Toda, Teizō

1937. *Kazoku kōsei* (*Structure of the Family*). Tokyo: Kōbundō.

Uozumi, Sōgorō (general ed.)

1960. *Nishinomiya-shi-shi* (*History of Nishinomiya City*). Nishinomiya: Municipal Office.

Wade, Richard C.

1959. *The Urban Frontier*. Cambridge, Mass.: Harvard University Press.

Yazaki, Takeo (trans. David L. Swain)

1963. *The Japanese City: A Sociological Analysis*. Tokyo: Japan Publications.

1968. *Social Change and the City in Japan*. Tokyo: Japan Publications.

Yokoyama, Sadao

1949. "Kinsei toshi shūraku no dōtaisei to shūdansei" ("Movement and Groupings in the Urban Community of the "Early Modern" Period). In *Gendai shakaigaku no shomondai* (*Problems of Modern Sociology*), pp. 523-46. Tokyo: Kōbundō.

Caste, Kinship, and Association in Urban India

William L. Rowe

Introduction

Mircea Eliade has written: "All the Indian royal cities, even the modern ones, are built after the mythical model of the celestial city where, in the age of gold, the Universal Sovereign dwelt. And like the latter, the King attempts to revive the age of gold, to make a perfect reign a present reality." As man constantly seeks re-enactment of Eliade's archetypes, he finds that "reality is conferred through participation in the 'symbolism of the Center': cities, temples, houses become real by the fact of being assimilated to the 'center of the world' " (Eliade, 1959: 5-9). The symbolism of the house, the temple, and the city are realities in the Hindu scheme of life: the village priest supervises the enactment of a ritual "house beginning ceremony" which symbolizes the safety and prosperity of the dwelling in the universe (Eliade, 1959: 19), and the most ancient of the Hindu scriptures instruct the ruler on the plan of a capital city (Mukerjee, 1961: 394-98).

The symbolic meaning of the arrangement of space is manifest as the village priest arranges the *mandap* for a ceremony (any, every ceremony) which is itself a representation of creation, of the temple, and of the celestial kingdom. The *mandap* is essentially a square, ritually cleansed area bordered with lines of rice flour and with corner posts usually of banana trees. Arranged within the *mandap* are the representations of the gods of the pantheon, each in his hierarchical place; the most high nearest the center and the sacrificial fire—the symbol of creation. So too, the temple itself recreates the order and meaning of the universe (Kramrisch, 1946), as does finally the capital city of the ruler. In the *Arthaśastra* of Kautilya, a text dated circa 300 B.C., the king is instructed on the apportionment of space in the capital radiating out from the palace. Each of the various castes has a locale, with the "heretics and Cāndalas (untouchable cemetery attendants) having a place of residence beyond the cemetery" (Kane, 1946, 3:181).

From very earliest times, the Indian city has provided a symbolic representation of the social order, both in its spatial arrangements and in its social structure. In the city we note arrangements reflecting the necessities of caste, kinship, and association, and these mirror concerns of the totality of Indian society. This is true whether we listen to a description of the golden city of Ayodhya in the *Ramayana* or explore the social arrangements in contemporary Bombay or Bangalore. Furthermore, the arrangements which we find at any given time are similar in content and purpose to the social and spatial arrangements in rural India, since "urban" and "rural" are simply different parts of the same system.[1] In the brief exploration of available historical sources and contemporary anthropological data which follow, I shall attempt to outline the persistent elements in the organization of two Indian cities, Bombay and Bangalore, from about the seventeenth century. In the second portion of the essay I will discuss contemporary rural migration to both cities and indicate some observable but nascent trends from caste and kinship as primary ties to those of voluntary association. Finally, I discuss how caste neighborhoods or locales become significant units in politics in the contemporary Indian city.

Founders of Cities and Villages[2]

The ideology of Hindu social organization (and in important respects both the Muslim and British conquerors subscribed to portions of this ideology) and spatial planning emanated from the same scriptural source

1. I intend to avoid an explicit discussion of the "folk-urban" continuum, but it is not a totally moribund concept. In some recent Indian demographic studies of cities the authors force the rather obviously unwilling data into the mold of the classical Chicago school. See Venkatarayappa, 1957, especially pp. 123-46. A recent and stimulating discussion of the antiquity of ideas about the polar attributes of the city and the countryside will be found in Baroja, 1963.
2. For materials on the ancient city and Hindu ideas of town and village planning I have drawn heavily on Kane and Mukerjee.

for the founders of villages and the founders of cities. Among other duties, the king was responsible for the apportionment of space, for allotting economic rewards, for adjudicating and upholding caste status, and for arranging to have the proper complement of economically and ritually necessary functional castes in the capital. The distinguishing mark of a town or city in the ancient texts (Kane, 1946, 3:182) was that *only* there did one find all the castes resident. It was in the city alone that the most specialized ritual castes, the learned Brahmins and astrologers, as well as the artisans producing luxury goods, could be maintained.

The founder of a village or petty kingdom of several villages (Cohn, 1962: 315-17) fulfilled the same role described for kings but on a minor scale. And the village socioeconomic system (also that of the rural "Little kingdom") reflected the arrangements of the city on a lesser scale. Frequently a dominant land-controlling caste (Kshatriya-warrior or Brahmin-priest) assumed the duties and obligations of ruler. (This ideology of village organization persists to the present day, as numerous recent anthropological works have indicated.[3]) As in the city, the headman or *panchayat* (council) of the dominant[4] village caste apportioned space, rights, and obligations to the various resident castes. Ideally each of the castes had its own *panchayat* which was responsible to the village *panchayat* for the conduct of members of the caste. In a like fashion, the caste *panchayat* negotiated with the village *panchayat* in matters affecting the welfare of the caste.

Networks of cultural "brokers" or specialists performing "hinge" functions between the city as a center and the village hinterland traditionally provided reinforcement for the ideology of social organization and its cultural content (Cohn and Marriott, 1958: Marriott, 1959).

The popular history of the founding of villages as well as cities frequently begins with military conquest, fortification of the newly won area, settlement of tributary (and necessary) castes, and regularization of political life within the social unit. Often, some religious sanction is required, such as the installation of a village godling-protector, or in the case of cities, of a deity of the higher pantheon (Mukerjee, 1961: 196). On occasion the tribal or caste deity of the conqueror is Sanskritized to

3. For example, several of the studies in *Village India* (McKim Marriott, ed.; Chicago: University of Chicago Press, 1955) describe such situations.
4. "Dominant caste" is used as conceptualized by Srinivas (1955:18) to refer to a caste "when it predominates numerically over the other castes, and when it also wields preponderant economic and political power. A large and powerful caste group can be more easily dominant if its position in the local caste hierarchy is not too low."

accord with the new regal status of the ruling lineage. All of these elements are important in the founding of Bombay and Bangalore, and some persist today as important cohesive forces.[5]

Bangalore

Bangalore was founded by a migrant agriculturalist-turned-warrior, Kempe Gowda, in the early sixteenth century.[6] As a tributary ruler under the Vijayanagar empire, he prospered and built a fort in Bangalore in 1537. Kempe Gowda planned the original city and Sanskritized the religious life of his caste, transferring worship from *Bire Deva,* a non-Sanskritic goddess (who was worshipped by amputation of the ring and little fingers of daughters of the caste) to Siva of the Sanskritic pantheon. In the seventeenth century the dynasty fell, and, following a series of military exchanges, Bangalore eventually became part of the kingdom of the Mysore rajas, where it remained until it became the capital and principal industrial city of Mysore State in 1947.

Although the record of Bangalore's social organization is somewhat sparse (when contrasted with data on Bombay City), we learn that under the Mysore ruler, Chikkadevaraja Wodeyar (1673-1704), many castes of artisans were settled in Bangalore.

> Not only merchants but also 12,000 families of weavers were securely established there, agreements (*kaulu-kararu*) were entered into with them and facilities afforded for the passage of bales of cotton to various parts of the country . . . (Rao I:350, describing events in 1687).

The ecology and reconstructed history of contemporary Bangalore suggest that as well as entering into compacts with various caste communities, the Raja designated specific sections of the city to the various priestly, merchant, and worker castes. We shall turn to the persistence of caste ecology when we discuss contemporary Bangalore. Because of the delightful and salubrious highland tropical climate, the British established

5. That the role of founder is a crucial one in the small market town is suggested by Richard G. Fox (personal communication). He notes that many of these towns had as a source of "community" only the fact of the local *zamindar* (landlord) who built the market. Once land reform destroyed the relationship, the settlement lost its community function and became "merely an amorphous collection of caste groups bounded by governmental, political and social institutions coming from the modern state."

6. Early history of Bangalore is covered in the *Imperial Gazeteer of India,* vol. VI, in Venkatarayappa, and in Rao, vol. I.

Table 1. Population Growth and Percentage of Migrants in the Population[1]

BOMBAY			*BANGALORE*		
Year	*Population*	*Per cent migrants (born outside Bombay)*	*Year*	*Population*	*Per cent migrants*
1662	10,000				
1677	50,000				
1716	16,000				
1744	70,000				
1816	161,550				
1864	816,562[2]	79.0			
1872	644,405	68.9	1871	142,513	
1881	773,196	72.2	1881	155,857	
1891	821,764	75.0	1891	180,336	
1901	776,006[3]	76.6	1901	159,046[3]	
1906	977,822	79.0	1911	189,485	
1921		84.0	1921	237,496	
1931		75.4	1931	306,470	34.7
1941	1,695,000	72.6	1941	496,760	34.9
1951	2,839,000[4]	72.1[5]	1951	939,000	36.6
1961	4,146,000[6]	64.2[7]	1961	1,208,000	

1. Sources: Edwardes, 1909; Census of India, 1931; Census of India, 1951.
2. First properly organized census.
3. Plague accounts for sudden loss of population; deaths and panic outmigration.
4. Figures for 1951 and afterward for "Greater Bombay."
5. 1.6 million of total population migrated to Bombay during decade 1941-51. Bogue and Zachariah, p. 39.
6. Davis, 1962.
7. The decreased influx, in percentage terms, is partially due to the incorporation of additional tracts of land by the Bombay Corporation.

a military-administrative base there in 1809.[7] By the late nineteenth century the separate, adjoining military cantonment area accounted for roughly half the population of the city. The persistence of caste ecology in modern "Greater Bangalore" is all the more noteworthy for the existence of (1) a separate colonial enclave for about 150 years and (2) a constant situation of a high percentage of immigrants in the city population. Today Bangalore is the industrial boom town of South India (see population figures, Table 1). Located at the meeting place of three dis-

7. Mysore remained as a princely state until 1947, but the English established a garrison in Bangalore in 1809. In 1881 the cantonment area was transferred to the British as an "assigned tract." It became part of Greater Bangalore following independence.

Table 2. Urban Linguistic Diversity (By Mother Tongue)[1]

BOMBAY		BANGALORE	
Language	*Per cent of city population*	*Language*	*Per cent of city population*
Marathi	42.5	Tamil	31.7
Gujerati	18.4	Kannada	23.7
Urdu	9.9	Telegu	17.8
Hindu	7.4	Hindustani	15.8
Konkani	4.5	Marathi	4.6
Telegu	2.4	Others	6.4
Sindhi	2.3		
Tamil	2.0		
Kannada	1.8		
Kachchhi	1.5		
English	1.2		
Punjabi	1.1		
Malayalam	1.1		
Others	3.9		

1. Source: Census of India, 1951.

tinct linguistic areas, as well as having a large population of Eurasians, Bangalore is both linguistically and culturally a heterogeneous city (see Table 2).

Bombay

Bombay's history has been more liberally recorded (by British, Portuguese, and Indian writers since the eighteenth century), yet many questions relating to its evolving social organization and culture cannot be answered.[8] Bombay as a city began with the English occupation in 1665, although the previous Portuguese and early Hindu periods have pertinence. Largely because of Bombay's magnificent harbor, it had long been coveted by the English, who in time acquired it as a portion of the Portuguese Infanta's dowry on the occasion of her marriage to Charles II.

Late seventeenth-century accounts provide a vivid picture of a heterogeneous, dangerous, and lively town of 10,000 population, settled somewhat precariously on seven distinct islands (see Map 1). Something of

8. For the early period, Burnell, Edwardes, Spear, and DaCunha have been found most useful. Although the nineteenth-century literature is extensive, ecology and social organization are frequently not explicitly dealt with. "Tourist Guides" which describe sections of the city and deal with the graphic are frequently more helpful than English works, which tend to concentrate on British social life or political activities.

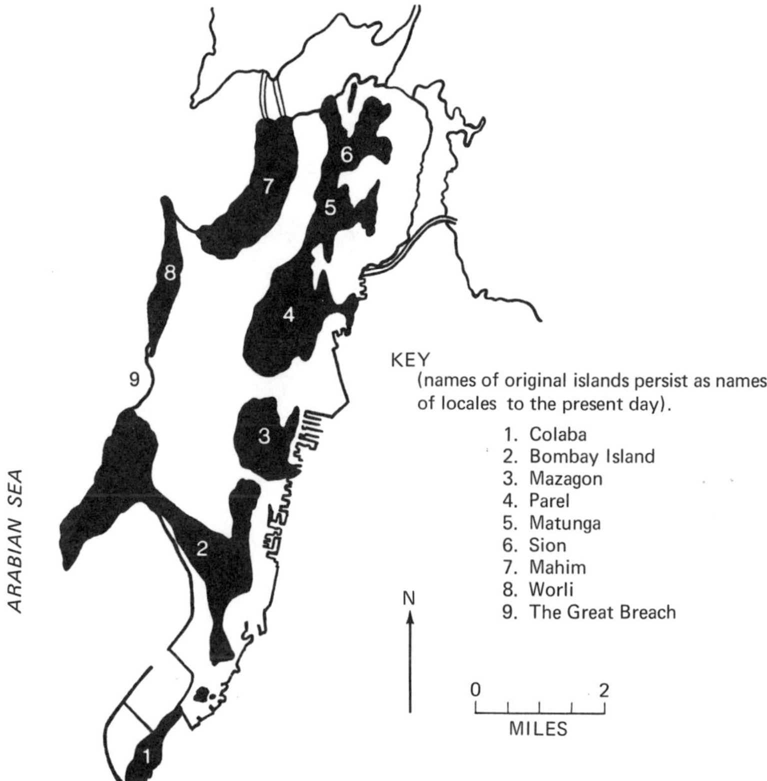

Shaded areas represent original islands (ca. 1665).
Remainder (within outline) is reclaimed land.
*Based on Sheppard: 56

Map 1.* The Seven Islands of Bombay and the Reclaimed Land

the conditions of the time are indicated in the statement of one visitor in 1698, "Two Mussouns (monsoons) are the age of a man" (Fryer, quoted in Burnell: xxi). Seaward were the possibilities of Danish or French attack, and on the mainland unsettled political conditions, with the Portuguese, Marathas, and the Mughul Empire as contestants.

Following several decades of political vicissitudes, but during which Bombay had grown considerably in both population and area,[9] a pattern of compacts similar to that mentioned above for the weavers who set-

9. Gradually the original separated islands of Bombay were joined through extensive reclamation projects. This development is shown in Map 1.

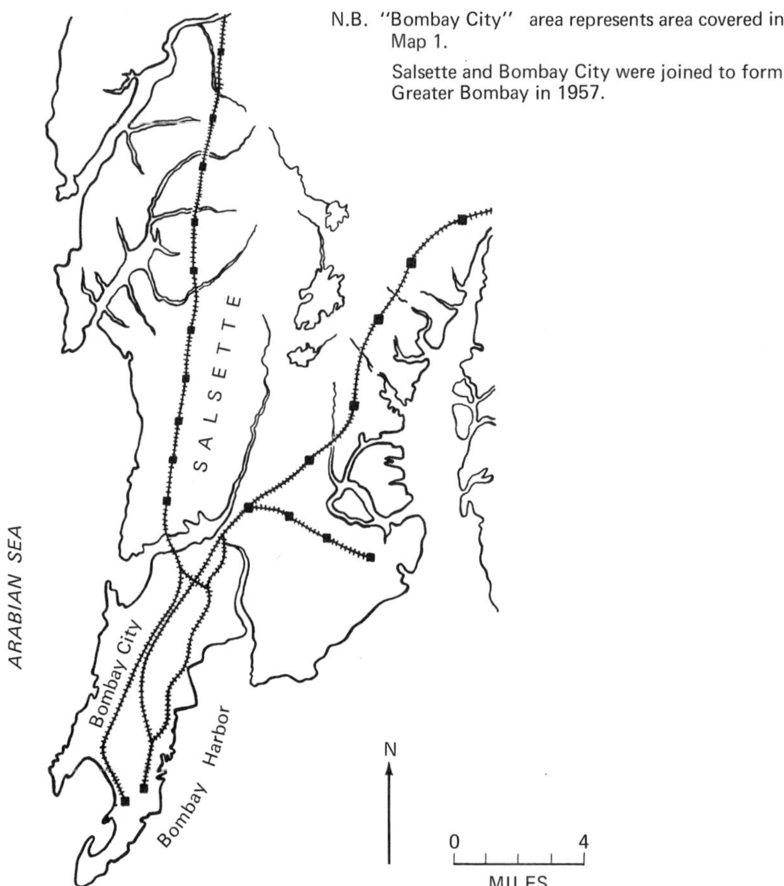

Map 2.* The Greater Bombay, 1962

tled in seventeenth-century Bangalore is noted. Nineteenth-century Indian and English writers alike seem to interpret the existence of those compacts between ruler (in this case Gerald Aungier, Bombay's early governor, 1671-77) and caste communities as an "invention" while, in fact, this kind of arrangement had an ancient history and in a sense was a necessary cohesive mechanism in a society composed of endogamous, ranked groups. The earliest settlers in Bombay had been the Bhandaris (toddy-tappers and later warriors), Palshikar Brahmins (priests), Pathare Prabhus (clerks), Agris (agriculturalists), and Kolis (fishermen).

In 1671 the leader of the Baniyas (traders) of Surat obtained assurances from the English relating to the status and facilities available to his caste community prior to their proposed migration to Bombay (DaCunha: 293). In 1677 Aungier entered into a compact with the Baniyas of Diu, who migrated at that time to Bombay. The Baniya leader of Diu, Neema Parrack, requested a patent under the seal of the East India Company "containing certaine favours wch he begs in relation to liberty and security in ye exercise of religion, trade, property and reputable residence on s^{d} island" (Malabari: 138).[10] In 1685 the Palshikar Brahmins secured an agreement from the British granting them the right of "presiding at the religious ceremonies of the Hindus of Bombay and of administering medicine to the sick" (Edwardes, 1:167). This patent was ratified in 1689 and again in 1723.

Partially as a reward for their military assistance at an earlier date, the Bhandaris were granted certain exclusive rights over the production and

10. The most important provisions of the patent or compact are given below (Malabari: 138):

> (2) That he wthye Brahminees or Ver of his cast shall enjoy ye free exercise of their religion wth^{in} their owne houses w^{t}hout ye molestation of any person w^{t}soever, that noe Eng^{s}man, Portuguez, or other Christian, nor Mahomitan, shall be permitted to live wthin their compund or offer to kill any living creature there, or doe ye least injury or indignity to y^{m}, and if any shall presume to offend y^{m} wthin ye limits of their said compound upon their complaint to the Govr or Dep^{ty} Govr ye offenders shall be exemplary punished; y^{t} they shall have liberty to burn their dead, according to their customs and also to use their ceremonies at their weddings, and y^{t} none of their profession of w^{t} age, sex or condition w^{t} everthey be, shall be forced to turne Christians, nor to carry burthens against their wills.
>
> (4) That in case there falls out any difference or suite in law between him or his Vakeell or attorneys or ye Banians of his caste, and any other persons remaining on the Island, ye Govr or Dept^{y} Govr shall not suffer him or y^{m} to be publiquely arrested, dishonoured or carryed to prison without first giving him due notice of ye cause depending, y^{t} he or they may cause justice to be done in an honest and amicable way, and in case any difference happen between him or his attorney, or any Banian of his owne caste, they may have liberty to decide it among themselves w^{t}hout being forced to go to law.
>
> (7) That in case any person be indebted to him and also to other Banians, and be not able to pay all his debts, his right may be preferred before other Banians.
>
> (9) That he or any of his family shall have liberty of egress and ingres to and fro ye fort or residence of ye Governor or Dept^{y} Govr, y^{t} they shall be recevied wth civil respect and be permitted to sit downe according to their qualities; y^{t} they shall freely use coaches, horses or pallanqueens and quitasals for their conveniency w^{t}out any disturbance; y^{t} their servants may weare swords and daggers, shall not be abused, beaten, or imprisoned except they offend agst ye law, and y^{t} in any case of his kindred or friends shall come to visit him or them from any other parts, they shall be used with civility and respect.

sale of toddy and other alcoholic drinks in an agreement concluded with the English in 1773 (Malabari: 421). In 1885 they contested a new tax on toddy and arrack, citing this earlier agreement (Hunter: 388-89). Pocock (70-71) citing Edwardes, notes that by 1909 the Palshikar Brahmins and the Prabhus had been pushed from the areas where they had formerly lived in some elegance and that these areas had been taken over by enterprising groups of merchants. The ecology of succession in zones of cities has been noted elsewhere (Caplow, 1961; O'Brien, 1961), but little has been specifically written of the significant history of succession in caste ecology in Indian cities.

Even the earliest accounts of the British period in Bombay seem to emphasize the importance of the trading and banking castes. For example, in 1711 John Burnell describes a spatially distinct "Black Town" (meaning Indian quarter in contrast to the English "Fort" area) existing in Bombay. He mentions twenty-four castes but especially indicates the vitality of the Baniyas and bankers. It is apparent as one attempts to chart successive ecologies of the city through time that the merchant and trading castes of all religious groups prospered tremendously even before the advent of industrialism. It is not mere coincidence that the first Bombayite to be knighted was a Parsi merchant.

Another great achievement of Aungier, the early Bombay governor, according to Malabari and others (e.g. Douglas, I:85-100) was his mandate that each caste community be self-governed by a *panchayat*, which in turn was responsible to the governor:

> He modelled the several races inhabiting the town and island of Bombay into so many orders of tribes, appointed over each a chief or consul to manage their affairs; in short, when he raised the fabric of self-government by inauguration of the *panchayat* system, he gave the people the means of procuring justice for themselves (Malabari: 116).

Yet as we have seen, this in fact was the traditional system, a form of arrangement described in the ancient texts, prevalent in village social structure and existent in Bombay itself at the time (see Gune, 1953). Malabari's account of "Some Interesting Trials" of the period 1661-1726 indicates the extent to which the *mukkadam* or caste leader was held accountable for the behavior of offenders brought before the courts (Malabari: 289-363). In other aspects of life too, the caste community was dealt with, and apparently thought of, as an entity. Edwardes notes that the Bombay Customs Master, in estimating amounts of grain and provisions upon the island in 1759, apportions the stores among the named (29) caste communities. Edwardes (I:143-273) and MacLean (215-75) both describe the specific caste *mohallas* or residential sections of the city, although by 1909, when Edwardes wrote, the city had greatly changed. In 1875 MacLean indicated that Malabar Hill was the domain of the British; while by 1909 "wealthy natives" had begun to leave caste localities and had built villas on Malabar Hill. Parel, once a fashionable residential area, had become engulfed by the new industrialism in north Bombay.

Patterns of Migration

MacLean's *Guide to Bombay* lists 16 cotton mills in operation in 1875, the first having been established in 1854. During the American Civil War (1861-65) the Bombay cotton industry had boomed. Although the crash at the conclusion of the war caused a temporary exodus of migrant mill workers, the pattern of industrial development was set, and MacLean lists 13 mills in construction ten years following the crash. By 1909 there were 143 mills with 17 per cent of the total population involved in the manufacture and sale of cotton (Edwardes I:411-12).

From the very beginnings of the city there had always been a high percentage of migrants in the population. Early writers emphasize this as a characteristic of Bombay. MacLean, referring to Hewlett's 1816 census, comments on the disproportionate percentage of males in the population and quotes Hewlett:

> the census was taken in the winter months of the year "when the fixed population is annually much augmented by an influx of men who come from their villages for the purposes of trade and in search of service, and who do not bring their wives and families with them" (MacLean: 86).

In 1842 it was estimated that the city had a floating population of 70,000 (Edwardes I:163) and, writing in 1875, MacLean says that there are at least 60,000 not included in the census figures because they are "floating population." Migrants to Bombay were at first derived from adjacent states and provinces, but gradually the area from which the city drew its recruits expanded until it included north and northeast India.

In 1909 Edwardes implies that migrants who are not Gujerati, Kanarese, or Marathi are a negligible fraction of the total. He refers to the North Indians as Pardesi Bhaya (pardesi means "one of another country," and Bhaya is a corruption of *bhaiya,* a form of greeting meaning "brother"), but indicates that they had not as yet become a crucial part of the work force. However, Ghurye states that there were more than 50,000 migrants from Uttar Pradesh (then United Provinces) in Bombay in 1911 and over 80,000 in 1931 (Ghurye, 1962: 276). In this early twentieth-century period of migration, the North Indians were apparently largely mill workers, probably primarily from various Muslim weaving and cotton-carding castes of Uttar Pradesh and Bihar. This situation was not unique to Bombay. Mukerjee, writing in 1940, states that from 75 per cent to 85 per cent of Calcutta's population is migrant, visiting their village homes once a year or more (Mukerjee: 400). (But, one must ask, what does "migrant" mean in this statement? Once we consider more than the demographic fact of rural-born city dwellers, we uncover an infinitely more complex situation. One finds a continuum, ranging from those migrants who are "in the city but not of it" to those who have become truly urbanized townsmen.)

Although large sections of the migrant group could and actually did quit the city at times of calamity, the city always regained its population. Both Bangalore and Bombay lost heavily during the years of the great plague epidemics at the turn of the century (see Table 1), and Bombay's floating population has characteristically responded to both "push" and "pull" economic and social factors, such as famine in the countryside, the economic crash following the American Civil War, the great depression of the 1930's, and the boom period of World War II. While conducting research in a North Indian village in 1956, I witnessed the sudden return from Bombay of migrants fleeing the intense political disturbances attendant on Gujerati-Maharashtrian conflict over the political future of Bombay City.

Given the ebb and flow of the migrant population and the very large percentage of migrants present in the city at any one time—and Bombay seems to have a fairly steady figure of around 75 per cent of the total population—it is remarkable that caste localities have persisted and that when they have moved, the caste seems to be found again as a coherent group in its new setting. Several qualifications, however, need to be suggested: Ghurye notes that area-of-origin (i.e. Uttar Pradesh, Jaunpur District, and so forth) is an influence in choice of residence, as well as caste (Ghurye, 1957: 212). Also certain nascent trends are discernible which indicate the influence of class rather than caste or kinship affiliation. The movement of the newly rich to Malabar Hill is such an example. However, the evidence overwhelmingly supports the contention that caste and kinship association have been dominant in the city throughout its history.

Characteristics of the City

To summarize the discussion thus far: The Indian city and village are traditionally planned on the same spatial and social pattern. There is ample evidence that this was thought necessary, and detailed instructions to founders of cities exist. Pocock's discussion (65-66) of urbanism suggests that a primary difference exists between African and Indian urbanization, the former being "purely a product of European interest and almost consciously and deliberately represent[ing] the alien culture of the West." A somewhat related comment by Mukerjee (1961: 396) suggests that the Indian cities most closely approximating the ideal, in terms of traditional criteria, will be found in South India where European influence has been least. Evidence has been presented suggesting that even in Bombay, which is perhaps the most "Western" of Indian cities, there is reason to note the similarity with the traditional pattern. Although less is known about Bangalore's history, the contemporary ecology of the city indicates that it too bears strong resemblances to a standard pattern, despite 150 years of active European influence.

Castes were settled by rulers (of both villages and cities); indeed rulers often actively sought castes considered to be essential to the economic, social, and ritual life of a community. Compacts defining rights, obligations, and forms of protection were frequently drawn up with the ruler and at least the key castes as contracting parties. That caste communities retained their internal structure in the city environment is attested to by the historical references to *panchayats* and headmen. We have also seen that the Indian city always had a substantial percentage of new migrants in its midst, and that this characteristic preceded modern industrialism.[11] This fact is a potent indicator of the strength and vitality of Indian social organization since caste, kinship, and place-of-origin have remained solid bases for the choice of residential area (*mohalla, pura, patti,* etc.) within the city.

Unfortunately neither the ethnographic nor the historical evidence is sufficiently complete at this time to give a firm outline of Indian urban

11. Census data on rural-born persons in the city as well as contemporary references to "floating population" seem to challenge purely economic interpretations of the growth of urban populations, as for example, in M. D. Morris (1965).

life.[12] Hence it will only be through empirical research that the relevance or generality of the above can be determined. However, in the following section, we present case studies of rural migrants to Bombay and to Bangalore, asking in each situation questions relating to the types of social relations retained by migrants in their villages, their forms of association in the city, and the degree to which new associational patterns seem to alter the total equilibrium of the rural-urban network.

Associational Patterns of Rural Migrants in the City

North Indians in Bombay:[13] *Village Background*

For the North Indian village (especially in the densely populated areas of eastern Uttar Pradesh and Bihar) the scale of migration to urban centers has tremendous importance.[14] At any given time about 10 per cent of the adult population of Village Senapur (in Jaunpur District, Uttar Pradesh, twenty-five miles north of Benares) is away in the *pardesh* (foreign country), as the villagers would say. During the winter season migration is greatest, since at this time not only are the "recurrent" migrants gone from the village, but there are also a large number of "temporary" migrants who go on an *ad hoc* basis to relatively nearby areas on short-term jobs.

12. Historical materials useful to the anthropologist attempting to reconstruct city life are not lacking, and it would be possible through the utilization of city census tracts (until 1931 when caste was last recorded) to learn much of what actually happened during the colonial period. In some areas family chronicles, temple records, etc. are available. For important recent contributions to an understanding of urban India see Fox, 1968, 1970; Gillion, 1968; Lynch, 1969; and Vatuk, 1972.

13. I have benefitted from the critical comments of F. G. Bailey, B. S. Cohn, H. Gould, L. Hazlehurst, S. Kannappan, P. Kolenda, J. J. Spengler, and G. Woodruff Marlowe on an earlier draft of this paper. Fieldwork was carried out in North India (see Rowe, 1960a for a description of the village setting) and in Bombay from August 1955 to August 1957. I am indebted to Shri Permanand Yadav for assistance in interviewing some of the migrants in Bombay. Financial support from the Cornell University India Research Project, the Center for South Asia Studies, University of California, Berkeley, and the Program in Comparative Studies on Southern Asia, Duke University is gratefully acknowledged.

14. Uttar Pradesh and Bihar states have the greatest percentage of outmigrants and, eastern U.P. is particularly heavy. The greatest number of U.P. migrants go to West Bengal; Bombay is in second place. The 1931 census lists 1,063,143 outmigrants from U.P. (Hutton:64). The 1951 census (Uttar Pradesh Part 1-B:20) states that 338,913 persons migrated to West Bengal and 295,237 to Bombay State, although for the latter one suspects that the vast majority went to Bombay City and its environs.

These temporary migrants are always low caste (which is not true of migrants generally) and in their view, and that of the village, are not *real* migrants. They are only temporarily supplementing farm income or view themselves as "target workers," in that their rationale for going out is to obtain a limited sum of cash for a specific purpose. Usually these men are not eager to go outside, even for temporary work, unless accompanied by their kinsmen, because the *pardesh* is, at best, beset with dangers. Accompanying kinsmen may be from the same village or may be, and frequently are, from villages of affinal connection. The marriage network is of tremendous importance as a supportive and controlling device once a villager has reached the *pardesh* (Rowe, 1960b). The social situation of some migrants in this category does not allow them to be other than "temporary," although their economic situation might provide a strong pull for "recurrent" migration. This type of villager cannot remain away except for the brief winter season because there is no one in the village who can adequately protect his economic and political position.

Although it is beyond the scope of this paper to discuss temporary migration further, it is important to note that this form of migration, and migration generally, is facilitated by the existence of strong kinship ties, ideally by membership in a cohesive joint family, and secondarily by good relations with men of one's own generation in other families of one's lineage.

Recurrent Migration

Recurrent migration involves men who live and work at great distances from home, sometimes for years. It is "recurrent" rather than "permanent" because these men traditionally go to the city without their wives and families and return home annually for visits of a month or six weeks. With few exceptions these men view migration to the city as a temporary solution to economic problems and maintain their involvement in the network of personal relationships in the village. In some cases they have worked for twenty-five to thirty years in Bombay, which is 900 miles from the village. Bombay attracts the greatest number of migrants from the village, with West Bengal taking second place. These two states attract most of the migrants from the state of Uttar Pradesh.

Migrants to the city either remit or bring home with them all of their income beyond their minimal living expenses. This income has a differential function for the various families and caste communities who have deputed migrants to the city. Some men are pulled to the city because it is here that money can be earned to improve the family position at home through purchase of additional land or farm animals or other capital expenditure.

The other class of recurrent migrants includes those men who go to the city because there is poverty at home and because there is simply no opportunity locally to earn sufficient money for basic needs such as food, clothing, and taxes. They still have some stake in the community in terms of ongoing relationships, house site, and probably claims to agricultural land or, in the case of artisans, to serve the group of families who are hereditary clientele (*jajmani*).

Permanent migration out of the village by an entire family does not occur often because, for most people, the tie in the village provides at least some sense of security, while the positions they can acquire in the city are seldom more than marginal. Significantly enough, the one caste group for which such permanent migration does occur is the Leatherworkers, a large untouchable and landless caste in the village. The Leatherworkers also exhibit a higher rate of intervillage migration (see Cohn, 1959a).

A study of household budgets of both classes of recurrent migrants indicates that, regardless of what the causes may have been for the first migrant trip to the city, the family unit tends to perpetuate the relationship. A survey of items in the material culture makes it manifest that new items such as lanterns and bicycles enter the village first as "luxury" goods brought home by the migrant, but that a decade later they have become "necessities." The whole equilibrium of families, especially those who are able to utilize city-earned income for capital expenditures, becomes dependent on having a migrant representative in the city.

This seems to be particularly true for the upwardly mobile middle-caste groups. In such cases pressure frequently is placed upon the migrant to remain in the city, or, if he returns for a visit, to curtail it. A number of the migrants in the city borrow from Bombay Baniyas so they can send money back to the village to satisfy family needs. They ultimately find themselves so far in debt that they are unable to consider leaving the city. The main point here is that, regardless of the original reason for going to the city, migration (which tends to be a family decision rather than an individual one) soon becomes a way of life both for the family and indeed for the village. In direct contradiction to the claim that "the city will destroy the village," it is our finding that, in economic terms at least, the city makes the continuance of the North Indian village possible.[15]

Analysis of family income and expenditure for one large middle-caste community in the village showed that over 35 per cent of the total annual income is derived from outside cash, largely from Bombay earnings. This caste, the Saltworkers, is one which is noted particularly for its upward striving. It would probably be accurate to state that those communities and families who send out migrants regularly (where there is not desperate economic need) are characteristically *nouveau riche.* In fact among the Saltworkers, almost all (85.4%) of the adult men have worked as recurrent migrants at some time during their lives. The trend towards migration has greatly increased in the years since World War II, due to greater urban opportunity and the growing rural demand for cash. Although it is still as true as it was in the past that "to be truly rich, one must be rich in sons as well as in land," this local saying now has a new meaning. In the past one's sons worked the land and provided the strength of arms necessary in times of political conflict. Now one's sons work in the city, making it possible for the family to purchase additional land—or perhaps its first land. A poor man with four sons can now send two off to the city and with the income attempt to change his class position. One of the more conservative elders of the village commented on such a *nouveau riche* household: "Oh yes, now they are sahibs, but only yesterday they were so poor that when X [of their house] died, they secretly carried the body to the river since they could not afford proper funeral ceremonies!"

Before turning to the lives of migrants in Bombay, we should briefly characterize the total social interaction of the village. Senapur is a Warrior-dominated village with a proud Warrior history as part of a prominent "Little kingdom." As such it satisfies most of the criteria for social and ecological arrangements which we discussed in the introduction to this essay. This Warrior domination has been benevolent in ethos and

15. Senapur, like the entire area which surrounds it, has almost doubled its population during the past sixty years, while its economic resources have, if anything, declined. Agricultural lands are over-worked and now give lower yields. In addition, manufactured goods have caused the technological displacement of weaving and cotton-carding castes as well as greatly reduced the need for such castes as potters, who now compete with cheap aluminum pots from the town bazaar. Since former pasturelands have been put into agriculture, the large caste of cowherders, too, has been partially displaced.

spirit, incorporating, at least in its ideal form, elaborate mechanisms of duty and obligation between the lords of the village and their dependents.

Although this ideal unity of the past has been under attack for several decades, the observer is still impressed with the degree of integration. The villagers are conscious of the challenges to authority characteristic of contemporary life, but the outsider cannot help note that challenge is in terms of the village structure, that is, it is an attempt to improve the position of one's group *vis-à-vis* other groups in the traditional village. In a very real sense, the urban migrants make challenge within the village a greater possibility. Migrants are aware of their crucial contribution to the "war chest" back home.

City Life

Once on board the "Bombay Express" at Benares, the villager assumes the identity of a *bhaiya* bound for a *chawl* (tenement) in north Bombay—to Dadar, Lower Parel, or Mahalakshmi; unless he is a Muslim, and then he will probably be en route to Nagpadi or Madanpura. These are the principal sections of the city where the North Indian migrants or *bhaiya* live. *Bhaiya* form a visible group by their dress, by their general lack of modernity in personal style, and of course, by their North Indian country dialect (*dehati*). There are nearly always a group of *bhaiya* together; no one really goes to the city alone. Migration is associational in every respect, as is life in the city (Lambert, 1962: 134-35).

Parel, as late as 1910 a fashionable residential area, is now an industrial slum of almost incredible population density. The area is heavily populated with *bhaiya*, and as one strolls with them in the evenings they point out *chawls* where the "Barbers of Y village live" or "the Cowherders of X village reside." It is almost as though the map of the North Indian district had been reproduced within the wards of the city.

The ecology of the area is symbolic of the social arrangements which the *bhaiya* have made, for they seem to have duplicated many of the core features of traditional life. But it is not entirely as though "they had brought the village with them to the city," as I first thought. The city is, and apparently always has been, arranged to receive groups as though, perhaps, they were new additional parts to an already existing mosaic.

The forty-six men from Senapur Village (from twelve castes) were found residing, with one exception, in tightly controlled kinship groups. Although some groups are composed of men entirely from Senapur, it is common for the groups to include men of the same caste from other villages, usually related in one way or another by marriage to Senapur. The principles of fictive kinship (see Freed, 1963) are such that groups can be assembled easily which have a "kinship ethos," although members actually may not have very close relationships. In the city, caste and kinship tend to fuse together, and beyond that there is an identity as belonging to Senapur Village. The ideal of all men of a village being *goan bhai,* or village brothers, has greater meaning in the city than almost anywhere else. Hence in the city relationships among men of different castes but of the same village may be much warmer and closer than in the village.

As *bhaiya* (with the exception of the few who move out of this category and become true townsmen) the migrants also share an identity which at times can be a source of support. This is true in Bombay City politics, as will be shown later. A negative aspect of the identity as *bhaiya* is the sense in which they are found in opposition to other ethnic and linguistic groups in Bombay. Local (Maharashtrian and Gujerati) people have a tendency to look down upon the *bhaiya* as crude countrymen, an attitude not lost on the *bhaiya.* Regardless of caste or achieved class position in the city, *bhaiya* have little meaningful contact with the local population. Both living and working situations tend to be removed from what might be described as acculturating mechanisms. *Bhaiya* (in all cases investigated) live with other *bhaiya* in areas dominated by *bhaiya.* The nature of the living groups, acting as they do to exercise effective social control over members, is such that they also limit new meaningful experiences.

Furthermore, there is a very strong correlation between village caste and occupational status and the occupation and earning power of the individual *bhaiya* in the city. Men from the landlord class (Warrior caste) average Rs 124 in their monthly city wages. Men from the artisan-specialist class (middle-level castes) average Rs 91.59, and the agriculturalists (low castes) average Rs 70.82 per month in the city. This perpetuation of the rural status hierarchy in the city is due to several factors. The high-caste and landlord groups arrive in the city literate and with more formal education than is usual among low castes, artisans and agriculturalists. Although high castes are not trained in any specific occupations which would bring lucrative rewards, they have been able, through kinship connections, to obtain the better jobs in the city (see Table 3). With only one exception all the migrants in the city had obtained employment through the assistance of kinsmen; but low castes can only help their low-caste kinsmen to obtain low-status, low-paying city jobs.

Table 3. Senapur Villagers in Bombay, by Caste and Occupation

No.	*Caste and Village Occupation*	*Bombay Occupation*	*Earnings In Rupees Per Month*	*Age*	*No. of Yrs. in Bombay*
1.	Warriors	Tram conductor	140.	44	15.
2.	(landlords)	Dairy worker	60.	29	14.
3.	"	Tram conductor	125.	35	13.
4.	"	Shopkeeper	125.	38	13.
5.	"	Tramways worker	120.	34	12.
6.	"	Messenger, travel company	185.	35	10.
7.	"	Tram driver	145.	38	8.
8.	"	College student & schoolteacher	184.	24	2.5
9.	"	Casual laborer	60.	20	1.
10.	Cowherders	Dairy worker	70.	24	12.
11.	(cowherders &	Unemployed	—	18	.3
12.	farmers)	Dairy worker	70.	28	10.
13.	"	Dairy worker	70.	26	5.
14.	"	Mill worker	100.	23	8.
15.	"	Dairy worker	70.	35	5.
16.	Grain Parchers	Grain shopkeeper	125.	45	31.
17.	"	Grain shopkeeper	125.	38	25.
18.	"	Grain shopkeeper	125.	33	30.
19.	"	Grain shopkeeper	125.	30	20.
20.	"	Shopkeeper	125.	44	25.
21.	"	Shopkeeper	125.	40	5.
22.	"	Parched-grain hawker	60.	19	10.
23.	"	Cook	100.	40	.5
24.	"	Railway policeman	100.	32	10.
25.	Barber	Barber	70.	40	13.
26.	"	Barber	60.	18	1.
27.	Saltworkers	Parched-grain hawker	150.	26	11.
28.	(farmers &	"	180.	21	8.
29.	earthworkers)	"	70.	29	7.
30.	"	"	90.	28	7.
31.	"	"	75.	31	7.
32.	"	Dairy worker	70.	28	4.
33.	"	Dairy worker	70.	21	3.
34.	(farmers & earthworkers)	Parched-grain hawker	60.	23	3.
35.	"	"	90.	23	3.
36.	"	"	47.50	14	2.
37.	"	"	35.	17	.5
38.	Barber-shopkeeper	Barber	150.	40	20.
39.	House servant	Grain hawker	70.	20	3.
40.	Oil Presser	Parched-grain hawker	65.	21	3.

Table 3. (*Continued*)

No.	*Caste and Village Occupation*	*Bombay Occupation*	*Earnings In Rupees Per Month*	*Age*	*No. of Yrs. in Bombay*
41.	Wine maker (shopkeepers)	"	60.	21	3.
42.	Leatherworkers (agricultural laborers)	Mill worker	85.	28	11.
43.	Washerman	Washerman	75.	20	1.
44.	Weaver	Mill worker	Unemployed	50	35.
45.	"	Shop worker	100.	40	15.
46.	"	Mill worker	105.	24	3.

Each residential migrant group has a leader who acts as a source of authority for the group and represents it in dealings with outsiders (landlords, police, merchants, employers) in much the same way the head of a family or the headman of a caste might function in the rural setting. Leaders tend to be older in years, to be senior in kinship, and to be more acculturated, usually having been present in the city a much longer time than other migrants in a group. Interviews with leaders indicated that they feel a considerable degree of responsibility for the welfare and safety of co-residents. Despite the attempt to enforce rural norms of appropriate caste, ritual, and moral behavior of migrants, there are lapses. But the group retains knowledge of these as secrets among its members. If they cannot control a member he may well be sent home since the group cannot be responsible for really serious breaches of conduct. In this sense, the Bombay "homeboy" group is quite effective in forestalling dangerous acculturation.[16]

Another way of dealing with the dangerous *pardesh* is through religion. Deities and godlings are frequently viewed as controlling a particular place. Hence, the village protector godling is carefully propitiated before leaving and upon returning to the village. In a like fashion the *bhaiya* go to the temple of Mombadevi, the patron goddess of Bombay,

16. Wilson and Mafeje's discussion of "homeboy" versus "townsmen" groups among migrants to Cape Town provides some interesting parallels to the case discussed here, one of the major contrasts being the strength of the village community in India as compared with the disintegrating situation on the Native Reserves in South Africa. Also see Mayer, 1963, for an analysis of a similar situation.

soon after their arrival and always just before leaving the *pardesh* for the return trip home. In both the village and the city then, deities control space and their worship provides an integrating mechanism for the diverse groups making up the population.

New Forms of Association

The discussion so far has emphasized some ways in which ancient ideas of village and town planning reflect cultural values and social structure, and how these ideas still provide a charter for rural and urban parts of the same society. It has been implied that it is this very similarity (through time and space) which facilitates the movement of individuals through the network of city and village experience.

Independent of the experiences of Senapur migrants, we know that a great deal of activity in the city is not controlled by primary relationships at all—that there is an enormous and growing involvement in many forms of voluntary association in Bombay. However, Senapur men in Bombay have relatively little contact with voluntary associations of any type, although Saltmakers did march with the Scheduled Castes Federation at election time, and several of the Tramways Workers reported some labor union activity. In general the Senapur *bhaiya* seem to be at the far end of the continuum of involvement in city life, since nearly all of them are so strongly identified with the rural village.

A brief survey of those voluntary associations in Bombay which arc large and affluent enough to have registered offices (see Table 4) indicates some ways in which associational activity is related to more traditionally based groups. Many of the associations in Bombay, and in other cities as well, are specifically organized for the promotion of the welfare of the endogamous caste.[17] Although only thirty-eight associations can be specifically identified as caste associations, there are probably others hidden in the educational and recreational category. From fieldwork among North Indians in Bombay, I know that there are also many others too improvident, small, or nascent to have become formally registered or to have rented office space in the city.

Caste associations function in a variety of ways to promote the inter-

17. Sangave has given an interesting account of caste associations and their activities for Kholapur City in Maharashtra, while Anderson (1963, 1964) has made a preliminary survey of caste associations in Hyderabad-Secunderabad, Andhra State. Also see Bose, 1960, for data on caste associations in Orissa, and Kothari and Rushikesh, 1965, for a case study in Gujerat.

Table 4. Voluntary Associations in Bombay, 1960[1]

Types of Associations	*Local*	*All-Indian*	*Other province, culture area*	*Total*
Caste associations	35	2	1	38
Professional, business, lobbyist groups, trade unions, etc.	61	4	0	65
Communal, religious, or ethnic community associations	11	1	9	21
Educational, cultural (art, music, and recreation)	93	7	1	101
Social service (including medical)	41	3	0	44
Neighborhood or *Mohalla* groups	3	0	1	4
Political party	6	1	0	7
Total	250	18	12	280

1. Based on *Thapar's Bombay Pocket Guide*, published by Indian Industrial Directory, 1960, pp. 67-115.

ests of their members, but those large enough to be listed in the city directory are the type which have sufficient funds and members to be engaged in cooperative housing, the operation of educational hostels, schools, scholarship funds, and so forth. Ghurye (1957: 212-14) feels that this type of caste activity has grown a great deal in recent years; it is surely an important adaptive mechanism of caste in the modern urban context (Gould, 1963a). That caste associations perform a bridging function between the residential caste unit and caste in its widest endogamous sense is indicated indirectly by Ghurye when he writes: "In fact it would be true to remark that only those cooperative housing societies have succeeded most which have restricted their membership to their caste-fellow" (1957: 212). It should be pointed out that cooperative caste housing is an interesting adaptation of caste ecology to modernity. It is also, of course, related to the ecology of succession, since the affluent or growing caste community which wishes to move out of an older, perhaps deteriorating, caste *mohalla* can do so without sacrificing caste exclusiveness characteristic of the old, defined area.

Although reform of caste practices, status preservation, or the acquisition of new and higher status may be a part of the function of the caste associations discussed above, they are less likely to be concerned with such matters than the associations of low and untouchable castes. In north Bombay I interviewed *bhaiya* leaders of several low-caste mobility movements (see Rowe, 1968) and collected information on several other associations. These associations provide a mechanism for the acculturation of low-caste *bhaiya* while they are learning the ways of the educated middle class. These upwardly mobile men had little contact with *bhaiya* such as the dairy workers or grain hawkers I knew. They had acquired enough education to achieve entrance into another occupational world, usually that of the clerk or schoolteacher. Their small *sabhas* (or caste associations), sometimes not more than an informal tea drinking club, gave them needed psychological support while in Bombay. These same men and the same associations are active in rural North India, although this is beyond the scope of discussion here. In one way the city branches of the associations are a training ground for the leadership of rural, low-caste mobility movements (see Cohn, 1959b).

In discussing caste associations it is difficult to avoid mentioning political activity of a formal sort, for the two are closely intertwined in Bombay City. The man who had been most active in *bhaiya* low-caste associations in Bombay from about 1920 until 1947 explained to me quite explicitly that *sabhas* were no longer of primary importance but that direct political activity was (also see Lynch, 1969). With adult franchise following independence, each ward in Bombay City increased in political importance. Since wards are often dominated by one or two caste or ethnic communities, the list of 132 Bombay Corporation councilmen clearly reflects the social ecology of the city. There are 14 North Indian members (Sharma and Jangam: 60-63), although in several wards where this group is third or fourth in the population rankings of resident groups it is not represented in the corporation.

In these two related ways, through caste associations and direct political activity, migrants to the city are being increasingly incorporated into the nation state. Some political scientists are pessimistic about the strength of integrative forces in an India composed of competing linguistic and caste groups (Harrison, 1960); others tend to present these forces as analogous to lobbies or interest groups in the West (Rudolph, 1960; Weiner, 1962). With the exception of M. N. Srinivas (1955) and F. G. Bailey (1963), few anthropologists have dealt with this topic in the urban setting. Understanding the political ramifications of the urban-rural network is of direct importance to our predictions about the type of societal integration likely to emerge in India.

Tamil Untouchables in Bangalore[18]

A great deal of the phenomenal population growth which Bangalore has experienced during the past thirty years (Table 1) can be attributed to the immigration of Tamil-speaking Pariahs (untouchables) from neighboring Madras State. Tamil migrants are spatially concentrated in the ninety-two jopadis (a slum neighborhood of mud huts) which are scattered throughout the city but are most likely to be located adjacent to industrial sites (Learmonth and Bhat, 1961, 1:283). As in Bombay, migrants tend to be found at lower levels in the labor force.[19] Evidence supporting the existence of spatial isolation of migrants is provided by Learmonth and Bhat (1961, I:283) and their associates, who report that 75 per cent of the population residing in *jopadis* (which they classify as "slum dwellings") are Tamil migrants. In a large survey of Bangalore households Gist (1954a, 1954b) reported that caste, education, and occupation are correlated—particularly at the polar ends of the caste hierarchy. It is not surprising then to find that untouchables exhibit a consistency in the several indices of their status: low ritual, occupational, and residential position. Map 4 illustrates the growth of Bangalore since about 1800 as a series of concentric rings. The latest, post-Independence growth is seen in a number of isolated industrial estates at some distance from the present city. Data on the social ecology of the city during the eighteenth and nineteenth centuries were not located, but we do have clear evidence of the contemporary ecology of caste and ethnic groups in Bangalore. Map 3 summarizes Gist's study showing that at the polar ends of the caste hierarchy, among the Brahmins and the untouchables, there is a high degree of spatial separation. Ritual and physical space are most clearly correlated for the Brahmin wards. Also a number of wards are

18. Gertrude M. Woodruff's excellent case study of life in a Tamil Pariah (untouchable) community in Bangalore provides the data for this discussion. The ecological and demographic studies of Noel P. Gist allow the case study to be placed in the broader perspective of Bangalore City.

19. For example, Hoselitz (1962:438) notes that there is a strong relationship between migrant status and a low position in the urban social structure. He suggests that in India the percentage of migrants in the labor force increases as skill of labor decreases. Bogue and Zachariah (1962:50) conclude that Calcutta has a disproportionately large share of migrants who are low-status, lower-paid, unskilled laborers. They state, "Industries where skill, high status, higher incomes and artisanship are involved tend to be reserved for Bengalis." They feel that the situation they describe for Calcutta is typical of Indian cities.

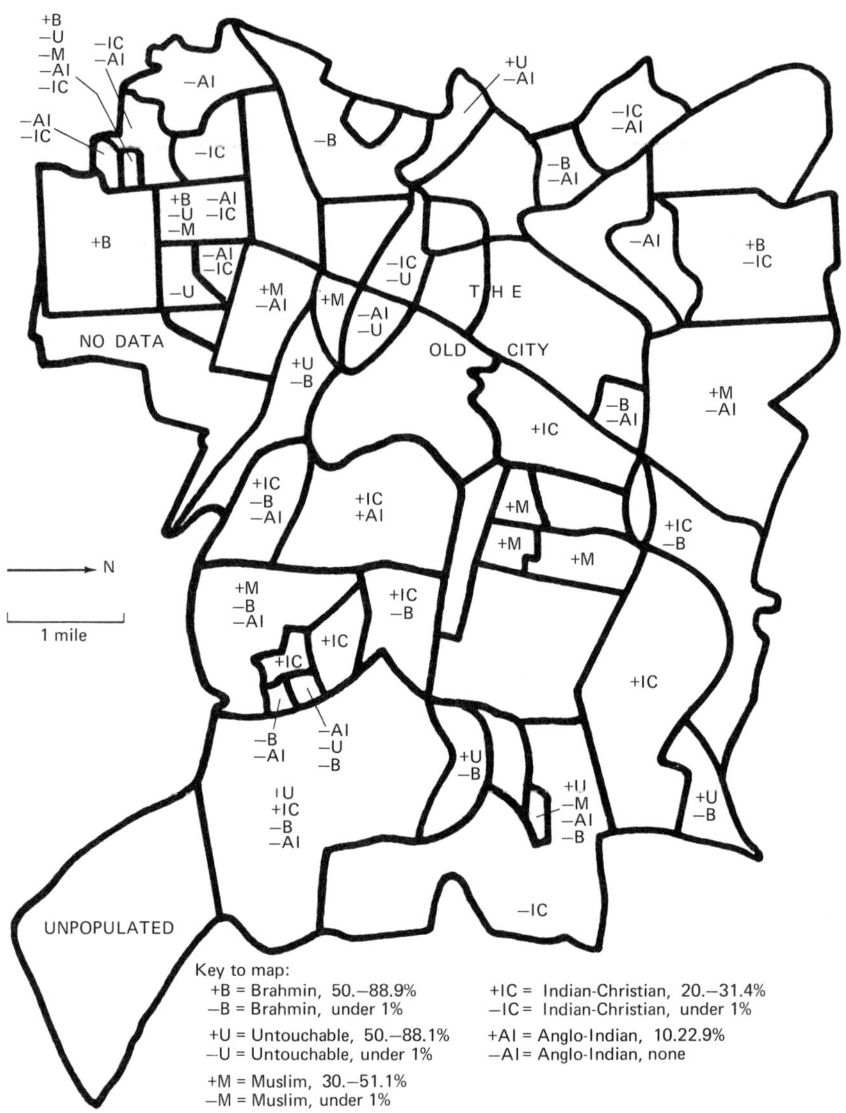

N.B. The ecological distribution of castes is marked showing high concentrations of residence and less than 1% residence in a ward.

*Based on Gist: 1957

Map 3.* Greater Bangalore, 1957

dominated by either Muslims or Indian Christians, while untouchable residence corresponds to the existence of *jopadis*. Map 3 has been constructed to emphasize residential *polarities* only. For example, the population of castes known as Non-Brahmins in South India is not represented on the map at all.

It can be surmised that residential caste areas existed in the old city (circa 1800), but at the present time the core of the old city no longer exhibits such a pattern. We hypothesize that through a process of eco-

N.B. Note that area covered by city in 1800 is now dominated by public buildings, mercantile activity.

Cantonment and most Europeanized sections of the city are in the 1900-1935 section.

Key to map:
N.I. = New Industrial zones added to the city since Independence.
H.M.T. = Hindustan Machine Tools
I.T.I. = Indian Telephone Industries
H.A.L. = Hindustan Aircraft Limited

◇ H.M.T.

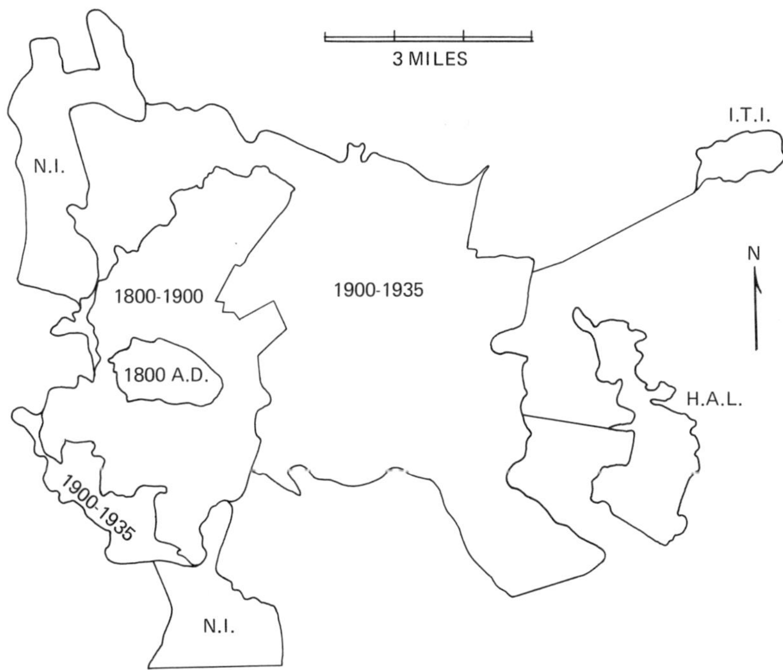

Map 4.* Development of Bangalore, 1800–Present

logical succession, new areas of the growing city became the ecological zones of various caste communities. This does not mean that caste-dominated streets may not now exist in the old city, since in many Indian towns and cities one does find compact areas dominated by artisans and specialized merchants. As in Bombay, we see the strength of caste as a factor in ecology, since many of the caste-specific wards are in the newer portions of Bangalore. It is relatively safe to assume that Brahmins, Muslims, and untouchables did exist as groups in the older city. What a comparison of Maps 3 and 4 tells us is that caste communities moved as units as the city grew. The ecology of succession and the addition of social groups is probably most clearly seen in the increasing number of untouchable *jopadis* since World War II.

Life in the Jopadi

Woodruff has provided a vivid picture of caste, kinship, and association in one Bangalore slum community which she calls "Cafe Street Jopadi." This settlement of 793 Tamil-speaking Pariahs (untouchables) from Madras State has existed as a separate community for about forty years. The rural origins of 62 per cent of the *jopadi* residents are a group of thirty villages in the Arcot District of Madras, about 125 miles from Bangalore.

This case study shows the rural-urban network providing a continuous stream of new and permanent recruits to the city. They arrive either as nuclear family units or as single men who shortly afterwards marry and fetch their wives to the city. In any event migrants, by and large, quickly establish families in the city. Commenting on the stability of individual and family life in the *jopadi*, Woodruff states: "The *jopadi* can have socially effective families because migration to the city does not disrupt the nuclear unit." A high proportion (43%) of the wives are also wage earners, and thirty-four children under the age of fifteen are employed.

This study and other data[20] lead us to categorize South Indian migra-

20. Ransom (1938) noted this for Madras in the 1930's and felt that because of family settlement in the city the adjustment process was easier than for the single migrant to Calcutta or Bombay (1938:3-4). The two case studies on Bangalore and Bombay are representative of two types of migration, as shown in numerous demographic studies on sex ratios in northern (Bombay and Calcutta) and southern (Bangalore and Madras) cities (See Woodruff: 42; Davis, 1951:135-40; and Census of India volumes). Overall sex ratios for Bombay make it the most "male city" in India. Davis (1951:139-40) gives evidence to show that Indian cities are becoming increasingly masculine. However, in 1911, of the 6,551 Bombay residents born in Jaunpur District, U.P., only 439 were women. Urban migration is more masculine the greater the distance covered.

tion to the city as permanent family migration, in contrast to the North Indian pattern of recurrent unaccompanied male migration. Woodruff's data and other anthropological descriptions of South Indian village life permit a number of contrasts and tentative generalizations.[21] Both ritual and spatial distance between Brahmins and untouchables is much greater in the south of India than in the north. Village life in the south tends to be such that the untouchable castes in their outlying settlements (*cheri*) have relatively little contact with the dominant caste. The people of the *cheri* are somehow less integrated into the total life of the multi-caste village, and hence their ties to the village are not as strong as low-caste village ties in the north. Another aspect which I suggest as important is the differing positions of low-caste women in the two areas. The rule of village exogamy in the north, in contrast to southern marriage patterns which emphasize the strengthening of already existing kinship ties through marriages, may have some pertinence in understanding differing attitudes towards bringing wives to the city. Among the northerners in Bombay, it was considered shameful to bring wives to the city where they could not be properly supervised or watched.

Certainly the total attitude towards urban migration is different for the two cases. In the North Indian village itself, there is at best ambivalence about going to the *pardesh* to work (except for a small upper-caste elite who have prestigious city jobs), as though this represented some form of failure. In contrast, Woodruff states that for the migrants from the Arcot Districts there is no stigma attached to migration.

Perhaps an even more fundamental contrast is in the eventual outcome of the two forms of migration. In Bombay, even those migrants who have statistically spent most of their lives in the city think of themselves as really being residents of Senapur Village. The city is always a temporary abode. Woodruff states that quite another pattern occurs among the Pariahs in the *jopadi*. They talk in a "stereotypic" fashion of retiring to the village, but she finds that the probability of this is slight. Only a very few *jopadi* residents send money back to village kin. Although a few men buy land to retire on, some look upon village land purchase purely as an investment and have no intention of returning to work on it. Woodruff notes that the adjustment of the city-born Pariah in the village setting is very poor. But there is a great deal of traffic between the rural *cheri* and the

21. Srinivas (1955), Gough (1955), and Béteille (1964) give a fairly consistent picture of this aspect of South Indian social structure.

urban *jopadi,* though permanent moves are customarily only in one direction, towards the city.

Forms of Association in the Jopadi

As is true elsewhere in India, the South Indian village Pariahs have a caste council with a traditional headman. This residential caste unit is frequently a part of a group of village caste communities in an area, a unit which in turn has a council and headman. In the city *jopadi,* attempts are made to reproduce this structure, but with varying degrees of success. Although Cafe Street Jopadi is a single-caste, single-language community, there was not sufficient cohesion to continue support of the traditional form of council and headman. Eventually an adaptive mechanism was devised—that of choosing a headman by lot. Woodruff notes that in some *jopadis,* especially multi-caste settlements, a modern form of association, the *changam* (similar to the *sabha,* the Hindi organizational form mentioned earlier), is utilized. The *changam* is characterized by a "democratic" structure, including a long list of office-bearers holding English titles. The value orientation of the *changam* also is toward the "modern."

In Cafe Street Jopadi, a *changam* was formed in opposition to the traditionally organized council and headman. This eventually led to a formal division of the community into two opposing factions. Significantly, after some early failures, a second *changam* was formed as a voluntary association tied to the wider political arena of the pan-Indian Scheduled Caste movement. The leader of the *changam* group succeeded in arranging for the removal of fifty-one families to a new Bangalore Corporation housing development located on the outskirts of the city. That this *changam* group was highly selective is shown in the following table (Woodruff: 137):

	Remaining jopadi residents (%)	*New housing development residents* (%)
Men with permanent jobs	47	68
Employees of Bangalore Corporation[1]	29	44
Male literacy	25	34
School-age boys in school	45	86

1. Considered the most secure employment.

All Cafe Street Jopadi residents have caste, language, and area of origin in common. But some groups form within the *jopadi* on the basis of further distinguishing criteria. Woodruff notes these as (1) common village of origin; (2) having the same employer; and (3) residence in the same house line or neighborhood within the *jopadi*. She states: "When there is an issue at stake, a leader emerges who can utilize the potential affiliations to form a faction" (Woodruff: 151).

Although certain religious practices symbolic of lineage solidarity in the rural village fall into disuse in the city, the *jopadi* does have a temple representing the community concern with the supernatural. Under the traditional *jopadi* form of council, it was the headman's duty to insure proper performance of certain key rituals designed to guarantee the well-being of the total *jopadi*. Hence, there was a transfer of ideas of ritual and social space to the city from the rural *cheri*. The other cohesive tie within the *jopadi* is the relationship all households have with a specific priest who officiates at all life-cycle rites.

The contrasts and similarities in the two (briefly presented) cases cannot be very strongly stated, since in both cases the data are concerned with tiny cells in a very large complex. However, both authors feel that their respective groups are representative of larger phenomena—North and South Indian migration patterns (see note 20). In both cases migration is associational (with caste brothers, kin, and other villagers), as are living patterns in the city. This is partially because "the city wants it that way," that is, the city is organized to accept and incorporate migrants in that fashion. This characteristic must also be seen in terms of rural social structure.

One of the contrasts which emerges from a comparison is the relatively minor "pull" the village has for the Pariahs and the quite opposite tendency for the *bhaiya*. One might ask, "To what degree is there a choice for the *bhaiya*? Is not their style of living in the city the only possibility?" But for the Pariahs too, income is low[22] and housing is difficult.

I think we would have to analyze the differing family systems, the degree of authoritative strength held by the extended family in both cases and, I suspect, the ties to other castes in the rural social system, as well as the extent of ties to land. These comparative questions can and should be

22. Woodruff states that in 1956 the average income in the *jopadi* was Rs 54 per month per family. Income ranged from a low of Rs 15 to Rs 190, but the highest frequency concentration was in the Rs 40-49 bracket (p. 100).

asked of the growing body of data on villages in the differing subcultures of India.

Conclusions: The City and Changing Forms of Association

In discussing the social ecology of the village and the city in India, emphasis has been placed on the spatial meaning of ecology, for this meaning emerges clearly when we *look* at either form of living. The sense in which spatial arrangements reflect values and social structure may be thought fanciful for some societies, but in Hindu life it is elegantly manifest, both in ideology and in physical reality. This relationship is visible in the many types of Indian community.

Few anthropologists seem to have utilized the graphic dimensions of the city. John Gulick did so in Tripoli, collecting drawings from his informants of their "images" or projections of what the city meant. Urban and human geographers have this concern, but the cultural and social anthropologist will naturally ask different questions of the data. In Indian urban studies this would surely be one of the rewarding approaches to the complexity of the data.

Considering the whole of modern Indian life, we might say that a social system, functional for a particular level or type of ecology, has gone awry. Recalling that Senapur and similar villages in northeastern India have almost doubled their populations in the past sixty years (without a corresponding change in the level of material resources), we could claim that the urban migrants have extended the resources of the village to include the city. In this adaptation—given the strength of regnant social patterns and values—the integrity of the village is maintained, despite the ecological imbalance, by defining the city as a new part of the village.

Only a few of the forms of association in Indian cities have been discussed. Caste and kinship as bases of residence and interaction have been examined at greater length since they still seem to be the most meaningful.[23] Also it is from these basic ties that we move to new forms of association. Religion and religious participation as an associational activity which gives the city some degree of integration has been studied in Madras City by Milton Singer (1958), but it is a field still virtually *terra*

23. Studies which document this include Dhekney, Mukerjee, and Singh (on Lucknow); the Bharat Sevak Samaj study of the slums of old Delhi; and Bopegamage on Delhi.

incognita. Some recent fiction (e.g. Jhavbala, 1960) deals with the meaning of religious association for the new townsman; but we are without a study of the great annual temple festivals of Indian towns. Baroja (1963: 33) mentions the Feast of Corpus Christi as an occasion when all the guilds of a town come together in an integrative rite, yet, since the ethnographic accounts of the last century, we have nothing about this very active and rich Indian cultural complex.[24]

Another area of research which must take the city as its central locale and which will be essential to an understanding of the Indian social fabric will be the study of Indian mercantile castes and guilds. Economists have been busily assuming (and writing) that the Hindu ethic prevented the development of modern industrial capitalism but, in lieu of substantial data, this question is a lively and important one open to empirical exploration.[25]

For several reasons, however, the area which seems most fascinating is that of changing forms of association. Here, one would hope for studies of caste associations, particularly at the stage of development when they become involved in the politics of the modern state. Banton suggests (in his chapter in this book) that tribes become the locus of new roles in the city, the tribe becoming emphasized as it becomes an urban political phenomenon. When more of the anthropologists in India leave the village and reach the city, we may well discover that castes (in some situations) in the Indian city have a similar nature. Harold Gould (1963b) and Kahl (1959: 70) both argue that one cannot study a *mohalla* or ward of a city as a "community" because urban segmentation of roles invalidates the notion of community. The actual lives of individuals in their city associations (both residentially in the single-caste *mohalla* and in occupational and other roles) must be investigated before "community" in the Indian city ward is dismissed. Given the very strong tendency for caste to be associated with residence, and for residential wards to have political status in the city, one could equally well argue that "community" does exist in the Indian city.

The city in India has historically represented the full cultural complex,

24. Mukerjee (1961) mentions the great festivals of the local deities for Indian towns, occasions on which the deity is paraded through all of the town or city. We are reminded of barrio and town-wide fiestas of this sort in parts of Latin America. Prof. McKim Marriot has made a major study of Wai, a sacred town in Maharashtra, but it has not yet been published.

25. See Hazlehurst (1966) for a study of mercantile groups in a Punjabi city. Richard Fox has studied a small market town in eastern Uttar Pradesh.

the most ideally worked out approximation of that which was valued. This was true when orthodoxy went from city to village; and it seems to be true today as "modernism" takes the same path.

References Cited

Anderson, Robert T.

1963. "Preliminary Report on the Associational Redefinition of Castes in Hyderabad-Secunderabad." *Kroeber Anthropological Papers,* No. 29.

1964. "Voluntary Associations in Hyderabad." *Anthropological Quarterly* 37 (4).

Bailey, F. G.

1963. *Politics and Social Change: Orissa in 1959.* Berkeley and Los Angeles: University of California Press.

Baroja, Julio Caro

1963. "The City and the Country: Reflections on Some Ancient Commonplaces." In J. Pitt-Rivers (ed.), *Mediterranean Countrymen.* Paris: Mouton and Co.

Béteille, André

1966. *Caste, Class and Power: Changing Patterns of Stratification in a Tanjore Village.* Berkeley and Los Angeles: University of California Press.

Bharat Sevak Samaj

1958. *Slums of Old Delhi.* Delhi: Atma Ram and Sons.

Bogue, Donald J., and K. C. Zachariah

1962. "Urbanization and Migration in India." In Roy Turner (ed.), *India's Urban Future.* Berkeley and Los Angeles: University of California Press.

Bopegamage, A.

1957. *Delhi: A Study in Urban Sociology.* Bombay: Bombay University Press.

Bose, Nirmal Kumar (ed.)

1960. *Data on Caste: Orissa.* Calcutta: Memoir No. 7, Anthropological Survey of India, Government of India.

Burnell, John

1933. *Bombay in the Days of Queen Anne.* London: Hakluyt Society.

Caplow, Theodore

1961. "The Social Ecology of Guatemala City." In G. T. Theodorsen (ed.), *Studies in Human Ecology.* Evanston, Ill.: Row Peterson and Co.

Census of India

1951. Volumes on Bombay, Uttar Pradesh, and Mysore.

Cohn, Bernard S.

1959a. "Madhopur Revisited." *The Economic Weekly,* Special Number, July 1959.

1959b. "Changing Traditions of a Low Caste." In Milton Singer (ed.), *Traditional India: Structure and Change.* Philadelphia: American Folklore Society.

1962. "Political Systems in Eighteenth Century India: The Banaras Region." *Journal of the American Oriental Society* 82(3):312-20.

Cohn, Bernard S., and McKim Marriott

1958. "Networks and Centers in the Integration of Indian Civilization." *Journal of Social Research* 1:1-9.

DaCunha, J. Gerson

1900. *The Origin of Bombay.* Extra Number, Vol. 20, *Journal of the Bombay Branch of the Royal Asiatic Society.*

Davis, Kingsley

1951. *The Population of India and Pakistan.* Princeton: Princeton University Press.

1962. "Urbanization in India: Past and Future." In Roy Turner (ed.), *India's Urban Future.* Berkeley and Los Angeles: University of California Press.

Dhekney, B. R.

1959. *Hubli City: A Study in Urban Economic Life.* Dharwar: Karnatak University.

Douglas, James

1893. *Bombay and Western India,* 2 vols. London: Sampson Low, Marston and Company.

Edwardes, S. M.

1909. *The Gazetteer of Bombay City and Island,* 3 vols. Bombay: Times Press.

Eliade, Mircea

1959. *Cosmos and History: The Myth of the Eternal Return.* New York: Harper Torchbooks.

Fox, Richard G.

1964. Personal communication.

1969. *From Zamindar to Ballot Box: Community Change in a North Indian Market Town.* Ithaca, N.Y.: Cornell University Press.

1970. *Urban India: Society, Space and Image.* Durham, N.C.: Duke University Studies on Southern Asia, No. 10.

Freed, Stanley A.

1963. "Fictive Kinship in a North Indian Village." *Ethnology* 2(1):86-103.

Ghurye, G. S.

1957. *Caste and Class in India.* Bombay: Popular Book Depot.

1962. *Cities and Civilization.* Bombay: Popular Prakashan.

Gillion, Kenneth L.

1968. *Ahmedabad: A Study in Indian Urban History.* Berkeley and Los Angeles: University of California Press.

Gist, Noel P.

1954a. "Caste Differentials in South India." *American Sociological Review* 19:126-37.

1954b. "Occupational Differentiation in South India." *Social Forces* 33:129-38.
1957. "The Ecology of Bangalore, India: An East-West Comparison." *Social Forces* 35:356-65.

Gough, Kathleen E.
1955. "The Social Structure of a Tanjore Village." In McKim Marriott (ed.), *Village India.* Chicago: University of Chicago Press.

Gould, Harold A.
1963a. "The Adaptive Functions of Caste in Contemporary Indian Society." *Asian Survey* 3(9):427-38.
1963b. *Review of Social Profiles of a Metropolis* (R. Mukerjee and B. Singh). *Eastern Anthropologist* 16(2):156-66.

Gulick, John
1963. "Images of an Arab City." *Journal of the American Institute of Planners* 29(3):179-98.

Gune, Vithal Trimbak
1953. *The Judicial System of the Marathas.* Poona: Deccan College Dissertation Series No. 12.

Harrison, Selig S.
1960. *India: The Most Dangerous Decades.* Princeton: Princeton University Press.

Hazlehurst, Leighton W.
1966. *Entrepreneurship and the Merchant Castes in a Punjabi City.* Durham, N.C.: Duke University Studies on Southern Asia, No. 1.

Hoselitz, Bert F.
1962. "The Role of Urbanization in Economic Development: Some International Comparisons." In Roy Turner (ed.), *India's Urban Future.* Berkeley and Los Angeles: University of California Press.

Hunter, Sir William Wilson
1892(?). *Bombay: 1885-1890.* London: Henry Frowde.

Hutton, J. H.
1933. *Census of India, 1931,* Vol. 1-India, Part I, *Report.* Delhi: Manager of Publications.

Imperial Gazetteer of India
1908. New Edition. London: Oxford University Press.

Jhabvala, R. Prawer
1960. *The Householder.* New York: W. W. Norton.

Kahl, Joseph A.
1959. "Some Social Concomitants of Industrialization and Urbanization." *Human Organization* 18(2): 53-74.

Kane, P. V.
1941. *History of Dharmasastra,* Vol. II (2 parts). Poona: Bhandarkar Oriental Research Institute.
1946. *History of Dharmasastra,* Vol. III. Poona: Bhandarkar Oriental Research Institute.

Kothari, Rajni, and Rushikesh, Maru
1965. "Caste and Secularism in India: Case Study of a Caste Federation." *Journal of Asian Studies* 25(1).

Kramrisch, Stella
1946. *The Hindu Temple*, 2 vols. Calcutta: Calcutta University.

Lambert, Richard D.
1962. "The Impact of Urban Society upon Village Life." In Roy Turner (ed.), *India's Urban Future*. Berkeley and Los Angeles: University of California Press.
1963. *Workers, Factories and Social Change in India*. Princeton: Princeton University Press.

Learmonth, A. T. A., and L. S. Bhat (eds.)
1961. *An Atlas of Resources*, 2 vols. Calcutta: Asia Publishing House and Statistical Publishing Society.

Lynch, Owen M.
1967. "Rural Cities in India: Continuities and Discontinuities." In Philip Mason, (ed.), *India and Ceylon: Unity and Diversity*. New York: Oxford University Press.
1968. "The Politics of Untouchability: A Case from Agra, India." In Milton Singer and B. S. Cohn (eds.), *Structure and Change in Indian Society*. Chicago: Aldine.
1969. *The Politics of Untouchability: Social Mobility and Social Change in a City of India*. New York and London: Columbia University Press.

MacLean, James MacKenzie
1876. *A Guide to Bombay: Historical, Statistical, and Descriptive*. Bombay: "Bombay Gazette" Steam Press.

Malabari, P. B. M.
1910. *Bombay in the Making (1661-1726)*. London: T. Fisher Unwin.

Marriott, McKim
1959. "Changing Channels of Cultural Transmission in Indian Civilization." *Proceedings of the Annual Spring Meeting, American Ethnological Society*, pp. 66-72.

Mayer, Philip
1963. *Townsmen or Tribesmen: Conservatism and the Process of Urbanization in a South African Town*. Cape Town: Oxford University Press.

Morris, Morris David
1965. *The Emergence of an Industrial Labor Force in India: A Study of the Bombay Cotton Mills, 1854-1947*. Berkeley and Los Angeles: University of California Press.

Mukerjee, Radhakamal
1961. "Ways of Dwelling in the Communities of India." In G. T. Theodorsen (ed.), *Studies in Human Ecology*. Evanston, Ill.: Row, Peterson and Co.

Mukerjee, Radhakamal, and Baljit Singh
1961. *Social Profiles of a Metropolis: Social and Economic Structure of*

Lucknow, Capital of Uttar Pradesh, 1954-56. Bombay: Asia Publishing House.

O'Brien, Robert W.

1961. "Beale Street, Memphis: A Study in Ecological Succession" in G. T. Theodorsen (ed.), *Studies in Human Ecology*. Evanston, Ill.: Row, Peterson and Co.

Patel, Kunj

1963. *Rural Labour in Industrial Bombay*. Bombay: Popular Prakshan.

Pitt-Rivers, Julian

1963. *Mediterranean Countrymen: Essays in the Social Anthropology of the Mediterranean*. Paris: Mouton and Co.

Pocock, David F.

1960. "Sociologies–Urban and Rural." *Contributions to Indian Sociology* 4:63-81.

Prabhu, Pandhari Nath

1956. "A Study on the Social Effects of Urbanization on Industrial Workers Migrating from Rural Areas to the City of Bombay." In *The Social Implications of Industrialization and Urbanization*. Calcutta: UNESCO Research Center on the Social Implications of Industrialization in Southern Asia.

Rajagopalan, C.

1962. *The Greater Bombay: A Study in Suburban Ecology*. Bombay: Popular Book Depot.

Rao, C. Hayavadana

1943. *History of Mysore (1399-1799)*, 3 vols. Bangalore: Government Press.

Ransom, C. W.

1938. *A City in Transition: Studies in the Social Life of Madras*. Madras: Christian Literature Society.

Ross, Aileen D.

1961. *The Hindu Family in Its Urban Setting*. Toronto: University of Toronto Press.

Rowe, William L.

1960a. *Social and Economic Mobility in a Low-Caste North Indian Community*. Unpublished Ph.D. Thesis. Ithaca, New York: Cornell University, September 1960.

1960b. "The Marriage Network and Structural Change in a North Indian Community." *Southwestern Journal of Anthropology* 16(3): 299-311.

1968. "The New Cauhans: A Caste Mobility Movement in North India." In James Silverberg (ed.), *Mobility in Caste in India*. The Hague: Mouton.

Rudolph, Lloyd I.

1960. "The Political Role of India's Caste Associations." *Pacific Affairs* 33: 1-22.

Sangave, Vilas A.
1961. "Changing Pattern of Caste Organization in Kolhapur City." *Sociological Bulletin* 11 (1 & 2): 36-59.

Sharma, B. A. V., and R. T. Jangam
1962. *The Bombay Municipal Corporation: An Election Study*. Bombay: Popular Book Depot.

Sheppard, Samuel T.
1932. *Bombay*. Bombay: The Times of India Press.

Singer, Milton
1958. "The Great Tradition in a Metropolitan Center: Madras." *Journal of American Folklore* 71 (July-Sept. 1958): 347-88.

Spear, Percival
1963. *The Nabobs: A Study of the Social Life of the English in Eighteenth-Century India*. London: Oxford University Press.

Srinivas, M. N.
1955a. "The Social System of a Mysore Village." In McKim Marriott (ed.), *Village India*. Chicago: University of Chicago Press.
1955b. "Castes: Can They Exist in the India of Tomorrow?" *Economic Weekly* 7:1230-32.

Thapar's Bombay Pocket Guide
1960. Bombay: Indian Industrial Directory.

Turner, Roy (ed.)
1962. *India's Urban Future*. Berkeley and Los Angeles: University of California Press.

Vankatrangaiya, M.
1953. *The General Election in the City of Bombay, 1952*. Bombay: Vora and Co. Publishers, Ltd.

Vatuk, Sylvia
1972. *Kinship and Urbanization: White Collar Migrants in North India*. Berkeley and Los Angeles: University of California Press.

Venkatarayappa, K. N.
1957. *Bangalore: A Socio-Ecological Study*. Bombay: Bombay University Press.

Weiner, Myron
1962. *The Politics of Scarcity*. Princeton: Princeton University Press.

Wilson, Monica, and Archie Mafeje
1963. *Langa: A Study of Social Groups in an African Township*. Cape Town: Oxford University Press.

Woodruff, Gertrude Marvin
1959. *An Adidravida Settlement in Bangalore, India: A Case Study of Urbanization*. Unpublished Ph.D. Thesis. Cambridge, Mass.: Radcliffe College, April 1959.

Urban Ethnicity and the Cultural Process of Urbanization in Ethiopia[1]

W. A. Shack

African towns are not "melting pots" for rural Africans with diverse tribal backgrounds. Even after living in an urban environment for periods of up to a generation or more, Africans in town retain their tribal identity and membership in the rural society. They think in terms of the hinterland: and a great deal of the social and economic activities of African townsmen are directed towards forming and keeping alive urban-based tribal institutions which function to maintain ties of kinship with the rural village where they ultimately propose to retire.

African towns are thus unlike American towns, or at least American towns as they are said to be, insofar as the urbanization of immigrants is concerned. Ethnic quarters do exist in large metropolitan areas in America such as New York, Chicago, and Philadelphia; the "little Italys,"

1. Field data upon which this essay is based were gathered during two periods of research among the Gurage in their tribal district and in Addis Ababa, Ethiopia. The first, between 1957 and 1959, was part of a study of tribal migration and social structure; the second, between 1962 and 1965, was part of a study of ritual and authority. This paper was written during tenure of grants awarded by the National Institute of Mental Health, Nos. 07141-02. Comments on an earlier draft were kindly made by Dr. J. Comhaire, Mr. G. Savard, Dr. J. Hamer and Professors A. Vilakazi and J. van Velsen. For the final form which this essay has taken, I gratefully acknowledge the assistance of my colleagues in the Wenner-Gren symposium where the views expressed here were first brought to their critical attention. In particular I wish to thank Professor J. Clyde Mitchell and Dr. Michael Banton for the many helpful suggestions concerning the theoretical position I have taken; their criticisms have been of immense value in making final revisions.

"Irishtowns," "Germantowns," and the like. But one of the characteristic features of the American urbanization process is that relatively rapid assimilation of immigrants is not only possible, but that in fact it does occur. There are exceptions; the particular ethnic and racial factors which restrict complete assimilation of Jews and Afro-Americans respectively into the mainstream of American society are obvious examples. In the main, however, ethnic group distinctions in American communities generally become increasingly less noticeable and important with each succeeding generation of immigrant families. This is not the rule in Africa. African townsmen generally do not lose their ethnic traits and tribal characteristics after several decades of active participation in the social, political, and economic spheres of urban society. "Industrial employment," as Watson (1958:6) has observed, "does not seem to affect the retention by Africans of their tribal identity, nor their adherence to their chiefs"; tribal ties and loyalty to chiefs are in fact enhanced. This has been shown in several studies to be generally true throughout African urban centers. It is contrary to Forde's opinion (1956:39) that tribal membership in towns, which has been called by various writers "tribalism," "supertribalism," and "urban tribalism," appears to be an "unstable short-lived phenomenon."

Sociologically, urban ethnicity, the term I use in this paper, suggests that separation from tribal life and entry into urban life, far from weakening the bonds between tribal members, on the contrary greatly strengthens them. Indeed, Mercier (1965: 490) has argued that the maintenance of ethnic allegiances in towns is not always divisive, but it can lead to greater integration. Urban associations and ceremonial cults based on ethnic membership both express and reinforce ethnic solidarity, which is commonly connected with competition for employment or trade. These features of urban ethnicity are manifested in several ways, its function varying from one African town to another, as the following examples illustrate. Among the Temne in Sierra Leone, one form of urban ethnicity is expressed in the organization of young men's companies which, as Banton (1957: 216) explains, "provides the individual a substitute lineage or kin group, and a new structure of urban leadership." It is further noted that one of the functions of these companies is to "combat the disorganization of a tribal society in a strange city." Of the ethnic associations formed by migrants from Eastern Nigeria, Little (1957: 582, 1965) writes that their main *raison d'être* is to foster and keep alive a person's attachment to his native lineage. In Central and East Africa, Mitchell (1957), Gluckman

(1960), and Southall (1961) all insist that ethnicity in towns is "primarily a means of classifying the multitude of Africans of heterogeneous origins who live together in towns"; ethnic classification is the basis on which new groupings are formed to meet the needs of urban life. Similarly, urban ethnicity in Addis Ababa manifests itself in ways not unlike what has been observed elsewhere in African towns. I discuss in this paper the role of urban membership and ethnic identity in the urbanization process of the Gurage, one of the principal urban migrant groups in Ethiopia.

There is common agreement that urban tribalism persists primarily because of the ambivalent position in which most Africans in town find themselves, and that the majority of town immigrants look to the tribal area for their ultimate social and economic security (cf. van Velsen, 1961: 233). Moreover, from the several studies relating to aspects of ethnicity in African towns, from Mitchell's pioneering work on the Kalela Dance (1957) to more recent analyses of neighborhood and small-group associations (Southall 1961), it is apparent that under urban influences African tribal societies do not necessarily become disorganized, secularized, and individualized. To these examples, Bruner's (1961) observations of urbanization and ethnic identity among the Toba Batak in North Sumatra provide supporting evidence from outside the African continent. In other words, a prolonged residence in the "atmosphere of town," as Mayer (1962: 591) has said, will not automatically change people, nor make them "urbanized." Some Africans in town are more "urban" than others; some African towns are more "urban" than others.

The sociological implications of ethnicity in towns are much greater, it seems, than if ethnicity were only a primary mode of classifying the heterogeneous masses whom a man meets into manageable categories. Important sociological questions regarding ethnicity in town appear to turn on at least three related issues: why ethnicity persists; the extent to which rural tribal institutions can be transferred effectively to towns; and the relationship of urban ethnicity to the cultural process of urbanization. These problems underlie the working assumption in the study of urban ethnicity presented here: that sociological explanations of this phenomenon are to be sought in the particular historical and sociocultural processes which have shaped the urban social structure and determined the relative social and economic roles and status positions of the several urban ethnic groups. By considering the historical and sociocultural variables as interdependent, such an approach attempts to view the wider field of urban social relations, both in time and form, within which the group selected for purposes of analysis interacts with other groups in the social system. It is from this starting point that the following descriptive analysis of ethnicity among the Gurage in Addis Ababa proceeds. Although the discussion here centers on the specialized occupational roles, status positions, and rural-urban kin relations of the Gurage, with more adequate data available it could also be demonstrated that similar forms of urban ethnicity are manifested in the social behavior of other ethnic groups in Addis Ababa: the Wallamo, Dorze, and Gimira, to mention only a few.

Before discussing Gurage urban ethnicity, I shall define briefly my use of the terms "urban" and "town," "tribalism," and "tribal" and "ethnic," as these appear in later sections of this paper. If African towns are defined as "urban" on the basis of being mainly non-industrial, relatively large in size, densely populated, and ethnically heterogeneous (cf. Bascom, 1955), Addis Ababa only, among other Ethiopian towns, measures up to these criteria. Hence, when I speak later of "Gurage in town," I shall have specific reference only to Gurage in Addis Ababa. It has already been pointed out that some writers refer to "tribalism in town" as a "system of categorization," but tribalism in town also implies the "manifesting of tribal ways of behavior in town"; I use the term "ethnicity" for "tribalism" mainly in the second sense. The terms "tribal and "ethnic" also need to be distinguished, since these are sometimes used to define similar kinds of social groups in town. The distinctions suggested by Epstein (1958: 231), based upon his analysis of tribalism on the Copperbelt, and Wallerstein (1960: 130), based on West African "ethnicity and nationalism," seem suitable for our purpose; thus "tribal" will refer to the group in the rural area, whereas "ethnic" will refer to the one in town. Lastly, in urban Ethiopia, if not in all African towns, ethnic groups are at the same time "subcultural groups," that is, cultural differences involve much more than simply linguistic variations (as is the case, for instance, among some Bantu-speaking groups in urban South Africa). I find it analytically useful, therefore, to introduce the term "subcultural groups," with specific reference to the cultural process of Ethiopian urbanization discussed in the final section of this paper.

The Urban Background: Historical and Sociocultural Perspectives

Urbanization in Ethiopia presents striking historical parallels with Japan (Yazaki, 1965). The old imperial feudal social structures served as models for modern urban development; the demographic plans of the urban capitals in Ethiopia and Japan were laid out according to the military, economic, and social resources necessary for effective functioning of imperial systems, at the apex of which stood the royal emperors whose authorities were divinely inspired. The traditional systems of authority, social ranking and occupational castes, land holding, and tribute and taxation, as well as the special sectors of society occupied by priests, merchants, artisans, minstrels, peasants, and the professional warriors and military adventurers: all of these factors contributed to shaping the non-Western indigenous character of pre-industrial urban development in Japan and Ethiopia. That so many of Ethiopia's traditional sociocultural features have survived into the modern period (and that they underlie the structure of urban roles today) is perhaps the single characteristic which sets Addis Ababa apart from other urban towns in Africa.

Emperor Menilek II founded Addis Ababa in the last quarter of the nineteenth century as the first permanent capital of Ethiopia (Pankhurst, 1961: 103). Some speculation still exists over the exact date that the city was established, but 1890 is the year most widely accepted by historians. Until 1898, when Menilek finally consolidated his rule over Ethiopia, Addis Ababa served not only as a seat of his Shoan-Amhara kingdom but also as a military camp from which his vast armies launched ruthless and devastating campaigns against petty-rival Amhara, Tigrean, and Galla kingdoms in Shoa and the northern provinces of Ethiopia. Later to fall under Amhara domination were the small Sidamo kingdoms in the southwest, the Nilotic tribes in the West Nile region, and the Gurage in southern Shoa province. With the pacification of most tribal groups achieved by 1900, intertribal warfare in Ethiopia practically ceased to exist. The Shoan-Amhara kingdom was established militarily and politically. Addis Ababa emerged as its religious and cultural center.

The Coptic Christian church-state oligarchy gave renewed impetus to the Amhara sociocultural system, which rapidly spread as the most pervasive religious and political force in the empire. The "Amhara system"[2] provided a sociocultural framework for the ranking of Ethiopia's diverse tribal groups into a hierarchical status structure based on cultural differ-

2. By "Amhara system" I mean that the sociocultural system was dominated by the Amhara tribal group but not exclusively so. Traditionally the Amhara system was built up on combined Amhara and Tigrean cultural elements, though in the popular mind, and in practice, the former has always taken precedence in considerations of socioeconomic and political status.

entiations between Amhara and non-Amhara groups, and the respective occupational roles the latter were expected to fill in the developing urban system; it ascribed a rank order of low-status occupational roles to tribal groups farthest removed culturally and "racially" from the traditional norms of the upper-status Amhara. These, the landed aristocracy, were mostly direct descendants and affinal kin of Amhara nobility, many closely connected to the imperial family; and, as followers of Menilek, nearly all had been directly involved in founding the new state. For the sake of political expediency, however, a sizable minority of Wollo, Galla, and Tigrean families from chieftain lineages had been assimilated into the upper-status group through arranged marriages, large grants of land, and military-political appointments in Menilek's government.

Urban social ranking and status differentiation of the various ethnic groups crystallized during the formative period of the capital. Noble provincial governors and warlords, each commanding large personal armies, brought to the city and settled their entourages of war prisoners, indentured serfs, and slaves. Important chiefs are reported to have brought to the capital as many as 100,000, or 150,000 men at any one time, and as late as 1912 it was not uncommon for a chief to bring upwards of 50,000 men with him (Pankhurst, 1961: 114). Most, but by no means all, of this uprooted, landless urban population, consisting of prisoners of war and slaves, were drawn from the defeated tribes in southern Shoa province and the West Nile region. Land confiscated from conquered tribes in these areas, and more often than not the tribesmen themselves were considered personal property of the governing nobility; the wealth the nobles accumulated through these sources entrenched not only their own status positions but that of their descendants of the present generation. To make settlement possible for the masses of displaced persons brought to Addis Ababa, in such a manner that their labor would be readily accessible, Menilek granted the nobility extensive tracts of land, while smaller plots were given to his royal servants, thus creating several military camps (*sefers*) within the boundaries of the city. Each *sefer* settlement or "neighborhood" was distinguished almost exclusively by the ethnic group which inhabited it; the *sefers* bore such names as "Wollamo *sefer*," "Gurage *sefer*," and so forth. This is a demographic feature of not a few urban *sefers* today (cf. Pons 1969: 6-10).

The provincial feudal system around which rural life was organized provided the political-economic model for local organization in urban *sefers*. The titled "lord" owned the land and the *sefer* was known by his name; *Negus* Tekle Haimanot, *Ras* Wolde Giorghis, *Ras* Tessemma, *Dejazmach* Wubie, *Dejazmach* Wossensegged, *Fitawrari* Hapte Giorghis, *Neggadiras* Haile Giorghis are typical names of *sefers* whose founders held prominent positions in Menilek's government (Pankhurst, 1962: 40).[3] A "village chief" (*shum*), elected from among the *sefer* elders, acted on behalf of the community as chief spokesman to the lord, especially in petitioning for redress of grievances. The principal duties of the *shum* entailed collecting tribute and tithes and supplying corvée labor from the community as the *sefer's* contribution to the development of urban public works. This was also based on the provincial model, for rural and urban economic development employed variations of a common system of utilizing human and natural resources. The rural one, possibly of great antiquity, but certainly flourishing in the late nineteenth and early twentieth centuries, was the *guebar* system[4] of serfdom, whereby tribute and taxation of the peasantry supported both provincial and central administrations. The urban variation, a modification of the *guebar* system for developing the new urban complex, made massive use of corvée and slave laborers. The vast majority of these were uprooted non-Amhara tribesmen brought to Addis Ababa between 1890 and 1910 specifically for the construction of public buildings, roads, private housing, and later the Addis Ababa–Djibouti (French Somaliland) railroad, completed in 1917. Other laborers were conscripted to serve the households of upper-status families as hewers of wood, water carriers, and domestic servants; for example, Emperor Menilek is reported to have used as many as 20,000 Wallamo tribesmen in his private employ.

By 1910, urban social rank and status had crystallized in terms of two closely linked factors: ethnicity and occupation. From the distribution of ethnic groups then in Addis Ababa, as listed in Table 1 below, urban stratification of this period can be broadly discerned. Of the total urban population, fewer than 10 per cent were from "Amhara provinces," that is, Amhara and Godjam (Gojjam), though perhaps about one-third of the

3. Most of the titles (italicized) indicate one of the several orders of Amhara military ranking, the English equivalents being somewhat as follows: *Ras*–"chief," "head," or "general"; *Dejazmach*–"leader of the rear guard"; *Fitawrari*–"leader of the advanced guard"; *Negus*–"king"; *Neggadiras*–"chief of the market (traders)."

4. The *guebar* system which before 1890 supported the northern Ethiopian kingdoms, and later the central government, was vastly complex; full understanding remains a problem of historical and sociological interest. The most adequate description of the system, especially as it obtained in the southern provinces, is given by Perham (1947).

Table 1. Distribution of Urban Ethiopian Population: 1910[a]

Ethnic Group	*Number*	*Per cent of Total*
Gallas	20,000	30.8
[b]Shanqella, Beni Shangul, etc.	15,000	23.1
Shoans	15,000	23.1
[b]Wallamo	5,000	7.7
Amharas	3,000	4.6
Somali, Danakil, [b]Kaffa, etc.	3,000	4.6
[b]Gurage	2,000	3.1
Tigre	1,000	1.5
Godjam	1,000	1.5
Total	65,000	100.0

[a] After Merab (1921 II: 116).
[b] From Southwest Ethiopia and the West Nile region. For "Danakil" read "Adal," e.g. in Table 2 below.

population designated "Shoans" could also be included as Amharas. However, it is doubtful if all 9,000 "Amhara" then in Addis Ababa shared upper-status positions equally, for even today ethnic factors are not in every case the single determinants of social ranking. No doubt the greater percentage of urban Amhara did enjoy higher socioeconomic status than the numerically larger population of lower-status non-Amhara, who chiefly constituted the occupational categories of merchants, itinerant traders, peasants, craftsmen, common laborers, domestic servants, and slaves.

The close relationship between ethnic and occupational factors in the system of social stratification in Addis Ababa, which was manifest at the turn of the century, is emphasized in the following passage from the observations of an early traveler:

> In those northern provinces . . . the prevailing view that work was dishonourable prevented large-scale migration to the capital for the purpose of seeking employment in manual occupations though these people could not of course fully avoid it in their own country. The greater part of the free Addis Ababa labour force was therefore recruited from the central and southern provinces and was largely composed of Gallas and Gurages, as well as a certain number of Falashas, or Jews, who as in earlier times seemed willing to enter professions held in disrepute by other northern Ethiopians. Something like a third of the population . . . were made up of Shanqellas, Beni Shanguls and Wallamos, who were mainly servants and slaves. The Gallas, most of whom came from the

surrounding countryside, made up the final third of the population (Pankhurst, 1962: 53).

Since 1910, when the above observations were made, few fundamental changes have taken place either in the attitudes towards work held by urban Ethiopians from the northern provinces, or in the general urban role structure and system of social ranking. The principal means of manipulating status positions, that is, through extensive rural and urban land holdings and obtaining prominent government appointments, which are mainly upper-status Amhara prerogatives, still remain largely inaccessible to lower-status non-Amhara groups in urban Ethiopia.

In comparison with urban development of African towns south of the Sahara (Forde, 1956), urbanization in Addis Ababa has, in some ways, taken a different trend. European influences have neither directly controlled Ethiopia's economic system nor shaped the urban social and political institutions along the lines of Western models, as in the former dependent African territories. Urban industrial growth in Ethiopia lags conspicuously behind the expansion in town of cottage industries and market trade and its wide variety of services. There is yet to emerge an

Table 2. Distribution of Urban Ethiopian Population: 1952[a]

Ethnic Group	*Number*	*Per cent of Total*
Amharas	161,627	52.7
Gallas	56,755	18.5
[b]Gurage	52,951	17.2
[b]Wallamo	12,233	4.0
Tigre	6,202	2.0
[b]Kambatta	3,328	1.1
[b]Dorze	2,775	0.9
[b]Kaffa	2,490	0.8
Hamassien	2,164	0.7
[b]Gimira	1,499	0.5
[b]Gamu Goffa	1,259	0.41
[b]Shanqella	1,244	0.40
[b]Kulo Konta	1,143	0.37
Somali	444	0.20
Adari (Harari)	429	0.15
Adal (Afar)	216	0.07
Total	306,759	100.00

[a] After Wang (1957: 57). Based on 1952 census report: Ministry of Interior.
[b] From southwest Ethiopia and the West Nile region.

Ethiopian equivalent to the Central African Copperbelt town complex; the handcrafts of potters, weavers, tanners, tinkers, silver- and goldsmiths, wood craftsmen, basketmakers, etc., are as essential to the daily activities of the urban masses in Ethiopia as to rural tribesmen. Addis Ababa is still today a vast non-industrial urban complex of heterogeneous ethnic groups; it is a collection of ethnic *sefers* with highly transient populations.

No very reliable census data are available from which accurate estimates of the rate of urban growth since 1890 can be made. But on the basis of the urban population estimates given in Tables 1 and 2, for the period between 1910 and 1952, urban growth increased approximately 472 per cent, or an average of 11.23 per cent annually. At any given time of the year the urban demographic pattern is altered by the migration habits of members of different tribal groups entering the city. Young people come mainly seeking education or odd jobs, whereas the majority of rural adults come because of a variety of social, religious, and politico-legal problems which can only be settled in town. They come in search of employment, to seek spiritual blessings at sacred shrines, or to obtain medical attention, while many hope to settle legal matters through the courts of higher appeal; such legal matters might ultimately necessitate petitioning the emperor directly. Some rural folk never return to their villages after either satisfying their personal problems or failing to settle them. Lacking job skills and often urban kin, many rural migrants eventually drift into begging alongside the aged, the infirm, and the homeless.[5]

Each of the sixteen urban ethnic groups represented in Addis Ababa and listed in Table 2 above speak distinct languages; some are more closely related than others, but most are mutually unintelligible. The national language, Amharic, which is also the *lingua franca* for non-Amhara groups, cuts across polyglotism, thus providing common ground for communication, especially in the urban area. Tribal dialects, however, are commonly spoken within the closed circles of urban ethnic communities, and to observe offspring of third-generation immigrants speaking fluently the tribal vernaculars of their parents is not unusual. While many of their predecessors came to Addis Ababa as military adventurers or under conditions of servitude, immigrants today are lured to the city be-

5. A survey conducted in 1958 on "beggars in Addis Ababa" disclosed that, apart from the aged and infirm, the majority of beggars had been made homeless as a result of the Italian occupation of Ethiopia (1935-41). This was chiefly true of beggars from southwest Ethiopia formerly attached to upper-status families who were either killed or fled the country. Of the 100 beggars in the sample, only 2 were Gurage.

cause it is the political, economic, and religious center of the empire; all of the five main road arteries extending into the hinterlands, the roads that migrants travel on foot or by rural transportation, radiate from a single point: Addis Ababa.

The demographic and social composition of *sefers* in Addis Ababa is strikingly like that of Ethiopia's rural villages. Kinship and ethnic factors rather than social class factors usually underlie residential settlement. Unlike most African towns, in Addis Ababa there are no neighborhoods occupied exclusively by one racial group; Europeans, Asians, Arabs, and non-Ethiopian Africans, who in all represent only 2.7 per cent of the urban population, live dispersed throughout the city. Social interaction between urban ethnic groups is limited by discriminatory factors, for outside the context of wage employment situations where individuals of different ethnic groups are thrown into contact, other fields of social relations are drawn primarily by kinship and ethnic boundaries, even where the European and Asian communities are concerned. In the main, social interaction, between Ethiopian lower-status groups especially, is conditioned by the different occupational roles which they play and which, in turn, bring them into varying networks of social relations, some competitive, others not. And it is within this field of urban social and economic relations that the significance of the occupational role as a factor promoting urban ethnicity can be seen in relation to the Gurage.

Gurage Patterns of Urban Tribalism

Urbanization of the Gurage began in 1889. Many were then brought to Addis Ababa as defeated tribesmen, and though some migrated as free laborers in the early 1900's, as late as 1925 most Gurage were indentured serfs and slaves in the *sefer* of *Fitawrari* Hapte Giorghis. But before turning to the patterns of urban ethnicity which subsequently developed among Gurage town dwellers and migrants, as manifested in forms of neighborhood groupings, labor undertakings, voluntary associations, and rural-urban relationships, I shall describe briefly the major features of Gurage tribal organization and those rural factors which have stimulated the migration of Gurage to town.

The Rural Background

The Gurage, linguistically related to the Amhara and Tigrean peoples, are settled agriculturalists who number about 500,000 persons and inhabit the semi-fertile mountainous fringes of the Central Ethiopian Plateau.[6] Broadly speaking their country lies between the Awash and Great Ghibie rivers, which form the northern and western boundaries, respectively, of the Gurage territory. The only form of modern communication between the tribal area and the rest of Ethiopia is the Addis Ababa–Jimma road, which intersects the western side of the territory. Rural transportation service narrows the normal 130-mile three-to-four-day walking distance some migrants travel between the countryside and Addis Ababa to a matter of six to eight hours by bus or lorry. In modes of production and social organization the Gurage form the easternmost extension of the Ensete Culture Complex in southwest Ethiopia (Shack, 1963a), the distinguishing cultural feature of the Cushitic Sidamo and related peoples. The staple food crop, intensively cultivated, is *Ensete edulis,* commonly called the "false banana"; but mixed farming of a few vegetables, cereals, pulses, and the rearing of cattle supplement the staple *ensete.* Cash crop cultivation is a minor activity, limited chiefly to the growing of coffee and *chat*[7] on minute plots which seldom exceed a few square meters. Within the village, the extended family and lineal kin form the basis around which communal agricultural and domestic activities are organized and for mustering financial assistance when social and economic crises arise.

The Gurage social and political system is typical of segmentary lineage organizations of shallow genealogical depth found elsewhere in Africa. The homestead and village are at the lowest levels of lineage segmentation; at the upper limits stand named patrilineal exogamous clans wherein political authority is vested in clan chieftainship. Gurage tribes are built up on the aggregate number of politically autonomous clans. Tribal affiliation, as with that of lineage and clan, is cross-cut by the several core rituals of the centralized religious system. Traditional religious ceremonies are the most important occasions for tribal gatherings, attracting Copts, Muslims, and a minority of Catholics. Marriage is commonly patrilocal, and polygyny is the norm even for Copts. However, since co-wives

6. Here and throughout this paper, for the sake of brevity, I refer to Gurage in the tribal district in the widest sense, ignoring internal tribal groupings. Field research among rural and urban Gurage has been primarily among the Western Gurage tribes: the Chaha, Ezha, Muher, Ennemor, Gyeto, Aklil, and Walani-Woriro. The Eastern Gurage tribal groupings consist of the Sodu, Silte, Urbarag, and Masqan. An analysis of ecology and social structure of the Western Gurage is in Shack (1965).

7. *Chat* (*Catha edulis* or *Celastrus edulis*) is a bush crop, the leaves of which are chewed almost habitually by Muslim Ethiopians for the pleasant insomnia and slight intoxication effected. *Chat* is one of the Gurage's principal cash crops.

are normally settled in separate villages, land shortage today has reduced polygyny from a once-common practice to a now common ideal. Indeed, the distinguishing demographic feature of the tribal lands is the high density of population; in some districts the average exceeds 240 persons per square mile, which by African standards of land use is considerable. Arable land to relieve population pressure and increase cash crop production to a profitable income level is scarce throughout Gurageland. These factors, coupled with new tax burdens since the Land Tax Act of 1929, have cumulatively generated demands for ready cash which the Gurage can meet only through wage labor migration.

For most Gurage men labor migration is a seasonal undertaking. The peak of migration is reached during the slack period of agricultural work when young men, single and married, are relieved from homestead confinement. The pattern by which some African migrant laborers sooner or later become permanent town dwellers after several successful seasons of short-term urban employment is similar for the Gurage (cf. Schapera, 1947; Prothero, 1957). Gurage migrant laborers who have been drained off by steady urban employment become the townsmen through whom rural kin ties are extended, and the network of rural-urban kin relationships is one aspect of urban ethnicity. However, in terms of the overall pattern of Gurage migratory labor, three categories of migrants can be briefly distinguished: "permanent," "seasonal," and "temporary." To Group I belongs the permanent migrant, with steady urban employment. If he is monogamous, his family usually lives in town; if polygynous, one wife remains in the tribal area. In Group II is the seasonal migrant, who migrates regularly for six to eight months (usually between mid-February to mid-October) after harvesting and planting ends, with semi-permanent or day-to-day employment in town. If he is married, his family never migrates. Group III includes the temporary migrant, who migrates occasionally, that is, whenever the opportunity arises for homestead responsibilities to be assumed by a relative, thus freeing the migrant to spend a few weeks in a wage-earning center; this pattern of migration is most common among young unmarried men.[8] Migration from the tribal area to rural provincial towns is mainly undertaken by men in Groups II and III, whereas by and large Group I migration is to Addis Ababa, the principal center for wage employment. Group I migrants, the townsmen, are also the source through whom potential employment is made possible

8. I summarize here only the essential features of Gurage labor migration; a more exhaustive report is in preparation.

for Group II and III migrants. But migrants in all categories usually return to their villages for the annual tribal religious festivals.

Urban Settlement Patterns

Urban Gurage are mainly concentrated in Tekle Haimanot municipal district (*wereda*), which incorporates, among others, Hapte Giorghis *sefer*, the original settlement of Gurage in Addis Ababa. Since 1910 the Gurage community has increased from about 3 per cent of the total urban population (Table 1) to 17.2 per cent of the 1952 estimated 306,759 urban Ethiopians (Table 2).[9]

In the context of the discussion later, on the participation of Gurage in the Amhara-dominated urban cultural process, it is necessary to note briefly the sociological significance of the reported increase in population size of urban Amhara since 1910, for this growth bears upon the question of urban status mobility. The urban Amhara population increase of about 262 per cent for the same period, from about 13.8 per cent of the 1910 total to 52.7 per cent of the 1952 total, throws some doubt upon the statistical reliability of "Amhara" as an ethnic category. It seems doubtful that Amhara labor migration would be the single factor to account for this sharp increase—essentially because of the traditional disdain northern Ethiopians have for manual work, which for non-skilled persons is the principal source of urban wage earning. It is more probable that a sizable percentage of urban non-Amhara have claimed "Amhara" origin in census reporting, particularly persons of mixed tribal parentage who very often disregard the father's tribal affiliation if it happens to be other than Amhara. Thus in certain urban situations, "Amhara" becomes a sociological rather than an ethnic category of grouping; any person who claims to be Amhara and

9. The Wang report is of considerable historical and socio-demographic importance to the study of population growth in Addis Ababa. Although the data were published more than a decade ago, it was the first as well as the last census giving the distribution of ethnic groups in Addis Ababa since Mérab's figures of 1921. Ethiopian government policy presently prohibits reporting an ethnic breakdown of the urban population. Hence, in the most recent official municipal census, the distribution of urban dwellers is listed accordingly:

Ethiopian Nationals	430,907
Foreigners	11,824
Not Stated	997
Total	443,728

(Source: *Report on Census Population: Municipality of Addis Ababa.* 10-11 September, 1961.)

to whom others react as though he were an Amhara, is by definition an "Amhara."

However, the steady increase of Gurage urban migration and settlement since the 1930's is reflected in their rural and urban areas. In a village surveyed by the present writer in 1958, of the 61 adult men normally present in 41 homesteads, 46 per cent were away in labor centers; and brief observations in other villages disclosed even higher percentages, with no apparent negative effects on community life (cf. Watson, 1958; van Velsen, 1961). Similarly, an urban survey conducted in 1962 in *Dejazmach* Dubale *sefer,* in Tekla Haimanot district, indicated that 73 per cent of the residents were Gurage families and three-fourths had migrated between 1930 and 1950.[10] As already mentioned, the demographic and social composition of urban *sefers* takes a form characteristic of rural villages, and the Gurage community in Dubale illustrates this.

As is true of most "Gurage *sefers,*" the Gurage inhabitants of Dubale migrated from the same tribal district; all 73 household heads are immigrants from Soddu, a tribal district in Eastern Gurageland. The composition of Dubale households approximates to three patrilocal forms of residence which commonly obtain in the tribal districts: single elementary families, extended families of father and father's brother, and families consisting of the children of other relatives. Only 7.3 per cent of Dubale men admitted to being polygamous, which is considerably less than the rural norm. With one exception, the tribal pattern of settling co-wives in separate villages is upheld in Dubale: three co-wives live in Soddu; one lives in Sidamo, a tribal province neighboring Soddu; three co-wives are settled in other urban *sefers;* one wife lives in Dubale but not with her co-partner; the whereabouts of two co-wives were not disclosed. Although marriage instability in the tribal districts is reported to be high, I have no reliable figures to support this. However, about 10 per cent of Dubale married women above the age of fifteen had been divorced. The normal pattern of marriage for Gurage townsmen, which holds for Dubale men, is that they invariably select their wives from the tribal area, they uphold the rules of clan exogamy, and village elders negotiate the marriage contract, with the ceremony taking place in the village. This is also the rule for prominent educated Gurage. On the other hand, intertribal marriages initiated by Gurage townsmen occur infrequently, but the attractiveness of Gurage women according to standards of the high-

10. Data reported here are based partly on an unpublished survey conducted by a socio-medical team comparing nutritional standards of migrant groups.

land Semitic peoples has long made them desirable as wives by men of other groups. This has led to a relatively high degree of female out-group marriages, and it affords many women a second opportunity for marriage; but on the whole few Gurage women ever contract upper-status marriages.

Neighborhood settlement patterns also affect the character of extra-kin associational groupings of town Gurage. Drinking and chatting, the principal forms of recreation, usually take place in Gurage-owned establishments frequented by close kinsmen and clansmen of the proprietor. Here tribal dialects of Guraginä are spoken publicly, whereas in other social contexts Amharic is the language of conversation. The social atmosphere of town bars, as in rural situations when men gather to drink, has the effect of equalizing status differences between drinking companions; town bars create a sense of belonging even for the recent, often barefoot, migrant. Such places also provide a social setting for exchanging gossip, passing on messages from rural folk to town kin, and transacting business. In not a few Gurage-owned bars, weekly *Iqub* meetings are held; the *Iqub* is one of the important types of rural voluntary "self-help" associations for financial assistance which Gurage now frequently organize in town.[11] Town bars attract both temporary migrants and seasoned immigrants, many of whom congregate nightly expecting to meet and form associations with fellow Gurage, or to obtain assistance with personal problems. Urban recreation centers and *sefers* alike provide the atmosphere for fusing the social and economic links in rural-urban kinship and

11. In the organization of an *Iqub* each member contributes an equal sum of money weekly, twice monthly, or on some agreed-upon regular schedule. The total is drawn by lottery according to the scheme of contributions until each member has won a drawing of the total *Iqub*. No member can receive a winning twice before each other member earns a draw. *Iqub* lotteries range from those formed by shoe-shiners who each contribute 10 cents to those of merchants who each pool $100 or more. Joining an *Iqub* provides for many Gurage the initial capital for starting a business in town. In the rural area, nearly every village has an *Iqub* for enabling a member to purchase additional livestock or wood for house construction, or to raise money for giving a large feast. The Gurage *Iqub* is similar to the *Nanamei Akpee,* or "mutual help" society in Accra, Ghana (see Little, 1957: 584). On other rural and urban self-help associations in Ethiopia, see Pankhurst and Eshete (1958) and Shack (1959a). No figures are available on the number of *Iqub* or other types of self-help associations formed by urban Gurage, or the extent to which associational membership cuts across *sefer* and kinship groupings. Broadly speaking: (a) *Iqubs* are frequently short-lived, being formed to achieve a specific aim, after which their membership is dissolved; (b) in every *sefer* one or more small *Iqubs* are usually found; (c) as a rule, the more ambitious the aims of the association, the greater the tendency for its membership to include persons having different clan and tribal affiliations.

friendship relations. And in rural and urban areas Gurage social relationships based on kinship have an economic coefficient: rural kinship behavior is a model of economic behavior in land activities; urban kinship behavior is a model of economic behavior in labor undertakings.

Urban Labor Undertakings

Urban occupational roles, as I have pointed out, are differentiated according to status and prestige models based on traditional Amhara sociocultural norms. In the general order of Amhara social ranking, high status is ascribed to administrative, ecclesiastical, and military roles, while low status, not necessarily in the following order, is ascribed to merchants, skilled and semi-skilled artisans, craftsmen, hawkers, domestic servants, and manual laborers. By and large most urban labor undertakings of individuals of lower-status ethnic groups, such as the Gurage, fall within the second category, and over the years the particular ethnic group as a whole has become identified with certain occupational specializations; for example, like the Dorze with weaving and the Wallamo with building construction. In the same way, market trade, cottage industries, domestic work, and manual labor are mainly, but not exclusively, the undertakings of urban Gurage, and they are more extensively engaged in market trade and the variety of services linked to it than any other Ethiopian urban group.

In Tekle Haimanot, the central market district (*merkato*), the Gurage total 43 per cent of the population (109,934). Here market goods and services upon which the overwhelming majority of urban Ethiopians depend flow primarily through Gurage merchants who, in the last decade, have nearly replaced the Arab and Indian small shopkeepers. With larger resources of working capital at their disposal than most Gurage merchants have, Arabs and Indians, as well as Europeans, still retain economic control over the vast amount of urban import and export trade. At the level of petty trade, however, Gurage merchants in the *merkato* and elsewhere in town get the better of competition with non-Gurage merchants, as they do in their markets in the tribal districts. For that matter, the only tribal area in Ethiopia, at least the only one that I am aware of, where itinerant Arab traders are not found, is Gurageland! In town, market goods are linked to other sectors of the urban economy chiefly by way of three Gurage channels of trade: to small Gurage-owned shops and *kiosks* spread throughout the city; to Gurage house-to-house merchants of sundry items and foodstuffs; to itinerant Gurage traders servicing the rural districts.

Gurage urban undertakings in trade or wage employment closely approximate the tribal pattern of the sex division of labor. Gurage men in town are typically occupied as meat sellers to Coptic and Muslim Ethiopians, merchants of produce, cereals, and pulses, bakers of European-type bread, owners of drinking houses, tailors of Ethiopian and European dress for men and women, weavers of traditional cloth, shoemakers, craftsmen of general leather goods including horse and mule saddles and trappings, mattress-makers, cane and wooden furniture craftsmen, and tinkers. Some haul wood and water. Gurage boys in particular are hawkers of sundry goods, shoe-shiners, news vendors, and food peddlers; older men are often skilled craftsmen in construction of stone houses and traditional *chiqa* (mud and straw) houses, still the most common type of urban dwelling. Many others are porters. And Gurage men often undertake work in town, like the Amhara, which they disdain in the tribal area, such as tanning and smithing, without any apparent loss of status or fear of social ostracism at home (Shack 1966: 8). As compared with other urban groups, few Gurage are employed in lower-grade municipal civil service, e.g. clerks, tax collectors, meter readers, and policemen. In part this is because of the general lack of formal education attained by most Gurage, and in part because Gurage are more attracted to labor undertakings where they have direct daily control over their earnings, even though small, which in turn can be manipulated for higher profit. Wage employment practically eliminates this.

On the periphery of Addis Ababa, Gurage tenant farmers on land owned by upper-status families are the main growers of European varieties of produce; this in turn is distributed and marketed by Gurage merchants and street peddlers in town. In some cases the farming and selling of produce is an extended family enterprise. So also with the vast eucalyptus forests which extend over the plateaux surrounding the city and are the principal source of wood for fuel and building construction; here tree felling, hauling, and reselling the lumber is a Gurage monopoly, with the capital for purchasing the rights to fell a plot of trees jointly invested by a kin group. At another level, intratribal monopolies of certain sectors of the urban economy, which are similar to those of the rural economic system, are reflected in special Gurage undertakings. Skilled masons and stone-dressers are Ennemor Gurage; the trade in spices, peppers, and *chat* are near monopolies of Silte and Soddu Gurage; market trade in fresh produce is the province of Ezha Gurage; Chaha Gurage are predominantly small-shop merchants in the *merkato* and elsewhere in the city.

Gurage women in town are primarily petty traders in spices, butter, *ensete*-food, and brewers of local beer and mead drinks; these are typical cash-earning activities for women in the tribal districts. Although prostitution is now often engaged in along with selling drinks, rarely does this occur among Gurage women in the tribal area. Gurage women have also created new sources of cash income by producing the paraphernalia required by Copts in their religious services, such as incense, candles, and prayer beads. They bake Amhara *enjera*-bread and Gurage *ensete*-bread, make pottery, and weave baskets. And both sexes of all ages are engaged extensively in market trade, men principally in the *merkato*, women in the numerous small street markets found in every *sefer*.

Individually owned enterprises are far less common among urban Gurage than joint ownership by a kin group. As with produce farmers and lumber merchants, part of the shopkeeper's initial capital is usually invested by rural kinsmen from savings accumulated from cash crop sales or earnings from wage labor migration. One Ennemor lineage, for example, is proprietor of four meat shops, and lineage members rotate periods of work in the town shops, so that some of them always remain in the village for tending the homestead and agriculture. Another lineage in Chaha has progressively invested in a leather craft shop, a bar-restaurant, and two clothing shops. Such cases are not the norm for most Gurage business undertakings, however. Few of their enterprises require large capital investment, they seldom expand beyond the small shop level, and most of their trade involves petty cash sales. But cumulatively Gurage merchants, and laborers as well, gain a considerable share of the expenditures of other urban Ethiopians, who themselves usually make only small purchases of foodstuffs and inexpensive non-luxury goods on a day-to-day basis. Urban kin group enterprises provide a wide range of work opportunities, skilled and non-skilled, for migrant and resident Gurage. The employment of one's kinsmen and utilizing kin ties to further economic interests generally account for the success of Gurage in competitive urban market trade and wage employment.

There is a direct correlation between urban relations and potential employment opportunities, on the one hand, and the low ratio of destitute urban Gurage, as compared with other temporary migrant and immigrant Ethiopian groups, on the other. Few town Gurage ever resort to begging; and this stands out sharply against the fact that asking for alms in the names of patron saints is institutionalized and sanctioned by the Coptic Church, and begging is a common refuge sought by many of the urban unemployed. Temporary unemployment of individual Gurage does occur from time to time and not infrequently, although it is seldom lasting. Urban ties, however, are not solely responsible for the relative economic security of Gurage townsmen. Of equal importance are Gurage attitudes towards undertaking employment that is disdained by other Ethiopians, especially the Northerners, as lacking status. No more graphic example of this could be cited than the fact that until nearly a decade ago, the word *kuli* (coolie) in Addis Ababa was synonymous with Gurage!

Urban Voluntary Associations

Gurage voluntary associations are one manifestation of rural-urban ties. But here they are separated in the context from the latter, which I discuss in the following section, because of their particular relationships to the problem of urban ethnicity.

The few societies that town Gurage organize for the purpose of savings and burial serve the same fundamental function as mutual benefit societies in West African towns described by Banton (1957) and Little (1957, 1960). Gurage have formed other types of "self-help" associations, however, which have a more direct relationship to urban ethnicity. These associations are organized by town Gurage not to better the urban conditions of fellow immigrants, as in the case of West African associations, but, on the contrary, to improve the living standards of rural kinsmen. Some of the rural improvement schemes undertake the building of health stations, schools, and roads in the tribal districts. The organizing committees which initiate and pursue these projects are formed by urban Gurage, and though they draw upon the assistance of rural tribesmen, the urban Gurage contribute the greater financial shares. The most ambitious programs organized so far involve building roads in the Eastern and Western tribal districts at respective costs of Eth. $2 million and Eth. $1 million (U.S. $800,000 and U.S. $400,000).[12] To underwrite these programs financially, town Gurage in hired labor pledge contributions of one month's salary, those self-employed the net profit of one month's earnings, and rural Gurage are assessed contributions on the basis of the size of their land and livestock holdings. Political and ritual dignitaries from the tribal area frequently attend weekly town meetings to encourage

12. An exhaustive account of the role of voluntary associations among urban Soddu Gurage in road construction schemes and other activities is presented by Gadamu (1972).

urban Gurage to make contributions; ritual dignitaries often add in the course of their solicitations threats of spelling curses on townsmen who seem reluctant to honor their pledges. Likewise, prominent town Gurage attend tribal meetings for the same purpose, and by appearing in the company of local chiefs they symbolize the identity that townsmen retain with rural kinsmen. Even town Gurage whose ties with the tribal area have practically ceased to exist in other ways assume a moral and economic responsibility in promoting rural self-help schemes.

Voluntary associations in West Africa have been described as serving diversified roles in the urbanization process (Little, 1957: 593): mutual aid and benefit, occupational and professional, craft guild, entertainment and recreational are typical ones. Little notes that these urban associations help the West African immigrant adjust to the more cosmopolitan ethos of the city, and they constitute as well a cultural bridge for the tribal individual which spans the rural and urban social universes. These appear not to be functions of Gurage voluntary associations, particularly those of the self-help type described above, and they have no specific urbanizing role to play for recent immigrants. Nor do they function in Wirth's (1938) terms as "fictional kinship groups" which cross-cut, or substitute for, urban kinship ties. For though the Gurage tribal kinship system with all of its social implications has not been transplanted to the urban area without alterations, the modified and reduced form which the rural kinship system has taken in the adjustment to urban conditions has neither weakened nor ceased to function among town Gurage. In short, Gurage voluntary associations which aim at improving the social and welfare conditions of tribal kin in the hinterland express two interrelated aspects of urban ethnicity. On the one hand, they represent a partial social and psychological detachment of a significant number of the association members from the urban society, within which complete sociocultural integration has not yet been achieved; on the other hand, they represent an idealization of the social and economic security that most urban Gurage endeavor to achieve, a security that is ultimately to be obtained by investment in the tribal land. Gurage voluntary self-help associations institutionalize urban ties with the tribal system.

Rural-Urban Relationships

Apart from the relationship between rural-urban kin ties in economic undertakings already noted, the values that urban Gurage attach to clan and tribal membership are expressed in other ways. Most town Gurage maintain a dual stake in the tribal area, in terms of investment in the patrilineal land and concern for the conduct of tribal affairs. They frequently send money and goods home. They buy additional land in the tribal district when possible and increase their livestock holdings. With additional savings some urban Gurage even erect an extra-large thatched hut on the village homestead, a traditional symbol of status, though they have no intention of ever living there. When clan chiefs hold important councils to pass new laws or to amend old ones, or to decide on serious offenses of theft, property damage, or homicide, urban clansmen are concerned; if a close kinsman is directly involved in the issue, they return to the clan district, take part in the litigation, and make contributions towards fines levied by the tribal council. Equally townsmen expect moral and financial support, if need be, from rural clansmen when one of their members runs foul of town law, an expectation which is usually fulfilled.

In this regard, Gluckman (1960: 58; 1961: 70) has stressed that the urbanized African is outside the tribe but not beyond the influence of the tribe, and that while in town he comes under different political authorities. This holds true no less for town Gurage; but at the same time their tribal political system is extended into town by way of those Gurage who maintain tribal citizenship, and town Gurage are not entirely beyond the influence of tribal authority. One tenet of the Gurage tribal politico-legal system is that all clan members are held equally responsible for any infraction of tribal law committed by a related clansman, whether the dispute is between members of the same clan or between Gurage of different clans or tribes. All clan members are obliged to defend him; and even succeeding generations are held liable until retribution is eventually made to an injured person of the same or a different clan. In the few cases of which I have record, and I take these not to be isolated instances, village property of townsmen who refused assistance to rural kin involved in clan disputes was partially confiscated by clansmen at home to help compensate the victim. Rural clansmen took this action even though the town Gurage was associated with the issue only indirectly, by virtue of his lineal relationship with one of the disputants (cf. Schwab, 1966: 104, 108). Other examples could be cited where the issues concerned homicide, theft, property damage, and conflicts over marriage. Without pressing the point further, there is sufficient evidence on the basis of Gurage rural-urban political relations to suggest that Gluckman's proposition could be reconsidered; and comparative studies might also demonstrate this to be the case with other societies who, like the Gurage, are organized on segmentary principles and have representative groups in towns.

Town Gurage are under dual systems of authority and social control: the one, tribal, regulates their behavior in terms of tribal norms and values insofar as the field of social relations in which town Gurage become involved with one another belongs to the rural socio-political system; this would include a range of social situations, from interlineal and clan disputes over land to theft and homicide. The other, urban, regulates their behavior in terms of the legal codes of the larger "Ethiopian" authority system in which town Gurage become involved in a different network of socio-political relations with fellow Gurage and other townsmen as well. Here the situations of interaction might range, for example, from paying municipal taxes to paying court fines for clashes with another townsman, or committing misdemeanors that are settled under the jurisdiction of urban courts and not under local councils composed of village elders and clan chiefs (cf. Epstein, 1958: 234). While, at first glance, the dual authority systems might appear to pose a contradiction of roles, from the point of view of town Gurage the systems are functionally operative, even though the Gurage may not always so consider them. Town Gurage depend upon the tribal authority system not only to regulate their domestic relations in the hinterland, but also to protect the land and property interests in which they have continually invested during a prolonged residence in town. To turn to the Ethiopian politico-legal system to settle conflicts in which town Gurage become involved with kin over issues that in their very nature are tribal and belong to the hinterland (issues, for example, of marriage and inheritance, or of interclan dispute) is tantamount to tribal treason; few risk endangering their standing in the tribal community in this way. On the other hand, the tribal authority system does not intrude into the domain of the urban authority system to the extent that it becomes involved in attempting to regulate the behavior of town Gurage in situations that clearly fall within the sphere of social control in the larger urban social system.

Gurage townsmen, because they *are* townsmen and not rural tribesmen, can opt to stand outside the binding network of traditional social and political clan relations and the ritual sanctions which enforce them. But by and large town Gurage do not; they retain clan membership and the concomitant obligations of tribal citizenship. There are two reasons, I would suggest, for this: first, moral suasion and a sense of duty; second, the important social, economic, and psychological security which obtains from clan and tribal membership. The combined effect of these is to reinforce the ties that town Gurage seek to maintain with rural affairs (cf. Watson, 1958: 8).

Lastly, the religious behavior of town Gurage as an expression of rural-urban relations deserves to be mentioned. Annual tribal rituals hold as much attraction for townsmen of long standing as for tribesmen. The compulsion to fulfill spiritual obligations no doubt provides the motivation for some Gurage to return home and participate in village religious festivities. For other Gurage, such occasions enable them to renew social contacts with rural kinsmen, when there is an invariable ritual of gift-giving; the economic success of townsmen is often indicated by the kinds of gifts presented to relatives at home. A case in point is the mid-September Christian *Mäsqal* ("finding of the Holy Cross") celebration, the largest religious ceremony in Gurageland, which was so even before the conversion of many Gurage to Christianity. Most men and women who are able to return to participate in village rituals; the bull slaughtered for the occasion is nearly always bought by returning kinsmen, or at least they bear a considerable share of the cost. The exodus of town Gurage to their tribal districts at *Mäsqal* is on a sufficiently large scale to necessitate provision of extra rural transportation; the increase in market sales owing to the purchase of gifts in the days preceding *Mäsqal* also indicates this. A similar increase in gift buying and departure of Muslim Gurage takes place annually for the pilgrimage to the shrine held in trust by their prophet. The tribute he is presented at the *Mulid* (birthday of the prophet-leader) celebration in part symbolizes the economic success of Muslim Gurage in town, for which their spiritual leader is given much credit. Annual tribal cult ceremonies in honor of traditional deities also attract a considerable number of urban men and women. Those Gurage unable to attend these, as well as the traditional feasts designed to placate their relations by marriage, will usually send gifts home. In another expression of urban religious behavior, some migrant Gurage make a ritual covenant (*gurda*) with a fellow migrant before leaving the village. The ritually binding element of the covenant calls for aid to be given by either party of the contract should the other suffer a personal or financial crisis while in town (Shack, 1963b).

Gurage women in town also keep up their religious ties with the village. They return to the village periodically (perhaps more frequently than men) for a variety of ritual needs which cannot be met satisfactorily in town. They consult ritual agents, renew spiritual requests at village shrines with petitions regarding fertility, and participate in possession cult rituals which have a bearing upon the stability of their marriage. In this regard, it would be of sociological interest to ascertain the frequency with which urban Gurage women feel compelled to undergo village rituals, and the ways in which their spiritual petitions differ, if at all, from rural Gurage women.

The Cultural Process of Ethiopian Urbanization

Urbanization, as Mitchell (1956: 695) has suggested, implies "participation in social relations in urban areas and the development of modes of behavior peculiar to urban situations." By extension, this also implies that the particular sociocultural patterns of an urban society affect to a great extent the character and scope of social relationships between individuals and groups, these relationships being expressed very often in political and economic situations. In this final section I shall view the Ethiopian process of urbanization in terms of this proposition, with specific reference to the Gurage and lower-status urban ethnic groups in general.

I have attempted to show so far that urban status positions of ethnic groups are determined on the basis of occupational roles which are scaled in terms of the dominant political and economic positions occupied by upper-status Amhara. The tendency is for the Gurage and lower-status ethnic groups generally to participate only in specialized kinds of urban economic undertakings, such as trade, marketing, and certain categories of non-prestigious labor; and they tend also to manifest fewer of the normative sociocultural modes of behavior fashioned by the dominant group. To put this another way, when ethnic groups are at the same time "ethnic-occupational groups," or ethnic groups who participate chiefly in a specialized sector of the urban occupational structure, the result is what Steward (1955: 43) has described as "differential levels of sociocultural integration." The urbanization process, then, is not only a product of diverse social relations between status groups, but it is also influenced by two concomitant variables of sociocultural integration: (a) the extent to which lower-status ethnic or "subcultural groups" have access to and/or reject the integrating norms of the dominant cultural groups; and (b) the extent to which the dominant cultural group limits the assimilation of subcultural groups by making inaccessible the sociocultural norms of integration.

Let us recapitulate the essential factors underlying urban status differentiation between Amhara and Gurage in terms of the argument just advanced. The manifest forms of Gurage urban ethnicity represent a mode of socioeconomic adaptation to culturally defined low-status occupational roles which the upper-status dominant group considers undesirable. The historical circumstances of military conquest and subsequent political domination of the Gurage resulted in the subordination of Gurage cultural norms and values to those of the Amhara; from the Amhara point of view, those of the Gurage were, by implication, "inferior." Once this sociocultural cleavage between Amhara and Gurage was established, it sustained itself in three ways: by the different values each group placed on its own culture; by the Amhara socioeconomic barriers against upward status movement; by the socioeconomic insecurity which Gurage experience in the urban situation. The Amhara-Gurage sociocultural cleavage supports Gluckman's (1958: 63) analysis of the cleavage in the Zulu-white social system, and even though these two systems make use of different categorical distinctions, the social function of the cleavage is identical in both cases. The Zulu-white cleavage is racial, whereas the Amhara-Gurage cleavage is set against an ethnic (cultural) background, for both Amhara and Gurage have Semitic origins, and no prominent physical or "racial" distinctions set one group apart from the other. But, to paraphrase Gluckman, the Amhara and Gurage set equal value on their respective cultures, that is, each group values its own culture higher; and these values tend constantly to increase, since they express the major sociocultural, political, and economic separation.

In the urban social system, lower-status non-Amhara who seek upward mobility must do so within the Amhara cultural framework of norms and values, and the process in which this takes place is commonly termed "Amharaization" by urban Ethiopians. As a cultural model, Amharaization can be distinguished from "Westernization" or "Europeanization," since these processes denote changes in individual and group modes of behavior in consequence of adopting Western or European sociocultural norms and values associated with education, technology, language, religion, and material goods. Most urban towns in Africa have undergone change in this direction. In constrast, in India and Japan, "Sanskritization" and "Shintoization" respectively might be considered cultural models of change comparable to the Ethiopian process. Amharaization differs from Westernization even more, on the grounds that the Amhara cultural model with its own set of norms and values has been adopted, and though "foreign" elements have been incorporated, the general trend of sociocultural change has been away from a Western model, and the Amhara model has shaped the structure of the urban social system.

Western forms of culture have not been rejected entirely by upper-status Amhara, however; in fact, eating and drinking Western foods and beverages, wearing Western dress, driving automobiles, reading Western periodicals and enjoying Western music and dance, building modern stone housing for personal use or lease, as well as working under Western bureaucratic institutions in government and private enterprises all attest to this. The overriding factor is that the more conspicuous forms of Western culture in urban Ethiopia have been reinterpreted, wherever possible, in the Amhara culture context, and they convey status and prestige among urban Ethiopians not because they are Western *per se*, but chiefly because dominant Amhara values are now associated with their use. In this regard, upper-status urban Amhara in particular, and Ethiopian townsmen on the whole, stand in sharp contrast to the people of Gwelo in Central Africa, who are said to have retained no status symbols of African origin that confer prestige, but to have accepted indiscriminately all accessible European status symbols (Schwab, 1961: 141). Similarly, Mitchell and Epstein (1959: 33) have pointed out that in African communities on the Copperbelt the concept of "Western civilization" or "the European way of life" provides a scale by which African townsmen there are able to measure prestige and so to ascribe social status to the many diverse individuals with whom they are thrown into association. This is not the case in Addis Ababa. The notion of a "civilized way of life" held by urban Ethiopians is not scaled in terms of being more or less "Europeanized" as it is among Africans on the Copperbelt or those in Stanleyville (Pons, 1956: 640; 1969: 257-74), for instance. The concept of "civilized" among urban Ethiopians, or as they commonly phrase it with the Amharic term, *silltane*, is associated with the obvious traits of Amhara culture, or Amharaization, which alone carries with it status and prestige.

Briefly, the social and cultural symbols of behavior broadly characteristic of Amharaization are as follows. Foremost is the habitual use of Amharic as the language of conversation rather than English or another foreign language, even in private circles. The traditional Amhara custom whereby the "will" of the king and other important dignitaries was always expressed through a third person, the *afa negus* (lit. "mouth of the king"), often has its overtones in contemporary situations. It is not uncommon to witness an upper-status Ethiopian speaking through an interpreter to a foreigner despite the Ethiopian's fluency in the particular

European language. In a related way, the problem of teaching English, the language of instruction in middle and secondary government schools, is aggravated by the failure of the vast majority of students to use English outside of classroom situations, as against the social acceptance and prestige values associated with speaking Amharic (Shack, 1959b: 418). On a social-value scale equal with language is religion. This includes the adoption of a Christian name at baptism, and active ritual and financial participation in the *sefer* church in which family membership has been traditionally held. No less important is the acquisition of extensive land holdings; *rest*-land by inheritance, or *gult*-land granted by the Emperor, or free-hold purchase; in any case the economic return from land ownership is derived from tenant or sharecrop farming systems. The long tradition of awarding important administrative positions and official titles as royal favors or merits for faithful government service is still symbolic of status mobility and Amharaization. Lastly, there is the arrangement of a prestigious marriage into the upper-status group, which usually entails combining land and other economic resources between families.

In the main, urban Gurage who have made attempts to acquire the cultural norms of Amharaization comprise no great number. Most Gurage have rejected them; and this, I suggest, is owing to the realities of the urban situation in which most of the socioeconomic, if not cultural, symbols of Amharaization are inaccessible, for the majority of urban Gurage speak Amharic and many are Copts as well. For lack of a satisfactory alternative to the Amhara cultural model—Amharaization—town Gurage place an emphasis on their own cultural model. They stress the use of Guraginä in conversation with fellow Gurage; they form kin-based urban settlements and neighborhood associations; they participate actively in tribal rituals; they invest in village development schemes; and they organize kin-based enterprises in the urban area.

It is clear from the foregoing that the Amhara sociocultural system is not a "national" sociocultural system in the sense that it is shared equally by all non-Amhara groups in the urban society. This perhaps could be said of other societies of similar cultural complexity and, indeed, Bruner (1961) has shown this to be the case for North Sumatra; even though here a "Western" model has been adopted, it fails to function in a national sense (cf. Vincent 1970: 253-55, 273-74). The social structure of Addis Ababa is a complex network of status positions based on the cultural norms of the Amhara, wherein occupational role is a major determinant of social ranking of each urban ethnic group, Gurage wealth or achievements notwithstanding. The core of Amhara national sociocultural traits fails to incorporate the differential cultural forms of non-Amhara groups. The stress placed upon Amhara sociocultural traits at the expense of those of non-Amhara groups is a dysfunctional factor in the integration of groups having diverse ethnic backgrounds through the cultural process of urbanization. In this regard, urban ethnicity in Addis Ababa emphasizes "separation" in much the same way that Wallerstein (1960) has observed for certain situations in West African towns; and thus urban ethnicity can, and perhaps does, inhibit national integration in Ethiopia. The strong emphasis laid upon promoting the sociocultural values of the dominant group also provides ground for the accentuation of ethnic exclusiveness and the crystallization of status positions based on subcultural differences.

To sum up, urban ethnicity among the Gurage reflects the lack of an urban status system alternative to that based on the Amhara sociocultural model, one by which wealth accrued from business and entrepreneurship, economic undertakings of the majority of well-to-do Gurage, would be an acceptable channel to higher status. In East Africa, Southall (1956: 574) describes a similar situation where the modified status system of the Ganda in Kampala alone provides the basis for the urban social structure and the status positions of other ethnic groups are ranked in accordance with it. As with non-Ganda, so also with Gurage: those who through education and professional training have acquired prominent administrative positions in the national and municipal governments are so few that a case for them can hardly be made. With the Gurage, this is partly compounded by the fact that, like other Ethiopians, a few make a concerted effort to lose ethnic identity by claiming to be "Amhara" once slight upward mobility has been achieved. But even if a few Gurage manage to become ethnically marginal in town, the opportunity for arranging an upper-status marriage, or for obtaining extensive rural or urban land holdings, either of which factors is a means by which status positions can be manipulated, exists even less for Gurage as a whole.

I do not wish to develop the point at length here, but I suggest that urban ethnicity establishes a socioeconomic status system within the Gurage community, its members being ranked according to the prestige values that Gurage themselves assign to occupational roles they commonly perform. In other words, differential status structures obtain between the Gurage community and the larger urban society. In the former, for instance, a successful Gurage entrepreneur can achieve the status of a "big man," whereas in terms of Amhara social ranking he might be "just a

Gurage." Similarly, status mobility which is closed to Gurage in the wider society is possible within their own community; in a single generation an ambitious Gurage can rise from itinerant trading to successful entrepreneurship, with all of the status concomitants this implies within the Gurage community. Urban status thus achieved can also be made evident in the rural society through increased land and livestock holdings; but the reverse is not always true. For a wealthy and important Gurage, by tribal standards that is, a village headman, chief, or ritual dignitary, will be reckoned as such only within the urban Gurage community but not outside of it. This phenomenon is strikingly comparable to St. Clair Drake's (1945) analysis of the differential status systems by which Afro-Americans are ranked in "Black Metropolis" and in the larger, dominantly white society.

The Gurage form of urban ethnicity is an extension of the rural social and economic network of kinship and tribal relations restructured in terms of the Amhara-dominated urban social structure. The economic well-being of individual Gurage has improved considerably since the era in which most of them were corvée and slave laborers. One reason is that an expanding urban market economy has created new semi-skilled occupational categories which Gurage eagerly fill. Another reason is that kinsmen in town now provide a relatively reliable means of temporary employment for seasonal migrants, who no longer need to rely solely upon "*kuli*" labor earnings as in the past. The old stereotype of the Gurage as street sweepers, hewers of wood, and water carriers still exists in the popular mind, however. In actual fact, relatively few Gurage are so employed today; these occupations are rapidly being taken over by new migrant groups, even low-status Amhara, as urban employment for unskilled workers becomes increasingly scarce, and as Gurage as a whole gain greater economic security in a variety of urban labor undertakings. Such security has also made town Gurage less dependent upon their rural kin, yet their ties with them have not been severed. On the contrary, the relationships of town Gurage with rural kinfolk are now manifested in new social, economic, and welfare benefits which accrue to tribal relatives. Lastly, as is true for other urban Ethiopians, Gurage voluntary associations, except church-oriented clubs and self-help societies of the type already described, associations which have no political aims, are proscribed by government policy. And when no other institutional channels exist for the expression of public opinion and for fostering economic interests, urban kin and tribal-based institutions become, as they have in

South African towns (Mayer, 1962: 582), the focal points of social action, particularly for lower-status groups like the Gurage. In short, the significance of urban ethnicity as an aspect of the cultural process of Ethiopian urbanization is twofold: on the one hand, urban ethnicity is a manifestation of the behavioral form of cultural opposition to Amharaization by non-Amhara groups, and on the other, it establishes a framework of ethnic group consciousness within which economic and social security is made possible in the urban society.

Because of the historical and sociocultural particularities of the urbanization process in Addis Ababa, any generalizations prompted by the Ethiopian material might prove to have limited correspondence with other towns in Africa and elsewhere, where forms of urban ethnicity have been reported. The relative absence of direct European and other foreign influences in Ethiopia might be considered factors which set Addis Ababa apart in some, but not all, ways from urban centers in West, East, and Central Africa. Yet the similarities seem greater than the differences; and at the risk of restating what might appear to be obvious, two generalizations follow which seem worthwhile for comparisons in cross-cultural studies of urban ethnicity:

1. Urban ethnicity obtains among subcultural groups in rigidly stratified societies, (a) where there is a direct relationship between occupational role, social status, and sociocultural integration; and (b) where the social integrating norms usually provided by a national sociocultural system have been substituted by those of a dominant ethnic (cultural) group.

2. The extent to which tribal institutions can be effectively transferred to an urban setting will depend largely upon the socioeconomic characteristics of the urban social structure. Thus, (a) where the industrial sector of the urban economy lags behind the rural-urban market sector, this is likely to give ground to (b) the perpetuation of rural socioeconomic institutions in the urban society based on kinship and ethnicity for the purpose of furthering local interests.

These propositions can be roughly linked with the central theme of this essay: that the dominant cleavage between Amhara and the several non-Amhara groups influences the behavior of the latter in terms not only of the total field of relations involving the dominant group but also of the behavior of one non-Amhara group to another. This cleavage, rephrased in words familiar to social anthropologists concerned with social and political relations in African tribal settings, becomes that of balanced or structural opposition between groups. It is seen to operate most clearly in urban situations where non-Amhara groups seek prestige, status, changes in occupational role, and sociocultural integration. At the same time, in the fields of economic and occupational competition, non-Amhara groups generally tend to act not as a combined opposition to Amhara, but to regroup themselves along ethnic (tribal) lines, with new cleavages being formed and enlarging as competition increases (cf. Banton, 1964). This kind of opposition and realignment of groups in response to changing urban stimuli does not lead to atavism; the urban social system is a single field of social relations composed of groups who share certain common ties which cross-cut other ties that make for opposition between them. Domestic relations, local groupings and associations, and labor undertakings such as market trade and cottage industries—economic activities which fall outside the principal wage economy—comprise the field of relations where structural opposition between non-Amhara groups originates in kinship and affinity, and these areas also form the basis for promoting their local interests. But the ties which cross-cut non-Amhara groups who at other times are in opposition are found in the field of relations where interaction involves industrial wage employment, the assimilation of selected aspects of Amhara cultural behavior, participation in "national" political and religious ceremonies, and partaking of the benefits of government-sponsored institutions of health and education. Social class and political alignments have yet to emerge as a category of social interaction among urban Ethiopians (cf. Cohen 1969: 190-98), but it seems safe to assume that when these have fully crystallized the urban ethnic factor will be largely overcome. In his brilliant analysis of ethnicity on the Copperbelt, from which this writing has drawn much inspiration, Epstein (1958: 227) has said that the "understanding of the urban social process in Africa requires a formulation in which inconsistency and disharmony are recognized." This essay has been an attempt to illustrate social processes of this nature which characterize the social system of Addis Ababa and continue to be the source of its dynamics.

References Cited

Banton, M.

1957. *West African City*. London: Oxford University Press for the International African Institute.

1964. "Social Alignment and Identity in a West African City." In H. Kuper (ed.), *Urbanization and Migration in West Africa*. Berkeley: University of California Press.

Bascom, W.
1955. "Urbanization Among the Yoruba." *American Journal of Sociology* 60:446-54.

Bruner, E.
1961. "Urbanization and Ethnic Identity in North Sumatra." *American Anthropologist* 63:508-21.

Cohen, A.
1969. *Custom and Politics in Urban Africa*. Berkeley: University of California Press.

Drake, St. Clair
1945. *Black Metropolis*. New York: Harpers.

Epstein, A. L.
1958. *Politics in an Urban African Community*. Manchester: Manchester University Press.

Forde, D. (ed.)
1956. *Social Implications of Industrialization and Urbanization in Africa South of the Sahara*. Paris: UNESCO.

Gadamu, F.
1972. Ethnic Associations in Ethiopia and the Maintenance of Urban/Rural Relationships: With Special Reference to the Alemgana-Walamo Road Construction Association. Unpublished Ph.D. Dissertation. London: University of London.

Gluckman, M.
1958. "An Analysis of a Social Situation in Modern Zululand." Manchester: Rhodes-Livingstone Paper, no. 28.
1960. "Tribalism in Modern British Central Africa." *Cahiers d'Etudes Africaines* 1:55-70.
1961. "Anthropological Problems Arising from the African Industrial Revolution. In A. W. Southall (ed.), *Social Change in Modern Africa*. London: Oxford University Press for the International African Institute.

Little, K.
1957. "The Role of Voluntary Associations in West African Urbanization." *American Anthropologist* 59:579-95.
1960. "West African Urbanization as a Social Process." *Cahiers d'Etudes Africaines* 3:90-102.
1965. *West African Urbanization*. Cambridge, Eng.: Cambridge University Press.

Mayer, P.
1962. "Migrancy and the Study of Africans in Towns." *American Anthropologist* 64:576-92.

Merab, P.
1921. *Impressions d'Ethiopie*, 3 vols. Paris.

Mercier, P.
1965. "On the Meaning of 'Tribalism' in Black Africa." In P. van den Berghe (ed.), *Africa: Social Problems of Change and Conflict.* San Francisco: Chandlers.

Mitchell, J. C.
1956. "Urbanization, Detribalization and Stabilization in Southern Africa: A Problem of Definition and Measurement." In D. Forde (ed.), *Social Implications of Industrialization and Urbanization in Africa South of the Sahara.* Paris: UNESCO.
1957. "The Kalela Dance." Manchester: Rhodes-Livingstone Paper, No. 27.

Mitchell, J. C., and A. L. Epstein
1959. "Occupational Prestige and Social Status Among Urban Africans in Northern Rhodesia." *Africa* 29:22-39.

Pankhurst, R. P., and E. Eshete
1958. "Self-help in Ethiopia." *Ethiopia Observer* 2:354-64.

Pankhurst, R. P.
1961. "Menelik and the Foundation of Addis Ababa." *Journal of African History* 2:103-17.
1962. "The Foundation and Growth of Addis Ababa to 1935." *Ethiopia Observer* 6:33-61.

Perham, M.
1947. *The Government of Ethiopia.* London: Faber and Faber.

Pons, V. G.
1956. "The Changing Significance of Ethnic Affiliation and of Westernization in the African Settlement Patterns in Stanleyville." In D. Forde, (ed.), *Social Implications of Industrialization and Urbanization in Africa South of the Sahara.* Paris: UNESCO.
1969. *Stanleyville: An African Urban Community Under Belgian Administration.* London: Oxford University Press, for the International African Institute.

Prothero, R. M.
1957. "Migratory Labour from North-Western Nigeria." *Africa* 27:251-61.

Schapera, I.
1947. *Migrant Labour and Tribal Life: A Study of Conditions in Bechuanaland Protectorate.* London: Oxford University Press.

Schwab, W. B.
1961. "Social Stratification in Gwelo." In A. W. Southall (ed.), *Social Change in Modern Africa.* London: Oxford University Press for the International African Institute.
1966. "Oshogbo—An Urban Community?" In H. Kuper (ed.), *Urbanization and Migration in West Africa.* Berkeley: University of California Press.

Shack, W. A.
1959a. "Native Institutions of Self-help in Ethiopia." London: Institute of Commonwealth Studies. Mimeographed.

1959b. "Organization and Problems of Education in Ethiopia." *Journal of Negro Education* 28:405-20.

1963a. "Some Aspects of Ecology and Social Structure in the Ensete Culture Complex in Southwest Ethiopia." *Journal of the Royal Anthropological Institute* 93:72-79.

1963b. "Religious Ideas and Social Action in Gurage Bond-Friendship." *Africa* 33:198-208.

1966. *The Gurage: A People of the Ensete Culture.* London: Oxford University Press for the International African Institute.

Southall, A. W.

1956. "Determinants of the Social Structure of African Urban Populations, with Special Reference to Kampala (Uganda)." In D. Forde (ed.), *Social Implications of Industrialization and Urbanization in Africa South of the Sahara.* Paris: UNESCO.

1961. *Social Change in Modern Africa* (ed.). London: Oxford University Press for the International African Institute.

Steward, J.

1947. *The Theory of Culture Change.* Urbana: University of Illinois Press.

Swedish Nutritional Survey

1963. "Swedish Pediatric Clinic." Addis Ababa. Unpublished.

van Velsen, J.

1961. "Labour Migration as a Positive Factor in the Continuity of Tonga Tribal Society." In A. W. Southall (ed.), *Social Change in Modern Africa.* London: Oxford University Press for the International African Institute.

Vincent, J.

1970. *African Elite: The Big Men of a Small Town.* New York: Columbia University Press.

Wallerstein, I.

1960. "Ethnicity and national integration in West Africa." *Cahiers d'Etudes Africaines* 3:129-39.

Wang, C. K.

1957. "The Population of Ethiopia's Metropolis." *Ethiopia Observer* 2:56-59.

Watson, W.

1958. *Tribal Cohesion in a Money Economy.* Manchester: Manchester University Press.

Wirth, L.

1938. "Urbanism as a Way of Life." *American Journal of Sociology* 64:1-24.

Yazaki, T.

1973. "The History of Urbanization in Japan." This volume, p. 139.

Distance, Transportation, and Urban Involvement in Zambia[1]

J. Clyde Mitchell

Anthropological studies have by tradition been intensive studies of small-scale communities and they have employed above all the methods of participant observation. Their approach has been configurational rather than statistical. There has been a tendency to see the units of studies as wholes rather than as relatively isolated elements bearing to one another relationships which might conveniently be stated in quantitative terms.

As anthropologists have turned their attention to towns and cities, the difficulties in their traditional approach to the study of society have become exacerbated. It is hardly possible to equate the idea of a "city" with that of a "tribe," if only because of the heterogeneity and complexity of cities and their relative dependence upon the larger societies of which they are essentially integral parts.

Anthropologists, however, have been able to make signal contributions to the understanding of city life by intensive studies of limited aspects of urban behavior into which they have been able to provide illuminating insights. But these insights are essentially hypotheses which by their very nature are difficult to test on a large scale. In this paper I use data derived from a social survey to test an hypothesis which had been formulated in the course of a classical type of anthropological enquiry.

The formulation to which I refer is that advanced by Philip Mayer in

1. I wish to express my gratitude to my colleagues of the Seminar on Urban Anthropology at Burg Wartenstein, September 1964, especially to Dr. E. Bruner, Dr. A. W. Southall, and to my wife Hilary Flegg Mitchell, for their helpful comments on an earlier draft of this paper.

connection with his study of migrants in the South African town of East London. Mayer (1962: 583) typifies the Xhosa in East London as a person who is able to combine frequent and easy home-visiting with a protracted stay in town. There are administrative restrictions on the movement of Africans between town and country in South Africa, and on their settlement in towns and this probably induces migrants to stay in towns while continuing to maintain intimate connections with their rural homes. This is particularly characteristic of the migrants whom Mayer calls "Red," who are traditionally and tribally oriented to a high degree. Such migrants maintain a close network of personal associations in East London. Within these cliques there are strong pressures on individual members to preserve an image of themselves as essentially rurally oriented. These people take every opportunity of returning to their rural homes in order to participate in social activities or merely to visit their kinsmen there. Significantly, however, Mayer points out that this type of clique does not exist to the same degree among migrants from rural areas near East London. He writes:

> These are the men who can go home for weekends, or fortnightly, having their homes in the East London or Kingwilliamstown magisterial districts. While in town they will, like other Red men, choose home friends as domestic or drinking companions. But otherwise they do not need the substitute gratification of an organized "home community in exile" because they are still able to participate directly and regularly in the social life of the home community itself (1964: 32-3).

In other words, Mayer argues that a migrant in town does not cease to be a member of his tribal community merely by moving into town. He points to "mechanisms which, as it were, keep open his particular place in some hinterland society—as a member of this or that family, lineage, age-set. . . . They require that during his stay in town he should maintain certain relationships in a latent state and discharge certain roles in absentia" (1962: 578). The migrant thus occupies statuses and has rights and responsibilities in both places simultaneously.

Although social contact between a townsman and his rural kinsmen and friends may be maintained by means of letters or messages borne by returning home-mates, a townsman is able to maintain his position in a rural social system more effectively if he is able to participate personally in rural activities and reinforce his bonds with the community by frequent personal visits. The degree to which the migrant is able to maintain position both in town and in the rural area, therefore, turns partly on the distance of this area from the town where the migrant is living, and partly on the efficiency of the transportation system which the migrant may use to get to and from the rural area. We therefore expect the migrants who come from the closest rural areas would be more deeply involved in rural activities. At the same time there would be no need for a migrant from a conveniently close tribal area to withdraw substantially from his urban commitments in order to maintain his rural links. A migrant coming from a more distant area would not be able to afford either the time for or the expense of frequent visits home, so if he were to maintain contact he would have to withdraw from the urban system of social and economic activities for comparatively long periods. We would therefore, expect some correlation between the distance of a migrant's rural home from the town where he is living and the extent to which he is involved in urban social relationships.

Quantification and the Testing of the Hypothesis

Testing an hypothesis of this sort, of course, is likely to present some difficulties. While it is possible to validate the connection between the involvement of migrants in town life and the proximity of their areas of origin to towns merely by describing the urban activities of migrants from areas both far from and near to those towns, it would be simpler if the variables could be expressed in quantitative form and the relationship tested statistically. One of the advantages of this latter procedure would be that the exceptions to the general pattern in the data and the discrepancies between what we expect and what we observe could provide the occasion for the elaboration of the research and call for explanations beyond the original hypothesis, enabling us to refine the hypothesis and deepen our understanding of the situation.

Yet our confidence in the generality of the analytical relationships among a set of variables will be encouraged if they are found to hold in a body of material collected with a different set of problems in mind and by using a different set of techniques of data collection. This will of necessity involve some reinterpretation and regrouping of variables so as to approximate them to the concepts underlying the hypothesis to be tested but which were not employed in the collection of the material to be used in testing it. In this sense, there is a limit to the extent to which general survey data may be used to test hypotheses derived from studies employing participant observation.

The hypothesis could best be tested with data which have been collected in terms of the original analysis. Yet there is some merit in making a virtue out of necessity by using material gathered in a general social survey to test the hypothesis, if it can be restated in quantitative terms. There is obviously a limit to the degree to which general social survey data can be used to test and refine hypotheses. Exceptions and discrepancies can be explained only by additional detailed and intensive enquiry of the sort which Mayer conducted in East London. But if these enquiries are carried out against a background of knowledge of the regularities in the data obtained from a social survey, they would be more pointed and more specific. There is no single way of assembling and interpreting sociological data. Participant observation, case studies, and social surveys are all equally important links in the chain of sociological analysis.

The Background to Urbanization

I use here material collected during a social survey of the African population of the Copperbelt of Zambia (formerly Northern Rhodesia) to examine the relationship between the distance of the rural homes of migrants from the Copperbelt and the degree to which these migrants are involved in town life. This material was collected between 1950 and 1954, that is, approximately a decade before Mayer published his study of East London and therefore before I knew of the postulated relationship between the ease of contact of town-dwellers with rural areas and their maintenance of links with people in those areas.

We would not expect, of course, that the specific economic, historical, social, and political circumstances pertaining to South Africa would apply to Zambia. The sociological generalization we would hope to establish would be that given roughly similar circumstances; then, the relationship between ease of contact and the maintenance of links would be similar. In fact, of course, rural-urban contacts in Zambia have been influenced by the social context in which they have occurred and this context must be taken into account in exploring the hypothesis.

The development of towns in Zambia dates effectively from the discovery of copper and other metals at the close of the nineteenth century.[2] A beginning was made at mining these deposits in the early years of the twentieth century, but extensive development was delayed until a railway line connected the copper mines with outlet ports in South Africa.

2. For a general historical background to the development of Zambia see Bradley (1952), Gann (1958), and Hall (1965). For a history of the copper mining industry relevant to this study see Baldwin (1964).

Table 1. Population of Copperbelt Towns. African and European. 1951-1963

	1951		*1956*		*1963*	
	African[a]	*Non-African*[b]	*African*[c]	*Non-African*[b]	*African*[b]	*Non-African*[d]
Bancroft	–	–	15,000	1,647	27,770	2,500
Chingola	20,500	2,602	25,000	4,919	50,690	5,800
Kalalushi	–	–	–	846	15,410	1,200
Kitwe	50,800	5,229	55,000	9,809	101,570	13,200
Luanshya	47,500	4,920	45,000	6,671	66,160	6,100
Mufulira	38,000	3,708	50,000	5,731	69,310	6,900
Ndola	26,800	3,418	55,000	8,794	76,800	12,100

a. Estimated from 1950 Demographic Survey.
b. From official census.
c. Rough estimate by Central Statistical Office.
d. Estimate by Central Statistical Office.

This railway line was built northwards from Bulawayo through Broken Hill, where the lead and zinc mines were, to the area where copper deposits lay on the Congo border, an area known today as the Copperbelt. The railway line, which reached Broken Hill in 1906 and Ndola in 1909, has had a profound influence on urban development in Zambia. In common speech, in fact, "on the railway line" is synonymous with "in the towns."

At the time the railway line was being built, the extent of the deeper copper deposits on the Copperbelt was probably unknown, and it was only between 1925 and 1927 that several deep-level mines were established. Large numbers of skilled European technicians and many thousands of unskilled African workers were attracted to these mines. Following an initial setback during the economic recession of the 1930's, development proceeded apace. The population of the Copperbelt thus grew rapidly—particularly during the period just before the 1939-45 war and, because of military requirements, during the war years.

Table 1 sets out the population of the towns of the Copperbelt between 1951 and 1963. Ndola had been established in 1902, but most of the other towns arose out of virtually uninhabited bush in 1926 and 1927. The towns of Kalalushi and Bancroft both developed after 1954. As a whole, therefore, the Copperbelt is barely more than thirty-five years old.

Plural Society and Dual Economy

The Africans among whom these towns suddenly materialized had remained until the closing years of that century relatively unaffected by the early-nineteenth-century economic and social revolution. It was then that British imperial expansion, motivated particularly by the quest for raw material, led to the European penetration into Central Africa.

The Europeans—planters, farmers, miners, traders, administrators, and missionaries—set themselves up in tiny outposts aloof from the indigenous inhabitants and followed as closely as circumstances could permit the way of life they had brought with them. The African tribesmen, for their part, continued in the way of life to which they were accustomed except where they were prevented from doing so by the administrative requirements of the European government. The two populations went about their daily affairs in apparent disregard of each other except for points of common interest, which arose particularly out of the suppression of tribal warfare and the slave-trade, in the spreading of the Gospel, or in economic relationships. These relatively limited points of contact led to the establishment of a society composed of separate and disparate groups with widely divergent social structures, standards of living, and value orientations. These groups were, however, linked by their common economic interests, as rulers and subjects, traders and customers, or masters and servants. Almost from the first day of penetration there developed a society based on a dual economy and essentially plural in character.

In the African population, the range of wants, which expanded rapidly with economic development, soon came to include money for taxes, school fees, fines, and licenses, as well as for consumer goods such as blankets, clothing, cooking utensils, hoes, ploughs, axes, and a variety of decorative trifles. The cash needed for these goods and services, however, could not easily be earned within the framework of a largely subsistence tribal economy. The only real alternative open to tribesmen was to seek wage-earning employment in labor centers which as a rule were far away and to stay there until they had accumulated the wealth they had set out to acquire.

Initially these labor centers lay outside Zambia, but with the expansion of mining, particularly after 1934, local opportunities for wage earning increased. Men migrated to the newly established towns for the express purpose of earning money to meet their immediate requirements. When these were met they returned directly to their tribal homes. From the outset, then, the mining industry was developed on the basis of circulatory labor.

Labor circulation is a social phenomenon of some complexity, the roots of which lie in various social, economic, and political circumstances. While undoubtedly economic factors lie at the basis of the extent and rate of labor circulation, a series of individual and personal factors combine to determine just who becomes a migrant and when.[3] In general the circulation of labor between wage-earning centers and tribal areas may be seen as one way in which tribesmen attempt to reap some of the benefit of Western economic endeavor without at the same time surrendering their position in the tribal social system from which they are temporary absentees. It is a phenomenon particularly characteristic of a dual economy and a plural society.

The Flow of Labor

In Zambia the commencement of large-scale mining created the main wage-earning opportunities for Africans. As with the case of many other enterprises established in tribal areas, at first little local manpower was attracted by the wage-earning opportunities the mines offered. In the early stages of the mining development, therefore, recruitment was the usual way of obtaining labor. During the 1929-32 recession, however, when the demand for labor fell sharply, labor recruitment was found to be unecessary, and in fact was never started again.

There were several factors in this changed situation. The most important, undoubtedly, was that there was available a large pool of labor which had been displaced from other areas further afield, such as Katanga, Southern Rhodesia, and South Africa. Also, no doubt, the gradually rising standard of living after the recession had ended, coupled with the rapidly increasing pressure of population on rural resources, made wage-earning essential for a larger proportion of the population than before. Lastly, the rapid extension of motor transport and the development of the road system made the journey to the Copperbelt from rural areas easier than it had been for a large number of laborers and their families.[4]

In 1951-54, the period to which the data analyzed in this paper refer, the adult population was drawn from a catchment area which extended to over 800 miles from the Copperbelt. Of a total of 8,787 adults (men

3. The causative factors and other aspects of labor circulation in Central Africa are discussed in Wilson, 1941-42; Watson, 1958; and Mitchell, 1959, 1961, 1969.

4. The influence of transportation routes and means of communication on the composition of Copperbelt towns and on labor migration is discussed in Niddrie (1954) and Mitchell (1954a).

and women) interviewed in a social survey of the five towns of Ndola, Luanshya, Kitwe, Chingola, and Mufulira,[5] 13.8 per cent had come from within 100 miles of the Copperbelt; 36.0 per cent from within 200 miles; 53.1 per cent from within 300 miles; 66.1 per cent from within 400 miles; 83.7 per cent from within 500 miles; 84.6 per cent from within 600 miles; 87.6 per cent from within 700 miles; and 93.9 per cent from within 800 miles. The majority of the population, therefore, was drawn from within 300 miles of the Copperbelt, but a considerable proportion came from further afield.

The Selective Effects of Distance

The accessibility of labor markets to areas of labor supply, by reason of efficient transport services, obviously influences the number of men who migrate. But accessibility is not the only factor involved, since more attractive opportunities in more distant labor centers may offset the disadvantages and cost of the longer journey to work.

It is possible to examine the selective effect of the Copperbelt on the places within its labor catchment area by comparing the proportion of men from different areas on the Copperbelt with the proportion of all absentees from those areas. It may be argued, for example, that if men migrated to labor centers purely at random, then the numbers of men from individual areas at any particular labor center would be proportional to the number of men absent from those individual areas.[6] Table 2 sets out the percentage of adult men on the Copperbelt from various areas of origin and the proportion of absentees as a whole from those areas, whether or not they have gone to the Copperbelt.

It is simple to compute an index of selection by expressing the Copperbelt proportion as a percentage of the proportion of absentees from an area of origin. Thus the percentage of adult men from the Ndola rural district on the Copperbelt as a whole was 6.58. But among all absentees from Zambian rural areas only 3.23 per cent came from Ndola rural district. Therefore there were proportionately more men from Ndola rural district on the Copperbelt than there were absentees as a whole from that district. The ratio of proportion of men from the Ndola rural district on the Copperbelt to the proportion of all absentees from that district is 6.58/

5. The field data referred to were collected in connection with a sociological study of the towns of Zambia which was one of the studies sponsored by the Rhodes-Livingstone Institute of Social Research, Lusaka.

6. This method was used by Pons (1956: 251) in his study of Stanleyville.

Table 2. Proportion of Adult Males on the Copperbelt from Areas Within Northern Rhodesia compared with Proportion of All Absentees from Those Areas

Areas	*Distance* (*i*)	*Per cent on Copperbelt* (*ii*)	*Per cent Absentees* (*iii*)	*Index of Selection* (*iv*)
Ndola	50	6.58	3.23	204
Fort Rosebery	135	9.42	7.03	134
Solwezi	160	2.92	2.24	130
Mkushi	170	3.49	2.74	128
Broken Hill	180	2.06	2.35	88
Serenje	240	4.79	3.06	157
Kawambwa	240	9.14	6.82	134
Luwingu	265	7.82	4.56	172
Kasempa	270	3.99	2.21	181
Lusaka	270	0.55	1.17	47
Mumbwa	280	1.38	1.39	99
Mwinilunga	280	2.30	1.64	141
Mporokoso	310	5.83	3.45	169
Kasama	315	6.63	4.91	135
Mpika	335	4.29	3.08	139
Kabompo	335	2.05	1.28	160
Southern Province	360	1.01	7.53	13
Abercorn	410	2.02	2.41	84
Petauke	415	4.55	6.63	69
Balovale	435	2.44	1.53	160
Chinsali	440	2.58	2.54	102
Isoka	450	2.32	2.42	96
Fort Jameson	525	7.25	10.76	67
Barotseland	555	2.13	10.00	21
Lundazi	680	2.46	5.04	49

Index of Selection = column (ii)/column (iii) × 100.
The number of absentees from areas was computed from Appendix 2 and Table 8 in Williams (1962). The figures refer to 1956. The figures in column (ii) refer to the period 1951-54. The difference in dates probably does not affect the results much.

3.23, which, as a percentage, is 204. Indices of selection of this sort from areas in Zambia which supply labor to the Copperbelt are set out in column (iv) of Table 2.[7]

If an area has an index of selection of 100, this indicates that the flow of manpower from it is as likely to go to the Copperbelt as not. The area, in effect, is located on a labor-flow watershed. We may therefore describe the

7. The index can be computed, of course, only for those areas for which the total numbers of absentees is known. Indices are presented here, therefore, only for areas within Zambia, since the requisite information is available for these areas.

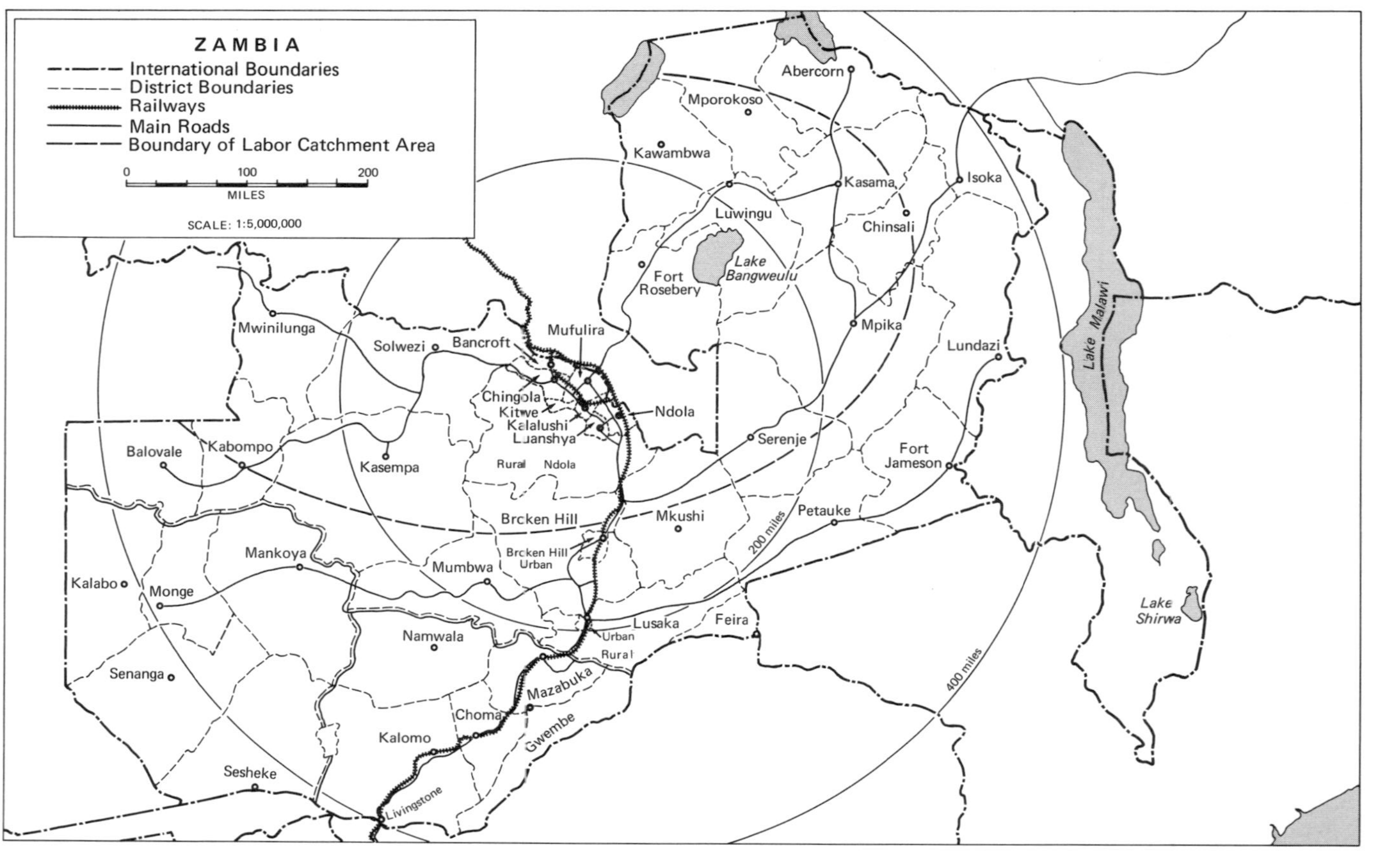

ZAMBIA
International Boundaries
District Boundaries
Railways
Main Roads
Boundary of Labor Catchment Area
0
100
200
MILES
SCALE: 1:5,000,000
Abercorn
Mporokoso
Kawambwa
Kasama
Isoka
Luwingu
Chinsali
Lake Bangweulu
Fort Rosebery
Lake Malawi
Mpika
Lundazi
Mwinilunga
Solwezi
Bancroft
Mufulira
Chingola
Kitwe
Kalalushi
Luanshya
Ndola
Serenje
Fort Jameson
Balovale
Kabompo
Kasempa
Rural
Ndola
Brcken Hill
Mkushi
Petauke
200 miles
Mankoya
Brcken Hill Urban
Mumbwa
Kalabo
Monge
Lusaka
Feira
Lake Shirwa
Urban
Rural
Namwala
Senanga
Mazabuka
400 miles
Choma
Kalomo
Gwembe
Sesheke
Livingstone

effective catchment areas of flow of labor to the Copperbelt by tracing a line through those places where the index of selection is approximately 100.[8] Using this method we find that the catchment area for Copperbelt labor in the period 1951-54 was contained within an arc drawn from Abercorn through Mpika, Mkushi, Mumbwa, and on westwards to Balovale (see map). In general, thus, the labor from the northern and western provinces of Zambia flows more to the Copperbelt than to other places. In some particular districts, such as Kasempa and Luwingu which have indices of 181 and 172 respectively, the flow is very heavily towards the Copperbelt.

These data suggest that the population from a certain defined area surrounding the Copperbelt tends to seek wage-earning employment on the Copperbelt rather than elsewhere, and that by the same token migrants from areas further afield tend to seek their fortunes elsewhere than on the Copperbelt. The nature and composition of the population on the Copperbelt is influenced in this direct way by the combined effect of the distance they must travel to get to the Copperbelt and, by implication, the efficacy of transportation services in that area. A more detailed examination shows that men who come from places near the Copperbelt exhibit different social characteristics from those who come from further afield. In order to avoid complications arising because of age differences, I have confined this examination of the social characteristics to men aged 25 to 34. Records covering 2,415 men of this age who were married had been obtained in a social survey between 1951 and 1954 covering a 10 per cent random sample of all African dwellings on the Copperbelt. The approximate distances from the Copperbelt of the areas from which the men had come were measured by the shortest route following road, rail, and river transport systems. These distances were measured from the administrative headquarters of the districts, in Zambia, or the largest local center in the provinces of Malawi, Tanzania, and the Congo. The distances from Angola, Mozambique, and Southern Rhodesia were estimated to be 390 miles, 700 miles, and 780 miles, respectively. The areas of origin were then grouped together into three zones, from each of which approximately one third of the sample of men came. These were areas of less than 200 miles, between 200 and 400 miles, and more than 400 miles from the Copperbelt. The attributes of men coming from these areas are tabulated in Tables 3a to h.

8. The line was in fact derived from a trend surface fitting the natural logarithm of the index of representation to a second-degree polynomial with the latitudes and longitudes of the centroids of the areas of origin of the migrants as values. The second-degree polynomial explained 83 per cent of the variance of the logarithm of the index of representation.

Table 3. Tabulations of Characteristics with Distance from the Copperbelt (Males aged 25-34)

	Miles distant 0-200	200-400	400+
Sample	823	761	831
a. *Conjugal state*			
Single	10.98	14.61	14.64
Married (wife in town)	70.69	61.38	52.47
Divorced	3.63	3.44	2.92
Widowed	0.13	0.14	0.35
Married (wife at home)	14.58	20.44	28.63
	100.00	100.00	100.00
b. *Polygynists*			
Two wives, one in rural area	1.23	1.04	1.54
Two wives, both in town	0.54	0.26	0.12
Two wives, both in rural area	0.13	1.04	1.91
c. *Length of continuous residence in present location*			
0-4 years	65.12	69.56	80.16
5-9 years	20.08	20.81	13.96
10-14 years	12.32	7.01	4.94
15-19 years	2.13	2.36	0.65
20-24 years	–	0.27	0.17
Over 25 years	0.13	–	–
	100.00	100.00	100.00
d. *Attitude to town life*			
Target Worker	56.03	59.98	64.85
Temporarily urbanized	37.90	35.07	32.20
Permanently urbanized	6.07	4.94	2.94
	100.00	100.00	100.00
e. *Proportion of adult life in town*			
Less than one third	34.49	42.22	60.92
Between one and two thirds	29.54	34.47	24.76
Over two thirds	23.98	15.50	10.36
Urban born	11.99	7.81	3.96
	100.00	100.00	100.00
f. *Occupation*			
Unskilled	68.41	67.85	66.44
Skilled	27.90	27.69	28.84
White-collar	3.69	4.46	4.52
	100.00	100.00	100.00

Sample	*Miles distant* 0-200	200-400	400+
g. *Monthly cash wage*			
Under 60s	39.87	37.66	35.12
60-120s	47.82	47.73	51.12
120-180s	6.97	7.74	6.28
180-240s	3.57	4.93	4.56
240s and over	1.77	1.93	2.92
	100.00	100.00	100.00
h. *Percentage who have never visited rural area by periods of absence from rural area*			
Period of Absence			
0-4 years	71.1	85.0	88.4
5-9 years	47.2	46.8	41.3
10-14 years	36.6	32.5	46.5
15-19 years	36.4	33.5	37.1
20 years and over	38.8	51.0	76.1
Average	54.0	59.0	63.1

Tables 3(a) to 3(h) demonstrate the distinct differences in the attributes possessed by men who have come varying distances to work on the Copperbelt. As might have been anticipated, the proportion of men who had their wives with them falls consistently from 70.7 to 52.5 per cent with increasing distance from the Copperbelt; the proportion of men who had left their wives in the rural areas rises correspondingly; while the proportion of men who had never married shows no trend with distance. This is not difficult to interpret. Migrants are unlikely to be able to bring their wives and families to town until they have had an opportunity to earn sufficient money to pay for the relatively high cost of their transport.[9]

The relationship between distance on the one hand and wage and occupation on the other is slight. There is a weak tendency for a greater proportion of unskilled labor to be drawn from areas near the Copperbelt than from far away. Naturally, therefore, the wages of those drawn from

9. It is interesting to note that Reader found exactly the opposite. He writes: "Those living closest to the city naturally tend least to have their wives with them since they can go home most often" (1961:56). The sex ratio on the Copperbelt has tended to equalize since 1954, so that the effect of distance on the proportion of men who have left their wives in the rural areas probably becomes less important since this study was made.

nearer areas are slightly lower than wages of men from the more distant areas. The mean wage for migrants from areas less than 200 miles from the Copperbelt was 77.8 shillings per month; from areas 200 to 400 miles away, 81.5 shillings per month; and from areas more than 400 miles away, 83.5 shillings per month. At first sight this may appear to be due to the continued residence in town of those migrants from the most distant places, who have better-paying jobs in the skilled and white-collar categories. In fact, however, migrants from the more distant places have spent on the average less time in the towns than those from nearer places.

The most striking differences occur, however, in connection with three related attributes which may be considered to reflect the degree of involvement in town life and which therefore bear directly on the hypothesis we wish to test. These are the length of time the men have lived continuously in the town they were in at the time of the survey (Table 3c); the proportion of time they have spent in urban areas as a whole since they turned fifteen years of age (Table 3c); and the attitude they have towards their continued residence in town (Table 3d).[10]

The interviewers were required to classify each person they interviewed into one of eight categories according to the attitudes evinced about continued residence in towns. These attitudes may be thought of as lying along a single continuum of increasing commitment to town life; the migrants may be grouped as follows:

A. Target workers
   1. Will return to rural area as soon as possible.
   2. Working to go back to rural area as soon as possible.
   3. Will return to rural area after a specific object is attained, e.g. money for a sewing machine, to buy cattle for bridewealth.

B. Temporarily urbanized
   4. Will return to rural area at some unspecified future date.
   5. Will stay in town but keep contact with rural area.
   6. Will return to rural area on retirement.

C. Permanently urbanized
   7. Think they will always stay in town.
   8. Born and bred in town: "It is as if it were my village."[11]

10. I have discussed these attributes more fully elsewhere. See Mitchell (1956: 707-9).

11. These types of town dwellers are discussed in Wilson (1941-42) and Mitchell (1951, 1954b).

All three of these attributes relating to urban involvement showed a marked variation with distance from the Copperbelt. From Table 3d we see that the ratio of those evincing attitudes of permanent urbanization to those reflecting "target worker" attitudes ranged from one to 9.1 in the nearest areas to one to 22.1 in the most distant areas. In Table 3e, which relates distance from the Copperbelt to the proportion of adult life spent in town, we find that the proportion of migrants who have spent less than one third of their adult life in town increases from 34.5 per cent among the migrants who have come from within 200 miles of the Copperbelt to 60.9 per cent among those who have come from more than 400 miles away. The same trend is to be seen in respect of the period of continuous residence in town (see Table 3c).

Further light may be thrown on this association by considering the proportion of migrants who had not visited their tribal areas since first leaving them. Since the period of absence from the tribal area obviously will affect the probability of a visit back being made, this factor must be held constant in any comparison between migrants from areas of varying distances from the Copperbelt. From Table 3h we see that among migrants who have been away from rural areas longest, the proportion of men who have never visited their tribal homes tends to be highest among those whose tribal homes are furthest away. For example, amongst those who have been away twenty years or more, 38.8 per cent from places nearer than 200 miles have never been back; 51.0 per cent from areas between 200 miles and 400 miles have never been back; and 76.1 per cent from places over 400 miles away have never been back. This is unlikely to be due to the greater cost of returning to more distant places, because we find that among those who have been away for fifteen to nineteen years the proportion who have not been back to their rural homes is the same, whether or not those homes are near at hand.

It should be noted, however, that since the cases examined here are all of men under thirty-five years of age, those who left their rural areas twenty years ago or more must all have been born in town or must have come as children. In fact 15.2 per cent were born in town; 5.6 per cent were brought to town before they were five years old, 29.3 per cent while they were between the ages of 5 and 9, and 50.0 per cent while they were between the ages of 10 and 14. This means that these men had grown up away from the rural areas and had little personal contact with them.[12] It

12. People who have been born on the Copperbelt usually associate themselves with the area of origin of their parents.

is not surprising, therefore, that in all as many as 56 per cent of them had not visited their rural areas.

A large proportion of these are undoubtedly people who have, in fact, little or no connection with the rural homes of their parents. They represent the category of townsmen who have known no other life than a town life and have no wish to live in the rural areas. They are stabilized in town and presumably committed to town life.

Yet distance affects the amount of contact town-dwellers have with their rural kinsmen even among those who have been in town since childhood. A greater proportion of men visited their tribal homes if these were near the Copperbelt than if they were further away. This trend is confined, however, to those who have been away from their rural homes for less than five years on the one hand, and more than twenty years on the other. It is understandable that in the first five years of their stay away from their rural areas, a smaller proportion of migrants will visit their rural homes if these are far away than if they are near at hand. A migrant in town is able to keep in contact more effectively with his rural kinsfolk and with others in his tribal area to whom he is bound by personal ties if he is, as we have already pointed out, able to visit them, and they him, easily, that is, when there are efficient means of transportation and frequent services between rural areas and towns. Therefore we may argue that children born and brought up in town are more likely to maintain relationships with their parents' rural kinsmen if these kinsmen live in places within relatively easy access of town than if they live in distant places where transport services are poor. Thus even among those brought up in town, visits to parents' home areas are most likely to be made where these areas can be reached easily.

Distance and Urban Involvement

It is clear from the material presented in the tables that there are variations in the social characteristics of migrants which vary systematically with the distance the migrants have traveled to get to town. Some of these characteristics, furthermore, may be looked upon as reflecting the migrants' involvement in town life and participation in urban institutions. The argument here is that whether or not a migrant has brought his wife to town with him, and the extent to which he has spent more time in the urban areas than in his rural home district and has lived for comparatively long unbroken periods in the towns and sees himself as living in the towns for a long time in the future, for example, reflect the degree to which the migrant has become implicated in urban, as against rural, living and has tended to center his interest and activities in town affairs—though not, of course, at the same time to the complete exclusion of an interest in rural matters. This is what, for want of a better term, I refer to as "urban involvement": it implies preponderant participation in activities and involvement in social relationships which are primarily centered in towns.

This concept should be distinguished from the closely related and similar concepts of stabilization, commitment, and urbanization. Stabilization is essentially a demographic concept and refers to the degree to which people are living for longer and longer periods in urban as against rural areas. A measure of stabilization could be derived from suitable demographic data, which need make no assumptions whatsoever about the nature of the social relationships of the population (Mitchell, 1956: 699, 1969a: 472-86; Mayer, 1961: 5).

Commitment is a psychological concept and refers to the degree to which people are emotionally and personally involved in urban living and are likely to remain living in town in the future. Although I have previously used the term "commitment" for what I would now call "involvement," the two concepts should be kept separate (Mitchell and Shaul, 1963). Commitment could probably be measured most effectively by techniques of attitude measurement and psychological testing aimed at revealing the motivation of migrants. Urbanization refers to the process whereby migrants adopt behavior patterns appropriate to urban life. It is a sociological concept not amenable to easy measurement.

Urban involvement, as I see it, will manifest itself in a number of empirically observable characteristics of migrants. A characteristic which would obviously discriminate between migrants who are comparatively deeply involved in urban living and those who are not would be the proportion of adult life a migrant has spent in town as against the country. Similarly a man who has brought his wife to live with him in town is likely to have his interest more centered in town than one who has not. Similar arguments might be used in connection with men who have been in the towns where they were living at the time of the survey for relatively long continuous periods and who evince a favorable attitude towards continued residence in town.

We can contrast the careers of two men of the same age in the following respects. One is married; he has his wife living with him in the town; he has spent a large *proportion* of his adult life, as well as a relatively long time actually, in town, and he evinces an attitude favorable to continued residence in town in the future. The other man has left his wife in the rural area, he has spent a relatively short part of his adult life and only a short time actually in towns, and evinces an attitude which reflects an unwillingness to continue living in town. We can thus argue that the former is more involved in urban living than the latter.

Some attributes related to socioeconomic status may be viewed in the same light. A person who follows an occupation which is particularly related to industrial and commercial activities, such as professional, white-collar, or skilled work, or who has a better-than-average education, is likely to find these attributes more advantageous to him in town than in the country and therefore is likely to be involved in urban living. A man earning a wage higher than the average in a situation where cash earning opportunities in the rural areas are meager is also likely to resist influences which might otherwise persuade him to return to his rural home. To people with these attributes urban life presents greater rewards, satisfactions, and potentialities than life in the rural areas.

An individual involvement in urban living, we may argue, will be reflected in the possession simultaneously of most, if not all, of the attributes we have mentioned. If so, we may look upon urban involvement, in the sense in which I have defined it, as an element common to all the attributes which we have selected (on commonsense grounds) as being likely to imply involvement in urban living. These attributes, however, will not all reflect an individual's involvement to the same degree; some will reflect it with greater fidelity than others. The problem thus becomes one of estimating the association of each attribute with the hypothesized underlying common factor, of urban involvement. If this can be accomplished, we may use these correlations as weights to apply to the combination of attributes any individual may exhibit to estimate the extent of his involvement in town living.

An effective technique for deriving such weights is factor analysis. The argument is that the set of intercorrelations among the sets of attributes possessed by all individuals may be represented by a limited number of unrelated factors. We may use the factor with which the urban involvement attributes correlate most highly to provide weights for attributes for the purpose of placing each individual on an urban involvement continuum.[13] The weights derived from this procedure were:

Proportion of time spent in town	0.37
Period of continuous residence in town	0.32
Wife living in town	0.18
Attitude to continued urban residence	0.12
Occupation	0.01
Wage	0.00
Education	0.00
Total	1.00

The first five attributes, together with their loadings, may be used to compute an index of urban involvement for every migrant, and from these indices a mean index of urban involvement for categories of migrants may be calculated; for example, for migrants from relatively near or from relatively distant places. This index is derived by using the weights to score the combination of the presence and the absence of attributes, so that a person who possesses all of the attributes would be given the highest index—in this case 100—and a person who possesses none of them would be given the lowest—in this case zero. The scores of the various other combinations of attributes fall between these two extremes.

It is now possible to compute from the individual scores a mean index of involvement for migrants from various areas of origin. These and the approximate distances of the areas from the Copperbelt are set out in Table 4.

The product-moment correlation coefficient between the index of urban involvement and distance is -0.68 ± 0.09. This shows that there is a moderately high linear relationship between distance and the index of urban involvement, and that the further away the area is the lower the index of urban involvement of the migrants from that area is likely to be.

This finding supports the contention that those migrants from rural areas within the range of fairly easy and frequent personal contact from

13. The procedure is set out in Mitchell and Shaul, 1964. In this case concomitance ratios were analyzed by the centroid method. The factor solution was rotated to simple structure manually. Analysis by principal components would probably have been preferable, but in the absence of access to a computer the centroid method was used since it could be done on desk calculating machines. Subsequently I was able to make a principal components analysis of the material yielding slightly different weights and to extend the validation of the indices slightly. See Mitchell (1969a).

Table 4. Mean Distance from Copperbelt of Area of Origin and Index of Urban Involvement

Area of Origin (*i*)	*Mean Distance* (*ii*)	*Index of Involvement* (*iii*)	*Expected Index* (*iv*)	*Difference* (*v*)	*C.R.* (*vi*)
Ndola	50	60.4	58.5	1.9	.27
Fort Rosebery	135	60.0	55.9	4.1	.58
Congo	150	49.5	55.5	−6.0	.85
Solwezi	160	42.5	55.2	−12.7	1.80
Mkushi	170	61.0	54.9	6.1	.86
Broken Hill	180	62.8	54.6	8.2	1.15
Serenje	240	56.0	52.8	3.2	.45
Kawambwa	240	54.2	52.3	1.4	.20
Luwingu	265	55.8	52.0	3.8	.54
Kasempa	270	50.0	51.9	−1.9	.27
Lusaka	270	53.2	51.9	1.3	.18
Mumbwa	280	57.0	51.6	5.4	.76
Mwinilunga	280	39.2	51.6	−12.4	1.75
Mporokoso	310	50.1	50.7	−0.6	.08
Kasama	315	54.5	50.5	4.0	.57
Mpika	335	59.4	49.9	9.5	1.34
Kabompo	335	47.8	49.9	−2.1	.30
Southern Province	360	42.1	49.2	−7.1	1.00
Angola	390	39.9	48.3	−8.3	1.17
Abercorn	410	49.8	47.7	2.1	.30
Petauke	415	47.4	47.5	−0.1	.01
Balovale	435	49.0	46.9	2.1	.30
Chinsali	440	43.6	46.8	−3.8	.45
Isoka	450	45.4	46.5	−1.1	.16
Fort Jameson	525	41.5	44.2	−2.7	.38
Barotseland	555	49.9	43.3	6.6	.93
Cent. Prov. Malawi	660	35.9	40.1	−4.2	.59
Lundazi	680	50.0	39.6	10.4	1.47
Tanganyika	730	16.5	38.0	−21.5	3.04*
S. Rhodesia	780	42.4	36.6	5.8	.82
North. Prov. Malawi	820	37.8	35.4	2.4	.34
South. Prov. Malawi	880	39.3	33.7	5.6	.79

Standard error of estimate = 7.07. Critical ratios over the 5 per cent level are marked with an asterisk.

town are able to involve themselves in urban activities and relationships more completely than those from areas so far distant that participation in affairs in them would involve a relatively protracted withdrawal from urban social relationships. Paradoxically, it is those who are most easily able to participate in rural affairs by reason of the proximity of their home areas to their places of employment who are best able to involve themselves in town life.

We may appreciate this regularity more fully, however, if we examine the exceptions to it. This is most easily done by using a regression equation to compute what we could expect the mean index of involvement to be for migrants coming from an area at any given distance from the Copperbelt and comparing this theoretical index with the index which has been empirically observed. Where the observed mean indices differ markedly from these theoretical indices, we may assume that special factors are operating and a special examination of these cases is called for. Column (iv) of Table 4 shows the expected index of urban involvement computed from the regression equation.[14] The ratio of the standard error of estimate to the difference between observed and expected index is set out in column (vi) of Table 4.

Here we see that the expected index differs from the observed index by an amount of more than 1.96 times the standard error of estimate for only one area, Tanzania, and approaches it for Solwezi and Mwinilunga. In all three cases the index of urban involvement in relation to distance from the Copperbelt is lower than we might have expected from the observed overall relationship between distance and the index of urban involvement.

These cases, departing as they do from the general run of the relationship, serve to point up further complexities in the relationship and suggest additional lines of enquiry. Initially we note that while the migrants from Tanzania show less involvement in urban living than we may have expected from the overall relationship between distance and involvement, those from Lundazi, an area only slightly nearer to the Copperbelt, have a mean index which is somewhat higher than the expected level, though statistically the difference is not significant. The differences in the attributes associated with involvement which we have used to compute the mean index are as follows:

	Lundazi per cent	Tanzania per cent
Proportion with more than median proportion of adult life in town	62.71	12.55
Proportion with more than five years continuous residence in town	25.73	8.06

14. Expected index = 59.97 − 0.02997 (Distance).

Proportion with wife in town	77.12	27.90
Proportion evincing positive attitude to continued residence in town	35.61	31.96
Proportion with semi-professional, white-collar, or skilled occupation	51.07	20.63

It is clear that the relationship between distance and urban involvement is not mechanical, and that in some circumstances special factors intervene. Insofar as the migrants from Tanzania are concerned, several accounts confirm that, in general, they do not involve themselves in urban activities when they are in town. Gulliver (1957: 44), for example, who studied Nyakyusa labor migration—and the Nyakyusa constitute the majority of the migrants from Tanzania on the Copperbelt—describes the situation thus:

> There are relatively few Nyakyusa who do not return home from the employment areas or who remain there for long periods. These people retain a great love for their own village life and tribal culture. They do not readily mix with other tribesfolk or learn other languages and customs; they have a particular indigenous way of life and set of values, including a system of age-village organization thought to be unique in Africa; their corporate life flourishes and is both a pleasure and a pride to them. Consequently they accept, and temporarily enjoy the necessity and advantages of employment in urban areas but they have no wish to remain there long, let alone to become urbanized wage-earners.

The Nyakyusa are drawn from the body of patrilineal East African peoples whose cultures and languages are markedly different from the matrilineal Central African peoples who predominate on the Copperbelt. In addition, like the migrants from the Congo, Angola, Mozambique, and Malawi, they are not Zambian nationals. They thus constitute an easily identifiable minority group in a population which is mainly Bemba-speaking. Epstein, describing the Nyakyusa on the Copperbelt, writes:

> . . . they have been generally despised by their fellow-workers of the local tribes, and in the past clashes between Nyakyusa and others were said to be common. Possibly because of this hostility, possibly because of linguistic differences, the Nyakyusa appear to live a life apart from the rest of the community. The impression of separateness is further emphasized in the fact that most Nyakyusa are not accompanied by their wives and thus tend to live contiguously in the mens' single quarters (Epstein 1958: 8-9).

Epstein points out also that the percentage of mine workers who were members of the mine workers' trade union was smaller than the average for all tribes (pp. 115-16),[15] a fact which could be interpreted as reflecting their being less involved in the social obligations of an industrial community than less distant peoples. From the point of view of the argument being presented here, it is significant that Epstein attributes the reluctance of the Nyakyusa to participate in a strike in 1955 partly to their lack of locally available rural kinsfolk from whom they could expect help with food during the strike (p. 238). This is an illustration of the very direct way in which the existence of a network of local support influences participation in social action in urban areas.

In the case of the Nyakyusa on the Copperbelt we have several factors operating conjointly. They are a cultural and linguistic minority group, and they appear to be deeply attached to rural communal life. But at the same time their rural homes are so far from the Copperbelt that in order to maintain their involvement in the rural society activities they must withdraw completely from town life and undertake the long and expensive journey back to their rural homes.

The data from Lundazi, however, appear to contradict this interpretation. Here the distance from the Copperbelt is almost the same as from Tanzania, but the migrants on the Copperbelt from this area appear on the whole, unlike those from Tanzania, to have immersed themselves in town living. We lack detailed ethnographic studies of the people of Lundazi district such as we have for the Nyakyusa, and are unable, therefore, to seek an explanation in terms of local conditions in the Lundazi area. A number of *ad hoc* explanations immediately suggest themselves: that the basic economic conditions in the Lundazi area are too poor to attract migrants back easily; that the people in the Copperbelt from Lundazi are those most heavily involved in urban life who have filtered through the intermediate towns of Fort Jameson, Lusaka, and Broken Hill en route to the Copperbelt[16]; and lastly that the relatively frequent

15. This is confirmed by the findings of a study which I made independently, before Epstein worked on the Copperbelt. In an analysis of the staff records of one of the mines made in September 1951, I found that of the 5,649 Africans employed, 2,331 or 43.0 per cent were paying trade union dues through the company. Among the 592 Nyakyusa mine workers, however, only 168 or 28.4 per cent were subscribing to the trade union through the company. The implication is that proportionately fewer Nyakyusa were contributing members of the trade union.

16. Some evidence that this may be true is provided by the mean indices of urban involvement of Lundazi migrants at Lusaka, where the stream first reaches the line of rail; at Broken Hill, which is a labor center intermediate between Lusaka and the

bus services from Fort Jameson to the line of rail, as against those from Tukuyu, may make it easier for migrants from Lundazi to remain in contact with their rural homes without withdrawing from urban life for extended periods. I put forward these ideas, however, not so much as explanations than as suggestions for further study.

Solwezi presents another anomaly in terms of the otherwise close association between distance and urban involvement, though not as definitive as Tanzania. Once again the degree of urban involvement, as shown by the frequency of the attributes we have chosen to indicate it, is lower for men from Solwezi than we would have expected in view of the district's proximity to the Copperbelt. Fort Rosebery is about the same distance from the Copperbelt as Solwezi, but the migrants from that district show a very different incidence of the attributes associated with urban involvement.

	Solwezi per cent	Fort Rosebery per cent
Proportion with more than median proportion of adult life in towns	44.96	69.68
Proportion with more than five years continuous residence in town	29.96	42.17
Proportion with wife in town	64.18	83.14
Proportion evincing a favorable attitude to continued urban residence	35.62	46.47
Proportion with semi-professional, white-collar, or skilled occupations	23.87	28.23

Migrants from two other areas west of the Copperbelt, Mwinilunga and Angola (and to a lesser extent Kabompo, Balovale and Kasempa), exhibit similar "lower than expected" indices of urban involvement, though not to the same degree as those from Solwezi.

Ethnographic studies in the Fort Rosebery area show that there has been a long history of labor migration to the Copperbelt (Richardson, 1959; Kay, 1960). There have been no comparable ethnographic studies

Copperbelt; and at the Copperbelt itself. These are 28, 39, and 50, respectively, suggesting that it is those more involved in town life in the urban population who migrate to the more distant labor centers. The numbers involved, however, are small and indices may not be too reliable.

conducted in the Solwezi area, so it is not possible to draw the contrast with Fort Rosebery. The general impression from the reports of District Commissioners, however, is that the areas to the west of the Copperbelt, Solwezi included, are relatively poorly developed economically. This implies that bus services probably operate less frequently along the roads leading west from the Copperbelt, whereas services through Fort Rosebery, which is one of the main routes of labor migration from the Northern Province to the Copperbelt, are much more frequent.[17] It would be much easier, therefore, for a person from Fort Rosebery living on the Copperbelt to visit his rural home and get back to the Copperbelt within a relatively short space of time than it would be for a person from Solwezi. In addition there is a constant ebb and flow of travelers and visitors between Fort Rosebery and the Copperbelt, so that migrants from that district would always be able to maintain contact through third parties with their rural homes even if they themselves did not travel. In short I argue that there is a general relationship between a migrant's involvement in urban living and the proximity of his place of origin to the town, which is intelligible in terms of what we know of the persistence of rural roles and statuses of African townsmen in colonial situations. Where the general relationship does not hold, then special local circumstances operate to obscure it.

Conclusion

The findings of this analysis of survey data, therefore, are consistent with Mayer's suggestion that the degree to which an individual is able to become caught up in urban life depends upon the extent to which he is able to maintain his participation in events and affairs in his rural home without finding it necessary to absent himself completely from the town for long periods.

An important determinant of the degree to which a person is able to do this is the physical distance of his rural home from the town and the efficacy of the transportation services connecting the town and the rural area. That mere geographical distance is not the sole factor is shown by the fact that migrants from areas approximately equidistant from town,

17. No statistics of passenger traffic are available from the reports of the Commissioner of Road Traffic, Lusaka, which may be used to substantiate this contention. I have been informed by the Secretary of the Central African Road Services that the information does not exist.

but differing in economic and social background, exhibit markedly dissimilar indices of urban involvement. By using methods of statistical analysis, we have been able not only to confirm the original hypothesis in general terms, but also to discover departures from it and thereby to point to areas and problems which call for additional studies, studies which are likely to illuminate further the as yet unelucidated relationship between the structure of social relationships and the characteristics of the demographically stabilized town population.

References Cited

Baldwin, R. E.
1966. *Economic Development and Export Growth: A Study of Northern Rhodesia. 1920–1960.* Berkeley and Los Angeles: University of California Press.

Bradley, K.
1952. *Copper Venture: The Discovery and Development of Roan Antelope and Mufulira.* Mufulira Copper Mines and Roan Antelope Copper Mines, Ltd.

Epstein, A. L.
1958. *Politics in an Urban African Community.* Manchester: Manchester University Press for Rhodes-Livingstone Institute.

Gann, L. H.
1958. *The Birth of a Plural Society: The Development of Northern Rhodesia under the British South Africa Company: 1894-1914.* Manchester: Manchester University Press for Rhodes-Livingstone Institute.

Hall, R.
1965. *Zambia.* London: Pall Mall Press.

Kay, G.
1960. *A Social and Economic Study of Fort Rosebery.* Rhodes-Livingstone Institute Communication No. 21.

Mayer, P.
1961. *Townsmen and Tribesmen.* Cape Town: Oxford University Press for Rhodes University Institute for Social and Economic Research.

1962. "Migrancy and the Study of African Towns." *American Anthropologist* 64: 576-92.

1964. "Labour Migrancy and the Social Network." In Holleman, J. F., Knox, J., Mann, J. W., and Heard, K. A. (eds.), *Problems of Transition: Proceedings of the Social Sciences Research Conference held in the University of Natal, Durban in July 1962.* Pietermaritzburg: University of Natal Press: 21-34.

Mitchell, J. C.

1951. "A Note on the Urbanization of Africans on the Copperbelt." *Rhodes-Livingstone Journal.* 12: 20-27.

1954. "The Distribution of African Labour by Area of Origin on the Copper Mines of Northern Rhodesia." *Rhodes-Livingstone Journal* 14: 30-36.

1956. "Urbanization, Detribalization and Stabilization in Southern Africa: A Problem of Definition and Measurement." In Forde, D. (ed.), *Social Implications of Industrialization and Urbanization in Africa South of the Sahara.* Tensions and Technology Series. Paris: UNESCO: 693-711.

1959. "The Causes of Labour Migration." *Bulletin of the Inter-African Labour Institute* 6: 12-46. Reprinted in *Migrant Labour in Africa South of the Sahara.* London: CCTA Publication No. 79 (1961): 259-80.

1961. "Wage Labour and African Population Movements in Central Africa." In Barbour, K. M., and Prothero, R. M. (eds.), *Essays on African Population.* London: Routledge and Kegan Paul: 193-248.

1969a. "Urbanization, Detribalization, Stabilization and Urban Commitment in Southern Africa: A Problem of Definition and Measurement." In Meadows, P., and Mizruchi, E. H. (eds.), *Urbanism, Urbanization and Change: Comparative Perspectives,* pp. 470-93. London: Addison-Wesley.

1969b. "Structural Plurality, Urbanization and Labour Circulation in Southern Rhodesia." In Jackson, J. S. (ed.), *Migration: Sociological Studies No. 2,* pp. 156-80. Cambridge, Eng.: Cambridge University Press.

Mitchell, J. C., and J. R. H. Shaul

1965. "An Approach to the Measurement of Commitment to Urban Residence." In Snowball, George J. (ed.), *Science and Medicine in Central Africa. Proceedings of the Central Africa Scientific and Medical Congress held at Lusaka, Northern Rhodesia, 26-30 August 1963.* London: Pergamon Press: 625-33.

Niddrie, D.

1954. "The Road to Work: A Survey of the Influence of Transport on Migrant Labour in Central Africa." *Rhodes-Livingstone Journal* 15: 31-42.

Pons, V.

1956. "The Growth of Stanleyville and the Composition of its African Population." In Forde, D. (ed.), *Social Implications of Industrialization and Urbanization in Africa South of the Sahara.* Tensions and Technology Series. Paris: UNESCO: 229-73.

Reader, D.

1961. *The Black Man's Portion: History, Demography and Living Conditions in the Native Locations of East London, Cape Province.* Cape Town: Oxford University Press for Institute of Social and Economic Research, Rhodes University.

Richardson, E. M.
1959. *Aushi Village Structure in the Fort Rosebery District of Northern Rhodesia*. Rhodes-Livingstone Institute Communication No. 13.

Watson, W.
1958. *Tribal Cohesion in a Money Economy*. Manchester: Manchester University Press.

Williams, S.
1962. *The Distribution of the African Population of Northern Rhodesia*. Rhodes-Livingstone Institute Communication No. 24.

Wilson, G. B.
1941-42. *An Essay on the Economics of Detribalization in Northern Rhodesia*. Part I. Rhodes-Livingstone Institute Paper No. 5.

Sociological, Cultural, and Political Characteristics of Some Urban Migrants in Peru

William Mangin

I bring together here some thoughts I have had about the urbanization process in Peru.[1] I have been particularly interested in migrants to the capital city, Lima, who have subsequently moved out to squatter settlements, called barriadas, that ring the city, and shall discuss the residents of one barriada that I will refer to as Benavides. I have also included some ideas about current social and political changes in Peru.

Urban centers have existed in Peru since before the Inca empire (Schaedel, 1951). In addition to sizable cities such as Chan Chan on the north coast and Cuzco in the southern highlands, there were many towns of 2,000 or more inhabitants in the area. That these older cities, as well as subsequent ones, have grown largely through migration from rural areas seems so commonplace an observation as hardly to need mentioning.

Many commentators, ranging from newspapermen to social scientists, however, as well as many government officials and urban planners, seem to view the present-day migrations from small towns and rural areas to Lima, Chimbote, Ilo, and other large Peruvian cities as a remarkable, temporary phenomenon. In spite of repeated claims that migration is ta-

1. My fieldwork in Peru in 1951-53 was financed by the Social Science Research Council and the Cornell-Peru Project. In 1957-59 I was financed by a grant from the National Institute of Mental Health of the U.S. government. In 1960 I worked two months in Peru financed by the Sullivan Institute of Psychoanalysis, in 1961 by the Maxwell School of Syracuse University. In 1962-64 I have worked in Peru for the U.S. Peace Corps. I have returned to Lima six times since 1964, the last visit being in 1971.

pering off and barriada invasions are over, government planners say that, although the rate of increase seems to be declining, migration continues, and in 1970 and 1971 two of the largest barriada invasions in the history of Lima took place. Dorich (1961), commenting on population growth in Peru between 1940 and 1957, shows the following figures:

Population Growth in Important Peruvian Urban Centers (In Thousands)

Urban Center	*1940*	*1957*	*Percentage Increase*
Lima	540	1,135	110
Callao	72	126	75
Arequipa	70	120	71
Piura	20	31	55
Cuzco	46	66	43
Puno	16	22	37
Huánuco	13	18	38
Chimbote	4	25	525
Ilo	1	10	900

Source: Ministry of Finance. Statistical Deaprtment.

The 1961 national census indicates that there are 1,769,323 people in Lima and about 64,000 in Chimbote. The head of the Office of Urban Planning in Chimbote estimated that there were over 80,000 inhabitants in 1964 and over 125,000 in 1971. Lima had over three million inhabitants in 1971. The country as a whole has a rate of population increase of well over 3 per cent, and the large cities are booming by the day.

The Lima-Callao area is the primary city and the governmental, "cultural," recreational, economic, and educational center of the country, and has about 20 per cent of the population. It is one of the busiest ports and the busiest air center in South America. The Chimbote figures indicate clearly that one would expect to find a small percentage of adult natives of the city but, even in Lima, the majority of the adult population is provincial-born (Stycos and Richards, 1963). The cities have grown largely through migration from the outside, mainly the mountain provinces (Dobyns and Vasquez, 1963; Bradfield, 1963).

The migrants come from all over the country and from all social classes, and they settle in all parts of the cities. The development of the fish meal industry on the north coast and of a steel mill in Chimbote and a copper smelter near Ilo have caused new centers to develop; but the largest concentration of migrants still come to Lima, and this paper will deal with a phenomenon related to migration to Lima.

Most migrants, like most Peruvians, are relatively poor, lower-class people. There is considerable economic, racial, and cultural variation within this segment, and there are enormous differences in the degree of urban sophistication. Upon arrival many of them settle in crowded parts of the older sections of Lima (Breña, La Victoria, Barrios Altos, Callao, Rimac, Surquillo), where they pay high rents for substandard houses and apartments. The stimuli of overcrowdedness and generally unhealthy, unpleasant, and expensive housing, plus large unoccupied areas of state-owned land on hillsides and river banks near the city, have led to the creation of invasion-formed squatter settlements, called barriadas, on these lands (Mangin, 1960a, 1963; Matos, 1961). At least 15 per cent of Lima's population is in barriadas, and 89 per cent of the heads of families in barriadas were born in the provinces, according to a 1956 census (Matos, 1961). The majority of the population in barriadas, again following the Matos 1956 census, is Lima-born, because of the large number of children under 10 (approximately 35 per cent of the barriada population). Large invasions along the Canta road and in the San Pedro sector of El Agustino hill in Lima in 1963 and 1964, plus numerous smaller invasions, increased the barriada population to about 250,000. Subsequent invasions to the north, south, and east of Lima, and filling in of existing barriadas, plus natural population increase have led some observers to estimate the barriada population in 1972 to be somewhere between 750,000 and a million.

The evolution of a barriada may be described as follows:

> Lima is changing rapidly, as are the barriadas, and it is difficult to compile a list of characteristics that will apply to all barriadas or to any one barriada over a period of time. It is possible, however, to describe an ideal type of barriada and indicate the direction of change. There is variation between barriadas, of course, but their histories are remarkably similar. A typical barriada, allowing for a few months' settling period, exhibits the following characteristics:
>
> 1. The overwhelming majority of the adults are provincial-born, and the majority of these are from the mountains. They are usually young people with children. There are few adolescents or aged.

2. Few residents have come to the barriada directly from the province but have resided for some time in Lima.

3. The residents are all "owners" of the lots and the straw-mat houses they themselves have constructed. In some cases there has been land speculation from the beginning, but generally speculators have been rare among the original settlers. There are no units that are not dwellings, and the usual household group is the nuclear family. In many cases the association will allow only nuclear families and married couples to build.

4. There is a feeling of separateness from the city, a feeling of being under attack, which is reinforced by the lack of municipal services and protection and by unfavorable public attitudes toward barriadas.

5. The residents generally feel very much a part of a community and there is a sense of belonging. There is considerable pride in achievement and in home ownership. A successful invasion is one of the few opportunities for lower class Peruvians to see a direct relationship between initiative, hard work and success.

6. The barriada associations (such as Fathers of Families of Mariscal Castilla, Defenders of Mirones, and House Owners of Santa Clara de Bella Luz) consist of self-appointed groups, usually the leaders and organizers of the original settlements, and leadership is based chiefly on the personality of the members plus kinship and regional loyalty.

The direction of change for each of the above items seems to be as follows:

1. Naturally, the percentage of provincial-born goes down as more children are born in a barriada. The heads of new families, both those who construct new homes and those who replace moving families, continue to be provincial-born, and many people come from the provinces to reside in the new house of a relative.

2. More people come directly to the barriadas from the provinces, often upon the advice and with the assistance of relatives and others from the same region.

3. Renting becomes more frequent, and many individuals sell, lease, or lend their houses, almost always without having clear title. The number of boarders goes up as does the number of extra people in the household. The open conflicts over lot ownership characteristic of the early period give way to litigation before the

barriada association or in the police stations and courts. The local associations continue to exert some control but the National Housing Authority and Lima city officials begin to play a part in zoning and title assignments. As the newly settled area becomes more valuable, outside individuals and groups, both public and private, begin to move in. Many families open stores and/or bars in their homes, a common provincial pattern, and some public buildings (schools, assembly halls, churches, offices for the barriada association, movies) are constructed. Many such structures are begun but never finished or finished only after long periods. Most houses are gradually converted from straw to cement and brick. The nuclear family is augmented by relatives of various degrees of closeness as well as by occasional non-kin. Desertion by husbands is common enough to make the woman-children household a frequently encountered phenomenon.

4. Generally the feeling of separateness lessens and services increase, but there is considerable variation on this point. In many cases, where there has been no continued pressure for the land from outsiders or where the inhabitants have successfully resisted such pressure, the area gradually becomes "urbanized" and blends into the city, as in the case of Zarumilla and parts of San Martin de Porres and Mirones. The electric company serves the area, branch banks and stores appear, movies are opened, bus lines operate, priests come, and finally the government recognizes the existence of the barriada for more than tax collection by appointing school teachers and, in one case, even appointing two mounted police to patrol an area of five square miles and 20,000 people.

5. "Belongingness" tends to be replaced by coresidence. The original settlers are swallowed up by the growing population, and some of them move out. The need for unity in defense against outside threats to the barriada lessens, and internal tensions increase. Many more people rent, and many of the older inhabitants, who were pleased with their situation at first, begin to complain of the surroundings, quarrel with their neighbors, and comment unfavorably on new arrivals ("too many brute-Indians," "too many brute-Negroes," and "too many bad people"). Many individuals also develop new, or reinforce old, relationships with outsiders on the basis of such ties as kinship, region, occupation, and politics.

6. The association takes on a more political character and, even

> though personality and regionalism continue to be important in the local elections, national politics and national issues play a larger part. The original leaders often move out (in which case they may or may not continue to exert influence) or, following a time-honored Peruvian tradition, a reform faction accuses them of stealing money and they, in turn, can choose to fight, flee, or sulk. As the barriada becomes more a part of Lima the association usually loses power.
>
> For most of the migrants the barriada represents a definite improvement in terms of housing and general income, and Lima represents a definite improvement over the economically and socially oppressive life of the mountain Indian, Cholo, or lower-class Mestizo.

In his 1956 census Matos (1961) asked for motives for coming to Lima. There were 17,426 provincial-born heads of families who gave 22,461 replies. Matos, using general headings, groups 61 per cent of the responses as indicating economic motives either drawing the person to Lima or pushing him out of the provinces; 23 per cent as social, largely family conflicts; 9 per cent as educational, usually for children; plus a few others. He found 10 per cent illiteracy among heads of families, and only 1 per cent declared themselves unemployed, although a large percentage of these were not fully employed (Matos, 1961).

At one extreme of the Peruvian social system is the White upper class, characterized by great wealth, high rates of intraclass endogamy, and out-marriage to foreigners, control of extractive industries, land, banking, and commerce as well as the government, and a lack of knowledge of life outside their own circle; and at the other extreme is the isolated Quechua-speaking Indian, characterized by loyalty to a local community, local endogamy, lack of knowledge of life outside of the community or hacienda (Mangin, 1957), and occupational and social ties to agriculture and land. Parenthetically, neither of these groups is numerically large, and neither is important in migration to cities. The upper-class group maintains itself with little change. The isolated Indian group is rapidly becoming less isolated, and thus is changing character by the day. Individuals from isolated Indian communities seldom migrate directly to Lima; they are likely to migrate to a coastal or tropical hacienda to earn money and then they or their children may move on to Lima, or they may move to one of the cities or towns in the mountains.

As Simmons has pointed out (1952), there are many subcultural divisions in Peruvian society, and for many years Creole culture (Simmons, 1955) was dominant. The major difference in the last few years has been the increasing effect of the mountain culture on modern Peruvian culture and the decreasing influence of Creole culture. The relatively stable Indian, Mestizo, and Creole types in Peru[2] are giving way in numbers and in influence to a transitional group, called by several writers "Cholos,"[3] and to modern Peruvian participants in the national culture.

In treating subcultural variation in a changing society such as Peru's, it must be pointed out that the types are not clear-cut, there is considerable overlap, and a large number of individuals are impossible to place. The Cholo group is composed of first-, second- or third-generation Indians who have left Indian communities and, generally, have left subsistence agriculture as a way of life. The values of nineteenth-century capitalism and twentieth-century socialism and communism seem to have great, if contradictory, appeal for many of them. They are plantation workers, truck drivers and owners, market workers, fishermen and fishing-boat owners, waiters, clerks and/or owners of small stores, salesmen, street vendors, university students, minor government officials, etc. They cover a wide range of occupations and political interests and cut across the lower class–middle class division. The aspirations of parents for children are unrealistically high, and uniformly directed toward economic and social change. They want their children to have more money than they have, different kinds of jobs (doctors, lawyers, teachers, etc.), and to live middle-class lives.

The Cholo group is concentrated largely in cities and towns and constitutes a significant part of the barriada population. In recent years I have detected a modification in the nature of the changes desired by this group. In a lecture delivered in 1958, I said of a barriada population:

> Children are encouraged to be as Creole or Peruvian as possible and there are few cases of parents who actively instruct their children in Quechua or in Indian culture. The trend in clothing, music preferences, amusements, beverages, food, courtship, etc., is all away from the Indian. Actually none has to actively teach this. Anticipatory socialization

2. For discussions of class and caste differences in Peru see Adams, 1959; Arguedas, 1952, 1957; Bourricaud, 1954; Hammel, 1961a; Mangin, 1955; Nunez del Prado, 1951; Rowe, 1947; Simmons, 1952, 1955; Tschopik, 1948, 1952; Pan-American Union, 1961.
3. Fried, 1961; Mangin, 1955; Schaedel, Escobar, and Nunez del Prado, 1959a, 1959b.

> is institutionalized. Parents, with the help of teachers, newspapers, priests, and peers, provide their children with new reference groups to which neither they nor the children belong.

I would still say that the remarks are applicable, but I now see a strong Quechua, mountain nationalism developing, which is affecting the national culture as well as revising the attitude of many Cholos toward Indian culture and reducing the shame attached to speaking Quechua and exhibiting publicly preference for Indian customs and tastes. Mountain culture is everywhere in evidence in Lima (Doughty, 1970) and is maintained more vigorously than ever by the many mountain regional associations in the city (Mangin, 1959). There are as many Quechua speakers now as ever before, and the number is constantly growing. There is also a tendency for educated upper- and middle-class Peruvians to equate interest in Quechua and Indian culture, especially in the field of education, with left-wing political movements, particularly communism and Trotskyism. There have been indications during the past few years that this has perhaps become a case of the self-fulfilling prophecy, and many Indian and Cholo individuals, completely unsophisticated politically, are identifying themselves as communists and Trotskyists. This is due in part to the appeal of the communist promise to change the social order, but, since most of the communist leaders are upper- and middle-class themselves and share the prejudices of those classes toward Cholos and Indians, they are not trusted. The constant identification by the press, many government officials, and upper-class spokesmen of Indian demands for land in the mountains and Cholo demands for land in city barriadas as "communist inspired," and the frequently made charge that Indian land invasions in the mountains and Cholo invasions in barriadas are "communist-led," has probably had more of an effect in the self-identification than the actual labor of the communists.

A 1964 story in *La Prensa*, a large Lima newspaper, cites a case of a mass meeting of Indians in the Cuzco mountain region cheering a call from one of the speakers to lynch "all those who wear ties." The distrust and resentment Indians feel toward Whites and Mestizos, particularly that felt by Indian women,[4] has been constant for centuries. What is new is the beginning of feelings of identification with vague political ends, a sense of being part of a large category ("Cholos," "Indians," "people of

4. In regard to the participation of women in land invasions in the Cuzco area, there was an interesting series of articles in the newspaper *Expreso* by Hugo Neira in February and March of 1963, incorporated in Neira, 1964.

the barriadas," etc.) rather than just a member of a family or local group, or at the most, a person from a particular region. In the past, family, local group, and regional loyalties have been about the only ones for Indians and Cholos. Presently, loyalty to Peru as a country is growing because of improved transportation and communication, plus the advent of a new administration, which, although dominated by basically elitist, White, upper- and middle-class architects, engineers, physicians, and businessmen, has conveyed a feeling of commitment and patriotic enthusiasm to much of the country.

Class consciousness and awareness of cultural and linguistic differences are also growing, along with the new sense of national unity. Many of the individuals most active in promoting Indian and Cholo identification are Whites. Many others are marginal men, often more at home in Spanish than Quechua, usually educated and acculturated to "Western" customs. The early 1960's, however, saw the emergence of many Cholo and Indian leaders, often in connection with land invasions and land title fights in country and city.

The large majority of the Indian population, as well as a large percentage of the Cholo population, is still uncommitted politically, however, and still not overly concerned with making common cause with any group in relation to any broad national issue except agrarian reform. The rural and urban land invasions of the sixties led to heightened interclass political tension that has abated somewhat, but by no means completely, with the rural land reforms and the urban policies of consolidating barriadas into the cities initiated by the military government in 1969 and 1970. The word "barriada" is no longer used in official sources. The new term is "pueblos jovenes," young towns.

The data for the following discussion were collected mainly by me during fieldwork in the communities described. I have also had access to large bodies of data collected by Cornell investigators on the rural community, and I have collaborated with a psychiatrist, Dr. Humberto Rotondo, and an anthropologist, Dr. José Matos Mar, in the employment of numbers of interviewers to administer various questionnaires in barriadas. I refer to the personally collected material in about the same terms as the questionnaire material, although I have found the former to be more reliable when dealing with complex matters. One of the problems with much of the questionnaire material has been the class appearance and bias of the interviewers. The psychiatrists and social workers were mostly upper- and upper-middle-class and very much Caucasian.

The university students were generally lower-middle and lower-class, and many of them rejected the Indian and Cholo culture. Both groups were hampered by political and social preconceptions, different in each case, but equally effective in preventing a relaxed interview situation and any degree of objectivity. There were, of course, notable exceptions, and practically all of the interviewers worked hard and conscientiously. Two incidents, typical of both rural and urban interviewing, will illustrate some of the difficulty without going further into the matter. One psychiatrist was obviously impatient with having to search for the specific individuals chosen in a sample. The interviewing he did was mainly on Sunday morning and he wanted to go home. He was also much more accustomed to having short, dark people seek him out for favors rather than the reverse. His remark was, "Why all the running around after these dopes? One Cholo is the same as another." A social worker who had worked in Lima slums for several years said, "I have never seen a highlander (*serrano*) who was not closed (*cerrado*). No matter who they are or how long they have been here they are closed people (*gente cerrada*)." The grain of truth in each of these cases is that the majority of Indians and Cholos probably would fit the comments when confronted by individuals with the appearance and attitudes of the investigators in question. In this regard, it is possible that a foreigner has a slight advantage in this type of interviewing, since he does not convey the same kinds of class-linked bodily and linguistic cues to the informants.[5]

The interviews and observations in Benavides were generally taken in houses, bars, street stands, buses, and on walks from the barriada to the city bus stop. On a few occasions family members were used as interpreters with older men and women who spoke little or no Spanish.[6] The major parts of the description and the census tables refer to the 1957-59 period. I have returned there for brief periods every year from 1959 to 1971.

5. There were instances of opposition to foreigners on occasion, and one informant said to a Peruvian investigator, "What is the matter with you people asking all these questions? You even sent a gringo around to bother me."

6. The home situation where most of the Benavides interviews took place was not always the best for concentration. Generally children and babies and dogs crowded the one- or two-room house. Alley and street noises provided a constant distraction. Many times an inquisitive and often suspicious and irate husband or wife rattled around in the cramped quarters. Squabbling between neighbors, especially mothers, over children's quarrels escalate rapidly in barriada blocks, and some interviews took place with fairly serious fights going on immediately outside the open door. I have over fifty references in my notes to husbands being drunk, and drunken husbands often interfered with their wives' interviews.

Occasional comparisons are made with rural mountain communities in general and a few with a specific Indian community, Vicos, where I have done fieldwork and have had access to material collected by members of the Cornell-Peru Project.[7]

The barriada has changed gradually from a visible, new settlement to a relatively established neighborhood of the district of Rimac.

The tables used refer to three different samples from the same population. In a census taken in 1959 we collected a form for each of the 561 households. Tables 1, 3, 4, 8, and 10 refer to the households. Tables 2, 6 and 7 refer to figures drawn from the lines of the form dealing with individuals in the households. Table 9 and the results of the adaption of the moral inventory tests refer to more intensive interviews done with a 2 per cent sample of Benavides adults.

The following composite case history gives some idea of the processes involved in recruiting and organizing for a barriada invasion and of life during the early stage in Benavides:[8]

> Fortunato Quispe, a Quechua-speaking Indian from an hacienda in the mountains of Peru, contracted himself out to a coastal sugar plantation for a year's work in order to earn some cash for a religious festival.
>
> After a year on the coast he took a wife and settled down on the plantation leaving his mountain home for good. He and his wife had seven children. When their oldest, Blas, was 18, he found himself with no job, no possibility of schooling, and under pressure from his father to leave and get a job. The small two-room adobe company house was hardly big enough for the parents and the seven children and the sugar company was mechanizing the plantation even as its resident population expanded rapidly. Blas, who had spoken mainly Quechua as a child, was, at 18, fully at home in Spanish. He had visited Lima, the capital city, twice, was an avid radio and movie fan and considered the life of the plantation town dull.
>
> Six months after his eighteenth birthday he and his friend, Antonio, took a truck to the Lima valley and took a bus from the

7. For information on the Vicos project see Adams and Cumberland, 1960; Holmberg, 1955, 1960; Mangin, 1955, 1960b; Patch, 1957; and Vasques, 1952, 1955.

8. The case history presented here was published elsewhere (Mangin, 1962) in essentially the same form. It seemed to be useful to include it in this paper because of the invasion description. The original source is out of print.

edge of the valley to the city. Having been there before, they knew how to get to the house of an uncle of Antonio's near the wholesale market district. The uncle had heard via the grapevine that they might come. He was renting a three-room house on a crowded alley for his own family of seven, and his maid and her child slept in the small kitchen. He was only able to put them up for one night. They moved into a cheap hotel and pension near the market, and through Antonio's uncle were recruited for a provincial club, Sons of Paucartambo, the native mountain district of Antonio's and Blas' fathers. Much of their social activity is still with members of the club, and their first orientation to life in Lima was from club members.

Antonio went to work for his uncle, and Blas, who had been robbed of all his clothing from the hotel, took a job as a waiter and clean-up man in a modest boarding house catering to medical and engineering students. He worked six-and-a-half days a week in the pension, taking Thursday nights and Sunday afternoons off. During his first year he saved a little money. He impregnated a maid from a neighbouring house, Carmen, and agreed to marry her sometime. Meanwhile, they rented a two-room one-storey adobe house in a large lot not far from the boarding house. The lot was packed solidly with similar houses and the walks between them were about five feet wide. They had filthy, constantly clogged common toilets and water taps for every ten houses, and the rent was high. They paid extra for electricity and for practically nonexistent city services.

Through a relative of one of the students Blas got a better job as a waiter in a rather expensive restaurant. In spite of the distance and the extra money spent for transportation it paid to take the job. With the arrival of a second child plus a boost in their rent, they found themselves short of money even though Blas' job was quite a good one for a person of his background.

Carmen, Blas' common law wife, had come to Lima at the age of fourteen from the southern highland province of Ayacucho. She had been sent by her mother and step-father to work as a servant in the house of a Lima dentist, who was also a land-owner in Ayacucho, and Carmen was to receive no pay. The dentist promised to "educate" her but, in fact, she was not only not allowed to go to school but was rarely allowed outside the house. During her third year with the dentist's family her mother, who had left her stepfather in Ayacucho, rescued her from the dentist's house after a terrible row. Her mother then found a maid's job for Carmen where she was paid. Carmen worked in several private houses in the next few years and loaned a large part of her earnings to her mother. Blas was her first serious suitor. Previously she had had little experience with men and when Blas asked her to come and live with him after she became pregnant, she was surprised and pleased.

In her own crowded house with Blas and their son she was happier than she had been since her early childhood with her grandmother. Although her work was hard, it was nothing like the work she had done in the houses in Lima. They were poor but Blas had steady work and they ate better than she had in any of her previous homes. Her infrequent arguments with Blas were usually over money. He had once hit her when she had loaned some of the rent money to her mother, but, on the whole, she considered herself well-treated and relatively lucky in comparison with many of her neighbours.

She did not have too much to do with her neighbours, mostly longer-time residents of Lima than she, and she was afraid of the Negroes in the area, having been frightened as a child in the mountains by stories of Negro monsters who ate children. She found herself being drawn into arguments over petty complaints about children trespassing, dogs barking and messing the sidewalk, husband's relative success or failure, mountain Indian traits as opposed to coastal Mestizo traits, etc. She was mainly occupied with her son and her new baby daughter, and the constant arguing annoyed Blas more than it did Carmen. Blas had also been disturbed by the crowded conditions. There was no place for the children to play, and the petty bickering over jurisdiction of the small sidewalk was a constant irritant. Thievery was rampant, and he had even lost some of his clothes, since they had to hang the washing outside above the alley. In Lima's damp climate, it often takes several days to dry clothes even partially.

He had been thinking of moving and, although Carmen was settled into a more or less satisfactory routine, she was interested as well. They carried on for another year and another child without taking any action. When their landlord told them that he was planning to clear the lot and build a cinema within six months, they decided to move. A colleague of Blas' in the restaurant had spoken to him about a group to which he belonged. The members were organizing an invasion of state land to build houses and they wanted fifty families. The group had been meeting irregularly for about a year and when Blas was invited they had forty of the fifty they sought.

The waiters' group came mainly from the same central highland region and their spokesman and leader was a bank employee who was also a functionary of the bank employees' union. The other major faction was a group of career army enlisted men, including several members of a band that plays at state functions, who were stationed near the proposed invasion site. About half of the group had been recruited as Blas was. Blas himself recruited a neighbour and another family from the Sons of Paucartambo, to which he still belonged.

They met a few times with never more than fifteen men present. They were encouraged by the fact that the government seemed to be tolerating squatter invasions. Several earlier invasion attempts had been blocked by the police and in many barriadas people had been beaten, some shot, and a few killed. The recent attitude in 1954, seemed tolerant, but under a dictatorship, or under any government, the law is apt to be administered whimsically and their planned invasion was illegal. Another factor pointing to haste was the loss of seven of their families who had found housing some other way. Blas was one of those suggesting that they move fast, because his eviction date was not far off.

Many barriada invasions had been arranged for the eve of a religious or national holiday. Their invasion site was near the area used once a year, in June, for a grand popular folk-music festival, so they decided to wait until that was over. The next holiday was the Independence Day vacation, July 28th, 29th, 30th; so they picked the night of the 27th. It would give them a holiday to provide a patriotic aura as well as three days off from work to consolidate their position. They thought of naming their settlement after the dictator's popular wife, but, after taking into account the vicissitudes of current politics, they decided to write to her about their pitiful plight, but to name the place after a former general-dictator, long dead, who freed the slaves.

A letter was drawn up for mailing to the dictator's wife and for presentation to the press. The letter stressed equally their respect for the government and their abandonment by the government. They had no hesitation about wringing the most out of the clichés concerning their status as humble, abandoned, lost, helpless and disillusioned but always patriotic servants of the fatherland.

During the last month word was passed from the active meeting-goers, still never more than 20 or 25, to the others and preparations were made. Each family bought its own straw mats and poles for the house, and small groups made arrangements for trucks and taxis. Each household was asked to get a Peruvian flag or make one of paper. No two remember the details of the invasion the same way, but about thirty of the expected forty-five families did invade during the night. A newspaper photographer was notified by the invaders and he arrived about the time the houses were being finished. The members had discussed previously what lots they would take, and how the streets were to be laid out and there was very little squabbling during the first day. By early morning when the police arrived there were at least thirty one-room straw houses flying Peruvian flags and the principal streets were outlined with stones.

The police told them they would have to leave. A picture and story appeared in two papers and by the 30th of July about twenty or thirty more families had come, including some of the old members. A few men, with the help of friends and relatives and, in at least one case, paid workers, had built brick walls around their lots. These families and a few other early arrivals, most of whom are still in the barriada in 1963, proudly refer to themselves as the original invaders and tend to exaggerate the opposition they faced. They were told to leave several times but no-one forced them. A resident, not one of the original invaders, was killed by the police in 1960 during an attempt to build a school on government land. The unfavourable publicity caused the government to desist and the residents cut a lot out of the hillside and built a school.

Blas and Carmen picked a lot about fifteen by thirty metres on the gradual slope of the hill on the principal street. The lot was somewhat larger than most subsequent lots, an advantage of being an original invader.

Blas and some friends quickly expanded the simple invasion one-room house to a three-room straw mat house and they outlined the lot with stones. He worked hard on Sundays and some nights, sometimes alone, sometimes with friends from the barriada or from outside. He soon managed to get a brick wall six-and-a-half feet high around his property.

Many of the residents of barriadas hurry to erect the walls around their lots and then take anywhere from one year to five or ten to finish the house. After about a year of working on the lot and making his "plan," Blas decided to contract a "specialist" to help him put up walls for four rooms. He paid for the materials brought by the "specialist" and helped out on the job. When the walls were done he roofed the rooms with cane, bricked up the windows and put in cement floors. With his first pay cheque, after finishing paying for the walls, Blas made a down payment on a large, elaborate cedar door costing about $45. With the installation of the door and wooden windows they finally felt like homeowners. They even talked of getting formally married.

About two years later, after a particularly damp winter during which his children were frequently sick, he decided to hire another "specialist" to help him put on a concrete roof. He hired a neighbour who had put on other roofs and he found out that the first "specialist" had sold him faulty cement and had also erected the walls in such a way that it would be difficult to put on a roof. It took considerable money, time and energy to rectify the mistakes and put on the roof, but when it was done it was a good job and strong enough to support a second floor some day. Meanwhile a straw mat room has been erected on the roof and Blas helps out with the houses of friends and neighbours against the day he will ask them to help with his second floor.

Skilled bricklayers and concreters abound in barriadas and the bulk of the construction in these places is cheaper than on contracted houses. Much of it is done through informal mutual aid arrangements and when contractors are hired they are generally very closely supervised. There is considerable cheating by contractors on materials and many of the specialists hired for roofing and electrical and plumbing installations are not competent. Transport of materials is often expensive but the personal concern of the builder often results in lower prices at purchase. Some barriadas have electricity from the central power plant and public water; the one in this story does not. The front room/shop combination they have in their house is not only fairly common in barriadas but throughout the provincial area of Peru.

Their principal room fronts on the street and doubles as a shop which Carmen and the oldest children tend. Blas is still a waiter and they now have five children. The saving on rent and the income from the shop make them considerably more prosperous than before, but, in spite of their spectacular view of the bright lights of the centre of Lima some twenty minutes away, Carmen has never seen the Plaza San Martin and has passed through the central business district on the bus only a few times. She has never been inside the restaurant where Blas works. She gets along with most of her neighbours and has the company and assistance of a fifteen-year-old half-sister deposited with her by her mother.

Blas and Carmen have a television set which runs on electricity bought from a private motor owner and they are helping to pay for it by charging their neighbours a small amount to watch. It also brings some business to the store.

Carmen and Blas bemoan the lack of sewage disposal, running water and regular electricity in the barriada, and they complain about the dust from the unpaved streets.

They are also critical of the ramshackle auxiliary bus which serves them, but, on the whole, they are not dissatisfied with their situation. They own a house which is adequate, Blas has steady work, their oldest children are in school, and Blas has been on the elected committee that runs barriada affairs and feels that he has some say in local government. Since local elections are unknown in Peru the barriadas' unofficial elections are unique. The committee passes judgement on requests from new applicants to settle in the barriada and cut new lots out of the hillside. They also decide on requests to sell or rent. Renting is against the rules of the association. Another important function is presenting petitions and requests to various government ministries for assistance. Until 1960 barriada residents had no legal basis for their ownership of lots. Any recognition by the government in the form of assistance or even taxation was an assuring sign. In 1960 the congress passed a law saying, in effect, that what could not be changed might as well be made legal, and residents of barriadas are to be given their lots. As of 1963 a few land titles had been given out by the government, but the people have been buying and selling for years with home-made titles.

The committees are also concerned with internal order. Barriadas are ordinarily quiet places composed mainly of hard-working family groups, but the public image is one of violence, immorality, sloth, crime, and revolutionary left-wing politics. Barriada residents are quite sensitive about this and the committees try to screen out potential trouble makers and control those present. They also try to get as much publicity as possible for the productive work done by barriada people.

The experience of this couple is probably happier than the average family but is certainly well within the "typical" range. They feel, in comparison to people like themselves and in terms of their own aspirations, that they have done well. When asked what they would do if they acquired a large sum of money, they both answer in terms of improving their present property and educating their children. There is some resentment of the children, and Blas beats the oldest boy for not doing well in school, and all five children are bedwetters, but they give the impression of a happy family and, although Carmen cried during several interviews, they smile frequently and seem to be getting along. Carmen speaks some Quechua with her neighbours and her half-sister, and has actually improved her Quechua since coming to the barriada. Spanish is the principal language, however, and neither she nor Blas have any strong interest in their children learning Quechua.

The children themselves learn some Quechua but they speak Spanish with their peers, and in a group of children it is difficult to distinguish those of recently arrived near-Indian migrants from those of the most *Criollo* coastal families. There is a certain amount of antagonism among the adult barriada dwellers over race, cultural difference, politics, and place of origin. The children, however, are strikingly similar in attitude and have very little of the mountain Indian about them.

The situation of Blas and Carmen is similar to that of many others. They have some friends, some relatives and some income, but they could be ruined by a loss of job or any chronic illness of Blas, and they are aware of it. If there is a potentially disruptive factor in their lives it is that the high aspirations they have for

> their children are vastly unrealistic. They are sacrificing and plan to sacrifice more for the education of the children to be professionals, doctors, teachers, people with comfortable lives, and in this they are similar to most interviewed barriada families. But it is highly unlikely that they will be, unless there are monumental and rapid changes in Peru (Mangin, 1963).

After sixteen years of building, Benavides still presents a remarkable appearance. The lower zone is built on the gently rising slope of a crescent-shaped hill. It contains eleven streets that are more or less straight and wide. Seven streets go up the hill and four go across. The lower area was settled first and contains the most substantial brick and adobe houses and most of the stores and bars. The other half of the population lives on the steep hillside around the lower part of the crescent. Cars and buses can traverse the eleven streets, but only footpaths serve the hillside. There are more straw houses on the hillside, particularly among the newcomers at the top, although there is almost constant construction work going on in all zones of the barriada.[9]

The different style of rock, the retaining walls, the hanging-garden effect of the house sites carved out of the hillside, the irregularity and precipitousness of some of the paths and stairways, and the variety of brick, straw, adobe, wood, metal, and cardboard construction make a spectacular, if not always attractive, sight. There is no foliage beyond an occasional potted and carefully tended tree by someone's house, and it is hot and dusty in the summer and cold and damp in the winter. The houses usually involve considerable investment of time, money, labor, and emotion and often show considerable ingenuity and skill. Shortly after the erection of the straw house the lots are walled in, giving an impression of crowding that is often not reflected inside the walled areas. Addresses within the barriada are by street and lot number in the lower part and by two zones, A and B, and lot number in the higher part. No mail is delivered, but a person can be located fairly easily by "passing the voice," and the association leaders make announcements by megaphone and public address systems.

For a stranger it is not always so simple. Not everyone knows everyone else. At the close of the study in 1959 I probably knew more about more individuals in Benavides than any resident did. Many feel that a stranger cannot want anything good, and they are often right. Many also know others by a nickname or simply as "neighbor," and many do not want to

9. John Turner has an excellent article that deals with many aspects of the development of Lima's barriadas (1963). See also Turner, Turner, and Crooke, 1963.

"compromise" themselves by singling another out in case the visitor is unwanted. Most people, however, were quite helpful during the interviewing and, except for the numerous hostile dogs and the steepness of some of the paths, we had little difficulty locating informants in the 2 per cent sample chosen and little difficulty entering the house and conducting interviews.

There is no running water, water must be purchased and stored in cylinders. It is one of the most frequent complaints in the barriada. There is no sewer system; fecal matter is carried to a hillside near an irrigation ditch and dumped. Some of it is carried away, some is eaten by dogs, and some stays. For some time it was dumped underneath a large sign erected by the government housing authority announcing the fact that sewer construction was in progress. No sewers have been built, but the sign has been removed. Garbage is collected daily by trucks from a nearby municipality, but the residents have to fill the trucks on the run because they often do not stop.

The nuclear family, including a minority of one-parent families once nuclear, is found in 528 out of 561 households. "Household" in this case refers to those inhabiting a separate dwelling. One hundred fifty-nine households have one or more "extra" persons, overwhelmingly kinsmen of one of the spouses. Unlike rural communities, the barriada has 17 individuals living alone.[10] Tables 1 and 2 show the number of persons

Table 1. Number of Persons Per House

No. of houses	*No. of persons*
17	1
28	2
52	3
94	4
119	5
83	6
55	7
47	8
28	9
20	10
18	11 or more
561	

10. The census in Benavides was taken under the direction of Alberto Cheng and myself, with the assistance of anthropology students from San Marcos University and students from the Lima School of Social Work. The coding was done by a Cornell research group under the direction of J. M. Stycos.

Table 2. Relationship of Residents of House Over 17 Years of Age to Head of House

Number	Relationship
560	Head
466	Mate
65	Sibling
29	Parent
14	Parent-in-law
51	Sibling-in-law
253	Child or stepchild
37	Nephew or niece
58	Other relative
22	Non-relative
1,555	

per house and the relationship of residents over 17 years of age to the head of the house.

The houses are close together in blocks in the lower section of the barriada, and on paths on the steep hillsides. The most common unit is the isolated nuclear family, but there are some cases of children who have built close to parents, siblings building close to each other, and in-laws of various kinds living near one another. The barriada was founded by an organized invasion in 1954, so the basic residence pattern can be said to be neolocal. There are several cases of married sons and daughters living with parents, and of unmarried daughters with children living with parents. Twenty-seven households consist of mother and children, 20 of mother, children, and others. Most of these 47 households, plus some of the others with a temporarily residing, easily replaceable male, are essentially matricentered extended families, a group frequently encountered among migrants to Lima.

The social groupings available beyond the nuclear family are many, and participation varies from not at all to considerable. Most of the heads of families belong to the barriada tenants' association, but few participate actively in it except at election time. Extended family groupings are very common, and there is considerable visiting back and forth between the barriada and other districts of Lima, and some between the barriada and the original provincial home. Regional clubs and informal groupings of friends who have migrated from the same region form an important basis of association, mutual aid, acculturation, etc. (Mangin, 1959), and there are other clubs available to join. For some men friendships formed at work are important. For others, unions or political parties provide opportunities for association.

The possibility of non-kinship groups being important is much greater than in rural communities, but kinship groupings are still the main basis of association for the migrants. In rural Peru, particularly among Indians, non-kinship groupings are rare. In Vicos the only such group is an informal association of army veterans who have organized for certain purposes, such as fiesta sponsorship. In the southern mountains, especially in Cuzco and Puno, peasant syndicates have acquired great importance and are largely non-kinship organizations. Unilinear kinship groupings found in some mountain Indian communities (Mangin, 1960b) have no counterpart in Benavides, but there is one "matrifocal family" with 12 households in the barriada and three others in different parts of downtown Lima, all connected through commonly descended female relatives.

Tables 3 and 4 show the persons in the house unrelated to the head of the house or the spouse and the relationship of children to the mated couple.

Of the 57 "Other" households, 37 had one, 14 had two, 5 had three,

Table 3. Persons in House Unrelated to Head of Household or Spouse

No. of Houses	*No. of persons*
16	1
2	2
2	3
2	4
539	0
561	

Table 4. Relationship of Children to Mated Couple

No. of houses	
360	Children of both spouses only
27	Children of both plus wife's
24	Mated couple but no children
10	Children of wife only
7	Children of both plus husband's
0	Children of husband only
57	Other
485	

and 2 had four children. These children were identified as "adopted," "servant," "nephew," or "niece." Whatever the actual relationship, most of these children seemed to be servants. In two known cases the children were virtual slaves given to the householders by their parents in payment of debts. In both cases the pretext was that the householder was going to educate the child in Lima. In neither case was this being done. Some of the "nephews" and "nieces" also seemed to be illegitimate children of one of the spouses.

The majority of the houses contain young adults and children. The tenants' council has some screening function in that new arrivals to the settlement are supposed to apply for a lot to the council, and most do. The council tends to reject single women or widows with children as applicants; they get practically no applications from single men or childless single women. This situation probably leads to a larger percentage of two-parent families in barriadas than in lower-class areas of the city, although no information is available to make the comparison.

Inheritance, by law and by consensus, should be bilateral, but as of 1959 only two individuals had acquired their lots through inheritance. Table 5 shows how each owner acquired his lot.

The first residents who invaded came in October of 1954. There were

Table 5. How Each Owner Acquired His Lot

252	Invasion
75	Ceded by the association
11	Gift from previous owner
2	Inheritance
10	Purchase
77	Occupation of abandoned site
7	"Owner"
2	Renting
4	Borrowing
98	Other
23	No answer
561	

The figures in Table 5 are derived from the fieldwork of 1959. They cannot be supplemented by figures from subsequent Peruvian censuses because the area is not distinguished. By 1964 there were some 75 new houses with an average of four persons each. They were in a new area round the corner of the hillside and were prevented from further expansion by police action. In 1970 there were only ten new houses since 1964, and in 1971 there were no new houses. The main growth occurred in the first few years and then slowed down.

many less than the 252 of Table 5 in the original group, but many who came during the subsequent year or so consider themselves to be invaders. There is a certain prestige attached to having been one of the original invaders, so many who actually were not report themselves as having been. No attempt was made to dislodge them after the first few days, unlike the case in many other barriadas, and the number swelled rapidly. Today there is disagreement about the number and identity of the original invaders, but some of the original leaders are widely acknowledged in the barriada and are still there. Many of the newer arrivals, however, have little knowledge of the pioneers and couldn't care less.

Most of the property holders either invaded the lot they occupy or acquired it by applying to the tenants' council. Legally the tenants' council has no right to distribute the land and none of the residents has a legal title. The land is owned by the state; the disposition of the considerable portion of public land invaded in this way will be one of the most explosive political issues in Peru for some time to come. Some land has been sold, some houses have been sold or rented, and land conflicts are common, involving lawyers, police, various government bureaus, and church organizations. It is probably fairly safe to assume that no prospective government in Peru will feel strong enough to evict the 200,000-plus squatters around Lima, or even the 561 households of Benavides; and there is always the possibility that the 1960 Law of Barriadas, which provides for the development of the areas and guarantees the property rights of the residents, will be implemented. As many Peruvians would point out, however, there is also always the possibility that it will not be implemented. Many laws, particularly those concerned with taxation and land distribution, are on the books but not implemented, and it is not only barriada residents who do not have clear titles. A clear title in Peru is a rare document; and title difficulties are probably as much of a stumbling block to land reform in rural areas and barriada reform in the cities as are the right-wing political objections. The Belaunde government of the sixties and the military government since 1968 both have tried to provide some kind of security for the residents of *pueblos jovenes*, but that security has not gone beyond giving a limited number of "provisional" titles.

Most of the couples were married or living together before coming to Benavides. I noted no feeling against marrying someone from the barriada in asking questions about attitudes toward the place. Out of the 471 households with a resident mated couple of the 561 censused, 338 reported themselves as "married," 131 as "conviviente," or consensual union, two had one of each, and the rest did not reply. There is probably a tendency to overreport marriage, but there is no reason to suppose that a formal marriage makes a union any more stable. An analysis of records of a sample of 65 families indicates that about half of the individuals had had more than one mate.

The importance of co-godparenthood, *compadrazgo,* varies with the family. Most people choose co-godparents from among their kinsmen, many others from the same province or district. Many choose from higher-status acquaintances in Lima, especially those from the same region. Many have also chosen neighbors from the barriada.

It is somewhat difficult to predict the family cycle for the barriada migrants. Most of them were born into Cholo or Mestizo families in rural areas and small towns of the provinces. Some men migrated alone or with friends during young adulthood. Most met their present mates in Lima, although many are from the same region as their mate. There is a strong tendency for relatives from the provinces to join the barriada families, particularly aged parents who abandon land in the provinces and can act as caretakers of grandchildren and property while both husband and wife work.[11]

In Benavides parents are frequently ambivalent about their children, and there is considerable tension in the parent-child relationship. Parents say, in response to a questionnaire as well as in conversations, that one should sacrifice all for one's children (and to a certain extent they do), but at the same time they restrict their children in many ways and seem to resent the apparent increase in opportunity for their children over themselves (Mangin and Cohen, 1964). They think that their children should take care of them during their old age but they don't expect that they will. Sibling relationships are strong, and the cooperative relationship seen in Vicos between a man and his wife's sister's husband is also seen in Benavides.[12]

There is considerable occupational variety in Benavides. Some individuals own property in the provinces, but no one lives solely from rent. The highest-paid men in the community seem to be an owner of a small store and a white-collar bank employee who is also a minor official of

11. For a report on a similar situation in a southern coastal city barriada, see Hammell, 1961b and 1964.

12. The importance of the mother's brother in Vicos was first called to my attention during the analysis of the composition of mutual aid work groups where the wife's brother was one of the most frequently represented individuals. He is also important as a co-godparent in Vicos.

the militant bank workers' union. Both men have run for political office in the barriada, and the bank employee was the president in 1963. The men and some of the women work in many different parts of the city, although each tends to know only the part of the city traversed on regular routes such as to work or to a relative's house. Some women who have lived in Benavides for years, overlooking the city, have only been to the modern center once or twice. Unlike rural Peru, where the father is apt to be working around home much of the time, Benavides is mainly a community of women, children, and old people on weekdays. The jobs of the men range from the above-mentioned to policemen, soldiers, construction workers, factory workers, garbage men, salesmen, servants, waiters, drivers, and others. Benavides provides many more models for its children than do the rural areas, as does the general exposure to the urban milieu.

Benavides is much less of a one-class community than Vicos. There are individuals in fairly comfortable economic circumstances as in many Indian communities, but in Benavides some of them are also middle-class in their clothing, attitudes, aspirations, and general consumer habits. They are the high-status people in the barriada. The range is from lower-middle to lower-class, with the coast-mountain division also being quite important. Coastal people are generally higher-status in Lima. Negroes are coastal and Creole and usually possess a high degree of urban sophistication in Benavides. There are about 70 Negroes in the barriada. Indians and mountain lower-class people often scare their children with stories of Negro witches who are cannibals; and Negroes often ridicule and look down on "serranos," highlanders, as country bumpkins.

There is a president elected each year with his council. Any resident male can run, and voting is in the mountain fashion of one vote for each head of a household. Members of the association vote. Membership is open to any resident head of a house who pays a small fee and joins. The campaigns are vigorous but the results are respected. The barriada presidents carry considerable power in their communities although they are not recognized officially. National political parties enter into barriada campaigns, and barriada politicians usually have some connection with a national party. In Benavides during the years of 1958, 1959, and 1960, candidates ran as independents with regional slogans because of local reaction to a bitter campaign fought on national political lines in which one of the candidates was killed in a fight. The "regional" candidates turned out to have national party connections anyway.

The prevailing popular Peruvian view of the migrant who settles in a barriada is that he is rural, Indian, Quechua-speaking, landless, lawless, jobless, and recently arrived. In this regard a look at some of the census data from Benavides in 1959 is interesting on several counts. The sketchy migration information in the census shows considerable urban experience before the barriada, and the information from the 2 per cent sample interviewed in more detail shows a great deal of urban sophistication on the part of the Benavides residents. Of 1,417 adults answering on the census, 290 either were born in Lima or had resided in Lima 20 or more years. Only 15 had been in Lima less than a year. Four hundred ninety-nine have been in Lima for from 10 to 20 years, 405 had been in Lima for over 4 years, and 223 (including the 15 mentioned as less than one year) had been in Lima less than 4 years (see Table 6). Although well over 90 per cent of the subjects migrated to Lima at some time, it is certainly not appropriate to refer to them as recent migrants.

Table 6. Years Spent in Lima by Those Over 17, Assuming June Arrival

15	Less than one year
75	1-1.9
133	2-3.9
131	4-5.9
156	6-7.9
118	8-9.9
276	10-14.9
223	15-19.9
290	20 and over
1,417	

There is also a popular misconception frequently expressed in newspapers and shown in cartoons to the effect that barriada residents come directly from their home towns in the mountains to barriadas. Matos' data from the 1956 census do not give specific information on this point but do indicate that there are stopovers. The data from the 2 per cent sample and general interviewing in Benavides show invariably that the migrants have stopped off at least in the city of Lima before coming to the barriada. Table 7 shows the migration history of those over 17 answering the question in the 1959 census of Benavides.

The language information also casts doubt on the stereotype. It is only fair to point out, however, that there is a tendency on the part of many Cholos and Mestizos to underreport Quechua knowledge and exaggerate

Table 7. Migration Pattern of Adults

Lima to Benavides	152
Home town—other—Lima—Benavides	153
Home town—other—Benavides	0
Home town—Benavides	8
Home town—Lima—Benavides	1,086
Other	13
No information	157
	1,417

Spanish skill, so that the following figures are probably slightly distorted. In response to a question on languages spoken, the following results were obtained. Three hundred and two said Spanish only, 3 said Quechua only, 40 said Spanish and Quechua but did not indicate which was primary, 168 said Quechua was their first language and Spanish second, one said Spanish first and Aymara second. Four gave no information. In spite of the presence of several families from the Tupe area no one claimed to speak Kauke. A few individuals said they spoke some English.

In response to a question on parents' language, 255 said Spanish only, 54 said Spanish as a first language plus Quechua, 81 said only Quechua, 135 said Quechua first and Spanish, 15 said Spanish and Quechua with no indication of a primary language, 4 said one parent Spanish the other Quechua, one said one parent Aymara the other Spanish. The remaining records had no information.

Grouping the informants and their parents in Table 8, we have the following result.

Table 8.

	Informant's Language	*Parents' Language*
Spanish only	302	255
Quechua only	3	81
Spanish and Quechua	251	203
Spanish and Aymara	1	1
No information or other	4	21

Many Benavides resident adults and their parents were agricultural workers before coming to Lima. In Table 9, with a reduced number answering, it is apparent that parents were more apt to be agriculturalists than the informants.

Table 9.

Former Occupation Before Lima	*of Informant*	*of Male Parent*
Unemployed	5	0
Not in labor force	23	0
Housework	3	1
Worker	8	6
Skilled worker	4	3
White-collar	0	0
Business	2	5
Military or police	0	0
Service	1	2
Transportation	1	0
Agriculture	130	299
No information	19	21

Table 10 shows that a good many of the householders own property in their home towns. Judging from the more detailed information from the 2 per cent sample and from general interviewing, few have great interest in their property and many of them left the mountains so as to avoid litigation and dispute over land.

The data on employment have not been adequately analyzed, but the rate of unemployment among heads of families is low. Only 2 individuals said they were unemployed. Many are so marginally employed as to be counted as unemployed, but in the vast majority of cases, someone in the house had a more or less steady, although often low, income; and in many houses two or three people had jobs. The barriada population in general performs a high number of the service and low-level factory jobs in Lima, and they cost the city practically nothing in terms of goods and services such as water, sewers, paved streets, lights, police, hospitals,

Table 10. Property Ownership in Home Town

None	237
Land	162
Building	21
Land and building	5
Land and animals	4
Land, building, and animals	15
Animals	1
Property unspecified	5
No information	16

schools, etc., because the city has provided them with practically none.

Benavides is a law-abiding community and there is little crime, prostitution, gambling, or violence. What violence there is is confined mainly to aggression by husbands against wives and children; the most frequent complaints made to the police in the nearby district of Rimac are by wives for this reason. In a comparison of anti-social conduct of minors between a Lima slum and Benavides, Rotondo and his associates (1961) found a high, varied record for the slum and a low, unvaried record for Benavides. Practically all of the barriada residents, and a large majority of Peruvians in general, are in precarious economic situations and are on the underprivileged end of a rigid and abusive class system. Criteria for getting, holding, and advancing in jobs are essentially particularistic and whimsical, and special favor, bribery and kickbacks are a normal part of almost everyone's universe. In response to some questions on an adaptation of a moral inventory test where the respondents were asked to disagree or agree with statements, the following results were obtained from the 2 per cent sample:

1. Almost everything can be fixed up in court if you have enough money. Agree——38. Disagree——20.
3. In general the police are honest.
   Agree——20. Disagree——32.
14. The law protects the rights of property owners at the expense of the rights of the people.
   Agree——44. Disagree——10.
19. A very poor man has the right to steal.
   Agree——16. Disagree——41.
24. Success in life is a question of pull.
   Agree——43. Disagree——15

As can be seen, there is a general lack of confidence in the courts and the police and the system as a whole. Even in the question on the poor man having the right to steal, it appeared upon investigation that many of the informants were thinking of poor men robbing them in the barriada and were not opposed to robbing rich people. In spite of these attitudes, however, they continue to play the system's rules, send their children to schools, pay their taxes, solicit help in an orderly fashion from government ministries, abide by the laws of the land, and expect orderly change.

The varied population of Benavides compared to the unvaried Indian population of Vicos reflects one of the basic differences between subcultures in Peru. Vicos is only one supplier of migrants and, at that, a very small one. As has been indicated, Indians seldom migrate directly to Lima but stop somewhere in between. But some of the young children of Vicosinos who move out will have as much in common with the barriada migrants as with their own parents, even as most of the barriada children will have as much in common with urban participants in the national culture as with their own parents.

Anticipatory socialization to new patterns is more advanced in Benavides than in Vicos because of a greater desire for change for their children on the part of the barriada parents, and a greater knowledge of the national culture because of their familiarity with Spanish and their proximity to the major disseminating center, Lima.

Benavides residents are increasingly aware of Peru as a country and increasingly nationalistic and political, but not as much so as native urban residents or many of the young migrants to Lima who become university students, union members, or government workers and reside in the center of the city.

In the barriada parents are often naively optimistic about upward mobility for their children through education, and they indicate frequently that they think they are better off than they were in the provinces and that their children will be better off than they are. They also see their children leading different lives as professionals, teachers, white collar workers, etc., with more comforts and a more secure class position.

They see the solution to their problems mainly in outside help. Out of 56 responses to a question about how the problems of the barriada should be solved, 46 said that some agency, usually "the government," should help. Out of the remaining ten answering, only three suggested that the residents should help themselves.

For the Vicosino, adult local interests are primary and aspirations are toward success in what Ralph Beals (1953) has termed as "internal prestige system" centering around local politico-religious office. There is a general lack of information about the outside world. Some individuals have been to Lima, some men have been in the army, many have been to coastal haciendas and more have been to Huaráz, the provincial capital, but at the same time few speak Spanish and few are particularly concerned with Peru as a nation. As yet, in spite of the ten years of the Cornell-Peru project, a large number of the Vicosinos, particularly the women, are ignorant of the national culture and only a handful of schoolchildren and fewer than 100 adults speak Spanish. The number of individuals who read Spanish in Vicos, in contrast to the high literacy rate of barriada residents, cannot be more than 20 or 25. In 1951 few recognized the national anthem. Now the army veterans recognize it and the schoolchildren sing it rather badly. Many in 1951 did not recognize the name of Odria, then dictator of the country. President Prado was not well known in Vicos and neither was Belaunde, but many more people know that there is a president and a government.

The Indians are generally dissatisfied with their economic condition, but many of them were more or less satisfied with the hacienda system. They see the solution to their problems, much like the barriada people, in the coming of a "good patron."[13] They see their children having basically the same sort of life they themselves have but, hopefully, with more eocnomic advantages. This hope has been stimulated by the Cornell-Peru Project's action to terminate the hacienda system and the expropriation and sale of the property to the people in 1962.

One of the Indian leaders, an army veteran, speaking to a meeting of Indian delegates and U.S. and Peruvian government functionaries in Vicos, warned that if things did not change Peru would go like "*China nacionalista.*" From a later conversation it was apparent that he meant China *comunista* and was thinking specifically of the fate of many Chinese landowners. This attitude is by no means typical, for, as I have said, most Vicosinos are still hazy about what Peru is, but such a speech would have been inconceivable in Vicos in 1952.

Despite the seeking for someone to depend on in problem-solving in both communities, the Cholos of Benavides and the Indians of Vicos show considerable initiative compared to other segments of the population. They both hold local elections, which have rarely been held in the cities and towns of Peru, where even national elections tend to be far apart. The people of Benavides invaded state land in the face of the threat of police action and economic loss to establish their settlement. The Vicosinos had been actively trying to get hold of their property and had made two attempts to buy or rent it before the advent of the Cornell-Peru Project. Indians in Junin, Ancash, Cuzco, and Puno have been taking the initiative and moving far ahead of some of their left-wing middle-class instigators to reclaim lost lands from hacienda owners (Neira, 1964). The Indians and Cholos also share a tremendous common advantage over

13. For contrasting views of Vicos and urban barriadas see Fried, 1959. For a view of a non-barriada slum see Rotondo *et al.*, 1963.

the traditional Mestizo and Criollo segments of Peruvian culture in that each type of community sets a high value on hard physical labor.[14] The lack of influence from Spanish colonial culture and the possession of the traits of hard work, thrift, sacrifice to educate children, and desire to own property will probably be of considerable assistance to both groups in the present rapidly changing Peruvian society.

References Cited

Adams, Richard N.
1959. *Miquiyauyo, a Community in the Andes.* Seattle: University of Washington Press.

Adams, Richard N., and Charles C. Cumberland
1960. "U.S. University Cooperation in Latin America: A Study Based on Selected Programs in Bolivia, Chile, Peru and Mexico." East Lansing, Mich.: Michigan State Institute of Research on Overseas Programs.

Arguedas, José Maria
1952. "El complejo cultural en el Perú y el primer congreso de Peruanistas." *America Indigena (Mexico)* 21:131-39.
1957. "Evolución de las comunidades indigenas." *Revista del Museo Nacional (Lima)* 26:1-74.

Beals, Ralph L.
1953. "Social Stratification in Latin America." *American Journal of Sociology* 58:327-39.

Bourricaud, François
1954. "Algunas caracteristicas originales de la cultura mestiza en el Peru." *Revista del Museo Nacional* (Lima) 23:162-73.

Bradfield, Stillman
1963. *Migration from Huaylas: A Study of Brothers.* Ithaca, N.Y.: unpublished Ph.D. dissertation, Cornell University.

Crooke, Patrick, and Carlo Doglio
1960. "Scuole e Comunità." *Comunità* (Rome) 84:28-57.

Dobyns, Henry F., and Mario Vásquez eds.
1963. *Migration e integracion en el Peru.* Lima: Editorial Estudios Andinos.

Dorich, Luis T.
1961. "Urbanization and Physical Planning in Peru." In *Urbanization in Latin America,* Philip Hauser ed., pp. 280-93, International Documents Service. New York: Columbia University Press.

14. For a perceptive analysis of attitudes toward physical labor and work performance among White and Mestizo Peruvians see Storm, 1948. For a dramatic example of the results of Cholo and Indian work patterns in the construction of schools in a rural area around Puno see Crooke and Doglio, 1960.

Doughty, Paul L.
1970. "Behind the back of the city: Provincial Life in Lima, Peru." In *Peasants in Cities,* Mangin (1970), 30-46.

Fried, Jacob
1959. "Acculturation and Mental Health Among Migrants in Peru." In *Culture and Mental Health,* Marvin Opler, ed. New York: Macmillan.
1961. "The Indian and *mestizaje* in Peru." *Human Organization* 20:23-26.

Goldrich, Daniel; Raymond B. Pratt; and C. R. Schuller
1967. *The Political Integration of Lower Class Urban Settlements in Chile and Peru.* Studies in Comparative International Development. St. Louis: Washington University.
1961a. *Wealth, Authority and Prestige in the ICA Valley.* Albuquerque: University of New Mexico Press.
1961b. "The Family Cycle in a Peruvian Slum and Village." *American Anthropologist* 63:989-1006.
1964. "Some Characteristics of Rural Village and Urban Slum Populations on the Coast of Peru." *Southwestern Journal of Anthropology* 20: 346-58.

Holmberg, Allen
1955. "Participant Intervention in the Field." *Human Organization* 14: 23-28.
1960. "Changing Community Attitudes and Values in Peru: A Case Study of Guided Change." In *Social Change in Latin America Today.* Harper, N. Y.: Council on Foreign Relations.

Lewis, Oscar
1966. "The Culture of Poverty." *Scientific American,* October, 19-25.

Mangin, William
1955. "Estratificacion social en el Callejón de Huaylas." *Revista del Museo Nacional* (Lima) 24:174-89.
1957. "Haciendas, *Communidades,* and Strategic Acculturation in the Peruvian Sierra." *Sociologus* (Berlin) 7:142-46.
1959. "The Role of Regional Associations in the Adaptation of Rural Populations in Peru." *Sociologus* (Berlin) 9:21-36.
1960a. "Mental Health and Migration to Cities: A Peruvian Case." *Annals of the New York Academy of Sciences* 84, Art. 17:911-17.
1960b. "Organizacion social en Vicos." *Etnologia y Arqueologia* (Lima) 1: 24-37.
1963. "Urbanization Case History in Peru." *Architectural Design* (London) 8:366-70.
1967. "Latin American Squatter Settlements: A Problem and a Solution." *Latin American Research Review* 2(3):65-98.
1971. Autobiographical Notes on a Rural Migrant to Lima," *Sociologus* 21(1):58-76.

Mangin, William, and Jerome Cohen
1964. "Cultural and Psychological Characteristics of Mountain Migrants to Lima, Peru." *Sociologus* (Berlin) 14:81-88.

Mangin, William (ed.)
1970. *Peasants in Cities*. Boston: Houghton Mifflin.
Matos Mar, José
1961. "Migration and Urbanization: The Barriadas of Lima." In *Urbanization in Latin America,* Philip Hauser, ed. New York: Columbia University Press.
1966. *Estudio de las barriadas Limeñas, 1955*. Lima: Universidad de San Marcos.
Neira, Hugo
1964. *Cuzco: Tierra y Muerte*. Reportaje al Sur. Lima: Problemas de Hoy.
Murdock, George P.
1949. *Social Structure*. New York: Macmillan.
Nunez del Prado, Oscar
1951. *Aspecto Economico de Viru, una communidad de la costa norte del Peru*. Cuzco: University of Cuzco.
Pan-American Union
1961. *Integracion economic y social del Peru central*. Mision Tecnica of Organization of American States, con 2 apendices. Washington: Pan-American Union.
Patch, Richard W.
1957. "An Hacienda Becomes a Community." Peru: American Universities Field Staff Letter.
Ramiro, Cardona G., ed.
1968. *Urbanizacion y Marginalidad*. Bogota: Asociacion Colombiana de Faculdades de Medicina.
Rotondo, Humberto, *et al.*
1961. "Un estudio comparativo de la conducta antisocial de menores en areas urbanas y rurales." *Archivos de criminologia, neuro-psiquiatria y disciplinas conexas* (Lima) 9:97-107.
Rotondo, Humberto; Baltazar Caravedo; and Javier Mariategui
1963. *Estudios de pisquiatria social en el Peru*. Lima: Ediciones del Sol.
Rowe, John H.
1947. "The distribution of Indians and Indian Languages in Peru." *Geographical Review* 37:207-15.
Schaedel, Richard P.
1951. "The Lost Cities of Peru." *Scientific American* 185 (2):18-23.
Schaedel, Richard P.; Gabriel Escobar; and Oscar Nunez del Prado
1959a. "Los recursos humanos del departamento de Puno." 5 PS/B/9. Lima: Plan Regional del Sur del Peru.
1959b. "La organizacion social en el departamento de Puno." 22 PS/F/49. Lima: Plan Regional del Sur del Peru.
Simmons, Ozzie G.
1952. "El uso de los conceptos de aculturación y asimilación en el estudio del cambio cultural en el Peru." *Peru Indigena* (Lima) 2 (4):40-47.
1955. "The *Criollo* Outlook in the Mestizo Culture of Coastal Peru." *American Anthropologist* 57:107-17.

Storm, Hans Otto
1948. *Of Good Family*. New York: William Morrow Co.
Stycos, Joseph, and Cara Richards de Dobyns
1963. "Fuentes de las migracion en la gran Lima." In *Migracion e integracion en el Peru*, Henry F. Dobyns and Mario Vasquez, eds. Lima: Editorial Estudios Andinos.
Tschopik, Harry, Jr.
1948. "On the concept of Creole culture in Peru." In *Acculturation in the Americas*, Sol Tax, ed., pp. 261-66. Chicago: University of Chicago Press.
Turner, John
1963. "Lima Barriadas Today." *Architectural Design* (London) 8:369-80.
1967. Barriers and Channels for Housing Development in Modernizing Countries." *Journal of the American Institute of Planners* 33:167-81.
Turner, John; Catherine Turner; and Patrick Crooke
1963. "Conclusions." *Architectural Design* (London) 8:389-93.
Valentine, Charles
1968. *Culture and Poverty*. Chicago: University of Chicago Press.
Vásquez, Mario
1952. "La antropologia cultural y muestro problema del Indio: un caso de antropologia aplicada." *Peru Indigena* (Lima) 2 nos., 5 y 6:7-158.
1955. "Cambios en la estratificación social en una hacienda Andina del Peru." *Revista del museo nacional* (Lima) 24:190.

Selectivity in Rural-Urban Migration: The Case of Huaylas, Peru[1]

Stillman Bradfield

Introduction

Latin America as a whole is urbanizing at a rapid rate. In 1960, about 50 per cent of the population of Latin America lived in cities of 2000 or more inhabitants. Almost 70 per cent of the population of the United States lived in cities of this size in 1960. Considering the disparities between the United States and Latin America in the amount of industrialization at that time, the Latin American urban concentration seems quite pronounced. Moreover, it is increasing rapidly. In 1940, 7.4 per cent of the total population of Peru was living in the capital city, Lima. Lima and its port, Callao, form the metropolitan area and together contained 19 per cent of the population of Peru in 1961 and 24.5 per cent in 1972. In 1961, there were 11 urban concentrations of 50,000 or more inhabitants, containing 27 per cent of the total population. In 1940, only 11.6 per cent of Peru's population resided in cities of 25,000 or more.

The rapid growth of the cities is due primarily to immigration and not to higher fertility or lower infant mortality in the urban areas. The rate of growth of the urban areas of Latin America is about twice that of rural areas (Davis: 148). Given the increasingly dominant position of cities and the fact that migration accounts for a large part of the increase in

1. The study was carried out under the direction of the Cornell-Peru Project and was financed by the National Institute of Mental Health, research grant M-5558 and Fellowship No. 5 Fl MH-17, 358-02. The data were reported in detail in the author's doctoral dissertation, Migration from Huaylas: A Study of Brothers, Cornell University, Ithaca, N.Y., September 1963. I am grateful to Leila A. Bradfield and David L. Westby and the members of the symposium for critical comments on this draft.

the size of cities, it is important to understand something of the nature of the migration to the cities. The purpose of the present work is to examine some of the dimensions of rural-urban migration in Peru. The most important stream of migration in Peru is from the rural areas of the highlands to the coastal cities. Migrants in this stream are involved in making most of the normal changes that have been noted in discussions of rural-urban differences (Kahl). They are also involved in a more general cultural change, from a culture heavily permeated with Indian and Spanish Colonial traditions to one that is markedly more European and modern. All studies agree that normal migration is always selective, but different studies indicate selectivity on different variables. The only characteristic that so far has stood all the tests is age. Migration streams are made up of younger people than the population as a whole, at the points both of origin and destination (Bogue: 504).

Studies of migration typically are of two types. Actuarial studies normally depend upon census data and are designed to make statements about the direction, volume, and velocity of migration streams and the characteristics by which migrants differ from the general population. A second type are studies on the causes of migration, emphasizing factors affecting the individual which "push" him out of a given area and those which "pull," or attract, him to some place of destination.

In some cases, a mass migration takes place as a result of political repression or a natural disaster that makes life in an area untenable. However, the normal case is one in which some people migrate, but the majority stay home. It is probable that many of the people who stay have been the recipients of the same information about opportunities elsewhere as those who migrate. Given exposure to the same pull factors, some respond by migrating and others do not. Similarly, many of the push factors normally used to explain why some migrate and others do not are general conditions which affect many more than those who respond to these pressures. It could be argued that, although the forces may be roughly the same for most of the people in a given area, not all can respond to them in the same manner. The young and single, without land and animals to tie them to the countryside, may be the ones who are freer to respond to the pressures. But it is hard to find communities where all people with a given set of characteristics have left for the city. The normal case is one in which a disproportionate share of a given group migrate, but many who have the same biographical characteristics remain at home. The major question that will concern us here will be: between men with approximately the same biographical characteristics, why did one of them migrate and the other not? After matching a group of migrants with a group of non-migrants as closely as possible, we will look for differences between the groups in terms of uncontrolled differences in biographical characteristics, their self-images, the conditions of migration, and their reasons for leaving.

Background of the Study

The data reported here were gathered in the fall of 1962. For a year prior to this time I had been working in Chimbote, an industrial boomtown on the north coast of Peru. The study in Chimbote was concerned mainly with migration to that city and the process of adaptation to urban life and work in modern industry. A survey of 10 per cent of the heads of households in Chimbote provided some clues as to the nature of the rural-urban migration, and the characteristics by which migrants differed from the general population.

One of the most surprising findings was that only 17 per cent of the informants reported having been agriculturists in their place of origin, and only 39 per cent said that their fathers were farmers. Almost half of the respondents said that they were born in provincial capitals, departmental capitals, or large cities. Fifty-five per cent said that they were born in district capitals (normally small villages), haciendas, or rural areas. Apparently, many of those born in the smaller areas were already outside agriculture before they migrated to the city. Two-thirds of the sample did not come to Chimbote directly from their place of origin, and most of them had been working in towns or cities, since only 4 per cent of the sample reported working in agriculture in the place they lived before coming to Chimbote. Chimbote is located about 415 kilometers north of Lima, near the border between the departments of Ancash and La Libertad. Three-quarters of the respondents were born in these two departments. About half of the sample were born in the highlands.

The data presented above provide some clues to the nature of the migration to the cities and to the process of selection that goes on in the small towns and villages, but does not enable us to really say how those who migrated were different from those who remained at home. A study of this problem involves work at a point of origin of the migration stream, as well as at the point of destination.

The Design of the Study

Huaylas, a district in the Callejon de Huaylas area of the Department of Ancash, was chosen as the base point for several reasons. The Cornell-Peru Project had been active in this area for more than a decade. Consequently, a large body of data had already been accumulated which would serve as a base for further study. Paul Doughty had spent a year and a half resident in Huaylas itself. While there, he conducted a census of the district and a sample survey which included migration histories of people then resident in Huaylas. He found that there had been a long history of outmigration from Huaylas, particularly to Lima and Chimbote. Three-quarters of the men resident in Huaylas had lived outside the district and had returned. Of those who had lived outside the district, 90 per cent had stayed out a year or more. Of those he interviewed, 34 per cent said they had relatives in Chimbote, and 61 per cent reported having relatives in Lima (Doughty, 1961: 2). With the basic migration patterns of the district already known, and with so many people reporting that they had relatives in these two cities, it seemed feasible to do a more specialized study limited to closely matched groups—one group living in Huaylas and the other living in Chimbote or Lima.

Simultaneous control on several biographical characteristics can be obtained in either of two ways. If a large random sample is used, control can be obtained in the analysis by matching cases on as many characteristics as is desired. But by so doing, the size of the sample dwindles sharply as each additional characteristic is subjected to control. Thus, of 1000 cases, as few as 25 or 50 may be equivalent to each other when controlled on as many as 5 variables simultaneously. The other way to obtain simultaneous control on several variables is to build the controls into the design, selecting only those respondents who fulfill all of the requirements.

The resources available did not permit a large survey of Huaylas, nor was one necessary in view of the work already done by Doughty. Interviewing pairs of brothers seemed to me most appropriate for the purposes of this study. Since the interest of the study at the point of origin of migration was in finding differences among men of approximately the same biographical characteristics which could explain why one had migrated to the city and the other had not, a study of brothers seemed to offer the types of controls desired. By limiting the study to brothers, we omit from consideration the migration behavior of women, and migration patterns of women are frequently different from those of men. Similarly, we shall have to ignore differences in age and sibling order which may be of considerable importance in the development of such characteristics as sibling rivalry and achievement motivation. Nevertheless, there are some positive advantages to limiting the study to pairs of brothers. Besides controlling on sex, by interviewing only pairs of brothers, we achieve maximum control on both the heredity and early environment of the respondents. In a number of studies it has been argued that the interaction of heredity and environment determines intelligence, so we will assume that men with the same parents and early environment are more similar to each other in intelligence than those from different backgrounds (see, for example, Anastasi, Ch. 4, pp. 101-31). Since both members of the pair were raised in the same family, they were both raised in the same socioeconomic class. It is assumed that they had more nearly equal opportunities to get an education than would be the case for a random group of non-brothers. Both brothers were probably exposed to more similar child-rearing techniques than would be the case with a group of non-brothers. We can assume that they were exposed to approximately the same sets of values and attitudes during childhood. Ecological control is also maximized by interviewing only pairs of brothers, since they were raised in the same household, in whatever part of Huaylas the family lived, whether rural or urban, low or high altitude.

Inasmuch as the two groups were selected on the basis of their similarities on all variables possible except age, sibling order, and migration pattern, it would be unrealistic to suppose that great differences between the two brothers would emerge from the analysis of the data. Nevertheless, a group of this sort offers the possibility of greater specificity in the differences in migration behavior among people of like background. Most studies on selective migration indicate differences in migration behavior among people with different characteristics. For example, Noel P. Gist, in his study in urban South India, found that Brahmins were more migratory than other caste groups (Gist: 821). Doughty found that migration from Huaylas was also disproportionately upper class. One of the criteria of class is education. In his census, Doughty found that only 11 per cent of the present population of Huaylas had completed primary school. Of the approximately 2,000 Huaylinos who completed primary school (the only schooling available in the district) during the years 1940-61, 75 per cent had migrated and were living outside Huaylas at the time of his survey.

With a group of brothers we can ask the question, is education related to migration among people with similar genetic and environmental backgrounds? That is, even between men of the same class background, are there differences in education that are related to migration patterns?

A questionnaire was administered by the writer and two anthropology students from the Universidad Nacional Mayor de San Marcos, Peru's national university. Both of these students had had previous experience with this technique, and both had worked with Doughty on his census and surveys in Huaylas. With the help of some of the leaders of various *barrios* of Huaylas, we made up a list of 102 pairs of brothers. In each case, these local leaders believed that one of the two was still resident in Huaylas and the other was either in Chimbote or Lima. All were adults of 20 years of age or more, since younger men and boys might not have the opportunity to migrate. We aimed at interviewing the entire population of brothers of whom one was resident in Huaylas and the other in Lima or Chimbote. We succeeded in locating and interviewing only 51 pairs. One of these interviews was missing several pages of information, so the pair was thrown out to give a final population of 50 pairs of brothers, or 100 cases.[2]

2. Of those lost, 3 pairs were lost because one of each pair refused to be interviewed. Another 35 pairs were lost because we succeeded in locating and interviewing only one of the pair. Ten men were interviewed in Lima whose brothers were no longer living in Huaylas. In Huaylas, 25 men were interviewed who could not give the addresses of their brothers in the cities. Considerable effort was made not only by the interviewers, but also by Huaylinos living in all three places to locate the men who were supposed to be living there, but we could not even find out whether the men really lived there or not. One man in Lima was chronically ill and too sick to be interviewed, so his brother was not approached. The remaining 13 pairs were lost because we could not locate the first man of the pair and, therefore, did not look for the other.

The results of the interviews lost through failure to find the other brother were compared with the results of the completed group. There is some reason to believe that the group lost was generally of higher class than the group that was completed, as the group that was not completed reported a higher percentage in the middle class and higher average incomes.

Comparing the completed group with men in the cities who did not qualify for the study because they had no brother in Huaylas, the impression gained was that the group interviewed omitted a disproportionate share of the men in the cities of high socioeconomic status. In Chimbote, I knew only 3 Huaylinos who were not eligible, but all 3 were of higher socioeconomic status than *any* of the men interviewed in Chimbote. In Lima-Callao, I met about 15 men who were the officials of the two District Associations of Huaylas, and as a group they were definitely of a higher socioeconomic status than the group interviewed. Only one of them qualified for inclusion by having a brother still resident in Huaylas. In all probability the group

The group of 50 pairs of brothers, one living in a city and the other in Huaylas, does not mean that there are two migration types–migrants and non-migrants. There are four migration types. Of the 50 living in Huaylas, 11 have never lived outside the district of Huaylas, and will be called "non-migrants." The other 39 men in Huaylas have lived outside but have returned and were living and working in Huaylas at the time of the survey. These will be called "returned migrants." The 50 men living in the cities are also of two types. There are 34 who left Huaylas and have never returned to live and work there. They are termed "convinced migrants." The other 16 men in the cities left Huaylas, worked outside, returned to live and work in Huaylas, then left again. These men are called "oscillating migrants." These terms describe the individual at the time of the survey; they represent a summary statement of the man's migration experience up to that point. Any man could in the future change his category by changing his migration behavior.

Given the nature of the group that was interviewed, care must be taken in generalizing the findings to other groups. As will be indicated later, Huaylas is in many ways a community quite atypical of the region. Within this community, respondents were selected on the basis of specific characteristics. The findings should be regarded as highly tentative and untested with regard to the migratory phenomena of the district as a whole and of other places. The study was intended to be exploratory in nature, not definitive; the search was for ideas, not for correct estimates of population distributions. It will be shown that in some ways the 50 men in Huaylas are representative of adult males in Huaylas. But no work has been done on the population of Huaylas that has migrated. We cannot know at this time, with a sufficient degree of accuracy, either the size or the characteristics of the adult male population of migrants from Huaylas. Therefore, it is not possible to define a larger universe from which we could say the group interviewed was drawn as a sample. Given these circumstances, tests of statistical significances are not defensible.

Before presenting the findings of the study, it would be useful to give a brief description of the three areas in which the respondents are living.

Huaylas

Doughty has described Huaylas as follows:

---

interviewed under-represents the emigration of men from the upper class of Huaylas. Even so, we shall find that the migrants who are included are disproportionately from the upper class.

> Huaylas is a political district comprising some 700 square kilometers located at the extreme northern end of the Callejon de Huaylas, an abrupt, deep river valley which runs down from south to north through the mountains of the department of Ancash. Geographically, the district is isolated from the rest of the Callejon towns and must be reached via a 17 kilometer road which winds precariously up the mountains from the edge of the Santa River. Roughly 85 percent of the population of Huaylas resides in a beautiful hanging valley ranging between altitudes of 2,600 meters to 3,100 meters above sea level (8,500 to 10,200 feet above sea level), and commanding a magnificent view of the Cordillera Blanca which flanks the Callejon de Huaylas along the eastern bank.
>
> The town of Huaylas occupies the southern rim of the valley and is laid out in the typical "grid" pattern of Spanish-American cities, around a central plaza on which border the church and municipality buildings. The *chacras* or cultivated fields invade the town, reaching the plaza itself along the northern edge. Elsewhere other *chacras* occupy vacant lots within the town limits. The town has a population of approximately 1136 (which is 20 percent of the total district population of 5495), the great majority of whom, like those who live in the other, non-urbanized areas of the district, dedicate their lives principally to farming activities. The town of Huaylas is the commercial center of the district as well as being the focal point for all other official activities of the population. Narrow, cobbled streets, electricity, a piped water system, two complete primary schools, and a good library comprise the urban facilities available to the inhabitants of the town.
>
> . . . Outside the town, the population is rather evenly dispersed over the countryside with each *barrio,* or political subdivision of the district, having a small hamlet of 15 or 20 houses as its center, "officially" verified by the presence of a rural primary school . . . Elsewhere, the houses are found in clusters of three or so or else singly. There are very few houses at altitudes much over 3,000 meters, and those are generally solitary.
>
> The economy, as indicated, is based primarily on agriculture, and even those persons who practice some other specialty farm as well. I know of only one man who practices no agriculture in Húaylas—but even he keeps chickens and *cuyes* (guinea pigs) (Doughty, 1961: 1-3).

The people of the district can be divided into three main groups. The upper class consists of the farmers with the most land, shopkeepers, professionals (such as schoolteachers), and government officials. The middle class are those engaged in self-sufficient farming who also usually have some other trade. The lower class are not normally self-sufficient in farming, and supplement their income through wage labor. The upper class is almost exclusively urban in residence, the middle class is both urban and rural, and the lower class is 90 per cent rural (Doughty, 1963: 121-40).

Chimbote

Chimbote is on the Pan American Highway in an offshoot of the Santa River Valley. The large, deep, well-protected bay provides the best natural harbor on the Peruvian coast. Chimbote is connected by railroad to Huallanca near Huaylas, where the road enters the Callejon de Huaylas. The area of Chimbote has 34 fishmeal and fish canning factories and Peru's only steel plant. The smoke from these factories gives the impression of a large industrial city. Indeed, Chimbote does have several characteristics of a city. On the basis of population alone it qualifies as a city. According to the 1961 census, Chimbote had a population of 63,970, by 1972 it had grown to 159,045. There is a great deal of traffic congested by buses, trucks, taxis, and cargo-carrying tricycles. There are also a few multistoried buildings and many hotels, one of them first class.

On the other hand, there are a number of characteristics normally associated with a city that are lacking. Until recently, the Pan American Highway and the main street in town were the only ones that were paved; the rest of the streets were rough dirt roads. Sewers, water, and electricity are available to only a quarter of the population in and near the center of town.

The first impression, then, is of a boom-town atmosphere. There are lots of newly established factories, temporary housing units, and a great many bars and restaurants that cater to the transient population.

There are very few natives of Chimbote. Over half of the 1962 population came between 1955 and 1961. In 1924 Chimbote had an estimated population of 2,000. By the time of the first national census in 1940, the population had increased to 4,243. A public health agency conducted a census in 1951 and found that the population had increased to 15,642. This agency conducted another census in 1955 and found 27,253 people in the urban zone. The second national census in 1961 established the figure of 63,970. Most of the influx in the period from 1943 to 1951 was associated with the activities of the Corporacion Peruana del Santa, a semi-autonomous, regional development corporation patterned on the TVA. Most of the increase since then has been attracted by the establishment and extremely rapid expansion of the fishmeal industry. In spite of having been there for ten to fifteen years, many of the high officials and white-collar workers of the fish factories and the CPS feel that they are there only temporarily. They hope to return, or move on, to Lima as soon as possible. Many of those who can afford to do so maintain their families in Lima, while they live in company housing in Chimbote. Chimbote was a small fishing village which has become an industrial boom town. It is now Peru's seventh largest city.

Lima

One of the most frequently heard descriptions, or definitions, of Lima is "Lima is Peru." This is not to say that Lima is typical of Peru, but rather that everything is concentrated in Lima. As is the case in most Latin American countries, there is a centralization of practically all institutions in the capital. Lima is the center of political power, economic power, educational and health facilities, and the chief entrepôt for foreign influence. It is also the main reception center for migrants. According to the 1940 census, the population then was 522,826. It was estimated at 1,045,000 in 1955, and the 1961 census counted 1,769,323 inhabitants in Lima. It has more than tripled in two decades. The better residential districts of Lima house virtually all of the country's wealthy, regardless of the geographical source of their wealth. Given the concentration of power, economic opportunity, modern Western styles of life, and all of the facilities that are desired in a city, it is no surprise that Lima acts as a magnet for the rural-urban migration streams in Peru.

Reasons for Emigration from Huaylas

The reasons for emigration from Huaylas are similar to those used to explain emigration from most agricultural areas. There is a combination of factors which serves to push people out and a set of pull factors to explain the attraction of the places to which they migrate. The land base in Huaylas is relatively fixed, given its technology and the water supply. As a result of a secular decline in the amount of water available for irrigation, some men feel that the base of their economy is actually shrinking. There is little incentive to get a good education in order to stay and make a better living in Huaylas, since there is little opportunity there. People who want a good education and a good living must, for the most part, leave Huaylas. People who want to have a substantially higher level of living than their parents must get out of Huaylas, regardless of their education.

It is widely recognized in Huaylas that the land will not support a growing population at higher levels of living.

The city offers a solution. The city can absorb more people of whatever training, and it offers them the chance to get ahead that they could never get in Huaylas. There is some migration, mainly on a seasonal basis, to coastal haciendas, but the majority of emigrants from Huaylas head for Lima, with a second stream to Chimbote. The attractions that the city holds for many rural people are probably quite universal. The main attraction is the possibility of a better-paying job. Beyond that, the city also offers a greater variety of jobs, more interesting jobs for the qualified, better educational, health, and recreation facilities—all the things that make a city more interesting and exciting than a rural village.

The group studied is representative of Huaylas in at least three important respects. In his study of the migration of Huaylinos, Doughty found that 76 per cent of the men in his sample had worked outside Huaylas. Of the 50 men in the present study who are living in Huaylas, 78 per cent are returned migrants. The distribution of relatives between Chimbote and Lima is also similar. In his survey, Doughty found that 34 per cent of his respondents said they had relatives in Chimbote, and 61 per cent said they had relatives in Lima (Doughty, 1961:2). Of the brothers living in the cities, 36 per cent live in Chimbote, 64 per cent in Lima. When language is the criterion, the group interviewed also has the same percentage of Indians as the general population—only 3 per cent. The high rate of outmigration to the cities, and the very low percentage of Indians in the district, make Huaylas somewhat atypical of the area.

Summary of the Findings

Although the population interviewed was selected with a view to *minimizing* the differences between men in the rural district and those in the cities, no system of controls could eliminate all differences, nor was it intended to. We expected to find differences in biographical characteristics between brothers that would be related to their migratory experience. We also expected that differences in personality traits would be related to migratory behavior.

Differences in Biographical Characteristics Between Brothers

Age was left largely uncontrolled in sample selection, and the distribution of the brothers by age is, for the most part, the expected pattern. The average age for the men in Huaylas at the time of the survey was 41.4, that for the men in Lima was 40.9, whereas the most migratory group of them all—the men in Chimbote—averaged 39.2 years of age. However, the largest group of men in the cities is the group in Lima, and they are, on the average, only six months younger than the men in Huaylas. The average positions in sibling order are consistent with the age data. The men in Huaylas are first with an average position of 2.7, the men in Lima are intermediate with an average position of 3.0 and the men in Chimbote are third with 3.9. The average number of siblings (both living and dead) per family was reported to be six and a half. Older brothers have a high propensity to migrate, but they also have a high propensity to return. Considering only those who have left Huaylas, 54 per cent of the older brothers are returned migrants, as compared with only 32 per cent of the younger brothers. There are no important differences between the brothers with respect to marital histories, except that men in the cities married an average of 4 to 6 years younger than those in Huaylas.

Various studies have indicated that rural-urban migrants are much more likely to be literate than the general population (see, for example, Husain: 59 and Matos Mar: 179). The relationship between the amount of education and subsequent migratory behavior of Huaylinos is very strong. Fifty-eight per cent of those who left Huaylas with less than four years of education became returned migrants. Those who had four to five years of school before leaving had a return rate of 45 per cent. Only 32 per cent of those who finished primary school before leaving have become returned migrants.

The more education a person had before leaving, the more likely he was to go to Lima, and stay there, rather than to Chimbote. The evidence indicates that the men who go to Lima are of higher class origin and of more urban origin within Huaylas than those who go to Chimbote. Further, and most important, small differences in the amount of formal education, even at the primary school level, make a considerable difference in subsequent behavior.

The amount of education is related to the age at which a man started work. Taking 13 years of age as the breaking point, we see that the older the man is when he takes his first job, the more likely it is that he will migrate and remain outside.

Self-Images

The respondents were asked to compare themselves with their brothers with regard to a list of 18 items. The intent of the list was to discover personality differences that were evident to the men before either of them left Huaylas.

The question read: "Comparing yourself with your brother, before one of you left Huaylas, which of you was the more ambitious, he or you?" The other 17 items followed this one, and the respondents were asked simply to indicate which of the two was "more" on that particular quality. If they could see absolutely no difference at all, they were scored "no difference." But they were asked at the beginning to indicate the difference even if they felt that the difference was small. On 5 of the 18 items, over 50 per cent of the respondents said that there was no difference between themselves and their brothers. These items have been eliminated from the analysis in Table 1. One was the question as to which of the two was more ambitious. The most common connotation of *ambicioso* is covetousness, and the most frequent response to the question was, "Neither of us has ever been *ambicioso*." Similarly, they found no difference in their honesty, on the grounds that to do so would imply that one of them was dishonest. The same principle applies to the question as to which was the lazier of the two. In general, neither of them was willing to say that one had demonstrated higher moral qualities, because of the invidiousness of the comparison. Finally, they said that there was no difference between themselves on the amount of dependence upon their relatives before leaving Huaylas. But, as will be shown later, they did see a difference when they were asked which had been the more independent of the two.

Comparing only on those items where 50 per cent or more of the respondents said that they could see a difference between themselves and their brothers, and omitting the "no difference" responses from the calculations, we will look first at the general pattern of the responses. The most general pattern is that each member of the pair showed a tendency to rate himself higher than his brother, and the men in Huaylas much more decisively so. On the top seven items, from 66 to 90 per cent of the men in Huaylas rated themselves higher than their brothers, and on three of these, over 80 per cent did so. On the other hand, from 59 to 80 per cent of the migrants rated themselves higher on the top seven items.

Given the inequalities that resulted from this tendency, it was necessary to put the responses in a rank order. Table 1 contains the top seven items for each group as measured by the percentage of those who saw a difference. The table presents the ranking and the percentages for the ranking by the migrant of himself and of his brother, and the same for the Huaylino. The table does not differentiate by migration type. The

Huaylinos are the fifty men living in Huaylas, and the migrants are the fifty men in the cities. Looking first at the columns that apply to the migrant (first and fourth), there are only four items on which both the migrant and the Huaylino agree that the migrant is the most outstanding in these respects. Both groups see the migrant as more daring, more independent, more intelligent, and the one who studied harder in school. Although the migrants claimed that they were more interested in their personal progress, and the Huaylinos are willing to give this their seventh ranking, we cannot say that there is agreement, because 66 per cent of the Huaylinos who saw a difference also ranked themselves seventh on this item.

Table 1. Ranking of Self and Brother on Personality Traits Evident Before Migration

	Migrant's Opinion of				*Huaylino's Opinion of*			
	Self		*Brother*		*Self*		*Brother*	
	Rank	*%*	*Rank*	*%*	*Rank*	*%*	*Rank*	*%*
1. More independent	1	80					4	51
2. More persistent	2	74			6	73		
3. More daring, audacious	3	70					1	85
4. More interested in personal progress	4	69			7	66	7	34
5. More responsible	5	64			5	75		
6. Studied harder in school	6	61					3	68
7. More intelligent	7	59	6	41			2	76
8. More interested in local affairs			2	54	1	92		
9. Cared more for family	7	59	6	41	2	90		
10. Participated more in fiestas			1	66	3	89		
11. More obedient to parents			5	44	4	81		
12. Worked harder			3	51			6	42
13. More interested in earning money			4	47			5	48
100% =		(50)		(50)		(50)		(50)

The columns ranking the Huaylino (second and third) indicate agreement that the Huaylino was more interested in local affairs, that he participated more in the fiestas of Huaylas, and that he was more obedient to his parents. The Huaylinos also claim strongly that they were the ones who cared most for the family, and the migrants are willing to rank them sixth on this characteristic. There is no agreement on this, however, since the migrants also claim this characteristic for themselves with 59 per cent of their vote.

Each group claims two characteristics for itself. Each sees itself as the more persistent and the more responsible. On the other hand, there are two characteristics that both groups are willing to assign to the other. They agree that the other worked harder and was more interested in earning money. That the brothers should both be willing to say that the other was the harder worker is a bit curious, since this is a characteristic that Doughty says is highly valued in Huaylas and one which other writers have also reported as important in the general area of the Calleion de Huaylas and probably the sierra as a whole.

The general trend that emerges from the analysis of these items bears out in part what one would expect to be the differences between the brothers. On four items which are important for achievement and personal progress in general, both groups agree that the migrant was stronger in these characteristics at the time of first migration. These are audacity, independence, intelligence, and studiousness. Both groups also agree that the Huaylino was stronger on three items that would tend to keep him in Huaylas, or bring him back there more readily than the ones who have stayed out. These are interest in local affairs, greater participation in local fiestas, and obedience to his parents. These seven characteristics are the only ones on which there is general agreement among all those who saw a difference between themselves and their brothers.

Having found differences between the brothers in terms of their biographical characteristics and personality traits, we need to turn now to the question, why did some of them leave Huaylas? Are the conditions under which the man left and his specific reasons for leaving related to his subsequent migratory behavior? The 11 men who have never left Huaylas will necessarily be dropped from consideration for the time being.

External Conditions and Migration

The decision to migrate is often dependent upon circumstances at the moment, which may impede migration or tend to push, or at least permit a man to leave when he was previously unable to do so. A number of questions were asked of the respondents to measure the effect of particular circumstances during the year they left Huaylas for the first time. They were asked if there had been a death in the family; how the crop yields were the year they migrated; whether or not there had been a drought;

whether or not they had received extra income, such as separation pay from a nearby hydroelectric plant; and who they traveled with on their first migration. The relationships found between the answers to these questions and subsequent migration patterns were at best only suggestive, not conclusive. There is some evidence that short-distance migration to Chimbote seems to have been either more pushed or permitted by circumstances of the year in which migrants left Huaylas for the first time than was the case for those who went to Lima. Moreover, both short-distance migrants to Chimbote and returned migrants show a greater tendency to have gone out as part of a family migration than was the case for migration to Lima. But with only two cities involved, there is no way of knowing whether it was the difference in distance or the difference in the character of the two cities that was most important. The differences may also be a function of the different class origin of migrants to the two cities. In this case we would say that a disproportionate share of the upper-class men went to Lima, and they are the ones least likely to be affected by these sorts of conditions.

Reasons Given for Leaving Huaylas for the First Time

It was felt that if the respondents were simply asked, "Why did you leave Huaylas?," we would get only one or two reasons, which would be economic. The most common response to an open-end question of this sort would probably be, "There was no futurc in Huaylas, I couldn't make a good enough living there, I wanted to earn more money, etc." On the other hand, if we were to present them with a wide range of choices and simply ask them whether or not they had thought about that before they left, we would get a lot of responses that were not true, and have no way of separating the valid from the false responses. Nevertheless, the list approach was used for the following reasons: it was assumed that what the respondent *said* he was thinking about is just about as interesting and important as what he *was in fact* thinking about. Moreover, since the average migrant left Huaylas for the first time twenty years ago, we could not expect that their memories would be fully responsive after such a lapse in time. The list approach aids recall.

The respondents were asked, "When you left for the first time to work outside your village, did you think a great deal, a little, or not at all about the following?" The most frequently cited response was "improving economic situation"—97 per cent said they thought about this and most of them reported having thought a great deal about it. After this item, most of the ten most frequently cited reasons indicated that the men felt attracted by the possibilities outside Huaylas more than being pushed by the realities of Huaylas. The question of insufficient land in Huaylas for the population was only the eighth most frequently cited reason.

When the data are sorted by migration type, we find that the similarities in reasons for leaving are much more important than the differences. Using only eleven items from a list of twenty-one, the top ten reasons for each group could be put in rank order. The results are essentially the same when the responses are arranged by present place of residence, matching the brothers. Therefore, the stated reasons for leaving Huaylas do not provide us with a useful tool with which to predict subsequent migratory behavior.

Reasons for Returning to Huaylas

A list of reasons for returning to Huaylas was also presented to the returned migrants and the oscillating migrants to see if they went back for different reasons. There was essential agreement among them that the most important single reason for returning was to help the family. Also, the most important group of reasons for both groups was dissatisfaction with the job that they held. But the differences are also striking. There are three items that, for the returned migrants, were among the ten most frequently cited which were not in the top ten for the oscillating migrants. Two of these items indicate a lack of ability to adapt to the life they had had, and the other indicates that they could not stand the pace on their jobs. On the other hand, the oscillating migrants cited three reasons with greater relative frequency than the returned migrants. All three of these indicate that the oscillating migrants also went back to take home their earnings—to buy land, pay debts or religious obligations.

Nevertheless, the most important conclusion we can reach on the basis of the evidence we have is that the similarities in the reasons and conditions of migration were more notable than the differences. At first glance, it appears that we could argue that this similarity is largely a function of the relative homogeneity of the population studied, and that if we had a representative sample of people from the region or, better still, from different regions, we would have found greater differences in the conditions of, and the reasons for, migration. But the very homogeneity of the group leads us in another direction. We found earlier that there were differences in both biographical characteristics and personality traits even within a group that includes only pairs of brothers. These differences were found to be closely related to the decision to migrate and, among those who did migrate, the decision to stay or to return to Huaylas. Personality factors are interrelated with the background factors and underlie the development of such factors as the amount of education and the age at which the man decided to leave Huaylas. On the basis of the evidence presented, the conclusion must be that it is personality and the development of characteristics before the time of migration which provide the best prediction of subsequent migration behavior.

Mobility Patterns by Place of Origin Within Huaylas

Rural or urban origin within Huaylas has a good deal to do with the acquisition of characteristics that are likely to lead to migration. Moreover, these initial advantages are preserved and increased over time. All of the men now in the cities who came from the urban part of Huaylas had at least four years of education before leaving, as compared with 82 per cent of their brothers who returned to Huaylas. Of the men from the countryside, 68 per cent of those now in the city had this much education before leaving, in comparison with only 50 per cent of their brothers who returned.

The characteristics of the men at the time of the survey indicate that the migrant has increased his advantage over his brother in Huaylas. The data also indicate that there are important differences between the men in the urban part of Huaylas and those in the rural areas. More importantly, perhaps, the men from the urban part of Huaylas have done much better in the cities than the men from the rural areas. Some indicators of the differences between the men in terms of their origins and their present place of residence are presented in Table 2.

Table 2. Socioeconomic Status at Time of Survey

	Brothers From:			
	Rural Zone Now In:		*Urban Zone Now In:*	
Percentage Reporting:	*Huaylas*	*City*	*Huaylas*	*City*
1. Has more than primary school education	13	23	37	53
2. In highest group on ownership of material items	6	55	58	84
3. Monthly income of 2,000 soles or more ($75.00)	0	43	32	63
4. Has had at least one white-collar job	18	23	35	68
100%	(30)*	(31)	(19)	(19)

* omits one schedule with incomplete information

On all four indicators of socioeconomic status, the men in the cities who are from the urban part of Huaylas are higher than all other groups. The advantage of urban residence in Huaylas clearly persists even though the men in the cities have been there for an average of 15 years. The two groups that are most similar to each other are the men in the cities from the rural areas and the men living in the urban part of Huaylas. The advantage of urban residence is also clear from a comparison of the two groups of men now living in Huaylas.

Another migration fact of considerable importance does not emerge from Table 2. Whereas 20 per cent of the population of the district of Huaylas lives in the urban zone, 38 per cent of the migrants are from the urban zone. Since migration is disproportionately from the urban part of Huaylas, and disproportionately from the upper class, there must be some "rural-urban" migration and upward social mobility going on within the district of Huaylas to replace the losses and maintain the relative strength of the social classes and the same distribution of population between the two zones. Doughty's census data, as well as that of the two national censuses indicate that this has indeed been the case.

Conclusions

The decision to focus the present study on pairs of brothers from one place of origin was based on the desire for special controls on the group studied. It was recognized that the special nature of the group would not make it possible to test hypotheses and extend generalizations beyond the group. The search was for ideas, so the findings can only be regarded as suggestive, not definitive. On the other hand, given the stringency of the controls, it may well be that the results obtained understate the differences that would exist in a "normal" population. At any rate, the findings indicate the possibility that findings of other studies may be specified further than they have been to date. In this section some of the findings of the present study will be presented as hypotheses which require testing by larger studies with representative samples from different areas.

The selectivity of normal rural-urban migration of men operates on a number of principles. Migration to cities is disproportionately from the most urbanized parts of the rural areas. That is, a disproportionate number of the migrants from a rural area, such as a district, consists of people from the villages. This suggests that the idea that migration to the cities is disproportionately urban in origin might be extended to much smaller units, not normally thought of as urban. It may well be that population centers of only a few hundred or a thousand inhabitants send a disproportionate number of migrants to the cities, when compared with the proportion coming from the surrounding countryside. A correlate of this is that migration to the largest cities is disproportionately from the most urbanized parts of rural areas, whereas migration to smaller cities and rural areas may originate disproportionately from the open countryside.

Social class factors related to migration are also related to residence. The upper class is concentrated in the villages, so if migration tends to be disproportionately from the urban centers, it may also be disproportionately from the upper class of the area. This is clearly the case in Huaylas. Educational opportunities in rural areas are also related both to social class and to residence, since the best, and sometimes the only, schools are located in the villages. All of these factors are closely interrelated: the villages contain the advantages of the most urban life found in rural areas; the upper class there lives in the village because of its advantages, and the advantages exist there because of the presence of the upper class. Achievement in education is enhanced by residence in the village. Contact with the outside world, and consequently knowledge of the outside world, are centered in the village. It is small wonder, then, that preparation for migration to the cities is enhanced by residence in the village rather than the countryside.

Migration streams generally consist of people who are younger than the population as a whole. The data of this study are consistent with this generalization, and suggest that further specification of the relationship between age and migration may be possible. *Within* the migration stream, those who left before their eighteenth birthday showed a greater tendency to remain outside. Permanency in migration appears to be related to age at time of first migration.

The instrument used in assessing differences in personality traits is admittedly crude. The data at hand suggest that there is a relationship between personality traits and migration, and that those best equipped for life in the city, and most likely to break away from home ties are, indeed, the ones who do migrate and remain in the city. In spite of the crudeness of the instrument, these differences assume particular significance when it is recalled that the group studied was controlled as much as possible on such things as heredity and early social environment—including both social class and residence within Huaylas. However, research with more sophisticated instruments on larger populations will be needed to specify the traits as well as test the relationship between personality traits and migration.

It appears that differential migration is more related to differences in biographical and personality characteristics than it is to the conditions or stated reasons for migration. Difficulties in adjustment to urban life are minimized by a selection process which sends to the cities the men who are already most urbanized and most likely to succeed in the city. Another selection process takes place in the cities (indicated by the 39 per cent of the group who are returned migrants) which sends back those who do not adjust.

In the most general sense, migration from an area constitutes a tax imposed upon that area. Huaylas bears all the costs of raising migrants up to about the age when it could begin to reap some return on its investment, and then they leave without paying off. It is difficult to estimate the real costs of this flight of human capital, as Huaylas cannot make effective use of it in any event.

The loss is not only on just so many units of its production of human beings; Huaylas also loses the most progressive element it produces via this process of rural-urban migration. In terms of quality, the best educated, the men who are best equipped to "go places," are those who do indeed go places. Those who are most likely to perpetuate the way of life of the area are those who stay or return. Those who return from the cities to live in Huaylas bring back some of the goods they have acquired, but most of them cannot apply whatever skills they may have learned in the environment of limited possibilities which confronts them in Huaylas.

Huaylas benefits from the outmigration only in limited ways. Some of the men in the cities send back money to help support their relatives—particularly their parents. Huaylas also benefits insofar as men in the cities serve as a "welcoming committee" to help the next group of migrants to get settled. This helps keep the rate of outmigration as high as it is by greatly facilitating the process. By stabilizing the population in Huaylas, heavy emigration helps prevent a steady decline in the level of living that would surely result from increasing pressure on a fixed land base, in the absence of a changing technology.

The cities benefit from the process for the same reasons that the countryside loses. The city receives men who are of working age, whom it did not have to bear any of the costs of raising. The city gets many of the most progressive men the rural areas have to offer. Migrants seem to adapt rather easily to life and work in the city. To the extent that they do not adapt, they tend to return to the countryside, so the city is not burdened with an undue number of misfits. Because the highlanders are generally eager to lose their identification with the sierra, they drop most of the traits that readily identify them as highlanders. Therefore, the city does not have to cope with the problem of a large, distinct minority group and resultant intergroup hostilities.

If it is generally true that rural-urban migration funnels a large share of the country's most progressive human material to the cities, this would seem to be a factor to consider in programs of economic development.

References Cited

Anastasi, Anne, and John P. Foley, Jr.
1949. *Differential Psychology*. New York: Macmillian Company.

Bogue, Donald J.
1959. "Internal Migration." In Philip M. Hauser and Otis Dudley Duncan, *The Study of Population, An Inventory and Appraisal.* Chicago: University of Chicago Press.

Davis, Kingsley, and Ana Casis.
1946. "Urbanization in Latin America." *The Milbank Memorial Fund Quarterly* 24 (2), April. Reprinted in Olen E. Leonard and Charles A. Loomis, *Readings in Latin American Social Organization and Institutions,* 1953, pp. 143-66. East Lansing: Michigan State University Press.

Doughty, Paul L.
1961. "Report on the Census and the Study of Peruvian Family Life in Huaylas, Peru." Lima: unpublished.
1963. *Peruvian Highlanders in a Changing World: Social Integration and Culture Change in an Andean District.* Unpublished Ph.D. thesis. Ithaca, N.Y.: Cornell University.

Gist, Noel P.
1954. "Selective Migration in Urban South India." *Proceedings of World Population Conference,* p. 821.

Husain, A. F. A.
1956. *Human and Social Impact of Technological Change in Pakistan.* 2 vols. Dacca, Pakistan: Oxford University Press.

Kahl, Joseph
1959. "Some Social Concomitants of Industrialization and Urbanization." *Human Organization* 18 (2).

Matos Mar, José
1961. "Migration and Urbanization: The Barriadas of Lima, An Example of Integration into Urban Life." In Hauser, Philip M., *Urbanization in Latin America.* New York: International Documents Service, Division of the Columbia University Press.

Kin and Non-Kin

Edward M. Bruner

The Problem

"Primitive societies have, and not without justification, been said to treat the limits of their tribal group as the frontiers of humanity and to regard everyone outside them as foreigners, that is, as dirty, coarse sub-men or even non-men: dangerous beasts or ghosts." Lévi-Strauss (1966:166) goes on to say that what is often overlooked is that an essential function of totemic classification is to break down this closing of the group and to promote the idea of a humanity without frontiers. He cites evidence of intertribal totemic divisions from Western Australia, and he describes how both the Menomini and Chippewa regard themselves as related to persons of the same totem even though those persons may belong to different tribes. We know that in many ethnographic areas the tribes within a localized region will extend the frontiers of humanity through totemic classification or other mechanisms which serve a similar purpose. On the Plains of North America the various tribes utilized the mechanism of father-son adoption to establish a basis of relating to one another, even to those with whom they were at war, and this applied to both nomadic and village groups. Examples could be multiplied throughout the world. There are other means of extension beyond totemic classification and father-son adoption; and these two should not be equated, since one is a classificatory scheme and the other a social mechanism, although if the latter is to be effective it too implies shared intertribal categorizations. But the point is that tribes within a region may share some system of categories or some social means of relating to peoples who are defined *a priori* as being different from themselves.

The problem is not restricted to the primitive world, for contemporary cities represent the example *par excellence* in which peoples of different tribes and ethnic groups and social categories come together and must establish some new bases of order and of interaction. Modern urban centers grow by migration more than by natural population increase, and those who have migrated to the cities of Africa, Asia, and elsewhere may confront, for the first time, a bewildering variety of kinds of persons different from themselves, speaking different languages, and practicing seemingly unintelligible social customs. Indeed, a modern context as opposed to a primitive one may be defined by the fact that it includes so many different kinds of people. The primitive world has been classically viewed as one bound by shared common understandings and by an established conception of the moral order. But with geographical mobility, the increase of world travel, and the entire onslaught of modernity, the contemporary context is characterized precisely by the mixing of people with varying cultural conceptions. It is the modern context to which anthropologists increasingly have been turning their attention.

As social scientists have told us for the past century, all peoples, everywhere, have one universally human characteristic—they try to make sense out of the world and put things in order, irrespective of how initially bewildering the situation may be. They impose their own system of categories, and if there are different kinds of people interacting, there are multiple systems operating simultaneously. It is not necessary that there be a common consensus as a basis of order, and Wallace (1961) has made a convincing case that the various participants in the system need only share what he calls partial equivalence structures. For purposes of interaction, they have to know only enough to predict the behavior of the other, but each must also have some system of categorization that makes sense to him.

Urbanization may be viewed from this perspective, as a process by which migrant peoples in cities come to terms with urban heterogeneity. This paper will attempt to apply this perspective to field data gathered among the Toba Batak of Indonesia. The Batak situation represents a general one that could be duplicated in many cities of Africa as well as in many areas of the world, so that the point of view utilized and the generalizations that emerge here may have relevance elsewhere. The Batak have migrated from a relatively homogeneous all-Batak village world, where every man is a person essentially similar to oneself and in which the basic culture pattern is shared by all, to a heterogeneous, multi-ethnic-group, large-scale urban world. In this paper we focus on the way the Batak view and make sense out of the new urban environment in which they find themselves and how, in the process, they extend the frontiers of humanity.

The Village Background

The Toba Batak are located a few degrees from the equator in North Sumatra in an area that may be divided into two main regions, the east coast and the Tapanuli highlands, which differ ecologically and historically. The east coast is a lowland area which rises gently in altitude toward the interior until coming to the Bukut Barisan, a mountain range running north–south from one end of Sumatra to the other. In the mid-nineteenth century the east coast was sparsely populated by indigenous Malay peoples, while the Tapanuli highlands were somewhat more densely populated by different Batak subgroups. In 1864 a Dutch planter discovered that tobacco—the famous Deli tobacco—could successfully be grown on the coast, which led to a radical transformation of the entire region. The east coast became a vast plantation area not only for tobacco but also for palm oil, rubber, and other commercial crops. Population density increased with the recruitment of Javanese and Chinese estate laborers, although the control of the estates and of the area remained firmly in the hands of Europeans. Malay sultans were nominally heads of government by what was politely known as "indirect" rule. Motor roads and a railroad were built, and the city of Medan, which in the early 1960's had a population of approximately one-half million, arose to serve the commercial interests of the planters and the administrative needs of the district. In 1957 the Dutch and other Westerners were forced to leave Sumatra as the estates were nationalized by the Indonesian government, but in the post-Sukarno period after 1965 many Westerners have returned.

No plantations were established in the Tapanuli highlands, and Europeans did not settle there. It remained an ethnically homogeneous rice-growing area regulated by Batak adat or customary law. An aerial photograph of Tapanuli in 1860 and a century later in 1960 would have shown the same small Batak villages with their distinctive high-pitched palm-thatched roofs surrounded by sawah, or wet rice fields. The physical landscape was changed very slightly, mainly by the addition of motor roads and metal roofs, although the social landscape was more extensively altered. But despite the changes that did occur there was no disruption of the basic mode of ecological adaptation nor of Batak relations to the land. The primary mode of subsistence was and remains rice agriculture.

One of the main consequences of colonialism was a vast increase in the Batak population, brought about by inoculations and modern medical and sanitary practices. The Dutch eliminated intervillage warfare and slavery. German missionaries introduced Christianity and Western education to Tapanuli in the late nineteenth century, and a relatively large number of educated Batak found employment on Western estates and with the Dutch government on the east coast.

The migration from the Tapanuli highlands began at the turn of the century. Since it had been the policy of the colonial government to restrict the movement of indigenous peoples, it was only after Indonesia achieved independence in 1949 that the migration became extensive (Cunningham, 1958). The Batak left their highland homeland literally by the hundreds of thousands, so that today there may well be more Batak outside than inside Tapanuli. They went to Medan (approximately 150 miles from the highlands) and to other areas on the east coast, and to more modern regions elsewhere in Indonesia where they could find employment and establish business. The Batak have a reputation throughout Indonesia as aggressive enterprising entrepreneurs. The Tapanuli highlands, however, remained undeveloped, providing few economic opportunities other than farming and small-scale trading. Very few urbanized Batak ever return there to live, even after retirement, but many come back for short visits to discuss lineage affairs, to look after their property, or to participate in village ceremonials.

The core of each Batak village is a localized patrilineage, the basic social unit in the Tapanuli highlands. Some members of the patrilineage of course have moved elsewhere to Medan and to other cities on the east coast, but they retain rights in their home village and they have the prerogative of returning at any time. Many of those who migrate continue to own a house and rice fields in their village even though they may be permanently established in the city. Ownership of village property in such cases eventually comes to have more symbolic than economic value. Not all residents of the village are members of the patrilineage. Some belong to more distantly related lineages or even to different clans, while others are men who have married daughters of the core lineage and who reside matrilocally. In the latter instances residence is often temporary, and usually there is some personal or economic reason for moving outside one's home village.

Throughout the Tapanuli highlands there is a rough correspondence between descent group and territory. Not only does each patrilineage have its defined locality, but larger descent units such as the named exogamous clans are also localized. The correspondence is never exact, and it is not possible to identify a man's village from his clan name alone, but by specifying the main patrilineal branch within the clan or, if necessary, the name of his grandfather, most Batak can identify a man's place of origin. In Batak thought, descent and territoriality are interrelated and are essential components of the social system.

Another essential component is marriage alliance. Every Batak marriage establishes a long-term relationship between the lineage of the bride, the wife-givers or *hula hula,* and the lineage of the groom, the wife-receivers or *boru.* The wife-givers have a superior status, and there is a systematic exchange of money, food, and other items of economic and symbolic importance at every transition point in the marriage. Birth, marriage, and death of the offspring of the couple are the most crucial occasions for ceremonial exchanges between the wife-giving and the wife-receiving lineages. If the Batak feel that a marriage has been successful, as measured by many children, good health, long life, and economic prosperity, or if there is some political reason for continuing the tie between the two lineages, then every effort will be made to renew the relationship in the next generation by marriage to a matrilateral cross cousin. Although the frequency of cross cousin marriage is decreasing, especially in the cities, some parents may apply considerable pressure on a son to marry a real or classificatory mother's brother's daughter.

The combination of localized lineages linked with one another through wife-giving and wife-receiving relationships creates a kinship grid binding all Toba Batak. Any two persons may trace their precise kinship relationship vertically through descent ties and horizontally through marriage alliances. As there are well over a million Toba Batak, an individual frequently encounters others who are complete strangers, but by utilization and sometimes manipulation of the basic ideas of descent, territory, and alliance, a kinship tie can be created. And except for transitory fleeting interactions, whenever two adult Batak strangers meet they always *martarombo* and *martutur,* which means that they go through a process utilizing the genealogy to establish some basis of kinship order. This happens in the village and the city, on Sumatra and Java, or wherever two

Toba Batak meet. They exchange such information as the name of their clan, the number of generations removed from the ancestral founder of the clan, the clan of their mother or wife or sister's husband, the name of their grandfather, and their home village. Some Batak are more skilled in these matters than others, and if two individuals are not very good at it they always have the alternative of asking their parents, or a clan elder, or one of the many recognized genealogical specialists.

All Batak engage in the process of exchanging information to establish a kinship tie, with the exception of those whom the society defines as being children, or not adults, which means those who are not yet married. Certainly there are mature unmarried persons; but if asked if they are married they invariably reply "not yet" rather than "no," implying that there is always the possibility of marriage, and they remain sociological children. Only married persons participate in Batak ceremonials, have a voice in lineage affairs, and have the right to full membership in the clan associations which arise in all urban centers. Young unmarried persons, and especially students, generally use first names in address, and most have only a minimal knowledge of Batak kinship and adat affairs, as they have only a minimal role in these activities. Most are well aware, however, that their role in Batak society will change appreciably after marriage, and even more after they have children of their own.

In the adult village world of the Tapanuli highlands, everyone is a Batak and a relative, and although customs vary slightly from place to place, the basic ideas are the same and the system of categorization is uniform. In Indonesia, all land is owned by the government in theory, but actually in Tapanuli and in comparable areas elsewhere the land is held by descent groups and cannot be sold to outsiders. No stranger may purchase land in Tapanuli, and only in exceptional circumstances could one live there. In 1957, when my wife and I moved to Tapanuli, we were the only non-Bataks then living in a village in the entire province, as far as we were aware. Within weeks after our arrival, a formal adat ritual was held in which my wife was adopted into the Simandjuntak clan as a daughter of the localized patrilineage, after which everyone addressed us in kinship terms and we reciprocated. The Batak had incorporated us into their system which defined everyone's rights and responsibilities. They certainly felt more comfortable after the adoption ceremony; and possibly it was the only way for a married couple to enter Batak village society on a long-term basis. The adoption ritual is also performed when a Batak man migrates to the city and marries a Javanese, or a Chinese, or a woman of any other ethnic group. Most frequently the non-Batak wife is brought back to Tapanuli and is adopted into the clan of her husband's mother, as if the man had married a matrilateral cross cousin. Robert Redfield's (1947) statement about the folk society does apply to the Batak: "The kin are the type persons for all experience."

The village Batak are not, however, to be equated with, say, Australian aborigines, to whom non-kin are non-people. The Batak are very much aware that there are other kinds of people in the world beyond Tapanuli. They trade with them, confront them on their territorial borders, and receive outside cultural influences, and this has probably been the case for a very long time.

Non-Batak do reside in the small administrative market towns along the main road in the Tapanuli highlands. Towns such as Balige and Tarutung have a few Chinese stores, a Chinese restaurant, and occasionally a Western missionary or mission medical doctor; and in the government offices of the police, the military, and the civil authority there are always some Indonesians of other ethnic groups such as Javanese or Menadonese. Except for the Chinese merchants, these non-Batak are usually temporary residents, rarely learn to speak the Batak language, and do not integrate in the village society that surrounds them. During the time that we lived in Tapanuli, not one non-Batak from the nearby town of Balige or elsewhere entered our village, aside from those whom we had invited, with the single exception of a German university student who appeared one day and announced that he was on a walking tour. Some effort is being made now to encourage tourists to come to Tapanuli—certainly the landscape has a rugged natural beauty and the Toba Lake is magnificent —but the tourist industry has not yet developed.

Although villagers may not have very many opportunities for interacting directly with non-Batak, they learn about them from a variety of sources. The primary means of communication are schools, mass media such as newspapers and radio, and word of mouth from parents and elders in the village and particularly from relatives who have migrated to the city and return for visits. Most children in Tapanuli attend primary schools; they receive instruction in the Batak language for the first three years and then in the national Indonesian language for the last three years. It is interesting to compare the themes contained in the Batak as opposed to the Indonesian schoolbooks. The first story in the Batak reading book tells of the teacher who asks the student for the name of his father, and after the student refuses the teacher compliments him and comments that in the Batak adat it is the height of disrespect to mention the name of one's father. The Indonesian books used in the final three years of elementary school reflect national themes and culture heroes. They tell about the fight for independence, about revolutionary leaders, about Java and the Ramayana. On a more advanced level, anthropology textbooks tell about ethnic differences, and there are many books written by Bataks on Batak culture and character which often contain comparative statements about other Indonesian groups. The most vivid descriptions, however, are provided by returning relatives.

What then are the main categories of classification of others held by villagers in Tapanuli? The major one is simply *halak hita*, "our people," meaning other Toba Batak. There are not many situations in which villagers think of themselves as Toba Batak, as it is not often that a contrast is called for on such a high level of generalization. Usually village people identify themselves by their localized patrilineage; the term *halak hita* is most frequently heard in terms of opposition to other Indonesians. All Batak villagers are aware that Indonesia as a nation consists of a number of different ethnic groups (*suku bangsa*), that each group has a home locality on one or another island, and that each has its own customs. From the perspective of Tapanuli, the ethnic groups of Indonesia as a nation are somewhat comparable to the Toba Batak descent groups, in that each has a common origin and locality, and each varies in dialect and adat (cf. Skinner, 1959).

For most of the main ethnic groups of Indonesia there are commonly accepted stereotypes. In general, the most prominent village attitude toward others is caution and distrust. The Javanese are *halus* or refined and civilized, but one never knows what they are really thinking. The Batak neighbors to the south, the Minangkabau of central Sumatra, are likely to use poison, and the Atjehnese to the north will draw a knife if provoked. Outside of Tapanuli one must be continually on guard, and black magic is an ever-present threat. Many Batak traders, some soldiers, and even some university students attending school in Java or abroad will carry amulets designed to serve as protection against poison or magic. One adult remembers the time when, as a child in her early teens, she was severely beaten by her parents for being so foolish as to accept food from a Javanese family.

On the other hand, when village Batak are away from Tapanuli, they sometimes take advantage of non-Batak strangers, since the adat rules and the Batak mechanisms of social control do not apply. Again, this is a further extension of a Batak pattern. Two classificatory brothers who live in the same village are both engaged in the pepper leaf (*gambir*) trade and are in direct competition in their commercial transactions. This poses no particular problem, for as one of them said, "We are brothers in the village and enemies in the marketplace." In their interactions in the marketplace they take account of the fact that they will again be brothers in the village; but this restraint does not apply to non-Batak strangers. The hostility and aggression which the Batak feel toward their brothers and lineagemates is controlled and channeled and even institutionalized in a village context, but toward strangers with whom one is in competition it is sometimes given rather uninhibited expression.

The final category of non-Batak is a *tuan,* which the dictionary translates as "mister" or "you," but which the Batak apply to Dutchmen or Americans or any high-status foreigner. In the village view all *tuan* have great wealth and tremendous power, hence one must be respectful in dealing with them. Before my wife's adoption ritual in the village, I was called a *tuan.* In one revealing incident, a villager who had for almost a year called me by the Batak kinship term *amang uda,* younger father, reverted to the term *tuan* in the heat of an argument, which indicates how it is possible to switch from one system of categorization to another, and also how tenuous is an outsider's incorporation into the Batak social order.

The Urban Context

Recent census data on the ethnic composition of Medan does not exist, but the most numerous peoples are the Toba Batak and other Batak subgroups such as the Mandailing, Angkola, Pakpak, Simelungun, and Karo; the Atjehnese, Minangkabau, and others from Sumatra; the indigenous Malays; the Javanese; and the Chinese and Indians. There are also some Sundanese, Madurese, Menadonese, Ambonese, Buginese, and probably representatives of a hundred other ethnic subgroups of Indonesia. Although Medan arose as a Dutch colonial city, the number of Westerners has never been large. The total population grew rapidly from 76,000 in 1930 to one half million in 1960, and there is every indication that the rate of growth has not decreased in recent years. In the colonial era there was some localization of ethnic groups to the extent that there was a Chinatown and a European section, but since Indonesian independence the lines have become blurred. Clearly, the Toba Batak are not concentrated in any one area of the city. The major sociological facts about Medan are its ethnic heterogeneity and also the fact that no one group has a numerical majority or a dominant position. It is a city of minorities.

The Toba Batak are regarded as aggressive intruders, even as "invaders," and there is considerable political and economic competition among the ethnic groups of Medan. Although in the colonial period most Batak entered Medan as white-collar workers, primarily clerks and teachers, today they occupy every available sociological niche and are found at every level of stratification. The Toba are mostly Christian who have their own church, the H.K.B.P. (Huria Kristen Batak Protestan), and services are held in the Toba Batak language. There are many different Christian denominations represented in Medan, and not all Toba Batak join the H.K.B.P.; but the most significant point of contrast is that most of the other Indonesian ethnic groups are Moslems. These factors contributed to the ethnic fighting that arose in Medan and in other Indonesian cities, particularly during the 1950's. There were severe conflicts between the Batak and the Atjehnese, the Minangkabau, and the Menadonese at different time periods, and a number of people were killed before the more responsible members of the respective communities could restore order. Most Toba Batak in Medan, of course, do have cordial and friendly relations with the non-Batak whom they meet in the neighborhood, at school, at work, and in the marketplace; almost every Indonesian strives for ethnic harmony and will go to considerable lengths to avoid open conflict; and the actual ethnic fighting involved only a very small number of persons. Nevertheless, all parties are aware that open fighting has occurred in the past and that it could recur.

The mechanisms of adaptation toward non-Batak that were utilized in Tapanuli are no longer effective in Medan. It would not be very realistic to attempt to adopt all urban strangers into clans, thereby extending the Batak system outward, as most others do not want to be incorporated into the Batak social order. They have their own customs and adat. There are Chinese traders in the Tapanuli highlands as well as in Medan, but there is a vast difference in the behavior of the two groups. The Tapanuli Chinese realize that they are in an alien land and they learn to speak the Batak language and adapt to the local culture. It is only good business to do so. But in Medan, the opposite occurs and it is the Batak who adapt to the Chinese. There are Toba Batak who were born in Medan and who have learned to speak Chinese because it helps them to obtain better bargains in their daily shopping. We have also observed that in the Sundanese city of Bandung on the island of Java, many members of the Batak community learn the Sundanese language.

When a Tapanuli migrant first comes to Medan, however, he has no firm basis in his previous experience for relating to non-Batak. He is equipped with a multiplicity of ethnic stereotypes which he has learned in the village, but the basic difficulty is that the stereotypes do not tell him very much about how to behave toward others. It is important to know that the Javanese are *halus* and refined; but this is a very gross characterization, it is not situationally specific, it does not prepare him for the variety of Javanese that he may meet, and does not differentiate between a Javanese prostitute and a Javanese governor. Stereotypes do not provide sufficiently detailed behavioral guides for social action. And he may confront some varieties of Indonesians, such as Balinese, for whom he has no stereotypes whatsoever.

Most Tapanuli migrants eventually learn, not immediately but over a period of months or even years, that they simply cannot behave as village Batak in Medan. The pressure for change comes not only from members of other ethnic groups but, even more, from the Toba Batak who are established long-term residents. If the Javanese and others are regarded as more *halus,* the Toba Batak are considered the opposite or *kasar,* which means coarse and crude. The village Batak realizes that others regard him as *kasar,* which he defines to himself as rough but frank and straightforward, and he is even proud of the characterization. But in Medan and more so in the cities of Java, he comes to realize that *kasar* is interpreted as being vulgar and uncivilized. Others say that the Toba Batak are barbarians who eat pork and formerly practiced cannibalism. Most Batak acknowledge that their ancestors a century ago did practice cannibalism, but it is a thing of the past, and they have subsequently become Christians. Members of other ethnic groups in Medan, however, have told us that in one or another remote area of the Tapanuli highlands there are Batak who still eat people. Group images have an existence independent of historical reality.

The village Batak and the new migrants may not be aware of it, but in Medan they will become more *halus.* They become less rough, they speak more softly, and they learn to adapt their behavior to contemporary Indonesian urban culture. The vast majority of Toba Batak who came to Medan are not there for purposes of temporary labor migration but have come to settle permanently, to raise a family, and to establish a life for themselves in the city.

The acquisition of knowledge about how to behave toward the other groups in Medan usually comes slowly, in stages, step by step. One boy in his early twenties who had been born and raised in Tapanuli arranged for a visit with urban relatives. He had never been to Medan before and could not yet speak Indonesian easily. When he got off the bus, he found someone who "looked like" a Batak, asked for directions to the house of his relative, and then spent most of his time in Medan inside the home, where they spoke Batak and ate Batak food. He never went out alone, and after a brief period he returned by bus to Tapanuli. It was a minimal urban experience, but it gave him an opportunity to sort out his impressions, to revise his preconceptions of the city, and to prepare for the next trip.

The example is important in another respect because no Tapanuli Batak enters "the city" as such. He moves along a network, through a system, occupies a particular social structure slot, and there is invariably someone else, most frequently a relative, to help interpret the urban experience in terms he can understand. No man has to recapitulate the experience of his group and learn about the city on his own. But the learning must occur in the city itself. The knowledge of urban ways is not readily transferable in the village, because it is not relevant there. An evening stroll in an urban area, an encounter with a Javanese neighbor, a bargaining session with a Malay fruit seller, a discussion in the coffee house with a Mandailing university student, all accompanied at first by a Batak interpreter and multiplied a thousand times, provide the basis for urban sophistication. The knowledge is acquired in context.

There are situations in which it is just not possible to become more cosmopolitan and sophisticated in stages, and in these instances every effort is made to accelerate the process. At the technological university in Bandung, ITB, the older Batak students will provide a short intensive period of instruction to entering Batak freshmen who have come directly from Sumatra. They are taught not only about university regulations, but also about local Sundanese behavior and expectations. The same function is frequently performed in Indonesian cities by Batak ethnic associations or by the Batak members of one's government bureau or business concern.

The degree of urban sophistication required is, of course, quite variable, and depends in part upon one's structural position in the city, age, sex, and the neighborhood in which one resides. A high-ranking military officer, an unemployed teenage boy, and a village woman who comes to

Medan to be married need to acquire different kinds of knowledge about the city and about ethnic heterogeneity. Because of the totality of their social roles, there are some whose behavior is rather narrowly prescribed, while others have considerable freedom and choice. There are those who live in Medan but who restrict their activities outside the home to all-Batak gatherings. It is possible to do so. They go to the H.K.B.P. ethnic church, join their all-Batak neighborhood mutual aid society, participate in the activities of their Batak clan association, and attend every Batak adat ceremonial to which they are invited. On these occasions, one talks, thinks, and acts Batak. Almost every Toba Batak in Medan participates in some of these activities some of the time, but for others it is equivalent to the totality of their social identity.

To summarize thus far, some individuals maintain an entrenched Batak position within the urban environment, while others, because of structural necessity or individual choice, reach out to members of other ethnic groups and thereby extend the boundaries of their own awareness and personality. Even siblings of the same sex vary in the ethnic mix encompassed within their egocentric networks. Those simplistic overgeneralized schemes which dichotomize the population into two "groups" of traditional vs. modern, or older generation vs. younger generation, or village-orientated vs. city-orientated, are totally inadequate as explanations. The Batak population cannot be segmented into two gross categories as if each actually represented a different population, for the problem occurs within each individual, and it is a question of how he categorizes and regards others in the urban world.

I propose a different and in many respects a more naive way of conceptualizing interpersonal relationships in the city. The initial distinction and the most fundamental binary opposition made by every Batak in every encounter is to differentiate others on the basis of ethnicity into Batak and non-Batak. By this I mean that whenever and wherever one Batak confronts another human being a decision is made, on an unconscious level, that the other is a Batak like oneself, or a non-Batak who is different than self. With some possible exceptions to be considered later, all Toba Batak, including those born in Tapanuli and those born in Medan, young and old, rich and poor, men and women, everyone, even when they are not aware of it, segment other persons into Batak and non-Batak.

As an illustration, the following conversation, recorded in our field notes, involves three women: an anthropologist (my wife, Elaine C. Bruner); the host woman in whose home the conversation took place and who is married to a wealthy Medan businessman; and her visiting relative from Tapanuli.

Anthropologist	Who do you see when you come to visit?
Visitor	Well, only these people here.
Anthropologist	Do you go anywhere else?
Visitor	Just to another close family on Bulan Street.
Anthropologist	How about the people in this neighborhood, around this house?
Visitor	Them? I don't dare.
Anthropologist	Why not?
Visitor	They are not our people (*halak hita*), they are strangers (*halak asing*).
Anthropologist	Can you tell what ethnic group they are from?
Visitor	No, how can one tell?
Anthropologist	Are they different?
Visitor	Sure.
Anthropologist	What is the difference?
Visitor	You can't trust them. They don't like us. They speak different, and they don't understand the way I speak.
Host	That's a village woman for you!
Visitor	Right!
Anthropologist	What about me?
Visitor	You are not a stranger. I met you years ago. I once danced next to you. You speak our language, so I dare to mix with you. Otherwise, I would have just stayed in the kitchen.

This example was selected because it presents only the minimal opposition between Batak and non-Batak, and no further differentiations are made within the latter class. Although the conversation occurred in the city, and although this woman has actually visited Medan many times, all non-Batak are lumped together as "them," in contrast with "us." There is a clarity in this village woman's thought that reveals a universal feature of all Batak thought, the opposition between Batak and non-Batak.

The most urbanized modernized Batak starts with the same basic binary opposition, with the one difference that he has acquired the conceptual equipment to make a multiplicity of finer classifications within the class non-Batak. In the perspective of this paper, to be urbanized may be equated with or measured by the degree of expansion of the scope of categorizations of non-Batak.

The question arises in any interaction of exactly how one distinguishes a Batak from a non-Batak, and beyond this, how one differentiates among other Indonesian ethnic groups. The main point is that ethnic identification is relevant information to all Indonesians, and proper identifications are made. Appearance provides one guide. Shades of skin color, hair style, facial contours, and body mannerisms enable some to specify ethnic affiliation. One informant claimed to be able to tell a Batak by looking at his face, and although his judgments proved to be surprisingly accurate, appearance alone is not always a good indicator. Name and language usage are more obvious and reliable clues. The Batak use their clan names, and this is invariably a positive means of identification. The Javanese and other ethnic groups also have characteristic identifiable names. The way that the Indonesian language is spoken and pronounced provides another clear indication of region of origin. There are ethnic jokes on the theme of how a Batak or a Javanese speaks Indonesian, and some persons can imitate the Indonesian language style of a variety of different peoples, to everyone's amusement.

A combination of factors such as appearance, name, and language evaluated simultaneously provides the basis for ethnic identification. In many situations there is no need to be subtle and one can ask a person where he comes from, or more directly, for the name of his ethnic group. College students in Medan, when they are not sure about someone's ethnic affiliation, just ask him. They need to know because it influences their behavior. If a Batak boy at a party sees an attractive girl, he may ask her to dance without first determining her ethnic group, and there may even be some excitement in purposeful concealment, but eventually he must find out. If she is a Batak, she may be his classificatory sister or a potential marriage partner, and if she is a non-Batak he acts differently—if he learns that she is, say, a Sundanese or an Atjehnese.

Batak adults in Medan usually speak to each other in their own language, use kinship terms in address and reference, and avoid any mention of personal names. In relating to non-Batak, they speak Indonesian, use appropriate Indonesian pronouns, and freely use names. It is remarkable how easily they can switch from one mental set to another, depending on context. In a conversation with a man in Medan who had migrated from our village in Tapanuli, he identified himself as the second son of the fourth grandfather, which referred to his genealogical connection to the founding ancestor of the localized patrilineage in Tapanuli. He asked about *ito,* his Batak kinship term for my wife, and introduced me to his children as their *amang boru.* I inquired about how he had heard of our arrival in Medan, and he replied from the family on First Street, a way of avoiding any mention of that family's name. Then we were joined by a non-Batak Indonesian, and my Batak friend referred to my wife as Mrs. Bruner and to himself by name as Monang Simandjuntak, thereby changing over from a Batak to an Indonesian frame of reference.

Positive ethnic identification is not just a matter of convenience or politeness in Medan but is rather an economic and political necessity. Particularly in situations of potential conflict or competition, it is sometimes essential for survival to know the other's ethnic group. A businessman needs to determine the extent to which he can drive a hard bargain, and a teenager must know when to back down if challenged in a neighborhood encounter. In these and other situations, ethnicity provides the initial basis of devising one's own strategy, based upon an evaluation of what might be called the ethnic limits, a calculation of how far you can go.

In one ethnically mixed middle-level kampong or neighborhood in Medan, the Batak children are given very explicit instructions from their parents regarding the appropriate behavior if a conflict develops. We interviewed the young children themselves, as well as the parents, and there was widespread agreement. One can fight with a Javanese, but the best strategy, they say, is to yell at him, and he will probably retreat. If there is the slightest argument with an Atjehnese or a Minangkabau, the standing instructions are to return home immediately and to report it to the parents, so as to prevent the conflict from spreading. Regarding the Karo Batak, who have had a history of tense relations with the Toba people, the instructions are to try to avoid them. As one mother overcommunicated to her children, "they only think of money, they are heartless, we hate them, they are slovenly and dirty."

Every individual interaction in Medan occurs within a larger framework of ethnic group relations in the city, and the behavior of a Toba Batak toward an Atjehnese or a Karo is very much influenced by the respective power positions of the groups involved. Mothers do not usually do a sociological analysis for the benefit of their children, but tell them to come home to avoid these groups; they provide recipes for behavior. Their instructions, however, represent a distillation of the group wisdom and knowledge in a particular context and locality.

The group wisdom in Medan, as I understand it, indicates lack of basic trust, says that we have no firm basis of predicting the behavior of some other groups under conditions of stress, and provides no established way of resolving conflicts. Avoid these people, it is said, because we do not know them, we do not know how they will act if there is trouble, and we have no way of settling disputes. With regard to the Javanese, the Batak seem to have established a more satisfactory working relationship, more so than with the adjacent groups from Sumatra. The stereotype of the Javanese is changing in Medan, and they are frequently referred to now as more honest and as sincere. But the Batak and the Javanese in Medan are not really in competition.

Intergroup relations might be easier if there were one dominant culture in Medan, or one national Indonesian standard of established and universal applicability. There is an emerging national Indonesian culture, of course, but no one would claim that it is fully developed yet or that it has replaced the many regional Indonesian culture patterns, belief systems, and languages. If there were one such generally accepted regional or national culture in Medan, then every group could shape its behavior in terms of it, and this might facilitate urban adaptation. But this is speculation, since such a situation does not yet exist.

The underlying fear in conflict situations involving members of different ethnic groups is not so much the possibility of direct expressions of aggression and fighting, for this can be seen and handled, but rather that someone whose real thoughts and reactions are not entirely apparent will use poison or magic against you or a member of your family. With a Minangkabau or a Sundanese it is difficult, the Batak say, to ascertain their true emotions, and one never knows how angry they may be or when they will resort to a supernatural means of seeking revenge. Throughout Indonesia, belief in magic is very real, in the rural and urban areas, and at all levels of society. There are auspicious and inauspicious days, there are men who can predict the future, and almost everyone has a story of an ailment that could not be cured by modern science but cleared up in a few days after the source of the trouble was diagnosed and exorcised by a *dukun* or medicine man. There are evil Toba Batak too who resort to magic and poison against their own people, but with another Batak there is at least a clearer understanding of what behavior might trigger a violent reaction.

Conclusion

In this paper, we have presented a brief sketch of some of the perceptions of Tapanuli Batak who migrate to Medan. The categories and stereotypes of other ethnic groups acquired in the village are not adequate to handle the variety and heterogeneity of peoples in the city. The most fundamental interpersonal binary opposition is between Batak and non-Batak, and with increasing urban experience over time there is an expansion in the scope of categorizations of non-Batak others. The process of categorical expansion is not uniform among all segments of the urban population; for some it is rapid and extensive, while for others it is minimal, depending upon structural position and personal inclination. In this perspective the major interpersonal consequence of urbanization consists of a breakdown and refinement of the category "stranger."

An expansion of the scope and quality of relationships within the class non-Batak does not imply that relationships within the class Batak remain static, for they change too. An opposition between Batak and non-Batak is identical to a distinction between kin and non-kin, for all Toba Batak are kinsmen, or potential kinsmen, and non-Batak are non-kin, unless they change their status by adoption. Batak kinship operates differently in a Tapanuli village than it does in an Indonesian city. In Medan there is a realignment of the significant units of social organization, an emergence of new social groups adapted to the urban context, and a transformation of the quality of Batak social relations, as I have documented elsewhere (Bruner, 1959, 1961, 1963).

The literature on kinship change as a consequence of modernization has been growing in recent years (e.g. Spoehr, 1947; Firth, 1964; Wolf, 1966; Singer, 1968), and this paper is related to that literature but it begins from an alternate perspective. From our point of view, the kinship change literature tells only half the story, in that it leaves out changing relationships to non-kin. A more complete picture would result from an examination of the total range of social relationships in the urban environment, including both kin and non-kin taken together.

Changes in the kin and non-kin domains are not independent of one another, but neither are they connected in a simple one-to-one manner so that an increase in one domain leads to a corresponding decrease in the other. The urban Batak in Medan do expand the scope of relations with non-kin, in that more specific and detailed categorizations are made and there is an increase in frequency of interaction with non-Batak strangers, but it does not follow that there is a concomitant contraction in the Batak kin domain. It is a process of addition, not substitution, and the quantity of social relations is not fixed. Those Batak who relate more to non-kin may be said to be more urbanized or modernized, but this does not mean that they become less Batak, or that they renounce their ethnic affiliation, or that they cut ties with their fellow villagers and clansmen. They are urban and Batak at the same time. From the perspective of the totality of social relations in village and city, however, urban kinship is less important as there are more relations with non-kin, or to put it another way, there has been more change in the role of kinship than in the kinship system itself. This is the case for the Toba Batak, but more generally the precise connections between changes in the kin and non-kin domains is a topic for empirical investigation.

In Indonesia, my hypothesis is that the basic opposition between Batak and non-Batak does have more general relevance in that a similar distinction is made by other ethnic groups. In West Java, the distinction is between Sundanese and non-Sundanese, and in Padang it is between Minangkabau and non-Minangkabau. The hypothesis claims that the initial differentiation in interpersonal relations in Indonesia is on the basis of ethnicity (Bruner, 1973).

There may be contexts in which the hypothesis does not apply, in which an Indonesian no longer perceives others as members of ethnic groups in opposition to his own. This would involve a fundamental reorientation of cognitive and emotional structure in which the frontiers of humanity were extended to all others, but I do not foresee that this will occur very frequently in Indonesia in the immediate future.

References Cited

Bruner, Edward M.

1959. "Kinship Organization Among the Urban Batak of Sumatra." *Transactions New York Academy of Science* 22(2): 118-25.

1961. "Urbanization and Ethnic Identity in North Sumatra." *American Anthropologist* 63(3): 508-521.

1963. "Medan: The Role of Kinship in an Indonesian City." In Alexander Spoehr (ed.), *Pacific Port Towns and Cities*. Honolulu: Bishop Museum Press.

1973. "The Expression of Ethnicity in Indonesia." In Abner Cohen (ed.), *Urban Ethnicity*. ASA Monograph. London: Tavistock.

Cunningham, Clark E.
1958. "The Postwar Migration of the Toba-Batak to East Sumatra." New Haven: Yale University Press. Southeast Asia Studies.

Firth, R.
1964. "Family and Kinship in Industrial Society." *Sociological Review* Monograph 8. Keele, Eng.: University of Keele.

Lévi-Strauss, Claude
1966. *The Savage Mind.* Chicago: University of Chicago Press.

Singer, M.
1968. "The Indian Joint Family in Modern Industry." In Milton Singer and Bernard S. Cohn (eds.), *Structure and Change in Indian Society.* Viking Fund Publications in Anthropology 47.

Skinner, G. William (ed.)
1959. *Local, Ethnic, and National Loyalties in Village Indonesia: A Symposium.* New Haven: Yale University Southeast Asia Studies.

Spoehr, Alexander
1947. "Changing Kinship Systems." *Anthropological Series, Field Museum of Natural History,* Chicago, 33:159-235.

Wallace, Anthony F. C.
1961. *Culture and Personality.* New York: Random House.

Wolf, Eric R.
1966. "Kinship, Friendship, and Patron-Client Relations in Complex Societies." In Michael Banton (ed.), *The Social Anthropology of Complex Societies.* London: Tavistock.

Urbanization and Fijian Cultural Traditions in the Context of Pacific Port Cities

R. R. Nayacakalou
and Aidan Southall

In terms of a worldwide context, urbanization is a most difficult concept to define because of the wide variety of its manifestations. It seems to us that anthropologists cannot develop a comprehensive definition of the concept until all its manifestations have been analyzed, for only then can those features which are truly general and distinctive be determined and made the basis of a comprehensive definition. Analysis, however, need not wait for such a stage to be reached.

From this point of view, we shall take the term to refer to the process by which more and more people come to live in towns and cities, following the definition adopted by the South Pacific Commission Urbanization Advisory Committee (1961). For this purpose we regard towns as distinct from rural settlements not simply in terms of size, but also in terms of their character as marketing and shopping centers for the surrounding countryside, their role as administrative centers, their formal constitution (in many cases) into statutory bodies with legal powers and perpetual succession, the apparent absence from their overall structure of a specifically kin basis, coupled with the development of a distinctively "urban" culture, the kinds of amenities available in them such as cinemas, eating houses, barber shops, etc., and, finally, the predominance of a regular non-agricultural means of livelihood among their inhabitants. It is in these ways that we suggest, for Fiji at least, and indeed for the Pacific region as a whole including Australia and New Zealand, that we can conceive of urbanization as involving a rural-urban drift. This would seem to be a workable concept in terms of which to discuss the Fijian material.

One of the most general features of Pacific island societies is the absence of pre-European cities. All the urbanization in the region today is a purely post-European phenomenon. It is astounding to reflect that, even so, Oceania (including Australia and New Zealand) is the most highly urbanized region in the world,[1] and this is entirely a development of the last century and a half or so. Since this phenomenon has developed so fast and is due to the introduction of an alien way of life, it is easy to see why problems of urbanization in Oceania call for an approach of the kind adopted here.

The earliest Fijian town was Levuka, which developed as a trading center and port of call in the first half of the last century. To its credit (or debit, as one looks at it), it was once said that no pilot was ever required there if the captain of the incoming vessel kept his eye open for empty gin bottles floating out to sea! It was the capital when Fiji became a British Crown Colony in 1874, but when Suva became capital in 1882, Levuka never again attained a position to compete for a share of urban growth comparable to that of Suva. Other towns sprang up at the crucial locations both on Viti Levu and Vanua Levu, the most important of which was certainly Lautoka, with a population of 7,420 in 1956 and growing at a fast rate. Suva, however, remains Fiji's largest and probably fastest growing urban center, with a population of 25,386 in 1946 and 37,371 in 1956, representing a growth of 47 per cent in ten years, assisted by extension of the urban area in 1952 from one to eight square miles.[2]

Fiji's towns contain differing proportions of the country's racial components, as may be seen from Table 1. This table also shows different degress of "urbanization" in the sense of urban residence. For instance, 10.9 per cent of the Fijians were living in urban areas in 1956, compared with 18.7 per cent among the Fiji Indians and 46 per cent among the "others." The last category includes other Pacific islanders, Chinese, and Europeans, all of whom are largely non-agricultural in occupation anyway.

1. J. V. de Bruijn writes: "Forty-seven per cent of Oceania's population reside in cities of 20,000 or more inhabitants as compared with forty-two per cent in North America, thirty-five per cent in Europe (excluding USSR), thirty-one per cent in the USSR and only thirteen and nine per cent in Asia and Africa, respectively. Of course Oceania's high degree of urbanization is due to the fact that in 1961 practically seventeen out of twenty Australians lived in towns of 1,000 or more inhabitants, while seventy-five per cent of New Zealanders were town dwellers. In Australia sixty per cent of the people are concentrated in cities of more than 100,000 inhabitants; in New Zealand this falls to forty-two per cent."
2. J. V. de Bruijn, *op. cit.*

The process of "urbanization," in the sense of an urban drift, affects the racial components differently. The population increase in the Indian component is absorbed largely in the form of a higher population density in the rural areas rather than in an urban drift. The Fijian increase, on the other hand, is largely absorbed into the towns. The Fijian population of Suva, for instance, increased by 51.8 per cent during the period 1946-56, i.e. by nearly double the national Fijian increase of 26 per cent over the same period.

Attempts to explain this urban drift have been diverse (Belshaw, 1963; de Bruijn, 1963). At the root of them lies the idea of a "push and pull" relationship—the attractions of going to town and the unattractiveness, in various forms, of staying in the village. The problem to which we wish to address ourselves here, however, is the more general one of what happens to the cultural tradition of a people as a result of urbanization. In a way the treatment of this question calls for the polarization of an "urban" and a "rural," and it may be that this is the reason why we took the position we did at the beginning of the paper. However, it seems a useful device and we propose to use it here, coming back later on to the question of polarization.

The ways in which the urban Fijians of Suva handled their relations with the new people with whom they came into contact in the urban situation were outlined in a previous paper (Nayacakalou, 1963). Kinship in particular was dealt with, as were the new types of alignment or association which developed in the urban situation. Here we wish to take the matter a little further and analyze the operation of the more basic cultural traditions that lie behind the variety of relations that one observes in the urban situation.

We shall mean by the cultural traditions of the Fijians those ideological tenets—more or less formal—by which they order their relations, either individually or in groups. Thus on the level of kinship, quite apart from the generally accepted norms of obligatory mutual assistance and the like, which are rather less formal, there are, e.g. ideological tenets requiring restrained behavior between brother and sister or between cross-cousins of the same sex, or between a man and his mother's brother or anyone standing in that kind of relationship. Such relations require some degree of formal handling in the sense of slow and deliberate speech and avoidance of joking or a tendency towards levity. These types of kinship relations are very often applied between whole groups by a process of extension. Thus a man marries a woman and immediately places all his brothers in a cross-cousin type of relationship with all the brothers of his wife. Formal behavior would then be required between two groups of brothers.

But certain groups also have their own special relationship, which may be of many different kinds. Included here are relationships of *tauvu,* which require that separated clans having a common ancestor adopt a joking relationship with one another, or those of *bati* or warrior, which requires that a chief's *bati* or warrior clan shall stand by and protect him in all circumstances, somewhat like a bodyguard. The chief is forbidden to eat fish in the presence of his *bati,* and the *bati* is forbidden to eat pork in the presence of his chief. At a higher level relations of this type are formalized on a political basis, i.e. in terms of the traditional political relationship between the members of two given tribes, such as subjection, in which case the superior is allowed to make certain demands upon the inferior, or such as relative independence, so that a demand of this kind cannot properly be made upon a non-vassal type of group. Thus in the island of Kadavu, containing seventy-two villages, fifteen *vanua* or autonomous political units are recognized in the records of the Native Lands Commission; but in ceremonies involving the whole of the island, the people themselves recognize only six of them, the less important ones being automatically absorbed into or subsumed under another in some known way for some particular purpose. Although these six are theoretically independent, one of them does achieve recognition as superior and is recognized by the others as such whenever all are juxtaposed in a common relationship with an outside unit of similar order. But the whole of Kadavu is within the area of jurisdiction of the chief of the kingdom of Rewa, and so are Serua, Namosi, Nadroga, and others which are themselves autonomous "kingdoms" on their own account.

Such customary "political" relations are common throughout Fiji and represent hierarchies in terms of which Fiji can be divided into two or more segments without losing the essential ties which link together those segments and which also provide the links within segments. Along with kinship and the other kinds of ties briefly outlined here, the political relations provide a criss-crossing network, which in the eyes of the individual provides essentially alternative ways to order his relations with his fellows. Fijians are rarely lost as to how to adapt to the company of another, much less in the case of groups as such. Two persons may treat one another as kinsmen, or as *tauvu,* or as superior and inferior, depending upon which set of relations is chosen. This is the nature of the set of ideological relationships to which we are here applying the term "cultural traditions." It is perhaps the more consciously formal part of those general rules by which the society is ordered. Its sanctions are found at least in part in the shaming of those who fail to conform either as being either stupid or untutored in the ways of the land. How does this cultural tradition fare in the urban environment?

On the level of kinship it has been shown previously that there is considerable solidarity among kin in Suva (Nayacakalou, 1963). The kinship basis of households is little different from that in rural areas—except that a greater proportion of urban households contain kinsmen other than parents or children, though on an average the number per household is less than in the rural areas. The difficulty encountered in the urban areas is, however, that the total number of households with whom one recognizes kin ties is drastically reduced compared to what it is in the rural areas, especially when it comes to mutual assistance such as at a wedding or a funeral. Hence the adoption of various devices, such as the inclusion of neighbors and "friends" acquired at work or at the club or in some other way. These are wholly non-traditional devices by which the urban Fijians make up for the lack of kinsmen in the urban areas for such gatherings or ceremonies. But there remains a solid core of cultural traditions by which people can also receive the sympathy of more people at a funeral and their support at a wedding ceremony. This is the "path" by which many people who are neither kinsmen nor "friends" come to the aid of other Fijians. Although these are mere extensions in a fictional way of the accepted tradition, they do acquire a binding force that is effective enough to form the basis of co-operation, particularly in the context of the wider political situation where the group in question sees itself threatened with domination by a more numerous out-group. The Fijians as a whole have a vested interest in the preservation of their indigenous culture; the urban Fijians need at least some aspects of it for security in an environment where the out-group is more numerous and there are few, if any, opportunities for establishing lasting relations with it.

One of the best demonstrations of persisting strength of these cultural traditions occurred in July 1964, when the Methodist Church in Fiji celebrated its independence from the parent body in Australia. The celebrations took place in Suva and lasted a week. People came in from all parts of the island group; they were boarded mainly by friends and relatives. They brought with them produce and handicraft, to sell to raise money for the Church. The Suva Fijians, through their chiefs, arranged for the performance of traditional dances by men and women and for songs and dances by schoolchildren and other groups; these arrangements were so thoroughly made that there was entertainment going on in Albert Park, the venue of the celebrations, throughout the day and night every day of the week. The entertainments were organized on the basis of three competing groups, the traditional political units of Bau, Rewa, and the Tovata, together with their respective allies and subjects. Everyone in Suva and from the rural areas knew his group and the chief of that group, and made his contribution accordingly. Considering that Suva is a modern city with the population dispersed over a wide area, it was a difficult job arranging to hold dance practices for the women, for instance, especially when there were as many as a hundred of them to be assembled at a time. But it was all successfully done and more than £17,000 ($42,000) was raised in the week. On occasions like this the solidarity and pride of the various groups in terms of their traditional political or kinship associations come fully into view, even though they might be living in an urban area.

The people's loyalty to the "cultural traditions" of their society is not the less strong for living in a city. They may have to modify them in certain ways, supplementing here and varying there, but they do hold on to the basic tenets as strongly as if they were living in the rural areas. What then is the difference between such behavior in the urban and in the rural context?

At first sight it may appear that the urban folk conform less well in certain respects. For example, they do not always have the traditional hall type of house in which to fit the social relations of superior and inferior, as can be done in a Fijian house in the village, which is constructed to accommodate such symbols of rank. It may well be that they vary tradition more. But it must be remembered that the rural areas, too, are having to vary tradition to suit circumstances. Population mobility is not only in the rural-urban direction, it also occurs between rural areas. In 1956, although 25 per cent of all Fijians were living outside their own provinces, only 10.9 per cent of them were living in urban areas. Thus the rural areas also have to improvise in order to accommodate non-kin into their kinship framework. They have to order their relations with the strange folk who come to live in their midst, utilizing the same set of cultural traditions we have been describing for the urban areas. Thus there is a common tendency for both urban and rural folk to try, in a situation of change, to order their social relations by drawing upon their common body of "cultural traditions." And it isn't as though the two were capable of being kept in watertight compartments. People move forwards and backwards between urban and rural either to visit or to stay. There is, therefore, considerable interrelation. The figures given in Table 1 are, from this point of view, open to objection on the ground that they greatly understate the degree of urbanization, for apart from the fellow who lives one yard outside the town boundary, there are also those who live in the village and commute daily to work in the town.

Thus on the level of the cultural traditions of a people, by which it orders its society, there seems to be little significance in a rural-urban polarization, for although there are outward differences in the way rural and urban people adapt to their respective environments, they are to a greater or lesser extent guided by basically the same set of ideas as to how their relations with their fellows ought to be ordered. In other words, there is a significant way in which rural and urban folk can be said to be part of a single framework of social relations, even though in other ways there are considerable differences in the details of their local adaptation.

The brute facts of demography and economy show that the position of Fijians in Suva City is quite distinctive, as is brought out more clearly if we compare it with the situation in other Oceanian cities and also take into account its political implications. The number of Indians in Fiji as a

Table 1. The Urban Population of Fiji, 1956

	Fijian	*Indian*	*All others*	*Total*
Ba Township	99	2,007	275	2,381
Nadi Airport	308	58	393	759
Nadi Township	123	1,434	96	1,653
Tavua Township	135	583	72	790
Vatukoula Township	2,902	847	1,296	5,045
Lautoka Town	1,902	3,908	1,610	7,420
Savusavu Township	109	109	97	315
Levuka Township	428	245	383	868
Nasea Township	191	1,210	194	1,595
Sigatoka Township	37	502	122	661
Vaileka Township	20	137	22	185
Suva City	9,785	19,321	8,292	37,371
Navua Township	46	575	12	633
Nausori Township	110	860	135	1,105
Totals	16,174	31,796	12,999	60,780
Totals for colony	148,134	169,403	28,200	345,737
% Urban	10.9	18.7	46.0	17.5

Source: 1956 Census

whole is greater than the number of Fijians (Table 1), constituting just half the total population, but in Suva Indians are far more dominant, being more than twice as numerous as Fijians. The Indians were brought to Fiji, as they were brought to Natal, and as they and the Chinese were brought to many other plantation economies in Asia, Africa, and the Caribbean, as indentured sugar workers. The history of the system is told by Gillion (1962). Indentured workers from another continent were thought more reliable (because more defenseless) than local labor. What Thurston said of Fijians in 1878 (Gillion, 1962: 2) is of more universal application: "No Fijian will go from home to be worked from morning till night, upon paltry pay, indifferent fare, and frequently anything but mild treatment, if he can avoid doing so." The fact that local people would not work as required reflects the continuing dilemma of the international plantation economy in the Third World through successive centuries of slave, indentured, and migrant labor. Indian demographic expansion in Fiji has led to the same kind of political dilemma as in Honduras or Mauritius, where the inevitably ethnic emphasis of colonial government precipitated the struggle for ethnic dominance as the crucial issue in the politics of independence.

As in East Africa, the British policy of "protecting" their colonial charges from direct competition with expansive immigrant groups was an ostrich policy which turned a blind eye to burgeoning problems until they defied any harmonious solution. In East Africa this is leading to the progressive squeezing out of the Indian population while the British Government curtails their right of entry to Britain as Commonwealth citizens. In Fiji it led to the situation in which Fijians delayed asking for an independence which threatened to swamp them with an immigrant majority vote. Although they were favored in civil service jobs, so that the Fijian population of Suva is of relatively high socioeconomic standing, this hardly compensates for the disastrous results of a policy which leaves economic life almost entirely in the hands of the immigrant majority. There are virtually no indigenous Fijian businessmen (Nayacakalou, 1964). Indeed, the Indians even succeeded in driving out the small retail businesses of the earlier European settlers, probably with the connivance of the larger European firms who supplied them (Gillion, 1962: 150).

There are thus two parallel channels of urban-rural relations, that of the Fijians and that of the Indians. The Suva Fijians constitute a rather well-established element in the urban population, 17 per cent of them having already been there for over 25 years by 1959. Shielded from much of the hurly-burly of either industrial or commercial life, they are still able to retain strong identity with the rural population. Indeed, even the immigrant Fijian population on the outskirts of Suva has a village-like organization with headmen and quarters by province of origin and local Christian congregations of various denominations, very much as in the countryside (Nayacakalou, 1963). However, official low-cost housing schemes have proved (as in most poor countries) beyond the means of those for whom they were intended, leading to unauthorized squatting and the development of shantytowns (Whitelaw, 1964).

The Suva Indian business families are equally closely tied to the all-embracing network of Indian retail trade throughout the country. There are a number of small centers of about 3,000 in population, said to be just as urban as much larger towns in India, though hardly more than large villages in size. They supply goods and services to a much wider hinterland than a village does, and are in fact the outposts of essentially urban operations, as is also true of the innumerable small Indian trading posts at crossroads throughout East Africa, which result from similar colonial policies of economic segregation. But in Fiji the hinterland of even these small towns is provided by the essentially industrialized sugar plantation rather than by rural communities (Chauhan, 1965). This urban quality is all the more marked in view of the fact that many of the indentured Indian laborers who came to Fiji are thought to have been the unemployed from great Indian cities such as Kanpur, Allahabad, Lucknow, and Agra (Gillion, 1962: 47). Nonetheless, the Indians of rural Fiji criticize those of Suva for their poor fulfillment of the obligations of kinship and hospitality (Mayer, 1961: 8).

Many of the same factors can be seen at work in other Pacific port towns and cities (Spoehr, 1963), but their combination in different proportions leads to very different results. Thus in Papeete, the Tahitian capital, the Chinese have come to dominate commerce as much as the Fijian Indians and have actually edged the Europeans out of the central part of the city previously occupied by them, but they remain a minority, self-segregated group. Papeete and Tahiti escaped the fate of Fiji because no labor-demanding resource as prosperous as Fijian sugar was developed there. The Polynesians remained almost as separate from the Chinese as the Fijians from the Indians, although many Chinese have Polynesian mistresses and a few emancipated young Chinese have married them. But the combination of French and Polynesian cultural proclivities and colonial policy led to a different ethnic and status structure

(Jullien, 1963). Despite the distinctiveness of the Chinese, there are otherwise no clearly drawn racial or ethnic lines corresponding to socioeconomic status differences. Though most Europeans are well off, some are poor, and most Polynesians are poor, but some are well off, while in addition there is a considerable population of mixed descent, not easily distinguished from either, and also intercalary in socioeconomic status. As in Suva, there is a rather stable element in the local population, 30 per cent of the Papeete Polynesians having been born in the city; yet in one sample it was found that 45 per cent had changed residence within one year (Kay, 1963). The Polynesian urban household is somewhat larger and more extended than its rural counterpart, mainly because of the housing shortage rather than by choice. Women outnumber men and are more stable, it is suggested, because they are tied by their child-rearing responsibilities and actually have fewer employment opportunities to cause changes of residence. This frequency of matricentric families lacking a stable father figure is linked to the emergence of youth gangs and delinquency and compared to similar manifestations which have been noted in the Caribbean, in American black ghettoes, and increasingly in depressed urban populations in many parts of the world.

The Chinese of Papeete are all the more turned in upon themselves by their exclusion from the civil service and near-exclusion from prestigious and influential organizations such as Rotary, Lions, and even the Chamber of Commerce. They cannot purchase but only rent land, on which they have developed vanilla plantations and truck gardening. They settle their own disputes through their own associations, six of which represent counties of origin in China and have their own clubhouses in Papeete, while several other associations represent different combinations of linguistic and ethnic origin with political orientation. Marriages are also celebrated within these clubs, which provide the most intensive channels of interaction and the dominant context of status recognition. It is no surprise that Chinese business is based on transactions of trust between kin, as the main solution to shortage of capital; that kinship and family solidarity is an aid and not a hindrance to success; and that it is even suggested that the desire to keep the family intact strengthens the motivation for economic expansion (Moench, 1963). There are many formal resemblances here with the situation of ethnically solidary, immigrant commercial groups all over Asia and Africa.

A slightly different blend of the same factors is found in Noumea, the capital of French New Caledonia, which is still much more dominated by a white colonial elite, although all the immigrant Polynesians consider themselves Europeans. The complement of this is that the local Melanesians remain a minority group in the city, numerically as well as socially and politically. They are mainly in casual, unskilled, and temporary employment, usually sending their children to the country because of overcrowding. They have the franchise but have not yet challenged white domination of the urban vote. Their situation reflects past labor policy, which brought 10,000 European convicts to supply unskilled labor in the nineteenth century; when this system was brought to an end in 1900 a combination of native forced labor (until 1945) and indentured immigrants from Indo-China and Indonesia was substituted. Until 1945, non-Europeans were not allowed in town without a permit, illustrating the tenacious segregationist tendencies of the colonial situation even where it is not a dominant feature of a particular colonial policy. Five main status categories are schematically distinguished (Guiart, 1963): (a) less than twenty highest-level expatriate technical, administrative, and financial experts, who control industry and banking and whose orientation is towards France; (b) the older white settlers with local assets in land and buildings, and the locally resident white directors of trading firms, who are almost a hereditary group, controlling the import-export business, the docking and transport industries and the liberal professions, together with the senior expatriate civil servants who try to identify with them, and a few Asian and Melanesian political leaders who are partially accepted; (c) the middle class of Chinese, Japanese, Vietnamese, North Africans, French, Germans, British, Italians, Norwegians, and Maltese—petty traders, lower civil servants, and white-collar workers, all considering themselves European, though including Indians from Malabar who are much darker than the local Melanesians; (d) the working class of the various Asian groups and Melanesians, quite a new category hardly more than ten years old; and (e) the bottom thousand or so of poor whites, unemployed Melanesians, and prostitutes. In this case, as in so many others, formal non-discrimination was enforced by the Metropolitan government in the face of opposition from local Europeans.

It is clear that the Pacific island cities, small though they are, represent the effect of highly diverse international forces, both in their extreme ethnic heterogeneity and their direct dependence on world market vagaries. Although Oceania appears on international tables as the most urbanized region of the world, the fact is that the figures are swamped by the relatively large populations of Australia and New Zealand, so that the situation of most of the Pacific is not reflected at all. However, the Pacific island cities are extremely dominant focal points in socioeconomic networks covering huge areas. Papeete's population of 22,000 is still more than a quarter of the total population of French Polynesia, which is spread over an area of islands and ocean the size of Europe. Papeete even operates informally as a kind of marriage market, in which Polynesians from great distances and diverse directions, who would otherwise never meet, have the chance to establish unions and often later go back to settle in the home of one of the partners. Nuku'alofa, the capital of Tonga, with a population of only about 16,000, also represents the strong population drift from the many islands to the main island and within it to its main city (Walsh, 1964). Nuku'alofa is unusual in that over 90 per cent of its population is Tongan, though much of it immigrant from other islands.

Most cities of the Pacific, from Fiji to Hawaii, have been swamped by a great diversity of foreigners from both Europe and Asia. Oram (1964) cannot tell Port Moresby from an Australian town until he sees the New Guineans in the market and the canoe anchorage. Perhaps New Guinea has a large enough population to confer distinctive characteristics on its cities in the long run, but in the multitude of smaller islands, even where some local cultural traditions seem to be preserved, as in Suva, it is in somewhat fragile defiance of the dominant ethnic forces and the economic and demographic facts.

References Cited

Belshaw, C. S.

1963. In Spoehr, *q.v.*

1964. *Under the Ivi Tree: Social and Economic Growth in Rural Fiji.* Berkeley: University of California Press.

Chauhan, I. S.

1965. "Town, Region and Nation: Study of a Small Town in Fiji." *Journal of Social Research* 8(2):1-25.

1967. "Networks in a Small Town." *Journal of Social Research* 10(1):33-37.

de Bruijn, J. V.

1963. "Urbanization in the South Pacific," *South Pacific Bulletin* 13(4): 20-24, 66-67.

Gillion, K. L.

Fiji's Indian Migrants: A History to the End of Indenture in 1920. London: Routledge & Kegan Paul.

Guiart, J.
1963. "Noumea, New Caledonia." In Spoehr, *q.v.*
Jullien, M.
1963. "Aspects de la Configuration Ethnique et Socio-Economique de Papeete." In Spoehr, *q.v.*
Mayer, A. C.
1961. *Peasants in the Pacific,* London: Routledge & Kegan Paul.
Moench, R.
1963. "A Preliminary Report on Chinese Social and Economic Organization." In Spoehr, *q.v.*
Nayacakalou, R. R.
1963. "The Urban Fijians of Suva." In Spoehr, *q.v.*
1964. "Traditional and Modern Types of Leadership and Economic Development among the Fijians." *International Social Science Journal* 16: 261.
Oram, N. D.
1964. "Urbanization–Port Moresby." *South Pacific Bulletin* 14(4):37-43.
South Pacific Commission
1962. *Technical Paper,* no. 137, Noumea.
Spoehr, A. (ed.)
1963. *Pacific Port Towns and Cities.* Tenth Pacific Science Congress. Honolulu: Bishop Museum Press.
Walsh, A. C.
1964. "Urbanization in Nuku'alofa, Tonga." *South Pacific Bulletin* 14(3): 33-37, 54.
Whitelaw, J. S.
1964. "Suva, Capital of Fiji." *South Pacific Bulletin* 14(3):33-38.

Urbanization and Regional Associations: Their Paradoxical Function

Kenneth Little

This article is concerned with the phenomenon of urbanization in a number of African countries. The term urbanization itself, according to Wirth (1938), refers to the cumulative accentuation of characteristics distinctive of the mode of life associated with the growth of cities. In the context we are about to consider many such indices of urbanism already exist. There are banks, churches, mosques, hotels, stores, restaurants, schools, offices, paved streets, rented housing, and electric power. In addition, a large proportion of the adult population works for wages, and, varying with a town's history and other circumstances, there is also intellectual sophistication. Frequently, an elite or intelligentsia has meeting places and clubs and engages in cultural activity. There are also political parties of a modern kind; and local affairs are managed by a municipality. These are characteristic features of the towns and cities which have grown as a result of industrialization, through European contact and settlement. Dakar, Lagos, Accra, Abidjan, and Brazzaville, as well as Nairobi and Johannesburg, are typical examples.

However, a large proportion of the population of such places are illiterate people from the countryside. They hail from many different ethnic groups and tribes, each speaking its own language and following its own customs. In some cases, as in Accra, more than sixty separate tribes may be represented. The migration and resettlement of these people implies the acquisition of a different technique of living and a different outlook from those of the rural conditions in which they were reared. What is the process whereby these men and women fresh from the rural areas give up their tribal loyalties and come to regard themselves as citizens of a larger world? What persuades them to depend no longer on the economic and social systems of their tribes or local communities? Recent studies of urban life in Africa prompt these questions. They have shown that prolonged residence in the atmosphere of the town does not automatically change country-bred people and make them into townsmen (cf. Meyer, 1961; Imoagene, 1967).

Townsmen Who Remain Migrants

There is, for example, the town of Lunsar in Sierra Leone, which has grown in response to a nearby iron-ore mine. Lunsar's population is multitribal, and nearly all its inhabitants are first- or second-generation migrants. The Temne, the principal group represented, come from rural villages where the way of life is based on subsistence rice farming. Traditionally, there is a clan system and people live domestically in extended families, venerate ancestral spirits, and believe in the existence of genii and bush spirits. The Temne living in Lunsar, however, have given up most of these practices. They take jobs at the mine or earn money in other ways. Mostly, their family units are small and they occupy rented housing. The children are brought up either as Moslems or Christians and are encouraged to do well at school. In the main, therefore, although some traditional customs persist, the Temne show great readiness to assimilate to urban and industrial conditions.

This is also the general trend in Lunsar, but the exception is Fulbe[1] migrants, who, being very strict Moslems, do not send their children to the locally available schools because they are run by Christian missions. The result is that the Fulbe, not being educationally equipped for anything but unskilled work at the mine, refuse jobs there because they regard such employment as degrading. Instead, they stick to traditional activities, such as cattle-trading, and organize themselves as far as possible on the lines of their communities back home in the Futa Jallon. Further, fortified by their religion and conscious of their distinctive outlook and occupation, the Fulbe hold themselves aloof from the other inhabitants of Lunsar. Many of them have rooms or houses in the town, but they take little or no part in its modern institutions (Butcher, 1964).

1. The Fulbe (sing. Pullo) are known as Fulani in Nigeria and Ghana; as Fulas in Sierra Leone and the Gambia; and as Foulahs and Peuls in the former French colonies.

Another African people who apparently reject urban values are the Tonga. They move a thousand miles and much more from the shores of Lake Nyasa to find work in the employment centers of Zambia, Rhodesia, and South Africa. Often, these men spend the best part of their adult lives in the town, but most of them retire to their villages in Tongaland. While working abroad, the majority of these labor migrants leave their families behind in the care of kinsmen or in-laws. A husband sends back money to his wife, and he also provides his relatives with financial help to pay a fine, damages, or bridewealth, and to buy clothes and other necessities. In return for those and other services, the man who is away expects his kinsfolk at home to protect his membership of and his place in Tongan society. He regards his contributions of cash and goods to the rural economy as a kind of insurance premium safeguarding, in particular, his own rights to land. Also, by letter-writing and by periodic visits home, he does what he can to keep in touch with local affairs. It means that the Tonga abroad in the towns look to the social and economic system of their tribal areas for their ultimate security (van Velsen, 1961).

This is so because of the kind of administrative and industrial system to which Tongan rural society is geared. Generally, wages in the towns are only adequate for quasi-bachelors. There is an acute shortage of housing and social services are lacking. In other words, Africans are induced to migrate as individual workers, but discouraged from settling with their families. The result is that the migrants in the towns are all urbanized, in the sense that they come under the urban authorities and live in an industrial urban cash economy. But their integration into the industrial urban situation is only partial, because it is in the tribal village, not the town, that are located the most important personal ties of these men in exile. Migration having become part of Tongan culture, they never cease to be migrants. The system does not encourage a different choice.

In part, this statement also applies to Xhosa migrants studied by Philip Mayer in the South African town of East London. The particular group he describes are known as the Red people through their custom of wearing a red blanket. This section of the tribe typically insists on remaining pagan and illiterate. Xhosa men in general seek urban employment as a matter of course, but unlike mission and school products of the same tribe, most of these Red people steadfastly refuse to internalize the values of white civilization (1962: 576-92).

East London lies so close to the rural hinterland that most migrants can make brief visits home during their prolonged stay in town. This home visiting is one factor which keeps the Red type of man faithfully Red during all his years in town. He continues to be bound to one specific Red family, lineage, and community in the country. Also, while in the town he restricts himself as far as possible to the company of home friends—residing with them and spending all his leisure time with these fellow exiles from his own place. The result is that on returning to his rural village, a Red migrant can fit in almost as if he had not been away.

In each of the above cases the migrant deliberately maintains a position for himself in tribal society. For the Tonga it may be argued that this decision is inherent in the social and economic system of the urban area in which they live and work. The situation, however, is different in both Lunsar and East London. There is less necessity for either the Fulbe or the Xhosa to remain traditional in outlook, because alternative opportunities exist. Basically, therefore, it is a question of the migrant's own attitude. Admittedly, as Mayer has pointed out, it is not easy for Red people to alter their behavior, because conservative kin and elders oppose this on moral grounds. Nevertheless, a minority of them do come to adopt and value town ways. The individual person, Mayer emphasizes, has a choice. Certain relations at work are thrust upon him, but outside working hours he voluntarily decides upon his associates. It is a question of social relations and cultural practices taken in conjunction. The individual who makes the step of adopting town ways must select new habits and also new companions and friends. He must be ready to accept in place of his people at home "real townsmen" as his reference group.

Regional Associations and Urbanization

Mayer discovered that these were the basic conditions of urbanization in East London. His suggestion is worth pursuing, because a person derives from his reference group his norms, attitudes, and values and the social objects these create. However, "real townsmen" are a more Westernized and sophisticated category than the ordinary migrant himself. They are people whom he customarily regards with suspicion and hostility. How, then, does he come to change his attitude and to aspire to relate his identity to such a different social group?

There is no single or simple answer. Nevertheless, a major factor in this regard is the function of regional associations, one of the paradoxes of urbanization. These organizations are an important product of the newly industrialized town. In its heterogeneous population the members of different tribes may be competing economically and politically for power in the local community. There are age-old enmities and alliances which divide or coalesce the various factions. Some of the most obvious in Ghana are the hostility of the Zabramas and the Gaos against the Hausas and the friendship between the Moshis and the Zabramas; the Fulani are not popular with any group. Although these peoples regard themselves as Moslems, Islam is not strong enough on its own to override their differences, so the migrants have only one thing in common: they are foreigners. As such they are shunned by the indigenous inhabitants, for whom any migrant is straightaway associated with the native of the Northern Territories: he is a "bushman," a naked barbarian. The migrants retort in similar terms and refer to the people of the Coast as "sons of Slaves"[2] (Rouch, 1954).

Antagonisms of this kind sometimes break out into open warfare, including riots and fights between the younger tribesmen. In order, therefore, to operate more effectively, migrants from the same town or district group themselves together; and in Nigeria, the Ibo were one of the first people to organize for mutual aid and defense. On moving into the towns of the West and the North, they formed associations to protect themselves from the hostile way in which they were received by the local inhabitants when they took jobs as clerks, policemen, traders, and laborers. Among the Ibo, such associations or "meetings" correspond roughly to the basic units at home—village, village group, and clan. Organizations of this kind are locally described in Nigeria and Ghana as tribal unions,[3] the term used in the French-speaking countries being *association d'originaires.* They are referred to in this way to distinguish them from associations which also practice mutual aid but whose members are united by other factors, such as age, occupation, or education. In fact, although the members of a particular union may speak of themselves as a people from

2. Similar attitudes have been noted in Freetown, where, until recently, the term usually applied to a tribal migrant was 'aborigine.' About the northern migrants' reaction in Ghana, Rouch adds the following: "The Zabrama . . . confident in his ancient civilization, regards the Coast man, whether in a dickey or a Jaguar, as a 'Gurunsi', a descendent of the slaves whom Babatu used to exchange for a kola-nut in the market . . . This proud attitude of the least *'kaya kaya'* in rags toward the lawyer or doctor who brushes him in his car is one of the most extraordinary facets of behaviour it is possible to see in the Gold Coast" (quoted in Little, 1965:86. See also Rouch, 1954).

3. Middleton (1969: 46-48) provides an interesting account of some of these Nigerian unions.

a given region or town, the basis of common origin is often more imaginary than real. Membership may not be withheld from persons who are not actually affiliated to the particular clan or even the particular tribe concerned (Little, 1965: 26-27).[4]

However, since the aim is to strengthen group solidarity by encouraging members' attachment to their native town or lineage, every effort is made to foster and keep alive an interest in the moral beliefs, language, song, and history of the tribe. Some associations go so far as to record these things in writing for the benefit of the younger generation who have never known the older customs. Social activities include an annual celebration and the organization of dances on festival days and of sports and games for the young people. Some of these unions also produce an annual magazine called an Almanac, in which their members' activities are recorded, and they make a special point of looking after and welcoming persons newly arrived from the country or returned from overseas. In these ways—through reception committees and by holding "send-off" parties—they provide means whereby the migrants to the city can maintain contact with their rural friends and relatives (*ibid.*: 29).

Another significant feature of these associations is their mixture of social elements. Although most members are illiterate, there are individuals of every class, including schoolteachers, doctors, and lawyers, as well as day laborers. Some educated people look down upon tribal associations

4. A somewhat similar practice has been reported from Indonesia, where Toba Batak migrants form urban clan associations in the large and rapidly growing city of Medan. These are simultaneously residence groups, descent groups, and voluntary associations. In order to join a man must live in Medan, and must be a descendant of the clan ancestor. However, social affiliation is further extended, as it is customary for each nuclear family to join both the clan association of the husband as well as the clan association of the wife. The unnamed children become members of the two associations and may participate in the groups. To put it another way, each urban clan association is open to both the male and the female members of the clan and their spouses, which doubles the membership and widens the scope of the relationships (Bruner, 1963).

It should be noted, however, that the nature of the affiliation is different. In the husband's clan group, the one that bears his name, the named couple have a superior status relative to the husband's sisters. The male members of the clan and their spouses are superordinate wife-givers (*hula-hula*), while the female members of the clan, with their spouses, are subordinate wife-receivers (*boru*). A man, of course, would also belong to his wife's clan group, which bears her maiden name, and, together with his wife, occupies an inferior status relative to his wife's father, her brothers, and by extension the male members of her clan. This is in keeping with the asymmetric alliance system which pervades all aspects of Batak society, both rural and urban (Bruner, 1964).

as parochial and backward-looking. Many others, however, have taken the lead in founding and directing them, and among the Ibo, in particular, affiliation is considered a duty. An Ibo living in a city who did not join would probably be ostracized by his fellow tribesmen. Explaining this attitude, an informant said, "You see, we all belong to this [union] once we come to a city. If you didn't, people will say you are not sociable and will not respect you. And if you didn't join, when you are in trouble, you won't have any one to help you. So you can see why all of us belong to it." (*ibid.*: 30, 33).

The immediate effect, therefore, of the regional association is to increase tribal consciousness by reminding people of their common origin. This sentiment is further strengthened by exhortations to fraternity. Members are actively urged to regard each other as brothers and sisters with the obligation to assist and sympathize with one another in every kind of difficulty.

On the other hand, the fact that the regional association is under educated leadership gives to certain of its activities a modern slant. This comes about because "progressively" minded young men see in resuscitation of the tribal spirit an opportunity of building up larger structures which may, in turn, be used to bring about social change. Under this dynamic influence, therefore, many associations set out to improve their home town, village, or state. Their names—the Calabar Improvement Society, the Anlo State Improvement Society, the Igbarra Progressive Union, etc.—reflect this aim. The idea is to provide up-to-date amenities—schools, hospitals, and roads—equal to those of the place to which the migrants have moved. This is done through home branches of the associations abroad, which are formed by returning members wishing to continue the comradely times they have enjoyed while away. Quite often, local chiefs and other notabilities help with funds, and the home association embarks on its own regular program of activities. There are football matches and dances to attract people from the larger towns; communal work, such as building bridges, repairing roads, etc., is also undertaken by the union. Sometimes, too, this diffusion of improvement unions to the countryside is only the first step in a wider process of development, involving several phases of integration. In Nigeria, these have included respectively the federation of all branches abroad of the same union; the federation of the federated branches abroad with their home branch; and the formation of an all-tribal federation (*ibid.:* 29-30, 33).

The procedure was for members originating from the same region to set up regional bodies to which representatives from the home town and clan associations were elected. These in turn set up the organization covering the whole tribe. Delegates from regional associations sat on the main committee, and once a year at the annual general meeting of this central organization any member could attend. It will thus be seen that the all-tribal federation had a pyramidal structure which began with the primary associations (the extended family among the Ibo) and passed upwards through the various levels of the social structure (clan) or of the territorial organization (division or province) of the tribe concerned. The first all-tribal federation to be organized was the Ibibio Welfare Union. This occurred in 1928, and since 1947 these larger all-tribal organizations have adopted the name of State Unions (Coleman, 1952; Acquah, 1958: 104-7).[5]

Regional Associations and Their Functions

Attention is drawn to the complex structure and modern aims of the regional association because of the obvious implications for urbanization. In the first place, the ordinary illiterate member is provided with a reference group. Not only is he brought into close personal contact with individuals of higher social status than himself, but interacting with them in an informal and sociable atmosphere encourages him to emulate different habits and ways. It makes him more amenable to new standards of dress and personal hygiene, the advantage being that he is no longer regarded as a country bumpkin but is able to keep pace with "real"

5. In view of their comprising every union of members of the same tribe it is not surprising that these Nigerian State Unions have obtained a power and influence far beyond their original objectives. They have played a particularly important part, for example, in the expansion of education. They ran their own schools and offered scholarships for deserving boys and girls. In some places, the monthly contribution of members for education was invested in some form of commercial enterprise, and appeals for money to build schools seemed to meet with an extremely ready response. One observer claimed that he saw an up-country union raise in six hours and in a single meeting over £16,000 for such purposes. Higher education has also been improved. In 1938, for example, the Ibibio State Union sent eight students, all in one day, to England and America; and several leading members of the Nigerian Eastern House of Assembly owe their training in British universities to State Union money. Even more ambitious plans have included the building of a national bank where people can obtain loans for industrial and commercial purposes; and, in this connection, some unions have economic advisers who survey trade reports for the benefit of members (Little, 1965: 33-34).

townsmen.[6] Moreover, although educated people are the associations' principal leaders, a host of minor offices and titles is generally available. These give even the most humble member an opportunity to feel that he "matters." They also assist him, through cooperation with the senior officials, to develop a more broad-minded attitude towards non-tribesmen. Similar factors stimulate an illiterate individual's acceptance of urban values by providing him with extra opportunities to be socially mobile in the wider community. Since the association is conceived of as a single family, richer members have the obligation of assisting those less well off. They are expected to stand as sureties and to use their influence with respect to jobs. Also (although at a higher level), there is the prestige which may accrue from holding office in an association itself. The significance of this kind of position has been shown by the part played by tribal unions in West African politics. Some Nigerian unions, for example, provided the nucleus of emerging political parties, thereby enabling the leaders of the associations concerned to move naturally into posts of national importance.[7] In addition, some well-known associations make it a practice to confer honorific titles such as Chief, Chief Patron, etc. Since the significance of these organizations is widely recognized, the recipients are singled out publicly as persons of special distinction. To be known as "Chief So-and-So" frequently marks a step upward for a commoner, even a professional man. Also, since it identifies the individual concerned with his ethnic group, it may be very helpful to an aspiring politician seeking traditionally minded supporters (Little, 1965: 162).

Another factor facilitating the rural individual's adjustment to town ways is the regional association's combination of modern and traditional activities. Quite often, its administration is organized in such a way that many of the officeholders concerned have Western titles, such as Doctor and Nurse. There may be further officials, such as Overseer, Solicitor, Lawyer, and so on. To a large extent these roles are make-believe, but their performance also involves some knowledge of urban patterns of conduct. In addition, members may be required to sit on committees.

6. In this connection Meillassaux (1968: *passim*) provides an illuminating description of the role of voluntary associations in assisting upward social mobility, as well as orientation to town life.

7. La Fontaine (1970: 153-69, 147-48), Little (1969: *passim*), and Parkin (1966: 90-94) throw light on the part played by voluntary associations in politics and in providing media for political ambition. La Fontaine's account in particular, provides a fascinating analysis of the role of ethnic associations as pawns in Leopoldville's (now Kinshasa's) "power game."

Finally, as already explained, regional associations advocate up-to-date amenities; they endeavor to spread "civilization." The fact, however, that these ideas are propagated within a familiar context makes the innovations seem less strange. On the association's premises a man can sit with his fellow countrymen, play and listen to traditional music, and eat traditional dishes without feeling anxious or ashamed about the ridicule of local people. Meetings themselves invariably begin with a prayer, and for every deceased member there is not only a funeral but a wake which everybody attends. Also, not only is every meeting or celebration a reminder of home ties and obligations, but social sanctions have a customary ring. A migrant's reputation for good or evil accompanies him to the town, and within the union abroad gossip regulates the personal conduct of members in the same way as it restricts behavior in the rural village.[8]

This is a further reason why regional associations are significant for urbanization. Other species of urban association also discipline their members; there are women's groups, for example, which not only upbraid members who create strife among other women but expel those who are constant troublemakers in the home. Regional associations, however, seem able to exercise an even stricter control. A Nigerian union in Freetown, for instance, decrees that no member shall take legal steps against any other member without first bringing the matter up to the hearing of the meeting. It also claims the right to submit evidence in court if its own arbitration is ignored by the complainant. Apparently this kind of ruling was so effective that in Nigeria Ibo people entirely deserted the courts except when drawn there by members of different tribes, or in the rare event of disloyalty on the part of a member of their own union (*ibid.*: 95). The members of another Nigerian tribal union resolved not to marry any girl of their town so long as the prevailing amount of money asked for bridewealth was not reduced (Little, 1957: 593).

Regional associations are able to arbitrate to this extent because they replace the social control exercised by neighbors, extended family, and

8. Chinua Achebe's description of a tribal union, although fictional, provides an interesting illustration of this kind of informal sanction. Obi Okonkwo, the hero of Achebe's novel *No Longer At Ease,* has returned to Nigeria after qualifying in the United Kingdom, where his studies were paid for by his fellow members. Being financially in low water, he needs time to repay the loan. The Union is proud of Obi's achievement and would probably have been generous had the rumor not got around that he is moving with a girl of 'doubtful' ancestry. She belongs to a special caste with whom Obi's people at home are strictly forbidden to marry or mate. This is pointed out to Obi in such certain terms that he has no alternative but to withdraw his request (Achebe, 1960, *passim*).

local community in the rural village. Since senior kinsmen and other traditional figures of authority are lacking from his immediate environment, it is to the head of his association that a person in trouble turns for help or advice.[9] His position is similar to that of a junior member of the lineage: he is dependent upon the favor and good will of the group's leaders.[10]

The result is that the role of regional associations is not confined to supervising private conduct. They frequently have in addition formal rules and regulations designed to govern the public behavior of members as well as their relations with each other. For example, a member who is reported for quarreling in the town, for abusing elderly people, or for putting curses on others, may be suspended, fined, or expelled. Similarly, where members are adulterous, are known to steal, or cause disorders at gatherings, they are warned to correct their behavior.

Regional Associations as an Adaptive Mechanism

We have examined urbanization as a process of adaptation on the part of country-bred people to new social norms and values.[11] In fact, nowadays, many individuals who settle in the city have previous experience of its attitudes and practices; they are already "urbanized" to an appreciable extent.

The extreme type of migrant is a different case; residence in the town does not automatically change his ways. It does, however, thrust him into

9. He consults first the secretary or the president of his union, who refers the matter to the committee, and if it is a question of money, the case is probably put before the entire association at its next meeting. Decisions involving the expenditure of cash are rarely taken without the consent of all the members and, in some cases, the society's money cannot be disbursed without a written order containing the principal officials' signatures. Alternatively, the person in difficulty may approach one of the society's patrons. The patrons are generally individuals of high standing who have been appointed on account of their local influence and in the expectation that they will use it on the society's behalf. If this appeal fails, it is quite common for the association itself to back a deserving member by paying his legal expenses in the event of the case going to court (Little, 1965: 91).

10. In fact, the association's practice of helping its own members is probably one of the main sources of control. It enables the officials concerned to exert their authority more readily, particularly as recalcitrant members are sometimes the most needy. The ultimate sanction, however, is expulsion. This penalty is effective because many migrants know that they have little hope of companionship outside their own tribe.

11. David Parkin (1966: *passim*) provides a very useful analysis of the function of associations in Uganda as an adaptive mechanism, and the "mechanisms" of adjustment through tribal unions have been examined in some detail in Sapele, Nigeria's timber-exporting port, by Imoagene (op. cit.).

a novel and unpredictable situation. It obliges him, since he cannot exist in isolation, to cooperate with other migrants. These people may, as in the case of the Fulbe, Zhosa, and Zabrama,[12] have established the sort of community to which he is well accustomed. In the absence, however, of migrants of his own kind, his only hope of affiliation may be with a tribal group whose interests run in a less traditional direction. Having no alternative to this, he seeks acceptance and so comes to disguise and perhaps, ultimately, to deny his rural connection.[13] He pays this price for social recognition.

This, perhaps, is the fundamental reason why regional associations are so effective as an adaptive mechanism. As explained, their function is not unique; many other urban associations assist the general socialization of the migrant. There are, for example, groups which concern themselves with their members' trading and occupational interests. A person can also belong to numerous entertainment societies and to the new syncretist cults and heterogeneous "churches" which have developed out of contact between Christianity and the indigenous religion. In addition labor unions, church associations, and various species of social club exist. Nearly all these associations provide their members with moral as well as material forms of support, including mutual benefit schemes.

This second kind of organization confines its membership to individuals of the same sex, or only admits people who have attained a certain standard of education or who engage in similar occupations. The members of such groups are brought together by a common interest in business, religion, or recreation, but these activities have usually a practical aim. They do not necessarily depend upon any underlying moral sentiment—still less do they involve any mystical bond of fellowship.

The regional association, on the other hand, may have as its goal modernization and improvement. Still, though it may be concerned to "civilize" its home town or village, its general norms are familiar to people who have been tribally reared. Above all, members are conceived of as tribal brothers irrespective of wealth or education. It is these considerations which make the regional association the most effective reference group, because, being composed of people with whom he feels the nearest

12. This point in the case of the Zabrama is illustrated by Rouch (op. cit.).
13. This point is evident in the "Creolization" of up-country people in Freetown. See Little (1951) and Banton (1957). Wallerstein (1960: 132-33) also provides illustrations of the practice of migrants identifying themselves with the dominant ethnic group of the town.

affinity, it is the migrant's best substitute for kinship—for the solicitude that he customarily experienced in the kinship circle. Therefore, like the lineage and the extended family in tribal society, the regional association serves as a buffer between the individual and the rest of the community.

Conclusion

These formulations lead us back finally to the "modern" or industrialized West African town and its social structure. Diagrammatically speaking, such urban communities are frequently divided, in part, by vertical lines. There are various ethnic, tribal, and religious groups, in each of which status is ascribed mainly in traditional terms, and so one tendency is for social organization to be segmental. At the same time, achieved as well as ascribed forms of status exist. These are based upon criteria of money income, wealth, and political power. Since these factors betoken differences in prestige, the town's population is economically and socially stratified, imparting to the picture a horizontal design. In addition, superior position in the hierarchy of embryonic classes is determined by an individual's education and by the extent to which his observed behavior is "modern" and he is able to provide social evidence of his wealth (Banton, 1957: 96-119; Little, 1965: 138-43).

It was for these reasons that we described the function of the regional association as paradoxical. On the one hand, its attitude is conservative and parochial, and by enhancing ethnicity causes its members to cohere more closely. On the other hand, since this increases the association's control over its members' actions, the association is enabled to supervise their public as well as their private conduct and so to reduce intertribal friction. Furthermore, the association also teaches its members urban standards and so facilitates their assimilation to the wider community. In thus paving the way for "urban" as distinct from "rural" status, it encourages not tribal but class consciousness.

This functional dualism is not contradictory; it merely reflects the fact that in urbanization the changes undergone have both negative and positive effects, because dis-integration and re-integration go hand in hand. They are simultaneous (Banton, 1957: 219). Along with other agencies, regional associations play their part in reconciling these opposing tendencies. Nor is their role confined to West Africa; there is comparable evidence from other developing countries as well. In Peru, for instance, practically every town of over 1,000 inhabitants seems to have a club in Lima, consisting of rural migrants (*serranos*). These urban clubs engage in many of the same activities as West African associations. Their members get together to work on a member's home, to repair a street or top an irrigation ditch, and provide material aid with a variety of simple cooperative tasks. As in West Africa, they also organize feasts and dances and sports and games for young people. Sometimes the patron saint's day of the home town is celebrated, and at other times a group from the club will return to the home town for a fiesta. Similarly, again, club members in Lima often defend local interests in the various government departments and are usually in the forefront of attempts to get new schools, roads, water services, sewers, clinics, and other public services and advantages for the town or district (Mangin, 1959).

Furthermore, many Lima customs are learned in the clubs, and unacceptable customs, or at least those marking the person as rural, Indian, and *serrano,* are discouraged. Sometimes a course in etiquette is offered; and, as in West Africa, a member of these associations has access to lawyers, doctors, and businessmen whom he might otherwise never meet socially. These individuals serve as go-betweens linking the association to Lima's civic and other institutions, providing useful contact with the officials of various ministries. In addition, the significance of a *serrano* achieving club office is emphasized by the club paper and the Lima papers, including the large dailies in their provincial sections (*ibid*). Obviously, there are wide cultural differences between Peruvian *serranos* and African tribal migrants. But both types of association impress on their members the importance of home ties,[14] and they are equally intermediate groups intercalated between the individual and the wider community and even the state.[15]

However, one further matter does need attention because, although regional associations are a characteristic feature of East as well as West African urbanism, the existence of strong ethnicity/tribalism vouched for by several observers of the Zambian Copperbelt[16] has not seemingly given rise to similar institutions in the latter area. Nor, even in West African cities,

14. This criterion needs to be emphasized because urban clan associations are often regarded as a species of regional association. Thus, as mentioned above (see note 4), there are associations in Medan whose members are recruited on a basis of clanship. However, Bruner also points out that in this Indonesian city kinship obligations are to a large extent the foundation upon which urban life is organized. In consequence, the clan association itself is, in effect, one of these kinship institutions (1964, *passim*).
15. See Wallenstein (op. cit., *passim*) for an elaboration of this point.
16. See Mitchell, 1956, and Epstein, 1958.

do all migrant groups necessarily form such organizations. Rather is there evidence, instead, for the idea that the regional associations' appearance may be governed by the presence or absence of certain structural factors. Thus, in Freetown, for example, whereas politically and economically disadvantaged Temne migrants found in the dancing *compins* they formed a means of resuscitating tribal *morale*[17] and securing more social recognition for themselves, among Mende immigrants associational participation of a similar kind was minimal by comparison. The reason, perhaps, was that not only had many more Mende people than Temne attended school, but the Government itself was largely controlled by Mende politicians. This meant that a Mende young man of ambition had readier means of improving his position occupationally and had not the same need to explore less orthodox channels of social mobility. Furthermore, whereas secret societies play a relatively small part in Temne traditional life, the well-known Poro society continues to exercise considerable influence over the ordinary Mende migrant. The Poro has always strongly opposed innovation, and so although its elders could not prevent an educated man joining a "progressive" association, they had power over illiterate Mende. The latter could be reminded of their vows as Poro initiates and threatened with supernatural reprisals if they showed disloyalty by taking part in what from the Poro elders' point of view were rival institutions.[18]

A situation of this kind—if the above analysis is correct—brings us finally to conclude that the regional association's function may be, in fact, less paradoxical than it seems. True, as we have stressed, regional associations provide an immediate outlet for ethnicity and tribalism, but their apparently deliberate attempt to keep traditional loyalties and sentiment alive is, perhaps, almost incidental. It simply conceals the regional association's real, though latent, function, which paramountly is—we suggest—to facilitate the conversion of country people into townspeople. This, in other words, means that regional associations are, in the last analysis, just as much a part of the urbanization process as schools, churches, masonic lodges, and other such recognizable "urbanizing" influences.

17. Since they were formed ostensibly for recreational purposes (including mutual benefit schemes) rather than on a basis of common origin, these dancing *compins* are not by definition regional associations. Nevertheless, since their underlying purpose was to reassert the Temne's position, the experience reported above provides a relevant illustration of the general argument (see Banton, 1957, for documentation of this point).

18. See Little, 1967, 159-65. For an explanation of the sanctions at the Poro's disposal see Little, 1965 and 1966.

References Cited

Achebe, Chinua
1960. *No Longer at Ease*. London: Heinemann.

Acquah, I.
1958. *Accra Survey*. London: London University Press.

Banton, Michael P.
1957. *West African City: A Study of Tribal Life in Freetown*. London: Oxford University Press for International African Institute.

Bruner, Edward M.
1963. "Medan: The Role of Kinship in an Indonesian City." In Spoehr, Alexander (ed.), *Pacific Port Towns and Cities*.
1964. "Voluntary Descent Groups in an Indonesian City." Paper presented at VII International Congress of Anthropological and Ethnological Sciences. Moscow, August.

Butcher, David
1964. *The Role of the Fulbe in the Urban Life and Economy of Lunsar, Sierra Leone*. Unpublished Ph.D. thesis, Department of Social Anthropology, University of Edinburgh.

Epstein, A. L.
1958. *Politics in an Urban African Community*. Manchester: Manchester University Press.

Imoagene, Stephen
1967. "Mechanisms of Immigrant Adjustment in a West African Urban Community." *Nigerian Journal of Economic and Social Studies* 9(1).

LaFontaine, Jean
1970. *City Politics: A Study of Leopoldville, 1962-1963*. Cambridge, Eng.: Cambridge University Press.

Little, Kenneth
1951. *The Mende of Sierra Leone*. London: Routledge and Kegan Paul.
1955. "The African Elite in British West Africa." In *Race Relations in World Perspective* Lind, A. (ed.), Honolulu: University of Hawaii Press.
1957. "The Role of Voluntary Associations in West African Urbanization." *American Anthropologist* 59 (4).
1965. *West African Urbanization*. Cambridge, Eng.: Cambridge University Press.
1965-66. "The Political Function of the Poro." *Africa* 35 (4) and 36 (1).
1967. "Voluntary Associations in Urban Life: A Case Study in Differential Adaptation." In M. Freedman (ed.), *Social Organization: Essays Presented to Raymond Firth*. Chicago: Aldine.

Mangin, William P.
1959. "The Role of Regional Associations in the Adaptation of Rural Populations in Peru." *Sociologus* (New Series) 9 (1).

Mayer, Philip

1961. *Townsmen or Tribesmen: Conservation and the Process of Urbanization in a South African City*. Oxford: Oxford University Press.

1962. "Migrancy and the Study of Africans in Towns." *American Anthropologist* 64.

Meillassaux, Claude

1968. *Urbanization of an African Community: Voluntary Associations in Bamako*. Seattle: University of Washington Press.

Middleton, J.

1969. "Labour Migration and Associations in Africa." *Civilisations* 19 (1).

Mitchell, J. Clyde

1956. "The Kalela Dance." *Rhodes-Livingstone Papers,* No. 27. Published on behalf of the Rhodes-Livingstone Institute by Manchester University Press.

Parkin, David

1966. "Urban Voluntary Associations as Institutions of Adaptation." *Man* (New Series) 1.

1969. *Neighbours and Nationals in an African City Ward.* London: Routledge and Kegan Paul.

Rouch, Jean

1954. *Migration in the Gold Coast.* English translation by P. E. O. and J. B. Haighan of "Migrations au Ghana (Gold Coast) (Enquête 1953-1955)." *Journal de la Société des Africanistes* 26. Accra, mimeographed.

van Velsen, J.

1961. "Labour Migration as a Positive Factor in the Continuity of Tonga Tribal Society." In *Social Change in Modern Africa.* Southall, Aidan (ed.), London: Oxford University Press.

Wallerstein, Immanuel

1960. "Ethnicity and National Integration in West Africa." *Cahiers d'Etudes Africaines* 3.

Wirth, Louis

1938. "Urbanism as a Way of Life." *American Journal of Sociology* 44 (8).

Bibliography on Urban Anthropology

Peter C. W. Gutkind

The publication of this volume is just one of many recent indications of the rapidly developing interest in urban anthropology, particularly in non-Western countries. Urban anthropology is now taught as a specialized subject in a number of universities, while each year the number of students with a serious interest in the subject increases. It is not overoptimistic to say that the future for urban anthropology looks bright.

This bibliography is not meant to be either comprehensive or highly selective. It springs from classroom use at McGill University, Montreal, where I first offered a course on the Urban Anthropology of Non-Western Towns and Cities in the academic year 1966/67. With the help of my students and various colleagues with a similar interest, I have revised this bibliography several times. Despite this, I have no doubt that many significant items have been left out, particularly those in rather out-of-the-way publications; while I have included some items which are either of secondary quality or are now rather dated. I could have included many references from Africana, a literature which reflects my own interests, but have not done so on the ground that I wanted to achieve a reasonably rounded regional presentation. African urban studies have produced a rich theoretical harvest; hence I hope that teachers and students alike will make a special effort to become acquainted with this literature. I have brought together over 900 references, which should be enough both for the beginner and the specialist.

I cannot claim that there is a particular "logic" behind the selection of the topical headings, or the sequence of their presentation. The topics have "emerged" over time in the course of classroom teaching. I have no doubt that a more systematic approach is desirable. But student and teacher alike can select whatever references they want and place them in a different order.

Some items could be placed in more than one category. But to prevent undue duplication, I have noted such references under the topic which appears to be the main concern of the author. The reader will also note that I have allocated chapters from books to various topical headings.

Nor can I defend the rationale of the almost total exclusion of material from Western countries except to say that these areas have been of primary concern to the sociologist. I accept the fact that this is a rather arbitrary and not very creative approach. However, production of a bibliography which covers both Western and non-Western cities and towns in any depth is a task still to be carried out.

To produce a bibliography without errors is one of those dreams which is destined to remain unfulfilled. I have given as complete references as were available to me, and I hope that the number of errors is small. Nevertheless, I herewith offer my apologies for any inconvenience which might be caused because an error has not been detected or a reference is not as complete as it should be. Should a further printing of this bibliography be contemplated, readers may wish to forward their additions and corrections to me.

Had it not been for Miss J. Wilson, our Department Secretary, and my wife, who typed various drafts of this bibliography, publication would have been impossible. I thank them both for their unrewarded labor.

1. What Is Urban Anthropology? Models for Urban Studies of Non-Western Areas

Anderson, N., "Urbanism and Urbanization," *American Journal of Sociology*, 65:1 (1959), 68-73.

Beals, R., "Urbanism, Urbanization and Acculturation," *American Anthropologist*, 53:1 (1951), 1-10.

Eddy, E. M. (ed.), *Urban Anthropology: Research Perspectives and Strategies*, Southern Anthropological Society Proceedings No. 2 (Athens: University of Georgia Press, 1968).

Epstein, A. L., "Urbanization and Social Change in Africa," *Current Anthropology*, 8:4 (1967), 275-84. (See also pp. 284-95.)

Forde, D., "Background and Approaches," in *Urbanization in African Social Change* (Edinburgh: Centre of African Studies, 1963), 1-6.

Ganguly, P. G., "A Model for Urban Studies," *Economic Weekly,* 13:37 (1961), 1467-70.

Gluckman, M., "Anthropological Problems Arising from the African Industrial Revolution," in A. W. Southall (ed.), *Social Change in Modern Africa* (London: Oxford University Press, 1961), 67-83.

Gulick, J., "Urban Anthropology: Its Present and Future," *Transactions of the New York Academy of Sciences,* 25:4 (1963), 445-58.

Gulliver, P. H., "Anthropology," in R. A. Lystad (ed.), *The African World: A Survey of Social Research* (New York: Praeger, 1965), 96-100.

Guterman, S. S., "In Defense of Wirth's 'Urbanism as a Way of Life,'" *American Journal of Sociology,* 74:5 (1969), 492-99.

Gutkind, P. C. W., "African Urban Studies: Past Accomplishments, Future Trends and Needs," *Canadian Journal of African Studies,* 2:1 (1968), 63-80.

Gutman, R., "Urban Studies as a Field of Research," *The American Behavioral Scientist,* 6:6 (1963), 11-16.

Hauser, P. M., "On the Impact of Urbanization on Social Organization, Human Nature and the Political Order," *Confluence,* 7:1 (1958), 57-69.

———, "Urbanization: An Overview," in P. M. Hauser and L. F. Schnore (eds.), *The Study of Urbanization* (New York: Wiley, 1965), 1-47.

Kamerschen, D. R., "Further Analysis of Overurbanization," *Economic Development and Cultural Change,* 17:2 (1969), 235-53.

Kuper, L., "Sociology–Some Aspects of Urban Plural Societies," in R. A. Lystad (ed.), *The African World: A Survey of Social Research* (New York: Praeger, 1965), 107-30.

Magubane, B., "Crisis in African Sociology," *East African Journal,* 5:12 (1968), 21-40.

Manheim, E., "Theoretical Prospects of Urban Sociology in an Urbanized Society," *American Journal of Sociology,* 66:3 (1960), 226-29.

Marris, P., "Motives and Methods: Reflections on a Study in Lagos," in H. Miner (ed.), *The City in Modern Africa* (New York: Praeger, 1967), 39-54.

Mitchell, J. C., "The Anthropological Study of Complex Communities," *African Studies,* 19:3 (1960), 169-72.

———, "Social Change and the New Towns of Bantu Africa," in G. Balandier *et al.* (eds.), *Social Implications of Technological Change* (Paris: International Social Science Council, 1962), 117-30.

———, "Theoretical Orientations in African Urban Studies," in M. Banton (ed.), *The Social Anthropology of Complex Societies* (London: Tavistock Publications, 1966), 37-68.

Morse, R. M., "The Sociology of San Juan: An Exegesis of Urban Mythology," *Caribbean Studies,* 5:2 (1965), 45-55.

Park, R. F., "The City: Suggestions for the Investigation of Human Behavior in the Urban Environment," *American Journal of Sociology*, 20:5 (1915), 577-612.

Pocock, D. F., "Sociologies: Rural and Urban," *Contributions to Indian Sociology*, 4 (1960), 63-81.

Reissman, L., "Urbanization: A Typology of Change," in S. F. Fava (ed.), *Urbanism in World Perspective: A Reader* (New York: Crowell, 1968), 126-44.

Safier, M., "The Urban System in Africa: Patterns of Disjunction and Integration," *African Urban Notes*, 2:3 (1967), 4-11.

Schnore, L. F., and Lampard, E. E., "Social Science and the City: A Survey of Research Needs," in L. F. Schnore and H. Fagin (eds.), *Urban Research and Policy Planning*, v. 1 (Beverly Hills: Sage Publications, 1967), 21-47.

Sjoberg, G., "Comparative Urban Sociology," in R. K. Merton, L. Broom, and L. S. Cottrell (eds.), *Sociology Today: Problems and Prospects* (New York: Basic Books, 1960), 334-75.

———, "The Rise and Fall of Cities: A Theoretical Perspective," *International Journal of Comparative Sociology*, 4:2 (1963), 7-20.

———, "Cities in Developing and in Industrial Societies: A Cross Cultural Analysis," in P. M. Hauser and L. F. Schnore (eds.), *The Study of Urbanization* (New York: Wiley, 1965), 213-63.

———, "Theory and Research in Urban Sociology," in P. M. Hauser and L. F. Schnore (eds.), *The Study of Urbanization* (New York: Wiley, 1965), 157-90.

Tilly, C., "The State of Urbanization," *Comparative Studies in Society and History*, 10:1 (1967), 100-13.

Wirth, L., "Urban Society and Civilization," *American Journal of Sociology*, 45:5 (1940), 743-55.

2. The Evolution of Urban Society

Adams, R. M., "The Origin of Cities," *Scientific American*, 230:3 (1960), 153-68.

Benet, F., "The Ideology of Islamic Urbanization," *International Journal of Comparative Sociology*, 4:2 (1963), 111-26.

Cahnman, W. J., "The Historical Sociology of Cities: A Critical Review," *Social Forces*, 45:2 (1966), 155-61.

Childe, V. G., "The Urban Revolution," *The Town Planning Review*, 21:1 (1950), 3-17.

Comhaire, J., and Cahnman, W. J., *How Cities Grew: The Historical Sociology of Cities* (Madison: Florham Park Press, 1959).

Jones, E., "Pre-Industrial Cities," in *Towns and Cities* (London: Oxford University Press, 1966), 38-51.

Mumford, L., *The City in History* (New York: Harcourt, Brace and World, 1961).

Sjoberg, G., "The Preindustrial City," *American Journal of Sociology*, 60:5 (1955), 438-45.

———, *The Pre-Industrial City* (Glencoe, Ill.: Free Press, 1960).

———, "The Origin and Evolution of Cities," *Scientific American*, 213:3 (1965), 54-63.

Weber, M., *The City* (New York: Collier Books, 1962).

3. The Older Non-Western Cities and Urbanism as a Traditional (Non-Western) Way of Life

Akinola, R. A., "Urban Tradition in Yorubaland," *Nigeria Magazine* (Lagos), 95 (1967), 344-50.

Bascom, W., "Urbanization among the Yoruba," *American Journal of Sociology*, 60:5 (1955), 446-54.

———, "Urbanism as a Traditional African Pattern," *Sociological Review*, 7:1 (1959), 29-43.

Crane, R. I., "Urbanism in India," *American Journal of Sociology*, 60:5 (1955), 463-70.

Dafalla, H., "Notes on the History of Wadi Halfa Town," *Sudan Notes and Records*, 46 (1965), 8-26.

Davis, K., "Colonial Expansion and Urban Diffusion in the Americas," *International Journal of Comparative Sociology*, 1:1 (1960), 43-66.

Eberhard, W., "Data on the Structure of the Chinese City in the Pre-Industrial Period," *Economic Development and Cultural Change*, 4:3 (1956), 253-68.

English, P. W., *City and Village in Iran: Settlement and Economy in the Kerman Basin* (Madison: University of Wisconsin Press, 1966).

Fishel, W. J., "The City in Islam," *Middle Eastern Affairs*, 7:6-7 (1956), 227-32.

Frankfort, H., "Town Planning in Ancient Mesopotamia," *Town Planning Review*, 21:2 (1950), 99-115.

Gakenheimer, R. A., "The Peruvian City of the Sixteenth Century," in G. H. Beyer (ed.), *The Urban Explosion in Latin America* (Ithaca: Cornell University Press, 1967), 33-56.

Hall, J. W., "The Castle Town and Japan's Modern Urbanization," *Far Eastern Quarterly*, 15:1 (1955), 37-56.

Hamdan, G., "The Pattern of Medieval Urbanism in the Arab World," *Geography*, 47:2 (1962), 121-34.

Horvath, R. J., "The Wandering Capitals of Ethiopia," *Journal of African History*, 10:2 (1969), 205-19.

Hoselitz, B. F., "A History of the Long-Term Development of the City," in G. H. Beyer (ed.), *The Urban Explosion in Latin America* (Ithaca: Cornell University Press, 1967), 18-33.

Kraeling, C. H., and Adams, McC., *City Invincible: A Symposium on Urbanization and Cultural Development in the Ancient Near East* (Chicago: University of Chicago Press, 1960).

Law, R. C. C., "The Dynastic Chronology of Lagos," *Lagos Notes,* 2:2 (1969), 46-54.

Lynch, O., "Rural Cities in India: Continuities and Discontinuities," in *India and Ceylon: Unity and Diversity,* P. Mason (ed.), (London: Oxford University Press, 1967), 142-58.

Miner, H., *The Primitive City of Timbucktoo* (Princeton, N.J.: Princeton University Press, 1953).

Morse, R. M., "Some Characteristics of Latin American Urban History," *American Historical Review,* 67:2 (1962), 317-38.

Pankhurst, R., "The Foundation and Growth of Addis Ababa to 1935," *The Ethiopian Observer,* 6:1 (1962), 33-61.

Philby, N. St. J. B., "Riyadh: Ancient and Modern," *Middle East Journal,* 13:2 (1959), 129-41.

Reed, R. R., "Hispanic Urbanism in the Philippines: A Study of the Impact of Church and State," *Journal of East Asiatic Studies* (University of Manila), 11 (March 1967), 143-63.

Silla, O., "Historic African Cities of the Soudanise [sic] Sahara," *Africa Quarterly,* 8:2 (1968), 146-57.

Smith, R., "Erin and Iwawun: Forgotten Towns of the Oke Ogun," *Odu,* 1:1 (1964), 17-32.

Smith, R. J., "Pre-Industrial Urbanism in Japan: A Consideration of Multiple Traditions in a Feudal Society," *Economic Development and Cultural Change,* 7:1 (1960), 241-57.

Snouck, C. H., *Mekha in the Latter Part of the Nineteenth Century* (London: Luzac, 1931).

Southall, A. W., "Kampala-Mengo," in H. Miner (ed.), *The City in Modern Africa* (New York: Praeger, 1967), 297-332.

Spate, O. H. K., and Ahmed, E., "Five Cities of the Gangetic Plain: A Cross Section of Indian Cultural History," *Geographical Review,* 41:2 (1950), 260-78.

Sternstein, L., "Krung Kao, the Old Capital of Ayuthaya," *Journal of the Siam Society,* 53 (1965), 83-121.

Stevenson, R. C., "Old Khartoum, 1821-1885," *Sudan Notes and Records,* 47 (1966), 1-38.

Trewartha, G. T., "Chinese Cities: Origins and Functions," *Annals of the Association of American Geographers,* 42:1 (1952), 69-93.

Un Groupe d'Etude de l'I.E.D.E.S., "La Société Urbaine Egyptienne," *Tiers Monde,* 2 (1961), 183-210.

Von Grunebaum, G. E., *Islam: Essays in the Nature and Growth of a Cultural Tradition, American Anthropologist,* 57:2, Part 2, Memoir 81 (1955), 141-58.
(On "The Structure of the Muslim Town.")

Wheatley, P., "The Significance of Traditional Yoruba Urbanism," *Comparative Studies in Society and History,* 12:4 (1970), 393-423.

Whitmer, J., "Study of the Ancient City of Damascus in Light of Present Problems," *Ekistics,* 77 (1962), 177-81.

Whittlesey, D., "Kano, a Sudanese Metropolis," *Geographical Review,* 27:2 (1937), 177-99.

Williams, D. S. M., "The City of Tashkent, Past and Present," *Royal Central Asia Journal,* 54:1 (1967), 33-43.

4. Urbanization in the Underdeveloped Countries: A General Overview

American University Field Staff, *City and Nation in the Developing World: Selected Case Studies of Social Change in Asia, Africa and Latin America. Readings,* v. 2, (New York: AUFS, 1968).

Awad, H., "Morocco's Expanding Towns," *Geographical Journal,* 130:1 (March 1964), 49-64.

Bellam, M. E. P., "The Colonial City: Honcara, a Pacific Island's Case Study," *Pacific Viewpoint,* 11:1 (1970), 66-96.

Berger, M. (ed.), *The New Metropolis in the Arab World* (New Delhi: Allied Publishers, 1963).

Bernus, S., *Niamey: population et habitat* (Niamey, Niger: Institut Français d'Afrique Noire, Gouvernement du Niger, Centre IFAN, 1962).

Beyer, G. H. (ed.), *The Urban Explosion in Latin America: A Continent in Process of Modernization* (Ithaca: Cornell University Press, 1967).

Breese, G., *Urbanization in Newly Developing Countries* (Englewood Cliffs, N.J.: Prentice-Hall, 1966).

——— (ed.), *The City in Newly Developing Countries: Readings on Urbanism and Urbanization* (Englewood Cliffs, N.J.: Prentice-Hall, 1969).

Browning, H. L., "Recent Trends in Latin American Urbanization," *Annals of the American Academy of Political and Social Sciences,* 316 (1958), 111-20.

Caldwell, J. C., "Urban Growth in Malaya: Trends and Implications," *Population Review,* 7:1 (1963), 39-50.

Chauhan, D. S., *Trends of Urbanization in Agra* (New York: Allied Publishers, 1966).

Comhaire, J., "Urban Growth in Relation to Ethiopian Development," *Culture et Développement,* 1:1 (1968), 25-39.

Cooper, E., "Urbanization in Malaya," *Population Studies,* 5:2 (1951), 117-31.

Davis, K., "Urbanization in India: Past and Future," in R. Turner (ed.), *India's Urban Future* (Berkeley: University of California Press, 1962), 3-26.

Davis, K., and Golden, H. H., "Urbanization and Development in Pre-Industrial Areas," *Economic Development and Cultural Change,* 3:1 (1954), 6-26.

Ducoff, L. J., "The Migrant Population of a Metropolitan Area in a Developing Country: Case Study of San Salvador," *Ekistics,* 13:79 (1962), 330-32.

Durand, J. D., and Pelaez, C. A., "Patterns of Urbanization in Latin America," in G. Breese (ed.), *The City in Newly Developing Countries: Readings on Urbanism and Urbanization* (Englewood Cliffs, N.J.: Prentice-Hall, 1969), 166-88.

Dwyer, D. J., "The City in the Developing World and the Example of Southeast Asia," *Geography,* 53:241 (1968), 353-64.

Dyer, D. R., "Urbanism in Cuba," *Geographical Review,* 47:2 (1957), 224-33.

Eames, E., "Urbanization and Rural-Urban Migration in India," *Population Review,* 9:1 & 2 (1965), 38-47.

Forde, D. (ed.), *Social Implications of Industrialization and Urbanization in Africa South of the Sahara* (Paris: UNESCO, 1956).

Gellar, S., "West African Capital Cities as Motors for Development," *Civilisations,* 17:3 (1967), 254-62.

Ghurye, G. S., "Cities in India," *Sociological Bulletin,* 2:1 (1953), 47-80.

Ginsburg, N. S., "Urban Geography and 'Non-Western' Areas," in G. Breese (ed.), *The City in Newly Developing Countries: Readings on Urbanism and Urbanization* (Englewood Cliffs, N.J.: Prentice-Hall, 1969), 409-35.

Gulick, J., *Tripoli: A Modern Arab City* (Cambridge: Harvard University Press, 1967).

Hallam, W. K. R., "The Great Emporium," *Nigeria Magazine,* 81 (1964), 84-97.

Harvey, M. E., "Bonthe: A Geographical Study of a Moribund Port and its Environs," *Bulletin of the Sierra Leone Geographical Association,* 10 (1966), 60-75.

Hauser, P. M. (ed.), *Urbanization in Asia and the Far East* (Calcutta: UNESCO, 1958).

——— (ed.), *Urbanization in Latin America* (Paris: UNESCO, 1961).

——— (ed.), *Handbook for Social Research in Urban Areas* (Paris: UNESCO, 1965), 91-115.

Heeren, H. J., "The Urbanization of Djakarta," *Economi Dan Kevnangan Indonesia,* 8 (1955), 696-736.

Herran, W. P., "Urbanization in Pakistan," *The Journal of Geography,* 63:7 (1964), 323-27.

Hoselitz, B. F., "The Role of Cities in the Economic Growth of Underdeveloped Countries," *The Journal of Political Economy,* 61:3 (1953), 195-208.

———, "Cities in Advanced and Underdeveloped Countries," *Confluence,* 4:3 (1955), 321-34.

———, "Urbanization in India," *Kyklos,* 13:3 (1960), 361-70.

Jenkins, G., "Africa as It Urbanizes," *Urban Affairs Quarterly,* 2:3 (1967), 66-80.

Johnson, A. W., "Abeokuta," *The Nigerian Geographical Journal,* 6:2 (1963), 89-95.

Kahl, J. A., "Some Social Concomitants of Industrialization and Urbanization," *Human Organization,* 18:2 (1959), 53-74.

Khan, F. K., and Massod, M., "Urban Structure of Comilla Town," *Oriental Geographer,* 6:2 (1962), 109-38.

Lee, Y. L., "The Port Towns of British Borneo," *The Australian Geographer,* 8:4 (1962), 161-72.

Leonard, O. E., "La Paz, Bolivia: Its Population and Growth," *American Sociological Review,* 13:4 (1948), 448-54.

Lybarger, L. H., "Urbanization in Pakistan," *International Review of Missions,* 55:219 (1966), 282-90.

Mangin, W., "Urbanization Case History in Peru," *Architectural Design,* 33:8 (1963), 366-70.

Mercier, P., "Urban Explosion in Developing Nations," *The Unesco Courier,* 7-8 (July-Aug. 1963), 50-55.

Milone, P. D., "Contemporary Urbanization in Indonesia," *Asian Survey,* 4:8 (1964), 1000-12.

Mohan, R. P., "Urbanization: Case Study of a Village in Uttar Pradesh," *Journal of Social Research,* 10:1 (1967), 14-17.

Morse, R. M., "Latin American Cities: Aspects of Function and Structure," *Comparative Studies in Society and History,* 4:4 (1962), 473-93.

———, "Urbanization in Latin America," *Latin American Research Review,* 1:1 (1965), 35-74.

Murphey, R., "New Capitals of Asia," *Economic Development and Cultural Change,* 5:3 (1957), 216-43.

———, "Urbanization in Asia," in G. Breese (ed.), *The City in Newly Developing Countries: Readings on Urbanism and Urbanization* (Englewood Cliffs, N.J.: Prentice-Hall, 1969), 58-75.

Nazeer, M. M., "Urban Growth in Pakistan," *Asian Survey,* 6:6 (1966), 310-18.

Neville, R. J. W., "An Urban Study of Pontian Kerchil, Southwest Malaya," *Journal of Tropical Geography,* 16 (1962), 32-56.

Ohadike, P. O., "Growth, Transitions and Problems of a Premier West African City (Lagos, Nigeria)," *Urban Affairs Quarterly,* 3:4 (1968), 69-90.

Oram, N. D., "Urbanization: Port Moresby," *South Pacific Bulletin,* 14:4 (1964), 37-43.

Panditratna, B. L., "The Urban Field of Colombo," *The Ceylon Geographer,* 16:1-4 (1962), 26-36.

Ragheb (Southall), I., "Patterns of Urban Growth in the Middle East," in G. Breese (ed.), *The City in Newly Developing Countries: Readings on Urbanism and Urbanization* (Englewood Cliffs, N.J.: Prentice-Hall, 1969), 104-26.

Reed, R. R., "Hispanic Urbanism in the Philippines: A Study of the Impact of Church and State," *Journal of East Asiatic Studies* (University of Manila), 11 (1967), 1-222.

Richards, J. M., "Desert City: An Account of Hail in Central Arabia," *Architectural Review,* 105:625 (1949), 35-41.

Sabanes, C. M., "Urbanization in Latin America," *International Review of Missions,* 55:219 (1966), 307-12.

Sable, M. H., *Latin American Urbanization: Guide to Literature and Organization in the Field* (Los Angeles: UCLA Latin American Center, 1967).

Sendut, H., "Contemporary Urbanization in Malaysia," *Asian Survey,* 6:9 (1966), 484-91.

Shiber, S. G., "The Urban Arab Scene," *Middle East Commerce* (Beirut), (15 Dec. 1961), 6-17.

Smith, T. L., "Urbanization in Latin America," *International Journal of Comparative Sociology,* 4:2 (1963), 227-42.

Sovani, N. V., *Urbanization and Urban India* (New York: Asia Publishing House, 1966).

Spoehr, A. (ed.), *Pacific Port Towns and Cities* (Honolulu: Bishop Museum Press, 1963).

Tandberg, O. G., "The Indo-Pakistanis' Importance for the Urbanization of Kenya," *Pakistan Geographical Review,* 17:2 (1962), 17-24.

Ullman, M. B., "Cities of Mainland China: 1953-1959," in G. Breese (ed.), *The City in Newly Developing Countries: Readings on Urbanism and Urbanization* (Englewood Cliffs, N.J.: Prentice-Hall, 1969), 81-103.

United Nations Economic Commission for Africa, "Size and Growth of Urban Population in Africa," in G. Breese (ed.), *The City in Newly Developing Countries: Readings on Urbanism and Urbanization* (Englewood Cliffs, N.J.: Prentice-Hall, 1969), 128-45.

Versluys, J. D. H., "Urbanization in Southeast Asia," *International Journal of Comparative Sociology,* 4:2 (1963), 40-51.

Weinryb, B. D., "The Impact of Urbanization in Israel," *Middle Eastern Journal,* 11:1 (1957), 23-36.

Wertheim, W. F., "Urban Characteristics in Indonesia," in W. F. Wertheim (ed.), *East-West Parallels: Sociological Approaches to Modern Asia* (The Hague: W. Van Hoeve, 1964), 165-81.

Wilkinson, T. O., "The Pattern of Korean Urban Growth," *Rural Sociology,* 19:1 (1954), 32-38.

Wingo, L., "Recent Patterns of Urbanization among Latin American Countries," *Urban Affairs Quarterly,* 2:3 (1967), 81-109.

5. The Demographic, Environmental and Economic Dimensions of Urbanism

Abiodun, J. O., "Central Place Study in Abeokuta Province, Southwestern Nigeria," *Journal of Regional Science,* 8:1 (1968), 57-76.

Ahmed, E., "A Note on the Size and Function of Towns in India: Uttar Pradesh, a Case Study," *Journal of Social Research,* 1:1 (1958), 54-58.

Arriaga, E. E., "Components of City Growth in Selected Latin American Countries," *Milbank Memorial Fund Quarterly,* 46:2 (1968), 237-52.

Beyer, G. H., *The Urban Explosion in Latin America* (Ithaca: Cornell University Press, 1967).

Burnright, R. G., Whetten, N. L., and Waxman, B. D., "Differential Rural-Urban Fertility in Mexico," *American Sociological Review,* 21:1 (1956), 3-8.

Chirot, D., "Urban and Rural Economies in the Western Sudan: Birni N'Konni and its Hinterland," *Cahiers d'Etudes Africaines,* 8:4 (1968), 547-65.

Davis, K., "The Origin and Growth of Urbanization in the World," *American Journal of Sociology,* 60:5 (1955), 429-37.

———, "The Urbanization of the Human Population," *Scientific American,* 213:3 (1965), 40-54.

Davis, K., and Golden, H. H., "Urbanization and the Development of Pre-Industrial Areas," *Economic Development and Cultural Change,* 3:1 (1954), 6-26.

El-Badry, M. A., "A Study of Differential Fertility in Bombay," *Demography,* 4:2 (1967), 626-40.

Farrage, A., "Demographic Trends," in M. Berger (ed.), *The New Metropolis in the Arab World* (New Delhi: Allied Publishers, 1963), 1-22.

Gibbs, J. P., and Schnore, L. F., "Metropolitan Growth: An International Study," *American Journal of Sociology,* 66:2 (1960), 160-70.

Gillin, J., "Houses, Food and Contact of Cultures in a Guatemalan Town," *Acta Americana,* 1:3 (1943), 344-59.

Hassan, R., "Population Change and Urbanization in Singapore," *Civilisations,* 19:2 (1969), 169-88.

Hoselitz, B. F., *Sociological Aspects of Economic Growth* (New York: Free Press, 1960), 159-84, 217-48.

Hoyt, H., "World Urbanization: Expanding Population in a Shrinking World," *Technical Bulletin* (Urban Land Institute), 43 (April 1962).

Hutchinson, B., "Fertility, Social Mobility and Urban Migration in Brazil," *Population Studies,* 14:3 (1961), 182-89.

Lopez, A., "Some Notes on Fertility Problems in a Columbian Semi-Urban Community," *Demography,* 4:2 (1967), 453-63.

McLoughlin, P., "The Sudan's Three Towns: A Demographic and Economic Profile of an African Urban Complex," *Economic Development and Cultural Change,* 12:1 (1963), 70-83; 2 (1964), 158-73; 3 (1964), 286-304.

O'Connor, A. M., "The Distribution of Towns in Sub-Saharan Africa," *Nkanga* (Kampala), 6 (1970), 4-12. (Special issue on "Urban Growth in Sub-Saharan Africa," J. Gugler, ed.)

Ohadike, P. O., *Some Demographic Measurements for Africans in Zambia,* University of Zambia, Institute for Social Research, Communication No. 5 (1969), 71 pp.

Onwuejeogwu, M. A., "The Typology of Settlement Patterns in Igbo Culture Area," *African Notes,* 6:1 (1970), 60-70.

Painter, N. W., and Murillo, E. C., "Demographic Characteristics of the Population," in C. P. Loomis *et al.* (eds.), *Turrialba, Social Systems and the Introduction of Change* (Glencoe, Ill.: The Free Press, 1953), 119-34.

Robinson, W. G., "Urbanization and Fertility: The Non-Western Experience," *Milbank Memorial Fund Quarterly,* 41 (1963), 291-308.

Sehgal, J. M., "The Population Distribution in Greater Bombay," *Asian Economic Review,* 8:2 (1966), 185-97.

Sendut, H., "City Size Distribution of Southeast Asia," *Asian Studies,* 4:2 (1966), 268-80.

Southall, A. W., "Urban Migration and the Residence of Children in Kampala," in W. Mangin (ed.), *Peasants in Cities: Readings in the Anthropology of Urbanization* (Boston: Houghton Mifflin, 1970), 150-59.

Spengler, J. J., "Africa and the Theory of Optimum City Size," in H. Miner (ed.), *The City in Modern Africa* (New York: Praeger, 1967), 55-89.

Thomas, B. E., "The Location and Nature of West African Cities," in H. Kuper (ed.), *Urbanization and Migration in West Africa* (Berkeley: University of California Press, 1965), 23-38.

———, "On the Growth of African Cities," *African Studies Review,* 13:1 (1970), 1-8.

Unikel, L., "The Process of Urbanization in Mexico: Distribution and Growth of the Urban Population," in Rabinovits, F. F., and Trueblood, F. M. (eds.), *Latin American Urban Research,* Vol. 1, (Beverly Hills: Sage Publications, 1971), 247-302.

United Nations, Bureau of Social Affairs, "Demographic Aspects of Urbanization in Latin America," in P. M. Hauser (ed.), *Urbanization in Latin America* (Paris: UNESCO, 1961), 91-117.

———, "World Urbanization Trends, 1920-1960 (An Interim Report on Work in Progress)," in G. Breese (ed.), *The City in Newly Developing Countries: Readings on Urbanism and Urbanization* (Englewood Cliffs, N.J.: Prentice-Hall, 1969), 21-53.

Ward, B., "The Process of World Urbanization," *Ekistics,* 18:108 (1964), 274-80.

Zarate, A. U., "Fertility in Urban Areas of Mexico: Implications for the Theory of the Demographic Transition," *Demography,* 4:1 (1967), 363-73.

6. The Composition of the Urban Population and Measures of Urbanism: General Conceptual Scheme

Abiodun, J. O., "Urban Hierarchy in a Developing Country [Nigeria]," *Economic Geography,* 43:4 (1967), 347-67.

Abu-Lughod, J. L., "Testing the Theory of Social Area Analyses: The Ecology of Cairo, Egypt," *American Sociological Review,* 34:2 (1969), 198-212.

Arensberg, C. M., "The Urban in Crosscultural Perspective," in E. M. Eddy (ed.), *Urban Anthropology: Research Perspectives and Strategies* (Athens: University of Georgia Press, 1968), 3-15.

Armstrong, W. R., and McGee, T. G., "Revolutionary Change and the Third World City: A Theory of Urban Involution," *Civilisations,* 18:3 (1968), 353-78.

Arriaga, E. E., "A New Approach to the Measurements of Urbanization," *Economic Development and Cultural Change,* 18:2 (1970), 206-18.

Beals, R. L., "Urbanism, Urbanization and Acculturation," *American Anthropologist,* 53:1 (1951), 1-10.

Bendix, R., "Concepts and Generalizations in Comparative Sociological Studies," *American Sociological Review,* 28:4 (1963), 532-39.

Bjeren, G., *Some Theoretical and Methodological Aspects of the Study of African Urbanization,* Research Report No. 9, The Scandinavian Institute of African Studies, Uppsala, 1971, 37 pp.

Bopegamage, A., "A Methodological Problem in Indian Urban Sociological Research," *Sociology and Social Research,* 50:1 (1966), 236-40.

Bose, A., "A Note on the Definition of 'Town' in the Indian Censuses: 1901-61," *Indian Economic and Social History Review,* 1:3 (1964), 1-11.

Briones, G., and Waisanen, F. B., "Educational Aspirations, Modernization and Urban Integration," in P. Meadows and E. H. Mizruchi (eds.), *Urbanism, Urbanization and Change: Comparative Perspectives* (Reading, Mass.: Addison-Wesley, 1969), 252-64.

Clignet, R., and Sween, J., "Accra and Abidjan: A Comparative Examination of the Theory of Increase in Scale," *Urban Affairs Quarterly,* 4:3 (1969), 292-324.

Cox, O. C., "The Preindustrial City Reconsidered," *The Sociological Quarterly,* 5:3 (1964), 133-44.

Drakakis-Smith, D. W., "Traditional and Modern Aspects of Urban Systems in the Third World—A Case Study in Hong Kong," *Pacific Viewpoint,* 12:1 (1971), 21-40.

Du Toit, B. M., "Cultural Continuity and African Urbanization," in E. M. Eddy (ed.), *Urban Anthropology: Research Perspectives and Strategies* (Athens: University of Georgia Press, 1968), 58-74.

Epstein, A. L., "Urban Communities in Africa," in M. Gluckman (ed.), *Closed Systems and Open Minds* (Chicago: Aldine, 1964), 83-102.

Fox, R. G., "Rationale and Romance in Urban Anthropology," *Urban Anthropology,* 1:2 (1972), 205-33.

Gamst, F. C., "Peasantries and Elites Without Urbanism: The Civilization of Ethiopia," *Comparative Studies in Society and History,* 12:1 (1970), 373-92.

Gibbs, J. P., "Measures of Urbanization," *Social Forces,* 45:2 (1966), 170-77.

Gibbs, J. P., and Martin, W. T., "Urbanization, Technology and the Division of Labor: International Patterns," *American Sociological Review,* 27:5 (1962), 667-77.

Goodman, A. E., "The Political Implications of Urban Development in Southeast Asia: The 'Fragment' Hypothesis," *Economic Development and Cultural Change,* 20:1 (1971), 117-30.

Graves, T. D., "Alternative Models for the Study of Urban Migration," *Human Organization,* 25:4 (1966), 295-99.

Greer, S., McElrath, D. L., Minar, D. W., and Orleans, P. (eds.), *The New Urbanization* (New York: St. Martin's Press, 1968).

Gugler, J., "On the Concept of Urbanization," (Kampala: East African Institute of Social Research, 1966). Paper No. 363, 8 pp.

———, "What is Urbanization? An Operational Approach," *African Urban Notes,* 4:1 (1969), 9-25.

———, "Life in a Dual System: Eastern Nigerians in Town, 1961," *Nkanga* (Kampala), 6 (1970), 24-34. (Special issue on "Urban Growth in Sub-Saharan Africa," J. Gugler, ed.)

Gulick, J., "The Outlook, Research Strategies and Relevance of Urban Anthropology: A Commentary," in E. M. Eddy (ed.), *Urban Anthropology: Research Perspectives and Strategies* (Athens: University of Georgia Press, 1968), 93-98.

Guterman, S. S., "In Defense of Wirth's 'Urbanism as a Way of Life,'" *American Journal of Sociology,* 74:5 (1969), 492-99.

Gutkind, P. C. W., "Orientation and Research Methods in African Urban Studies," in D. G. Jongmans and P. C. W. Gutkind (eds.), *Anthropologists in the Field* (Assen, Neth.: Van Gorcum, 1967), 133-69.

Hackenberg, R. A., and Hackenberg, B. H., "Secondary Development and Anticipatory Urbanization in Davao, Mindanao," *Pacific Viewpoint,* 12:1 (1971), 1-20.

Hanna, W. J., "The Integrative Role of Urban Africa's Middleplaces and Middlemen," *Civilisations,* 12:1-2 (1967), 12-29.

Hanson, R. C., and Simmons, O. G., "The Role Path: A Concept and Procedure for Studying Migration to Urban Communities," *Human Organization,* 27:2 (1963), 152-58.

Hauser, P. M. (ed.), "Comprehensive Urban Studies," in *Handbook for Social Research in Urban Areas* (Paris: UNESCO, 1965), 91-191.

Horvath, R. J., "In Search of a Theory of Urbanization: Notes on the Colonial City," *East Lakes Geographer,* 5 (1969), 69-82.

Hoselitz, B. F., "Generative and Parasitic Cities," *Economic Development and Cultural Change,* 3:3 (1955), 278-94.

Inkeles, A., "The Modernization of Man," in M. Weiner (ed.), *Modernization: The Dynamics of Growth* (New York: Basic Books, 1966), 138-50.

Jones, E., "The Process of Urbanization," in *Towns and Cities* (London: Oxford University Press, 1966), 13-37.

———, "What is a Town?" in *Towns and Cities* (London: Oxford University Press, 1966), 1-12.

Leeds, A., "The Anthropology of Cities: Some Methodological Issues," in E. M. Eddy (ed.), *Urban Anthropology: Research Perspectives and Strategies* (Athens: University of Georgia Press, 1968), 31-47.

Magubane, B., "Some Methodological and Ideological Problems in the Study of Social Change in Africa, as Reflected in the Studies of Migrant Labour," University of East Africa Social Sciences Council Conference 1968/69, Sociology Papers v. 2, (Kampala: Makerere Institute of Social Research, c. 1969), 245-59.

———, "A Critical Look at Indices Used in the Study of Social Change in Colonial Africa," *Current Anthropology,* 12:4-5 (1971), 419-31. (Commentaries on article, 431-45)

Mangin, W., "Introduction," in W. Mangin (ed.), *Peasants in Cities: Readings in the Anthropology of Urbanization* (Boston: Houghton Mifflin, 1970), xiii-xxxix.

McCall, D. F., "Dynamics of Urbanization in Africa," *Annals of the American Academy of Political and Social Sciences,* 298 (1955), 151-60.

McCulloch, M., "A Social Survey of the African Population of Livingstone," *The Rhodes-Livingstone Papers,* 26 (1956), 82 pp.

Meadows, P., "The City, Technology and History," in P. Meadows and E. H. Mizruchi (eds.), *Urbanism, Urbanization and Change: Comparative Perspectives* (Reading, Mass.: Addison-Wesley, 1969), 10-19.

Merriam, C. E., "Urbanism," *American Journal of Sociology,* 45:5 (1940), 720-30.

Miner, H., "The Folk-Urban Continuum," *American Sociological Review,* 17:5 (1952), 529-37.

Mitchell, J. C., "A Note on the Urbanization of Africans on the Copperbelt," *The Rhodes-Livingstone Papers,* 12 (1951), 20-27.

———, "African Urbanization in Ndola and Luanshya," *Rhodes-Livingstone Communication,* 6 (1954).

———, "Urbanization, Detribalization and Stabilization in Southern Africa," in D. Forde (ed.), *Social Implications of Industrialization and Urbanization in Africa South of the Sahara* (Paris: UNESCO, 1956), 693-711.

———, "Theoretical Orientations in African Urban Studies," in M. Banton (ed.), *The Social Anthropology of Complex Societies* (London: Tavistock Publications, 1966), 37-68.

Mukherjee, R., "Urbanization and Social Transformation in India," *International Journal of Comparative Sociology,* 4:2 (1963), 78-110.

Murvar, V., "Some Tentative Modification of Weber's Typology: Occidental Versus Oriental City," *Social Forces,* 44:4 (1966), 381-89.

Okediji, F. O., "Review" of K. Little, "West African Urbanization: A Study of Voluntary Association in Social Change, *The Nigerian Journal of Economics and Social Studies,* 8:3 (1966), 500-8.

Plotnicov, L., *Strangers to the City: Urban Man in Jos, Nigeria* (Pittsburgh: University of Pittsburgh Press, 1967), 3-27.

Pocock, D., "Sociologies: Urban and Rural," *Contributions to Indian Sociology,* 4 (1960), 63-81.

Pons, V., *Stanleyville: An African Urban Community under Belgian Administration* (London: Oxford University Press, 1969), 257-74.

Redfield, R., "The Folk Society and Culture," *American Journal of Sociology,* 45:5 (1940), 731-42.

———, "The Folk Society," *American Journal of Sociology,* 52:4 (1947), 293-308.

Reissman, L., "Urbanism and Urbanization," in J. Gould (ed.), *Penguin Survey of the Social Sciences 1965* (Harmondsworth, Eng.: Penguin Books, 1965), 36-55.

———, "Urbanization: A Typology of Change," in S. F. Fava (ed.), *Urbanism in World Perspective: A Reader* (New York: Crowell, 1968), 126-44.

Rollwagen, J. R., "A Comparative Framework for the Investigation of the City-As-Context: A Discussion of the Mexican Case," *Urban Anthropology,* 1:1 (1972), 68-86.

Ryder, N. B., "The Cohort as a Concept in the Study of Social Change," *American Sociological Review*, 30:6 (1965), 843-61.

Schnaiberg, A., "The Modernizing Impact of Urbanization: A Causal Analysis," *Economic Development and Cultural Change*, 20:1 (1971), 80-104.

Sjoberg, G., "The Rise and Fall of Cities: A Theoretical Perspective," *International Journal of Comparative Sociology*, 4:2 (1963), 107-20.

Sovani, N. V., "The Analysis of Over-Urbanism," *Economic Development and Cultural Change*, 7:2 (1964), 113-22.

Srinivas, M. N., "Social Anthropology and the Study of Rural and Urban Societies," in *Caste in Modern India* (Bombay: Asia Publishing House, 1962), 136-47.

Thrupp, S. L., "The Creativity of Cities," *Comparative Studies in Society and History*, 4:1 (1961), 53-64.

Trigger, B., "Determinants of Urban Growth in Preindustrial Societies," in P. J. Uko, Tringham, R., and Dimbley, G. W. (eds.), *Man, Settlement and Urbanism*, (London: Duckworth, 1972), 575-99.

Trivedi, H. R., "Emergence of Semi-Urban Pockets in Rural Areas," *The Indian Journal of Social Work*, 27:4 (1967), 378-80.

———, "The 'Semi-Urban Pocket' as Concept and Reality in India," *Human Organization*, 28:1 (1969), 72-77.

Weaver, T., and White, D., "Anthropological Approaches to Urban and Complex Society," in T. Weaver and D. White (eds.), *The Anthropology of Urban Environments* (Washington, D.C., Society for Applied Anthropology), Monograph 11 (1972), 109-25.

Wheatley, P., " 'What the Greatness of a City is said to be': Reflections on Sjoberg's 'Preindustrial City.' " *Pacific Viewpoint*, 4:2 (1963), 163-88.

Williamson, R. C., "Some Factors in Urbanism in a Quasi-Rural Setting: San Salvador and San Jose," *Sociology and Social Research*, 47:3 (1963), 187-200.

Wilson, M., and Mafeje, A., *Langa: A Study of Social Groups in an African Township* (Cape Town: Oxford University Press, 1963), 13-46.

7. The Ecology of Urban Growth and Social Ecology

Abu-Lughod, J., "The City is Dead—Long Live the City: Some Thoughts on Urbanity," in S. F. Fava (ed.), *Urbanism in World Perspective: A Reader* (New York: Crowell, 1968), 154-65.

Akinola, R. A., "The Ibadan Region," *Journal of the Geographical Association of Nigeria*, 6:2 (1964), 102-15.

Berry, B. J. L., and Rees, P. H., "The Factorial Ecology of Calcutta," *American Journal of Sociology*, 74:5 (1969), 445-91.

Boxer, B., "Space, Change and *Feng-Shui* in Tsuen Wan's Urbanization," *Journal of Asian and African Studies*, 3:3-4 (1968), 226-40.

Caplow, T., "The Social Ecology of Guatemala City," *Social Forces*, 28:2 (1949), 113-33.

Caplow, T., Stryker, S., and Wallace, S. E., *The Urban Ambience: A Study of San Juan, Puerto Rico* (Totowa, N.J.: The Bedminster Press, 1964).

Cressey, P., "The Ecological Organization of Rangoon, Burma," *Sociology and Social Research,* 40:2 (1956), 166-69.

Deffontaines, P., "The Origin and Growth of the Brazilian Network of Towns," *Geographical Review,* 23:3 (1938), 379-99.

Dotson, F., and Dotson, L. O., "Ecological Trends in the City of Guadalajara, Mexico," *Social Forces,* 32:4 (1954), 367-74.

———, "Urban Centralization and Decentralization in Mexico," *Rural Sociology,* 21:1 (1956), 41-49.

Gist, N. P., "The Ecology of Bangalore, India: An East-West Comparison," *Social Forces,* 35:4 (1957), 356-65.

Hamdan, G., "Some Aspects of the Urban Geography of the Khartoum Complex," *Bulletin de la Société de Géographie d'Egypte,* 32 (1959), 89-120.

———, "The Growth and Functional Structure of Khartoum," *The Geographical Review,* 50:1 (1960), 21-40.

———, "Capitals of the New Africa," *Economic Geography,* 40:3 (1964), 239-53.

Hance, W. A., "Economic Location and Functions of Tropical African Cities," *Human Organization,* 19:3 (1960), 135-36.

Hanna, W. J., and Hanna, J. L., *Urban Dynamics in Black Africa: An Interdisciplinary Approach* (Chicago: Aldine-Atherton, 1971), 13-25.

Hansen, A. T., "The Ecology of a Latin American City," in E. B. Reuter (ed.), *Race and Culture Contacts* (New York: McGraw-Hill, 1934), 124-42.

Hawthorn, H. B., and Hawthorn, A., "The Shape of a City: Some Observations on Sucre, Bolivia," *Sociology and Social Research,* 33:1 (1948), 87-91.

Hayner, N. S., "Oaxaca, City of Old Mexico," *Sociology and Social Research,* 29:2 (1944), 87-95.

———, "Mexico City: Its Growth and Configuration," *American Journal of Sociology,* 50:4 (1945), 295-304.

———, "Mexico City: Its Growth and Configuration, 1345-1960," in S. F. Fava (ed.), *Urbanism in World Perspective: A Reader* (New York: Crowell, 1968), 166-77.

James, W. R., "Port Sudan's Overspill," *Sudan Society,* 4 (1969), 5-26.

Keyfitz, N., "The Ecology of Indonesian Cities," *American Journal of Sociology,* 66:4 (1961), 348-54.

Mabogunje, A., "The Growth of Residential Districts in Ibadan," *Geographical Review,* 52:1 (1962), 56-77.

McGee, T. G., *The Southeast Asian City: A Social Geography of the Primate Cities of Southeast Asia* (New York: Praeger, 1967).

Morgan, W. T. W. (ed.), *Nairobi, City and Region* (Nairobi: Oxford University Press, 1967).

Penalosa, F., "Ecological Organization of the Transitional City: Some Mexican Evidence," *Social Forces,* 46:2 (1967), 221-29.

Sadek, D., "The Morphology of Damascus," *Bulletin de la Société de Géographie d'Egypte,* 28 (1955), 93-98.

Schnore, L. F., "On the Spatial Structure of Cities in the Two Americas," in P. M. Hauser and L. F. Schnore (eds.), *The Study of Urbanization* (New York: Wiley, 1965), 347-98.

Sendut, H., "The Structure of Kuala Lumpur, Malaysia's Capital City," *The Town Planning Review,* 36:2 (1965), 125-38.

Singh, R. L., "Mirzapur: A Study in Urban Geography," *Geographical Outlook,* 1:1 (1956), 16-27.

Stanislawski, D., "The Anatomy of Eleven Towns in Michoacan," in G. A. Theodorson (ed.), *Studies in Human Ecology* (Evanston, Ill.: Row Peterson, 1961), 348-55.

Wolfe, M., "Recent Changes in Urban and Rural Settlement Patterns in Latin America," *International Social Development Review,* No. 1 (1968), 55-62.

8. Patterns of Urban Life: The Scale of Urban Systems

Abrahams, R. G., "Kahama Township, Western Province, Tanganyika," in A. W. Southall (ed.), *Social Change in Modern Africa* (London: Oxford University Press, 1961), 242-53.

Acharya, H., "Urbanizing Role of a One-Lakh City," *Sociological Bulletin,* 5:2 (1956), 89-101.

Bose, N. K., "Calcutta: A Premature Metropolis," *Scientific American,* 213:3 (1965), 90-102.

Brokensha, D. W., *Social Change at Larteh, Ghana* (Oxford: Clarendon Press, 1966).

Cook, R. C., "The World's Great Cities: Evolution or Devolution," *Population Bulletin,* 16 (1960), 109-30.

Datta, S., "The World's Cities: Calcutta," *Encounter,* 8:6 (1957), 35-45.

Fosbrooke, H., and Young, R., *Smoke in the Hills: Political Tension in the Morogoro District of Tanganyika* (Evanston, Ill.: Northwestern University Press, 1960), 119-40.

Fryer, D. W., "The 'Million City' in Southeast Asia," *Geographical Review,* 43:4 (1953), 474-94.

Ginsburg, N. S., "The Great City in Southeast Asia," *American Journal of Sociology,* 60:5 (1955), 455-62.

Gutkind, P. C. W., "The Small Town in African Urban Studies," *African Urban Notes,* 3:1 (1969), 5-10.

Harris, M., *Town and Country in Brazil* (New York: Columbia University Press, 1956).

Harrison-Church, R. J., "Urban Problems and Economic Development in West Africa," *The Journal of Modern African Studies,* 5:4 (1967), 511-20.

Harvey, M., "Sierra Leone's Largest Provincial Town," *Sierra Leone Studies,* 18 (Jan. 1966), 29-42.

———, "Kabala–The Northern Frontier Town," *Sierra Leone Studies,* 21 (July 1967), 63-79.

———, "Makeni: A Geographical Study of a Growing Northern Town and Its Environs," *Sierra Leone Geographical Journal,* 11 (1967), 26-42.

Hoyt, H., "Growth and Structure of Twenty-One Great World Cities," *Land Economics,* 42 (Feb. 1966), 53-64.

Jefferson, M., "The Law of the Primate City," *Geographical Review,* 29:2 (1939), 226-32.

Linsky, A. S., "Some Generalizations Concerning Primate Cities," *Annals of the American Academy of Geographers,* 55 (1965), 506-13.

Loomis, C. P., *et al.* (eds.), *Turrialba, Social Systems and the Introduction of Change* (Glencoe, Ill.: The Free Press, 1953).

Mountjoy, A. B., "Million Cities: Urbanization and the Developing Countries," *Geography,* 52:241 (1968), 365-74.

Nash, M., *Machine Age Maya, the Industrialization of a Guatemalan Community* (Glencoe, Ill.: The Free Press, 1958).

Patil, R. K., and Talati, K. M., "Trends in Urbanization in Surat City: A Case Study," in Papers read at the 39th Annual Conference of the Indian Economic Association (1958).

Ragahana, R. G., "Problems of Urbanization in the Metropolitan Cities in India," *Journal of Social Research,* 5 (1962), 133-44.

Ranson, B. H. A., "The Growth of Moyamba," *Bulletin Sierra Leone Geographical Association,* 9 (May 1965), 54-62.

———, *A Sociological Study of Moyamba Town, Sierra Leone* (Zaria, Nigeria: Institute of Administration, Ahmadu Bello University, 1968), 110 pp.

Sadek, D., "Medium Sized Towns in the Urban Pattern of Modern Egypt," *Bulletin de la Société de Géographie d'Egypte,* 34 (1961), 111-24.

Service, E. R., and Service, H. S., *Tobati: Paraguayan Town* (Chicago: University of Chicago Press, 1954).

Wagley, C., *Amazon Town: A Study of Man in the Tropics* (New York: Macmillan, 1953).

Whitten, N. E., *Class, Kinship and Power in an Ecuadorian Town* (Stanford: Stanford University Press, 1965).

9. Urbanism: The Sociocultural Focus, the Urban Milieu

Abegglen, J. C., *The Japanese Factory: Aspects of Its Social Organization* (New York: Free Press, 1958).

Achebe, C., *No Longer at Ease* (London: Heinemann, 1960).

Anderson, E. N., "Some Chinese Methods of Dealing with Crowding," *Urban Anthropology,* 1:2 (1972), 141-50.

Bascom, W., "The Urban African and His World," *Cahiers d'Etudes Africaines,* 4:14 (1963), 163-85.

Blacking, J., "The Myth of Urban Man," in H. L. Watts (ed.), *Focus on Cities,* Proceedings of a Conference, Institute for Social Research, University of Natal, 1968 (Durban: Institute for Social Research, University of Natal, 1970), 228-38.

Camara, C., *Saint-Louis du Sénégal: Evolution d'une ville en milieu africain* (Université de Dakar: Institut Fondamental d'Afrique Noire, 1968).

Duodu, C., *The Gab Boys* (London: Deutsch, 1967).

Ekwensi, C., *People of the City* (London: Heinemann, 1963).

Gulick, J., "Old Values and New Institutions in a Lebanese Arab City," *Human Organization,* 24:1 (1965), 49-52.

Gutkind, P. C. W., "The African Urban Milieu: A Force in Rapid Change," *Civilisations,* 12:2 (1962), 167-91.

Le Tourneau, R., "Social Change in the Muslim Cities of North Africa," *American Journal of Sociology,* 60:6 (1955), 527-35.

Lévi-Strauss, C., "Crowds," *New Left Review,* 15 (May-June 1962), 3-6.

Mack, R. W., "Race, Power, and Class in an Urban Plantocracy: Barbados," in S. Greer *et al.* (eds.), *The New Urbanization* (New York: St. Martin's Press, 1968), 72-88.

Meier, R. L., and Hoshino, I., "Cultural Growth and Urban Development in Inner Tokyo," *Journal of the American Institute of Planners,* 35:1 (1969), 2-9.

Mohsin, M., "The Tenor of Indian Urbanism: With Particular Reference to Chittaranjan," *Sociological Bulletin,* 12:2 (1963), 50-65.

Murphy, R., "The City as a Center of Change: Western Europe and China," in P. C. Wagner and M. W. Mikesell (eds.), *Readings in Cultural Geography* (Chicago: University of Chicago Press, 1962), 330-41.

Nash, M., *Machine Age Maya: The Industrialization of a Guatemalan Community* (Glencoe, Ill.: The Free Press, 1958), 13-20.

Nwoga, D. I., "Onitsha Market Literature," in W. Mangin (ed.), *Peasants in Cities: Readings in the Anthropology of Urbanization* (Boston: Houghton Mifflin, 1970), 175-91.

Peattie, L. R., *The View from the Barrio* (Ann Arbor: University of Michigan Press, 1968).

———, "The Structural Parameters of Emerging Life Styles in Venezuela," in Leacock, E. B. (ed.), *The Culture of Poverty: A Critique* (New York: Simon and Schuster, 1971), 285-98.

Powdermaker, H., "Social Change Through Imagery and Values of Teen-Age Africans in Northern Rhodesia," *American Anthropologist,* 58:5 (1956), 783-813.

Reader, D. H., "Urbanism and the Industrial Continuum," *Psychologica Africana,* 10 (1963), 136-50.

Redfield, R., and Singer, M. B., "The Cultural Role of Cities," *Economic Development and Cultural Change,* 3:1 (1954), 53-73.

Schak, D. C., "Determinants of Children's Play Patterns in a Chinese City: The Interplay of Space and Values," *Urban Anthropology,* 1:2 (1972), 195-204.

Schwab, W. B., "Oshogbo—An Urban Community," in H. Kuper (ed.), *Urbani-*

zation and Migration in West Africa (Berkeley: University of California Press, 1965), 85-109.

Singer, M. B., "The Great Tradition in a Metropolitan Center: Madras," *Journal of American Folklore,* 71:281 (1958), 347-88.

Sternstein, L., "The Image of Bangkok," *Pacific Viewpoint,* 12:1 (1971), 68-74.

Taylor, R. B., "Conservatism in a Zapotec Town," *Human Organization,* 25:2 (1966), 116-21.

Van Den Berghe, P. C., *Caneville: The Social Structure of a South African Town* (Middletown, Conn.: Wesleyan University Press, 1964), 31-64.

Van Der Veur, K., and Richardson, P., "Education through the Eyes of an Indigenous Urban Elite," *New Guinea Research Bulletin,* 12 (August 1966), 100 pp.

Van Hoey, L., "The Coercive Process of Urbanization: The Case of Niger," in S. Greer *et al.* (eds.), *The New Urbanization* (New York: St. Martin's Press, 1968), 15-32.

Wirth, L., "Urbanism as a Way of Life," *American Journal of Sociology,* 144:1 (1938), 1-24.

10. Rural-Urban Balance and Interdependence

Barrows, W. L., "Rural-Urban Alliances and Reciprocity in Africa," *Canadian Journal of African Studies,* 5:3 (1971), 307-25.

Benet, F., "Sociology Uncertain: The Ideology of the Rural-Urban Continuum," *Comparative Studies in Society and History,* 6:1 (1963), 1-23.

Bogue, D., and Zachariah, K. C., "Urbanization and Migration in India," in R. Turner (ed.), *India's Urban Future* (Berkeley: University of California Press, 1961), 27-54.

Chauhan, D. C., "Town, Region and Nation: Study of a Small Town in Fiji," *Journal of Social Research* Bihar (India), 8:2 (1965).

Davis, J., "Town and Country," *Anthropological Quarterly,* 42:3 (1969), 171-85.

Dewey, R., "The Rural-Urban Continuum: Real But Relatively Unimportant," *American Journal of Sociology,* 66:1 (1960), 60-66.

Dowling, J. H., "A 'Rural' Indian Community in an Urban Setting," *Human Organization,* 27:3 (1968), 236-40.

Goddard, S., "Town-Farm Relationships in Yoruba Land: A Case Study from Oyo," *Africa,* 35:1 (1965), 21-29.

Gould, H. A., "The Peasant Village: Centrifugal or Centripetal?" *Eastern Anthropologist,* 13:1 (1959), 3-16.

Harris, M., *Town and Country in Brazil* (New York: Columbia University Press, 1956), 274-89.

Hauser, P. M., "Observations on the Urban-Folk and Urban-Rural Dichotomies as Forms of Western Ethnocentrism," in P. M. Hauser and L. F. Schnore (eds.), *The Study of Urbanization* (New York: Wiley, 1965), 503-17.

Holleman, J. F., "Town and Tribe," in P. Smith (ed.), *Africa in Transition* (London, 1958), 62-70.

Hoselitz, B. F., "Kotla-Mubarakhpur, an Urban Village," *Urban and Rural Planning Thought,* 1:1 (1958), 41-54.

Hutton, C., "Rates of Labour Migration," *Nkanga,* 6 (1970), 13-23. (Special issue on "Urban Growth in Sub-Saharan Africa," J. Gugler, ed.)

Imoagene, S. O., "Urban Involvement and Rural Detachment," *Nigerian Journal of Economic and Social Studies,* 10:3 (1968), 397-411.

Kaplan, D., "City and Countryside in Mexican History," *America Indigena,* 24:1 (1964), 59-69.

Kilby, P., "Balancing Town and Country," *West Africa,* 2465 (29 August, 1964), 975.

Lambert, R. D., "The Impact of Urban Society upon Village Life," in R. Turner (ed.), *India's Urban Future* (Berkeley: University of California Press, 1962), 117-40.

Leeds, A., and Leeds, E., "Brazil and the Myth of Urban Rurality: Urban Experience, Work, and Values in 'Squatments' of Rio de Janeiro and Lima," in A. J. Field (ed.), *City and Country in The Third World: Issues in the Modernization of Latin America* (Cambridge, Mass.: Schenkman, 1970), 229-85.

Lewis, O., "Tepotzlan Restudied: A Critique of the Folk-Urban Conceptualization of Social Change," *Rural Sociology,* 18:2 (1953), 121-34.

Lopreato, J., *Peasants No More* (San Francisco: Chandler, 1967).

Mazzarelli, M., "Intercommunity Relations in British Honduras," *Human Organization,* 26:4 (1967), 222-29.

McGee, T. G., "The Rural-Urban Continuum Debate, The Pre-Industrial City and Rural-Urban Migration," *Pacific Viewpoint,* 5:2 (1964), 159-81.

Mills, A. R., "A Comparison of Urban and Rural Population in the Lunsar Area," *Sierra Leone Studies,* Part I, 20 (Jan. 1967), 173-90; Part II, 21 (July 1967), 12-51.

Miner, H., "Urban Influences on the Rural Hausa," in H. Kuper (ed.), *Urbanization and Migration in West Africa* (Berkeley: University of California Press, 1965), 110-30.

Nader, L., "Communication Between Village and City in the Modern Middle East," *Human Organization,* 24:1 (1965), 18-24.

Redfield, R., *The Folk Culture of Yucatan* (Chicago: University of Chicago Press, 1941), 19-57.

———, *A Village That Chose Progress: Chan Kom Revisited,* (Chicago: University of Chicago Press, 1950). (Re-issued 1962.)

Roussel, L., "Measuring Rural-Urban Drift in Developing Countries: A Suggested Method," *International Labour Review,* 101:3 (1970), 229-46.

Schnaiberg, A., "Rural-Urban Residence and Modernism: A Study of Ankara Province, Turkey," *Demography,* 7:1 (1970), 71-85.

Sjoberg, G., "Rural-Urban Balance and Models of Economic Development," in N. J. Smelser and S. M. Lipset (eds.), *Social Structure and Mobility in Economic Development* (Chicago: Aldine, 1966), 235-62.

Srinivas, M. N., "Industrialization and Urbanization of Rural Areas," in *Caste in Modern India* (Bombay: Asia Publishing House, 1962), 77-86.

Strickon, A., "Hacienda and Plantation in Yucatan: An Historical-Ecological Consideration of the Folk-Urban Continuum in Yucatan," *America Indigena,* 25:1 (1965), 35-63.

Williamson, R. C., "The Rural Urban Continuum and Social Class: A Salvadorean Sample," in K. G. Specht (ed.), *Studium Sociale* (Cologne: Westdeutscher Verlag, 1964), 690-704.

Young, F. W., "Location and Reputation in an Inter-Village Network," *Human Organization,* 23:1 (1964), 36-41.

Yuan, D. Y., "The Rural-Urban Continuum: A Case Study of Taiwan," *Rural Sociology,* 29:3 (1964), 247-60.

11. Migrancy and Migrants and the Urban System

Abou El Ezz, M. S., "Some Aspects of Migration in Cairo," *Bulletin de la Société de Géographie d'Egypte,* 32 (1959), 121-41.

Abu-Lughod, J., "Migrant Adjustment to City Life: The Egyptian Case," *American Journal of Sociology,* 67:1 (1961-62), 22-32.

Balan, J., "Migrant-Native Socio-Economic Differences in Latin American Cities: A Structural Analysis," *Latin America Research Review,* 4:1 (1969), 3-29. (Commentaries: 31-51.)

Banton, M., *West African City: A Study of Tribal Life in Freetown* (London: Oxford University Press, 1957).

Bock, E. W., and Iutaka, S., "Rural-Urban Migration and Social Mobility: The Controversy on Latin America," *Rural Sociology,* 34:3 (1969), 343-55.

Bradfield, S., "Some Occupational Aspects of Migration," *Economic Development and Cultural Change,* 14:1 (1965), 61-70.

Brandao-Copes, J. R., "Aspects of the Adjustment of Rural Migrants to Urban-Industrial Conditions in Sao Paulo, Brazil," in P. M. Hauser (ed.), *Urbanization in Latin America* (New York: UNESCO, 1961), 234-46.

Brody, E. B., "Migration and Adaptation: The Nature of the Problem," *American Behavioral Scientist,* 13:1 (1969), 5-13.

Browning, H. L., and Feindt, W., "Selectivity of Migrants in a Metropolis in a Developing Country: A Mexican Case Study," *Demography,* 6:4 (1969), 347-57.

Browning, H. L., and Waltrant, F., "The Social and Economic Context of Migration to Monterrey, Mexico," in Rabinovits, F. F., and Trueblood, F. M. (eds.), *Latin American Urban Research,* v. 1 (Beverly Hills: Sage Publications, 1971), 45-70.

Butterworth, D. S., "A Study of the Urbanization Process among Mixtec Migrants from Tilantengo in Mexico City," *America Indigena,* 22:3 (1962), 257-74.

Caldwell, J. C., "Determinants of Rural-Urban Migration in Ghana," *Population Studies,* 22:3 (1968), 361-77.

Chatterjee, M., "Stabilization of Immigrants in Indian Towns: The Case of Bombay," *Sociological Bulletin* (India), 20:2 (1971), 145-58.

Chauhan, D. S., *Trends of Urbanization in Agra* (New York: Allied Publishers, 1966), 285-392.

Cohen, A., "The Migratory Process: Settlers and Strangers," in *Custom and Politics in Urban Africa: A Study of Hausa Migrants in Yoruba Towns* (London: Routledge & Kegan Paul, 1969), 29-50.

Doughty, P. L., "Peruvian Migrant Identity in the Urban Milieu," in T. Weaver and D. White (eds.), *The Anthropology of Urban Environments,* Washington, D.C., Society for Applied Anthropology, Monograph 11 (1972), 39-50.

Ducoff, L. J., "The Migrant Population of a Metropolitan Area in a Developing Country: A Preliminary Report on a Case Study of San Salvador," in *International Population Conference,* v. 1 (New York: Union Internationale pour l'Etude Scientifique de la Population, 1963), 428-35.

Dwyer, D. J., "The Problem of In-Migration and Squatter Settlement in Asian Cities: Two Case Studies, Manila and Victoria-Kowloon," *Asian Studies,* 2:2 (1964), 145-69.

Eames, E., "Some Aspects of Urban Migration from a Village in North Central India," *Eastern Anthropologist,* 8:1 (1954), 13-26.

———, "Urbanization and Rural-Urban Migration in India," *Population Review,* 9:1-2 (1965), 38-47.

Eisenstadt, S. N., "Analysis of Patterns of Immigration and Absorption of Immigrants," *Population Studies,* 7:2 (1953), 167-80.

Elizaga, J. C., "Internal Migrations in Latin America," *Milbank Memorial Fund Quarterly,* 43:4 (1965), 144-61.

———, "A Study of Migration to Greater Santiago," *Demography,* 3:2 (1966), 352-77.

Elkan, W., "Circular Migration and the Growth of Towns in East Africa," *International Labour Review,* 96:6 (1967), 581-89.

Flinn, W. L., "The Process of Migration to a Shantytown in Bogota, Colombia," *Inter-American Economic Affairs,* 22:2 (1968), 77-88.

———, "Rural-To-Urban Migration: A Colombian Case," Land Tenure Center, Research Publication 19 (Madison: University of Wisconsin, n.d. about 1966), mimeo, 42 pp.

Geiser, P., "Some Differential Factors Affecting Population Movement: The Nubian Case," *Human Organization,* 26:3 (1967), 164-77.

Gist, N. P., "Selective Migration in South India," *Sociological Bulletin,* 4:2 (1955), 147-60.

Graham, J. D., "A Case Study of Migrant Labor in Tanzania," *African Studies Review,* 13:1 (1970), 23-33.

Gugler, J., "The Impact of Labour Migration on Society and Economy in Sub-Saharan Africa: Empirical Findings and Theoretical Considerations," *African Social Research,* 6 (Dec. 1968), 463-86.

———, "On the Theory of Rural-Urban Migration: The Case of Sub-Saharan

Africa," in Jackson, J. A. (ed.), *Migration,* Sociological Studies No. 2 (Cambridge, Eng.: Cambridge University Press, 1969), 134-55.

Hanna, W. J., "The Study of Urban Africa," *Journal of Local Administration Overseas,* 5:2 (1966), 124-27.

Hanna, W. J., and Hanna, J. L., *Urban Dynamics in Black Africa: An Interdisciplinary Approach* (Chicago: Aldine-Atherton, 1971), 27-47.

Harrison, R. S., "Migrants in the City of Tripoli, Libya," *Geographical Review,* 57:3 (1967), 397-423.

Harvey, M., "Implications of Migration to Freetown: A Study of the Relationship Between Migrants, Housing and Occupation," *Civilisations,* 18:2 (1968), 247-69.

Herrick, B., "Urbanization and Urban Migration in Latin America: An Economist's View," in Rabinovits, F. F., and Trueblood, F. M. (eds.), *Latin American Urban Research,* v. 1 (Beverly Hills: Sage Publications, 1971), 71-81.

Hickman, J. M., and Brown, J., "Adaptation of Aymara and Quechua to the Bicultural Social Context of Bolivian Mines," *Human Organization,* 30:4 (1971), 359-66.

Hill, G. W., "The Adjustment of Rural Migrants in an Urban Venezuelan Community," *Migration News,* 12:2 (1963), 1-6; 12:3 (1963), 7-14.

Hitchcock, N. E., and Oram, N. D., "Rabia Camp: A Port Moresby Migrant Settlement," *New Guinea Research Bulletin,* 14 (Jan. 1967), 126 pp.

Humphrey, N. D., "The Cultural Background of the Mexican Immigrant," *Rural Sociology,* 13:3 (1948), 239-55.

Hutchison, B., "The Migrant Population of Urban Brazil," *America Latina,* 6:2 (1963), 41-72.

Imoagene, S. O., "Mechanisms of Immigrant Adjustment in a West African Urban Community," *The Nigerian Journal of Economic and Social Studies,* 9:1 (1967), 51-66.

Jürgens, H. W., Tracey, K. A., and Mitchell, P. K., "Internal Migration in Liberia," *Bulletin of the Sierra Leone Geographical Association,* 10 (1966), 39-59.

Khuri, F. I., "A Comparative Study of Migration Patterns in Two Lebanese Villages," *Human Organization,* 26:4 (1967), 206-13.

Lee, S. E., "A Theory of Migration," *Demography,* 3:1 (1965), 47-57.

Lewis, O., "Urbanization without Breakdown: A Case Study," *Scientific Monthly,* 75:1 (1952), 31-41.

Little, K., *West African Urbanization: A Study of Voluntary Associations in Social Change* (Cambridge, Eng.: Cambridge University Press, 1965), 85-102.

MacDonald, L. D., and MacDonald, J. S., "Motives and Objectives of Migration: Selective Migration and Preferences toward Rural and Urban Life," *Social and Economic Studies,* 17:4 (1968), 417-34.

Mangalam, J. J., and Schwarzweller, H. K., "General Theory in the Study of Migration: Current Needs and Difficulties," *International Migration Review,* 3:1 (1968), 3-18.

———, "Some Theoretical Guidelines Toward a Sociology of Migration," *International Migration Review,* 4:2 (1970), 5-21.

Mangin, W. (ed.), *Peasants in Cities: Readings in the Anthropology of Urbanization* (Boston: Hougton Mifflin, 1970).

Mayer, P., "Migrancy and the Study of Africans in Towns," *American Anthropologist,* 64:3 (1962), 576-92.

Mitchell, J. C., "The Causes of Labour Migration," *Bulletin Inter-African Labour Institute,* 6:1 (1959), 12-46.

———, "Structural Plurality, Urbanization and Labour Circulation in Southern Rhodesia," in *Migration,* Jackson, J. A. (ed.), Sociological Studies No. 2 (Cambridge, Eng.: Cambridge University Press, 1969), 156-80.

Okali, C., "A Study of Migration," *Bulletin of Rural Economics and Sociology,* 1:1 (1964), 87-88.

Oram, N. D., "The Hula in Port Moresby," *Oceania,* 39:1 (1968), 1-35.

Osoba, S. O., "The Phenomenon of Labour Migration in the Era of British Colonial Rule: A Neglected Aspect of Nigeria's Social History," *Journal of the Historical Society of Nigeria,* 4:4 (1969), 515-38.

Padilla, E., *Up from Puerto Rico* (New York: Columbia University Press, 1958).

Peterson, W., "A General Typology of Migration," *American Sociological Review,* 23:3 (1958), 256-66.

Phillips, D. G., "Rural-to-Urban Migration in Iraq," *Economic Development and Cultural Change,* 7:4 (1959), 405-21.

Pool, I., "Maoris in Auckland: A Population Study," *Journal of the Polynesian Society,* 70:1 (1961), 43-66.

Prabhu, P., "Social Effects of Urbanization on Industrial Workers in Bombay," *Sociological Bulletin,* 5:2 (1956), 127-43.

Prothero, R. M., "Migrant Labour in West Africa," *Journal of Local Administration Overseas,* 1:3 (1962), 149-55.

———, "Migrants," in R. M. Prothero (ed.), *Migrants and Malaria in Africa* (Pittsburgh: University of Pittsburgh Press, 1965), 25-46.

———, "Perspective on Migration," in *The Year Book of World Affairs, 1966* (London: Stevens, 1966), 169-85.

Rehfisch, F., "A Study of Some Southern Migrants in Omdurman," *Sudan Notes and Records,* 43 (1962), 50-104.

Rempel, H., "The Rural-to-Urban Migrant in Kenya," *African Urban Notes,* 6:1 (1971), 53-72.

Schultz, T. P., "Rural-Urban Migration in Colombia," *Review of Economics and Statistics,* 53 (1971), 157-63.

Senior, C., "Migration as a Process and the Migrant as a Person," *Population Review,* 6:1 (1962), 30-41.

Shannon, L. W., and Shannon, H., "The Assimilation of Migrants to Cities: Anthropological and Sociological Contributions," in L. F. Schnore and H. Fagin (eds.), *Urban Research and Policy Planning,* v. 1 (Beverly Hills: Sage Publications, 1967), 49-75.

Sternstein, L., "A First Study of Migration in Greater Bangkok Metropolitan Area," *Pacific Viewpoint,* 12:1 (1971), 41-67.

Tannous, A. I., "Emigration: A Force of Social Change in an Arab Village," *Rural Sociology*, 7:1 (1942), 62-74.

van Kemper, R., "Rural-Urban Migration in Latin America: A Framework for the Comparative Analysis of Geographical and Temporal Patterns," *International Migration Review*, 5:1 (1970), 36-47.

Warriner, D., "Problems of Rural-Urban Migration: Some Suggestions for Investigation," *International Labour Review*, 101:5 (1970), 441-51.

Whetten, W. L., and Burnright, R. G., "Internal Migration in Mexico," *Rural Sociology*, 21:2 (1956), 140-51.

Wilkenning, E. A., "Comparison of Migrants in two Rural and an Urban Area of Central Brazil," Research Publication No. 35, Land Tenure Center, University of Wisconsin, November 1968, 36. Mimeo.

Wood, E. W., "The Implications of Migrant Labour for Urban Social Systems in Africa," *Cahiers d'Etudes Africaines*, 8:29 (1968), 5-31.

Zachariah, K. C., "Bombay Migration Study: A Pilot Analysis of Migration to an Asian Metropolis," *Demography*, 3:2 (1966), 378-92.

12. "Townsman or Tribesman"

Adams, R. N., "Rural Labor," in J. J. Johnson (ed.), *Continuity and Change in Latin America* (Stanford: Stanford University Press, 1964), 49-78.

Balan, J., "Are Farmers' Sons Handicapped in the City," *Rural Sociology*, 33:2 (1968), 160-74.

Bopegamage, A., "Village Within a Metropolitan Area," *Sociological Bulletin*, 5:2 (1956), 102-10.

Butterworth, D., "Two Small Groups: A Comparison of Migrants and Non-Migrants in Mexico City," *Urban Anthropology*, 1:1 (1972), 29-50.

Harries-Jones, P., "Tribes in Town," in W. V. Brelsford (ed.), *The Tribes of Zambia* (Lusaka: Government Printer, 1968), 2nd ed., 124-46.

Mair, L., "New Townsmen," in *New Nations* (London: Weidenfeld and Nicholson, 1963), 128-59.

Mangin, W. (ed.), *Peasants in Cities: Readings in the Anthropology of Urbanization* (Boston: Houghton Mifflin, 1970).

Mayer, P., *Townsmen or Tribesmen: Conservatism and the Process of Urbanization in a South African City* (Cape Town: Oxford University Press, 1961).

———, "Labour Migrancy and the Social Network," in J. F. Holeman *et al.* (eds.), *Problems of Transition* (Pietermaritzburg: Natal University Press, 1962), 21-34.

Powdermaker, H., *Copper Town: Changing Africa* (New York: Harper and Row, 1962), 291-305.

Reader, D. H., "Detribalization in South Africa," *Scientific South Africa*, 3:5 (1966), 29-31.

———, "Tribalism in South Africa," *Scientific South Africa*, 3:4 (1966), 15-18.

Richards, A. I., "Multi-Tribalism in African Urban Areas," in *Urbanization in*

African Social Change (Centre of African Studies: University of Edinburgh, 1963), 43-51.

Wilson, M., and Mafeje, A., *Langa: A Study of Social Groups in an African Township* (Cape Town: Oxford University Press, 1963), 47-73.

13. Patterns of Urban Life: Ethnicity and Social Organization

Banton, M., *West African City* (London: Oxford University Press, 1957), 96-120.

Bates, R. H., "Approaches to the Study of Ethnicity," *Cahiers d'Etudes Africaines,* 11:44 (1971), 546-61.

Bernus, Suzanne, "Particularismes ethniques en milieu urbain: l'exemple de Niamey," *Université de Paris Mémoires de l'Institut d'Ethnologie,* 1 (1963), 262.

Betts, R., "The Establishment of the Medina in Dakar, Senegal, 1914," *Africa,* 41:2 (1971), 143-52.

Broom, L., "Urbanization and the Plural Society," *Annals of the New York Academy of Sciences,* 83:Art. 5 (1960), 880-86.

Bruner, E. M., "Urbanization and Ethnic Identity in North Sumatra," *American Anthropologist,* 63:3 (1961), 508-21.

Clarke, C., "Caste among Hindus in a Town in Trinidad: San Fernando," in B. M. Schwartz (ed.), *Caste in Overseas Indian Communities* (San Francisco: Chandler, 1967), 165-99.

Cohen, A., *Custom and Politics in Urban Africa: A Study of Hausa Migrants in Yoruba Towns* (London: Routledge and Kegan Paul, 1969).

Crissman, L. W., "The Segmentary Structure of Urban Overseas Chinese Communities," *Man,* 2:2 (1967), 185-204.

Crowley, D. H., "A Katangese Territorial Post in Transition," *Journal of Asian and African Studies,* 1:3 (1966), 177-82.

Davenport, R., "African Townsmen? South African Natives (Urban Areas) Legislation through the Years," *African Affairs,* 68:271 (1969), 95-109.

Du Toit, B. M., "The Isongoma: An Adaptive Agent Among Urban Zulu," *Anthropological Quarterly,* 44:2 (1971), 51-65.

Epstein, A. L., *Politics in an Urban African Community* (Manchester: Manchester University Press, 1958), 224-40.

Fallers, L. A., "Introduction," in L. A. Fallers (ed.), *Immigrants and Associations* (The Hague: Mouton, 1967), 7-16.

Freedman, M., "Immigrants and Associations: Chinese in Nineteenth Century Singapore," *Comparative Studies in Society and History,* 3:1 (1960), 25-48.

Gillin, J., "Race Relations Without Conflict: A Guatemalan Town," *American Journal of Sociology,* 53:5 (1948), 337-43.

Gist, N. P., "Caste Differentials in South India," *American Sociological Review,* 19:2 (1954), 126-37.

Gluckman, M., "Tribalism in Modern British Central Africa," *Cahiers d'Etudes Africaines,* 1 (Jan. 1960), 55-70.

Gussman, B. W., *Out in the Midday Sun* (London: Oxford University Press, 1963).

Hanna, W. J., and Hanna, J. L., *Urban Dynamics in Black Africa: An Interdisciplinary Approach* (Chicago: Aldine-Atherton, 1971), 105-43.

Hassan, R., "Interethnic Marriage in Singapore: A Sociological Analysis," *Sociology and Social Research,* 55:3 (1971), 305-23.

Hodder, B. W., "Racial Groupings in Singapore," *Malayan Journal of Tropical Geography,* 1 (1953), 25-36.

Hurt, W. R., "The Urbanization of Yanktown Indians," *Human Organization,* 20:4 (1962), 226-31.

Irelan, L. M., *et al.*, "Ethnicity, Poverty, and Selected Attitudes: A Test of the 'Culture of Poverty' Hypothesis," *Social Forces,* 47:4 (1969), 405-13.

Khuri, F. I., "The African-Lebanese Mulattos of West Africa: A Racial Frontier," *Anthropological Quarterly,* 41:2 (1968), 90-101.

Kilson, M. D. de B., "The Ga and Non-Ga Populations of Central Accra," *Ghana Journal of Sociology,* 2:2 (1966), 23-28.

———, "Variations in Ga Culture in Central Accra," *Ghana Journal of Sociology,* 3:1 (1967), 33-54.

Knowlton, C. S., "A Study of Social Mobility Among the Syrian and Lebanese Community of Sao Paulo," *The Rocky Mountain Social Science Journal,* 2:2 (1965), 174-92.

Kuper, L., "Structural Discontinuities in African Towns: Some Aspects of Racial Pluralism," in H. Miner (ed.), *The City in Modern Africa* (New York: Praeger, 1967), 127-50.

Lambert, R. D., *Workers, Factories and Social Change in India* (Princeton, N.J.: Princeton University Press, 1963), 141-68.

Lever, H., "Ethnic Preferences of White Residents in Johannesburg," *Sociology and Social Research,* 52:2 (1968), 157-73.

Little, K., "Some Urban Patterns of Marriage and Domesticity in West Africa," *Sociological Review,* 7:1 (1959), 65-82.

Mitchell, J. C., "The Kalela Dance," *Rhodes-Livingstone Papers,* 27 (1956).

———, *Tribalism and the Plural Society: An Inaugural Lecture* (London: Oxford University Press, 1960).

Mitchell, J. C. (ed.), *Social Networks in Urban Situations: Analyses of Personal Relationships in Central African Towns* (Manchester: Manchester University Press, 1969).

Moench, R., "A Preliminary Report on Chinese Social and Economic Organization in the Society Islands," in A. Spoehr (ed.), *Pacific Port Towns and Cities* (Honolulu: Bishop Museum Press, 1963), 75-89.

Morrill, W. T., "Socio-Cultural Adaptation in a West-African Lebanese Community," *Anthropological Quarterly,* 35:4 (1962), 143-57.

———, "Immigrants and Associations: The Ibo in Twentieth Century Calabar," *Comparative Studies in Society and History,* 4:4 (1963), 424-48.

Neville, W., "Singapore: Ethnic Diversity and its Implications," *Annals of the Association of American Geographers,* 56:2 (1966), 236-53.

Oram, N. D., "Social and Economic Relationships in a Port Moresby Canoe

Settlement," *New Guinea Research Bulletin*, 18 (1967), 59 pp.

Paden, J. N., "Urban Pluralism, Integration, and Adaptation of Communal Identity in Kano, Nigeria," in Cohen, R. and Middleton, J. (eds.), *From Tribe to Nation in Africa* (Scranton, Pa.: Chandler, 1970), 242-70.

Parkin, D. J., "Tribe as Fact and Fiction in an East African City [Kampala]," in P. H. Gulliver (ed.), *Tradition and Transition in East Africa* (London: Routledge and Kegan Paul, 1969), 273-96.

Plotnicov, L., "Who Owns Jos? Ethnic Ideology in Nigerian Urban Politics," *Urban Anthropology*, 1:1 (1972), 1-13.

Proudfoot, L., "Mosque Building and Tribal Separatism in Freetown East," *Africa*, 29:4 (1959), 405-15.

Rabushka, A., "Integration in Urban Malaya: Ethnic Attitudes among Malays and Chinese," *Journal of Asian and African Studies*, 6:2 (1971), 91-107.

Ratha, S. N., "Caste and Occupation in two Periurban Assamese Villages," *The Eastern Anthropologist*, 21:2 (1968), 155-66.

Rosen, L., "Muslim-Jewish Relations in a Moroccan City," *International Journal of Middle East Studies*, 3:4 (1972), 435-49.

Rosenthal, D. B., "Deference and Friendship Patterns in Two Indian Municipal Councils," *Social Forces*, 45:2 (1966), 178-92.

Sakumoto, R. E., "Residential Segregation in a Multi-Ethnic Metropolis: Honolulu," in S. Greer *et al.* (eds.), *The New Urbanization* (New York: St. Martin's Press, 1968), 169-78.

Seibel, H. D., "Some Aspects of Inter-Ethnic Relations in Nigeria," *The Nigerian Journal of Economic and Social Studies*, 9:2 (1967), 217-28.

Skinner, G. W., *Leadership and Power in the Chinese Community of Thailand* (Ithaca: Cornell University Press, 1958). (Monograph of the Association of Asian Studies, 3.)

Topley, M., "The Emergence of Social Functions of Chinese Religious Associations in Singapore," *Comparative Studies in Society and History*, 3:3 (1961), 289-314.

Welsh, D., "The Growth of Towns" in Wilson, M., and Thompson, C. (eds.), *The Oxford History of South Africa (South Africa 1870-1966)*, v. 2 (Oxford: Clarendon Press, 1971), 172-243.

Whitten, N. E., *Class, Kinship and Power in an Ecuadorian Town* (Stanford: Stanford University Press, 1965), 89-113.

Willmott, W. E., "Congregations and Associations: The Political Structure of the Chinese Community in Phnom-Penh, Cambodia," *Comparative Studies in Society and History*, 11:3 (1969), 282-301.

Winder, R. B., "The Lebanese in West Africa," *Comparative Studies in Society and History*, 4:3 (1962), 296-333.

14. Urbanism, Social Structure and Social Relationships

Anderson, H., "The Urban Way of Life," *International Journal of Comparative Sociology*, 3:2 (1962), 175-88.

Banton, M., "The Restructuring of Social Relationships," in A. W. Southall (ed.), *Social Change in Modern Africa* (London: Oxford University Press, 1961), 113-25.

———, "Social Alignment and Identity in a West African City," in H. Kuper (ed.), *Urbanization and Migration in West Africa* (Berkeley: University of California Press, 1965), 131-47.

Berreman, G. D., "Social Categories and Social Interaction in Urban India," *American Anthropologist,* 74:3 (1972), 567-86.

Epstein, A. L., "Gossip, Norms and Social Network," in J. C. Mitchell (ed.), *Social Networks in Urban Situations: Analysis of Personal Relationships in Central African Towns* (Manchester: Manchester University Press, 1969), 117-27.

Gould, H. A., "Some Preliminary Observations Concerning the Anthropology of Industrialization," *Eastern Anthropologist,* 14:1 (1961), 34-47.

Levy, M., "Some Sources of the Vulnerability of the Structures of Relatively Nonindustrialized Societies to Those of Highly Industrialized Societies," in B. F. Hoselitz (ed.), *The Progress of Underdeveloped Areas* (Chicago: University of Chicago Press, 1952), 113-25.

Mitchell, J. C., "Types of Urban Social Relationships," in R. Apthorpe (ed.), *Present Inter-Relations in Central Africa Rural and Urban Life* (Lusaka: Rhodes-Livingstone Institute, 1958), 84-87.

Southall, A. W., "Introductory Summary," in A. W. Southall (ed.), *Social Change in Modern Africa* (London: Oxford University Press, 1961), 31-45 and 217-30.

Vatuk, S., "Reference, Address, and Fictive Kinship in Urban North India," *Ethnology,* 8:3 (1969), 255-72.

Wirth, L., "Urbanism as a Way of Life," *American Journal of Sociology,* 44:1 (1938), 1-24.

15. The Basis of Urban Structure: Kinship-Based Networks

Adams, B. N., "Kinship Systems and Adaptation to Modernization," *Studies in Comparative International Development,* 4:3 (1968-69), 47-60.

Aldous, J., "Urbanization, the Extended Family and Kinship Ties in West Africa," *Social Forces,* 41:1 (1962), 6-12.

Ames, M. M., "Class, Caste and Kinship in an Industrial City of India," *Asia,* 15 (Summer 1969), 58-71.

Bettison, D. G., "Changes in the Composition and Status of Kin Groups in Nyasaland and Northern Rhodesia," in A. W. Southall (ed.), *Social Change in Modern Africa* (London: Oxford University Press, 1961), 273-85.

Boswell, D. M., "Personal Crises and the Mobilization of the Social Network," in J. C. Mitchell (ed.), *Social Networks in Urban Situations: Analysis of Personal Relationships in Central African Towns* (Manchester: Manchester University Press, 1969), 245-96.

Bruner, E. M., "Kinship Organization Among the Urban Batak of Sumatra," *Transactions of the New York Academy of Sciences,* 22 (1959), 118-25.

———, "Medan: The Role of Kinship in an Indonesian City," in A. Spoehr (ed.), *Pacific Port Towns and Cities* (Berkeley: University of California Press, 1963), 1-12.

Eames, E., "Corporate Groups and Indian Urbanization," *Anthropological Quarterly*, 43:3 (1970), 168-86.

Goode, J. G., "Latin American Urbanism and Corporate Groups," *Anthropological Quarterly*, 43:3 (1970), 146-67.

Gouellain, R., "Parenté et affinités ethniques dans l'écologie du 'Grand Quartier' de New-Bell, Duala," in A. W. Southall (ed.), *Social Change in Modern Africa* (London: Oxford University Press, 1961), 254-72.

Hunt, E., "The Meaning of Kinship in San Juan: Genealogical and Social Models," *Ethnology*, 8:1 (1969), 37-53.

Jitodai, T. T., "Migration and Kinship Contacts," *Pacific Sociological Review*, 6:2 (1968), 49-55.

Khuri, F. I., "Kinship, Emigration and Trade Partnership among the Lebanese of West Africa," *Africa*, 35:4 (1965), 385-95.

Oram, N. D., "Social and Economic Relationships in a Port Moresby Canoe Settlement," *New Guinea Research Bulletin*, 18 (July 1967), 59 pp.

Pearse, A., "Some Characteristics of Urbanization in the City of Rio de Janeiro," in P. M. Hauser (ed.), *Urbanization in Latin America* (Paris: UNESCO, 1961), 191-205.

Peattie, L. R., "The Kinship Network," in *The View from the Barrio* (Ann Arbor: University of Michigan Press, 1968), 40-53.

Schwab, W. B., "Urbanism, Corporate Groups and Culture Change in Africa below the Sahara," *Anthropological Quarterly*, 43:3 (1970), 187-214.

Service, E. R., and Service, H. S., *Tobati: Paraguayan Town* (Chicago: University of Chicago Press, 1954), 133-83.

Vatuk, S. J., "Trends in North Indian Urban Kinship: The 'Matrilateral Asymmetry' Hypothesis," *Southwestern Journal of Anthropology*, 27:3 (1971), 287-307.

Vogel, E., "Kinship Structure, Migration to the City, and Modernization," in R. Dore (ed.), *Aspects of Social Change in Modern Japan* (Princeton, N.J.: Princeton University Press, 1967), 91-111.

Whitten, N. E., *Class, Kinship and Power in an Ecuadorian Town* (Stanford: Stanford University Press, 1965), 114-47.

Wilson, M., and Mafeje, A., *Langa: A Study of Social Groups in an African Township* (Cape Town: Oxford University Press, 1963), 74-90.

Young, M., and Wilmott, P., *Family and Kinship in East London* (London: Penguin Books, 1962), 17-118.

16. The Basis of Urban Structure: Associations and Social Networks

Anderson, R. T., "Voluntary Associations in Hyderabad," *Anthropological Quarterly*, 37:4 (1964), 175-90.

Bates, R. H., "Trade Union Membership in the Coppermines of Zambia: A Test of Some Hypotheses," *Economic Development and Cultural Change*, 20:2 (1972), 280-98.

Bogdan, R., "Youth Clubs in a West African City," in P. Meadows and E. H.

Mizruchi (eds.), *Urbanism, Urbanization and Change: Comparative Perspectives* (Reading, Pa.: Addison-Wesley, 1969), 223-41.

Bopegamage, A., "Neighbourhood Relations in Indian Cities," *Sociological Bulletin,* 6:1 (1957), 34-43.

Chauhan, I. S., "Networks in a Small Town," *Journal of Social Research,* 10:1 (1967), 33-36.

Cheng, H., "The Network of Singapore Societies," *Journal of the South Seas Society,* 6 (1950), 10-12.

Dotson, F., "A Note on Participation in Voluntary Associations in a Mexican City," *American Sociological Review,* 18:4 (1953), 380-86.

Epstein, A. L., "The Network of Urban Social Organization," *Rhodes-Livingstone Journal,* 29 (June 1961), 29-62.

Gutkind, P. C. W., "African Urbanism, Mobility and the Social Network," *International Journal of Comparative Sociology,* 6:1 (1965), 48-60.

Hanna, W. J., and Hanna, J. L., *Urban Dynamics in Black Africa: An Interdisciplinary Approach* (Chicago: Aldine-Atherton, 1971), 145-65.

Henderson, R. N., "Generalized Cultures and Evolutionary Adaptability: A Comparison of Urban Efik and Ibo in Nigeria," *Ethnology,* 5:4 (1966), 365-91.

Jacobson, D., "Friendship and Mobility in the Development of an Urban Elite African Social System," *Southwestern Journal of Anthropology,* 24:2 (1968), 123-38.

Kapferer, B., "Norms and the Manipulation of Relationships in a Work Context," in J. C. Mitchell (ed.), *Social Networks in Urban Situations: Analysis of Personal Relationships in Central African Towns* (Manchester: Manchester University Press, 1969), 181-244.

Li, Yih-Yuan, "Chinese Voluntary Association and Leadership Structure in a Malayan Town," *Bulletin of the Institute of Ethnology,* 20 (1965), 1-45.

Little, K., "The Role of Voluntary Associations in West African Urbanization," *American Anthropologist,* 59:4 (1957), 579-96.

———, "Some Traditionally Based Forms of Mutual Aid in West African Urbanization," *Ethnology,* 1:2 (1962), 196-211.

———, "The Urban Role of Tribal Associations in West Africa," *African Studies,* 21:1 (1962), 1-9.

———, *West African Urbanization: A Study of Voluntary Associations in Social Change* (Cambridge, Eng.: Cambridge University Press, 1965).

———, "Voluntary Associations in Urban Life: A Case Study of Differential Adaptation," in M. Freedman (ed.), *Social Organization: Essays Presented to Raymond Firth* (London: Cass, 1967), 153-65.

Lukhero, M. B., "Tribalism in Urban Voluntary Associations," in A. A. Dubb (ed.), *The Multi-Tribal Society* (Lusaka: Rhodes-Livingstone Institute, 1962), 49-59.

Mangin, W., "The Role of Regional Associations in the Adaptation of the Rural Population in Peru," *Sociologus,* 9:1 (1959), 23-35.

Meillassoux, C., *Urbanization of an African Community: Voluntary Associations in Bamako* (Seattle: University of Washington Press, 1968).

Middleton, J., "Labour Migration and Associations in Africa: Two Case Studies," *Civilisations,* 19:1 (1969), 42-50.

Mitchell, J. C., "The Concept and Use of Social Networks," in J. C. Mitchell (ed.), *Social Networks in Urban Situations: Analysis of Personal Relationships in Central African Towns* (Manchester: Manchester University Press, 1969), 1-50.

Nash, M., *Machine Age Maya: The Industrialization of a Guatemalan Community* (Glencoe, Ill.: The Free Press, 1958), 82-91.

Parkins, D. J., "Some Ideas on the Concept of Neighbourhood in the Towns," Conference Proceedings (Kampala: East African Institute of Social Research, June 1963), 12 pp.

Pendleton, W. C., "Ethnic Group Identity Among Urban Africans in Windhoek, South West Africa," *African Urban Notes,* 5:1 (1970), 1-14.

Pons, V., *Stanleyville: An African Urban Community under Belgian Administration* (London: Oxford University Press, 1969), 127-73.

Rogler, L. H., "The Growth of an Action Group: The Case of a Puerto Rican Migrant Voluntary Association," *International Journal of Comparative Sociology,* 9:3-4 (1968), 223-34.

Suzuki, P., "Village Solidarity among Turkish Peasants Undergoing Urbanization," *Science,* 132:3431 (1960), 891-92.

Weightman, G. W., "Community Organization of Chinese Living in Manila," *Philippines Social Science and Humanities Review,* 19 (1954), 25-39.

Wheeldon, P. D., "The Operation of Voluntary Associations and Personal Networks in the Political Processes of an Inter-Ethnic Community," in J. C. Mitchell (ed.), *Social Networks in Urban Situations: Analysis of Personal Relationships in Central African Towns* (Manchester: Manchester University Press, 1969), 128-80.

17. Patterns of Urban Life: Social Stratification and Class Structure

Adams, R. N., "A Change from Caste to Class in a Peruvian Town," *Social Forces,* 31:3 (1953), 238-44.

Aronson, D. R., "Ijebu Yoruba Urban-Rural Relationships and Class Formation," *Canadian Journal of African Studies,* 5:3 (1971), 263-79.

Banton, M., "Role Congruence and Social Differentiation Under Urban Conditions," in A. Leeds (ed.), *Social Structure, Stratification and Mobility* (Washington: Pan-American Union, 1967), 177-200.

Beals, R. L., "Social Stratification in Latin America," *American Journal of Sociology,* 58:3 (1953), 327-39.

Buechler, H. C., "The Ritual Dimension of Rural-Urban Networks: The Fiesta System in the Northern Highlands of Bolivia," in W. Mangin (ed.), *Peasants in Cities: Readings in the Anthropology of Urbanization* (Boston: Houghton Mifflin, 1970), 62-71.

Chekki, D. A., "Social Stratification and Trends of Social Mobility in Modern India," *Sociologus,* 21:1 (1971), 146-63.

Comhaire-Sylvan, J. and Comhaire-Sylvan, S., "Urban Stratification in Haiti," *Social and Economic Studies,* 8:2 (1959), 179-89.

Davies, I., and De Miranda, S., "The Working Class in Latin America: Some Theoretical Problems," in R. Miliband and J. Saville (eds.), *The Socialist Register, 1967* (London: Merlin Press, 1967), 239-56.

Doughty, P. L., "Behind the Back of the City: 'Provincial' Life in Lima, Peru," in W. Mangin (ed.), *Peasants in Cities: Readings in the Anthropology of Urbanization* (Boston: Houghton Mifflin, 1970), 30-46.

Ellis, R. A., "Color and Class in a Jamaican Market Town," *Sociology and Social Research,* 41:4 (1957), 354-60.

Elmer, M. C., "The Growth of a Middle Class in Venezuela," *Social Science,* 38 (June 1963), 145-47.

El-Sayed El Bushra, "Occupational Classification of Sudanese Towns," *Sudan Notes and Records,* 50 (1969), 75-96.

Evers, H. D., "The Formation of a Social Class Structure: Urbanization, Bureaucratization and Social Mobility in Thailand," *American Sociological Review,* 31:4 (1966), 480-88.

Folan, W. J., "A Comment on Race, Class and Status Differences in Marida, Yucatan, Mexico," *Anthropologica,* 9:1 (1967), 43-50.

Fraenkel, M., *Tribe and Class in Monrovia* (London: Oxford University Press, 1964), 196-229.

Gamble, D. P., "Occupational Prestige in an Urban Community (Lunsar) in Sierra Leone," *Sierra Leone Studies,* 19 (July 1966), 98-108.

Glick, P. B., "Melanesian Mosaic: The Plural Community of Vila," in L. Plotnicov and A. Tuden (eds.), *Essays in Comparative Social Stratification* (Pittsburgh: University of Pittsburgh Press, 1970), 95-117.

Goldrich, D., Pratt, R. B., and Schuller, C. R., "The Political Integration of Lower Class Settlements in Chile and Peru," *Studies in Comparative International Development* (St. Louis: Washington University, Social Science Institute, 1967-68).

Hall, S. K., "The Manifestations and Perception of Social Class among an Urban African Group," in H. L. Watts (ed.), *Focus on Cities,* Proceedings of a Conference, Institute for Social Research, University of Natal, 1968 (Durban: Institute for Social Research, University of Natal, 1970), 262-70.

Harris, M., *Town and Country in Brazil* (New York: Columbia University Press, 1956), 96-146.

Hawthorn, H. B., and Hawthorn, A. E., "Stratification in a Latin American City," *Social Forces,* 27:1 (1948), 19-29.

Hayner, S., "Differential Social Change in a Mexican Town," *Social Forces,* 26:4 (1948), 381-90.

Heisler, H., "A Class of Target Proletarians," *Journal of Asian and African Studies,* 5:3 (1970), 161-75.

Hino, S., "Social Stratification in a Swahili Town," *Kyoto University African Studies,* 2 (1968), 51-74.

———, "The Occupational Differentiation of an African Town," *Kyoto University African Studies,* 2 (1968), 75-107.

Humphrey, N. D., "Social Stratification in a Mexican Town," *Southwestern Journal of Anthropology,* 5:2 (1949), 138-46.

Hutchison, B., "Class Self-Assessment in a Rio de Janeiro Population," *America Latina,* 6:1 (1963), 53-64.

Jacobs, M., Farzanegan, F., and Askenasy, A. R., "A Study of Key Communicators in Urban Thailand," *Social Forces,* 45:2 (1966), 192-99.

Jacobson, D., "Culture and Stratification Among Urban Africans," *Journal of Asian and African Studies,* 5:3 (1970), 176-83.

Kahl, J. A., "Social Stratification and Values in Metropoli and Provinces," *America Latina,* 8:1 (1965), 23-36.

Knowlton, C. S., "A Study of Social Mobility among the Syrian and Lebanese Community of Sao Paulo," *The Rocky Mountain Social Science Journal,* 2:2 (1965), 174-92.

Leeds, A., "Brazilian Careers and Social Structure: An Evolutionary Model and Case History," *American Anthropologist,* 66:6 (1964), 1321-47.

Lloyd, B. B., "Education and Family Life in the Development of Class Identification among the Yoruba," in P. C. Lloyd (ed.), *The New Elites of Tropical Africa* (London: Oxford University Press, 1966), 163-81.

McElrath, D., "Societal Scale and Social Differentiation: Accra, Ghana," in S. Greer *et al.* (eds.), *The New Urbanization* (New York: St. Martin's Press, 1968), 33-52.

Mitchell, J. C., "The African Middle Classes in British Central Africa," in *The Development of a Middle Class in Tropical and Sub-Tropical Countries* (Brussels: International Institute for Differing Civilizations, 1957), 222-32.

Mitchell, J. C., and Epstein, A. L., "Occupational Prestige and Social Status Among Urban Africans in Northern Rhodesia," *Africa,* 29:1 (1959), 22-40.

Nett, E. M., "The Servant Class in a Developing Country: Ecuador," *Journal of Inter-American Studies,* 8:3 (1966), 437-52.

Oberg, K., "Some Historical Aspects of the Conversion of Rural Classes to Urban Classes," in A. Leeds (ed.), *Social Structure, Stratification and Mobility* (Washington: Pan-American Union, 1967), 204-21.

Parathasarathy, V. S., "Caste in a South Indian Textile Mill," *Economic Weekly,* 10:33 (1958), 1083-86.

Ratinoff, L., "The New Urban Groups: The Middle Classes," in S. M. Lipset and A. Solari (eds.), *Elites in Latin America* (New York: Oxford University Press, 1967), 61-93.

Riessman, L., "Class, the City and Social Cohesion," *International Review of Community Development,* 7 (1961), 39-51.

Schwab, W. B., "Social Stratification in Gwelo," in A. W. Southall (ed.), *Social Change in Modern Africa* (London: Oxford University Press, 1961), 126-44.

Singh, B., *Urban Middle Class 'Climbers': A Study in Social Mobility,* Monograph No. 7 (Bombay: J. K. Institute of Sociology and Human Relations), 1958.

Straus, M. A., "Social Class and Farm-City Differences in Interaction with Kin in Relation to Societal Modernization," *Rural Sociology,* 34:4 (1969), 476-95.

Straus, M. A., and Winkelman, D., "Social Class, Fertility and Authority in Nuclear and Joint Households in Bombay," *Journal of Asian and African Studies,* 4:1 (1969), 61-74.

Taira, K., "Urban Poverty, Ragpickers and the 'Ants' Villa in Tokyo," *Economic Development and Cultural Change,* 17:2 (1969), 155-77.

Van Den Berghe, P. L., *Caneville: The Social Structure of a South African Town* (Middletown, Conn.: Wesleyan University Press, 1964), 151-96.

Vogel, E. F., *Japan's New Middle Class: The Salary Man and his Family in a Tokyo Suburb* (Berkeley: University of California Press, 1963).

Wagley, C., *Amazon Town: A Study of Man in the Tropics* (New York: Macmillan, 1963), 102-44.

Weightman, G. H., "Systems of Social Stratification in Three North Lebanese Towns," *Asian Studies,* 4:3 (1966), 491-99.

Weightman, G. H., and Rihani, Z., "Social Stratification and Adolescent Academic Performance in a Lebanese Town," *Comparative Education Review,* 11:2 (1967), 208-16.

Whiteford, A. H., *Two Cities of Latin America: A Comparative Description of Social Classes* (Beloit, Wis.: Beloit College, 1960).

Whitten, N. E., *Class, Kinship and Power in an Ecuadorian Town* (Stanford: Stanford University Press, 1965), 43-88.

Williamson, R. C., "Some Variables of Middle and Lower Class in Two Central American Cities," *Social Forces,* 41:2 (1962), 195-207.

———, "Social Class and Orientation to Change: Some Relevant Variables in a Bogota Sample," *Social Forces,* 46:3 (1968), 317-38.

Wilson, M., and Mafeje, A., *Langa: A Study of Social Groups in an African Township* (Cape Town: Oxford University Press, 1963), 137-52.

18. Patterns of Urban Life: Family Organization and Marriage Patterns

Ames, M. M., "Modernization and Social Structure: Family, Caste and Class in Jameshedpur," *Economic and Political Weekly* (Bombay), 4:28-30 (1969), 1217-24.

Brandel, M., "Urban *Lobolo* Attitudes: A Preliminary Report," *African Studies,* 17:1 (1958), 34-50.

Caldwell, J. C., "The Erosion of the Family: A Study of the Fate of the Family in Ghana," *Population Studies,* 20:1 (1966), 5-26.

Clement, P., "Social Patterns of Urban Life," in D. Forde (ed.), *Social Implications of Industrialization and Urbanization in Africa South of the Sahara* (Paris: UNESCO, 1956), 368-438.

Clignet, R., "Urbanization and Family Structure in the Ivory Coast," *Comparative Studies in Society and History,* 8:4 (1966), 385-401.

Cohen, A., "The Migratory Process: Prostitutes and Housewives," in *Custom and Politics in Urban Africa: A Study of Hausa Migrants in Yoruba Towns* (London: Routledge & Kegan Paul, 1969), 51-70.

Desai, I. P., *Some Aspects of Family in Muhuva: A Sociological Study of Jointness in a Small Town* (Bombay: Asia Publishing House, 1964).

Frazier, E. F., "The Negro Family in Bahia, Brazil," *American Sociological Review,* 7:4 (1942), 465-78.

Freed, S. A., and Freed R. S., "Urbanization and Family Types in a North Indian Village," *Southwestern Journal of Anthropology,* 25:4 (1969), 342-59.

Freedman, W., *Chinese Family and Marriage in Singapore* (London: H.M.S.O., 1957).

Gamble, D. P., "The Temne Family in a Modern Town (Lunsar) in Sierra Leone," *Africa,* 33:3 (1963), 209-25.

Giel, R., and Van Luijk, J. N., "Patterns of Marriage in a Roadside Town in Southwestern Ethiopia," *Journal of Ethiopian Studies,* 6:2 (1968), 61-69.

Goode, W. J., "Industrialization and Family Change," in B. F. Hoselitz and W. E. Moore (eds.), *Industrialization and Society* (Paris: UNESCO-Mouton, 1963), 237-55.

Gutkind, P. C. W., "African Urban Family Life and the Urban System," *Journal of Asian and African Studies,* 1:1 (1966), 35-42.

Hammel, E., "The Family Cycle in a Peruvian Slum and Village," *American Anthropologist,* 63:5 (1961), 989-1006.

Harris, M., *Town and Country in Brazil* (New York: Columbia University Press, 1956), 147-78.

Hayner, H. S., "Notes on the Changing Mexican Family," *American Journal of Sociology,* 7:4 (1942), 489-97.

Izzett, A., "Family Life Among the Yoruba, in Lagos, Nigeria," in A. W. Southall (ed.), *Social Change in Modern Africa* (London: Oxford University Press, 1961), 305-15.

Jacobson, H. E., "Urbanization and Family Ties: A Problem in the Analysis of Change," *Journal of Asian and African Studies,* 5:4 (1970), 302-7.

Kapadia, K. M., "Rural Family Patterns: A Study in Urban-Rural Relations," *Sociological Bulletin,* 5:2 (1956), 111-26.

———, "The Family in Transition," *Sociological Bulletin,* 8:2 (1959), 68-99.

Kubat, D., and Bosco, S. E., "Marital Status and Ideology of the Family Size: Case of Young Men in Urban Brazil," *America Latina,* 12:2 (1969), 17-34.

Lee, M. Y., Kwon, T. H., and Kim, C. K., "Family-Size Value in a Korean Middle Town, Ichon Eup," *Journal of Marriage and the Family,* 30:2 (1968), 329-37.

Levin, R., "Marriage in Langa Location," *Communications from the School of African Studies* (University of Cape Town), 17 (Sept. 1947).

Lewis, O., "Urbanization without Breakdown: A Case Study," *The Scientific Monthly,* 75:1 (1952), 31-41.

———, *Five Families* (New York: Basic Books, 1959). (1962 edition by Wiley.)

———, "Mother and Son in a Puerto Rican Slum: Felicita, Part I," *Harper's Magazine,* 231:1387 (1965), 71-84; "Portrait of Gabriel: A Puerto Rican Family in San Juan, Part II," 232:1388 (1966), 54-59.

Marris, P., *Family and Social Change in an African City* (London: Routledge & Kegan Paul, 1961).

Mazuoka, J., "Urbanization and the Family in Japan," *Sociology and Social Research,* 32:1 (1947), 535-39.

Morrison, M. J., "Family Types in Badlapur," *Sociological Bulletin,* 8:2 (1958), 45-56.

Nash, M., *Machine Age Maya: The Industrialization of a Guatemalan Community* (Glencoe, Ill.: The Free Press, 1958), 40-59.

Norbeck, E., *Changing Japan* (New York: Holt, Reinhart and Winston, 1965), 57-79.

Okraku, I. O., "The Family Life-Cycle and Residential Mobility in Puerto Rico," *Sociology and Social Research,* 55:3 (1971), 324-40.

Parkin, D. J., "Types of Urban African Marriage in Kampala (Uganda)," *Africa,* 36:3 (1966), 269-85.

Pauw, B. A., *The Second Generation: A Study of the Family Among Urbanized Bantu in East London* (Cape Town: Oxford University Press, 1963).

Pethe, V. P., "Life Cycle of Families in an Urban Community," *Sociological Bulletin,* 12:1 (1963), 39-46.

Powdermaker, H., *Copper Town: Changing Africa* (New York: Harper and Row, 1962), 151-219.

Roberts, B., "The Social Organization of Low-Income Families," in I. L. Horowitz (ed.), *Masses in Latin America* (New York: Oxford University Press, 1970), 345-82.

Rosen, B. C., and Berlinck, M. T., "Modernization and Family Structure in the Region of Sao Paulo, Brazil," *America Latina,* 11:3 (1968), 75-96.

Ross, A. D., *The Hindu Family in Its Urban Setting* (Toronto: University of Toronto Press, 1961).

Safa, H. I., "From Shanty Town to Public Housing: A Comparison of Family Structure in Two Urban Neighborhoods in Puerto Rico," *Caribbean Studies,* 4:1 (1964), 3-12.

Singer, M., "The Indian Joint Family in Modern Industry," in M. Singer and B. S. Cohen (eds.), *Structure and Changes in Indian Society* (New York: Viking Fund Publications in Anthropology No. 47, 1968), 423-52.

Sjoberg, G., "Familian Organization in the Pre-Industrial City," *Journal of Marriage and Family Living,* 18:1 (1956), 30-36.

Straus, J. H., and Straus, M. A., "Family Roles and Sex Differences in Creativity of Children in Bombay and Minneapolis," *Journal of Marriage and the Family,* 30:1 (1968), 46-53.

Straus, M. A., and Winkelmann, D., "Social Class, Fertility and Authority in Nuclear and Joint Households in Bombay," *Journal of Asian and African Studies,* 4:1 (1969), 61-74.

United Nations Bureau of Social Affairs, "Effects of Urbanization on Family Life in the ECAFE Region," in P. M. Hauser (ed.), *Urbanization in Asia and the Far East* (Calcutta: UNESCO, 1958), 209-29.

Wagley, C., *Amazon Town: A Study of Man in the Tropics* (New York: Macmillan, 1963), 145-86.

19. Patterns of Urban Life: Economic Activities

Belshaw, C. S., "Port Moresby Canoe Traders," *Oceania,* 23:1 (1952), 26-39.

Bray, J., "The Craft Industries of a Traditional Yoruba Town [Iseyin]," *Transactions, Institute of British Geographers,* 46 (March 1969), 173-87.

Brookfield, H. C. (ed.), *Pacific Market-Places: A Collection of Essays* (Canberra: Australian National University Press, 1969).

Callaway, A., "From Traditional Crafts to Modern Industries," *Odu,* 2:1 (1965), 28-51.

Carson, W. H., "The Social History of an Egyptian Factory," *The Middle East Journal,* 11:4 (1957), 361-70.

Cohen, A., *Custom and Politics in Urban Africa: A Study of Hausa Migrants in Yoruba Towns* (London: Routledge & Kegan Paul, 1969).

Dawson, J., "Traditional Values and Work Efficiency in a West African Mine Labour Force," in *Urbanization in African Social Change* (Centre of African Studies: University of Edinburgh, 1963), 196-206.

De Young, M., "An African Emporium: The Addis Märkato," *Journal of Ethiopian Studies,* 5:2 (1967), 103-22.

Dhekney, B. R., *Hubli City: A Study of Urban Economic Life* (Dharwar, India: Karnatak University, 1959).

Dutt, A. K., "Daily Shopping in Calcutta," *Town Planning Review,* 37:3 (1966), 207-16.

Elkan, W., "The East African Trade in Wood Carvings," *Africa,* 28:4 (1958), 314-23.

Fong, N. K., Lian, T. C., and Wikkramatileke, R., "Three Farmers of Singapore: An Example of the Mechanics of Specialised Food Production in an Urban Unit," *Pacific Viewpoint,* 7:2 (1966), 169-97.

Geertz, C., "Social Change and Economic Modernization in Two Indonesian Towns: A Case in Point," in E. E. Hagen (ed.), *On the Theory of Social Change* (Homewood, Ill.: Dorsey Press, 1962), 385-407.

———, *Peddlers and Princes: Social Change and Economic Modernization in Two Indonesian Towns* (Chicago: University of Chicago Press, 1963).

Harris, M., *Town and Country in Brazil* (New York: Columbia University Press, 1956), 44-95.

Hazlehurst, L. W., *Entrepreneurship and the Merchant Castes in a Punjabi City,* Monograph No. 1 (Durham, N.C.: Duke University Press, 1966).

Isaac, B. L., "Business Failure in a Developing Town: Pendembu, Sierra Leone," *Human Organization,* 30:3 (1971), 288-94.

Jarrett, H. R., "Lunsar: A Study of an Iron Ore Mining Center in Sierra Leone," *Economic Geography,* 32:2 (1956), 153-61.

Koll, M., *Crafts and Cooperation in Western Nigeria: A Sociological Contribution to Indigenous Economics* (Freiburg: Arnold-Bergstraesser-Instituts, 1969), v. 27.

Le Cour Grandmaison, C., "Activities économiques des femmes dakaroises," *Africa,* 39:2 (1969), 138-52.

Lloyd, P. C., "Craft Organization in Yoruba Towns," *Africa,* 23:1 (1953), 30-44.

Marris, P., *Family and Social Change in an African City* (London: Routledge & Kegan Paul, 1961), 67-81.

———, "Individual Achievement and Family Ties: Some International Comparisons," *Journal of Marriage and the Family,* 29:4 (1967), 763-71.

Nash, M., *Machine Age Maya: The Industrialization of a Guatemalan Community* (Glencoe, Ill.: The Free Press, 1958), 21-32.

Nyirenda, A. A., "African Market Vendors in Lusaka, with a Note on the Recent Boycott," *Rhodes-Livingstone Journal,* 22 (1957), 31-63.

Nypan, A., *Market Trade: A Sample Survey of the Traders in Accra,* African Business Series, 2 (Legon, University College of Ghana, 1960).

———, "Market Trade in Accra," *The Economic Bulletin,* 4:3 (1960), 7-17.

Oguntoye, O. A., *Occupational Survey of Old Bussa* (Ibadan: Nigerian Institute of Social and Economic Research, 1968), 59 pp.

Oram, N. D., "Culture Change, Economic Development and Migration among the Hula," *Oceania,* 38:4 (1968), 243-75.

Oram, N. D., and Hitchcock, N. E., "Rabia Camp: A Port Moresby Migrant Settlement," *New Guinea Research Bulletin,* 14 (Jan. 1967), 3-43.

20. Patterns of Urban Life: The Political Dimension

Ajayi, J. F. A., "Political Organizations in West African Towns in the Nineteenth Century: The Lagos Example," in *Urbanization in African Social Change* (Centre of African Studies: University of Edinburgh, 1963), 166-73.

Ashraf, A., *The City Government of Calcutta: A Study of Inertia* (New York: Asia Publishing House, 1967).

Ballard, J., "The Porto Novo Incidents of 1923: Politics in the Colonial Era," *Odu,* 2:1 (1965), 52-75.

Bayer, D. L., "Urban Peru—Political Action as Sellout," *Trans-Action,* 7:1 (1969), 36, 47-54.

Boissevain, J., "Poverty and Politics in a Sicilian Agro-town," *International Archives of Ethnography,* 50 (1966), 198-236.

Bujra, A. S., *The Politics of Stratification: A Study of Political Change in a South Arabian Town* (London: Oxford University Press, 1969).

Bulmer-Thomas, I., "The Political Aspects of Migration from Country to Town —Nigeria" (Brussels: International Institute of Differing Civilizations, 1952), 476-84.

Burks, A. W., "The City, Political Change and Modernization in Japan," *International Journal of Comparative Sociology,* 7:1-2 (1966), 29-51.

Callaway, B., "Local Politics in Ho and Aba," *Canadian Journal of African Studies,* 4:1 (1970), 121-44.

Cantori, J., "Islam, Political Legitimacy and the Istiglal Party of Morocco," *African Urban Notes,* 5:1 (1970), 15-21.

Cohen, A., "Politics of the Kola Trade: Some Processes of Tribal Community Formation Among Migrants in West African Towns," *Africa,* 36:1 (1965), 18-36.

———, "The Ritualization of Political Authority" and "Political Ethnicity in Contemporary African Towns," in *Custom and Politics in Urban Africa: A Study of Hausa Migrants in Yoruba Towns* (London: Routledge & Kegan Paul, 1969), 161-82 and 183-214.

———, "The Politics of Ritual Secrecy," *Man,* 6:3 (1971), 427-48.

Cornelius, W. A., "Urbanization as an Agent in Latin American Political Instability: The Case of Mexico," *American Political Science Review,* 63:3 (1969), 833-57.

———, "The Political Sociology of Cityward Migration in Latin America: Toward Empirical Theory," in Rabinovits, F. and Trueblood, F. M. (eds.), *Latin American Urban Research,* v. 1 (Beverly Hills: Sage Publications, 1971), 95-147. (See also Bibliography, 125-47)

———, "A Structural Analysis of Urban Caciquismo in Mexico," *Urban Anthropology,* 1:2 (1972), 234-61.

Daland, R. T., "Urbanization Policy and Political Development in Latin America," *American Behavioral Scientist,* 12:5 (1969), 22-33.

Diaz, M. N., *Tonala: Conservatism, Responsibility and Authority in a Mexican Town* (Berkeley: University of California Press, 1966).

Dorjahn, V. R., "The Extent and Nature of Political Knowledge in a Sierra Leone Town," *Journal of Asian and African Studies,* 3:3-4 (1968), 203-15.

Epstein, A. L., *Politics in an Urban African Community* (Manchester: Manchester University Press, 1958).

Flinn, W. L., and Camacho, A., "The Correlates of Voter Participation in a Shantytown *Barrio* in Bogota, Colombia," *Inter-American Economic Affairs,* 22:4 (1969), 47-58.

Fox, R. G., *From Zamindar to Ballot Box* (Ithaca: Cornell University Press, 1968).

Goldrich, D., "Peasants' Sons in City Schools: An Inquiry into the Politics of Urbanization in Panama and Costa Rica," *Human Organization,* 23:4 (1964), 328-33.

Goldrich, D., Pratt, R. B., and Schuller, C. R., "The Political Integration of Lower-Class Urban Settlements in Chile and Peru," *Studies in Comparative International Development,* 3:1 (1967-68), 22 pp.

Gutkind, P. C. W., "African Urban Chiefs: Agents of Stability or Change in African Urban Life?" *Anthropologica,* 8:2 (1966), 249-68.

Hanna, W. J., and Hanna, J. L., "The Political Structure of Urban-Centred African Communities," in H. Miner (ed.), *The City in Modern Africa* (New York: Praeger, 1967), 151-84.

———, "Influence and Influentials in Two Urban-Centred African Communities," *Comparative Politics,* 2:1 (1969), 17-40.

———, *Urban Dynamics in Black Africa: An Interdisciplinary Approach* (Chicago: Aldine-Atherton, 1971), 167-201.

Harries-Jones, P., " 'Home-Boy' Ties and Political Organization in a Copperbelt Township," in J. C. Mitchell (ed.), *Social Networks in Urban Situations: Analysis of Personal Relationships in Central African Towns* (Manchester: Manchester University Press, 1969), 297-347.

Harris, M., *Town and Class in Brazil* (New York: Columbia University Press, 1956), 179-207.

Harroy, J. P., "The Political, Economic and Social Role of Urban Agglomerations in Countries of the Third World," *Civilisations,* 17:3 (1967), 166-85.

Havens, A. E., and Flinn, W. L., "The Power Structure in a Shantytown," in *Internal Colonialism and Structural Change in Colombia* (New York: Praeger, 1970), 93-107.

Horowitz, I. L., "Electoral Politics, Urbanization and Social Development in Latin America," *Urban Affairs Quarterly,* 2:3 (1967), 3-35.

Hoskins, G., "Community Power and Political Modernization: A Study of a Venezuelan City," unpublished Ph.D. thesis. Urbana: University of Illinois, 1967.

———, "Power Structure in a Venezuelan Town: The Case of San Cristobal," *International Journal of Comparative Sociology,* 9:3-4 (1968), 188-207.

Institute of African Government, Lincoln University, Conference on the Government of African Cities, April 18-19, 1968. (Note contributions by Mittlebeeler, Werlin, Jarvis, Adam, Hanna, and Skinner.)

Jain, S. P., "Leadership Pattern in a North Indian Community," *Sociology and Social Research,* 55:2 (1971), 170-80.

Jenkins, G., "An Informal Political Economy," in J. Butler and A. A. Castagno (eds.), *Transition in African Politics* (Boston University Papers on Africa) (New York: Praeger, 1967), 166-94.

Kapur, M., "Municipal Elections in a Small Punjab Town: A Case Study of Cbheharta Municipal Elections," *Quarterly Journal of Local Self-Government Institute* (Bombay), 36 (Oct. 1965), 157-76.

La Fontaine, Jean, *City Politics: A Study of Leopoldville, 1962-63* (Cambridge, Eng. Cambridge University Press, 1970).

Mangin, W., "Poverty and Politics in Cities of Latin America," in W. Bloomberg and H. Schmandt (eds.), *Power, Poverty and Urban Policy* (Beverly Hills: Sage Publications, 1968), 397-432.

Marr, D., "Political Attitudes and Activities of Young Urban Intellectuals in South Viet-Nam," *Asian Survey,* 6:5 (1966), 249-63.

Nehwati, F., "The Social and Communal Background of 'Zhii': The African Riots of Bulawayo, Southern Rhodesia in 1960," *African Affairs,* 69:276 (1970), 250-66.

Nelson, J. M., "Migrants, Urban Poverty, and Instability in Developing Nations," *Occasional Papers in International Affairs*, 22 (Cambridge: Harvard University, 1969), 81.

———, "The Urban Poor: Disruption or Political Integration in Third World Cities?" *World Politics*, 22:3 (1970), 393-414.

Nowak, T., and Snyder, K., "Urbanization and Clientelist Systems in the Philippines," *Philippine Journal of Public Administration*, 14:3 (1970), 259-75.

Ottenberg, S., "The Development of Local Government in a Nigerian Township," *Anthropologica*, 4:1 (1962), 121-61.

———, "The Social and Administrative History of a Nigerian Township," *International Journal of Comparative Sociology*, 7:1-2 (1966), 174-96.

Pachai, B., "An Outline of the History of Municipal Government at Cape Coast," *Transactions of the Historical Society of Ghana*, 8 (1965), 130-60.

Pratt, R. B., "Parties, Neighborhood Associations, and the Politicization of the Urban Poor in Latin America: An Exploratory Analysis," *Midwest Journal of Political Science*, 15:3 (1971), 495-524.

Pye, L. W., "The Political Implications of Urbanization and the Development Process," in G. Breese (ed.), *The City in Newly Developing Countries: Readings on Urbanism and Urbanization* (Englewood Cliffs, N.J.: Prentice-Hall, 1969), 401-6.

Ray, T. F., *The Politics of the Barrios of Venezuela* (Berkeley: University of California Press, 1969).

Roberts, B., "Politics in a Neighbourhood of Guatemala City," *Sociology*, 2 (May 1968), 185-203.

———, "Urban Poverty and Political Behavior in Guatemala," *Human Organization*, 29:1 (1970), 20-28.

Rogler, L. H., "To Be or Not To Be Political: A Dilemma of Puerto Rican Migrant Associations," in E. B. Brody (ed.), *Behavior in New Environments: Adaptation of Migrant Populations* (Beverly Hills: Sage Publications, 1970), 425-36.

Rosenthal, D. B., "Administrative Politics in Two Indian Cities," *Asian Survey*, 6:4 (1966), 201-15.

———, "Factions and Alliances in Indian City Politics," *Midwest Journal of Political Science*, 10:3 (1966), 320-49.

———, *Limited Elite: Politics and Government in Two Indian Cities* (Chicago: University of Chicago Press, 1970).

———, "De-Urbanization, Elite Displacement, and Political Change in India," *Comparative Politics*, 2:2 (1970), 169-201.

Sangave, V. A., "Changing Patterns of Caste Organization in Kolhalpur City," *Sociological Bulletin*, 11:1-2 (1961), 36-59.

Schneider, P., "Honor and Conflict in a Sicilian Town," *Anthropological Quarterly*, 42:3 (1969), 130-54.

Schwartz, N. B., "Conflict Resolution and Impropriety in a Guatemalan Town," *Social Forces*, 48:1 (1969), 98-106.

Simpson, G. E., "Political Cultism in West Kingston," *Social and Economic Studies,* 4:2 (1955), 133-49.

Skinner, G. W., *Leadership and Power in the Chinese Community of Thailand* (Ithaca: Cornell University Press, 1958).

Smock, D. R., "Urban-Rural Contrasts in Political Values in Eastern Nigeria," *Journal of Asian and African Studies,* 6:2 (1971), 81-90.

Somjee, A. H., "Periurban Politics in India," *Asian Survey,* 3:7 (1963), 324-31.

Somjee, A. H. (ed.), *Politics of a Periurban Community in India* (New York: Asian Publishing House, 1964).

Stamp, P., "Urbanization in East Africa and Its Political Implications," *African Urban Notes,* 4:4 (1969), 50-55.

Stren, R., "Factional Politics and Central Control in Mombasa," *Canadian Journal of African Studies,* 4:1 (1970), 33-56.

Tangris, S., "Urbanization, Political Stability and Economic Growth," in R. Turner (ed.), *India's Urban Future* (Berkeley: University of California Press, 1962), 192-212.

Thompson, R. A., "Stochastics and Structure: Cultural Change and Social Mobility in a Yucatec Town," *Southwestern Journal of Anthropology,* 26:4 (1970), 354-74.

Torres-Trueba, H. E., "Factionalism in a Mexican Municipio," *Sociologus,* N. S. 19:2 (1969), 134-52.

Van Den Berghe, P. L., *Caneville: The Social Structure of a South African Town* (Middletown, Conn.: Wesleyan University Press, 1964), 65-122.

Vengroff, R., "Urban Government and National Building in East Africa," *The Journal of Modern African Studies,* 9:4 (1971), 577-92.

Vincent, Joan, *African Elite: The Big Men of a Small Town* (New York: Columbia University Press, 1971).

Wallerstein, I., "The Political Role of Voluntary Associations in Middle Africa," in *Urbanization in African Social Change* (Centre of African Studies: University of Edinburgh, 1963), 151-65.

———, "Migration in West Africa: the Political Perspective," in H. Kuper (ed.), *Urbanization and Migration in West Africa* (Berkeley: University of California Press, 1965), 148-59.

Walsh, A. H., "Urban Local Government in French-Speaking Africa," *African Urban Notes,* 4:4 (1969), 1-34.

Ward, R. E., "Urban-Rural Differences and the Process of Political Modernization in Japan: A Case Study," *Economic Development and Cultural Change,* 9:1 (1960), 135-65.

Weiner, M., "Violence and Politics in Calcutta," *Journal of Asian Studies,* 20:3 (1961), 275-81.

———, "Urbanization and Political Protest," *Civilisations,* 17:1-2 (1967), 44-52.

Whitten, N. E., *Class, Kinship and Power in an Ecuadorian Town* (Stanford: Stanford University Press, 1965), 170-94.

Wiebe, P., "Elections in Peddur: Democracy at Work in an Indian Town," *Human Organization,* 28:2 (1969), 155-59.

21. Patterns of Urban Life: Religious Activities

Chambers, M., "Jesus of Oyingbo," *New Society*, 80 (April 9, 1971), 13-15.

Dore, R. P., *City Life in Japan* (Berkeley: University of California Press, 1958 and 1965), 291-393.

Fiawoo, D. K., "Urbanization and Religion in Eastern Ghana," *Sociological Review*, 7:1 (1959), 83-97.

Freedman, M., and Topley, M., "Religion and Social Realignment Among the Chinese in Singapore," *Journal of Asian Studies*, 21:1 (1961), 3-23.

Geertz, C., "Religious Belief and Economic Behavior in a Central Javanese Town: Some Preliminary Considerations," *Economic Development and Cultural Change*, 4:2 (1956), 134-58.

Gonzalez, N. L., "Social Functions of Carnival in a Dominican City," *Southwestern Journal of Anthropology*, 26:4 (1970), 328-42.

Harris, M., *Town and Class in Brazil* (New York: Columbia University Press, 1956), 208-41.

Hwang, C. H., "Men in Their Oikoi: Urbanization in Taiwan," *International Review of Missions*, 55:219 (1966), 291-97.

Ikado, F., "Trend and Problems of New Religions: Religion in Urban Society," *Journal of Asian and African Studies*, 3:1-2 (1968), 101-17.

Jain, S. P., "Religion and Cast Ranking in a North Indian Town," *Sociological Bulletin*, 20:2 (1971), 134-44.

Kent, L., "Of Ancestors and Ognuni: Yorubaland in Harlem," *The Village Voice* (New York), (21 Dec. 1967), 3 and 15.

Mayer, P., "Some Forms of Religious Organization Among Africans in a South African City," in *Urbanization in African Social Change* (Centre of African Studies: University of Edinburgh, 1963), 113-26.

Nash, M., *Machine Age Maya: The Industrialization of a Guatemalan Community* (Glencoe, Ill.: The Free Press, 1958), 60-74.

Parrinder, E. G., *Religion in an African City* (London: Oxford University Press, 1953).

Patnaik, N., "Puri: Impact of Socio-Economic Change on a Religious Complex," *Economic Weekly*, 15:32 (1963), 1361-62.

Perira de Queiroz, M. I., "Brazilian Messianic Movements: A Help or a Hindrance to 'Participation,'" *International Institute for Labour Studies Bulletin*, 7 (June 1970), 93-121. (See 110-21.)

Roberts, B. R., "Protestant Groups and Coping with Urban Life in Guatemala City," *American Journal of Sociology*, 73:6 (1968), 753-67.

Samarin, W. J., "Religion and Modernization in Africa," *Anthropological Quarterly*, 39:4 (1966), 288-97.

Schwab, W. B., "The Growth and Conflict of Religion in a Modern Yoruba Community," *Zaire*, 6:8 (1952), 829-35.

Service, E. R., and Service, M. S., *Tobati: Paraguayan Town* (Chicago: University of Chicago Press, 1954), 184-200.

Thomas, N. E., "Functions of Religious Institutions in the Adjustment of African Women to Life in a Rhodesia Township," in H. L. Watts(ed.),

Focus on Cities, Proceedings of a Conference, Institute for Social Research, University of Natal, 1968 (Durban: Institute for Social Research, University of Natal, 1970), 282-90.

Wagley, C., *Amazon Town: A Study of Man in the Tropics* (New York: Macmillan, 1963), 215-56.

Wilson, M., and Mafeje, A., *Langa: A Study of Social Groups in an African Township* (Cape Town: Oxford University Press, 1963), 91-112 and 108-12.

22. The Urban System and Specific (Occupational) Social Groupings

Abegglen, J. C., *The Japanese Factory: Aspects of Its Social Organization* (Glencoe, Ill.: The Free Press, 1958).

Ampene, E., "Obuasi and Its Miners," *Ghana Journal of Sociology*, 3:2 (1967), 73-80.

Baker, T., and Bird, M., "Urbanization and the Position of Women," *Sociological Review*, 7:1 (1959), 99-122.

Belshaw, C. S., Port Moresby Canoe Traders," *Oceania*, 23:1 (1952), 26-39.

Bettison, D. G., "The Private Domestic Servant of Blantyre-Limbe," *The Nyasaland Journal*, 12:1 (1959), 36-45.

Bhattacharya, S. S., "The Shoe Shiners of Patna," *Sociological Bulletin*, 18:2 (1969), 167-74.

Bonilla, F., "The Urban Worker," in J. J. Johnson (ed.), *Community and Change in Latin America* (Stanford: Stanford University Press, 1964), 186-205.

Dorjahn, V. R., "Tailors, Carpenters and Leather Workers in Magburaka," *Sierra Leone Studies*, 20 (Jan. 1967), 158-72.

Eberhard, W., "Social Mobility Among Businessmen in a Taiwanese Town," *Journal of Asian Studies*, 21:3 (1962), 327-39.

Elkan, W., *An African Labour Force* (Kampala: East African Institute of Social Research, 1956).

Fabrega, H., "Begging in a Southeastern Mexican City," *Human Organization*, 30:3 (1971), 277-87.

Falade, S., "Women of Dakar and the Surrounding Urban Area," in D. Paulme (ed.), *Women of Tropical Africa* (London: Routledge and Kegan Paul, 1963), 217-29.

Gould, H. A., "Lucknow Rickshawallas: The Social Organization of an Occupational Category," *International Journal of Comparative Sociology*, 6:1 (1965), 24-47.

Hellmann, E., *Sellgoods: A Sociological Survey of an African Commercial Labour Force* (Johannesburg: Institute of Race Relations, 1953).

Hodge, W. H., "Navaho Urban Silversmiths," *Anthropological Quarterly*, 40:4 (1967), 185-200.

Lukhero, M. B., "The Social Characteristics of an Emergent Elite in Harare," in P. C. Lloyd (ed.), *The New Elites of Tropical Africa* (London: Oxford University Press, 1966), 126-37.

McCall, D., "Trade and the Role of Wife in a Modern West African Town," in A. W. Southall (ed.), *Social Change in Modern Africa* (London: Oxford University Press, 1961), 286-99.

Mkele, N., "The Emergent African Middle Class," *Optima,* 10:4 (1960), 217-26.

Nyirenda, A. A., "African Market Vendors in Lusaka," *Rhodes-Livingstone Journal,* 22 (Sept. 1957), 31-63.

Oberschall, A., "Lusaka Market Vendors: Then and Now," *Urban Anthropology,* 1:1 (1972), 107-23.

Preston-Whyte, E., "The Adaptation of Rural-Born Female Domestic Servants to Town Life," in H. L. Watts (ed.), *Focus on Cities,* Proceedings of a Conference, Institute for Social Research, University of Natal, 1968 (Durban: Institute for Social Research, 1970), 271-81.

Southall, A. W., "The Concept of Elites and Their Formation in Uganda," in P. C. Lloyd (ed.), *The New Elites of Tropical Africa* (London: Oxford University Press, 1966), 342-66.

Textor, R. B., *From Peasant to Pedi-Cab Driver,* Cultural Report Series, South East Asia Studies No. 9 (New Haven: Yale University Press, 1961).

Thomas, F. C., "The Libyan Oil Worker," *Middle East Journal,* 15:3 (1961), 264-76.

23. Views of the Urban World: The Collectivity

Anderson, N., *The Urban Community: A World Perspective* (New York: Holt, 1959), 1-46 and 207-32.

De Jong, D., "Images of the City," *Journal of the American Institute of Planners,* 28:4 (1962), 266-76.

Gulick, J., "Images of an Arab City," *Journal of the American Institute of Planners,* 29:3 (1963), 179-98.

Harris, M., *Town and Country in Brazil* (New York: Columbia University Press, 1956), 242-73.

Heisler, H., "The Enclave Society and Nationbuilding in Zambia," in *Urban Agglomerations in the States of the Third World: Their Political, Social and Economic Role,* International Institute of Differing Civilizations (Brussels: Editions de l'Institut de Sociologie, Université Libre de Bruxelles, 1971), 412-35.

Mascarenhas, A., "The Impact of Nationhood on Dar es Salaam," *East African Geographical Review,* 5 (April 1967), 39-46.

McCulloch, M., "Attitudes to Town Life," *Rhodes-Livingstone Papers,* 26 (1956), 57-65.

Mitchell, J. C., "African Images of the Town: A Quantitative Exploration," *Manchester Statistical Society* (Jan. 1969), 31 pp.

Peattie, L. R., "The Intellectual World of La Laja," in *The View From the Barrio* (Ann Arbor: University of Michigan Press, 1968), 105-17.

Powdermaker, H., *Copper Town: Changing Africa* (New York: Harper and Row, 1962), 223-305.

Reina, R. E., "The Urban World View of a Tropical Forest Community in the Absence of a City: Peten Guatemala," *Human Organization,* 23:4 (1964), 265-77.

Service, E. R., and Service, H. S., *Tobati: Paraguayan Town* (Chicago: University of Chicago Press, 1954), 217-77.

Siegel, B. J., "The Role of Perception in Rural-Urban Change: A Brazilian Case Study," *Economic Development and Cultural Change,* 5:3 (1957), 244-56.

Simmons, O. G., "The Criollo Outlook in the Mestizo Culture of Coastal Peru," *American Anthropologist,* 57:1 (1955), 107-17.

Singer, M., "The Great Tradition in a Metropolitan Center: Madras," *Journal of American Folklore,* 71:281 (1958), 347-88.

24. Urbanism and the Individual

Berque, J. *et al., The Role of the Human Factor in the Development of the Newly Independent Countries, with an Annotated Bibliography* (Paris: UNESCO, 1967).

Biesheuvel, S., *Basic Personality of African and Madagascan Populations* (London: Scientific Council for Africa South of the Sahara, 1960).

Clignet, R., "Environmental Change, Types of Descent and Child Rearing Practices," in H. Miner (ed.), *The City in Modern Africa* (New York: Praeger, 1967), 257-96.

Danziger, K., "Independence Training and Social Class in Java, Indonesia," *Journal of Social Psychology,* 15:1 (1960), 65-74.

———, "Parental Demands and Social Class in Java, Indonesia," *Journal of Social Psychology,* 51:1 (1960), 75-86.

———, "Social Change and Child Training in Underdeveloped Areas," in J. F. Holleman *et al.* (eds.), *Problems of Transition* (Durban: Natal University Press, 1964), 103-26.

De Ridder, J. C., *The Personality of the Urban African in South Africa* (London: Routledge & Kegan Paul, 1961).

Hanna, W. J., and Hanna J. L., *Urban Dynamics in Black Africa: An Interdisciplinary Approach* (Chicago: Aldine-Atherton, 1971), 49-73.

Hotchkiss, J. C., "Children and Conduct in a Ladino Community of Chiapas, Mexico," *American Anthropologist,* 69:6 (1967), 711-18.

Kahl, J., "Three Types of Mexican Industrial Workers," *Economic Development and Cultural Change,* 8:2 (1960), 164-69.

Kaye, B., *Bringing Up Children in Ghana* (London: George Allen and Unwin, 1962).

Levine, R. A., Klein, N. H., and Owen, C. R., "Father-Child Relationships and Changing Life-Styles in Ibadan, Nigeria," in H. Miner (ed.), *The City in Modern Africa* (New York: Praeger, 1967), 215-55.

Lewis, O., *The Children of Sanchez* (London: Secker and Warburg, 1962).

Mangin, W., "Similarities and Differences Between Two Types of Peruvian Communities," in W. Mangin (ed.), *Peasants in Cities: Readings in the Anthropology of Urbanization* (Boston: Houghton Mifflin, 1970), 20-29.

———, "Autobiographical Notes on a Rural Migrant to Lima, Peru," *Sociologus,* 21:1 (1971), 58-76.

Mayer, I., "Town Children and Country Children," in P. Mayer, *Townsmen or Tribesmen* (Cape Town: Oxford University Press, 1961), 270-82.

Miner, H., and De Vos G., *Oasis and Casbah: Algerian Culture and Personality in Change* (Ann Arbor: Museum of Anthropology, University of Michigan, 1960).

Munro, D., "Environment and the Intellectual Growth of Pre-School Urban African Children," *Bulletin* (University of Zambia), 1 (1966), 31-36.

Powdermaker, H., "Social Change Through Imagery and Values of Teen-Age Africans in Northern Rhodesia," *American Anthropologist,* 58:5 (1956), 783-813.

Prothro, E. T., *Child Rearing in the Lebanon* (Cambridge, Mass.: Harvard University Press, 1961).

Sen, S. N., "Calcutta's Lonely Crowd," *The Economic Weekly,* 11:8 (1959), 282-84.

Van Der Veur, K., and Richardson, P., "Education Through the Eyes of an Indigenous Urban Elite," *New Guinea Research Bulletin,* 12 (August 1966).

Wohl, R. R., and Strauss, A. L., "Symbolic Representation and the Urban Milieu," *American Journal of Sociology,* 63:5 (1958), 523-33.

25. Social Psychological Factors in Urban Life

Althabe, G., "Psychological Conclusions to a Study of Unemployment in Brazzaville in 1957," in F. R. Wickert (ed.), *Readings in African Psychology from French Sources* (East Lansing: African Studies Center, University of Michigan, 1967), 209-17.

Dawson, J., "Urbanization and Mental Health in a West African Community," in A. Kiev (ed.), *Magic, Faith and Healing: Studies in Primitive Psychiatry Today* (New York: Free Press, 1964), 305-42.

Fried, J., "Acculturation and Mental Health among Indian Migrants in Peru," in M. K. Opler (ed.), *Culture and Mental Health* (New York: Macmillan, 1959), 119-37.

Hammond-Tooke, W. D., "Urbanization and the Interpretation of Misfortune: A Quantitative Analysis," *Africa,* 40:1 (1970), 25-39.

Maclean, C. M. V., "Hospitals or Healers: An Attitude Survey in Ibadan," *Human Organization,* 25:2 (1966), 131-39.

Mangin, W., "Mental Health and Migration to Cities," *Annals of the New York Academy of Sciences,* 84:17 (1960), 911-17.

———, "Urbanization Case History in Peru," *Architectural Design,* 8:33 (August 1965), 366-70.

———, "Tales from the Barriadas," in W. Mangin (ed.), *Peasants in Cities: Readings in the Anthropology of Urbanization* (Boston: Houghton Mifflin, 1970), 55-61.

Mangin, W., and Cohen, J., "Cultural and Psychological Characteristics of Mountain Migrants to Lima," *Sociologus,* 14:1 (1964), 81-88.

Marwick, M., "The Continuance of Witchcraft Beliefs," in P. Smith (ed.), *Africa in Transition* (London: Reinhart, 1958), 106-14.

Murphy, H. B. M., "Culture and Mental Disorder in Singapore," in M. K. Opler (ed.), *Culture and Mental Health* (New York: Macmillan, 1959), 291-316.

Okediji, F. O., "Some Social Psychological Aspects of Fertility Among Married Women in an African City," *The Nigerian Journal of Economic and Social Studies,* 9:1 (1967), 67-79.

Press, I., "The Urban *Curandero,*" *American Anthropologist,* 73:3 (1971), 741-56.

Scotch, N. A., "A Preliminary Report on the Relation of Socio-Cultural Factors to Hypertension Among the Zulu," *Annals of the New York Academy of Sciences,* 84:17 (1960), 1000-9.

Swartz, M. J., "Interpersonal Tensions, Modern Conditions and Changes in the Frequency of Witchcraft/Sorcery Accusations," *African Urban Notes,* 4:1 (1969), 25-33.

Tsuang, M. T., and Rin, H., "An Evaluation of Social and Migration Factors among Psychiatric Out-Patients in the University Hospital," *Journal of the Formosan Medical Association,* 60:1 (1961), 30-36.

Weinberg, S. K., "Culture and Communication in Disorders and Psychotherapy in West Africa," *African Urban Notes,* 5:1 (1970), 22-28.

26. Adaptation and Reaction to Urbanism as a Way of Life

Ablon, J., "Relocated American Indians in the San Francisco Bay Area: Social Interaction and Indian Identity," *Human Organization,* 23:4 (1964), 296-304.

———, "The Social Organization of an Urban Samoan Community," *Southwestern Journal of Anthropology* 27:1 (1971), 75-96.

Antia, F. P., "India's Urban Population, the City Dweller: A New Deal," *Population Review,* 7:1 (1963), 3-32.

Banton, M., "Adaptation and Integration in the Social System of Temne Immigrants in Freetown," *Africa,* 26:4 (1956), 354-68.

Butterworth, D. S., "A Study of Urbanization Process among Mixtec Migrants from Tilaltongo in Mexico City," *America Indigena,* 22:3 (1962), 257-74.

Dawson, J., "Traditional Values and Work Efficiency in a West African Mine Labour Force," in *Urbanization in African Social Change* (Centre of African Studies, University of Edinburgh, 1963), 196-206.

Field, A. J., *Urbanization and Work in Modernizing Societies* (Detroit: Glengary Press, 1967).

Gatheru, R. M., *Child of Two Worlds* (London: Routledge & Kegan Paul, 1964).

Gonzales, N. L., "Black Carib Adaptation to a Latin Urban Milieu," *Social and Economic Studies,* 14:3 (1965), 272-78.

Hill, G. W., "The Adjustment of Rural Migrants in an Urban Venezuelan Community," *Migration News*, 12:2 (1963), 1-6; 12:3 (1963), 7-14.

Howton, F. W., "Cities, Slums and Accculturative Process in the Developing Countries," in P. Meadows and E. H. Mizruchi (eds.), *Urbanism, Urbanization and Change: Comparative Perspectives* (Reading, Pa.: Addison-Wesley, 1969), 431-47.

Lopes, R. B., "Aspects of the Adjustment of Rural Migrants to Urban Industrial Conditions in Sao Paulo, Brazil," in P. M. Hauser (ed.), *Urbanization in Latin America* (Paris: UNESCO, 1961), 234-48.

Martin, H. W., "Correlates of Adjustment among American Indians in an Urban Environment," *Human Organization*, 23:4 (1964), 290-95.

Murphey, R., "City and Countryside as Ideological Issues: India and China," *Comparative Studies in Society and History*, 14:3 (1972), 250-67.

Nash, M., *Machine Age Maya, the Industrialization of a Guatemalan Community* (Glencoe, Ill.: The Free Press, 1958), 92-111.

Oram, N. D., "Rabia Camp and the Tommy Kabu Movement," *New Guinea Research Bulletin*, 14 (Jan. 1967), 3-43.

Parkin, D. J., "Urban Voluntary Associations as Institutions of Adaptation," *Man*, 1:1 (1966), 90-94.

Peattie, L. R., *The View from the Barrio* (Ann Arbor: University of Michigan Press, 1968).

Plotnicov, L., "Nativism in Contemporary Nigeria," *Anthropological Quarterly*, 37:3 (1964), 121-37.

Price, J. A., "The Migration and Adaptation of American Indians in Los Angeles," *Human Organization*, 27:2 (1968), 168-75.

Salisbury, R. F., and Salisbury, M. E., "The Rural-Oriented Strategy of Urban Adaptation: Siane Migrants in Port Moresby," in T. Weaver and D. White (eds.), *The Anthropology of Urban Environments*, Washington, D.C., Society for Applied Anthropology, Monograph 11 (1972), 59-68.

Scotch, N. A., "Magic Sorcery and Football among the Urban Zulu: A Case of Reinterpretation under Acculturation," *Journal of Conflict Resolution*, 5:1 (1961), 70-74.

Suzuki, P., "Encounters with Istanbul: Urban Peasants and Rural Peasants," *International Journal of Comparative Sociology*, 5:2 (1964), 208-16.

Weinberg, S. K., "Urbanization and Male Delinquency in Ghana," *Journal of Research in Crime and Delinquency*, 2:2 (1965), 85-94.

———, "Delinquency and Urbanization in Ghana," *Estudios de Sociologia*, 9 (1965), 139-54.

Wyllie, R. W., "Ritual and Social Change: A Ghanaian Example," *American Anthropologist*, 70:1 (1968), 21-33.

27. Patterns of Urban Life: The Social Organization of the Slum

Back, K. W., *Slums, Projects and People—Puerto Rico* (Durham, N.C.: Duke University Press, 1962).

Barakbah, S. M., "The Problem of Illegal Settlers in Urban Areas of Kedah

State, Malaysia," *Journal of Administration Overseas,* 10:3 (1971), 200-209.

Bharat, S. S., *Slums of Old Delhi* (Delhi: Atma Ram, 1958).

Bonilla, F., "Rio's Favelas: The Rural Slum Within the City," *Dissent,* 9:4 (1962), 382-86.

Brisseau, J., "Les Barrios de Petare," *Les Cahiers d'Outre-Mer,* 16 (1963), 5-42.

Bryce-Laporte, R. S., "Family Adaptation of Relocated Slum Dwellers in Puerto Rico: Implications for Urban Research and Development," *The Journal of Developing Areas,* 2:4 (1968), 533-40.

———, "Urban Relocation and Family Adaptation in Puerto Rico: A Case Study in Urban Ethnography," in W. Mangin (ed.), *Peasants in Cities: Readings in the Anthropology of Urbanization* (Boston: Houghton Mifflin, 1970), 85-97.

Casasco, J. A., "The Social Function of the Slum in Latin America: Some Positive Aspects," *America Latina,* 12:3 (1969), 87-111.

De Jesus, M., *Beyond All Pity: My Life in the Slums of Sao Paulo* (London: Souvenir Press, 1962). (American edition: *Child of the Dark.*)

Descloitres, P., *L'Algérie des Bidonvilles* (Paris: Mouton, 1961).

Dietz, H., "Urban-Squatter Settlements in Peru: A Case History and Analysis," *Journal of Inter-American Studies,* 11:3 (1969), 353-70.

Dwyer, D. J., "The Problem of In-Migration and Squatter Settlement in Asian Cities: Two Case Studies, Manila and Victoria-Kowloon," *Asian Studies,* 2:2 (1964), 145-69.

———, "Urban Squatters: The Relevance of the Hong Kong Experience," *Asian Survey,* 10:7 (1970), 607-13.

Epstein, D. G., "The Genesis and Function of Squatter Settlements in Brasilia," in T. Weaver and D. White (eds.), *The Anthropology of Urban Environments,* Washington, D.C., Society for Applied Anthropology, Monograph 11 (1972), 51-58.

Frankenhoff, C. A., "Elements of an Economic Model for Slums in a Developing Economy," *Economic Development and Cultural Change,* 16:1 (1967), 27-36.

Hammel, E. A., "Some Characteristics of Rural Village and Urban Slum Populations on the Coast of Peru," *Southwestern Journal of Anthropology,* 20:4 (1964), 346-58.

Hellmann, E., *Rooiyard: A Sociological Survey of an Urban Slum,* Rhodes-Livingstone Paper No. 13 (1948).

Hollingshead, A. B., and Rogler, L. H., "Attitudes Toward Slums and Public Housing in Puerto Rico," in L. J. Duhl (ed.), *The Urban Condition* (New York: Basic Books, 1963), 229-45.

Juppenlats, M., *Cities in Transformation: The Urban Squatter Problem of the Developing World* (St. Lucia, Queensland, Australia: University of Queensland Press, 1970).

Laquian, A., *Slums are for People* (Manila: DM Press, 1968).

Leeds, A., "The Significant Variables Determining the Character of Squatter Settlements," *America Latina,* 12:3 (1969), 44-86.

Lewis, O., *Five Families: Mexican Studies in the Culture of Poverty* (New York: Basic Books, 1959).

———, "The Culture of Poverty," in J. J. TePaske and S. N. Fisher (eds.), *Explosive Forces in Latin America* (Columbus: Ohio State University Press, 1964), 149-73.

———, "Even the Saints Cry," *Transaction*, 4:1 (1966), 18-23.

Manaster, K. A., "The Problem of Urban Squatters in Developing Countries: Peru," *Wisconsin Law Review*, 23:1 (1968), 23-61.

Mangin, W., "Latin American Squatter Settlements: A Problem and a Solution," *Latin American Research Review*, 2:3 (1967), 65-98.

———, "Squatter Settlements," *Scientific American*, 217:4 (1967), 21-29.

Mangin, W., and Turner, J. C., "The Barriada Movement," *Progressive Architecture*, 49:5 (1968), 154-62.

Marchand, B., "Les Ranchos de Caracas: contribution à l'étude des Bidonvilles," *Les Cahiers d'Outre-Mer*, 19 (1966), 105-43.

Matos Mar, J., "The Barriadas of Lima: An Example of Integration into Urban Life," in P. M. Hauser (ed.), *Urbanization in Latin America* (New York: UNESCO, 1961), 170-90.

McEwen, A. M., "Stability and Change in a Shanty Town: A Summary of Some Research Findings," *Sociology*, 6:1 (1972), 41-57.

McVicar, K. G., "Pumwani—The Role of a Slum Community in Providing a Catalyst for Culture Change in East Africa," in H. Berger (ed.), *Ostafrikanische Studien* (Nürnberg: Wirtschaft-und Sozialgeographischen Instituts der Friedrich-Alexander-Universität, 1968), 157-67.

Patch, R. W., "Life in a Callejon," *American Universities Field Staff, Report Service*, 8:6 (1961), 24 pp.

Pearse, A., "Some Characteristics of Urbanization in the City of Rio de Janeiro," in P. M. Hauser (ed.), *Urbanization in Latin America* (New York: UNESCO, 1961), 191-205.

Peattie, L., *The View from the Barrio* (Ann Arbor: University of Michigan Press, 1968).

Portes, A., "The Chilean Urban Slum: Types and Correlates," *Land Economics* 47:3 (1971), 235-48.

———, "Rationality in the Slum: An Essay on Interpretative Sociology," *Comparative Studies in Society and History*, 14:3 (1972), 268-86.

Rogler, L. H., "Slum Neighborhoods in Latin America," *Journal of Inter-American Studies*, 9:4 (1967), 507-28.

Safa, H. I., "From Shanty Town to Public Housing," *Caribbean Studies*, 4:1 (1964), 3-11.

———, "The Social Isolation of the Urban Poor," in I. Deutscher and E. J. Thompson (eds.), *Among the People* (New York: Basic Books, 1968), 335-52.

Salmen, L. F., "A Perspective on the Resettlement of Squatters in Brazil," *America Latina*, 12:1 (1969), 73-95.

Schulman, S., "Latin American Shantytown," *New York Times Magazine* (16 Jan. 1966), 30-38.

Sebag, P., "Le Bidonville de Borgel," *Cahiers de Tunisie*, 6:23-24 (1958), 267-309.

Seeley, J. R., "The Slum: Its Nature, Use and Users," *Journal of the American Institute of Planners*, 25:1 (1959), 7-14.

Solzbacher, R. M., "East Africa's Slum Problem: A Question of Definition," in J. Gugler (ed.), *Urban Growth in Sub-Saharan Africa, Nkanga,* 6 (1970), 45-52.

Stokes, C. J., "A Theory of Slums," *Land Economics*, 38:3 (1962), 187-97.

Szulc, T., *The Winds of Revolution: Latin America Today—and Tomorrow* (New York: Praeger, 1963), 49-54.

Turner, J. F. C., "Lima's Barriados and Corralows, Suburbs vs. Slums," *Ekistics*, 19:112 (1965), 152-55.

United Nations, "Uncontrolled Urban Settlement: Problems and Policies," in *Urbanization: Development Policies and Planning* (International Social Development Review No. 1) (New York, 1968), 107-28.

28. Patterns of Urban Life: Conflict and Accommodation and Authority

Bettison, D. G., and Apthorpe, R. J., "Authority and Residence in a Peri-Urban Social Structure—Ndirande, Nyasaland," *The Nyasaland Journal*, 14:1 (1961), 7-39.

Comber, L. F., *An Introduction to Chinese Secret Societies* (Singapore: Straits Times Press, 1957).

Epstein, A. L., "The Role of African Courts in Urban Communities of the Northern Rhodesian Copperbelt," *Rhodes-Livingstone Journal*, 13 (1953), 1-17.

———, "Tribal Elders to Trade Unions," in P. Smith (ed.), *Africa in Transition* (London: Reinhardt, 1958), 97-105.

Gutkind, P. C. W., "Accommodation and Conflict in an African Peri-Urban Area," *Anthropologica*, 4:1 (1962), 163-73.

———, "African Urban Chiefs: Agents of Stability and Change in African Urban Life," *Anthropologica*, 8:2 (1966), 249-68.

Mafeje, A., "A Chief Visits Town," *Journal of Local Administration Overseas*, 2:2 (1963), 88-99.

Nkosi, L., "Zulu Tribal Fights," *New Society*, 5:125 (1965), 6-9.

Paden, J. N., "Communal Competition, Conflict and Violence in Kano," in R. Melson and H. Wolpe (eds.), *Nigeria: Modernization and the Politics of Communalism* (East Lansing: Michigan State University Press, 1971), 113-44.

Quarcoo, A. K., "Social Control in Madina," *Ghana Journal of Sociology*, 2:2 (1966), 8-14.

Wilson, M., and Mafeje, A., *Langa: A Study of Social Groups in an African Township* (Cape Town: Oxford University Press, 1963), 153-71.

Werlin, H. H., "The Nairobi City Council: A Study in Comparative Local Government," *Comparative Studies in Society and History*, 8:2 (1966), 181-98.

29. Urban Life, Social Problems, and Planning Policy

Anderson, N., *The Urban Community: A World Perspective* (New York: Holt, 1959), 182-206.

Ashton, G. T., "The Differential Adaptation of Two Slum Subcultures to a Colombian Housing Project," *Urban Anthropology*, 1:2 (1972), 176-94.

Barber, C. R., *Igbo-Ora, a Town in Transition: A Sociological Report on the Ibarapapa Project* (Ibadan: Oxford University Press, 1966).

Batson, E., "Relative Poverty in a Peri-Urban Area: A Report from the Cape Flats, Vleiland Survey," *Journal for Social Research*, 9 (May 1958), 37-49.

Bollens, J. C., and Schmandt, H. J., "The Metropolitan Trend in London, Ibadan, Tokyo and Sao Paulo," in S. F. Fava (ed.), *Urbanism in World Perspective: A Reader* (New York: Crowell, 1968), 525-40.

Breese, G., "Some Dilemmas in Poverty, Power and Public Policy in Cities of Underdeveloped Areas," in W. Bloomberg and S. Schmandt (eds.), *Power, Poverty and Urban Policy* (Beverly Hills: Sage Publications, 1968), 465-89.

Bulsara, J. F., *Problems of Rapid Urbanization in India* (Bombay: Popular Prahashan, 1964).

Carleback, J., "Juvenile Prostitutes in Nairobi," *East African Studies*, 16 (Kampala: East African Institute of Social Research, 1962).

Chang, S. D., "Peking: The Growing Metropolis of Communist China," *The Geographical Review*, 55:3 (1965), 313-27.

Chauhan, D. S., "Social Costs of Migration," *Journal of Social Sciences* (India), 1:2 (1958), 29-51.

Church, R. J. H., "Urban Problems and Economic Development in West Africa," *The Journal of Modern African Studies*, 5:4 (1967), 511-20.

Clifford, W., *Physical Handicap Amongst Africans in Broken Hill*, Social Welfare Research Monograph No. 2 (Lusaka: Northern Rhodesia [Zambia]: Government Printer, 1960).

Daland, R. T., "Urbanization Policy and Political Development in Latin America," *American Behavioral Scientist*, 12:5 (1969), 22-33.

Delgado, C., "Three Proposals Regarding Accelerated Urbanization Problems in Metropolitan Areas: The Lima Case," *American Behavioral Scientist*, 12:5 (1969), 34-45.

Dema, I. S., and Den Hartog, A. P., "Urbanization and Dietary Change in Tropical Africa: Food and Nutrition in Africa," (Accra: FAO/WHO/OAU), 7 July 1969, 31-63.

Desai, I. P., "Small Towns: Facts and Problems," *Economic Weekly*, 16:16 (1964), 725, 727, 729-30.

Doxiadis Associates, "The Town of Tema, Ghana: Plans for Two Communities," *Ekistics*, 77 (March 1962), 159-71.

Drake, St. C., and Omari, T. P. (eds.), *Social Work in West Africa*, Department of Social Welfare and Community Development (Accra: Government Printer, 1963).

Friedmann, T., "The Role of Cities in National Development," *American Behavioral Scientist*, 12:5 (1969), 13-21.

Gore, M. S., Mathur, J. S., Laljani, M. R., and Takulia, M. S., *The Beggar Problem in Metropolitan Delhi* (Delhi: Delhi School of Social Work, 1959).

Gupta, J. P., "Rural-Urban Migration and Community Development: A Major Social Issue of Urbanization," *Civic Affairs*, 12 (1965), 30-31, 33-35, 37-39.

Gutkind, P. C. W., "The Energy of Despair: Social Organization of the Unemployed in Two African Cities: Lagos and Nairobi," *Civilisations*, 17:3 (1967), 186-214; 17:4 (1967), 380-405.

Harries-Jones, P., "Marital Disputes and the Process of Conciliation in a Copperbelt Town," *Rhodes-Livingstone Journal*, 35 (June 1963), 29-72.

Harris, B., "Urbanization Policy in India," *Papers and Proceedings of the Regional Science Association*, 5 (1959), 181-203.

———, "Urban Centralisation and Planning Development," in R. Turner (ed.), *India's Urban Future* (Berkeley: University of California Press, 1962), 261-76.

Haynor, N. S., "Crimogenic Zones in Mexico City," *American Sociological Review*, 11:4 (1946), 428-38.

Hoselitz, B. F., "Urbanization and Town Planning in India," *Confluence*, 7:2 (1958), 115-27.

———, "The Cities of India and Their Problems," *Annals of the Association of American Geographers*, 49:2 (1959), 223-31.

Hughes, C. C., and Hunter, J. M., "Urbanization and Disease in Africa," *African Urban Notes*, 4:2 (1969), 20-36.

Jakobson, L., and Prakash, V., "Urbanization and Regional Planning in India," *Urban Affairs Quarterly*, 2:3 (1967), 36-65.

Khalaf, S., *Prostitution in a Changing Society: A Sociological Survey of Legal Prostitution in Beirut* (Beirut: Khayats, 1965).

Kirchherr, E. C., "Tema 1951-1962: The Evolution of a Planned City in West Africa," *Urban Studies*, 5:2 (1968), 207-16.

Knoop, H., "Some Demographic Characteristics of a Suburban Squatting Community of Leopoldville: A Preliminary Analysis," *Cahiers Economiques et Sociaux*, 4:2 (1966), 119-49.

Lai, D. C. Y., and Dwyer, D. J., "Tsuen Wan: A New Industrial Town in Hong Kong," *Geographical Review*, 54:2 (1964), 151-69.

Leeson, J., "Paths to Medical Care in Lusaka, Zambia (Some Preliminary Findings)," *African Urban Notes*, 4:2 (1969), 8-19.

Madavo, C. E., "Making the Cities 'Work,'" *Africa Report*, 16:8 (1971), 18-22.

Nair, B. N., "Urbanization and Corruption," *Sociological Bulletin*, 9:2 (1960), 15-33.

Nath, V., "Planning for Urban Growth," *The Indian Journal of Social Work*, 27:2 (1966), 119-46.

Okediji, F. O., "A Survey in the City of Lagos: Socio-Economic Status and Attitudes towards Public Health Problems," *International Journal of Health Education,* 13:2 (1970), 72-82.

Oram, N. D., "Health, Housing and Urban Development," *Papua–New Guinea Medical Journal,* 8:2 (1965), 41-51.

Peattie, L. R., "Social Process and Economic Development," in *The View from the Barrio* (Ann Arbor: University of Michigan Press, 1968), 130-44.

Pioro, Z., "Research on Urban Plant and Administration," in P. M. Hauser (ed.), *Handbook for Social Research in Urban Areas* (Paris: UNESCO, 1965), 192-214.

Qutob, I. Y., "Social Implications of Urbanization Trends in Arab Cities," *Journal of the Pakistan Academy for Rural Development, Comilla,* 5:1 (1964), 1-8.

Raymaekers, P., "Pre-Delinquency and Juvenile Delinquency in Leopoldville," *Inter-African Labour Institute Bulletin,* 10:3 (1963), 329-57.

Riddell, J., "The Housing Needs of Developing Countries: Some Recent Trade Union Initiatives," *Civilisations,* 15:1 (1965), 31-40.

Safier, M., "United Nations Survey on Urban Land Policies and Control Measures in Africa," *African Urban Notes,* 3:4 (1968), 30-42.

Salmen, Lawrence F., "A Perspective on the Resettlement of Squatters in Brazil," *America Latina,* 12:1 (1969), 73-95.

Sandesara, J. C., "Migration and Metropolitan Living: A Study of Indian Cities," *Economic Weekly,* 16:19 (1964), 807-10.

Scaff, A. H., "Urbanization and Development in Uganda: Growth, Structure and Change," *Sociological Quarterly,* 8:1 (1967), 111-21.

Shafi, S. S., "Planning for Urban Growth," *Civil Affairs,* 12 (September 1964), 1-10.

Smith, B. C., "New Bussa, a New Town on the Niger," *Urban Studies,* 4:2 (1967), 149-64.

Stren, R. E., "Limitations on Local Planning in Kenya: The Case of Mombasa Municipality," *African Urban Notes,* 4:4 (1969), 35-49.

Turner, J. F. C., "Uncontrolled Urban Settlement: Problems and Policies," in G. Breese (ed.), *The City in Newly Developing Countries: Readings on Urbanism and Urbanization* (Englewood Cliffs, N.J.: Prentice-Hall, 1969), 507-43.

Turner, R., "The Future of Indian Cities," *Asian Survey,* 1:1 (1961), 29-37.

United Nations, "Urbanization and National Development," in *Urbanization: Development Policies and Planning* (International Social Development Review No. 1) (New York, 1968), 79-88.

United Nations Bureau of Social Affairs, "Urbanization and Crime and Delinquency in Asia and the Far East," in P. M. Hauser (ed.), *Urbanization in Asia and the Far East* (Calcutta: UNESCO, 1958), 230-50.

United Nations Economic Commission for Africa, "Leopoldville and Lagos: Comparative Study of Conditions in 1960," in G. Breese (ed.), *The City in Newly Developing Countries: Readings on Urbanism and Urbanization* (Englewood Cliffs, N.J.: Prentice-Hall, 1969), 436-60.

Venter, H. J., "Urbanization and Industrialization as Crimogenic Factors in the Republic of South Africa," *International Review of Criminal Policy,* 20 (1962), 59-67.

Watts, K., "Small Town Development in the Asian Tropics: Problems and Possibilities," *Town Planning Review,* 34:1 (1963), 19-26.

Zachariah, K. C., and Sebastian, A., "Juvenile Working Migrants in Greater Bombay," *The Indian Journal of Social Work,* 27:3 (1966), 255-62.

30. Urbanization and Social Change: General Patterns and Social Surveys, Regional and Continental

Acquah, I., *Accra Survey* (London: University of London Press, 1958).

American Universities Field Staff, Inc., *City and Nation in the Developing World: Selected Case Studies of Social Change in Asia, Africa and Latin America* (New York: AUFS, 1968).

Baer, G., *Population and Society in the Arab East* (London: Routledge and Kegan Paul, 1964), 177-203.

Berger, M. (ed.), *The New Metropolis in the Arab World* (New Delhi: Allied Publishers, 1963).

Bopegamage, A., *Delhi–A Study in Urban Sociology* (Bombay: University of Bombay, 1957).

Bose, N. K., *Calcutta, 1964: A Social Survey* (Calcutta: Lalvani Publishing House, 1968).

Braithwaite, L. E. S., "Population, Migration and Urbanization," in G. Cumper (ed.), *Report of the Conference on Social Development in Jamaica* (Kingston: Standing Committee on Social Services, 1961), 63-69.

Caplow, T., "The Modern Latin American City," in S. Tax (ed.), *Acculturation in the Americas* (Chicago: University of Chicago Press, 1952), 255-60.

Carpenter, D. B., "Urbanization and Social Change in Japan," *The Sociological Quarterly,* 1:3 (1960), 155-66.

Chabot, H. T., "Urbanization Problems in Southeast Asia," *Transactions of the 5th World Congress of Sociology,* 3 (Louvain, Belg.: International Sociological Association, 1964), 125-31.

Churchill, C. W., *The City of Beirut: A Socio-Economic Survey* (Beirut, Lebanon: Economic Research Institute of the American University of Beirut, 1954).

Damle, Y. B., "The Nature of Urbanization in India," *Bulletin of the Tribal Research Institute* (Gahendwara), 3 (1963), 1-4.

De Briey, P., "Urban Agglomeration and the Modernization of the Developing States," *Civilisations,* 16:1 (1966), 1-25.

De Bruijn, J. V., "Urbanization in the South Pacific," *South Pacific Bulletin,* 13:4 (1964), 20-24 and 66-67.

Deffontaines, P., "The Origins and Growth of the Brazilian Network of Towns," *Geographical Review,* 23:3 (1938), 379-99.

Dickson, K. B., "The Determinants of Urban Growth," in *A Historical Geography of Ghana* (Cambridge, Eng.: Cambridge University Press, 1969), 239-65.

East Africa Royal Commission 1953-1955, *Report,* CMD 9475 (London: H.M.S.O., 1955), 200-250.

Fava, S. F. (ed.), *Urbanism in World Perspective: A Reader* (New York: Crowell, 1968).

Field, A. J. (ed.), *City and Country in the Third World: Issues in the Modernization of Latin America* (Cambridge, Mass.: Schenkman, 1970).

Forde, D. (ed.), *Social Implications of Industrialization and Urbanization in Africa South of the Sahara* (Paris: UNESCO, 1956).

Friedman, J., "Cities in Social Transformation," *Comparative Studies in Society and History,* 4:1 (1961), 36-103.

Gellar, S., "West Africa Capitals as Motors for Development," *Civilisations,* 17:3 (1967), 254-62.

Germani, G., "Inquiry into the Social Effects of Urbanization in a Working Class Sector of Greater Buenos Aires," in P. M. Hauser (ed.), *Urbanization in Latin America* (Paris: UNESCO, 1961), 206-33.

Goel, O. P., "Urban Structural Pattern in Africa," *Journal of African and Asian Studies,* 1:2 (1968), 206-19.

Guha, M., "Social Institutions in a Municipal Ward in Calcutta," *Man in India,* 42:3 (1962), 181-94.

Hagmuller, G., "A Noose around the City: To Live in Slums, Bidonvilles, Barriadas and Favelas will be the Rule Rather Than the Exception by the End of This Century," *Ceres* (FAO Review), 3:6 (1970), 44-47.

Hale, G. A. (ed.), "Sudan Urban Studies," *African Urban Notes,* 6:2 (1971). (Special Issue on Sudanese Urbanism.)

Hamdan, G., *Studies in Egyptian Urbanism* (Cairo: The Renaissance Bookshop, 1959).

International Institute of Differing Civilizations, *Urban Agglomerations in the States of the Third World: Their Political, Social, and Economic Role* (Brussels, Editions de l'Institut de Sociologie, Université Libre de Bruxelles, 1971).

International Union of Local Authorities, *Urbanization in Developing Countries: Report of a Symposium* (The Hague: Martinus Nijhoff, 1968).

Jacobson, H. E., "Some Aspects of the Structure and Organization of a Philippine Provincial City, Cebu City, and the Philippines," *Pacific Viewpoint,* 10:1 (1969), 55-59.

Jacoby, E. H., "The Coming Backlash of Semi-Urbanization: The Peasants in the Large Cities Who Constitute a Gigantic Pressure Group for Change Within the Very Precincts of Political Power," *Ceres* (FAO Review), 3:6 (1970), 48-51.

Kahl, J. A., "Some Social Concomitants of Industrialization and Urbanization," *Human Organization,* 18:2 (1959), 53-74.

Kaye, B., *Upper Nankin Street, Singapore* (Singapore: University of Malaya Press, 1960).

Kennedy, M. J., "Panjabi Urban Society," in S. Moran (ed.), *Pakistan: Society and Culture* (New Haven: Human Relation Area File, 1957), 81-103.

Lambert, R. D., *Workers, Factories and Social Change in India* (Princeton: Princeton University Press, 1963).

Lebeuf, J. P., "Centres urbains d'Afrique équatoriale française," *Africa,* 23:4 (1955), 285-97.

Leslie, J. A. K., *A Survey of Dar es Salaam* (London: Oxford University Press, 1963).

Le Tourneau, R., "Social Change in the Muslim Cities of North Africa," *American Journal of Sociology,* 60:6 (1955), 527-35.

Little, K., "The Study of Social Change in British West Africa," *Africa,* 33:4 (1953), 274-84.

Loomis, C. P. *et al.* (eds.), *Turrialba, Social Systems and the Introduction of Change* (Glencoe, Ill.: The Free Press, 1953).

Mabogunje, A. L., *Urbanization in Nigeria* (London: University of London Press, 1968).

McGee, T. G., "Catalysts or Cancers? The Role of Cities in Asian Society," in L. Jakobson and V. Prakash (eds.), *Urbanization and National Development* (Beverly Hills: Sage Publications, 1971), 157-81.

McNulty, M. L., "Urban Structure and Development: The Urban System of Ghana," *Journal of Developing Areas,* 3:2 (1969), 159-76.

Malik, R. A., "Cities of the Upper Indo-Gangetic Plain," *Pakistan Geographical Review,* 20:1 (1965), 61-72.

Meister, A., "The Urbanization Crisis of Rural Man: The Shantytown Is the Crucible in Which the Peasant Must Adapt to the Ways of the City," *Ceres* (FAO Review), 3:6 (1970), 40-43.

Middleton, J., *The Effects of Economic Development on Traditional Political Systems in Africa South of the Sahara* (The Hague: Mouton, 1966), 31-48.

Mills, A. R., "A Comparison of Urban and Rural Population in the Lunsar Areas," *Sierra Leone Studies,* Part I, 20 (Jan. 1967), 173-90; Part II, 21 (July 1967), 12-51.

Mohsin, M., *Chillaranjan: A Study of Urban Sociology* (Bombay: Popular Prahashan, 1964).

Morgan, W. T. W., "Urbanization in Kenya: Origins and Trends," *Transactions Institute of British Geographers,* 46 (March 1969), 161-72.

Morse, R. M., "Recent Research on Latin American Urbanization: A Selective Survey and Commentary," *Latin American Research Review,* 1:1 (1965), 35-74.

———, "Sao Paulo: Case Study of a Latin American Metropolis," in Rabinovits, F. F. and Trueblood, F. M. (eds.), *Latin American Urban Research,* v. 1 (Beverly Hills: Sage Publications, 1971), 151-86.

Mukherjee, R. K., and Singh, B., *Social Profiles of a Metropolis* (Bombay: Asia Publishing House, 1961).

Panditratna, B. L., "The Trend of Industrialization in Colombo City, the Capital of Ceylon," *Pakistan Geographical Review,* 20:2 (1965), 145-55.

Prakash, V., *New Towns in India,* Monograph 8, Program in Comparative Studies in Southern Asia (Durham, N.C.: Duke University, 1969).

Raper, A. F., *et al., Urban and Industrial Taiwan: Crowded and Resourceful* (Taipei: National University, 1954).

Rycroft, W. S., and Clemmer, M. M., *A Study of Urbanization in Latin America* (New York: The United Presbyterian Church in the U.S.A., 1963).

Safier, M., "Urban Growth and Urban Planning in Sub-Saharan Africa," *Nkanga,* 6 (1970), 35-44. (Special issue on *Urban Growth in Sub-Saharan Africa,* J. Gugler, ed.)

Sen, S. N., *The City of Calcutta: A Socio-Economic Survey 1954-1955 to 1957-1958* (Calcutta: Bookland, 1960).

Singh, R. L., *Bangalore: An Urban Survey* (Varanadi: Tara Publications, 1964).

Southall, A. W., "The Growth of Urban Society," in S. Diamond and F. Burke (eds.), *Transformation of East Africa: Studies in Political Anthropology* (New York: Basic Books, 1966), 463-93.

Sovani, N. V., *Social Survey of Kolhapur City* (Poona: Gokhale Institute of Politics and Economics, 1952).

Turner, J. C., "Barriers and Channels for Housing Development in Modernizing Countries," in W. Mangin (ed.), *Peasants in Cities: Readings in the Anthropology of Urbanization* (Boston: Houghton Mifflin, 1970), 1-19.

Turner, R. (ed.), *India's Urban Future* (Berkeley: University of California Press, 1962).

United Nations, "A Demographic and Socio-Economic Survey of the Metropolitan Areas of San Salvador, El Salvador, Mexico, D. F.," Economic Commission for Latin America, Doc. E/CN. 12/CCE/233/TAO/LAT (Jan. 1961).

———, "Population Distribution, Urban Growth and Planning in some Middle Eastern Countries," in *Urbanization: Development Policies and Planning,* International Social Development Review No. 1 (New York, 1968), 63-67.

———, "Recent Changes in Urban and Rural Settlement Patterns in Latin America," in *Urbanization: Development Policies and Planning,* International Social Development Review No. 1 (New York, 1968), 55-62.

———, "Urban-Rural Population Distribution and Settlement Patterns in Asia," in *Urbanization: Development Policies and Planning,* International Social Development Review No. 1 (New York, 1968), 48-54.

Versluys, J. D. N. (ed.), *The Social Implications of Industrialization and Urbanization* (Five Studies in Asia) (Calcutta: UNESCO Research Center, 1956).

Walsh, A. C., "Urbanization in Nuku'alofa, Tonga," *South Pacific Bulletin,* 14:2 (1964), 45-50.

Watts, H. L. (ed.), *Focus on Cities,* Proceedings of a Conference Organized by the Institute for Social Research, University of Natal, Durban, 8th-12th July, 1968 (Durban: Institute for Social Research, University of Natal, 1970).

Whitelaw, J. S., "Suva, Capital of Fiji," *South Pacific Bulletin,* 14:3 (1964), 33-37 and 54.

Whitten, N. E., *Class, Kinship and Power in an Ecuadorian Town* (Stanford: Stanford University Press, 1965), 28-42.

Willner, A. R., "Social Change in Javanese Town-Village Life," *Economic Development and Cultural Change,* 6:3 (1958), 229-42.

Winnie, W. W., *Latin American Development, Theoretical, Sectoral and Operational Approaches* (Los Angeles: UCLA Latin America Center, 1967), 149-66.

Yazaki, T., *The Japanese City: A Sociological Analysis* (Tokyo: Japan Publications Trading Company, 1963). See also review by O. Shunsuke, *Journal of Asian Studies,* 24:1 (1964), 122-29.

31. The Technique of Microanalysis of the Urban System of Network and Neighborhood

Bopegamage, A., "Neighbourhood Relations in Indian Cities—Delhi," *Sociological Bulletin,* 6:1 (1957), 34-42.

Caplow, T., Stryker, S. and Wallace, S. E., *The Urban Ambience: A Study of San Juan, Puerto Rico* (Totowa, N.J.: Bedminster Press, 1964).

Chauhan, I. S., "Three Families in a Small Town: A Study in Social Change," *Journal of Social Research,* 8:1 (1965), 83-90.

Dore, R. P., *City Life in Japan* (Berkeley: University of California Press, 1958 and 1965).

Guha, M., "Ward 19: Calcutta," *Man in India,* 44:1 (1964), 11-21.

———, "The Definition of an Indian Urban Neighbourhood," *Man in India,* 46:1 (1966), 59-65.

Hino, S., "Neighborhood Groups in African Urban Society: Social Relations and Consciousness of Swahili People of Ujiji, a Small Town of Tanzania, East Africa," *Kyoto University African Studies,* 6 (1971), 1-30.

Kay, P., "Aspects of Social Structure in a Tahitian Urban Neighbourhood," *The Journal of the Polynesian Society,* 72:4 (1963), 325-71.

Kaye, B., *Upper Nankin Street, Singapore* (Singapore: University of Malaya Press, 1960).

Lewis, O., "The Culture of Poverty in Mexico City: Two Case Studies," *The Economic Weekly,* 12:23-25 (1960), 965-72.

Pons, V., "Two Small Groups in Avenue 21: Some Aspects of Social Relationships in a Remote Corner of Stanleyville," in A. W. Southall (ed.), *Social Change in Modern Africa* (London: Oxford University Press, 1961), 205-16.

———, *Stanleyville: An African Urban Community under Belgian Administration* (London: Oxford University Press, 1969), 174-212.

Southall, A. W., "Introductory Summary," in A. W. Southall (ed.), *Social Change in Modern Africa* (London: Oxford University Press, 1961), 25-30.

32. Research Methods in Urban Studies

Bopegamage, A., "A Methodological Problem in Indian Urban Sociological Research," *Sociology and Social Research,* 50:2 (1966), 236-40.

Chattapadhyaya, K. P., "City Surveys: Methods and Analysis of Data," *Journal of Social Research*, 5:1 (1962), 10-22.

Gamble, D. P., "Sociological Research in an Urban Community (Lunsar) in Sierra Leone," *Sierra Leone Studies*, 17 (June 1963), 254-68.

Gutkind, P. C. W., "Orientation and Research Methods in African Urban Studies," in D. G. Jongmans and P. C. W. Gutkind (eds.), *Anthropologists in the Field* (Assen, Neth.: Van Gorcum, 1967), 133-69.

Hauser, P. M. (ed.), *Handbook for Social Research in Urban Areas* (Paris: UNESCO, 1965).

———, "Observations on the Folk-Urban and Urban-Rural Dichotomies as Forms of Western Ethnocentrism," in P. M. Hauser and L. F. Schnore (eds.), *The Study of Urbanization* (New York: Wiley, 1965), 503-17.

Hellmann, E., "Methods of Urban Field Work," *Bantu Studies*, 9:3 (1935), 185-202.

Kaye, B., *Upper Nankin Street, Singapore* (Singapore: University of Malaya Press, 1960), 277-93.

Lewis, O., "Further Observations on the Folk-Urban Continuum and Urbanization with Special Reference to Mexico City," in P. M. Hauser and L. F. Schnore (eds.), *The Study of Urbanization* (New York: Wiley, 1965), 503-17.

Mitchell, R. C., "The Problems and Possibilities of Measuring Social Attitudes in African Social Surveys," *African Urban Notes*, 3:3 (1968), 4-16.

Peil, M., "Methodological Lessons of the Medina Survey," *Ghana Journal of Sociology*, 2:2 (1966), 23-28.

Pelto, P. J., "Research Strategies in the Study of Complex Societies: The 'Ciudad Industrial' Project," in T. Weaver and D. White (eds.), *The Anthropology of Urban Environments*, Washington, D.C., Society for Applied Anthropology, Monograph 11 (1972), 5-20.

Schwab, W. B., "An Experiment in Methodology in a West African Urban Community," *Human Organization*, 13:1 (1954), 13-19.

———, "Looking Backward: An Appraisal of Two Field Trips," *Human Organization*, 24:4 (1965), 373-80.

Silberman, L., "The Urban Social Survey in the Colonies," *Zaire*, 8:3 (1954), 279-99.

Van Velsen, J., "Some Methodological Problems of the Study of Labour Migration," in *Urbanization in African Social Change* (Centre of African Studies, University of Edinburgh, 1963), 34-42.

33. Bibliographies

Ajaegbu, H. I. (ed.), *African Urbanization: A Bibliography* (London: International African Institute, 1972), 84 pp.

Brand, R. R., *A Select Bibliography on Accra, Ghana, A West African Colonial City (1877 to 1960)*, Monticello, Ill., Council of Planning Librarians Exchange Bibliographies, No. 242 (1971).

Breese, G., *Modernization and Urbanization: Existing and Potential Relation-*

ships in the Third World, Monticello, Ill., Council of Planning Librarians Exchange Bibliographies, No. 70 (1969).

Brunn, S. D., *Urbanization in Developing Countries: An International Bibliography,* Latin American Studies Center Research Report No. 8 (East Lansing: Michigan State University, 1971).

Department of Social Anthropology, University of Edinburgh (compiled by), *African Urbanization: A Reading List of Selected Books, Articles and Reports* (London: International African Institute, 1965), 27 pp.

Hale, S., "An Urban Bibliography of the Sudan: 1900-1971," *African Urban Notes,* 6:2 (1971), 150-181 (Special Issue on Sudanese Urbanism).

Hanna, W. J., and Hanna, J. L., *Urban Dynamics in Black Africa, an Interdisciplinary Approach* (Chicago: Aldine-Atherton, 1971), 215-378.

Laquian, A. A., and Dutton, P., *A Selected Bibliography on Rural-Urban Mirants' Slums and Squatters in Developing Countries,* Monticello, Ill., Council of Planning Librarians Exchange Bibliographies, No. 182 (1971).

Moller, T., and Mundt, G., "Ausgewahlte Neuere Literatur zur Urbanisierung in Tropisch-Afrika" (Selected New Literature on Urbanization in Tropical Africa), *Afrika Spectrum,* 2 (1971), 84-92.

Sable, M. H., *Latin American Urbanization: A Guide to the Literature, Organizations and Personnel* (Metuchen, N.J.: Scarecrow Press, 1971).

Vaughan, D. R., *Urbanization in Twentieth Century Latin America: A Working Bibliography.* Institute of Latin American Studies, Population Research Center (Austin: University of Texas Press, 1970).